# Cybersecurity: The Essential Body of Knowledge

**Dan Shoemaker and
Wm. Arthur Conklin**

**COURSE TECHNOLOGY**
CENGAGE Learning

Australia • Brazil • Japan • Korea • Mexico • Singapore • Spain • United Kingdom • United States

## COURSE TECHNOLOGY
### CENGAGE Learning

**Cybersecurity: The Essential Body of Knowledge**

**Dan Shoemaker and Wm. Arthur Conklin**

Vice President, Editorial, Career Education & Training Solutions: Dave Garza

Director of Learning Solutions: Matthew Kane

Executive Editor: Steve Helba

Managing Editor: Marah Bellegarde

Product Manager: Natalie Pashoukos

Developmental Editor: Jill Batistick

Editorial Assistant: Jennifer Wheaton

Vice President, Marketing, Career Education & Training Solutions: Jennifer Ann Baker

Marketing Director: Deborah S. Yarnell

Senior Marketing Manager: Erin Coffin

Associate Marketing Manager: Shanna Gibbs

Production Manager: Andrew Crouth

Senior Content Project Manager: Andrea Majot

Senior Art Director: Jack Pendleton

Library of Congress Control Number: 2011924924

ISBN-13: 978-1-4354-8169-5

ISBN-10: 1-4354-8169-0

**Course Technology**
20 Channel Center Street
Boston, MA 02210
USA

Cengage Learning is a leading provider of customized learning solutions with office locations around the globe, including Singapore, the United Kingdom, Australia, Mexico, Brazil, and Japan. Locate your local office at: **international.cengage.com/region**

Cengage Learning products are represented in Canada by Nelson Education, Ltd.

For your lifelong learning solutions, visit **www.cengage.com/coursetechnology**.

Purchase any of our products at your local college store or at our preferred online store **www.cengagebrain.com**

Visit our corporate website at **cengage.com**.

# Brief Contents

# Contents

## CHAPTER 6

CHAPTER 7
# The Data Security Competency .................................................. 149

## CHAPTER 8
## The Digital Forensics Competency . . . . . . . . . . . . . . . . . . . . . . . . . . . . . . . . . . . . . . . **173**

## CHAPTER 9
## The Enterprise Continuity Competency . . . . . . . . . . . . . . . . . . . . . . . . . . . . . . . . . . . . . **193**

CHAPTER 13
# Network and Telecommunications Security . . . . . . . . . . . . . . . . . . . . . . . . . . . . . **285**

CHAPTER 14
# Personnel Security . . . . . . . . . . . . . . . . . . . . . . . . . . . . . . . . . . . . . . . . . . . . . . . . **305**

## CHAPTER 15
# Physical Security . . . . . . . . . . . . . . . . . . . . . . . . . . . . . . . . . . . . . . . . . . . . . . . . . . . . . . . . **327**

## CHAPTER 16
# Procurement . . . . . . . . . . . . . . . . . . . . . . . . . . . . . . . . . . . . . . . . . . . . . . . . . . . . . . . . . . . . **349**

# Preface

## Getting to Know the Field

Electronic information is a critical part of our culture. In fact, it might be said that electronic information has created that culture. Yet no matter where the technology has taken us, the fact remains that what happens in cyberspace has tangible impacts on each of our lives. Therefore, it is as important for us to be secure in cyberspace as it is to be secure in our physical world.

The problem is that it is very difficult to ensure security in cyberspace. Cyberspace is intangible, borderless, and anonymous, so it provides unfettered access for faceless people to cause mischief anywhere in the world. Nonetheless, since cyberspace is such an indispensible part of our everyday lives, we have no other option than to take substantive steps to ensure our security. The crucial question is, "What are the right steps to take?"

This book presents a comprehensive set of practices that are designed to ensure security in cyberspace. Those practices were developed over the latter part of this decade by the U.S. federal government. Given that pedigree and the currency of its ideas, this framework provides very authoritative advice about how to create practical cybersecurity. Even so, it is hard to truly understand how to apply a complicated framework like this, by simply studying its contents. It is much better to experience the nuances of cybersecurity practice through an actual attempt to establish the process. That attempt is captured in a story about a fictional company. The story illustrates the actual problems that such a company might encounter in attempting to secure itself in the real world.

Although it is the authors' hope that the reader will find the story enjoyable, the story was not written to entertain. It is provided to help the reader personally experience the problems, pitfalls, and politics that are a part of the concrete process of implementing cybersecurity. Many of the things that happen to the characters in the story come from actual situations. It is hoped that the reader will be able to appreciate the true scope and depth of the issues involved in implementing a practical cybersecurity process by undergoing the same experience. Moreover, the fact that a lot of the actual learning is conveyed through the story makes this book different from other textbooks.

## Scope of the Text

Every textbook encompasses a body of knowledge. The one that was chosen for this book is the Department of Homeland Security's compendium of best practice, *Information Technology (IT) Security Essential Body of Knowledge (EBK): A Competency and Functional Framework for IT Security Workforce Development*. The EBK is a product of the Department of Homeland Security's National Cyber Security Division (DHS/NCSD).

Because Homeland Security is a federal entity, it is able to reach across all sectors to assemble a national body of experts. Given that reach, the experts who helped formulate the EBK were drawn from the logical places in our society: government, business, and academe. The input from each of those sectors was pulled together into a national baseline of essential knowledge and skills that, in the eyes of the people who prepared it, encompasses the universal things that IT security practitioners need to know in order to do their jobs correctly.

The EBK is an umbrella framework; it integrates all of the professional practices that are associated with the body of knowledge for cybersecurity into a single model for practical application. Umbrella frameworks typically catalog the contents of a profession by dividing the field into subsets. Given that classic approach, the EBK categorizes the field of cybersecurity into 14 separate areas of knowledge.

However, the EBK goes one step further. It links the contents of those 14 areas to 10 common cybersecurity roles and then makes recommendations about the four standard functions that each of those roles might perform. That connection between practice, role, and function creates a much more detailed and in-depth picture of the specific requirements of cybersecurity work.

# Intended Audience

This book was written to provide a comprehensive understanding of the field of cybersecurity. One of the advantages of the EBK model is that it does *not* define security as a set of specific implementation steps, or even a single profession. Instead, it provides a full assortment of competencies for a range of professional roles and functions. These roles and competencies can then be tailored and adapted to any relevant situation. Thus, the audience for this material could legitimately be anybody who wants to gain an understanding of the knowledge and competencies appropriate to his or her personal, career, or disciplinary area of interest.

From the standpoint of higher education, the audience might include everybody from students who want to explore security as a career, to instructors who want to teach a cybersecurity course. Consequently, the audience for some parts of this book might include every type of teacher or student, from introductory programming and business analysis all the way up to graduate study in strategic policy and organizational process architecture courses.

People in the practical world who might also benefit from this knowledge would include everybody from managers and technical workers to specialists such as auditors, physical security practitioners, and IT staff. From a career standpoint, the EBK was specifically designed to align with the competencies necessary to meet the education and training requirements of such federal laws and regulations as FISMA and DoD 8570. The competencies defined for each functional role in the EBK might also be considered to constitute the body of knowledge needed to acquire the commercial certifications required to progress down a career path in cybersecurity.

# Organization of the Text

There are a number of other umbrella frameworks for cybersecurity. The most popular examples are probably the International Standards Organization's (ISO) ISO 27000 series of standards, the CISSP-CBK, and ISACA's COBIT. The primary difference between the EBK and these other approaches is not in the specification of competencies, since all of these standards generally look the same. Rather, it is the categorization and application of cybersecurity competencies into a flexible and highly extensible role and function model. As a result, the text is organized to help the reader understand how those roles and competencies can produce any number of practical outcomes.

The EBK is ideally suited to educators because of its purpose. Unlike the other umbrella frameworks, the EBK was specifically designed to provide detailed advice about the knowledge requirements for cybersecurity work. It serves as an authoritative model for what has to be taught in every type of awareness, training, or educational situation.

The presence of competencies in a role-based framework also lets organizations mold the advice of the EBK into a custom solution that could fit their specific real-world needs. The tangible realization of the EBK's recommendations is determined by the roles that are involved and the particular circumstances. Given that flexible application, the organization can shape a routine, best-practice solution that has been customized to its precise needs. More importantly, the organization can easily modify its approach as circumstances change by modifying the roles or their competency definitions.

The presentation is divided into three parts. Part one comprises three chapters. Those three chapters give the reader an understanding of current cybersecurity issues and the generic problems involved in trying to secure a complex organization. Chapter One will introduce the practical context and pedigree of the EBK. Chapter Two will introduce a systematic tailoring process to apply the EBK in a real-world company. This explanation is necessary because, unlike ISO 27000, the EBK is not built around a formal implementation process. Thus, its role and competency recommendations have to be adapted to a given application. The process for doing that is presented in Chapter Two. Chapter Three will introduce the process that is used to customize a general set of EBK recommendations for a specific setting. Because the recommendations of the EBK are meant to apply to all situations, they are expressed at a relatively high level of application. Consequently, a process is required to turn the concepts in the EBK into specific work instructions that are applicable to a particular group of people in a given situation. That process will be detailed in Chapter Three.

The second major part of this text introduces the 10 roles embodied in the EBK. There are three different types of roles, which represent three levels of cybersecurity work. Those levels range from the three executive roles at the top, down through four functional security roles in the middle, to three related ancillary roles at the bottom of the hierarchy. Each of the three levels will be presented in its own chapter and each role within each chapter will be given its own context and discussion. The outcome from the discussion in those three chapters should be a thorough understanding of the standard roles that do cybersecurity work, as well as the organization and management of those roles.

The final, and by far the lengthiest, part of this text contains the competency recommendations. Since there are 14 of these areas, there are 14 chapters in this section. Each chapter will itemize the EBK recommendations for that competency area. The chapter will then discuss what those recommendations mean in terms of the activities required, as well as the steps that have to be taken to ensure that those activities are properly implemented and managed.

Each of the competency areas encompassed in the EBK represents an entire body of knowledge in and of itself. For this reason, the discussion in these chapters will be aimed at providing a comprehensive understanding of the major concepts in each area, rather than a detailed presentation of the current developments in each area, which could be endless and constantly changing. The aim is to ensure sufficient understanding to allow the reader to explore in detail any areas of interest.

The objective of all of these chapters is to enable a reader to develop a comprehensive cyber-security solution from the recommendations that are contained in the EBK framework. Of course, all of these chapters are elaborated and tied together by the story that runs throughout the book. We have also provided evaluation material at the end of each chapter to reinforce learning through pertinent questions and cases. A full case is presented in an Appendix at the end of the book. The case is a detailed scenario that describes how our fictional company operates. It provides additional information that couldn't be included in the chapter-based story lines. The information covers the company's various components, their purposes, and how the company does business. The case is meant to support the Hands-On Projects at the end of each chapter. In addition, it provides context that will help the reader see where the various roles and competencies fit into the story.

# Features

To ensure a successful learning experience, this book includes the following pedagogical features:

- *Running Story* — A story about a fictional company and the problems it faces securing itself in the real world, which runs throughout the book. The story is meant to help the reader understand all of the problems, pitfalls, and politics which are a part of the normal process of building cybersecurity into a real-world corporation.

- *Chapter Summary* — A bulleted list that gives a brief but complete summary of the chapter.

- *Key Terms* — A list of all new terms and their definitions in each chapter.

- *Questions from the CIO* — Review questions that assess the reader's understanding of the key topics covered in each chapter.

- *Hands-On Projects* — These projects help readers apply the knowledge gained from each chapter.

# Instructor's Materials

## Instructor Resources CD

A variety of teaching tools has been prepared to support this textbook and to enhance the classroom learning experience. (The Instructor Resources CD is also available online at www.cengage.com.)

- *Electronic Instructor's Manual* — The instructor's manual that accompanies this book includes additional material to assist in class preparation, including suggestions for classroom activities, discussion topics, and additional activities.

- *Solutions* — The instructor resources include suggested solutions to the Questions from the CIO at the end of each chapter.

- *PowerPoint presentations* — The book comes with Microsoft PowerPoint slides for each chapter. They are included as a teaching aid for classroom presentation, to make available to students on the network for chapter review, or to be printed for classroom distribution. Instructors, please feel free to add your own slides for additional topics you introduce to the class.

- *ExamView®* — ExamView, the ultimate tool for objective-based testing needs, is a powerful test generator that enables instructors to create paper, LAN, or Web-based tests from test banks designed specifically for their Cengage Course Technology text. Instructors can use the ultra-efficient QuickTest Wizard to create tests in less than five minutes by taking advantage of Cengage Course Technology's question banks, or they can customize their own exams from scratch.

- *Figure Files* — All figures and tables in the book are reproduced on the Instructor Resources CD in bitmap format. Similar to the PowerPoint presentations, they are included as a teaching aid for classroom presentation, to make available to students for review, or to be printed for classroom distribution.

ISBN: 1-4354-8170-4

# About the Authors

**Dan Shoemaker** is a senior research scientist at the Center for Cybersecurity and Intelligence Studies, a National Security Agency (NSA) Center of Academic Excellence, at the University of Detroit Mercy. He is a professor in computer and information systems at UDM and was the chair of the department for twenty-five years. He also holds a visiting professor appointment at London South Bank University in London. Dr. Shoemaker is co-chair of the Secure Software Assurance Workforce Training and Education working group within the NCSD and he is one of three domain editors for the Software Assurance Common Body of Knowledge. He was a member of the working group that developed the EBK for NCSD and has published extensively in the field of information security. Dr. Shoemaker is an author and lecturer whose talks on cybersecurity and software engineering-related topics have taken him throughout the United States, Canada, and Europe. He founded the International Cybersecurity Education Coalition (ICSEC), which connects higher education institutions located in Michigan, Ohio, and Indiana. Additionally, Dr. Shoemaker is a past recipient of the Michigan Homeland Security annual statewide award for educators (2007).

**Wm. Arthur Conklin** is an assistant professor and director of the Center for Information Security Research and Education in the College of Technology at the University of Houston. He received his Ph.D. in Business Administration from the University of Texas at San Antonio. He holds Security+, CISSP, CSSLP, IAM, and IEM certifications. His research interests include the use of systems theory to explore information security, specifically in cyber physical systems. He has an extensive background in secure coding and is a co-chair of the DHS Software Assurance Forum, a working group for workforce education, training, and development.

# Acknowledgments

Two people provided the essential support that is needed to produce a book of this magnitude. The first is my wife, Tamara, who has been the usual rock on which all of my efforts are founded. The second is my editor, Jill Batistick, who has contributed far beyond the call of duty both in terms of ideas, including the initial idea for the story, and also in guiding me through the twists and turns of the development process. I would not have made it without their exceptional contributions and I thank them sincerely. I would also like to thank my executive editor, Steve Helba, who has proven for all time that he has the patience of Job and the understanding of a saint, as well as my product manager, Natalie Pashoukos, who kept me organized with my nose to that proverbial grindstone for two exciting years.

# Reviewers

Wasim Al-Hamdani
Professor of Cryptography and Information Security
Kentucky State University
Frankfort, KY

Scott Dawson
Networking Instructor
Spokane Community College
Spokane, WA

Dean Farwood, MCT
Information Technology Program Director
Heald College
San Francisco, CA

Roger Findley
Information Assurance Instructor
Laramie County Community College
Cheyenne, WY

Michael H. Goldner, J.D.
CISSP, CEH, CHFI, MCSE/Security
Dean – Academic Affairs
ITT Technical Institute
Norfolk, VA

Dianna Jones, B.S., M.S.I.T.
Associate Dean
ITT Technical Institute
San Bernardino, CA

Randy Weaver, MCSE Security, CISSP
IT Technical Lead
Corinthian Colleges, Inc.
Everest College Phoenix
Phoenix, AZ

# chapter 1

# Information Security Is Important

## The Story Begins: Zero Hour

*The attackers struck at 3:00 A.M. on a bitterly cold Tuesday in New York City. It was mid-morning and snowing in Kiev, late morning and beastly hot in Mumbai, and the middle of the afternoon on a windy day in Beijing. The attack was driven by a botnet that investigators later estimated at an unprecedented 1.3 million zombie machines. The first warning came when the automated sensors, located on the perimeter of the company's network, began to process the signature of an incoming distributed denial of service (DDoS) SYN flood.*

*A SYN flood is characterized by the brute force transmission of requests for access to the target network, with the aim of overwhelming its capacity to receive them. Fortunately, the company's network was designed to address all reasonable expectations in the event of a SYN flood. Each server had enough bandwidth and router throughput built into it to resist a typical DDoS. In addition, the network was also protected by a rarely seen feature called a "hot" server. The purpose of this device was to "out horsepower" any attempt to fill up the primary server. It was an expensive solution indeed, but the company couldn't afford any downtime on its network.*

*As the primary server's resources began to erode, the network's automated defenses came on-line. That response would have worked under normal conditions, but nobody could have anticipated a botnet as powerful as the one that was driving this attack. As both sets of servers toppled, the organization's entire global network ground to a halt. Within an instant, the company's financial operations worldwide completely evaporated, manufacturing and logistical control disappeared, and managers everywhere were suddenly and very literally in the dark.*

# Assuring Information: Failure Is Never an Option

Computerized information is so tightly bound within the fabric of our society that its trust-worthiness and **availability** has to be assured in order for our basic social functions to operate properly. For example, one only has to imagine the impact on a bank's customers if the information in the bank's databases was corrupted or lost. But information is also a virtual entity, and as a result, the average corporate executive has a hard time getting a feel for its actual worth. It is also difficult for CEOs to justify the tangible effort and expense of protecting such an intangible asset in tough economic times.

Even though information has value and can directly impact people's lives, it is hard to relate in specific, personal terms to how the theft or destruction of information would affect each individual in any given situation. And it is usually challenging and costly to ensure reliable and systematic protection for something as dynamic and intangible as an information base. The rapidly evolving field of cybersecurity was specifically created to address that problem.

## Body of Knowledge

The field of cybersecurity is concerned with creating and sustaining processes that will identify emerging threats as well as provide the most practical and cost-effective **countermeasures** to address them. Cybersecurity is an emerging discipline; ten years ago, the notion of a discipline that was entirely dedicated to the protection of computerized information might be an oddity. But now, especially with the critical role that the Internet plays in every aspect of our lives, the formal study of effective ways to assure **confidentiality**, **integrity**, availability, authentication, and non-repudiation of digital information has moved to the forefront of our national priority list.

That priority is summarized by the Comprehensive National Cybersecurity Initiative (CNCI, 2008), which was authorized in 2008 by President Bush. It bundles mutually supporting government initiatives into a single coordinated effort to ensure the security of cyberspace and includes the establishment of a coordinated national capability to identify and remediate computer vulnerabilities. In order to underwrite that aim, the CNCI also seeks to specifically expand research and education in the methods and technologies to "deter hostile or malicious activity in cyberspace" (CNCI, 2008).

Yet, even with its newfound national prominence, there is still a lot of disagreement about what legitimately constitutes the right set of actions to deter that hostile activity. The field of cybersecurity could potentially include concepts from a number of disciplines that might reasonably fall within its boundaries. That includes such diverse areas as:

- Business management, which contributes concepts like security policy and procedure, continuity planning, personnel management, and contract and regulatory compliance
- Traditional technical studies of computer security, such as computer science, which contribute knowledge about ways to safeguard the processing of information in its electronic form
- Networking, which adds essential recommendations about how to safeguard the electronic transmission and storage of information

- Software engineering, which adds process considerations like configuration management and lifecycle process security

- Law and law enforcement, which contribute important ideas about intellectual property rights and copyright protection, privacy legislation, cyber law and cyber litigation, and the investigation and prosecution of computer crimes

- Behavioral studies, which address essential human factors like discipline, motivation, training, and certification of knowledge

- Ethics, which considers the personal and societal implications of information use and information protection

All of these fields could potentially contribute something to the overall purpose of information protection. As such, it would seem logical to incorporate the principles and methods from each area into the total body of best practice for cybersecurity. At this point there is still discussion about where the line ought to be drawn, or where the focus within those boundaries ought to be. That is where two simple common sense principles come into play.

## Two Common Sense Assumptions for Cybersecurity

The first assumption has to do with the fact that information can exist at the same time in many places and in many forms. The second assumption is more comprehensive. It is called the "complete protection" principle. Logically, under this rule protection isn't adequate if any part of it can be exploited. The condition that makes that kind of protection hard to achieve is the fact that information has to be available to the people who need to use it. In most organizations this condition implies that information needs to be dispersed. That is, information has to exist in many different places at the same time in order for it to be immediately accessible to the people who need it. For instance, the same piece of information can exist on a number of local paper records and also be present in several central databases. The problem for security is that every one of those places has to be identified and secured in order to ensure that that particular generic item of information is kept safe. Otherwise, a **compromise** of an instance of the item in one location will compromise all other instances of the same item in all other places.

The normal way to make certain that a compromise does not happen is to put technical or behavioral **controls** in place to ensure the security of all items that have to be protected. In order to operate properly, those controls have to be coordinated from within a single consistent framework. The operational term for the process of establishing and maintaining that framework is **governance**. In its simplest form, governance ensures that the company is able to manage all of its information-related functions through a single coordinated approach. That approach ensures the deployment and subsequent sustainment of a set of mutually supporting controls, or countermeasures. The governance function integrates those countermeasures into a single coherent means that will theoretically address every known area of exploitation. It should be obvious from this requirement that the governance approach has to be designed to meet the needs of each specific situation. In doing that, the designer will have to take into consideration all relevant principles for building effective protection.

# The Attack Builds: Hours 20 to 36

*Prior to the attack, the company had thought that it had all of its bases covered. The incident response team had been thoroughly drilled in all feasible restoration procedures. There was a detailed and well-documented incident response plan (IRP), which embodied specific strategies for coping with DDoS attacks. The IRP had been rigorously tested on a regular basis and had proven effective. That plan was activated as soon as the team assembled.*

*The first step required the network operations management of the affected systems to contact the immediate upstream traffic control centers. The aim was to trace and filter the attack requests out of the saturated links. However, because of the power of the botnet that was driving this attack, it was necessary to jump up the hierarchy to the root servers. Unfortunately, three of those servers were located in places where language and culture affected response time: Beijing, Novosibirsk, and the United Arab Emirates. The resulting cultural and timing differences added an extra seven hours to the resolution of the problem.*

*Once the affected linkages had been identified, the traffic flow data was analyzed in order to come up with a filtering solution. The team decided that the affected links were filterable, so it developed a carefully designed ingress filtering response. That response was implemented at the various traffic control centers and it almost immediately began to bring the attack under control. The return of control was welcome news to the company's senior executives, because all corporate functions had been shut down for approximately 30 hours at that point.*

*Although it was clear that this massive denial of service attack was going to cost the company a lot of money, the quick and efficient reaction of the incident response team had ensured that it was at least a survivable incident. By noon of the second day, connectivity was back up and the system was fully available. The system staff, which had been awake for almost a day-and-a-half at that point, was being relieved in phases and the chief information officer (CIO), who had been living on gallons of coffee and far too many furtive cigarettes, was beginning to feel a little bit like her old self again. All of the data links seemed to be working, all interrupted processing had been restored, and the staff was rolling the system up to the designated data restoration point.*

*Then the bad news came. The technical operations manager got the word first. While trying to do the rollback, his staff had discovered that the last 36 hours had actually been just one massive head-fake. While the system staff was dealing with the attack, a number of internal events had taken place within the critical company networks. It was never determined exactly where the rogue code had come from, but it was suspected that during the chaos of the attack, somebody had just walked into the affected server rooms and accessed a USB port to run a series of software routines from a small portable hard-drive.*

*Whatever the exact source, this second attack was absolutely fatal. Ironically, the actual target had never been the networks. Instead, it had been every piece of proprietary data, of any value, that the company owned. The data included all of the company's present and future product designs, all of its strategic plans, and worse, all of its customer and financial data. The thieves had not only stolen all of that information, they had then wiped all record of it from both virtual and local static storage. Although there were backups at the cold-sites, those were a week out of date. The CIO didn't need an in-depth analysis of the business implications to understand what had just happened. She took a couple of minutes to gather her thoughts and then slowly began the long walk up to the CEO's office to tell him that the company was effectively out of business.*

# Instilling Order in a Virtual World

The problem with protecting information is that it is nothing more than a proxy for something of value in the real world. The value of a piece of information might be derived from the importance of the idea, or the criticality of the decision, or it can represent simple things like your bank account number. Until the tangible value of information is known, it is hard to talk about the concrete mechanisms for protecting it.

The first problem for information security professionals is to figure out which items of information are of value, and which ones are not. Given the fact that most organizations are awash in information, this is not like finding a needle in a haystack. It is more like trying to find the right needle in a much larger pile of needles. So the first step in any cybersecurity process is to get it properly organized.

That would be relatively easy if you could actually see the information. But since information is both virtual and easily changeable, it is essential that the people responsible for assuring information follow a disciplined and well-defined process. That process has to reliably ensure that the information of any potential value is identified, assessed, and prioritized. If that identification, assessment, and prioritization is comprehensive and correct, a properly organized cybersecurity process can be created.

## Coordination of Efforts and Intent

In order for a defense to be effective, all of the requisite countermeasures have to be in place and properly coordinated. This might seem like a self-evident statement, but the fact is that information protection in most organizations will most likely only embody those measures that fall within the specific area of interest and expertise of the people responsible for the approach.

Accordingly, the approach will more often than not include only those countermeasures that the designers feel are necessary to secure their particular area of responsibility. For instance, if assurance is a responsibility of the network people, they are likely to install a firewall and electronic intrusion detection system (IDS). But electronic countermeasures alone will not protect a company from an authorized but rogue insider. So a company that relies only on a firewall and IDS solution would be vulnerable to insider theft.

Moreover, a defense that only reflects the focus and interests of a single field will almost certainly have exploitable holes in it. This can be a fatal flaw for any organization, because any competent attacker will simply scout around for the holes that they know must exist. That is why it is important to involve all of the fields necessary for electronic, personnel, and physical security in the design process. If a number of disparate fields are involved, it is important to ensure a comprehensive approach to security within the organization as a whole.

Consider that IT installs technical countermeasures, but it rarely has the responsibility to deploy accompanying physical security controls. Further, while the physical security team might deploy a complete set of physical protection measures, those rarely work in conjunction with the electronic access control measures employed by IT to control external user access to their systems. In most organizations, physical and electronic security involve two entirely separate and independent areas. As a result, the overall information security solution is likely to have holes in it simply because the electronic and physical access control measures are not properly coordinated.

Ensuring effective alignment between the countermeasures developed by the various security specialties might be difficult. But, to make matters even more challenging, most instances of information exist simultaneously in more than one form. For example, bank account balance information can be kept electronically, but the same information can also be written down in a checkbook, or just remembered. Therefore, the only way to ensure adequate security is to identify both the critical items of information (note here that we say "critical," not "all"), as well as where they reside.

A reasonably accurate inventory of the important information that the organization considers valuable and where it is kept is important. This inventory will allow security designers to establish the right set of procedural, environmental, technical, and human controls to secure all critical items of information. Besides targeting the right information items, these controls also need to ensure that the protection applies to all instances of the information item wherever it is kept across the entire organization.

Any workable solution has to be practical. That is, the overall array of protection measures has to operate within a well-defined and economically feasible management infrastructure. That infrastructure should reflect the assurance needs of the business as well as its business requirements. The controls themselves must provably address the known threats they are designed to target. Finally, the protection scheme itself should be assured to be trustworthy over time, so that it evolves as the asset base and the threat environment evolve.

## Information Diversity and Dispersion

Any information asset is a potential target for control. But information is dependent on the hardware and system assets, applications, facilities, and personnel that store and process it. With the exception of hardware, personnel, and facilities, all of these other assets are intangible, and not easily accounted for.

In order to have proper security, it is important to designate the information that will be controlled. But in most companies, information flows back and forth across organizational boundaries, both virtual and physical. Worse, the business processes in a complex organization can be diverse, ranging from high finance to loading dock information. Moreover, those processes are usually dispersed to a wide range of locations. The need to ensure information in highly diverse and widely dispersed settings gets us back to the problem of intangibility.

It is easy to account for the flow of parts from an inventory, or even the physical flow of dollar bills from a teller's till. That is because these are tangible items that can be seen and accounted for. Transactions can be made based on the ability of the person on the spot to actually see and control what has taken place. Information cannot be controlled that way. Even though it flows to and from a single point, usually a server, that server can be accessed from an infinite number of locations thanks to the Internet. That access is also in the virtual world. For instance, the whole point of a network is to provide remote access for users. The problem with controlling that access lies in determining whom to trust. The responsibility of the cybersecurity process is to ensure that that determination is correct.

Effective control of access requires the ability to ensure that access is only granted to trusted people. That implies the need for a system that embodies tangible controls and managerial factors into a tangible framework. That framework is operationalized through explicit control objectives and rules, which are shaped into a formal approach for ensuring trust. The creation of a comprehensive, well-coordinated, organization-wide set of rules and procedures is commonly the responsibility of upper-level management.

## Picking up the Pieces: Hours 36 to 72

*Understandably, the CEO, who was a lawyer by training, wanted answers. The CIO explained that the information that was sitting in electronic files had been more than adequately protected. It had been placed behind multiple firewalls of increasing strength. Those electronic measures were there to prevent it from being stolen by any external agent. Unfortunately, nobody had thought about exercising the same amount of diligence when it came to the employees.*

*Later in the day, a cursory audit of the logs made it clear that eight system employees had been acting suspiciously for some time. They had been working together during times the rest of the system staff was not at the facility. During those times, they had been accessing various sensitive files that they were not all authorized to see. They were able to do that because they were also sharing valid access tokens among themselves that should have been kept restricted only to each individual employee. At the same time, they were making unauthorized changes to some of the code in critical applications. They were able to do that because one member of their group had the right level of privilege and they were signed on under his account. Even more suspicious, one member of the group had been present at each of the company's distributed server sites at the precise time of the attack, which is the reason why the company's forensic investigators concluded that the theft had resulted from a physical exploit.*

*These eight people had come to the company through an outsourced labor contractor. Contract employees had been used over the past couple of years to cut down on permanent IT staff costs. The contractors, in turn, had hired some eager people, perhaps too eager given the salaries that were being offered, to substitute for the company's existing, highly paid system staff. Because of their duties, three of these people had been given root level access to all of the company's IT resources. Of course, the company had no reason to think that these new people were not trustworthy, since it was assumed that any responsible contracting agency would have thoroughly vetted a person it sent to do work in a sensitive position. Thus, all eight new employees were given some form of elevated privilege along with the keys to the system's security protection.*

*Sadly, that assumption proved fatally incorrect. In fact, the contracting house, which had cut its overhead costs to the bone in order to underbid all of its competitors, had done nothing more than run an ad in a trade journal and then screened the resulting flood of applicants for their technical skills. As a result, what the company got was a highly organized ring of technically superb cyber-thieves. The organization that they were working for was never determined. Even while the company was still struggling to restore operations after the DDoS attack, the thieves themselves had all flown out of several east coast airports in the United States to various locations in Eastern Europe. And of course, the material that they had stolen had evaporated into cyberspace.*

*What was finally determined was that whoever was responsible had been carefully planning the exploit for months prior to its execution. In fact, given the eventual outcome, which was bankruptcy for the company, the event seemed almost like a "contract hit," which was aimed at eliminating a competitor. The placement of the individuals was no accident, nor was the smokescreen attack a coincidence. Likewise, the perpetrators seemed to know in advance that the lack of coordination between the various functions in the organization responsible ensuring the trustworthiness of all employees would make their job easy. They had obviously studied their target carefully before executing such a coordinated strike.*

# Strategic Governance Processes

As a fundamental condition of doing business, cybersecurity is far too broad and important to be a simple technological problem. Cybersecurity has to be founded and sustained by an organization-wide strategic governance process. The goal of that process is to develop and integrate every requisite technology and management control into an organization-wide and sustainable system, which is able to meet the assurance needs of each specific organizational application.

## Creating a Strategic Governance Process

The role of cybersecurity is to ensure that information resources that are needed to underwrite a particular business strategy are kept confidential, correct, and available. The process of assurance itself has to fit within the day-to-day business model and it should always add some value to the enterprise's overall purposes. One of the common complaints about the day-to-day actions of any cybersecurity process is that those activities adversely impact business processes. Cybersecurity is also costly. Therefore, one of the most important mandates in the development of an overall cybersecurity solution is that the process cannot get in the way of effective and efficient business operation.

The aim of formal governance is to maintain an optimum and secure relationship between each of the company's business processes and their respective information security functions. In practice, the governance process develops the specific policies, organizational structures, practices, and procedures needed to achieve effective assurance. Operationally, that involves the definition of explicit procedural and technical controls for any given requirement. These controls should ensure the effective management and operation of all cybersecurity functions.

The comprehensive organizational control structure, which is the operational incarnation of this process, must always be appropriate to the security requirements of the entity being controlled. It must also be consistently executed. Thus, the control structure itself embodies a carefully designed and explicitly maintained set of electronic and managerial control behaviors, the outcomes of which can be observed and documented. The controls themselves are rarely standalone. They are normally integrated along with a range of other types of control to produce a verifiable state of sustainable assurance.

In order to make sustainment practicable, the coordination and management of the overall cybersecurity should be located at the policy development and enforcement level of the organization. Executive-level decision makers are the only people who have the authority to create, administer, and enforce policies and procedures across the entire organization.

## Strategic Planning and the Strategic Governance Process

Because cybersecurity is a strategic process, the people at the top have to sponsor and directly engage in the **strategic planning** to ensure an acceptable degree of protection. The problem is that most top executives do not think that something as operationally routine and often technical as cybersecurity is their problem, so they shift that responsibility down to the managers of the functional areas. That is a mistake, because nobody at the managerial level has the authority to enforce security outside of their own areas. As a result, the assurance measures that are implemented by managers for their areas are likely to represent a piecemeal, and therefore exploitable, defense.

In day-to-day practice, defenses that are weak or exploitable represent a growing problem for organizations across the spectrum of government, business, and academe. The number and type of attackers is growing in size and sophistication. In the 1990s, a typical attack was something like a criminal trespass, or website defacement. The victims tended to be entities such as government institutions, and attackers themselves were inclined to be counterculture types who worked alone and on the fringes of society.

That situation has changed, as the Internet has become the medium of choice for commerce. Now, instead of being motivated by a desire to prove their art, attackers are motivated by financial gain and political ends. As a consequence, the old stereotypical image of the kid living on candy while doing 72-hour hacks in his mom's basement has been replaced by a much darker and more complex persona, one who is well organized and much more focused on serious long-term trouble. For instance, there are organized groups who perpetrate large-scale raids on financial institutions for the purpose of theft. In fact, the opportunities for financial gain from cyber-crime are so great that well-established organized crime syndicates have taken to the business of electronic crime with the same zeal and enthusiasm as they did in the past with traditional physical crimes.

This new criminal business does not involve guns and strong-arm tactics. Instead, it involves all of the potential ways that information can be obtained and exploited, ranging from sophisticated hacking to dumpster diving. That raises the final concept of "due care," which is sometimes called "due diligence." Due care is nothing more than the ability to demonstrate that all reasonable precautions were taken to prevent harm resulting from something that you are legally responsible for. The problem is that up to this point, there has never been a standard definition of what constitutes due care in the information protection realm. Now it is possible to judge whether a company has been legally negligent in the way it handles an individual's personal information.

# The Story Concludes: A New Paradigm

*The company emerged from receivership under a new leadership team that was dedicated to ensuring that the events that took place under the previous leadership would never happen again. Most of the blame for that debacle had landed on the back of the former CEO, who was immediately dismissed. The old CEO was chiefly held responsible for the cost-cutting strategy that had let the disaster occur in the first place. The shareholder committee had been careful to make sure that his successor understood the inherent value in protecting the company's critical information. The person the committee eventually chose had nothing like the profile of the company's prior leadership.*

*First and foremost, the new CEO's professional background was neither in the law, like the last one, nor in finance, as were the two prior CEOs. Instead, the new CEO's MBA was in strategic management from the Krannert School at Purdue. This gave him a couple of advantages. First, he had the vision to see across corporate functions and over long periods of time. Second, he had also earned Purdue's certification in cybersecurity. So he understood what it actually took to secure an organization and he was entirely dedicated to making that happen. Accordingly, he had barely unpacked his potted fern and his desk-set when he began forming the taskforce.*

*The CIO was still holding down her post as chief technology officer. She had been absolved of most of the blame for the catastrophic events of the past, mainly because she was able to produce a contract with the prior CEO that said that she was only responsible for maintaining the integrity and availability of the network. And her performance during the actual DDoS attack had been heroic. Nevertheless, the new management team made it clear that she was now under a completely different set of marching orders. Her new contract read, "The CIO is accountable for the protection of all information of value from all reasonable sources of harm," which meant that she was now responsible for any losses of any type that might occur on her watch.*

*The problem with this new paradigm was that the CIO had a magnificent academic and professional grounding in the management of technology processes and nothing else. The harm from the last attack had originated from a breakdown in personnel security, and she was at a loss as to how to build an integrated defense-in-depth that factored in human-centered actions. The mere mention of other sources of threat, such as legal and regulatory violations, supply chain breakdowns, and physical security threats were simply out of her realm of understanding. In fact, she didn't know how she was going to ensure that her people would even be able to recognize and respond to threats that were not of the electronic variety. What she needed was a plan and a process. Under the new CEO's urgent direction, she decided to formulate a process improvement team from across all sectors of the company. Their mission was to develop a cybersecurity infrastructure and attendant process for the company.*

*Right away, the team ran into a wall, in that the members were not able to agree on the scope of responsibility for the project. The technical people on the team were certain that the problem involved nothing more than the implementation of an automated policy management system that would ensure that all organizational policies were enforced by the system. That view infuriated the team's management people, who pointed out 17 different ways that security could be breached by exploits that would not involve policy management; these ways included social engineering and human error. To back up their argument, they cited the fact that the last disaster had been at the hands of people who would have actually implemented the policy management system.*

*The technical people righteously responded that it was not possible to think of everything, nor did the company have the resources to ensure against every possible contingency. So considerations like monitoring and controlling human behavior were out of scope. The CIO, whose job depended on the criterion "no lost data of value," was frustrated by the unproductive wrangling. She assigned her two most trusted aides to answer a practical, but essential, question: Was there a commonly accepted high-level, expert framework that could be used to guide the development of complete and correct best practice governance framework for the company? After much consideration and research, her team answered, "Yes."*

# A Standard Model for Ensuring Best Practice in Cybersecurity

In simple, operational terms, the cybersecurity process involves nothing more than following a coherent set of best practices to protect all assets of value within a particular organization. The problem lies in the term "best practice." As might be expected, the best practice actions that one group might view as appropriate may not be deemed appropriate by another group. Therefore, it is essential to adopt a commonly accepted definition of correct practice as a point of reference to guide any subsequent actions. The ideal would be to have that framework endorsed by a universally recognized and legitimate third party.

In the case of cybersecurity, that best practice framework ought to encompass all of the legitimate actions necessary to ensure a reasonable state of reliable long-term security. That framework should encompass all logical actions to ensure adequate security. If it were necessary to prove that all reasonable actions had been taken, all that would be required would be proof that the activities specified in the framework had been consistently performed. Many other professions, such as law or medicine, have a commonly agreed on definition of what it takes to meet the minimum standard of due care. Those help set the boundaries of ethical practice as well as guide the correctness of actions within those boundaries. Up to this point, however, the problem for cybersecurity professionals is that a generally accepted framework didn't exist.

So the question becomes, "What criteria should a model for best practice in cybersecurity meet?" Ideally, a model for good cybersecurity practice would be universal in its application. Its correctness would be commonly accepted within the practitioner community. The model's recommendations would embody all of the currently understood correct actions for ensuring the confidentiality, integrity, availability, authentication, and non-repudiation of information. Moreover, those recommendations would be expressed in a form that would allow competent practitioners to tailor a practical and economically feasible system that would protect all of the information of value under their care.

The **Department of Homeland Security's** compendium of best practice is titled *The Information Technology (IT) Security Essential Body of Knowledge (EBK): A Competency and Functional Framework for IT Security Workforce Development*, and it attempts to satisfy all of those requirements. The EBK makes an authoritative, formal statement about what an individual has to know in order to fulfill the requirements of a range of roles in an organization.

The EBK is a product of the Department of Homeland Security's **National Cyber Security Division (DHS-NCSD)**. Because DHS-NCSD is a federal government entity, it is able to reach across all sectors to assemble a national body of experts. Given that reach, the experts who worked on the EBK were drawn from all of the concerned sectors of our society: governmental, business, and academic. That input was then pulled together into a single "national baseline representing the essential knowledge and skills" that all IT security practitioners should possess (EBK, 2008).

## The DHS Essential Body of Knowledge

The EBK is an **umbrella framework**, in the sense that its intention is to define the complete set of competencies associated with work. However, the EBK goes a step further by linking those competencies to a group of common security roles and a set of functions associated with those roles. That gives individual practitioners a standard set of recommendations about the activities that should be implemented in order to fulfill the requirements of each of those roles.

There have been other attempts to create an inclusive, top-level framework for best practice in cybersecurity. One of the better known examples of framework models of this type is the International Standards Organization's (ISO) ISO 27000 series of standards. In particular, ISO 27001 and ISO 27002 offer a valid model for the definition of an information security management system (ISMS). However, the processes and control objectives that are embodied in those two standards are relatively high-level and neither of those two were intended to define the common roles and knowledge requirements for cybersecurity professionals.

There are models that *do* define personal requirements for practitioners. These include the common body of knowledge (CBK) for the **Certified Information System Security Professional (CISSP)** and the Information System Audit and Control Association's (ISACA) Control Objectives for IT (COBIT). Specifically, the International Information Systems Security Certifications Consortium's (ISC2) CISSP and ISACA's **Certified Information Security Manager (CISM)** provide a perfectly acceptable CBK for information security professionals. Unfortunately, they are totally different and competing models and therefore they cannot be considered to be commonly accepted across the profession.

The aim of the EBK was to standardize the concepts and terms of the profession. These are arrayed into 14 areas of common practice:

1. Data security
2. Digital forensics
3. Enterprise continuity
4. Incident management
5. IT security training and awareness
6. IT systems operation and maintenance
7. Network security and telecommunications
8. Personnel security
9. Physical and environmental security
10. Procurement
11. Regulatory and standards compliance
12. Risk management
13. Strategic security management
14. System and application security

These 14 areas define the entire range of appropriate activities for securing information. The EBK also factors the activities in these 14 areas into specific professional practice requirements for 10 standard roles. Those 10 roles range from "CIO" to "acquisition specialist." In addition to specifying the acceptable actions for each of these professional roles, the EBK specifies the appropriate actions for each role in terms of four standard activities that each role might perform. The standard functions that could be carried out by each role are manage, design, implement, and evaluate (MDIE). This degree of direction establishes the EBK as an ideal conceptual framework to guide the development of a practical cybersecurity solution.

## Finding an Appropriate Model

*The EBK began to look like an appropriate model to guide the development of the company's new information security system. That assertion set off a series of last-ditch firefights as the various adherents to other models defended their positions. The ISO 27000 proponents pointed out that their model had been around in an assortment of forms, specifically as British Standard 7799, since 1995, which gave it credibility. However, most of the people involved in the discussion felt that was actually a negative, since the right model would have gotten more traction by now. At the same time, none of the adherents of the other proprietary frameworks could point to any organization that had actually based their cybersecurity processes on one of their standards.*

*The main objection to the EBK was that it was too new and untested for the company to stake its continuing survival on. That was considered a valid point, so the committee decided to investigate further. It formed a small task group from its members. The aim of the group was to identify any evidence that the EBK might potentially fit into emerging regulatory or statutory trends or might have a broader application.*

## The National Strategy to Secure Cyberspace

The **National Strategy to Secure Cyberspace** was created in 2003 to "engage and empower Americans to secure the portions of cyberspace that they own, operate, control, or with which they interact." The specific purpose of the EBK is to implement the education and training requirements of the National Strategy to Secure Cyberspace.

As part of that strategy, the National Cyber Security Division facilitates all national efforts to enhance cyber security. Among those duties, Priority III of the Strategy states that, "DHS will encourage efforts that are needed to build foundations for the development of security certification programs that will be broadly accepted by the public and private sectors."

This mandate is important, since there has never been a commonly accepted definition of the standard body of knowledge for security professionals. As a result, there has always been the possibility that essential security attributes, knowledge, or skills might have been left out of the definition of the field. This raises the prospect that the cyber security professionals we have been producing might not have all of the know-how they will need to respond to every relevant problem, which is a serious national security concern. Consequently, the committee that developed the EBK was specifically tasked to ensure that it represented the most valid and authoritative definition possible of the contents of the field.

In addition, because the competencies in the EBK are defined for a wide range of roles and functions, it is also possible for any given organization to relate those competencies to its own particular set of job categories and career tracks. As such, the EBK not only provides an encyclopedic definition of the knowledge that is contained in the field, it also provides a guideline for how to apply those elements in specific, real-world instances.

## The National Security Professional Development Program

The other important national initiative to which the EBK contributes is the **National Security Professional Development Program** (NSPD). The Program was created by executive order on May 17, 2007. Its specific aim is to "promote the education, training, and experience of current and future professionals in national security positions in executive departments and agencies."

The Program embodies a national strategy, which is meant to ensure that all people who work in security are exposed to "integrated education, training, and professional experience opportunities" (NSPD, 2007). Thus, the practical aim of this initiative is to ensure that security professionals are capable of performing their duties by enhancing the level of their general knowledge, skills, and experience. As such, the National Security Professional Development program is meant to apply to a range of security disciplines, not just electronic security professionals.

Because all of the Cabinet agencies, from Defense to the State Department, will participate in the NSPD, it is considered a Cabinet-level initiative. The Director of the Office of Personnel Management has been specifically tasked to establish and enforce an integrated approach by coordinating, "to the maximum extent practicable," the programs and guidance issued by each department (NSPD, 2007).

The strategy establishes a common platform of knowledge that will then ensure an integrated approach to security education and training across the spectrum of government agencies. Specifically, the head of every agency is required to document its current security education programs and then establish new programs as needed to address any gaps that might be identified. The EBK fits into this initiative in the sense that it is responsible for providing the measuring stick that will be used to judge whether each security education program is complete. As such, its mandate includes all professional development, training, and education programs across the entire federal domain.

## The Federal Information Security Management Act (FISMA)

The third national initiative that the contents of the EBK contribute to is the E-Government Act (P.L. 107-347), which was signed into law in December 2002. This Act formally recognizes the importance of information security to the economic and national security interests of the United States. Title III of P.L. 107-347 is entitled the **Federal Information Security Management Act** of 2002 (**FISMA**).

FISMA is an omnibus regulation for the federal government and its agencies. Its intent is to define all of the necessary controls and procedural protections required to ensure information security in all of the federal space. FISMA requires every federal agency to develop, document, and implement an enterprise-wide program to secure information and information systems that support the operations and assets of every federal agency. The scope of that mandate includes those systems provided or managed by agency contractors, or other sources. FISMA is a piece of legislation; therefore, as is the usual case with legislation, the actual means of implementing the federal law is left up to the **National Institute of Standards and Technology (NIST)**. NIST is charged with developing and issuing standards, guidelines, and other publications to direct how federal agencies will implement applicable federal laws.

NIST's role is to establish the specific form of the response. Under that mandate, it has developed several Federal Information Processing Standards (FIPS) to specify and elaborate on the implementation requirements for FISMA. The primary applicable Standard is entitled FIPS 200. This Standard, along with the accompanying FIPS that is used to classify the material that falls under FISMA, entitled FIPS 199, defines all of the general requirements for satisfying FISMA requirements. The controls that underlie those general requirements are specified in the NIST 800-53 Standard.

According to NIST, all information within the federal government (other than that information that has been determined as classified) and all federal information systems (other than those information systems designated as national security systems) falls under FIPS 200. In order to meet the requirements of this Standard, agencies must tailor their information security practices to their organization's particular mission, operations, and needs. The provision in FIPS 200 that is relevant to the EBK is the section that requires that managers and users of organizational information systems are made aware of the security risks associated with their activities and of the applicable laws, executive orders, directives, policies, standards, instructions, regulations, or procedures related to the security of organizational information systems. Organizations demonstrate compliance with this provision by documenting that the organization's personnel are adequately trained to meet their assigned information security-related duties and responsibilities.

## Chapter Summary

- Cybersecurity centers on devising tangible means to counter threats.
- Information is both an invisible and a dynamic resource.
- It is necessary to take inventory and label information in order to make it visible.
- Information is actually a proxy for things that have real-world value.
- The cybersecurity process has many facets.
- The cybersecurity process has to be coordinated to be effective.
- Coordination involves deploying and then maintaining an appropriate set of technical and managerial controls.
- Effective control ensures trusted access to information.
- Practical cybersecurity requires executive sponsorship.
- Criminal elements add a new dimension of threat to information.
- Standard models are important roadmaps for organizations to follow.
- The EBK is a national-level model for cybersecurity.
- The EBK relates well to other national initiatives to ensure cyberspace.

## Key Terms

**Availability** A state of cybersecurity where all necessary information is accessible at the time it is needed.

**Certified Information Security Manager (CISM)** A certificate of personal competency in information security management granted by the International Systems Audit and Control Association (ISACA).

**Certified Information System Security Professional (CISSP)** A certificate of personal cybersecurity competency granted by the International Information Systems Security Certifications Consortium (ISC2).

**Compromise** A breakdown in organizational control leading to the loss of or harm to data.

**Confidentiality** A state of cybersecurity where information is protected from unauthorized access.

**Controls** Technical or managerial actions that are put in place to ensure a given and predictable outcome.

**Countermeasures** Technical or managerial actions taken to prevent loss of a defined set of information items.

**Department of Homeland Security (DHS)** Federal agency charged with the overall protection of the national infrastructure.

**Federal Information Security Management Act (FISMA)** Title three of the E-Government Act which mandates all procedural protections to ensure information security in all of the federal space.

**Governance** A condition that ensures that all organizational functions are adequately coordinated and controlled, typically enabled by strategic planning.

**Integrity** A state of cybersecurity where information can be shown to be accurate, correct, and trustworthy.

**National Cyber Security Division (DHS-NCSD)** The division of DHS specifically tasked by the National Strategy with the protection of the U.S. cyber infrastructure.

**National Institute of Standards and Technology (NIST)** The body responsible for developing and promulgating standards for federal programs and federal government agencies.

**National Security Professional Development Program (NSPD)** The national strategy to ensure that all federal employees are adequately trained to carry out cybersecurity tasks.

**National Strategy to Secure Cyberspace** The national strategy to ensure the total protection of the American cyber infrastructure.

**Strategic planning** The act of translating an organization's intended direction into specific steps along a particular timeline; strategic planning affects the entire organization for a significant period.

**Umbrella framework** A comprehensive set of standard activities intended to explicitly define all required processes, activities, and tasks for a given field, or application.

# Questions from the CIO

The CIO requires you to brief her on the current status of your investigation. This will be an important part of your continuing work on this project since it is important to be able to summarize what the organization has learned in its continuing attempts to improve itself. Consequently, the CIO would like you to answer the following questions for her:

1. Why should we spend money to secure personnel and facilities when the information itself is always kept in electronic format?

2. More important, are all items of information always kept in electronic format? Is it possible that the same information could be kept in other forms simultaneously?

3. How can we go about making certain we know where all of our information is kept? What are the considerations we would have to keep in mind and how can we be certain that we can continue to keep track of information we know we have?

4. What can we do to make sure that we always have all of our bases covered when it comes to protecting information? What parts of the organization are always involved?

5. How should we include the cybersecurity function in the overall strategic governance process?

6. What is an infrastructure and how does it help ensure that the process works? How do you build one?

7. What are some of the potential models for developing an infrastructure? What are some of the advantages and disadvantages of each model?

8. Why should we pay more attention to cybersecurity now? What has changed since 2001? Is it all in the area of national security, or are there other players we need to consider? Why should we consider them?

9. What is the regulatory climate? What laws and other initiatives do you see affecting the overall requirements for cybersecurity?

10. What is the role of the federal government in defining how we do cybersecurity work? Where does this seem to be headed? What are the trends?

# Hands-On Projects

The committee has finally made its determination about the various differences between FIPS 200, ISO 2700, and COBIT. You are the person designated to report those findings. The committee would like you to do the following in preparation for briefing the CEO:

1. Make a list of the elements that are the same for all of these models.

2. Make a list of the elements that are present in two of the models.

3. List the unique elements that only exist in one of the models.

4. Explain why these frameworks all have the same common elements.

5. Explain why not all frameworks agree on the elements where there is a difference.

6. Explain why the unique elements exist for each framework.

# chapter 2

# A Global Roadmap for Security

## Narrowing the Search: More Questions

*The CEO was not happy. He had last met with the security policy group back in the winter, when he had made it abundantly clear that he wanted them to confirm that the model they were proposing would not be another passing fancy. In fact, he had told them that he honestly didn't care whether anybody else ever actually adopted the EBK. But he did want it confirmed that all of the ideas that were in it were both valid and correct. That was why they were all back together again in his 44th floor Manhattan suite, where the atmosphere was heavy with anticipation.*

*The main source of the CEO's ire was the fact that the team had decided to stake its entire claim on the fact that the EBK was directly plugged into three national initiatives. In his mind, that argument was a non-starter from the beginning, since each of the initiatives they were citing was aimed at securing systems in the federal space. He just wanted to be thoroughly sold on the EBK before he made a business decision to implement it. And this time he wanted them to show him a little better focus, in that he wanted concrete proof that the EBK provided the coherent, conceptually valid, and properly vetted strategic roadmap needed to formulate substantive security architecture. With that pronouncement hanging over their heads, the members of the group set off to wrestle with the question of the EBK's provenance.*

*The one problem that the people around the table had had with the EBK was with its original purpose. Based on evidence from the EBK itself, the team knew that the model was intentionally developed to define the training and education requirements for every relevant security position in a government entity. There was nothing in the EBK to support the idea that its role definitions also would apply in a conventional business organization.*

*However, after thinking about that question for a while, the group decided that validation of the roles defined in the EBK might be arrived at logically. Most governmental organizations are bureaucratic and hierarchical, which also describes the structure of most large business organizations. In effect, there is nothing special about the management structure of a government organization. In fact, in the mind of most of the group, if the truly distinctive issues for government, such as classification and clearance, were left out of the consideration, the feature that best characterized both types of organizations was their size and complexity. Given that similarity in both structure and purpose, the group felt that it was safe to conclude that the EBK was an appropriate basis for defining any security role in any type of large, multifaceted organization.*

*Like most strategic practice standards, the EBK was created by facilitating input from the expert community. The process of obtaining and verifying that input was both painstaking and comprehensive, taking place over a period of three years. As a result of the effort that was put into producing a valid set of security functions, the EBK contains what is recognized to be a coherent and correct set of behaviors based on expert opinion. Those behaviors are meant to ensure* **best practice** *in most security situations. From the standpoint of the specific application of the EBK to that particular company, the fact remained that the EBK was a general model. Therefore, the executive team still faced the problem of translating the EBK's generic recommendations into tangible and practical actions to secure that particular company.*

*For many of the company's stakeholders, identifying a comprehensive set of best practices was a long way from actually having a concrete approach in hand to implement overall organization-wide security in their particular bailiwick. So the team went off again, to answer two fundamental questions. The first was, "Within our current understanding, does the EBK specify all of the practices necessary to ensure real-world protection for this particular company?" Or in simple terms, "Can we adopt the EBK and be confident that all of our information protection needs will be met?" That was a simple question compared to the next one, which was, "Can the knowledge that is in the EBK be implemented?"*

*The people on the study team were no fools. They understood that the recommendations of the EBK had to be translatable into behaviors that could be consistently and reliably executed. Otherwise, they were just opening themselves up to the same type of situation that had put the company in Chapter 11 in the first place, in the sense that it was undisciplined security practice that had caused the problem. They also realized that the model's components had to provide a practical foundation to build tangible and effective organizational governance and control processes. The study team set out to determine, beyond the slightest shadow of doubt, whether the EBK actually could serve as a practical roadmap to information security.*

*The first and most obvious concern for the team was that of applicability. Answering that question would have been a priority even if the CEO hadn't made it one. Essentially, the team members had to ask themselves, "What are we really trying to accomplish by adopting and implementing this particular model?" By a process of elimination, the members decided that no national security work was involved, so there was no need to think about shaping the solution to comply with governmental regulations like FISMA and DIACAP. They also decided that the information that they were trying to protect did not require a rigorous classification scheme, so it wasn't necessary to concern themselves with hierarchical access control models like Bell-LaPadula.*

*What they were left with was the simple priority of protecting the company's information from the sort of criminal activity that had driven it into receivership in the first place. That narrowed the scope of their consideration a lot, but it still didn't answer the question, "Was the EBK the right model to ensure that purpose?" In order to address this question, the team had to demonstrate that the EBK could do three things. First, there had to be recommendations in the EBK that would allow the company to identify and then formulate a substantive and effective set of measures to ensure that the company's information was adequately protected. The CIO in particular was interested in proving that to herself, since her job was now riding on protecting all data of value.*

*Second, the EBK would have to provide a means to identify all relevant threats. From an assurance principles point of view, that requirement probably traces back to Sun Tzu. The company's emphasis in this particular instance was less on addressing all threats than it was on ensuring that only the threats that represented substantive harm were addressed. Essentially, the company wanted to have the ability to ensure that it was spending exactly as much as it needed to spend and not a cent more. Finally, the team had to demonstrate that it was possible to generate explicit policies, procedures, and work instructions from the EBK that would ensure the most comprehensive governance solution possible.*

# EBK Competency Areas

In order to ensure an adequate and reliable level of assurance, all of the behaviors that will eventually comprise an underlying, real-world security solution have to be described in practical terms and then integrated into a single, robust set of day-to-day practices. The problem is that the larger and more complex the organization, the more difficult it is to identify and inter-relate all of those required elements into a proper security system. That is where a standard conceptual model, which recommends all of the potential elements of a security solution and their relationships, comes in handy.

The aim of a high-level model like the EBK is to provide a strategic framework that specifies all of the commonly accepted activities and inter-relationships associated with good security. The EBK specifies a detailed and commonly accepted set of required security competencies. All of these competencies are properly related within a standard framework. That framework provides a template that will help any adopting organization tailor its own suitable set of substantive practices. If the tailoring is done correctly, the resulting practices will, in effect, be correct because they are derived from the general structure of the EBK model. In essence, the EBK dictates the generic elements and relationships that have to be present for organizations to create their own specific, but also provably effective, security practices.

The intent of the EBK is to present the most comprehensive possible listing of the competencies that could potentially help an organization become more secure. Some of these competencies are in the traditional areas of information technology, like network security and system and application security. However other competencies represent a broader view of information security, such as procurement and strategic security management. Taken as a whole, the 14 security competency areas of the EBK comprise a multifaceted array of things to think about when building a defense against all credible forms of potential attack.

All of the behaviors that the creators of the EBK deemed necessary to ensure fundamentally proper security were categorized into 14 competency areas. These competency areas were defined using commonly accepted standards as the point of reference. In order to make the investigation as exhaustive as possible, the recommendations that were derived from those standards were also filtered through a range of stakeholders across the IT industry.

The work of actually vetting and compiling the competencies was done by a group of subject matter experts (SME). That group was formulated under the sponsorship of the Department of Homeland Security's National Cyber Security Division (DHS-NCSD). A range of industry, governmental, and academic participants who had either participated in the formulation of information security standards or policy, or who had notable efforts in information security, was brought to Washington DC in the fall of 2005 to participate in working groups. These groups produced a draft version of the standard which was socialized around the country for review and revision. The final version of the EBK represents the final product of that process.

In essence, each competency area represents a required component of good security practice. The EBK then specifies a detailed set of security behaviors for each competency area. These behaviors represent the actual practices that can be considered appropriate to achieve each area's basic purposes. By using the detailed specification of practices that the EBK provides, a company can model its own tangible security infrastructure. At the same time, the company can assure itself that its approach incorporates commonly accepted best practice, because it can tailor its tangible activities to the practices that are specified in the EBK.

## Fifty-three Critical Work Functions

All of the underlying practices that a company institutes as standard operating procedure have to be tailored to reflect the implementing organization's specific business environment. For instance, common functions like password management and physical access control are specified in the EBK. Those functions will also most likely be a necessary component of every organization's eventual security solution. However, the actual behaviors associated with each of those functions will no doubt be different in a high-security government environment as opposed to a low-tech manufacturing facility.

The EBK assumes that in order to properly tailor and implement each practice, an explicit specification of the actual behaviors and outcomes needed to ensure proper performance has to be provided. The experts who formulated the EBK included the specific behaviors that they deemed necessary to ensure correct security practice within each competency area. These behaviors were extracted from a wide range of commonly accepted security standards and best practices. The analysis of those standards produced 53 critical work functions (CWF). Each of those CWFs encompassed multiple tasks. Because there are always a number of possible ways to fulfill the purpose of each common work function, explicit work practices are not specified by the EBK. Instead, it is assumed that work practices will be created to fit each specific situation.

Because many of these CWFs are integrated in the real world in order to achieve larger purposes, the developers of the EBK were able to factor all 53 CWFs into 14 competency areas. In order to differentiate each competency area's individual purpose and aims from those of all of the other areas, each competency area was given a functional definition. Those definitions are listed in Section 4.0 of the EBK. The EBK also takes the additional step of breaking each of those competency areas into four standard types of functional activity. These activities are considered to be common to all information security work. Those activities are manage, design, implement, and evaluate (MDIE).

## Fourteen Competency Areas

The distilled advice from all sources essentially guarantees a broad representation of all of the potential activities that might legitimately be considered to be an appropriate element of each individual competency area. As a result, the EBK can be considered to contain the most authoritative possible representation of security practices and their clarifying **terminology**. The EBK provides a list of those 14 competency areas:

1. *Data Security*—techniques aimed at ensuring electronic data
2. *Digital Forensics*—techniques aimed at evidence collection after an adverse event
3. *Enterprise Continuity*—techniques aimed at ensuring the continuing functioning of the enterprise after an adverse event
4. *Incident Management*—techniques specifically aimed at responding to incidents as they occur
5. *IT Security Training and Awareness*—techniques aimed at ensuring the competency of the members of the organization
6. *IT Systems Operations and Maintenance*—techniques aimed at ensuring continuous secure functioning of the enterprise
7. *Network Security and Telecommunications*—techniques aimed at ensuring the continuing secure functioning of all information communications
8. *Personnel Security*—techniques aimed at ensuring secure practice by the employees of the organization
9. *Physical and Environmental Security*—techniques aimed at ensuring secure physical practice within a secure space
10. *Procurement*—techniques aimed at ensuring that purchased goods and services are delivered in a secure state
11. *Regulatory and Standards Compliance*—techniques aimed at ensuring that the enterprise does not violate a regulation, standard, or law related to security
12. *Risk Management*—techniques for ongoing assessment and assurance of identified risk
13. *Strategic Security Management*—strategic methods for ensuring that the organization maintains a secure infrastructure
14. *System and Application Security*—techniques for ensuring that the operating environment of the machine and all of its associated applications remains secure

# Getting Real: Focusing on Implementation

*Based on the best expert opinion available, the team reported that the EBK competency categories contained all of the large elements necessary to ensure security within its current understanding. They also reported that those competencies were elaborated by a long list of keywords and work requirements, which would make the practical steps required to tailor those competencies into a specific implementation much easier.*

*Therefore, because they could successfully answer the two practical questions that they had posed to themselves, the group's members agreed that the company had found the right roadmap. The actual mechanism that would be employed to organize those competencies into a working system was still unresolved. Some of the ISO 27000 adherents pointed out that the beauty of their model was that it was built around a well-defined implementation process that produced a standard, certifiable information security management system (ISMS). The EBK did not embody an implementation process, nor did it have a method for evaluating whether the final product was correct.*

*One of the junior associates on the team made his move at that point. He was the one who had done most of the basic analysis of the EBK and so he was by far the best-informed member of the team when it came to the inner workings of the model. He was also an ambitious fellow, who was in no mood to wait his turn while other, less capable people had their say. He pointed out that the EBK was the most flexible model, since its implementation guidance is role based, rather than being based around a static implementation process like ISO 27000 uses. That is, the EBK provides specific advice as to how to perform the functions of a generic set of security roles. That advice would allow the company to tailor a precise specification of the day-to-day work practices of each of the employees involved with its security.*

*This was reassuring to the CIO, who was beginning to think that her group was trying to fit a square peg into a round hole. She had accepted the fact that the EBK was the best model to define required competencies. But she was getting uneasy with the idea of basing a real-world security system on a structure that was founded on nothing but competency requirements. That was because there was no guarantee that those competencies could be fitted into the existing personnel framework.*

*It was obvious to her that the essence of success was in the ability to translate the generic security activities defined in the EBK into an explicit policy and procedure framework for the various existing roles in the company. The devil was going to be in the details of documenting the necessary practices for each role. And so the development of standard, competency-based work practices, which could be associated with each competency area, was going to turn that implementation process into a much safer bet.*

*The CIO immediately promoted the ambitious junior associate to "chief security architect," which was the position that he had been angling for in the first place. The CIO then sat back and relaxed, since she also knew that she had found the perfect scapegoat should anything go wrong. The security architect, on the other hand, cracked open his well worn copy of the EBK and got down to business. He knew that, thanks to the role definitions in the EBK, he was well on his way to the first of many successes.*

# Roles in the EBK

Information security work involves a very wide range of potential activities. There are a number of potential roles that are associated with ensuring an organization. Those roles typically involve a cluster of associated competencies. The roles that are defined in the EBK are the outcome of an exhaustive job/task analysis, which involved a wide variety of IT job titles and their related security responsibilities. That analysis was done by the Department of Defense (DoD, 2005). The aim of the analysis was to identify and then characterize all of the forms of cybersecurity work that took place, specifically within the DoD. Ten security roles, along with a related set of general competency requirements, were identified in the study that supported the development of DoD 8570.

The 10 roles in the EBK represent job functions rather than job titles. These functions range across the IT security workforce. In order to avoid getting caught up in the myriad job titles that actually exist for equivalent jobs, the EBK takes a role-based approach to the definition of the work to be done. It is up to the individual organization then, to assign a job title that is equivalent to the functions specified by a given EBK security role. The title is likely to vary across organizations, but the required competencies and accountabilities will essentially remain the same.

The standard tasks associated with the roles can be mapped to virtually any organization. However, since most organizations have their own job titles, the process is not as simple as just dropping the EBK's tasks into an existing job description. Instead, the first step in the **mapping** process is to equate the EBK role definitions with whatever the organization presently calls that role. That might require bundling a number of existing job descriptions into a single EBK role.

For instance, the security professional role might encompass a number of existing job titles like risk or system analyst, contract compliance auditor, or even physical security officer. Conversely, the mapping might require factoring the activities of an existing job description into more than one role. Some of the activities of the CIO, for example, might actually fit better under the compliance officer. Or the activities of the people in purchasing might be better spread across the security professional and the procurement specialist functions. The general concept of the mapping process is outlined in Figure 2-1.

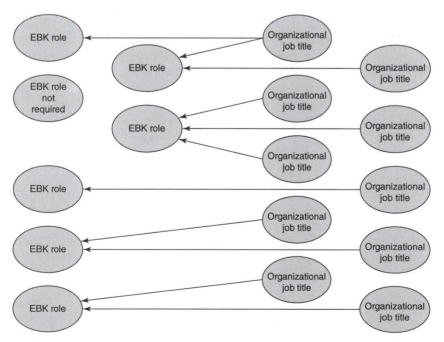

**Figure 2-1**  The mapping of existing job titles to EBK roles

© Cengage Learning 2012

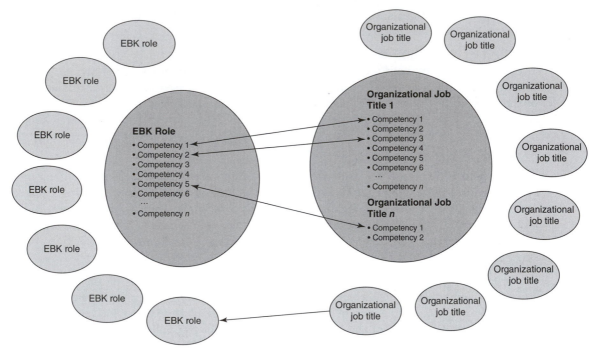

**Figure 2-2** Aligning EBK competencies with organizational job requirements

© Cengage Learning 2012

It is also possible that, in a practical application of the model, specialized EBK roles like digital forensic professional or the procurement professional will not have anything mapped to them. This makes sense in the light of the highly focused nature of these roles. In the event that no analogous job description exists, it is important to examine the competency requirements that are listed for the role. The aim would be to ensure that these competencies are either not required, or are adequately covered by other, successfully mapped job titles. Whatever the actual situation, the aim of the mapping is to understand how each of the existing job titles fits within the standard role definitions provided by the EBK. That is because the role definitions contribute specific competencies. And it is those competencies that form the ultimate basis for the duties required in every practical implementation.

Sufficiency of coverage can be ensured by comparing the competency requirements of the role as itemized in the EBK with the assigned job responsibilities of a given position. If any meaningful differences are identified in that comparison, then the gaps that exist must be filled by instituting practices that will ensure the required competencies have been institutionalized. This approach is used for all remaining job titles, mapped to defined roles in the EBK. Figure 2-2 illustrates how EBK competencies might be aligned with the job titles that have been mapped to the EBK roles.

# Organization of Roles in the EBK Framework

The EBK documents 10 roles. These roles are organized into three groups: executive, functional, and corollary. The roles constitute an itemized listing of the competencies that comprise proper security practice for a given real-world job. As a result, a company that can map its particular job titles to the EBK's role and competency matrix can, in effect, document that it is following a standard definition of correct practice. In actual practice though, that correctness hinges on the ability to document "**completeness.**"

Completeness is a relative term. The simple rule of thumb is that the security is complete if all of the job functions associated with security can be mapped to an EBK role and work requirement, and that all role and work requirements in the EBK are satisfied by the mapping.

The rationale behind completeness rests with the overall integrative purpose of the EBK. In practice, the EBK can be used to guide the development and implementation of a security solution across a wide spectrum of organizations. That is because the EBK was developed from a broad set of commonly accepted security frameworks, including elements of COBIT, ISO 27000 series, the CISSP body of knowledge, as well as a whole host of best practices including those promoted by NIST through the 800 SP series of technical publications. By distilling and integrating all of the relevant security behaviors from each of these models, the EBK creates a single compendium for defining effective security.

## Executive Roles

The three executive roles are probably the easiest to associate with a specific person within the corporation, as they are common functions in most companies and are generally, by their nature, single positions. The following three executive roles are defined by the EBK:

- Chief information officer
- Information security officer
- IT security compliance officer

The role of the CIO is, in some form or another, likely to be present in any large organization. This is probably the easiest role to justify, as every organization requires some form of executive leadership for an important asset like information, which is what the CIO role represents. The CIO is by definition the chief decision maker for the IT operation.

The role of information security officer is specific to the security function. It can go under various titles, but perhaps the most common one is chief information security officer, or CISO. This role is the chief strategic manager of the IT security operation and as such, it is for the most part responsible for all decision making with respect to the overall implementation and operation of the IT security function.

The IT security compliance role is primarily responsible for ensuring that the IT function has all necessary security controls in place and that those controls are operating properly. In larger organizations, the IT security compliance role also ensures that the company meets all legal and regulatory requirements. As a consequence of the Sarbanes-Oxley Act of 2002, this role has moved more into the forefront of corporate awareness. Because its primary area of responsibility is audit and control, this role can have a diverse range of titles, including such apparently non-IT unrelated titles as director of corporate controls and even manager of internal audit.

## Functional Roles

The roles that the EBK lists in the functional category encompass many of the operational responsibilities of the IT security function. These roles are more closely related to the actual performance of day-to-day IT work than to the executive roles. Consequently, they tend to be associated with the establishment and sustainment of the information security system. The functional roles defined in the EBK are:

- Digital forensics professional
- IT security engineer
- IT systems operations and maintenance professional
- IT security professional

The digital forensics professional is a highly specialized role that is expressly oriented toward the collection and analysis of digital evidence. It has come on the corporate radar of late because of the huge increase in cyber-crime. As such, the competencies of the digital forensics professional tend to incorporate both investigative and computer-related skills.

The IT security engineer is typically the architect of the IT security solution. This individual is usually responsible for the design and development of the company's specific IT security response. The position combines some of the strategic decision-making characteristics of the executive role with the creativity of engineering design.

The IT systems operations and maintenance professional role does what the name implies. Once the security solution has been implemented, it has to be maintained as a long-term organizational function. This role is primarily responsible for that mainte-nance. Competencies within the IT systems operations and maintenance professional role tend to cluster around incident reporting as well as response and change management.

The IT security professional role is differentiated from the IT security engineer role in the same way that the doers are differentiated from the designers. Thus, IT security professionals are not so much focused on long-term concerns as they are on ensuring the proper day-to-day performance of the security system. The role of the IT security professional is to work within a security solution, which has been established by the engineer. What this implies is that the IT security professional role will be populated by the vast majority of the company's professional IT security staff.

## Corollary Roles

The remaining category contains the corollary roles. This group typically supports the infor-mation security function, rather than executing it directly. Even though all of these roles have a direct impact on the overall security of the organization, they have not been traditionally associated with the classic aspects of information security work. The corollary roles defined in the EBK are:

- Physical security professional
- Privacy professional
- Procurement professional

The competencies in the physical security professional role assure the integrity and security of the *physical* elements of the system. Although the field itself employs many examples of advanced technology, the principles of physical security are generally not front-and-center when it comes to designing and implementing an IT security solution. This is an unfortunate reality in most organizations. Groups that tolerate such a dysfunctional division of responsibility should note that any electronic protection can be compromised by physical access alone.

The privacy professional ensures that personally identifiable information (PII) is kept confidential. PII typically represents only a percentage of the overall cybersecurity holdings of an organization. Nevertheless, PII is particularly attractive to thieves because it facilitates such criminal acts as identity theft. PII's critical importance tends to justify the use of a professional with the particular skill set to ensure against loss, or harm, which is the responsibility of the privacy professional role.

Finally, because there is an increasing tendency for business to outsource functions, there is a commensurate need for professionals to ensure that the procurement of goods and services is done securely. The role of the procurement professional is to ensure that all relevant security controls are set up and working properly and that all goods and services purchased by the company are free of latent security hazards. Because the actual development of goods and services is done outside the organization, a role dedicated to ensuring that anything brought into the company is secure cannot be overlooked.

# Common Functions

The roles and their associated competencies are broken down further into constituent activities, or functions that these roles might commonly perform. Those common functions represent the generic actions that each role might perform to establish, sustain, and then improve each of the competency areas. The use of common functions to organize the competencies allows the EBK to specify the actions required for individual roles much more precisely. Such a level of detail also makes both the intent and the application of the competencies for each role much easier to understand. More importantly, any resultant implementation of those practices will be better targeted. The common functional elements in the **EBK framework** are illustrated in Figure 2-3.

These functions are arrayed into four groups: manage, design, implement, and evaluate (EBK, 2008):

- **Manage functions** are those related to supervision and administration of the competency area, such as overseeing technical and operational activities from the highest levels. These functions ensure security system currency with the changing environment.

- **Design functions** are those that relate to the conceptualization and development of security-related functionality. Included are technical architectural as well as work process design aspects.

- **Implement functions** are those that involve tasks associated with the establishment of the operational security measures, including programs, policies, and procedures.

- **Evaluate functions** are equivalent to internal audit of security functionality, including activities to assess the effectiveness of policies, procedures, programs, or controls in achieving security objectives.

Each group is discussed in turn in the following pages of this chapter.

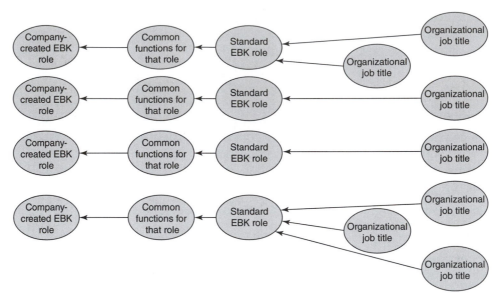

**Figure 2-3**  Mapping current organizational job titles to company-created EBK roles

© Cengage Learning 2012

## The Story Continues: It's Never As Easy As It Seems

*The newly minted chief security architect immediately put his knowledge of the EBK to use. He knew that the best way to get upper management's attention was to identify some existing problems within the company's protection scheme. So he set out to document whether the work practices specified for each of the competency requirements in the EBK model were actually being performed in real life.*

*Since he couldn't look at every role, he selected a couple of the more prominent ones. He knew that if he could demonstrate that there were essential functions that were not being carried out for key roles, it would be easier to convince his superiors to make changes.*

*His first visit was to the CIO role. He chose that role for its obvious importance to the company. But he was also aware that the CIO considered him her personal scapegoat; he hoped that he could find some holes in her game which he could then document for the edification of her superiors. With this purpose in mind, he decided to examine how well the CIO was doing with respect to the enterprise continuity competency. He chose enterprise continuity because he knew that the fallout from the prior disaster had been greatly exacerbated by breakdowns in the way the company ensured continuity of operations. Additionally, he knew that any identified weaknesses in the current way the company ensured its continuing operation would get everybody's undivided attention.*

*The CIO's role in enterprise continuity is classified in the EBK as a manage function. The manage function ensures that the particular competency area remains effective within the existing environment. That implies that the CIO has the overall responsibility for ensuring the effectiveness of enterprise continuity. In essence then, the CIO is the person accountable for ensuring that all enterprise continuity activities are both correct and sustainable. Sample statements from the EBK for what the CIO should be responsible for included:*

- *Define the enterprise continuity of operation's organizational structure and staffing model*
- *Define emergency delegations of authority and orders of succession for key positions*

*Besides the CIO role, the newly minted "chief security architect" also decided to look at the EBK's IT systems operations and maintenance professional role. He chose that role because the majority of the company's system people fell into that category. Most of the requirements for that role are embodied within the EBK's IT systems operations and maintenance competency, which requires all four common functional categories: manage, design, implement, and evaluate. Thus, based on the specifications of the EBK for that role and its competency requirements, sample practices for the IT systems operations and maintenance professional would be expected to include:*

## Manage

- *Establish communications between the security administration team and other security-related personnel (e.g., technical support, incident management)*
- *Integrate security administration team activities with other security-related team activities (e.g., technical support, incident management, security engineering)*

## Design

- *Develop personnel, application, middleware, operating system, hardware, network, facility, and egress security controls*
- *Develop security administration change management procedures to ensure that security policies and controls remain effective following a change*

## Implement

- *Establish a secure computing environment by applying, monitoring, controlling, and managing unauthorized changes in system configuration, software, and hardware*
- *Ensure that information systems are assessed regularly for vulnerabilities, and that appropriate solutions to eliminate or otherwise mitigate identified vulnerabilities are implemented*
- *Ensure security performance testing and reporting, and recommend security solutions in accordance with standards, procedures, directives, policies, regulations, and laws (statutes)*

## Evaluate

- *Assess system and network vulnerabilities*
- *Assess compliance with standards, procedures, directives, policies, regulations, and laws (statutes)*

*Unfortunately, as soon as he got into the actual specifics of the assessment, the chief security architect realized that there was something missing. Even though the recommendations of the EBK model appeared to be pretty straightforward and easy to document, they were not stated in a way that could be accurately assessed in the operational environment. For instance, it was clear that the company was assessing its systems and networks for vulnerabilities once in a while; however, the specific timing, methods for doing that, and problem reporting lines had never been specified or standardized in the form of company-wide operating procedure. So it was impossible to judge whether the practical purposes of that recommendation had actually been met.*

*As a result of the lack of implementation detail, it was obvious to the security architect that one last step was required before the company could use the EBK model. The company had to be able to create a set of concrete organizational policies, procedures, and operational practices, which would state in unambiguous terms how it planned to implement and carry out each of the EBK's generic recommendations. It was also plain to the chief security architect that that step would always be necessary if the EBK would ever be useful in real life. The concepts in the EBK are too high level in their actual focus to be applied without tailoring.*

*The primary purpose of the EBK is to specify a complete, coherent framework of generic best practices for any organization. In order to be as universally applicable as possible, the concepts in the model have to be defined in comparatively high-level and relatively abstract terms. Nevertheless, those high-level concepts would have to be turned into a set of concrete day-to-day actions in order to have a substantive implementation. Thus, the final step in the implementation process was going to require the formulation of a task team, whose aim would be to write unambiguous work instructions to substantiate the recommendations of the EBK for that particular company. Each of those individual work instructions would have to document the company's preferred approach to the four Ws: who, what, where, and when for each required recommendation. Plus, for the purposes of selling the entire system, the architect felt it might be a good idea to add an H, for "how."*

## Converting Roles, Competencies, and Functions into an Actionable Plan

The tailoring process is a standard mechanism that the organization adopts to transform the general aims of any generic model into a set of concrete actions that will define, in each instance, how the work will be done. Every company's approach to tailoring is shaped by its business culture and environment. So in that respect, all tailoring methods are implicitly unique. The only rule with tailoring is that the approach that is eventually selected has to be executed as standard operating procedure for that particular situation.

Both technological and management factors are considered in the process of tailoring. The explicit day-to-day practices that are the outcomes of the tailoring process are the real-world behaviors that operationalize the overall purposes of the high-level framework. The aim of the tailoring process is to drill-down from the framework's abstract view of the question, in order to define an explicit set of behaviors that align with the needs of the particular situation. That drilling-down process then ensures that each individual requirement, which is specified in the framework, is documented in such a way that the behaviors needed to fulfill the purposes of that requirement are embedded within the organization's standard operational practice.

The company-wide information security system, which a tailoring process eventually produces, integrates all necessary controls for all relevant recommendations into a single comprehensive solution. Each specific work practice that is tailored from the EBK is likely to have a set of technical and managerial controls associated with it. These controls constitute the actions that the organization feels will best achieve its security aims. As a result, the entire specification of all of the technical and managerial behaviors for all relevant EBK recommendations can be considered to represent the official information security solution for that company.

Each control has to be documented individually in order to put it into practice. The documentation of all controls then serves as the practical handbook for the day-to-day execution of the information security process. The one condition that must be satisfied in this process is that each constituent control has to be traceable to the recommendation that it implements. Ensuring traceability validates the purpose of each of the controls. But more important, it ensures accountability, because it identifies the person responsible for executing the control. Consequently, the documentation has to specify precisely how each step will be carried out, who will carry it out, and when it will be executed. Also, in order to ensure quantitative management, the documentation for each control should also define a set of metrics, which will allow the company to verify performance.

## The Importance of Planning

It takes a great deal of exhaustive planning in order to establish the necessary controls to ensure company-wide security, particularly in a large and complex organization. As a result, the overall information security approach is typically expressed through three types of standard organizational planning documents. The following documents communicate the precise steps that will be taken to build and sustain an effective information security effort:

- Management plan
- Design and implementation plan
- Evaluation plan

The management plan lays out the planned behaviors that the organization feels will satisfy the intent of the management functions described in the EBK. In other words, the management plan defines a set of explicit actions that the organization plans to take, to ensure that each EBK role properly executes its requisite management functions. The plan specifies the behaviors required to satisfy each function, as well as how each of those behaviors will be performed, monitored, and assessed.

The design and implementation plan defines the behaviors that the organization thinks will satisfy the EBK's recommendations regarding the design and implementation of common functions that are a part of each competency area. Because the design and implementation common functions itemize the activities that will constitute the day-to-day security activities of the organization, the design and implementation plan is really the practical operations manual for the organization's security system.

Finally, the evaluation plan documents how the company will assure performance. The evaluation plan is written to ensure the consistent execution of the behaviors that are specified in the management and the design and implementation plans. The evaluation plan also has to specify the provisions to assure the continuing trustworthiness of the overall security process. Because that involves assessment, those plans have to specify who will be responsible for doing the actual evaluation and when the evaluation will be done, as well as the specific measures that will be used to assess performance.

# The Story Evolves: Learning How to Make Adjustments

*The specification of the behaviors required to flesh out the company's security system was a six-month nightmare. But it was particularly hard on the chief security architect. In fact, he was beginning to wonder why he had ever thought that creating a security system from the EBK was a good idea in the first place. The process of guiding the definition and documentation of all necessary and appropriate behaviors, in order to satisfy the competency requirements of each of the 10 roles, was difficult enough. But at the same time, he had to ensure that traceability was maintained between all of the practical behaviors that his team had developed and incorporated into the company's policy and procedure manual, and the abstract recommendations of the EBK. That kind of exacting detail typically meant that his workday was 16 hours long. And since the company was global, the process of tailoring all of the security requirements for each of the installations in the company had kept him constantly wondering what time zone he was in.*

*Nonetheless, all of the plans were complete and the operational handbook had been established for all of the installations. The architect was just beginning to think about the prospect of getting reacquainted with his wife and kids when the gods of irony, who had been overseeing the situation from the beginning, handed him another one of their little surprises. In this case, the bombshell came in the form of a telephone call from the Singapore data center. The gist of the conversation was that after rolling the plan out, it didn't seem to fit the situation in the Far East. Specifically, their operation had established roles and competencies that were either not covered by the plan, or the plan assumed that a role or competency existed that had no operational justification. Moreover, the director of the Singapore center was not buying the idea that he had to change his well-established and effective process to fit the needs of an abstract model, no matter what kind of "alleged" best practices it might contain. So it was back to the drawing board one more time for the chief security architect and his staff.*

## Adapting the EBK to the Actual Situation

Although the EBK was developed using the most authoritative sources available, it was never intended to provide the single monolithic definition of secure practice. Instead, the assumption behind the EBK is that its core framework of roles and competencies are a valid and coherent baseline representation of fundamental security requirements. The actions derived from those basic requirements could legitimately serve as a foundation for formulating a correct security response. Nonetheless, before this can be accomplished, the concepts in the EBK have to be adapted to fit the unique needs of a given situation.

Once a company has surveyed its operation, it is more than likely to discover that in order to satisfy obvious security needs, it will need to add roles and competencies that do not exist in the basic model. Examples of such a need might be the addition of a biometric specialist role for high-tech access control, or a physical network infrastructure specialist, or even a strategic supply chain manager. Since the original assumption was that the changing nature of any security situation will require adaptation of the basic model, the EBK framework was purposely designed to be easy to expand. Figure 2-4 is a simple conceptual representation of the evolutionary cycle of that process.

The EBK expands in two logical dimensions. First, additional roles that could be added as new security requirements are identified. The biometric professional role is an example of this. Unlike the digital forensics professional, there is currently no role for the management, design, implementation, and evaluation of biometric security solutions. However, as biometrics becomes an essential part of access control, more and more organizations might require the services of a biometrics professional. In that case, the structure of the EBK makes it easy to add that standard role to the 10 basic roles that are presently contained in the model.

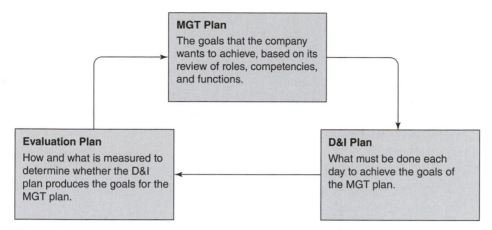

**Figure 2-4** The process of ensuring a relevant application of the EBK

© Cengage Learning 2012

Also, additional competencies can be added to a role, or even defined as an entirely separate competency category. That would be the case if, for example, the requirements for that unique competency extend across multiple EBK roles. Biometrics is a good example of that, in that the competency itself is becoming an increasingly important player in every aspect of the access control process, from networks to physical access.

The EBK is built directly on established methods and best practices, which have been garnered from both the public and private sectors. The ability to add roles and competencies within the overarching framework of the model makes unique situations easier to adapt to. It also ensures that organizations will always be able to integrate activities to meet their specific security needs, while still maintaining the logical coherence of the basic structure of the model.

As was the case with the company in this scenario, if an institution adopts the EBK as its information security framework, there are likely to be some specific instances where the EBK has to be modified to fit that particular organization's operation. Because the EBK is built on logical associations between its elements, unless those modifications are done using the established framework of the model as a point of reference, the potential exists to create dysfunctional gaps by installing practices that do not interact correctly with the rest of the elements of the security solution. Therefore the logic of any modification or change has to be closely examined.

For instance, it is important to continue to understand job titles within the standard role definition framework of the EBK. EBK roles are generic in nature and by design are broadly defined in order to cover several job titles in different industries. In the case of a firm with a substantial investment in biometrics, they may have individuals who are biometric engineers, whose responsibilities include the design, implementation, and maintenance of biometrics for access control. So rather than add a specific role for this type of job, consideration should be given as to whether the aim is to add a full-out biometrics capability or to simply ensure better security through biometrics. If the competencies that are required are uniquely biometric, than there might be justification for adding a new role. However, if the actual knowledge requirements are more for security than biometric engineering, then this particular requirement might be better incorporated under the security engineer role. In every case, where the need for an additional role is indicated, it is important to first determine whether the competencies that make up that role might actually fit under an existing role.

# Chapter Summary

- The EBK is a rational framework containing the basic elements of information security.

- The EBK maintains the elements of security in their logical relationship to each other.

- The EBK is easy to modify because it is possible to add roles and competencies that fit within the logical structure of the model.

- The EBK framework is an adaptable model intended to guide implementation of a practical security system through its role and competency definitions.

- The concept behind the relationships built into the EBK framework was developed through extensive study and expert advice.

- The EBK contains 14 competency areas that create a baseline for a secure organization.

- Each of the competencies can be mapped into 10 security roles.

- The roles and competencies can be applied to a practical setting by using the EBK framework as the point of reference.

- Existing organizational job titles have to be mapped to the EBK role definitions in order to implement the model.

- The common functions of the EBK allow an organization to specify the precise management, design, implementation, and evaluation requirements for each role.

- The framework is expected to be expanded by the addition of appropriate new roles or competencies to fit the particular situation of the organization.

- The EBK framework is operationalized by assigning technical and managerial controls to accomplish the intents of its activity recommendations for each role.

# Key Terms

**Best practice** The commonly accepted best way to perform a task.

**Completeness** A state in which all necessary criteria and requirements have been satisfied. In the case of the EBK, it refers to the mapping requirements for competencies.

**Design functions** In the EBK, these relate to the design of security related functionality; these can be technical, architectural, or work process related.

**EBK framework** The overall conceptual model for the EBK.

**Evaluate functions** In the EBK, these are equivalent to an internal audit of security functionality to assess the effectiveness of policies, procedures, programs, or controls in achieving security objectives.

**Implement functions** In the EBK, these involve tasks associated with the implementation of operational security measures, including programs, policies, and procedures.

**Manage functions** In the EBK, these are management activities such as overseeing technical and operational work from the highest levels. These functions ensure security system currency with the changing risk and threat environments.

**Mapping** Making an explicit and documented connection between two entities.

**Terminology** The terms used for a given purpose by a particular field, or in a specific context.

# Questions from the CIO

The CIO requires you to brief her on the current status of your investigation. This will be an important part of your continuing work on this project since it is essential to be able to summarize what the organization has learned in its continuing attempts to improve itself. Consequently, the CIO would like you to answer the following questions for her:

1. The EBK was designed as a model of the knowledge required to do training and education. What in its structure makes it also applicable to creating and evolving security systems?

2. What three things does any model for security have to ensure? Specifically, why these three and what is the overall outcome if these three conditions are all met?

3. Why is coordination so important to security? What exactly has to be coordinated and how should that be done?

4. What is the relationship between a role and a competency? How do roles facilitate the development and implementation of specific practices for any organization?

5. What benefit does the specification of competencies by common function represent? How will that make the resultant security system more effective? What would the situation be if the competencies for a role were not specified by common function?

6. What exactly is completeness and why is it important to security? How do you know whether you have achieved completeness? What is the role of traceability in that process?

7. Tailoring seems like an expensive step. Why do the recommendations of the EBK have to be tailored? What would be the outcome if tailoring weren't done?

8. Why is it necessary to add entire roles and competencies to the basic EBK model? What would necessitate the addition of a role and competencies and how should that be done? What part does the base model play in the process?

9. What are institutional specific additions? Why would they be necessary in order to ensure a coordinated security response? Is there a process that would allow unique, or location-specific, practices to be conducted in a way that would continue to ensure systematic security?

10. What specific benefits does the EBK provide to any organization? Why are those particular benefits important to the overall organization? Specifically, what is it about the EBK that makes it particularly useful as an implementation model for information security?

# Hands-On Projects

**HANDS-ON PROJECTS**

Using the EBK, map the security jobs from an organization that you select (it could be where you work or where you go to school) to the generic roles itemized in the EBK. Ensure that you have:

- Identified all relevant job titles within your organization
- Accounted for each of these under a given generic role, and then see how complete your mapping is. Are there any job titles that do not have equivalent roles? Are there roles where job titles could not be assigned?

# chapter 3

# Adapting Best Practice:
# Tailoring a Solution That Fits

## The Story Changes Venues: The Road to Singapore

*The architect got off the plane at Changi airport on a day that was unusually hot and humid, even for Singapore. The flight from Los Angeles had been a 20-hour nightmare. His main interest at that point was a shower, a cold beer, and some sleep, in that approximate order. The last thing he wanted to see was the little sign with his name on it, since that meant he was going to work, not to bed. The data center was located near the National University of Singapore, which was on the other side of the island from Changi. As the architect's limo ghosted its way along the East Coast Parkway past the shiny skyscrapers of the new city, he had some time to think about the challenge that he had just created for himself.*

*He had known from the beginning that getting his rather ambitious plan off the ground was going to be a problem. Being the highly motivated fellow that he was, he had thought that he could just power through it with hard work and a good eye for detail. The procedure manual that he and his team had created from the EBK was indeed a masterpiece of specification. Nonetheless, he now recognized that the success of his manual rested on one faulty assumption, which was that procedure was a universal thing.*

*Both he and his staff had just assumed that a practice that was applicable in one culture could always be applied in exactly the same way everywhere else. What they found instead was that the actual execution of any practice was always in the eye of the beholder. And since everybody has different views about the right way to do something, simply providing a list of practices without tailoring the requisite behavior to those differences was going to represent an exercise in "close-but-not-close-enough."*

*That fact should have been obvious from the beginning. People see and do things differently, because their own unique experiences and the influence of their environment shape their behavior. And since the way that people understand a task will dictate how they perform it, it is inevitable that most routine tasks will be executed differently between individuals and sometimes by each person. Unfortunately, without the ability to ensure the consistent execution of a process, there is no way that any given outcome can be guaranteed. Lack of consistency would not be a problem if real-world security didn't require predictable outcomes that rested on the disciplined execution of the steps of the process. It was that lack of discipline that was killing the architect's well-designed plans.*

*As his car slid across the Singapore River, past Raffles and the other vestiges of colonial Britain, the architect came to a resolution. He decided that fitting the company's new, standard, security procedures to the specific context of each site constituted the key to his success. So from that point on, his trip was going to be dedicated to creating and then validating a standard process that could ensure that the practices contained in the company procedure manual could be effectively adapted to the unique situation of each individual site. As a starting point he decided that he would have to get out on the table all of the underlying assumptions that each participant at the Singapore site had about the purpose and outcomes of each of the practices in the manual.*

*The architect believed that the single key ingredient in understanding and adapting practices was to get every implicit assumption clarified. He knew that the problem he was having with implementing consistent, standard operating procedures revolved around the fact that the people responsible for executing those procedures brought their own assumptions to the party. The architect was also astute enough to realize that the presence of a diverse range of assumptions was going to make the outcome of any standard processes unpredictable. As the person responsible for ensuring consistent security, the last thing he wanted was everybody going off in different directions based on their personal assumptions.*

*The architect decided that besides the specification of the practices themselves, he was going to have to devise a process to adapt the generic security practices in the company procedure manual to the specific environment in which the security system was operating. The fact that the practices were derived directly from the security manual guaranteed that they would fit the requirements of best practice, while the adaptation would ensure that those practices would be both understandable as well as acceptable to the people who were responsible for executing them. In simple terms, the architect knew that he would have to identify all of the factors that might potentially influence how a practice was performed and then factor them into the process of implementing the substantive security procedures for that site. Consequently, the architect decided that his aim in Singapore would be to find out exactly how easy it would be to adapt the standard practices in the procedure manual to fit the cultural norms and perspectives of the Singapore data center.*

*His take-away from that effort would be a standard tailoring process that would serve as a basis for effectively adapting the generic recommendations of the company's procedure manual to all of the other sites. The problem was that he and his team had translated the security concepts in the EBK into a set of company-wide best practices. However, those practices had produced inconsistent and fundamentally unacceptable results as soon as the company had tried to put them into use outside the culture of its east coast operations. Singapore was the biggest fire at the moment, but other fires were burning brightly, from the high-assurance computing operations in Belfast to the high-dollar day trading operation in Sydney. There were also serious problems brewing in the company's advanced manufacturing facility in Oregon, and since it was one of the company's "crown jewels," he knew that that site would be his next stop after Singapore.*

*As the car worked its way along the old West Coast road, the architect watched the high-tech buildings that were Singapore's future slide by on the right; at the same time, he noted the teeming docks that represented its maritime past on his left. He wondered how long it had been since he had seen so much contrast in cultures in one small place. In the architect's mind, the montage of the docks next to the silent modern buildings on the National University campus perfectly represented his problem of reconciling cultures. That led him to note that he had his work cut out for him if he wanted to maintain his new-found status as the guy who gets picked up at the airport by limousine. He had three weeks to develop a standard approach that would tailor an explicit and capable set of work instructions that everybody in the building, which was slowly materializing outside the limo's front window, could reliably execute.*

*He rubbed his hands on his face, partly to push away fatigue and partly to erase the memory of his most recent video conference with the people in Singapore. The meeting, while professional, also revealed serious communication problems between his U.S.-based group and the Singapore team. He had noted, with some concern, the Singapore director's defensive manner and speech during the entire conference. Everybody could tell that all was not well within that installation, and his manual—rather than helping the people on the Singapore team be more secure—was actually contributing to stress and depleting valuable energy and time. As he stepped out of the oppressive heat and into his company's cool, modern, high-tech environment, he set his mind to one task—creating a process that would ensure that a range of behaviors, as opposed to only one behavior, could be used to satisfy the specific purpose of each EBK-based standard operating procedure.*

*It had been six years since he had last been in Singapore. But even with his rusty recollections, he knew that the generic security practices in his procedure manual would have a long way to go to fit the norms of the hot, humid, and alien environment he was stepping out into. He made up his mind that his new organization-wide process would easily and without undue stress translate generic corporate procedure into practices that were workable for a given operation. It was particularly critical to solve the problem here in Singapore, because the data center was beginning to run into integrity problems and customers were taking notice. The Singapore data center was a multimillion dollar operation. Yet in the past three months, it had experienced four serious attacks. It was only through sheer luck that one of those had not made the Straits Times. The architect knew that they might not be so lucky if another attack occurred.*

# Walking the Talk

The EBK contains a comprehensive digest of generic security activities. As the architect soon discovered, that comprehensiveness can represent both an advantage and a real disadvantage. The advantage of such a broad range of generic practices is that companies whose personnel have been rigorously trained in them can be confident that they have instituted effective best practices down to the level of the individual employee. In addition, because each practice exists within a coherent conceptual framework, the company can also be reasonably certain that all of the practices that are derived from it will be properly coordinated.

The disadvantage of such a wide-ranging set of practices rests with the need to document them at the right level of detail. From a usability standpoint, in order to make the EBK generally applicable, the purpose and intent of each of those practices has to be specified at a fairly high level of generic description. As a result, in order to put the contents of the EBK into practice, its recommendations have to be clarified down to a level of practical application that the people responsible for executing those recommendations can understand. In practical terms, each generic recommendation has to be translated into substantive work instruction, which specifies the precise behaviors needed to achieve a given purpose. In addition, these behaviors have to fit the mind-set of the individuals who are accountable for their performance, in order for those individuals to execute them in a way that achieves their intended aims. Because the situation or context will vary from site to site, it is to be expected that the behaviors that are specified to achieve the same generic outcome will look different from one site to the next.

The problem of cultural variability has to be resolved if the recommendations of the EBK are ever going to be put into practice. Logically, the best way to assure a predictable outcome is to establish a single approach that will ensure that any action taken to achieve a given purpose will actually accomplish, and continue to accomplish, the intended outcome. In essence, a common, organization-wide oversight and coordinating function has to be established in order to ensure that any set of standard operating instructions, which are designed to achieve a given purpose, will reliably achieve that particular purpose. That requirement is shown in Figure 3-1.

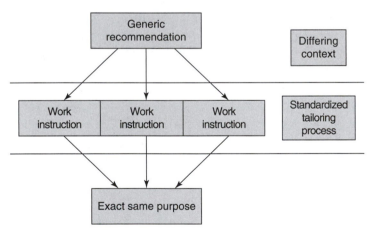

**Figure 3-1** Application of a standardized tailoring process to produce the same outcome

© Cengage Learning 2012

The aim of such a universal coordination and control process is to ensure that an appropriate set of work instructions is created and maintained traceable to the generic purposes that they are meant to implement. This coordination and control process must maintain the traceability between each individual work instruction and the purposes of the generic recommendation it implements. Work instructions are expressed at a much greater level of detail than the procedures they implement. It is those work instructions that give the implementation process the required flexibility. Essentially, work instructions are developed that can reasonably achieve the general purposes of a given procedure in that particular instance. As long as the work instructions achieve a given purpose they are correct, no matter how different they might be from one instance of application to another. This is illustrated in Figure 3-2:

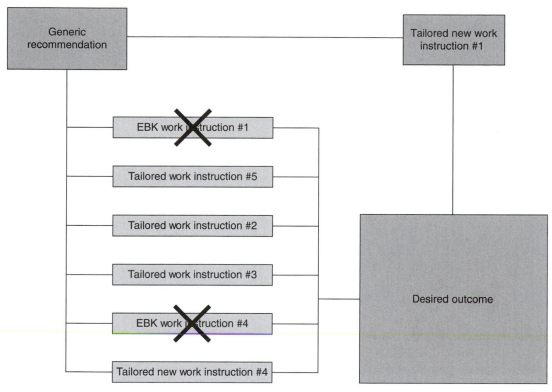

**Figure 3-2** Generating practical work instructions from generic recommendations

The effectiveness of the work instruction has to able to be assessed in order to ensure its consistently effective performance. As a result, a substantive set of criteria for evaluation has to be provided with each work instruction. Those criteria have to produce evaluation data that can be observed and recorded. They must also allow managers to judge, by direct observation, whether the actions of the work instruction continue to satisfy the purpose for which it was written. Each work instruction should be documented by describing:

1. The behaviors required
2. How each behavior will satisfy the purpose it is referenced to
3. The observable outcomes that can be used to evaluate performance
4. The interrelationships with other work instructions that underlie the generic purpose

For example, if there were frequent physical security breaches, documentation at this level would itemize the precise steps that would to be taken to correct this problem, such as visitor accompaniment, or gates and guards. The evaluation outcomes would also describe the empirical means that would be used to tell whether the recommended steps were successful, such as "no unaccompanied visitors," or "all people seeking access are processed at the gate." Finally, if there are other related work instructions, such as "all visitors must sign in for accompaniment," or "all entrants at the gate must be on the access list," the mechanism for coordinating the linkages between the two related work instructions would also be specified.

---

# The Story Progresses: A New Day in Singapore

*It was not hard to get agreement from the local site managers to undertake the tailoring process, as there had already been several disturbing incidents that could have resulted in a minor loss of data. Since the CIO had made it clear that any reports of a loss would be a firing offence, local management was committed to never having to make that report. The Singapore data center handled most of the processing for the company's Far East operations, and the five different cultures, ranging from Australian to Chinese, made the work relationships in that center decidedly complex. It was clear that some "outside the box" thinking was going to be required in order to ensure that the intended outcomes specified in the procedure manual were understood and implemented in practice.*

*The architect had made it clear that his new strategy was going to be to satisfy the intended outcomes of the practices contained in the manual, rather than execute its contents in a rote fashion. So the first tactical judgment that the Singapore team made was to throw out the set of work instructions that had been developed for the stateside operation. Those instructions were probably appropriate for people living on the east coast of the United States, but the local team felt that none of those instructions were useful in Singapore. As a general strategy, the team decided to test the architect's theory that a set of local work instructions could be written that would satisfy the exact same purpose and intent as the stateside recommendations, but they would be tailored directly to the Singapore data center's operating environment. Since the outcomes in the manual were derived directly from the EBK, everybody involved in the process had bought into the idea that all the work instructions from the company's procedure manual could be adapted to fit the realities of the Singapore data center.*

*Because time was short, rather than make the lengthy and resource-consuming commitment to develop work instructions for the entire operation, they decided to use the EBK to customize a standard set of work instructions for a sample of the local job titles at the Singapore data center. These job titles were already mapped to the company's standard security roles, competencies, and common functions by means of the overall process that was followed to establish the security response there. The issue was going to be to then prove that it was possible to maintain the original purpose and intent of each EBK element while still satisfying the special requirements of the local context.*

*Because ensuring understanding was the chief concern, the first logical step was to identify and inventory all of the company job titles that might be related to EBK roles. The purpose of this step was to identify those people who needed to be interviewed in order to determine their understanding of the specific activities their **role** would be asked to carry out. Identifying the security-related stakeholders required the team to go through the Singapore Data Center's organization chart for that installation and list all current job titles that could conceivably have some fundamental connection to IT security. Given the structure of the EBK's role specifications, which were arranged from executive to corollary, the team worked on the most senior **job title** first. It was assumed that the list of actual job titles that were identified could then be directly compared with the standard roles in the EBK, using the actual work functions performed by each of those job titles as the basis for the comparison. Figure 3-2 illustrates that.*

# Developing Solutions from the EBK

Every individualized security process that is tailored from a set of standard operating procedures will be unique by definition. That is because the tailoring process will always be influenced by three standard considerations, which comprise the general factors that influence the form of any concrete security response. These general factors are context, scope, and feasibility. Context dictates the assumptions and underlying conditions that apply to that specific security setting. Scope is derived from context. It defines what will be protected and what will not, as well as the priority of the protected items. In that respect, scope serves as the basis for the definition of the defense in depth scheme.

Both context and scope have to be explicitly defined before any consideration can be given to the form of the security countermeasures. Once the process of generally defining those countermeasures has begun, the first consideration has to be whether they are economically and technically feasible. The fine tuning that must take place in order to strike a feasible balance between the implementation of the measure and the economic, technical, and social realities of the situation, is what ensures that every **security solution** will be unique.

## Context

The first factor that has to be understood and explicitly dealt with is overall context. It is vital to gain a complete and detailed understanding of the environment that the security system will operate in prior to its detailed design. Since the security system has to interface with its surroundings, the solution has to be fitted to the requirements of those surroundings, not the other way around. The security system functions day-to-day within the relevant social, economic, and technical variables of the context. Therefore, the first step in the implementation process has to be to discover what operating variables might affect that functioning. For instance, a rigorous system of controls that is best suited to a high-security context would most likely be counterproductive if it were imposed on a typically low-tech manufacturing context. The opposite would also be true. Thus, for the sake of ensuring an effective fit between the security system and its setting, it is necessary to identify and document all of the factors that constitute that setting.

Context is a critical first step in tailoring. That requirement is often overlooked because the participants in the planning are likely to assume that all of the other members of the organization have the same motivation and commitment to security that they do. Consequently, during the process of developing that security response, these implicit, and often incorrect, assumptions may never be made explicit. The result is that important behavioral considerations, which could have a critical impact on the success or failure of the overall security system, might never be identified or factored into the eventual set of required security practices.

A simple example of that might be a solution that requires extremely complex passwords, which would better ensure security, but which would be extremely aggravating to the individual user because they would be difficult to remember. The inevitable consequence of hard-to-remember passwords in conventional businesses would be that individual users would write them down and leave them in handy places, simply because they needed the memory boost. Of course, leaving a written record of a password in an easily accessible place also defeats the intent of a strong password system. These kinds of behavioral factors should be considered in the design of any security system.

## Scope

The next step involves the specific actions that are taken to establish the security perimeter. It is important to define clearly where the security scheme will apply, because whatever countermeasures that will be deployed will demand resources. The greater the extent of the protected space, the greater the resource requirements. Documenting the scope of the protected space involves clarifying such practical issues as detailing the specific aspects of the operation that will be secured, who should be responsible for carrying out each of the security functions within the protection scheme, what reporting lines will be followed, and who will eventually be accountable for the overall success of the process.

The detailed definition of the organizational boundaries of protected space is an essential step in the proper management of the system which will eventually be implemented. Because the decisions about what will reside in the protected space can be political as much as they are rational, that definition has to be the result of a formal organizational process. That process should be supported by and referenced to any relevant, commonly accepted authorities such as standards, regulations, or even internal policies. Moreover, in order to ensure that the currently defined scope continues to remain effective, an appropriate set of measures to assess and judge the performance security system should also be provided.

Even though this part of the process sounds more like a conceptual exercise than a concrete activity, unique and meaningful boundaries have to be established for each processing, communications, storage, and information resource component that will have to be protected, and those inter-relationships have to be made explicit. A thorough and precise mapping of the protected items in secured space is required, because it ensures that all of the relevant functions necessary for security are actually being carried out.

In practice, there is rarely a one-to-one match between the specifications of the generic activities, which a document like the EBK provides, and the actual work responsibilities that might fall under a given job title in the real world. So the overall aim of the process should be to determine whether all of the generic security requirements, which have been derived from the EBK, have been satisfied by real-world behaviors. The amount of documentation required to ensure the relationship between an ideal **model** and the realities of its implementation is extensive.

## Availability of Resources

Once all required components have been identified, it is then necessary to estimate whether what has been proposed can be implemented within the real-world resources that the organization has allocated for that solution. A lot of security systems fail because they are not feasible within the resources available to execute them, or are just technically infeasible. Consequently, the viability of the solution within resource constraints has to be confirmed. That requires the company to estimate all of the resources required in order to both establish as well as maintain the desired level of security. It also requires planners to look at how the technology is progressing, in order to ensure that whatever technologies will be required in the future will be available.

# The Singapore Team: Turning Concepts into Practice

*The team had already made the decision not to do a total mapping of the Singapore operation. Instead, it decided to test its theories by trying them out in a few areas of the company. The architect had developed the hypothesis that the team at each site could ensure the same result using a different set of work instructions. His aim was to prove that hypothesis by mapping out the actions of an important EBK role. As a first cut, he chose to define the specific actions of the chief information security officer (CISO) role for the Singapore site. This role was chosen because of its key position in the information security hierarchy. It was also felt that a comparison of standard CISO actions from site to site might be informative.*

*The second example that he selected was the **software development** professional title. This title was chosen because it constituted the bulk of the IT staff at the Singapore center. The problem was that none of the generic roles in the EBK could be equated directly to that specific job title. Instead, software development professionals at the Singapore site held titles like software development analyst, and database administrator. Moreover, their primary responsibility was not to security. Nonetheless, because of the functions that they performed, software development professionals were important, since they represented the front line in the battle to ensure the security of the operation. Thus, it was important to find out whether the EBK security competencies could be embedded in some formal fashion into the job definitions of the various software development functions at that installation.*

*In effect, trying to equate a necessary role at that particular facility to an EBK generic role reversed the mapping process. It required the team to fit the security behaviors that were itemized in the architect's policy and procedure manual to an existing set of work functions at that particular site. However, if the tailoring process was going to be of any practical use, a means had to be found to specify an applicable set of security actions for all of the existing roles in the data center. Many of the complaints about the procedure manual had their basis in the architect's overt attempt to hammer the facility's existing roles into new and unfamiliar organizational shapes. However, if the new approach worked, the organization would be able to keep its conventional operational roles while still following new and more effective security practices.*

*Another advantage of selecting those two positions was that they provided insight into the workings of the two most important role categories in the EBK: executive and functional. Besides constituting the bulk of the 10 roles defined by the EBK, these are the categories responsible for the management and execution of the IT security function. As such, if it were possible to demonstrate that the security procedures recommended for these two categories could be successfully mapped, it would imply that it was possible to prepare a specification of standard operating procedure that would be applicable to the Singapore site while remaining compatible with the procedures developed for the stateside operation.*

*The team decided to start with the CISO. This role is termed Information Security Officer (ISO) in the EBK. In effect, the CISO role is a straightforward mapping from the EBK to a single job title. The software development professional mapping was going to require a bit more work, as the standard work functions associated with people who did that work were not as clearly associated with the standard role definitions listed in the EBK. Consequently, the mapping of the actual work functions performed at the site to the security practice specifications of the EBK was going to take considerable background research.*

# The Chief Information Security Officer

The CISO role is an upper management position with wide ranging responsibilities associated with the overall information security positioning of an organization. In simple terms, the **CISO function** can be seen as providing the leadership for the entire information security operation within an organization. A detailed set of work practices can be derived directly from the EBK for that role by simply following these standard steps:

1. First, the organization has to relate one, or several, of its actual job titles to the EBK role. In most organizations, the comparable job title for the CISO will also be chief information security officer. Nonetheless, in all cases there will typically be a person, or persons, who are responsible for the work functions that the EBK associates with the CISO role. Given the likely presence of such an individual, that person, or those persons, must be formally identified. Then the organization has to document the standard activities and practices that are performed in the CISO function, as well as any organizationally sanctioned criteria for judging performance.

2. Once the appropriate job titles are identified, their competency requirements have to be inventoried and listed for comparison with the recommended competency requirements of the EBK. The organization uses Section 4 of the EBK to develop the list of required competencies for any given role. Those required competencies are further classified by each EBK **functional perspective** (manage, design, implement, and evaluate). The detailed information from Section 2 of the EBK is then used to document the specific work function requirements for each of those competencies. This documentation is also organized by functional perspective.

3. The organization then compares the practices in its current operation with the recommendations of the EBK. At this point, there should be two sets of functions: the ones currently practiced by the organization and the activities that the EBK recommends *should* be practiced. The aim is to identify gaps or work functions that are not in proper alignment with each other. The organization can then use that comparison to adjust how it actually performs that role. The aim is to modify the organization's current practices in such a way as to ensure that the execution of the CISO function is as closely aligned as possible to the best practice recommendations of the EBK.

4. Finally, once the current job's practices are properly aligned with the EBK's recommendations, it is possible to draft a new set of standard operating procedures for the CISO role. These procedures provide a detailed specification of the practices and accountabilities for the tailored CISO role as it will exist within the organization. It takes into consideration all of the cultural and environmental factors that might influence those practices and accountabilities. Since those standard operating procedures operationalize a set of practices that were derived directly from the recommendations of the EBK, it can be assumed that the harmonized version of these two represents the best current practice possible for that role.

# Tailored Operating Procedures for the CISO Role

The generic set of activities for the CISO role are specified in Section 4 of the EBK. These activities are listed by competency area and functional perspective in the table below:

| Competency | Required functional perspective |
|---|---|
| Data security | Manage, design, evaluate |
| Digital forensics | Manage, design |
| Enterprise continuity | Manage, evaluate |
| Incident management | Manage, design, evaluate |
| IT security training and awareness | Manage, evaluate |
| Personnel security | Manage |
| Physical and environmental security | Manage, evaluate |
| Procurement | Manage, design, evaluate |
| Regulatory and standards compliance | Manage, design, evaluate |
| Security risk management | Manage, design, evaluate |
| Strategic security management | Manage, design, implement, evaluate |
| System and application security | Manage, evaluate |

Section 2 of the EBK itemizes 14 generic security competency areas that comprise a complete set of competencies associated with IT security work. In effect, the work functions within these competencies represent a standardized set of recommended professional practices for IT security. These work functions are further classified into four functional perspectives: manage, design, implement, and evaluate. The aim of the entire section of the document is to suggest a template of best practices, as they apply to 10 common IT security roles.

That template captures and defines the most appropriate best practice responsibilities for each specific role. Both the role and the competency specification were developed at a very high level by DHS, in order to establish a generic set of recommendations for IT security professionals as a whole. In order to apply these competencies, they have to be tailored into explicit work instructions. This section provides an example of a tailoring process and its outcomes, and it presents an example of how generic recommendations can be tailored to fit a given situation.

The first example involves a relatively easy transition from a role that is specified in the EBK to a single job title that would be likely to exist within the given situation. That is the role of the site's ISO. The work functions for the ISO role are specified in Section 2 of the EBK, which defines the following generic responsibilities for the data security competency, for the ISO:

Data security (manage)

- Ensure that data classification and data management policies and guidance are issued and updated
- Specify policy and coordinate review and approval
- Ensure compliance with data security policies and relevant legal and regulatory requirements
- Ensure appropriate changes and improvement actions are implemented as required

Data security (design)

- Develop data security policies using data security standards, guidelines, and requirements that include privacy, access, retention, disposal, incident management, disaster recovery, and configuration
- Identify and document the appropriate level of protection for data
- Specify data and information classification, sensitivity, and need-to-know requirements by information type
- Create authentication and authorization system for users to gain access to data by assigned privileges and permissions
- Develop acceptable use procedures in support of the data security policy
- Develop sensitive data collection and management procedures in accordance with standards, procedures, directives, policies, regulations, and laws (statutes)
- Identify an appropriate set of information security controls based on the perceived risk of compromise to the data
- Develop security-testing procedures

Data security (evaluate)

- Assess the effectiveness of enterprise data security policies, processes, and procedures against established standards, guidelines, and requirements, and suggest changes where appropriate
- Evaluate the effectiveness of solutions implemented to provide the required protection of data
- Review alleged violations of data security and privacy breaches and identify improvement actions required to maintain the appropriate level of data protection

# Wrapping Up in Singapore: Tailoring the CISO Role

*The architect had been in Singapore for a month and he could not see himself ever adjusting to the climate or, in all honesty, the culture there. Being put up for all of that time at a place like the Raffles Hotel should have brought out the colonial planter in him, but he hated Singapore Slings, and the strange dissonance between place names that were faintly reminiscent of an English village and the frantic and explicitly alien atmosphere of the queen city of the Pacific Rim was driving him nuts. He was in a big hurry. He concluded that the team's decision to write a set of work instructions for the ISO role was going to work and pay big dividends when it did. Moreover, the Singapore team's efforts were giving them a much better feel for how to conduct the process of tailoring the actual substantive work instructions for that site. More importantly, it was beginning to become clear that that tailoring process could be consistently applied across the entire organization. One unintended and frankly unexpected outcome emerged which might be more beneficial in the long run. The architect was also getting a much better understanding of the politics of the tailoring process itself.*

*The first question that team members had to answer when they started the tailoring process was, "What actual job title fits the ISO role?" It was immediately obvious that the analogous title for the ISO role at the Singapore data center was CISO. The overall accountabilities were the same for both the EBK role definition and the actual job title, and they both served the same general purpose. Moreover, the CISO at the Singapore data center was the single individual accountable for the management, design, and evaluation of the overall data security process, which made it much easier to assign the generic requirements of the EBK's ISO role to that job title.*

*Nevertheless, the deadline was fast approaching to make a decision about whether it was even possible to tailor out separate work instructions that achieved the same purpose. Moreover, the architect was getting tired of his diet of Singapore noodles and Tiger beer. So for the sake of meeting that deadline, rather than attempting to specify all of the requisite competencies and perspectives for the entire role, the architect decided to just tailor a model set of requirements for the data security competency for the ISO position. That particular competency was chosen because it was felt that in many ways, data security constituted the primary responsibility of the CISO at the Singapore data center, and data security was where they had been having their problems.*

# Example: Model EBK-Based Procedures for Two Positions

The essence of good tailoring lies in the organization's ability to integrate a complex set of activities into a single, standard set of actions to accomplish a well-established and well-known purpose. In order to do this, the recommendations of the EBK have to be tailored through two stages. First, the extremely generic practices of the model itself have to be turned into practical policies and procedures that can serve as a coherent management framework. Then those high-level policies and procedures have to be adapted to the specific perceptions and environmental factors of a particular place where they are to be applied.

In some instances that adaptation process might not represent much change. In situations where cultural norms are widely divergent, the eventual practices required might be much different from the way the work is conventionally done. In every case, however, it is essential that the intents and purposes of each EBK recommendation be fulfilled by an appropriate set of explicit work instructions.

The chief litmus test for whether a tailoring, or adaptation, has been effective is the simple determination whether whatever has been specified in terms of practices achieves the intended outcomes of the recommendation and is consistently executed by the people in that role.

What follows is an example of the tailoring process for a set of practices that are based on the generic recommendations of the EBK. In real life these sample specifications would be drilled down to a point where the conditions of their performance would be both explicit and clearly understood. In this example, the following set of work instructions might be specified for the CISO role:

*Generic instruction* – Ensure that data classification and data management policies and guidance are issued and updated. The CISO will be specifically accountable to:

1. Specify, coordinate, and review all of the policies that govern the identification and labeling of all of the data in the organization; this will be documented in a policy and procedure manual that will be updated annually.

2. Ensure that all data classification policies are defined and documented where relevant within that plan; this will be documented in the strategic plan, which will be updated annually.

3. Ensure that all of the guidelines for implementing those policies are documented and maintained; guidelines will be published annually in the form of a policy and procedure manual.

4. Ensure that all policies are kept current; this will be done by means of a review team formulated from representatives of all five sectors served by the data center and chaired by the CISO. Meetings will be held on a no less than monthly basis.

*Generic instruction* – Specify policy and coordinate review and approval. The CISO will be expressly accountable to:

1. Develop a comprehensive governance infrastructure; this infrastructure will be developed through a strategic planning exercise involving all five sectors served by the data center and chaired by the CISO. Establishment of the infrastructure will be the first priority of the process.

2. Develop governance mechanisms to coordinate all data security functions; this mechanism will be facilitated through coordinator roles at all five sectors served by the data center and overseen by the CISO. The delegated coordinators will be reviewed quarterly for performance.

3. Ensure that all relevant data management policies are defined and documented in the governance infrastructure for each site; this will be facilitated by the site coordinator role. Policies will be reviewed annually for understandability and relevance.

*Generic instruction* – Ensure compliance with data security policies and relevant legal and regulatory requirements. The CISO will be expressly accountable to:

1. Enforce compliance with all data security policies and relevant legal and regulatory requirements; enforcement will be supported by internal audit. The CISO will be the ultimate decision maker.

*Generic instruction* – Ensure appropriate changes and improvement actions are implemented as required. The CISO will:

1. Formulate and chair a committee that will hold monthly reviews of data security policies and procedures in order to certify that these policies and procedures conform with common organizational standards for configuration management.

*Generic instruction* – Develop data security policies using data security standards, guidelines, and requirements that include privacy, access, retention, disposal, incident management, disaster recovery, and configuration. The CISO will be specifically accountable for ensuring that data security policies and procedures:

1. Conform to organizational standards for data privacy; this will be ensured by monthly review against the relevant standards, which will be carried out by the data security group composed of representatives of all five sectors served by the data center.

2. Conform to organizational standards for controlled access; this will be ensured by monthly review against the relevant standards, which will be carried out by the data security group composed of representatives of all five sectors served by the data center.

3. Conform to organizational standards for secure retention and disposal; this will be ensured by monthly review against the relevant standards, which will be carried out by the data security group composed of representatives of all five sectors served by the data center.

4. Conform to organizational standards for incident management and disaster recovery; this will be ensured by monthly review against the relevant standards, which will be carried out by the data security group composed of representatives of all five sectors served by the data center.

5. Conform to the acceptable use policies for each of these areas; this will be ensured by monthly review of all relevant acceptable use policies, which will be carried out by the data security group composed of representatives of all five sectors served by the data center.

*Generic instruction* – Identify and document the appropriate level of protection for data. The CISO in conjunction with the CIO will be specifically accountable for:

1. The identification, coordination, and evaluation of the annual protection needs for every item of data in the organizational inventory; this will be supported by the data security advisory group under the oversight of the CISO.

2. Development of a governance and control model based on perceived risks to the data; this will be supported by the data security advisory group under the oversight of the CISO and reviewed annually.

*Generic instruction* – Specify data and information classification, sensitivity, and need-to-know requirements by information type. The CISO will be accountable to:

1. Specify the data classification, sensitivity, and need-to-know requirements for each information type in the inventory; this will be supported by the data security advisory group under the oversight of the CISO.

2. Establish and maintain a security testing process to ensure that all classification, sensitivity, and need-to know requirements are being met; this will be supported by the data security advisory group under the oversight of the CISO.

*Generic instruction* – Create authentication and authorization system for users to gain access to data by assigned privileges and permissions. The CISO will be specifically responsible for the process of:

1.  Creating and maintaining an authentication and authorization system; this will be used to ensure access. The actual account management will be done by the data security group under the supervision of the CISO.

2.  Assigning privileges to each user; the actual account management will be done by the data security group under the supervision of the CISO.

3.  Ensuring that the proper privileges have been assigned to each user; the actual account management will be done by the data security group under the supervision of the CISO.

*Generic instruction* – Develop sensitive data collection and management procedures in accordance with standards, procedures, directives, policies, regulations, and laws (statutes). The CISO will be specifically accountable to:

1.  Develop, manage, and maintain a process that will ensure that the collection and retention of sensitive data complies with applicable standards, procedures, directives, policies, regulations, and laws; this will be done by the data security advisory group under the supervision of the CISO.

2.  Assess the effectiveness of security policies and procedures through continuous operational testing; this will be done by the data security advisory group under the supervision of the CISO.

3.  Develop and implement changes to policies, where appropriate; these changes will be executed by the data security advisory group under the supervision of the CISO.

*Generic instruction* – Develop security-testing procedures. The CISO will be specifically accountable to:

1.  Assess the type and source of all breaches; this assessment will be done by the data security advisory group under the supervision of the CISO.

*Generic instruction* – Evaluate the effectiveness of solutions implemented to provide the required protection of data. The CISO will be expressly accountable to:

1.  Evaluate the operational performance of security controls throughout all sites to ensure that they comply with all security policies and plans; this will be executed by the coordinator at each site, through the oversight of the data security committee and under the supervision of the CISO.

*Generic instruction* – Review alleged violations of data security and privacy breaches and identify improvement actions required to maintain the appropriate level of data protection. The CISO will be expressly accountable to:

1.  Monitor operational processes on a continuous basis in order to ensure the day-to-day functioning of the IT security system and the identification and investigation of all risks; this will be executed by the coordinator at each site, through the oversight of the data security committee and under the supervision of the CISO.

# Another Aspect: Tailoring a Process from Parts of Jobs

In practice, there are likely to be instances where the situation just doesn't fit the recommendations of the EBK. Nonetheless, the principle discussed here still applies. The aim of any tailoring process is to define the set of work instructions that have the greatest chance of accomplishing the purposes of the recommendation. The recommendation provides the point of departure for specifying the right set of work instructions. However, if there is not a single well-defined role in the company responsible for carrying out the work, those work instructions have to be apportioned to existing roles that achieve the same purpose. In many cases, that might involve roles that are not part of the EBK definitions, or it might even involve apportioning the work to a number of related positions that work together to achieve the same common end.

In this example, software development professionals perform a diverse set of activities that can be associated with a number of different job titles within the Singapore data center. However, there is no standard role defined for the software development professional in the EBK. Since this role has significant potential to impact the overall safety and security of the organization, it is important to ensure that the software development professional is guided by a tailored set of standard work practices. That can be done by mapping recommended practices for related EBK roles to that particular job function. This would be perfectly acceptable as long as the intents and purposes of the overall EBK model are achieved.

In their conventional forms, software development professionals can perform a number of traditional tasks, ranging from requirements analyst, program designer, coder, and tester, all the way to documentation specialist. Consequently, unlike the CISO role, there is no obvious fit between this type of work and any one of the specific role definitions of the EBK. However, there are ways that the common knowledge and skills required for software development work can be associated with EBK definitions. This can be done in such a way that a new standard role can be built, even if that role does not have a specific analog among the 10 common EBK roles. Specifically, the generic competency requirements for the EBK's system and application security role can be equated to a range of job functions that are traditionally done by software development professionals.

The actual competencies that are required to ensure secure code are less than perfectly fitted to any specific competency area within the EBK. However, the work functions in the EBK competency for system and application security appear to be aimed at the same general purpose, which is to produce code that cannot be exploited. If the system and application security competency were selected as the base competency area then, the next step in the process would be to identify a common EBK role that could be associated with that competency. Two of the roles in the EBK that appear to have a significant number of work functions, which fall within the system and application security competency, are the operations and maintenance professional and the IT security engineer roles. Given the purpose of ensuring secure software, an association between systems and application security and the company's operations and maintenance and security engineering professionals makes good intuitive sense, so these two will be used to illustrate the mapping process.

From Section 4 of the EBK, the IT systems operations and maintenance professional (SOMP) and the IT security engineer (SE) roles map to the system and application security competency in the following way:

- Operations and maintenance professional/system and application security: *implement*
- IT security engineer/system and application security: *design, implement, evaluate*

Because of the composite nature of the mapping, which combines two roles, it is important to examine and extract the relevant work functions from the two areas. Thus, the integrated set of standard work functions for this example would be:

EBK Section 2.1.2 Design

- Develop data security policies using data security standards, guidelines, and requirements that include privacy, access, retention, disposal, incident management, disaster recovery, and configuration
- Identify and document the appropriate level of protection for data
- Specify data and information classification, sensitivity, and need-to-know requirements by information type
- Create authentication and authorization system for users to gain access to data by assigned privileges and permissions
- Develop acceptable use procedures in support of the data security policy
- Develop sensitive data collection and management procedures in accordance with standards, procedures, directives, policies, regulations, and laws (statutes)
- Identify an appropriate set of information security controls based on the perceived risk of compromise to the data
- Develop security-testing procedures

EBK Section 2.1.3 Implement

- Perform the data access management process according to established guidelines
- Apply and verify data security access controls, privileges, and associated profiles
- Implement media control procedures, and continuously monitor for compliance
- Implement and verify data security access controls, and assign privileges
- Address alleged violations of data security and privacy breaches
- Apply and maintain confidentiality controls and processes in accordance with standards, procedures, directives, policies, regulations, and laws (statutes)

EBK Section 2.1.4 Evaluate

- Assess the effectiveness of enterprise data security policies, processes, and procedures against established standards, guidelines, and requirements, and suggest changes where appropriate
- Evaluate the effectiveness of solutions implemented to provide the required protection of data

- Review alleged violations of data security and privacy breaches
- Identify improvement actions required to maintain the appropriate level of data protection

---

# Defining Requirements for a Non-EBK Role

*The architect literally had his bags packed when he got the news that there were a few "wild cards" among the necessary roles at the data center. Chief among those were the software developers, both application programmers, and also the maintenance grunts. The architect was not happy to postpone his departure, but because his idea of tailoring the work to the intention of the EBK recommendation had seemed to work for all of the currently existing job titles, he thought that this new wrinkle would not mean an extended stay. To his surprise, he found that for a change he might have actually over estimated the amount of work required.*

*He called the tailoring team together in the first floor conference room at the data center. Even though it was the largest room and it had the biggest table, the department heads for IT still crowded the space. The architect's first observation on entering was that there were certainly a lot of people doing IT work at that facility—maybe too many. Because this part of the tailoring was going to require input from everybody, he quickly got down to the business of securing everybody's agreement to participate. That participation was necessary because a lot of analytic work would have to be done in order to ensure that the mapping of recommended activities to roles was accurate. He knew the EBK role and competency recommendations by heart, so he knew that the first step would be to weed out the recommendations from both competencies that did not apply to software development work.*

*The architect quickly discovered that like a lot of other systems analysis processes, this was done iteratively. The problem was that it was often hard to tell at first glance what the intended outcome of the recommendation was until some of the actual work instructions had been specified. For the purposes of practical implementation, the aim was to decide on the smallest number of competency elements that could be responsibly included in the final definition of the software professional role. The sections that follow are examples of work functions from the two roles that the team felt did not apply to the EBK.*

*Design elements that were eliminated:*

- *Develop data security policies using data security standards, guidelines, and requirements that include privacy, access, retention, disposal, incident management, disaster recovery, and configuration*
- *Develop acceptable use procedures in support of the data security policy*
- *Develop sensitive data collection and management procedures in accordance with standards, procedures, directives, policies, regulations, and laws (statutes)*

*Implementation items that were eliminated:*

- *Address alleged violations of data security and privacy breaches*
- *Perform the data access management process according to established guidelines*
- *Apply and maintain confidentiality controls and processes in accordance with standards, procedures, directives, policies, regulations, and laws (statutes)*

*Evaluation elements that were eliminated:*

- *Assess the effectiveness of enterprise data security policies, processes, and procedures against established standards, guidelines, and requirements, and suggest changes where appropriate*

- *Review alleged violations of data security and privacy breaches*

- *Identify improvement actions required to maintain the appropriate level of data protection*

*The team felt that all of these work functions were either management elements that would not fall under the duties of the software development professional, or that they belonged to other job titles.*

*However, the members of the team stressed that the inclusion and elimination of work functions was a matter of informed justification on their part, and that a different group might produce a different list. The aim of the tailoring process is to produce a specification that everybody within that particular environment can live with; that caveat, when attached to the document, was sufficient qualification for the architect. The final set of work functions looked like this:*

*Design*

- *Identify and document the appropriate level of protection for data*

- *Specify data and information classification, sensitivity, and need-to-know requirements by information type*

- *Create authentication and authorization system for users to gain access to data by assigned privileges and permissions*

- *Identify an appropriate set of information security controls based on the perceived risk of compromise to the data*

- *Develop security-testing procedures*

*Implement*

- *Apply and verify data security access controls, privileges, and associated profiles*

- *Implement media control procedures, and continuously monitor for compliance*

- *Implement and verify data security access controls, and assign privileges*

*Evaluate*

- *Evaluate the effectiveness of solutions implemented to provide the required protection of data*

*The work instructions produced by the team for the titles that fell under the software development professional composite category were:*

*Generic instruction – Identify and document the appropriate level of protection for data. The software development professional will be specifically accountable to:*

1. *Identify all data that will fall within the protected space for any systems that they are working on; this will be documented in the strategic plan, which will be updated annually.*

2. *Define a data dictionary and associated sensitivity requirements; ensure that these requirements are documented and maintained. Requirements will be updated annually in the data dictionary.*

Generic instruction – *Specify data and information classification, sensitivity, and need-to-know requirements by information type. The software development professional will be specifically accountable to:*

1. *A merged data dictionary will be maintained by the company. It will be overseen by a team of software development professionals formulated from all five sectors served by the data center. Meetings will be held on a no less than monthly basis.*

2. *The merged data dictionary will maintain all classification, sensitivity, and need-to-know specifications for every item of data in the dictionary. It will be overseen by a team of software development professionals formulated from all five sectors served by the data center. Meetings will be held on a no less than monthly basis.*

Generic instruction – *Create authentication and authorization system for users to gain access to data by assigned privileges and permissions. The software development professional will be specifically accountable to:*

1. *Install and operate an account management process that will ensure that the appropriate privileges are assigned to each authorized user; this process will be common across all sectors and will be overseen by a committee of software development professionals formulated from all five sectors served by the data center. Meetings to evaluate the effectiveness of the process will be held every quarter.*

2. *Create authentication and authorization controls for data that will ensure that users only gain access to data that their privileges allow; this will be done in accordance with the requirements of the account management process. Audit logs for user accounts for every system that each professional is responsible for will be reviewed on a monthly basis for appropriate use.*

Generic instruction – *Identify an appropriate set of information security controls based on the perceived risk of compromise to the data. The software development professional will be specifically accountable to:*

1. *Perform risk assessments, develop security functional requirements, and install security functions that will be appropriate to all identified risks; the risk assessment and prioritization process will be common across all sectors and will be overseen by a committee of software development professionals formulated from all five sectors served by the data center. Meetings to evaluate the effectiveness of the risk assessment will be held every quarter.*

2. *Maintain audit surveillance over all systems in order to identify unforeseen risks; audit logs will be evaluated on a monthly basis in order to identify any emerging threat.*

Generic instruction – *Develop security-testing procedures. The software development professional will be specifically accountable to:*

1. *Develop appropriate security testing procedures for every application within the professional's area of responsibility; the effectiveness of these procedures will be evaluated both by the professional and the supervisor on a quarterly basis.*

2.  *Develop security-testing procedures to address any new or emerging threat for every application within the professional's area of responsibility; the need for any new procedures will be evaluated both by the professional and the supervisor on a quarterly basis.*

Generic instruction – *Apply and verify data security access controls, privileges, and associated profiles. The software development professional will be specifically accountable to:*

1.  *Develop an appropriate and cost-effective set of security access controls; these controls will appropriately enforce all user and automated process privileges assigned to the entity seeking access. The effectiveness of these procedures will be evaluated both by the professional and the supervisor on a quarterly basis.*

2.  *Routinely verify the continuing effectiveness of access controls for every application under the responsibility of the software development professional; verifications must be done by each individual professional on a monthly basis. Supervisors will confirm effectiveness on a quarterly basis.*

Generic instruction – *Implement media control procedures and continuously monitor for compliance. The software development professional will be specifically accountable to:*

1.  *Inventory all media associated with protected data and control that inventory for each application; inventories will be updated by the professional on a monthly basis.*

2.  *Implement and install controls to ensure protection of all media under the responsibility of the software development professional; controls will be inspected for effectiveness by each professional on a monthly basis. Supervisors will confirm effectiveness on a quarterly basis.*

3.  *Maintain continuous assurance of the effectiveness of all installed controls; inspections will be done on a monthly basis to confirm this.*

Generic instruction – *Implement and verify data security access controls, and assign privileges. The software development professional will be specifically accountable to:*

1.  *Implement an appropriate set of access controls for all protected data; controls will be inspected for effectiveness by each professional on a monthly basis. Supervisors will confirm effectiveness on a quarterly basis.*

2.  *Maintain continuous assurance of the effectiveness of all installed controls; inspections will be done on a monthly basis to confirm this.*

Generic instruction – *Evaluate the effectiveness of solutions implemented to provide the required protection of data. The software development professional will be specifically accountable to:*

1.  *Create and operate an evaluation process that will ensure that the appropriate controls are in place system-wide; this process will be common across all sectors and will be overseen by a committee of software development professionals formulated from all five sectors served by the data center. Meetings to evaluate the effectiveness of the process will be held every quarter.*

2.  *Evaluate the effectiveness of all controls for protected data; audit logs for user accounts for every system that each professional is responsible for will be reviewed on a monthly basis for appropriate use.*

# Chapter Summary

- The EBK is a framework that specifies the complete set of competency areas and role requirements for information security.

- The EBK is designed to aid management in determining the appropriate security activities of all relevant employees in the organization.

- The EBK actually embodies two types of knowledge—the knowledge that is required by individual employees to achieve a given security purpose and the knowledge that is needed by a specific organizational role to carry out its security functions.

- The primary principle behind the EBK's application is that any set of specific work activities may be appropriate as long as they achieve the purpose and intent of a given EBK recommendation.

- In order to carry the recommendations of the EBK into practice it is necessary to understand the specific perceptions and assumptions of the workers in a given place.

- Tailoring involves adapting EBK practices to the actual requirements of the target environment. Successful tailoring is demonstrated by evidence that the tailored practice meets the specific intent of the EBK recommendation.

- Given that tailoring is successful if the intention of the EBK is met, it is also possible to map its recommendations to roles that are not a formal part of the model. This mapping must demonstrate that the role achieves some purpose of the EBK.

- EBK roles can be applied to a diverse set of potential job titles utilizing a role and competency framework. This makes the EBK useful in practical terms.

# Key Terms

**CISO function** Usually the highest-level administrative position in the information security hierarchy, responsible for overall policy development and leadership of the IT security operation.

**Data security** A competency area of the EBK related to ensuring the confidentiality, integrity, and availability of enterprise data.

**Digital forensics** A specialized competency area of the EBK focused on the evidence gathering function, specifically targeted toward the collection of electronic evidence.

**Enterprise continuity** A competency area of the EBK related to ensuring the continuing survival of the business and that its data assets will be preserved in the event of a disaster.

**Functional perspective** A dimension of the EBK focused on the various potential responsibilities of an EBK role. Common function perspectives are manage, design, implement, and evaluate

**Incident management** A dimension of the EBK focused on the specific steps designed to deal with a known event, typically supported by risk assessment and planning.

**IT security training and awareness** A dimension of the EBK focused on ensuring that the workforce has adequate skills to perform assigned security functions.

**Job title** A specific title used by an organization to describe a standard function carried out by an assigned person.

**Model** A comprehensive conceptual framework used to describe the elements of a generic process or entity.

**Personnel security** A dimension of the EBK focused on ensuring that workers within the organization can be trusted, built around authentication, authorization, and monitoring.

**Physical and environmental security** A dimension of the EBK focused on ensuring the security of the space within a security perimeter, also known as secured space.

**Procurement** A dimension of the EBK focused on ensuring that products and services acquired by the organization are secure.

**Regulatory and standards compliance** A dimension of the EBK focused on ensuring that the organization complies with all relevant laws, directives, regulations, and standards.

**Role** A generic area of security work, delineated by a common set of skills and functional purposes.

**Security risk management** A dimension of the EBK focused on the identification, analysis, and mitigation of risks.

**Security solution** A specific architecture of controls designed to mitigate a given set of risks within a particular organizational context.

**Software development** The lifecycle process devoted to the creation of software; typically involves specification, design, code, test, and acceptance of software products.

**Strategic security management** A dimension of the EBK focused on the development of strategies and policies to govern organizational directions for some defined period.

**System and application security** The area of the EBK devoted to securing the lifecycle process by which system and application software is developed and sustained.

# Questions from the CIO

The CIO requires you to brief her on the current status of your investigation. This will be an important part of your continuing work on this project, since it is essential to be able to summarize what the organization has learned in its continuing attempts to improve itself. Consequently, the CIO would like you to answer the following questions for her:

1. Work practices are dependent on culture and environment for their successful execution. Explain in detail why that is the case. Also, explain how that might affect the idea of a common standard for performing a given process.

2. Every work instruction should specify the observable means that will be used to confirm that it is being carried out. How can a work instruction be made explicit? What has to be specified in order to do that? Why is it important that a work instruction be observable?

3. Why is the identification of job titles from the most senior to the least senior an issue in using the EBK? Or in simple terms, what is it about the EBK's structure that encourages using that approach?

4. What is the relationship between work instructions and resources? What is it about resources that might impact the form, rigor, or extent of a work instruction and why is that the case?

5. Is it possible to map a role that has no apparent analogue in the EBK to its recommendations? What would be the basis for doing that, and how would the process be approached?

6. Why is it important to define the smallest number of competency elements for a given role? What part of the process would benefit from a smaller number of competencies? What is the general approach to ensuring the shortest list possible?

7. The original purpose of the EBK was to specify knowledge for security training and education. What would have to be done in order to adapt that purpose to one of specifying the minimum knowledge requirements for a security system?

8. There are three general factors involved in the tailoring of a correct set of work instructions. What are those and specifically how do resources fit into the consideration for each of these?

9. Feasibility is an important issue in security system formulation. What are the two different dimensions of feasibility that might affect the development of a real-world solution?

10. Acceptance and understanding are also issues in security system development. How would acceptance and understanding affect the development of a security system? Are these the same considerations, or do they affect the process differently? What would the best approach be to ensuring both?

## Hands-On Projects

HANDS-ON PROJECTS

Select two of the positions from the Case in Appendix A. Tailor and map each of those to the role definitions in the EBK. Ensure that:

- There is a proper justification for each EBK role associated with the position
- All of the EBK competencies associated with these roles are listed for that job title

# chapter 4

# Defining the Company's Executive Roles

## Meanwhile, Back in the States....

*The return flight to Los Angeles was a lot more satisfying than the flight out, because the architect was coming back to the States with a newly validated process. The two months he had spent in Singapore had involved 14-hour workdays in what, for him, was an alien and relatively unpleasant environment. By the time he left Singapore, he knew that his approach would successfully bridge the gap between the theoretical and the practical. More important, since the process had succeeded in a place like Singapore, he was reasonably certain that it would work in any other location where the company did business.*

*The architect had seen the tailoring produce behaviors in Singapore that were materially different than what might have been expected if the data center had been located in Detroit. Nonetheless, in the time he had been at the Singapore site, the architect had been able to validate that each of those behaviors would fulfill the requisite purpose of one of the standard operating procedures in the company manual. And, since those standard operating procedures were derived directly from the best practice recommendations of the EBK, he was also reasonably certain that the Singapore data center was now on a much better security footing.*

*Finally, and perhaps more important from the architect's point of view, once the local work instructions that implemented those behaviors were developed and documented, he was able to assign a suitable set of security duties to each of the EBK roles that were present in that facility. The architect was especially pleased by that new ability, since it would then be possible to make each of the company's security workers accountable for explicit security actions that could be directly observed and subsequently evaluated. Likewise, the enhanced visibility would let the company's managers oversee the process better, which would help leverage trust between upper management and the security function.*

*Being able to generate that trust was a big deal for the architect, because he knew that nobody at the corporate level had any confidence in the security operation. Notwithstanding the obvious fact that it had been a breakdown in security that had sunk the company in the first place, the esoteric nature of the security function itself did not exactly engender trust. In fact, all of that technology-centered activity had made upper management increasingly more suspicious of the value of the entire operation; the technology itself made the security process opaque to the lay managers.*

*Those managers wanted some sort of concrete way to be able to objectively judge the performance of the security operation. Up to that point, upper-level management had been in the untenable position of not being able to tell for certain whether the situation was actually secure. There was no visible evidence to base those judgments on, which was obviously not the way to inspire confidence in the function. Since the architect was also acutely aware that he had become the "face" of the security function in upper-management's eyes, he knew that had a personal stake in making sure that the people in the executive suite were comfortable with the performance of the entire security operation.*

*In fact, the need to provide conventional executives with an accurate measure for judging performance was one of the primary reasons why the architect had wanted to have an explicit set of work instructions in the first place. It was his intention to ensure that the behaviors meant to satisfy each security requirement were defined in a way that could be observed and understood by everybody in the company, and therefore objectively evaluated. So he set out to create a behaviorally based accountability scheme for all of the security roles in the organization.*

*To fulfill that goal, the architect had made certain that a standard set of observable actions was specified for each of the security roles at the Singapore site. Those specifications then provided a tangible yardstick to assess each individual's effectiveness. By aggregating the results of all of the individual assessments at the site, it was possible to see how well the security operation was doing as a whole, as well as to identify the places where expectations were not being met.*

*The architect knew that such a detailed level of control had not been available to upper management before, and so he also expected that his new system would get noticed. As his last act before getting on the flight back to the U.S., the architect did a simple attitudinal survey to find out whether enhanced understanding of the responsibilities involved in the security process would lead to better security at the Singapore data center. What he found was that the ability to understand the process in objective, behavioral terms had increased the overall execution of the process as well as the confidence of the local executives in their security operation.*

*As he sat in the first class boarding lounge at Changi, he came to the conclusion that besides tailoring work instructions for each of the other sites, he would also have to come up with a standard way to ensure that each relevant EBK role at each of those sites would have explicit work instructions assigned to them. If he was going to be responsible for defining every one of the company's security roles, it would cement his status as the key guy in the process, not the **CIO**. Ambitious fellow that he was, that was a satisfying thought. On the flight back over* *the Pacific, the architect settled into his first class seat, ordered a glass of that scotch with a blue label that all of his friends told him marked "success."*

## Assigning Competencies to Roles

Unlike all of the other standard information security models, the EBK contains a specification of required competencies for 10 generic roles. ISO 27000 provides a definition of best practice for 11 security principles, while the commercial bodies of knowledge, such as the Certified Information System Security Professional (CISSP) **Body of Knowledge** (**BOK**), define individual knowledge requirements for IT staff. None of these other models factors their standardized knowledge elements into defined, representative roles for information security work.

The EBK uses those role and their associated **competency** definitions to satisfy its basic purpose, which is to provide a practical specification of security training and education requirements. The roles themselves basically encompass a variety of security job titles, ranging from CIO and CISO to physical security specialist. In actual practice, each of the roles is, in effect, a label that can be applied to a cluster of jobs, or job titles. No matter what the real title of a job, the decision about where it fits is based on whether the intent of that job title fits the common purposes of an EBK role. If that is the case, then the job title can be equated to that role.

Every job title within a given role category can be assumed to require the same general set of competencies. Given that assumption, the EBK provides a specification of the basic competencies that are required for each of 10 security roles within an IT security organization. The requisite practices, which are assigned to each role, are drawn from the 14 competency areas of the EBK. These practices are further broken down into four fundamental areas of IT practice: manage, design, implement, and evaluate.

For the purpose of easier and more logical presentation, the EBK factors the roles themselves into three **perspectives**: executive, functional, and corollary. Each of those perspectives represents an aspect of security work. Combined, they are meant to span the gamut of the entire cybersecurity process. There are three roles identified by the EBK within the **executive perspective: chief information officer**, information security officer/chief security officer, and **IT security compliance professional**.

## Assessing the Role of the Boss

*Up to the time of the disaster, the primary focus of the company's CIO had been developing and implementing generic information technology policies, and ensuring the satisfactory performance of the company's multitude of information systems. In the old company, the CIO reported to the board by way of the chief executive officer (CEO). After the events that had led to the company's demise, the shareholders had insisted on having the CIO report directly to the board. Strategic plans were drawn up that placed the CIO on the same footing as the CEO, the chief financial officer (CFO) and the chief operating officer (COO). Since the information technology function had been proven so integral to the company's actual survival, this elevation of the CIO role was seen as an essential first step in getting the issues associated with IT security out on the table as the company plotted its course into the future.*

*Given her newfound status, the CIO had a new set of accountabilities. She was not just responsible for the development of **policy** and policy directions for the information technology function any more. She was now also responsible for leadership in the evaluation of all new and emerging technologies as they impacted **risk** to the business. Additionally, the CIO was responsible for the management of all information technology processes, in terms of both performance evaluation and the development of substantive risk identification and **mitigation** strategies. That required her to establish and oversee a formal IT security measurement program, which included the evaluation of the degree that each individual unit in the company complied with all information technology policies and regulatory requirements, as well as all appropriate operation and use requirements.*

*The task that the board assigned to the architect was to establish whether that list of accountabilities was complete and detailed enough to be effective. If it was not, the architect was empowered to redefine the CIO role on the same successful model as he had used for the Singapore project. That new responsibility was particularly gratifying to the architect since, even before the Singapore situation had blown up, he had always planned to create a template of "ideal" practice that could be used to evaluate the CIO role. Notwithstanding the underlying political motives that were driving his original interest in creating performance criteria for his boss, the architect knew that it was critically important to the company that the single leadership position at the top of the technology food chain be held accountable. The CIO was the one person responsible for creating and maintaining a secure overall operation. So the architect opened the EBK to section four. Then he and his team began the process of developing a best practice definition for the role of the corporate CIO.*

# Defining the Role of the Chief Information Officer

The CIO is typically the highest-level position for information technology in the organization. It is the one that is accountable for overall leadership in the company's cybersecurity process.

In the past, the CIO title was assigned to the person who was responsible for policy formulation and general overall management of just the IT function. However, as information technology has become more central to the business operation, the responsibility itself has become one of ensuring proper alignment between business processes and the underlying information technology platform. The EBK dictates 10 specific responsibilities for the CIO function. Those are:

- Management of data security
- Management of enterprise continuity
- Management of incidents
- Management of IT security training and awareness
- Management of physical and environmental security
- Management and design of procurement processes
- Management and evaluation of regulatory and standards compliance
- Management and evaluation of **risk management** programs

- Management, design, and evaluation of the strategic management process
- Management of the system and application security process

## The CIO and Management of Data Security

The first competency that is specified for the CIO role is management of data security. In conventional terms, this competency typically involves management activities that are associated with ensuring reliable protection of the company's data. The EBK specifies that this capacity must encompass organizational data in "all forms of representation (electronic and hardcopy) and it applies throughout the life cycle of that data." Because the intent of the EBK is standardization rather than regulation, the actual steps that might be taken to perform any function within the **generic role** definitions are not made explicit. Given the implications of the CIO role, it is clear that the management of data security would at least include the following activities.

As is typical in the management of all IT **operations**, the CIO should be responsible for development of policy. That includes the creation of a governance **infrastructure** that embodies all of the relevant policies. Within that framework, the CIO should also coordinate the review of existing policies and the approval of new ones. In that respect, the CIO would normally have accountability for establishing and updating the policies for all security related work, such as the policies for data classification labeling and management activities within the company. Finally, the CIO is ultimately responsible for ensuring that data security policies and relevant legal and regulatory requirements are adhered to and that appropriate changes are implemented as required.

## The CIO and Management of Enterprise Continuity

The CIO is also responsible for establishing and maintaining an explicit set of policies and procedures which are aimed at ensuring the survivability of the organization's data and information systems. In essence, this means that the CIO is accountable for ensuring that all of the data that is needed to perform all essential business functions is protected from all reasonable threats. That includes harm from natural events, like hurricane or flood. It also includes manmade disasters like fire or terrorism. In conventional practice, this general responsibility area involves the business continuity, business recovery, **contingency planning**, and disaster recovery functions.

In order to ensure enterprise continuity, the organization typically establishes a formal, enterprise-wide continuity management function. The CIO's responsibility is not so much to manage that function, as it is to coordinate how it is developed, deployed, and sustained. That includes taking care of the practical business issues, such as ensuring sufficient resources are available and establishing the continuity management infrastructure. The CIO also supervises the assignment of personnel to key positions and the delegation of authority and order of succession for each task.

On the proactive side, the CIO is responsible for the direction of the contingency planning and **risk** management operations. That typically requires the identification and prioritization of critical functions and data as well as the establishment of a formal oversight program, including the inspections and audits to ensure effective, measurement based performance. It also involves overseeing any changes that might result from lessons learned from that monitoring function.

## The CIO and Incident Management

Incident management is a critical role for the CIO because it involves mitigating any active or likely attacks, intrusions, or harmful events that might threaten the confidentiality, integrity, or availability of the organization's data. In many respects, the CIO's ability to establish an effective incident management program will determine the organization's overall ability to fulfill its business purpose.

Typically, the CIO is the one responsible for instituting the incident management program. In effect, the CIO is accountable for creating the architecture within which the various stakeholders define the specific incident response plan and then perform their defined incident management tasks. That involves providing specific direction about the ways the incident response team will interact with the rest of the organization. It also involves allocating all of the resources necessary to ensure that the incident management program is capable of responding to foreseen incidents.

Finally, the CIO is responsible for ensuring that the information response function evolves with the changing threat picture. That requires the CIO to coordinate the inspections and reviews necessary to get real-world performance based information about current incident response capability, as well as to utilize that knowledge to make changes as needed to ensure a continuous and robust response.

## The CIO and IT Training and Awareness

If the organization expects to maintain its overall assurance capabilities, then it has to ensure that all of its personnel are knowledgeable. That basically involves the training and awareness function. In essence, training and awareness encompasses all of the methods utilized to enhance security awareness, as well as to ensure and maintain the security skills and knowledge of the workforce. That can range from simple coaching activities, which are aimed at ensuring that all workers understand the security aspects of their duties, all the way up to formal instruction in particular areas of focused concern.

The CIO's role in this is to ensure the successful establishment of a formal awareness, training, and education (AT&E) function within the enterprise. That includes developing and allocating resources appropriate to the mission of the AT&E program, as well as the establishment of an oversight program to ensure that the AT&E function meets all requisite performance goals and continues to evolve as requirements change. The CIO is also ultimately responsible for enforcement of compliance with AT&E standards across the organization.

## The CIO and Physical and Environmental Security

Because of its cross-organizational scope, one of the most difficult areas to manage is physical and environmental security protection. Essentially, the organization has to ensure that all of the necessary controls are in place to make certain that all physical structures within the secure space are protected from all potential threats. That mandate encompasses all of the people, equipment, facilities, and workspaces where data is kept.

As with the other functions, the CIO is specifically responsible for creating and maintaining the general governance approach and coordinating the various actors within that framework. That includes inventorying, valuating, and prioritizing all of the assets that require explicit protection.

Physical security is particularly problematic for the information systems people, because there are also typically well-established physical security operations within most organizations which pre-date the data security function. It is the particular task of the CIO to ensure that all traditional security functions specifically address the cybersecurity needs of the organization. That integration must be complete and comprehensive. As with the other programs, the CIO is also responsible for establishing an oversight and enforcement process to ensure continuous physical protection.

## The CIO and Management of Procurement

Procurement involves outside parties, so it is essential that the organization be able to know which vendor to trust. As a result, it is necessary for the customer organization to establish a formal set of policies and procedures to ensure a trusted relationship with all of the outside entities that will provide products, goods, and services. These policies are normally oriented toward identifying any potential risks in the vendor relationship. However, with the advent of web-based contracting, automated contract negotiation, and automated contract preparation systems, the problems with establishing trust become much more complex. That is because the people involved in those trust relationships are often remote and in some cases faceless.

In actual execution, secure procurement typically implies a formal set of procedures to ensure that the contracts, plans, and subsequent interactions with the supplier minimize risk by facilitating the maximum amount of communication and understanding. Characteristic procurement activities include the creation of a formal management infrastructure, the development of criteria to evaluate supplier bids and proposals, and ongoing processes to ensure a trustworthy and dependable relationship with the company's suppliers. The CIO's role in developing those plans is usually limited to oversight and coordination of the various parties involved. That can include everybody from the technical staff, through development managers and legal and financial executives, all the way up to the CIO of the vendor organization.

In that respect, the CIO is the person who is ultimately responsible for ensuring that the products and services that are purchased by the IT function are trustworthy. The CIO has to make certain that the features of the eventual purchase are properly aligned with the organization's security requirements. Consequently, the CIO is responsible for ensuring that sufficient review and analysis was done to attest that the business goals of the organization are reflected in the acquisition and that appropriate changes and improvement actions are implemented as required.

The CIO is the person who is eventually responsible for ensuring that risk is considered at every step in the acquisition process. That consideration can range from assuring that standard language to contain risk is present in all contracts and specifications, all the way to the definition of measurement and enforcement mechanisms. This latter duty implies that the CIO is also responsible for ensuring that the supplier understands the organization's commitment to security and its security requirements. Since much of the acquisition process is guided by the contract, the CIO is also responsible for ensuring that the specifications for goods and services that are place in that contract are correct and comply with all laws and regulations. That includes specification of acceptable use policies to all parties, including sub-contractors.

Unlike the other categories, where the CIO is only responsible for the oversight of the function, the CIO position traditionally gets down to developing the actual procedures that will govern the procurement process. That is because the CIO is the only person high enough in the organization to dictate company-wide secure practice. Also as the primary information technology officer in the organization, it is the CIO who has the greatest stake in ensuring that all purchased information technology products and services are safe and secure. Thus, the CIO will normally take a more direct hand in developing the actual procedures to administer the contract.

The CIO will also be more involved in evaluating and accepting delivered products. In essence, the CIO will normally be responsible for developing the actual measures to monitor and ensure that acquisitions fit with overall security policies. In that respect, the CIO is responsible for the development of the actual management policies and procedures regarding supplier behavior during the contract period, including acceptable use and connection procedures. In the end, it is the CIO's task to make certain that all due diligence has been done to ensure that the procurement process complies with all commonly accepted standards for proper security practice.

## The CIO and the Management and Evaluation of Legal, Regulatory, and Standards Compliance

**Legal and regulatory compliance** is one of the more dynamic areas of security. The requirements for the organization can vary considerably, depending on the legal and regulatory environment. In general, legal and regulatory compliance refers to the formal procedures that the organization follows to ensure that its information security practices comply with all applicable laws, regulations, standards, policies, and statutory requirements.

The CIO's role in the development of regulatory and legal compliance procedures is to ensure that any risks that might be associated with the violation of a given contract, law, regulation, or statute are first identified and then evaluated. That requires the CIO to maintain a comprehensive understanding of the legal and regulatory climate that the organization functions within. Once the risks are understood, it can be assumed that it is then possible to develop a reasonable and appropriate set of compliance policies.

The policy development process is overseen by the CIO; as a result, the CIO typically has final accountability for its success or failure. But the CIO does not actually carry out any of the information gathering and risk analysis activities. Instead, the CIO supervises and coordinates the activities of the group of people who do. That group includes all of the legal, business, and technology stakeholders who are directly responsible for ensuring the actual compliance with all licensing, regulatory, and legal requirements.

Since the availability of adequate resources is a necessary precondition for the policy and procedure formulation process, the CIO is directly responsible for ensuring that all requisite financial and personnel resources are available. In conjunction with this responsibility, the CIO is also accountable for ensuring that the overall legal and regulatory compliance program is evaluated in order to monitor its ongoing effectiveness. This requires the CIO to oversee the creation of a reliable set of objective measures of performance, as well as supervise their administration and use.

The CIO is directly responsible for ensuring that all applicable laws, regulations, standards, and contract practices have been identified and are addressed by a designated manager. In doing that, the CIO is also responsible for ensuring overall awareness of risks associated with violation of any of those statutes. That frequently means that the CIO must maintain a relationship with all of the relevant industry and governmental regulatory agencies within the organization's business space. That allows the CIO to keep informed on all pending changes to laws, regulations, and standards. The CIO also keeps relationships with industry interest groups for the same reason.

Finally, because of the importance of this area to the overall wellbeing of the organization, it is necessary for the CIO role to make certain that the actual governance controls that are embedded in the compliance program are effective. As a result, the CIO is accountable for directing a process of continuous improvement to ensure that all compliance processes, procedures, and controls remain effective. This is an everyday responsibility, in that control assessment and improvement must be embedded in the normal operational processes of the company. The CIO role is responsible for ensuring that these routine activities are always being carried out.

## The CIO and the Management and Evaluation of Security Risk Programs

It should be possible to identify and mitigate every risk to the organization; however, given the number of potential threats and the dynamic nature of the **threat environment**, that is an impractical goal. Therefore, the organization has to develop and deploy a program that can evaluate risk likelihood and impact and come up with effective strategies for mitigating those that pose the greatest threat. The security risk management program is a process that the organization adopts to ensure that priority risks are addressed at an affordable price.

The CIO is responsible for establishing that program. Risk management is always driven by the business context. It involves a formal risk assessment process that is intended to allow decision makers to understand what threatens their business goals. The CIO is then responsible for devising effective mitigation strategies and responses and then making subsequent changes to the risk management infrastructure that will enable it to address meaningful threats as they emerge. The CIO underwrites the overall effort by providing sufficient financial and human resources.

The CIO also ensures that all risk mitigation approaches are correctly implemented and persistently followed. In order to ensure success, the CIO must be able to assess the effectiveness of the risk management program and implement changes where necessary. That requires continuous review of risk management controls, policies, and procedures, as well as the tools and techniques adopted as part of the formal response. Finally, in conjunction with upper management, the CIO is accountable to make the right decision about how much residual risk to accept. This decision is normally based on an assessment of the general threat and vulnerability picture and an estimate of the harm that might ensue from any unmitigated risks that could compromise the information assets and systems that have been identified as critical, or priorities, for the company.

## The CIO and the Management of the Strategic Management Function

Strategic management is not just an information security function. The organization charts its course and maintains its overall direction by means of the strategic management process. Interfacing with the overall strategic management function of the company might be the single most critical competency required for the CIO role. Being able to make good strategic decisions demands that the CIO be able to analyze the internal and external business environment in sufficient depth to be able to understand all of the potential advantages and barriers to success. That requires the use of such mechanisms as customer analysis, competitor analysis, market analysis, and industry environmental analysis. It also requires the performance of internal business analyses that address financial performance, **performance measurement,** quality assurance, risk management, and organizational capabilities/constraints. The goal of these analyses is always to ensure that an organization's IT security principles, practices, and systems are kept in line with the overall obligations, aims, and purposes of the company.

It is the CIO's task to establish and oversee the strategic management process for cybersecurity in the organization. That requires the development of a comprehensive and coherent infrastructure of policies and processes to provide security for all relevant systems, networks, and data. This is done by aligning business processes, IT software and hardware, local and wide area networks, people, operations, and projects with the organization's overall **security strategy**. The aim is to ensure that appropriate changes and improvement actions are implemented as required.

The security response of the organization must be appropriate to the threat environment. It must be fully integrated so that the information security, physical security, personnel security, and other security components of that solution are aligned into an enterprise-wide, information security architecture. Since the creation and oversight of such a comprehensive architecture is organization-wide and strategic, only somebody at the CIO level can be made responsible for its development and oversight. Therefore, in most situations the CIO is accountable for ensuring that the enterprise's security architecture is developed and continuously managed and supported by the organization's strategic planning process.

A process is also required to ensure the efficiency, effectiveness, and maturity of the controls that make up the information security architecture. That includes implementing the measures necessary to determine if a process for developing security controls and processes is adequately integrated into the long-range planning process. Performance management might also include reviewing security funding to ensure that investment accurately aligns with security goals and objectives. This is a financial management process rather than a security one, and it can only be carried out at the CIO level. However, aligning investment with trends is a critical step to ensuring that security investments match the evolution of the organization's security needs.

## The CIO and the Management of System and Application Security Programs

System and application security is a traditional role in day-to-day information security work. Ensuring system and application security typically involves devising steps to build security into the system or software during its actual development. Building security in is far more preferable to trying to strap security onto an existing system once it is completed. As the title suggests, this is a management process rather than a technical one. Application and system security encompasses all of the necessary lifecycle activities that are taken to ensure that the application is built right prior to release. The aim of application and system security is to ensure that the organization's software does not pose a threat to the enterprise because of inherent **vulnerabilities**. Much of the application and system security process revolves around risk assessment, risk mitigation, and the implementation of security controls within both the process and the product.

The CIO's main task is to create a secure engineering environment and then ensure that the engineering procedures within that environment are followed correctly. That typically involves the development of policies for development and sustainment of applications and systems and then the education of IT security personnel sufficient to ensure that they understand what they have to do. The CIO's responsibility also involves continuous assessment of the effectiveness of the overall process. As the organization discovers which practices work best, it is the responsibility of the CIO to ensure that those are integrated into day-to-day operation and then make certain that appropriate changes and improvement actions are implemented as required.

**4**

## Assessing the Architect's New Role

*After six months and what had seemed like one bruising corporate battle after another, the CIO decided that she couldn't put it off any longer. So she bowed to the inevitable and called the architect into her office one bright Friday morning in May. There she broke the news that the board had decided that, since he had been in effect functioning as the single person in the organization responsible for information security, he might as well have the title. Accordingly, without actually drawing a sword and knighting him on the spot, the CIO invested the architect with an official new organizational title, chief information security officer, or CISO.*

*The new CISO had been waiting a long time to hear those words. It made all of the red-eye flights and the backbreaking hours he had spent overseeing development of the company's comprehensive security process seem worthwhile. The problem was that, although the EBK itself actually specifies a well-defined set of work functions for the CISO role, the actual position had never existed within the company up to this point. So the architect's first step in the process was to put together the job description and set of responsibilities for his own position as CISO.*

*The architect wanted to make sure that he defined his new job in terms that would be generic enough to give him plenty of wiggle-room, should the company's security situation change. At the same time, he wanted that definition to be explicit enough that it would allow him to prove that he was meeting all requirements for the job. Also, the actual EBK label for the role itself was "information security officer." But, the architect liked the sound of chief so he chose the more common title of CISO.*

*Even though the title was a comparatively new designation, the competencies that the EBK defined for the information security officer involved rather conventional security activities. For instance, like all types of security chiefs, the information security officer (ISO) role was specifically responsible for developing and implementing the strategy for the security function. In order to implement that strategy, the ISO had to develop a strategic plan for cybersecurity and then oversee and coordinate the actual execution of the plan. Moreover, as part of the operational responsibility to ensure proper execution of that strategy, the ISO was also specifically accountable for the development, documentation, and subsequent enforcement of all of the company's security policies and procedures.*

*The new ISO, or CISO as he chose to designate himself, appreciated the fact that he was now responsible for the day-to-day conduct of all aspects of the information security function. He had never shied away from overall leadership positions in the past. In fact, this very trait had brought him to his current status. Since the new CISO was now part of the upper management team, he was able to work directly with the CIO in the development of the company's technology strategy. That relationship put him in the position of being able to help provide policy direction that would support the deployment of appropriate technologies which were both safe and secure.*

*Because he was ambitious, he would have preferred to report directly to the CEO. However, given the CIO's larger responsibility for technology policy, he also understood that while security had a critical role in that policy, it was not the same as having to ensure the ongoing alignment of the information technology function with the business case. So instead of insisting on a new reporting line, the CISO worked to ensure that his personal turf was well defined.*

# Leading the Data Security Function: The Information Security Officer

The ISO role is typically the highest-level position in the organization that has specific accountability for information security. The role is a relatively new position in corporate culture, dating back perhaps 15 years in conventional industry practice. It reflects the increasing interest that most companies have in ensuring the confidentiality, integrity, and availability of their data.

The ISO role is not a hands-on function per se. Instead, the ISO oversees the work of the other information security professionals in the organization. In order to ensure that the work is properly directed, the ISO typically develops the policies for the information security function. In that capacity, the ISO provides the leadership in ensuring that the information security strategy is implemented as planned.

That leadership obligation includes the planning and deployment of all of the programs that support the overall information security strategy, such as business continuity and disaster recovery planning, secure software assurance, risk management, AT&E programs, and all legal and regulatory compliance responses. The ISO is also the person most likely to be accountable for measurement and assessment of the performance of the information security function. The EBK dictates the following 11 specific competencies for the ISO function:

- Manage, design, and evaluate data security
- Manage and design digital forensics
- Manage and evaluate enterprise continuity
- Manage, design, and evaluate incident management
- Manage and evaluate IT security training and awareness
- Manage and evaluate physical and environmental security
- Manage, design, and evaluate procurement

- Manage, design, and evaluate regulatory and standards compliance
- Manage, design, and evaluate risk management
- Manage, design, implement, and evaluate strategic management
- Manage and evaluate system and application security

## The Information Security Officer and the Management of Data Security

In most organizations, the ISO role is the one that is primarily accountable for the overall implementation and operation of the data security function. As the EBK defines it, data security is a process rather than a condition; somebody in the organization has to have specific responsibility for creating and overseeing the actual processes and practices used to secure data. That is the role of the ISO. The ISO provides leadership in the design of all of the organizational and technical controls that are utilized in the data security process. The ISO then manages those controls in day-to-day operation. Finally, the ISO has the job of evaluating the performance of the entire data security process and making recommendations for changes to the controls and the technology that underlies it.

The ISO is also responsible for performing the following actions. First, all of the data in the organization has to be identified and labeled in order to build a protection plan. Therefore, it is the duty of the ISO to ensure that all of the requisite data identification, classification, and management policies are created and in place and that all of the guidelines for implementing those policies are maintained. Because this is detailed and tedious work, the ISO role does not do the actual classification of the data. That activity is left to the data security staff. However, the ISO is responsible for the development, coordination, and review of all of the policies that govern how the data will be identified and classified by that staff. The ISO also ensures that the identification and classification policies are kept current. A decision about how current and relevant those classification policies have to be is typically supported by an assessment of risk. That assessment is done on an ongoing basis with the aim of ensuring that all of the company's identification and classification policies and practices remain effective.

Finally, the ISO is directly accountable for the execution of the data security process. It is an obligation of the ISO role to enforce compliance with all data security policies and relevant legal and regulatory requirements. The basis for most of this enforcement lies in standards. Consequently, the ISO is also responsible for ensuring that all of the company's data security policies conform to organizational standards for privacy, controlled access, secure retention and disposal, incident management, disaster recovery, and configuration management. Lastly, the ISO develops and oversees the acceptable use policies, which are needed to ensure routine compliance in each of these areas.

Operationally, the ISO is the role responsible for developing the specific administrative procedures to coordinate all of these functions. In its practical form, this function is typically termed an cybersecurity infrastructure, because it is the framework that holds together the various components of information security and allows them to work with one another. In order to create a properly functioning infrastructure, it is necessary to understand what the protection requirements are for each individual item of data in the organization's inventory of data assets. The ISO is typically responsible for identifying those protection requirements and is accountable for instituting a process to document the precise classification, sensitivity, and need-to-know requirements for each item of data in the inventory. Then the ISO is responsible for the design and implementation of a logical set of information security controls based on perceived risks to the data. Finally, in order to ensure that the system is operating properly, the ISO is also responsible for the development and ongoing execution of the security testing process.

The ISO also oversees the creation of the authentication and authorization systems, which are utilized to control access. This is primarily accomplished by assigning privileges to each user. Because proper authorization relies on the correct assignment of privileges, the ISO is also responsible for ensuring that the correct set of privileges have been assigned to each user. Since privilege rests on data sensitivity, the ISO is responsible for the development of organizational procedures to ensure that sensitive data collection and retention complies with applicable standards, procedures, directives, policies, regulations, and laws.

Finally, the ISO is responsible for assessing the effectiveness of data security policies and procedures. In essence, it is the responsibility of the ISO to maintain the appropriate level of data protection through a coherent policy and procedure framework. Once those policies and procedures have been created, the ISO maintains their continuing correctness through a rational change process. The ISO also evaluates the functioning of the overall cybersecurity system in order to ensure its ongoing effectiveness. The ISO typically fulfills that responsibility by performing regular and systematic evaluations of the type and source of all breaches.

## The ISO and the Management and Design of Digital Forensics Programs

Since the ISO is directly responsible for information security, that role is also responsible for investigation of any breaches or other violations that might occur. This type of investigative activity falls under the general heading of **forensic investigation**. There are numerous digital investigation and analysis techniques used for acquiring, validating, and analyzing electronic data. These techniques are all employed to reconstruct events related to security incidents. Although the ISO is not accountable for performing those actual investigations, the ISO role does provide the leadership in their management and design.

As the first step in the process, the ISO has to build a forensic investigation capability. That normally involves assembling all the necessary resources, both personnel, technical, and financial, to operate a forensic program. The ISO also has to organize a specialist team to do the actual forensics work. These cannot be conventional IT staff. Instead, the team has to be composed of investigators who are trained in evidence gathering in both IT and network environments.

Digital forensics is not like normal forensic investigation; most of the evidence is electronic, or virtual. Therefore, it is also the responsibility of the ISO to ensure that the specialized requirements of the investigative process are met. That includes laboratories that provide the equipment and tools to do virtual evidence gathering. Since the evidence is both sensitive and difficult to secure, the ISO is also responsible for taking all necessary precautions to ensure that access to that laboratory is strictly controlled. Finally, since digital investigation relies on the supporting technology, it is also the duty of the ISO to ensure that the forensic tools and processes in that laboratory are maintained appropriate to the investigative requirements of the company.

The ISO provides leadership in the process by defining the policies for the recovery, preservation, and analysis of evidence. The ISO also ensures that the reporting and archiving of evidence complies with all relevant standards, regulations, and laws. The ISO is responsible for establishing the detailed policies and procedures that define the evidence gathering process. Along with that, the ISO specifies all of the necessary requirements for the toolsets that are used in the actual investigations, both on-site and in mobile settings.

Additionally, the ISO is responsible for defining the investigative process. This is typically done by overseeing the creation of a policy and procedure handbook that defines investigative procedure in detail, including how to recover and analyze the data, preserve evidence, and report results. Because the investigation often involves civil or criminal liability, it is important that all procedures comply with relevant statutes. Thus, the ISO also ensures that the investigative process acts in accordance with all relevant standards, regulations, or laws and that the chain of custody and disposal procedures is legal and correct.

The ISO is also responsible for ensuring the continuing professional capability of the investigators themselves. So the ISO role oversees compliance with all applicable licensing or certification requirements. That might include periodic audits of staff credentials to make certain that they are in accordance with statutes. It might also include specialized training and oversight of investigators to ensure that they are capable prior to assigning them to cases.

Finally, when building a forensic capability there is a specific need to foster understanding of forensics' role within the general organization. That is because forensics has an investigative focus, which can sometimes center on the organization's own workers. Due to that focus, forensics people can sometimes look more like police, than fellow employees, to the rest of the IT staff. So the ISO has to ensure proper integration of the forensics staff into the overall IT function. Since the investigation of workers can raise human relations issues, it is also the specific duty of the ISO to ensure that everybody understands that forensics is just doing its job if it opens a case against an individual within the company.

## The ISO Role and the Management of Enterprise Continuity

The ISO is primarily responsible for creating and maintaining the organization's continuity and disaster recovery function. Since enterprise continuity is such a critical part of any business, this operation has to be established with the full cooperation of all stakeholders. The ISO is the person who is responsible for identifying and coordinating the stakeholders and formulating the continuity of operations plan. Once the plan is set, it is the ISO who acquires the necessary financial and human resources to implement it. The ISO is also responsible for maintaining the continuity process as correctly as possible over time. This is accomplished by ensuring that the continuity plan is placed under the control of a formal change management process.

The ISO is the person responsible for creating and overseeing the contingency planning and risk management operations. These typically require the ISO to define and obtain agreement on the scope of operations of the enterprise continuity function. The job of defining the scope of operations also applies to the disaster recovery function. The proper definition of scope is ensured by aligning the priorities of the business operation with the specific steps for continuity and disaster recovery. This involves the formulation of a priority list of critical business functions. These are then referenced to a set of specific actions to ensure continuity for each function in priority order. Once these actions have been instituted, the ISO also identifies and implements a set of quantitative performance measures to ensure that the continuity process functions as intended.

The ISO is responsible for creating the organizational framework and staffing for continuity. In order to fulfill that obligation, the ISO should personally oversee the assignment of staff to key positions as well as define the chain of succession should one of those staff be unavailable. The ISO then arranges the awareness and training activities to ensure that all continuity procedures are fully understood by all participants.

## The ISO and Incident Management

The ISO is also responsible for incident management. In that respect, the ISO is the person accountable for ensuring that all threats, attacks, intrusions, or harmful events are both identified and effectively mitigated. Since the whole point of cyber-security is to ensure against harmful events, incident management is a key accountability of the ISO role. As the chief executive officer for security, the ISO is responsible for formulating and overseeing the organization's incident management program. That means that the ISO must actively identify and work with stakeholders to define the specific plans for incident response and then develop the resources to underwrite the program. That responsibility involves establishing and then managing the incident response team. This means that the ISO must actively define and then manage how that team will work with the rest of the organization and any external entities who might be involved.

Operationally, the ISO is responsible for ensuring that the incident response team coordinates its efforts with other security functions on both the technical and physical security side of the organization. The ISO oversees the day-to-day functioning of the incident response team by deploying measures to obtain quantitative performance based data about current incident response capability. Then the ISO implements specific changes to the process to meet changing conditions as needed. That can include instituting such practices as new drills, or designing and implementing procedures to counter a new threat. It can also include changes in standard operating procedure that are implemented based on lessons learned from an incident.

## The ISO and the Management of IT Training and Awareness

The ISO has to ensure that the security staff is capable. This is typically done by instituting a formal AT&E program for all security staff. Awareness ensures a minimum level of security knowledge by all members of the organization. If a short-term response to a particular problem is required, the necessary skills can be provided by the training program. If a more substantial response is required, it can be addressed by an education program.

The aim of both training and education is to enhance the security skills and knowledge of the workforce. The AT&E program typically instructs workers about their security responsibilities and teaches them about information security processes and procedure. If the process functions correctly, it will ensure that personnel are adequately knowledgeable. The AT&E program should be designed to ensure that all security workers, as well as the general workforce, are able to perform their duties as optimally as possible. The members of the security staff must have the knowledge to fulfill their particular roles. At a minimum, all of the company's workers have to know the acceptable behaviors for their jobs.

The ISO's role in the process is to design and oversee the overall development of the awareness training and education AT&E function. That requires the identification of business requirements and the establishment of enterprise-wide policies for AT&E. No matter who does the eventual teaching or training the ISO is the executive who allocates and maintains resources appropriate to ensure that the AT&E function is executed properly. In addition, the ISO is accountable for ensuring that the AT&E function meets all requisite performance goals. The ISO manages the evolution of the program and ensures that it evolves as requirements and conditions change and evolve.

## The ISO and the Management of the Physical and Environmental Security Function

The ISO's role in the management of physical and environmental security is to oversee the development of all of the necessary controls to ensure that the physical infrastructure of the IT organization is secure and that all physical access points have been controlled. That includes ensuring that all of the equipment, facilities, and workspaces where data are kept are free of exploitable vulnerabilities.

The ISO is the role specifically accountable for ensuring that the IT security, human resources, physical security, and operations security management are brought together in a forum that produces a fully integrated, holistic, and coherent physical security plan. That includes the definition and establishment of a secure perimeter and defense in depth. It also includes the assurance that all assets within the controlled space are allocated explicit mechanisms for their protection. All of the elements of the plan must be maintained complete and its application must be provably comprehensive at all times. In support of that latter goal, the ISO is responsible for creating a formal quantitative measurement process to chart progress, as well as establishing a rational sustainment process to ensure that the protection scheme is always kept relevant and effective.

## The ISO and the Management of Acquisitions

The role of the ISO in conventional procurement is to ensure that the procurement process includes all necessary security related activities. That may touch on any of the standard activities associated with procurement, such as request for proposal (RFP) development or bid evaluation. But it will always involve monitoring procurement plans, contracts, and service level agreements (SLA) for compliance with organizational security policy. The ISO works with the various internal and external stakeholders in order to fulfill those duties. For example, the ISO might coordinate IT security professionals, software engineers, and even lawyers to ensure that the organization's procurement processes are safe and secure.

The ISO is the lead administrator when it comes to the acquisition of security related products and services. The ISO ensures that the specification of the features of the eventual purchase will correctly meet the organization's specific security requirements. In order to fulfill that obligation, the ISO conducts reviews and performs analyses to certify that security purchases satisfy all requirements as specified.

The ISO is responsible for ensuring that procurements are aligned with security requirements. Thus, the ISO ensures that the appropriate security requirements are always included in acquisition plans and that the correct set of evaluation elements are specified for all contracts and service level agreements. The ISO ensures that the acquisition of security related products is consistent with the business case and works with the company's lawyers to ensure that the organization's contracts do not violate any applicable standards, laws, or regulations.

Ensuring the proper level of contractor security generally includes the development and implementation of third party security policies. The ISO is then responsible for ensuring that all contractors understand and comply with the organization's security policies. The ISO role is responsible for all of the elements of organizational control with respect to the contractor's subsequent execution of security policies and procedures. That includes definition of an acceptable use policy for all contractors. It also includes the requirement to develop a relevant set of measures to ensure accurate reporting of performance. Finally, the ISO is responsible for all operational aspects of vendor management when it comes to the security process, including access by third parties to the organization's network. In that respect, it is the ISO who does the necessary background work to ensure that each supplier is technically competent and that that competency continues to meet all security requirements.

In order to facilitate execution of security duties among all contractors, the ISO develops and then embeds reasonable security requirements into all specifications of requirements and ensures that those security requirements are reflected in the specific contracting language. This applies to the purchase of conventional IT products and services as well as security products. The ISO manages that part of the contract oversight process that relates to all security products and services. The ISO also does the acceptance evaluation of all security products and ensures that all software being procured is free from exploitable vulnerabilities.

## The ISO and the Management and Evaluation of Legal, Regulatory, and Standards Compliance

The ISO is specifically responsible for ensuring that the organization's information processing and information retention functions do not violate any relevant standard, procedure, directive, policy, regulation, or law. In order to ensure fulfillment of that obligation, the ISO has to establish an enterprise-wide program to ensure compliance. The assurance of compliance is primarily a coordination task. It requires the ISO to identify and supervise the activities of every person who might be involved in the licensing, regulation, or legal compliance process.

The specific duty of the ISO is to identify the major risk factors involving compliance and then develop appropriate strategies to reduce the potential for regulatory risk. Consequently, the ISO has to be up-to-date on all applicable laws, regulations, standards, and best practices. The obligation to remain current requires the ISO to stay in touch with all relevant agencies and other external groups who might affect the organizational compliance process. The primary reason for the latter requirement is that the ISO has to be proactive in dealing with changes or trends in the external compliance environment.

As is the case with other areas, it is important for the ISO to be able to monitor the operational performance of the compliance function. The need for performance monitoring requires the ISO to establish a quantitative measurement program in order to ensure adequate understanding of the compliance situation. The ISO must be able to assess the effectiveness of all program controls for compliance. This assessment must be done on a regular basis in order to implement changes or improvements as required.

## The ISO and the Management and Evaluation of Security Risk Programs

No matter how conventional the situation, every organization has to develop and deploy a formal program to evaluate risk. This program has to comprise a substantive mechanism to identify and assess the impact of threats. Ideally, that program will be able to identify all risks and prepare a mitigating solution for each as they occur. However, that level of response is usually impossible, given the number of threats in the average organization's environment and the associated cost of mitigating every one of them. Therefore, every organization requires an intelligent risk management program, which will ensure that risks that pose the greatest threat are identified and then dealt with at an affordable cost.

The ISO is the person who establishes the risk management program. That program is always based on the business case for the enterprise. Operationally the ISO has to implement and then assess the effectiveness of the risk management program and implement changes where required. The ISO is responsible for performing regular threat and vulnerability assessments in order to identify all security risks. The aim is to install and update all necessary security controls. That requires the ISO to review the day-to-day performance of the technical and procedural controls that comprise the risk management system.

In support of this, the ISO establishes a substantive risk assessment procedure, which will allow decision makers to understand the impacts of identified risks on the businesses goals and objectives. There should be sufficient risk based data available to allow the decision maker to decide how much residual risk to accept and to guide the organization in steps to mitigate unacceptable risks. The ISO uses the assessment of residual risk to identify any necessary changes to risk management policies and processes. The purpose of this final step is to maintain those policies and processes relevant to the emerging risk and threat environment.

## The ISO and the Management, Design, and Evaluation of Strategic Management Programs

Most organizations achieve their long-term goals through a strategic management process. Strategic management is a large-scale governance process that charts the company's long-term course. The aim of strategic management is to determine the most productive path from among all of the potential directions the company might take. Overall strategic management is not just a security concern; it also involves the organization as a whole and is shaped by the business environment.

In the case of the security of information, the aim of the strategic management process is to reduce the organization's risk exposure by maintaining a systematic set of technical, physical, and personnel controls. In an operational sense, strategic management ensures that those controls are both effective and in line with the company's overall purpose. Then a tangible set of security controls is implemented and embedded in the overall operating structure of the organization. A single, well-defined information security management system reduces risk to the organization by ensuring comprehensive protection for the organization's information assets. The system itself is composed of all of the electronic, physical, personnel, and supporting security functions. The system is maintained in alignment with the organization's changing priorities and purposes by the strategic management process.

Alignment requires planning. Thus, much of strategic management involves the development of information security management plans that integrate all necessary security controls into a single, unified system. The ISO's particular role in the strategic planning process is to ensure that the right technical and managerial controls are combined into a functioning information security management system. The ISO is also directly accountable for managing the performance of the selected controls in operational use. Proper management includes defining and adopting performance measures to determine the efficiency and effectiveness of each control in the system. In conjunction with that assessment, the ISO also has the responsibility to ensure that objective data is utilized to maintain the correctness of the control set over time. Thus, the ISO is the one position in the organization that is responsible for ensuring that all controls within the information security management system are maintained effective. In that respect, the ISO is also responsible for making any required changes to that control set.

The integration of security controls and processes into the long-term management of the enterprise is a critical balancing task for the ISO. That is because the maintenance of a tangible set of security controls is fundamentally a resource management issue. For that reason, part of the ISO's job is to make certain that the organization's overall investment planning process incorporates considerations of security. It is the role of the ISO to maximize the organization's long-term security investment portfolio against the current threat picture and the organization's security priorities.

The ISO is also responsible for securing and administering the resources that are needed to guarantee the continuous acceptable performance of the control system. In support of that responsibility, the ISO collects and analyzes performance data in order to ensure that the information security system maximizes the use of security resources. Thus, it is an ongoing duty of the ISO to review security funding levels to determine if they are capable of sustaining a systematic security response. If the funds cannot maintain acceptable levels of security, then the ISO makes the recommendations for change.

In most organizations, the ISO is also the person responsible for the actual allocation of funds for security, so it is important that that position focus on assuring an adequate funding stream from the enterprise. At the same time, the ISO should also on make certain that all investments in security are cost-justified. That means that the ISO should regularly review the costs and benefits of each major investment and report on the performance of each investment to the people responsible for overall management of the organization.

## The ISO and the Management of System and Application Security Programs

The ISO is in the best position to ensure that practical information security is integrated into the software and systems development lifecycle (SDLC). The aim is to make certain that enterprise software does not contain exploitable vulnerabilities due to design or coding defects. That goal is supported by such activities as risk assessment and reviews and inspections to evaluate whether the SDLC complies with all applicable standards.

This is a primarily technical activity, so the ISO is usually the person responsible for developing the approach. The first step is to make sure that security is built in from the start by ensuring that there is a capable security-engineering program in place. Achieving a competent security engineering function requires the specification of procedures to build security into the SDLC. It should be noted that those procedures are in addition to the classic software quality assurance (SQA) methods. SDLC security procedures might include such additional activities as third party testing, certification, and even external audit.

In order to build security into the development process, the ISO typically designs and plans the security components that will be integrated into the SDLC. This is usually communicated through a developer's guide. The guide instructs programmers and other people involved in the security of applications and systems how to ensure secure code within the traditional SDLC. In order to ensure understanding, the ISO is responsible for the creation of a mechanism that will assure that developers are fully informed about security issues as they arise. The ISO also collaborates with project management to make certain that security activities are incorporated into the project management process as well as to ensure that any necessary changes are implemented as required.

# Ensuring the Corporate Commitment to Security: A New Breed of Security Manager

*The new CISO was sitting on a stool at his favorite after-hours watering hole thinking about the team he was about to form. Up to the present, he had relied on staff that had been pulled together from various other functions in the corporation. That was not a novel approach, since the company had always addressed any new crisis by forming ad-hoc task teams. Such teams were an amazingly cost effective way of dealing with the sort of issues that came and went on the corporate landscape, since the people on the team were just reassigned back to their original units when the emergency had passed.*

*On the other hand, a fire-fighting approach just didn't cut it with the new company CEO. He was painfully aware of the fact that cost-cutting and ad-hoc approaches had been the fundamental cause of the last disaster, and he wasn't about to make the same mistake. He was committed to more industrial strength methods. The expansion of the responsibilities of the CIO and the creation of a CISO role were the first steps in enforcing that commitment. But he knew that there was still a lot of organizing to do before he could declare the company to be reasonably safe. For now, however, his main concern was sustainability.*

*The CEO believed that the only way to ensure a state of continuously effective security was to establish an internal monitoring function, whose only task was to confirm that security was maintained at the right level of effectiveness. That belief was transmitted down to the CIO in no uncertain terms, and her commitment to keeping the CEO happy was the reason why the CISO was now sitting there thinking about hiring a sidekick. He knew that he could handle the development, deployment, and refinement of the security concept, but he felt that the task of also monitoring its day-to-day effectiveness was going to be a bridge too far.*

*He needed a person who was close to his level in the executive ranks, but whose only accountability would be to ensure that everything was functioning as it should be in the day-to-day exercise of security discipline. Essentially, what the CISO was looking for was an enforcer who could assure that every relevant individual in the company was complying, on a routine basis, with all pertinent security plans, policies, and procedures. Since the aim of that role was going to be to enforce compliance, he decided that the right label was **security compliance officer**, or **SCO**.*

*Because the SCO essentially constituted the "IT security police", the CISO felt that it was critical that the role be located at the executive rather than the managerial level. The point of that placement was to give the position corporation-wide authority for enforcement of security requirements. The CISO had been doing some reading on the subject of security discipline, and the literature in that field had been clear that the only way to ensure reliable execution of routine security tasks was through uniform supervision and enforcement of accountability across the board in the organization.*

*Given the requirement for consistent enforcement, that oversight process had to have some teeth in it. Otherwise the company's workers, who were likely to have a couple of inconvenient security tasks added their daily duties, might not be motivated to do their requisite duty. Fortunately, the CISO had worked with one individual who seemed perfect for the job. The woman was currently the manager of internal audit for the financial operation, and she had a fantastic eye for detail, a love of rules and regulations, and the personal instincts of a hungry wolverine.*

# Enforcing the Rules: The IT Security Compliance Officer

In some organizations, the IT SCO might be called the internal security auditor. Whatever the title, this role provides guidance and third party assessment of the organization's compliance status with respect to all relevant contracts, standards, laws, or regulations. That compliance, as defined by the EBK, can apply to both internal and external requirements. The basic role of the SCO is to oversee, evaluate, and ensure the organization's conformity with all regulatory, contractual, policy, and operational directives.

Individuals in this role perform a variety of functions with respect to assessment and compliance. Activities performed by the SCO include leading and conducting internal investigations into compliance issues and helping the various units in the organization comply with internal policies and procedures. The SCO also supports the third party compliance agents during audits. In order to fulfill this role, the SCO routinely evaluates compliance concerns for all 14 competencies. That includes:

- Evaluate data security
- Evaluate digital forensics
- Evaluate enterprise continuity
- Evaluate incident management
- Evaluate IT security training and awareness
- Evaluate IT systems operations and maintenance
- Evaluate network and telecommunications security
- Evaluate personnel security
- Evaluate physical and environmental security
- Evaluate procurement
- Design, implement, and evaluate regulatory and standards compliance
- Implement and evaluate risk management
- Evaluate strategic management
- Evaluate system and application security

## The SCO and Data Security Compliance

The role of the SCO is to ensure the enterprise's compliance with all data security policies and relevant legal and regulatory requirements. The SCO is not involved directly in the data security process beyond the evaluation of it; however, evaluation is an important task, given the consequences of a breach in confidentiality due to non-compliance with some law or regulation.

Besides assessment of the process, the SCO also works to maintain process integrity by ensuring that appropriate changes and improvement actions are implemented as required. Operationally, the SCO ensures that data classification and data management policies and procedures are issued and updated. The SCO also manages the enterprise's review and approval process when data management policies are disseminated. Finally, if a breach does occur, the SCO reviews all of the data concerning the breach and provides an incident report.

## The SCO and Compliance for Digital Forensics

The SCO ensures that the forensics process meets all legal standards and regulations. This is a critical task, since forensics work can often involve legal ramifications. Ensuring that the forensics process meets all mandatory requirements obliges the SCO to certify the effectiveness of the forensic examination procedures and accuracy of forensic tools. In order to do this, the SCO must attest to the degree of accuracy and appropriateness of the testing processes and procedures. The SCO also examines the penetration testing and vulnerability analysis results in order to identify risks and to implement the right patching response.

The SCO must also validate forensic tool sets used by the organization. Based on the results of these validations, assessments, and reviews, the SCO is accountable for implementing appropriate changes. The SCO must also review all forensic findings and documentation for their accuracy, applicability, and completeness. In order to do this, the SCO must authenticate the correctness of the analysis and reporting process using accepted methods for verifying suitability and suggests changes where appropriate.

Additionally, the SCO ensures that the forensics staff has the proper level of capability. Finally, the SCO has the responsibility to certify the continuing capability of the forensics process by recurrently assessing the quality assurance program, peer review process, and the audit proficiency testing procedures utilized by the forensics team. Based on those findings, the SCO will suggest changes to ensure effectiveness.

## The SCO and the Evaluation of Enterprise Continuity for Compliance

The SCO has responsibility for ensuring that due diligence has been done in establishing the enterprise continuity process. This is also an important function because should disaster strike, it is necessary to be able to document to all of the parties involved in the recovery process that all reasonable measures were taken to ensure the minimum amount of harm. The primary responsibility for the SCO is to test the crisis management response through targeted tests and exercises. Typical duties include assessment of the continuity response plan, and the associated operational training, to identify areas for improvement.

The SCO also evaluates the overall effectiveness of the enterprise continuity function, its processes, and its procedures in order to make recommendations for change.

In order to fulfill this responsibility, the SCO has to develop performance measures aimed at assessing the effectiveness of the various parts of the continuity process. The SCO also keeps track of any regulatory or mandatory changes to laws or standards governing continuity and ensures that the organization's response plan is kept current.

### The SCO and the Evaluation of Incident Management for Compliance

The SCO is responsible for ensuring that the incident management process remains effective through direct regular assessment of the value of incident response activities. That evaluation is done through tests, training, and exercises. The primary means of assessment is penetration testing. Because communication is such a critical element of incident response, the SCO also assesses the effectiveness of formal communication channels, both among the incident response team as well as with any associated internal and external organizations.

### The SCO and the Evaluation of IT Systems Operations and Maintenance for Compliance

The SCO is responsible for ensuring that all relevant security controls are in place and operating correctly during the IT systems operation and maintenance phases. In order to do this, the SCO audits the system and network for vulnerabilities and accounts for the strategic impact of all implemented security technologies. The responsibility to ensure the ongoing value of IT security is satisfied by regularly reviewing the performance and correctness of all functional security controls. The evaluation of those controls is based on, or references, all applicable standards, procedures, directives, policies, regulations, and laws.

In addition, the SCO is accountable for the performance of security administration technologies. In order to fulfill this responsibility, the SCO creates a relevant set of performance measures which are designed to ensure optimal performance of security technologies. This is a narrower assignment than overall security measurement, because in this case, the focus of the measurement and data gathering is strictly to ensure the effective operation of the technology.

### The SCO and the Evaluation of Network and Telecommunications Security for Compliance

The SCO is responsible for the evaluation and certification of network security. In order to do this, the SCO evaluates and calculates the risks to the enterprise of any identified network vulnerabilities. That requires the acquisition and assessment of routine operational data. The evaluation is done using measures that the SCO has to develop. These measures produce routine operating data, which the SCO can then analyze and report on. The SCO then ensures that capable and appropriate solutions are put in place to eliminate or otherwise mitigate any identified vulnerabilities.

Operationally, the SCO ensures that all anti-malware systems are operating as intended and that the functional processing requirements of the network have been satisfied. This is normally done through an independent verification and validation of the transmission capability. The SCO is responsible for arranging and overseeing that process and reporting the results.

## Evaluation of Personnel Security for Compliance

The SCO does not implement or manage the personnel security program. That is generally a human resources responsibility. Instead, the SCO routinely reviews the effectiveness of the personnel security program organization-wide. This is a particularly important task, given the impact of insider threats. The compliance function is essentially on the front-lines of personnel security when it is auditing the performance of the controls in the personnel security operation. The aim is to continuously identify and recommend changes that will improve personnel security practices organization-wide.

The SCO helps to maintain the effectiveness of the personnel security operation by evaluating the relationships between the known threat picture and the formal personnel security procedures that have been established to address it. The ideal would be to find that all threats to personnel security are addressed by effective personnel security controls. Operationally, the SCO accomplishes this task by periodically reviewing the personnel security program in order to determine whether it complies with all relevant policies, procedures, standards, directives, regulations, and laws.

## The SCO and the Evaluation of IT Training and Awareness for Compliance

The SCO is the person responsible for ensuring that information security personnel are receiving the appropriate level and type of training. This is accomplished through an evaluation of the effectiveness of the IT security awareness and training program. That evaluation essentially assesses the current performance of the security process. Where there are security breakdowns, each individual incident has to be studied in order to generate lessons learned. If it is found that the situation could be mitigated by new or better training, the knowledge gained from those lessons is factored back into improved training methods. The primary items assessed for training and awareness are the actual teaching materials. The aim of the evaluation is to ensure that the materials that support the awareness and training program encompass all current IT security issues and legal requirements and meets stakeholder needs.

## The SCO and the Evaluation of Physical and Environmental Security for Compliance

The SCO is not specifically responsible for physical security; however that role *is* responsible for ensuring that the overall physical and environmental security policies and associated controls are in place and remain continuously effective. If it is found that a policy is not effective, or is not in place to address a known physical security threat, it is the responsibility of the SCO to make recommendations for improvement. Those recommendations are primarily supported by the review of data that are generated from physical security incident reports. Any relevant standards can also be used as yardsticks for assessing compliance with best practice.

The SCO assesses the effectiveness of physical and environmental security controls by performing routine maintenance tests, which frequently take place in the field. The SCO also evaluates any procurement that has physical security implications and reports any adverse findings to management. Finally, the SCO routinely compiles, analyzes, and reports on the effectiveness of all of the performance metrics that are used to assess physical security performance.

## The SCO and the Evaluation of Procurement for Compliance

The violation or deviation from a contract, law, or regulation can lead to adverse consequences for a company. Therefore, an important duty of the SCO in the procurement process is to monitor all acquisitions for compliance with the requirements of contracts, regulations, or laws. The SCO is responsible for the evaluation of the effectiveness of the procurement function in ensuring the security of all purchased products. That does not normally entail the SCO actually being involved in the purchasing process. What it involves instead is the reviewing of memoranda of agreement, memoranda of understanding, and/or SLAs to ensure that minimum levels of IT security have been included. Those minimum levels are typically defined by executive management as part of strategic planning. The evaluation process also involves reviewing all contract documents, such as statements of work or requests for proposals, for inclusion of the standard set of IT security activities defined by the overall IT security plan. This determination is guided by the company's defined IT security policies, procedures, and practices.

From an operational and managerial standpoint, the SCO also conducts detailed reviews on the overall effectiveness of the investment when it comes to security. These analyses are driven by the business case that underlies the security investment. In terms of the business case, the SCO role also assesses and evaluates the effectiveness of the vendor management program. The primary focus of this evaluation is on the ability of the procurement function to ensure the security of all transactions with outside vendors and contractors. This evaluation also assures that the general procurement process aligns with established company policy.

Additionally, the SCO conducts vetting activities to ensure that vendors are operationally and technically competent to receive third party information, connect and communicate with company networks, and/or deliver and support secure applications. The SCO is also responsible for identifying and evaluating all relevant IT security trends with respect to procurement.

The process of vendor evaluation should particularly focus on identifying any new practices for mitigating the security risks associated with supply chain management. It is vitally important to assure the supply chain, because automated procurement systems have brought a whole new host of Internet-based threats into the supply chain management process. The consequence is that companies who previously never had to worry about being breached through weaknesses in their vendor supply chain now need to have procedures in place to protect themselves from attacks that might originate from their own vendor community. This is not strictly an electronic problem. In order to deal with it, consideration has to be given to potential harm from vendor personnel as well as failures in vendor procedures. Consequently, the SCO role not only has to patrol the company space; it also has to identify all reasonable threats from the people whom the company deals with.

## The SCO and the Design, Implementation, and Evaluation of Legal, Regulatory, and Standards Compliance Processes

Because compliance is the primary duty of the SCO, this role is particularly involved with legal, regulatory, and standards compliance. The SCO is responsible for developing the enterprise's compliance strategies, policies, plans, and procedures. Those strategies and plans must always be developed in accordance with established standards, procedures, directives, policies, regulations, and laws.

The SCO specifies the specific control elements of the enterprise's information security compliance program. The SCO also develops a plan of action and associated mitigation strategies, which are designed to address any identified program deficiencies. The latter activity is carried out by documenting the results from routine information security audits and recommending specific remedial action policies and procedures. In support of that reporting process, the SCO has to create a routine compliance reporting process that produces objective evidence that requisite control processes exist and are effective.

It is the role of the SCO to monitor, assess, and report on the information security compliance practices of all automated personnel and IT systems. Monitoring is achieved by compiling, analyzing, and reporting the outcomes of performance measures that have been established for each of those systems. The aim is to assess the effectiveness of the enterprise's established compliance program controls against all applicable standards, policies, procedures, guidelines, directives, regulations, and laws. In addition, the SCO assesses the effectiveness of the information security compliance process and procedures for process improvement and implements change where appropriate.

For compliance reporting purposes, the SCO is also responsible for maintaining ongoing and effective communications with key stakeholders. To fulfill this element of the role, the SCO conducts internal audits that are aimed at determining whether information security control objectives, controls, processes, and procedures are operating as expected and are effectively applied and maintained. This assessment is always done in accordance with enterprise policies and procedures.

## The SCO and the Implementation and Evaluation of Security Risk Programs for Compliance

Since non-compliance with standards, policies, procedures, guidelines, directives, regulations, and laws represents a specific risk to the organization, it is the duty of the SCO to develop and apply controls to support the general risk management program in the area of compliance. The SCO provides input during the consideration of how to properly balance the risks and benefits of policies, plans, procedures, and associated technologies for risk mitigation. The aim of the SCO's involvement is to ensure that compliance risks are factored into the overall risk management process.

Because the SCO's duties are also focused in ensuring operational security this position is responsible for conducting routine threat and vulnerability assessments to identify compliance based security risks as they arise. That information is then fed back into the overall development of security controls. The CISO normally oversees the actual development and change process for controls; however, the SCO typically provides input to the development and change process in order to ensure that all compliance issues have been addressed. Practically, there are usually more risks associated with the development of controls than can actually be mitigated. In that respect, it is the SCO role that is responsible for identifying all of the potential contractual and regulatory impacts that might shape the development of company-wide priorities. The SCO role also works with stakeholders within the company to ensure that the risk management program remains consistent with organizational policies regarding mitigation and acceptance of risk.

The SCO also typically initiates the necessary changes to risk management policies and procedures, in order to ensure that they remain current with the emerging risk and threat environment. The SCO role is the position responsible for assessment of the effectiveness of the overall risk management program. In order to identify the need for any changes to that program, the SCO routinely audits the execution of the risk management process and provides recommendations for changes to controls, policies, procedures, tools, and techniques for risk management.

Additionally, the SCO is responsible for monitoring any residual risk that might remain after the security program has been implemented. Residual risks are known risks that have been accepted without providing a specific mitigation. Typically, they are accepted rather than addressed, because they do not represent a significant threat. Because that situation can change over time, residual risk has to be monitored. It is the responsibility of the SCO to routinely assess known residual risks in order to identify any emerging threats associated with those risks. The SCO reports any emerging threats to the role responsible for developing security controls, typically the ISO. The SCO then works to ensure that the updated controls represent the correct response.

## The SCO and the Evaluation of Strategic Management Programs for Compliance

The primary role of the SCO with respect to strategic management is to determine whether the requisite security controls and processes have been adequately integrated into the investment planning process for IT. The determination of adequacy is usually based on IT portfolio and security strategic requirements. In order to assess adequacy, the SCO reviews the funding strategies within the overall IT portfolio to determine whether the level of investment in security correctly aligns with the company's overall security goals and objectives. If it is determined that the investment in security does not reflect the organization's stated aims, the SCO makes adjusted funding recommendations that are intended to balance investment with risk.

In the operational sense, the SCO regularly assesses the integration of security strategy with overall business strategy in order to ensure that these are properly aligned. Where these goals are not in alignment, the SCO makes recommendations for bringing the two strategies into proper alignment. Finally, in order to base these recommendations on objective evidence, the SCO has to develop a company-wide measurement program. The purpose of that program is to assess the goals of each major company initiative against the execution of the security program. The general aim is to ensure the continuing alignment of that security program with organizational goals and priorities.

## The SCO and the Evaluation of System and Application Security Programs for Compliance

In the technical domain of system and application security, it is the general role of the SCO to assess and evaluate electronic system compliance with corporate policies and architectural requirements. To meet this responsibility, the SCO audits the effectiveness of the automated controls that have been installed in each system to ensure operating system and application security. This assessment is typically supported by automated toolsets, which are designed specifically to test how all automated features are performing. Effectiveness can also be judged by conducting audits of system logs and tables. Using all of these methods, the SCO routinely audits all of the automated system controls in order to determine whether they have are achieving their purpose and then collects, analyzes, and reports the results.

Operationally, the SCO reviews the implementation of all new and existing risk management technologies within the routine operation of the system. The purpose is to ensure an optimal enterprise risk posture. To achieve that ideal state, the SCO reviews all security technologies to ensure that they support secure engineering across all SDLC phases. The SCO role also collects lessons learned in order to better support the integration of information security into the SDLC. The SCO is also responsible for assessing system maturation through the SDLC and its readiness for promotion to the operational stage.

## Chapter Summary

- The EBK assigns competencies to roles, which is unique among models.
- Each EBK role encompasses a number of different job titles, which are associated to the role by the fact that each job title achieves the same common purpose.
- There are three categories of roles (executive, functional, and corollary).
- There are three functional roles within the executive category (CIO, CISO, and SCO).
- Each of the functional roles in the executive category is important to security.
- The chapter explains the duties and competencies of the CIO.
- The chapter details the relationship between the CIO and the rest of the IA team.
- The chapter explains the role of ISO, often called the CISO in practice.
- There is a central relationship between the CISO and the information security management process.
- The SCO has a specialized role in a company.
- Compliance is an executive level, rather than an operational, responsibility.
- The SCO has a central role in ensuring security.

## Key Terms

**Body of knowledge (BOK)** A collection of knowledge elements all related to the same purpose and which describe the practices for accomplishing a well-defined goal or doing a specific type of work.

**Chief information officer (CIO)** The highest-level position in the information processing function; typically sets policy for the overall operation.

**Competency** A description of a specific behavior, or set of behaviors, that a person should be able to carry out in order to be considered "competent."

**Contingency planning** Planning based on responding to scenarios; in the case of security, this is also known as "disaster planning."

**Executive perspective** The policy layer perspective; most commonly involved in the development of strategic plans.

**Forensic investigation** The steps taken to gather and analyze digital evidence.

**Generic role** Categorization of common functions and purposes into a single role label, which is a unique feature of the EBK.

**Infrastructure** An architecture comprising all necessary components to accomplish a given purpose.

**IT security compliance professional** An executive position strictly devoted to ensuring compliance with policy, laws, directives, or regulations.

**Legal and regulatory compliance** Specific practices to ensure that the organization complies with all applicable laws, regulations, directives, and standards.

**Mitigation** Specific steps taken to decrease the impact of a given threat.

**Operations** The day-to-day functioning of an organization's, mostly routine, well-defined practices.

**Performance measurement** Objective assessment process designed to provide quantitative data about the performance of a process.

**Perspective** As applied within the EBK, a perspective encompasses a given set of roles. There are three EBK perspectives, which represent policy, management, and operational layers.

**Policy** An organization-wide directive on a given issue, which applies to all employees of the organization for a significant period of time.

**Risk** Likelihood that an identified weakness will be exploited by a known threat.

**Risk management** The process of placing a coherent set of countermeasures to mitigate all identified risks based on asset vulnerability and identified threats.

**Security compliance officer (SCO)** The executive who is responsible for ensuring the compliance of all aspects of the organization involved in information processing, or cybersecurity with laws, regulations, or directives.

**Security strategy** The specific organization-wide approach to security; this is more directionally focused than it is detailed.

**Threat environment** The specific threats that are known to exist within a specific organizational context.

**Vulnerabilities** Weaknesses, where threats are known to exist.

---

# Questions from the CIO

The CIO requires you to brief her on the current status of your investigation. This will be an important part of your continuing work on this project, since it is essential to be able to describe all of the ramifications of the functions of the key executive personnel. Consequently, the CIO would like you to answer the following questions for her:

1. How do organizational placement and reporting lines affect the ability of the security function to be effective? Why would reporting to the board of directors be advantageous?

2. How is it possible to group a cluster of potential job titles under a single generic label? What do those titles have in common that makes it possible to group them under a single label?

3. The CIO role is responsible for alignment. What are the generic functions that have to be aligned in every business, and why is it important to have that alignment?

4. What is the relationship between policy formulation and the CIO role? What is the specific responsibility of the CIO when it comes to policy? Why are general policies important in ensuring reliable security?

5. The CIO is responsible for implementing the overall cybersecurity process. That typically requires setting up some form of organizational governance system or architecture. What is this system composed of and what form does it take in actual practice?

6. What specific duties does the ISO perform? What differentiates the duties of the ISO role from those of other security professionals in the organization? What are the leadership responsibilities of the ISO? How are they different from those of the CIO?

7. What function does the ISO perform with respect to controls? How does the ISO use controls to ensure security? What are the specific tasks that the ISO carries out to ensure that controls are implemented correctly?

8. Risk is an important factor in security. What is the ISO's role in managing risk? What specific tasks does the ISO perform to satisfy that responsibility in the area of risk?

9. The SCO's role is heavily leveraged by the audit function. How does audit allow the SCO to do his or job? What is typically audited? How does the information gained from the audit help enforce security?

10. The SCO is responsible for routine threat and risk evaluations. Why is this type of activity logical for that role? How does threat and risk factor into the day-to-day assurance of proper security system performance? What is the SCO's specific set of tasks in identifying and assessing risk?

# Hands-On Projects

Using the Case in Appendix 1, develop a detailed strategic management plan for the executive roles for the company. Ensure that the following requirements are satisfied:

- There is a comprehensive job description for each role.
- All responsibilities for policy, management, and operational practice are specified.
- The organization has a mechanism in place to prove compliance with any anticipated regulations or laws.
- The continuity process is defined and roles are assigned.

# chapter 5

# Defining the Company's Functional Security Roles

## Building the Information Security Team

*The Singapore Airlines Airbus 380 deposited the CISO at the gate the next day at noon. He knew it was noon because his watch said so. But, seeing as he had crossed the International Date Line on the 20-hour flight, he was not sure precisely which day it was noon of. And of course, that was the exact moment when both his cell phone and his Blackberry went off. It was company headquarters, and they wanted him immediately. He hopped a cab at JFK, and because it was lunchtime, he covered the 18 miles to midtown in a mere hour and a half. He was not happy with the CIO when he got there.*

*The "emergency" centered on how to handle the three executive positions. He had never thought about creating a general policy for how to deploy those roles, because only one person could occupy each position at any given time. Under the CISO's own tailoring process, there was the implication that customized work instructions had to be developed at each site for each of the three executive roles. That was a nice idea in theory, but the vision of local CIOs reporting to corporate CIOs and local CISOs reporting to corporate CISOs was too convoluted to even think about, let alone implement. A policy decision was required. The CISO's problem with the CIO was that she could have easily made that decision while he was gone. Instead, she had left it up to him.*

*Obviously, the CIO was getting a little nervous about his rapid rise in the company. He knew that; this was the first big policy decision of his new tenure as CISO, and there were going to be some visible ramifications if he made the wrong choice. He grabbed a high-powered energy drink from the refrigerator in his office suite, mainly to clear the cobwebs from the 20-hour flight, and began to think about his company's corporate structure, demographics, and culture. He knew from his experience in Singapore that the eventual success of the response was going to have to take into account those three variables.*

*The staff size for the information security function at the local operations was relatively small, and the reporting lines at each site were tied directly to the central administrative office. The CISO was convinced that the most efficient way of instituting executive leadership was to set the policy direction from a single source. Of course, the CISO also recognized that what worked best in the particular instance of his company did not necessarily mean that the executive function should always be centralized. Nor did it imply that the security functions at the local sites were unmanaged. It simply meant that the security governance for this particular company would operate most efficiently if the executive roles were centralized in New York.*

*At the same time, the CISO also knew from his Singapore experience that the details of the security system were best developed and implemented at each site. Fortunately, he already had a model that he knew would let him reliably centralize policy while distributing the actual implementation. He already had the policy-making roles in place in the form of his new executive roles. What was left was the definition and staffing of a set of functional security roles at each site.*

*The four functional security roles are ideally suited to the creation and management of a specific security response for a given application. As the name implies, the functional roles are the ones that essentially do the hands-on management and operational work in a specific situation. So while the executive roles set policy, the functional roles are responsible for the implementation of that policy.*

*Everybody who was involved in the process was well aware that the functional roles were the ones that did the specialized security work. The precise details of how the functional roles would be defined and executed would form the concrete information security response for each site, and the company as a whole in aggregate. The CISO's guiding assumption had always been that different behaviors could be shaped to produce the same outcome. The notion of common definitions for each **functional role**, which could be tailored to fit the specific needs of each site, fit neatly into his overall game plan.*

*The EBK identifies four specific roles in the functional category: **digital forensics professional, IT security engineer, IT security operations and maintenance professional**, and **IT security professional**. The first step in the practical process of implementation was to identify and bundle each of the unique job titles in the company's organization chart under an appropriate role category. Unfortunately, as soon as the CISO's task team started the bundling process, it was apparent that an inordinately large number of job titles could conceivably fit under each individual role at each of the sites.*

*Initially, it had seemed logical to assume that each site would have the same general set of job titles; however, this was not the case. Slight differences in the work culture had produced an array of different and non-standard position titles at each site. The result was that there were a dissimilar number of security functions at every location, all with slightly different labels. Moreover, each of those titles had slightly different job tasks associated with them. It was clear that the process of sorting site-specific titles into their appropriate roles was going to take considerably more time than anticipated.*

*The team responsible for sorting this out had started the individual customizing process at each site with the digital forensics professional. There was some logic to starting with that role. Besides the obvious fact that it was first on the list in the EBK, the job titles associated with the digital forensics professional were the least common and the most distinctive across the company. So they were easier to identify and bundle under the digital security professional role. Since digital forensics was not as directly involved in day-to-day security work as the other roles were, it was simpler to work out the inevitable bugs in the assignment of standard work functions for that role. This could be done without disrupting the ongoing security process at the site.*

*The compliance officer, who was particularly expert at evidence gathering, was given the responsibility of overseeing the process of defining how the digital forensics role would fit. In addition, because the forensics process was particularly critical to determining legal compliance, it was decided that operationally all of digital forensics professionals at each of the sites would report directly to the compliance officer, rather than to the CISO.*

## The Digital Forensics Professional Role

The specific purpose of the digital forensics professional is to gather **electronic evidence** that supports any investigation of wrongdoing involving a computer device. The investigations themselves can encompass any instance of theft or harm, or even unintentional misuse. The digital forensics professional gathers evidence from any computers or digital media that might be implicated in the wrongdoing and supports any legal or regulatory action. The general public uses the terms "**computer forensics**" and "digital forensics" interchangeably. Since the EBK designates this role as the "digital forensics" professional, that label will be used here.

Typically, the digital forensics professional works with criminal investigators to process evidence of criminal activity. This person might also be required to gather evidence in support of **civil litigation**. In criminal or civil court cases, the digital forensics professional is responsible for guaranteeing the integrity and accuracy of the evidence gathered. Additionally, this person establishes and guarantees the integrity of the subsequent **chain of custody**.

Evidence gathered by the digital forensics professional is often in the form of hidden or erased files, encrypted items, passwords, and digitally transmitted or network data. This person also has a role in disaster recovery, for example, in rebuilding lost files. These various duties require the digital forensics professional to be able to analyze any digital artifact and capture, record, and report any evidence that might be contained in it.

Examples of digital artifacts include computers or computer systems. They can also involve separate storage media, electronic documents such as e-mail, and even packet stream and packet analysis. The ability to work with all forms of electronic media implies a high level of technical knowledge that enables the digital forensics professional to obtain and process all the evidence that is necessary to understand a given series of digital events. The characterization of those events has to be expressed in scientific or empirical terms. Because the evidence itself is digital, the actual process of discovery is typically supported by tools. Therefore, the digital forensics professional must also be able to execute all necessary, tool-based analytic procedures as well as operate all of the actual tools required to collect, process, preserve, analyze, and present digital evidence.

Digital forensics operations can be extremely resource intensive, in that they require highly trained digital forensics specialists and dedicated equipment. This equipment is rarely used outside of situations that are, by definition, exceptional. Therefore, digital forensics operations are often outsourced, or established as stand-alone functions that can be shared among a number of potential customers. Consequently, the digital forensics professional role normally operates independent from the rest of the cybersecurity roles. The relationship with the rest of the cybersecurity roles is typically in an external, or in-house, consulting capacity. That shared arrangement can mitigate the digital forensics functions resource demands. Nonetheless, it also means that, in ordinary settings, the digital forensics professional does not have a direct reporting line to anybody but the organization's executive managers.

One further complication is that the digital forensics examiner might need a formal license to practice, granted by the state or another licensing authority. Licensing is frequently required because forensics has legal implications. The licensure is similar to the way that private investigators or certified public accountants are licensed. The EBK specifies the following competencies for the digital forensics professional, who holds one of the four functional security roles in the modern enterprise, as shown in Figure 5-1.

- Manage, design, implement, and evaluate the digital forensics function
- Implement incident management processes
- Design, implement, and evaluate IT system operation and maintenance processes
- Design and implement network and telecommunications security
- Evaluate procurement processes
- Implement risk management processes

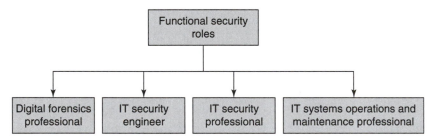

**Figure 5-1**  Functional security roles
© *Cengage Learning 2012*

## Daily Tasks

The digital forensics competency encompasses all of the knowledge and skills required to obtain, authenticate, and investigate electronic data from all relevant **incidents** and to recreate the events of the incident from the data. The digital forensics competency area is the primary responsibility of the digital forensics professional. Logically the digital forensics competency has the greatest number of task requirements for the digital forensics professional.

The general duty of the digital forensics professional is to design, implement, and then execute the most effective digital forensic procedures possible to obtain the necessary forensic evidence. The digital forensics professional ensures that the most advanced and appropriate forensics tools are available to support the investigatory process. In order to meet the overall conditions for investigative capability, the digital forensics professional must understand all legal requirements and practical restrictions as they apply to the criminal investigation process.

The legal responsibility for collecting and preserving evidence in a manner that meets all local statutory requirements is absolute when it comes to the prosecution of crime and the pursuit of civil remedies. Therefore, the digital forensics professional also has to make certain that the necessary technological processes are established to ensure that digital evidence is collected in a legally acceptable fashion. Examples of this latter responsibility include ensuring that policies and procedures exist for copying electronic media in a way that assures a legally correct and accurate image. Those policies should also encompass all of the equipment and tools that might be needed to perform all necessary digital investigation functions.

**Assurance of the Physical Requirements of the Investigation** In order to set up a proper digital forensics function, the digital forensics professional has to ensure that the actual equipment that performs the digital forensics investigations is both available as well as capable of supporting the digital forensics function. Moreover, because the gathering of electronic evidence often requires a highly controlled physical environment, the digital forensics professional is also responsible for ensuring that the electrical, thermal, acoustic, and physical security requirements of the digital investigation space are continuously satisfied.

In conjunction with this latter responsibility, the digital forensics professional is responsible for making certain that the software requirements of the digital forensics lab are kept up to date, including ensuring the software configuration of the forensic laboratory and mobile toolkit software.

Finally, because digital forensics investigations are based on technology, the digital forensics process and its equipment always have to evolve with that technology. The problem is that technology evolves at a rapid pace. One additional responsibility of the digital forensics professional is to stay on top of change as it occurs and make appropriate changes to the technology as needed.

**Assurance of the Procedural Requirements of the Investigation** As well as ensuring the maintenance of the physical requirements of the digital forensics function, there is a more critical responsibility for the digital forensics professional. That responsibility is to ensure the existence and integrity of all requisite policies for the identification, acquisition, and preservation of electronic evidence, the procedures for data recovery and analysis, and the means for reporting and archiving forensically examined material.

Because of the legal ramifications of digital forensics work, these policies must be in accordance with all relevant standards, procedures, directives, policies, regulations, and laws. The digital forensics professional is also responsible for the satisfaction of all federal, state and local legal requirements, as they apply to the forensic investigation process itself.

Examples of specific activities that fulfill that responsibility would be in such areas as ensuring that formal chain of custody procedures conform to applicable legal requirements for the particular environment. Other examples might include ensuring that policies are present for secure disposal, or retirement of media that is part of the investigative process. Because requirements will vary from place to place, this is not an easy task. It requires familiarity with local laws and regulations, as well as an understanding of how those apply to the digital investigative process for that environment.

**Assurance of Staff Capability** From the standpoint of ensuring staff capability, the digital forensics professional is responsible for all training and education programs that ensure the ongoing competency of any personnel who are involved in the forensics process. That activity can include mentoring, training, testing, and **professional certification** and periodic re-examinations. It also includes specific efforts to ensure expertise in such common tasks as use of forensic analysis equipment, technologies, and procedures. This duty is typically supported by any ongoing quality assurance program that ensures the capability of the digital forensic laboratory, as well as any peer review processes and any mandated audit or proficiency-testing procedures to identify where changes would be appropriate.

## Operational Duties

Operationally, the digital forensics professional must be able to coordinate investigations and other legal interactions with all appropriate corporate entities such as legal advisors and security managers. In investigations that involve external entities, such as governmental and law enforcement groups, the digital forensics professional must be able to assist in the collection and preservation of all pertinent evidence. As is the case with any other external investigation, evidence collection and chain of custody is typically dictated by the investigating body. Therefore, one other responsibility of the digital forensics professional is to ensure that all required activities are known and that they conform to all mutually agreed on and formally defined practices.

Besides investigative responsibilities, the digital forensics professional also contributes to operational efforts to protect networks and computer systems from vulnerabilities and weaknesses. The digital forensics professional contributes to this process by developing meaningful evidence to support operational risk analysis and patch management processes.

This evidence is typically derived from the results of **penetration testing** and vulnerability analysis, which in itself is carried out by the incident management function. Where vulnerabilities are discovered, the evidence that the digital forensics professional has developed will help support recommendations for remediation. This evidence is usually gathered from the organization's intrusion detection systems and intrusion prevention systems, as well as all of the conventional network and system monitoring and logging systems.

Forensic investigations for both computer and network equipment require a similar skill set. Nonetheless, there are enough differences between the two types of technologies that every digital forensics team ought to be composed of specialists with particular competencies in each of those areas of investigation. In addition to being able to practice specialized skills, the individual digital forensics professional must also be able to function effectively as a team member.

# The Digital Forensics Professional and the Assurance of the Integrity of Forensic Investigations

The digital forensics professional is responsible for ensuring the effectiveness of the forensic investigation processes and the accuracy of forensic tools. Where problems are identified, it is the responsibility of the digital forensics investigator to implement changes as required. Overall, the digital forensics professional is responsible for reviewing all forensic processes and their outcomes for validity, reliability, applicability, reproducibility, and completeness.

The digital forensics professional also assesses the effectiveness, accuracy, and appropriateness of testing processes and procedures and suggests changes where appropriate. In addition, this professional must be able to assess the digital forensic staff to ensure that members have the appropriate knowledge, skills, and abilities to perform forensic activities. The digital forensics professional also validates the effectiveness of the overall analysis and reporting process, and implements changes where appropriate based on the results of this validation, assessment, and review process.

In order to ensure the integrity of the investigative process, the digital forensics professional creates and then ensures the ongoing suitability of a formal baseline standard for the forensic work. A continuously documented record of the correctness of the forensic analysis process is important because the effectiveness of the procedures and tools utilized for forensic investigation cannot subsequently be called into question. Consequently, the digital forensics professional conducts evaluations to determine whether proper chain-of-custody practices have been followed. The aim is to ensure that all pertinent standards, procedures, directives, policies, regulations, and laws for maintaining the integrity of forensic evidence have been observed.

The digital forensics professional is also primarily responsible for the collection and retention of any audit data that is used to support the technical evaluation of any instance of accidental violation, intentional misuse, or outright criminal behavior. If the behavior is criminal in nature, the digital forensics investigator is also responsible for reporting any relevant audit data in such a way that it can be used by corporate security, or any appropriate law enforcement agency, to apprehend the criminal. In order to facilitate the criminal investigative process, the digital forensics professional is responsible for assessing, extracting and then coordinating and reporting any relevant investigative evidence obtained from all of the forensic data collected.

## Incident Management Controls

Incident response has distinct forensic overtones; forensic data is important if the organization hopes to understand incidents and build defenses that will avoid reoccurrences or prevent incidents from happening in the first place. The digital forensics professional assists in the process of incident response by doing forensic analysis of incidents and reporting the findings of that analysis to response management. Since the lessons learned from each incident point to more effective ways of identifying, containing, eradicating, and recovering from future events, the knowledge and understanding that the digital forensics professional can provide is vital to the overall mission of protecting the organization.

Operationally, the digital forensics professional is involved in the collection, processing, and preservation of evidence from every meaningful incident. This person also coordinates, integrates, and leads the evidence collection team's response to requests from internal and external groups, especially in cases where the incident is likely to require litigation. Because forensic examinations take place after an incident occurs, that data collection and analysis process happens after the fact. In that respect, the digital forensics professional is not strictly speaking responsible for the operational monitoring of networks and systems for intrusions. However, in the typical execution of the incident response plan, it is the digital forensics professional who is called on to do the scientific evidence gathering. The digital forensics professional collects, analyzes, and reports data based on the investigation of the incident. The results of that investigation are reported using standard reporting procedures, which the forensics professional is normally responsible for defining.

The digital forensics professional also helps the organization prevent incidents by identifying potential vulnerabilities. That support is provided through penetration testing and other types of proactive incident response exercises. It is the responsibility of the digital forensics investigator to ensure that the organization learns from all incidents. This aim is satisfied by ensuring that all analyses of relevant evidentiary data get to the right decision maker, who can then use the analyses to incorporate effective responses into future organizational plans.

# On the Job with a Digital Forensics Professional

As the name implies, the IT systems operation and maintenance function is an ongoing operational process that is guided by the policies and procedures established as part of the organization's operating plan. The purpose of the systems operation and maintenance function is to maintain, monitor, control, and protect IT infrastructure and assure the day-to-day functioning of the information technology process in the organization. Operationally, the digital forensics professional establishes a secure computing environment by ensuring that all information systems are assessed regularly for vulnerabilities, and by implementing the appropriate solutions to eliminate or otherwise mitigate identified vulnerabilities.

Unlike incident response, which requires direct involvement in the investigation of the incident, the role of the digital forensics professional in system operations is to implement a standard evidence-based process to confirm that the routine operation of the system conforms to all relevant security policies and procedures. The process must also be able to provide empirical proof that the standard system operation and maintenance process conforms to any relevant standards, procedures, directives, policies, regulations, or laws that might be relevant to a forensic investigation. The digital forensics professional also tests and certifies all strategic security technologies to ensure their integrity and correctness.

Because vulnerabilities might be inserted during the maintenance process, the digital forensics professional also has to make certain that a basic forensic audit of each system is regularly done. The data that supports forensic audits is usually developed as part of conventional operational testing. This requires the digital forensic professional to perform routine forensic audits of the software and systems operation using a well defined set of organizational procedures. These procedures must comply with all applicable standards, directives, policies, regulations, and laws for conduct of a forensic audit process.

Additionally the digital forensics professional participates in the analysis of formal change requests in the routine change approval process. These requests for change to a system or its software are submitted as part of the day-to-day operational management process. In support of that process, the digital forensics professional performs tests to ensure that all proposed changes to system software and hardware, as well as the performance of all contracted or outsourced work, are correct and do not introduce unanticipated vulnerabilities.

The digital forensics professional also performs proactive security tests to ensure that the system is adequately protected against all foreseen methods of attack. In order to do this, the digital forensics professional prepares test scripts, criteria, and procedures in order to ensure a satisfactory level of protection. These scripts, criteria, and procedures are then administered in conjunction with the routine system operation and maintenance testing processes; mitigations are suggested from the outcomes of the processes.

If the testing uncovers areas of subsequent weakness, the digital forensics professional recommends changes to those procedures or to the affected technology. Since the aim of these recommendations is to enhance the security of the overall system, that advice is typically provided outside of the reporting that is part of the routine operational testing of hardware and software. Furthermore, given their level of importance, these recommendations should normally be accompanied by the quantitative evidence that supports them.

Targets for the forensic investigative process typically include critical points of failure, such as the authentication and authorization function, the organizational continuity and disaster recovery plan, and the specific security controls, processes, policies, and procedures utilized by the organization. The digital forensics professional also identifies ways the system can be improved from the results of forensic examinations. Specifically, the forensics professional advises managers on the effectiveness of the organization's control functions with respect to conventional IT personnel, application, system software, or physical security operations. It should be noted that in the case of individual personnel, direct forensic investigation has implications with respect to privacy rights. These rights must be considered at the time a forensic examination is established.

## Network and Telecommunications Security

The system data that is used by the digital forensics professional is often a primary target for attack. It is therefore logical that this position should play a significant role in ensuring the security of basic network and telecommunications services. The digital forensics professional ought to be able to provide direct input into the development of the network and telecommunications security process. Specifically, the digital forensics professional should help shape the design of network security policies and the development of overall strategic plans for the network.

Input to policy and planning is justified because forensic investigations generate highly focused data about day-to-day security operations. These investigations provide forensic audit data, which is typically derived from system logs and the ongoing security testing process. The digital forensics professional documents all of the outcomes of these logs, tests, and forensic audits in standard network security reports. The data contained in those reports can then be used to design more effective network security controls.

Operationally, the digital forensics professional has a continuing obligation to prevent and detect attacks and intrusions. This duty is typically satisfied by performing routine forensic audits and tests of security controls. The digital forensics professional tests networks to determine whether they have been tampered with. This testing is aimed at proving that the messaging process is confidential and free from eavesdroppers and that the network itself is properly authenticated to outside users. The digital forensics professional also tests and confirms the effectiveness of the security control on the network and tests the security technologies within the entire network domain.

## Evaluation of Procurement Processes for Forensic Concerns

Because purchased products should be thoroughly vetted prior to their integration into the operating environment of the organization, the digital forensics professional also plays a part in ensuring the security of the procurement process. The primary involvement of the digital forensics professional in routine procurement is in the evaluation of the supply-chain management process and its products for security risks. In addition to vetting the supply chain and its products, the digital forensics professional also plays a role in the assessment and evaluation of the effectiveness of the vendor management program. The digital forensics professional does that by collecting detailed evidence which describes the performance of that process.

The digital forensics professional might also play a part in evaluating specific vendors, on or off site. This would be done by conducting forensic audits and penetration tests to verify that the vendor complies with all contractual requirements and is operationally and technically competent to maintain security. If vulnerabilities are discovered, the digital forensics professional can also provide sufficient evidence to support appropriate mitigations or improvements to the vendor's security processes.

## Risk Management Procedures

Because the identification and assessment of risks should be based on evidence, the digital forensics professional plays a part in the risk management process. In that capacity, the digital forensics professional should do routine forensic audits and security tests to identify and assess risks to information assets. Forensic data to support risk management can also be developed from the results of personnel, facilities, and equipment security audits and tests. Cost-effective recommendations about ways to mitigate the identified risk can then be developed from that evidence, which contributes to the business case for security.

Operationally, the digital forensics professional provides data to support in the development of the specific controls for risk mitigation. These controls are part of the risk management program. As with the maintenance and operation and network security functions, the digital forensics professional can provide input to the development of policies, plans, procedures, and technologies to mitigate the known risks. This advice is obtained from the evidence developed from routine and targeted audits and tests. The role of the digital forensics professional is to collect data from the actual threat and vulnerability assessments that are used to identify security risks. Based on the results of the analysis of this data, the digital forensics professional can provide advice that decision makers can use to update security controls.

# Designing the Security Response: The IT Security Engineer

*The CISO was perched on the arm of the CIO's expensive Modern Line couch looking out the window of her corner office at the helicopter traffic over the East River. The thought in the back of his mind was that he would like to be sitting behind that desk one of these days. But that would have to wait. He had more important matters to attend to first, mainly the creation of a staffing profile for the far-flung security operations that reported to him.*

*He felt that the highly visible activity of tailoring the old security staff positions into a logical and structured framework had gotten him a long way toward his eventual goal, which was the CIO's job. Nevertheless, he was also aware that there was going to be a lot of politics involved in the re-shuffling of the various job titles. So he needed the CIO's full support. And that was what he was in her office to get. Sitting on the edge of the couch put him a head taller than the CIO, who was sitting across from him behind her custom desk like the Queen of England herself. The CISO knew that he had to get her approval for the strategy he had devised, so he was being his usual charming self.*

*The CIO and the CISO were both of the opinion that the definition of the forensics professional role was more of a test run than an actual exercise in deployment. The reformatting of the* digital forensics role into a structured set of responsibilities had gone well. That was mainly because there were relatively few employees in the entire corporation who fell under that designation, and most of them were located at the corporate offices in New York. So they were easy to reach and convince. Both the CIO and the CISO agreed that the next step in the process would be much more complex and potentially risky. That was the task of documenting the primary role in the development of the information security response itself.

The overall strategy was built around the assumption that the forensics professional would be the easiest to create, because it had a relatively limited set of purposes and duties. On the other hand, the next role was responsible for the detailed design and implementation of the whole information security response at each site, which implied a much broader focus and skill set. The EBK label for that position was "IT security engineer." Whatever the actual title, the position itself was responsible for designing an appropriate security solution for their specific setting. Following the conceptual work, that role would then maintain the resulting day-to-day response.

The company had decided that each site needed to have practitioners who fulfilled each of the roles in the functional category. But it wasn't easy to distinguish between the role of the IT security engineer and the rest of the roles in the security team, all of whom had some form of operational responsibility. The main difficulty was that many of the responsibilities of that role appeared to overlap with those of the CISO position above it and the IT security professional positions underneath it. The reason why it was particularly hard to differentiate between the role of the IT security engineer and that of the CISO and the IT security professional roles was that all of them have some form of direct involvement in the design, implementation, and management of the IT security solution.

Where the IT security engineer differed from the CISO role was in focus. The CISO is responsible for the information security solution for the entire company. Consequently, the focal point of that role is much more in the realm of overall policy and strategy development. That is also the reason why it was logical for the company to have only a single CISO position. On the other hand, the IT security engineer is accountable for implementing all of the details of a workable, day-to-day solution for a particular location. The level of detail required to customize a solution like that requires a much more immediate presence on-site. That is the reason why the company felt that the decision to locate an IT security engineer position at each site was justified. It also was the basis for the decision not to have a CISO at each site. Instead, the executive team decided that each IT security engineer would function as the CISO's representative and alter ego at each particular site. Because the IT security engineer was local, yet had responsibility for implementing the overall security model, that decision also had the added advantage of extending management control over security down to the project level at each location.

Since this role was responsible for implementing the overall security concept as provided by the CISO, the company felt that only a single IT security engineer could be justified at each site. That was because the IT security engineer position is responsible for the overall implementation of the company's security concept for that particular place. And as the old adage about cooks and broth goes, too many engineers are likely to produce a less than ideal solution. On the other hand, since most of the actual day-to-day security work would be done by the information security professional role, it was expected that there would be a lot of people in the security professional positions at each site. And so it was decreed that they would all report to the IT security engineer.

*In fact, the difference between customizing the concept and executing the resultant security solution served as the main distinction between the IT security engineer and the IT security of operations and IT security professional roles. The former role in effect was the sole designer, implementer, and overseer of the solution, whereas the latter roles were responsible for doing the actual, day-to-day, hands-on work that was prescribed in that solution.*

*Finally, the team felt that it was important for all of the members of the corporation to understand that the IT security engineer was not a classic "engineer" in the sense that the position did not design and build concrete artifacts, nor was the body of knowledge in the field based around mathematics. The team members wanted people to understand that IT security engineers were specifically oriented toward integration and customization of processes and virtual tools. Their purpose then, was to build comprehensive IT security solutions using whatever cross-disciplinary knowledge was required.*

# The IT Security Engineer Role

The general activities of the IT security engineer role were process and practice based rather than technical. In that respect, the EBK specifies five competency areas for this role:

- *Data security*—design, evaluate
- *IT operations and maintenance*—design, implement
- *Network and telecommunications security*—design, implement
- *Risk management*—implement
- *System and application security*—design, implement, evaluate

## Data Security Processes

The IT security engineer is the role that is responsible for the detailed design of the security solution within each security setting. Where the executive positions might be responsible for the general definition of what is required in the way of security, the IT security engineer is responsible for ensuring that those requirements are implemented in practical terms at each site.

The person performing the IT security engineer role has to know and understand the meaning of all relevant corporate policies. That is because it is the IT security engineer's responsibility to ensure that the ultimate implementation of those policies can be traced back to what the policy makers originally intended to accomplish. Likewise, because policies change over time, the IT security engineer also has to maintain a continuing knowledge of corporate directions. The latter requirement ensures that new policies within the engineer's particular area of responsibility are correctly addressed.

The primary capability for this position is the ability to create a comprehensive information security solution which is appropriate to the area of responsibility of the engineer. In order to be able to do that, the IT security engineer has to coordinate all of the activities that go into building a working day-to-day security solution. That includes development of the design of the overall information security system, overseeing its implementation, and evaluating the results. The general goal of the IT security engineer is to produce a solution that will ensure effective privacy, secure access, retention, and disposal, as well as effective incident management, while adhering to all applicable data security standards, guidelines, and requirements.

The IT security engineer achieves this goal by following a formal process aimed at producing a security system that achieves the protection aims of the EBK's 14 principles. Since that protection scheme is primarily aimed at securing the organization's data, the first step is to identify, document, and label all data assets of any value, along with each of those item's protection requirements. The next step is to assess the risk to that data and then specify the sensitivity/protection requirements for each type. From this understanding, the IT security engineer would be expected to identify an appropriate set of information security controls.

The resultant control set is then based on the perceived risk of compromise to the data. Those controls comprehensively enforce the authentication and authorization of **privileges** to each user seeking access to the system. They should always be appropriate to the environment that they were designed to control. For instance, in the case of a highly secure facility, the controls might enforce classification policies, which are defined by government regulation, whereas in a general unregulated facility those controls would support a much more relaxed policy. That authorization is based on user identity and privileges. The controls are implemented based on the organization's data security policies, which the IT security engineer must help ensure are in accordance with all relevant standards, procedures, directives, policies, regulations, and laws.

The IT security engineer then audits and tests those controls on a regularly scheduled basis. Using the results from the routine audits and tests, the IT security engineer evaluates the effectiveness of the organization's data security policies, processes, and procedures. Conclusions about effectiveness are typically based on how well those activities achieve the purposes of the recommendations of the EBK, or any other global security standard that is used for guidance, such as ISO 27000, or FIPS 200. Given the all-inclusive nature of those standards, documented proof of satisfactory performance of the control set can be implicitly assumed to indicate that the general goal of security is being met in that instance.

The IT security engineer evaluates the effectiveness of the control set in relation to the requirements of the appropriate standard or guideline and suggests any needed modifications or changes. Those recommendations are based on the outcome of ongoing audits and tests. Since these tests will also reveal potential weaknesses, violations of data security, or privacy requirements, the IT security engineer is also in an ideal position to identify any improvements that are required to maintain the company's desired level of data protection.

## IT Systems Operations and Maintenance Processes

Everyday security activities always have a reasonable share of design built into them. Therefore, the IT security engineer is the person who has the primary responsibility for designing the exact processes used to continuously maintain, monitor, control, and protect the general IT infrastructure and the information that resides within it. That job is addressed by the steps the IT security engineer takes to ensure that the routine security activities that are built into that infrastructure are always kept in proper alignment with the company's current business case. The actions that are involved in assuring that alignment have to be embedded in the conduct of day-to-day operations.

The issues that have to be considered in designing a correct set of day-to-day security practices are not the same as the concerns that underlie the design of the overall security solution. That is because the practices that are required to fulfill the routine security needs of the organization are usually dependent on the willingness of the conventional workforce to perform them on a disciplined basis. Functional design criteria like simplicity and ease of use become major factors at the operational level.

The problem comes from the fact that the conventional workforce's primary interest is not in computer security, particularly if that security function requires additional work. As a result, people are likely to find ways of "getting around" or not performing their basic security duties. The design problem that this represents is how to arrange those practices to be as simple and understandable as possible. In addition to being simple and easy to use, **operational security** has to be facilitated by an awareness program, which is carefully designed to reinforce the importance to the workforce of disciplined execution of basic security tasks.

**Security Management** The IT security engineer is responsible for the creation of a management scheme to ensure that the wide range of routine security duties is reliably performed. The IT security engineer typically documents the practical management requirements for those duties in an operational security plan, which specifies in detail how to carry out all relevant information security practices at that particular site. The aim of the plan is to ensure continuous effectiveness and integrity of the system of security controls, processes, policies, and procedures that are established for day-to-day operation.

Since ensuring the security of the overall information processing function is one of the important responsibilities of the IT security engineer, that role is obligated to specify a comprehensive set of technical security practices. These technical practices are typically specified in an operational security plan and must ensure a secure computing environment. In order to ensure the proper level of security in that plan, the IT security engineer is responsible for drilling down to the right level of specification of day-to-day security practices. Getting to that proper level requires the ability to think the solution through to its fundamental level of execution in actual application. That is not a simple matter of listing a set of security activities, since there are a number of highly technical processes and controls involved, all of which are related to ensuring secure applications, systems, networks, and automated access.

In addition to ensuring that the system is properly implemented, the IT security engineer is also responsible for ensuring that the elements of the system are evolved in a way that maintains their basic security and integrity. The assurance of change is typically part of the overall IT configuration management process. However, the IT security engineer is expected to collaborate with the configuration manager in order to ensure that the security aspects of change to the technology are correctly implemented and maintained and that all new, or added, security technologies are properly authorized and installed. Accordingly, the IT security engineer is responsible for ensuring that every planned change conforms to all requisite security policies. In order to satisfy this final requirement, the IT security engineer has to establish a baseline of software and hardware configuration items that are related to security. The IT security engineer then works with the configuration manager to ensure that unauthorized change to those items does not take place.

**Technical Security** In order to be considered properly organized, all technical controls for security should be integrated into a coordinated and harmoniously functioning system. What is more challenging is the fact that the correct functioning of those controls has to be assured throughout the lifecycle of their use. Thus, in order to assure their continuous effectiveness, the IT security engineer has to establish a process that can regularly verify the performance of all of the operational security technologies embedded in the organization's information processing function.

In addition, the overall secure operation of the information processing function itself has to be confirmed. The assurance of day-to-day security in operation is typically underwritten by controls that embody three different types of assurance activity. The first of these control types is the automated assurance controls, which are built into the technology itself. These controls ensure that undesirable events that can be identified at the system level are automatically intercepted and mitigated. Since these controls are a fundamental part of the information processing function, they can provide an immediate response to adverse events.

The problem with these controls is that they have to be pre-programmed with patterns of known malicious behaviors. As a result, attackers are always looking to develop new or modified behaviors that will not be recognized, and therefore not responded to, which could allow harmful access to the system. For this reason, a second type of control is required. That control is the examination of system logs by human auditors in order to identify unanticipated or novel activities. Although this degree of oversight can be extremely effective, these human audits take time, and so the potential harm that they uncover has usually already occurred.

That leads to the third type of system assurance, which is the execution of targeted tests such as penetration tests and ethical hacks. The aim of these types of tests is to identify areas of weakness before they can be exploited by people with malicious intent. Because they are executed from the attacker's perspective, these tests can be extremely effective in identifying new or unknown security problems in the system. Because they have to be targeted on some specific aspect of system functioning, they are only capable of looking at a small percentage of the overall functionality at any one time.

## Network and Telecommunications Security Processes

Along with securing the overall operational IT system's activities, another primary responsibility of the IT security engineer is the assurance of the security of basic network and telecommunications services. That duty includes maintaining the equipment on which all of those services reside. Examples of the typical duties of the IT security engineer with respect to network and telecommunications security include the development of perimeter defense strategies, defense-in-depth approaches, and the assurance of data encryption technology and techniques.

Like the IT function itself, network operations support the organization's general business case, and so the IT security engineer should provide input to the development of corporate level strategic plans for network operations. That includes the definition of host-based security plans and domain level security controls for the organization as a whole, as well as the standard operations and maintenance security procedures for the network. In conjunction with corporate level planning, the IT security engineer should also provide advice in the development of long-range plans for corporate telecommunications. The goal is to ensure that all forms of transmission media achieve the organization's security aims.

As with all other policy creation processes, corporate planning for telecommunications and network development should reflect the standards, procedures, directives, policies, regulations, and laws that apply. At a minimum, the IT security engineer is responsible for ensuring alignment between the organization's plans and the constraints of those items. In order to ensure continuing alignment, the IT security engineer is also responsible for developing the appropriate network security and telecommunication audit processes, guidelines, and procedures to ensure compliance.

Operationally, when it comes to the company networks, the role of the IT security engineer is to prevent and detect intrusions, protect against malware, and subsequently mitigate any identified vulnerabilities. The IT security engineer also ensures, through the design, implementation, and management of network domain security controls, that messages are confidential and free from tampering and repudiation. In addition, the IT security engineer monitors and assesses the network for security vulnerabilities and threats. This monitoring is done by all appropriate technical and non-technical means. The primary mechanism that is employed in the monitoring process is conventional testing and audit tracking/reporting. The IT security engineer also tests and verifies strategic network security technologies for effectiveness.

## Risk Management Procedures for the Company

The IT security engineer is responsible for ensuring that a coherent set of processes, procedures, and technologies are installed to support the day-to-day management of risks. Operationally, the security engineer performs threat and vulnerability assessments to identify security risks, and then regularly updates the security controls identified through those assessments.

The general aim of the risk assessment process is to provide the organization with a cost-effective approach to identifying and assessing the risks to its information assets. Those risks can be inherent in any part of the organization, including its personnel, facilities, and equipment. As risks to information are identified, the IT security engineer develops and manages reasonable mitigation strategies. In order to ensure the proper balance between risk and cost, the IT security engineer also does the routine risk versus functionality tradeoff assessments in order to determine where to draw the line in terms of cost versus benefit. The IT security engineer then works with stakeholders to ensure that the mitigation and management approach that is implemented is consistent with the level of risk that the organization is willing to accept.

As with every other aspect of the implementation process, any decisions about risk originate from the organization's security policies. Thus, the IT security engineer also has to be involved in an advisory capacity to the strategic policy-making and planning processes of the organization. The IT security engineer has to be involved in executive level planning, because that role is the one that is specifically responsible for maintaining an acceptable balance between the threat and the cost of the mitigating risk management controls.

## System and Application Security

Because of the technical nature of the controls, the IT security engineer plays a significant role in ensuring IT systems and applications. That responsibility for assurance applies throughout the **system development lifecycle (SDLC)**. Therefore, the IT security engineer works to ensure that the organization's systems and software are reasonably free of threats and risks.

Much of the responsibility of the IT security engineer revolves around ensuring that system and application security processes comply with corporate policies, as shown in Figure 5-2. That typically involves assessing how well the organization's systems and application operations align with those policies. If a discrepancy in alignment is identified, then the IT security engineer is the person responsible for developing the appropriate risk mitigation strategies. Risk mitigation at this level typically involves selecting, implementing, and evaluating the right set of new security controls for the process.

On a day-to-day operational basis, the primary duty of the IT security engineer is to document and maintain all of the organization's formal IT and application security controls. The IT security engineer also performs process quality assurance reviews to ensure that the technical practices used to develop and maintain applications and systems are being followed. As

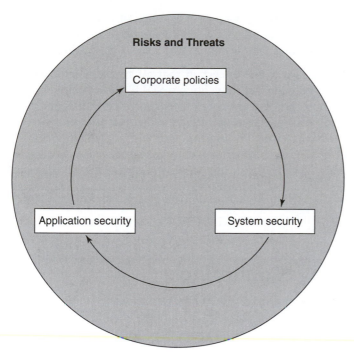

**Figure 5-2**  Policies, security, risks, and threats

© *Cengage Learning 2012*

part of the oversight responsibility, the IT security engineer also implements and tests the backup-and-restore procedures that are part of routine system operation. If any software security standards or regulations are involved, it is also the duty of the IT security engineer to ensure any necessary compliance.

**Software Security Plan** Because the IT security engineer is responsible for ensuring that all of the policies that apply to the organization's systems and applications are being followed correctly, this person also has to make certain that the appropriate policies, standards, and practices exist. The IT security engineer works with executive level policy makers to create a coherent set of strategies and attendant policies to guide the organization's application and system security process. The security engineer then derives the specific requirements for system and application security from that overall direction. Those specific requirements are typically captured in a  software security plan.

The IT security engineer identifies a relevant set of policies and standards to ensure the security of the organization's portfolio of software assets and then tailors a detailed set of practices from these policies. These detailed practices are used to ensure the security of the organization's software processes. In conjunction with the development of policy and practice, the IT security engineer also reviews new and existing security technologies to ensure that the IT platform remains secure.

**Assurance of the Development Process** The IT security engineer ensures that all necessary security requirements, controls, and procedures have been built into the development process. That includes taking the steps necessary to ensure the integration of effective risk management into the overall SDLC. Along with the assurance of effective risk management, the IT security engineer also confirms that the SDLC conforms to all standards, policies, procedures, guidelines, directives, regulations, and laws that affect the organization.

Operationally, the IT security engineer makes certain that all specified information security practices are being properly executed in the conventional SDLC. This position then regularly assesses the effectiveness of those practices in order to ensure their consistent performance. The IT security engineer also verifies how well specific security strategies that underlie the development process are working. The IT security engineer may subsequently redesign those strategies and controls if they do not perform as required. Because configuration management is an important part of application and system security, the IT security engineer also has to ensure that all necessary configuration management practices are being followed. Finally, this position is also responsible for verifying the security aspects of the development process and providing recommendations for improvement.

# The Perils of Day-to-Day Monitoring

*The CISO was feeling very smug, which, given his normal high opinion of himself, was satisfied indeed. He had been indulging himself in the pleasure of hiring the individuals who would act as his second-in-command at every one of the company sites. Because of the responsibility for the design and development of the individual security response at each site, there was only one IT security engineer for each location. So in the CISO's mind, the IT security engineer role was his designated representative in the overall process. He intended to ensure that every one of those people would serve to tighten his grip on the security operations of the company.*

*As he leafed through the stack of resumes that were sitting on his new custom-designed desk, which not coincidentally was an exact duplicate of the one the CIO was sitting at two doors down, he was looking for two qualities. The first was the ability to develop a concept and bring it to fruition. The second was the leadership skills to ensure that all of the rest of the employees in the security operation worked as a disciplined team. Of course, the CISO was also looking for people who exhibited the proper amount of dog-like devotion, but he couldn't exactly put that in the job description, particularly with the CIO involved in the hiring process.*

*And since he always thought ahead, he was also beginning to think about how to best organize the next level down, which was the IT Security Operations and Maintenance Professional category. Since that group was more or less responsible for actually doing the day-to-day work of security, the CISO wanted to make sure that whoever occupied that particular role knew exactly what they were required to do. Moreover, there were already numerous workers in that category. So the CISO felt that it was vital to ensure that all of them were working as efficiently as possible, which of course would also make him look better in the eyes of the company's directors.*

*In general, the CISO felt that the IT security of operations professional role could be summed up in two words: "monitoring" and "communication." In doing that monitoring work, the IT security of operations professional was the one role most likely to be able to spot problems as they occurred. As far as communication was concerned, the fact that the IT security of operations professional served as the advance lookout for the entire security operation meant that it was important for the person in this role to be able to get the word about emerging threats back to whoever was steering the ship. The CISO approached the definition of that role under the assumption that the establishment of clear and effective reporting lines would be critical. Moreover, since the IT security of operations professional also typically oversaw changes to the technology, the CISO also felt that it was important to have clear lines of communication to the technical people who were responsible for making the appropriate changes.*

*Finally, the CISO felt that it was essential to establish a clear and precise reporting line between that function and the risk mitigation decision-making process. When it came to risk in particular, the CISO wanted to make sure that the IT security of operations people were tied into the decision-making process. That meant that the CISO had to be certain that everybody who fell into the IT security of operations professional category was given a clear and comprehensive statement of duties. He continued sifting through the resumes.*

# On the Job with an IT Security Operations and Maintenance Professional

The EBK specifies nine operational competencies for the IT Security Operations and Maintenance Professional, as discussed in the list below. These competencies complement those of the IT Security Professional, who is discussed in the last section of this chapter.

1. Implement and evaluate operational aspects of data security
2. Implement operational aspects of digital forensics
3. Design and implement operational aspects of enterprise continuity
4. Design, implement, and evaluate operational aspects of incident management
5. Manage, design, implement, and evaluate IT systems operations and maintenance process
6. Manage, design, implement, and evaluate operational aspects of network and telecommunications security
7. Evaluate operational aspects of procurement
8. Implement operational aspects of risk management
9. Implement operational aspects of system and application security

## Data Security

The IT security operations professional has principal hands-on responsibility for maintaining the continuing assurance of the confidentiality, integrity, availability, and privacy of the organization's data. This professional is the person who is most directly involved in the actual practice of assuring data in all forms of media. This responsibility is ongoing and day-to-day.

The primary responsibility of this position is to reliably carry out its requisite assurance practices, the outcome of which is the assurance that data is controlled at all times. Although control procedures are established by other roles, the IT security of operations professional is the person who has hands-on responsibility for the disciplined performance of every control.

In particular, the IT security of operations professional is responsible for issuing and enforcing access privileges, which these controls subsequently enforce. This role is also primarily responsible for the assurance of the security and integrity of all data storage media. The IT security of operations professional maintains the controls that enforce confidentiality. The latter responsibility is carried out in accordance with any relevant standard, policy, regulation, or law. The IT security of operations role is the first to respond to incidents and violations.

Finally, the IT security of operations role is responsible for operational security testing, which is done to evaluate the effectiveness of the organization's assurance controls. The role also ensures continuing adherence to established data security policies. In that respect, the IT security of operations professional also works with the digital forensics professional to investigate breaches or violations, and recommends improvements to operational data protection procedures based on the outcomes of a digital forensics examination.

## Digital Forensics

Because the IT security of operations professional is often the first on the scene at incidents, this role plays a part in digital forensics. Specifically, the IT security of operations professional assists the digital forensics professional in the collection and preservation of forensic evidence at the point of occurrence. Also, the IT security of operations professional might implement a remediation based on the recommendations of forensic study.

Since the IT security of operations professional does the operational testing of the organization's intrusion detection systems, this role is the one that generates the raw data used by forensics to identify vulnerabilities. Because the role is on the front lines in data capture, the IT security of operations is also involved in the chain of custody associated with incident investigations.

The primary role of the IT security of operations professional when it comes to the forensics professional is to execute routine audits and then provide audit data in support of the forensic investigation process. The IT security of operations professional then works in conjunction with forensics professionals to support the efforts of law enforcement. Additionally, since the IT security of operations professional is on the front-end of the data collection process, this role assists in reporting the findings of forensics investigators. The person in this position should therefore be cross-trained in the use of forensic analysis equipment and procedures.

## Enterprise Continuity

Enterprise continuity relies on the organization's ability to maintain disciplined, routine security processes, like backups and archiving. Since these processes are sustainment activities, they have to be planned and implemented as operational procedures. Planning to ensure that the organization is taking the steps necessary to assure business continuity, business recovery, disaster recovery, and incident handling requires the participation and input of IT security of operations professionals.

What is more, the maintenance of the continuity of operations plan is also supported by day-to-day operational testing, training, and disaster exercise programs. The role of the IT security of operations professional in that maintenance is to perform all of those functions and then evaluate the effectiveness of the continuity of operations plans using the outcomes of those exercises.

## Incident Management

In addition to ensuring the organization's long-term continuity, the IT security of operations professional is also responsible for the day-to-day execution and maintenance of the organization's incident management function. In that respect, the IT security of operations professional is on the front lines in the organization's response to incidents; it is the responsibility of the IT security of operations role to ensure that all procedures for incident management are clear and appropriate and that the incident management team is always ready to respond.

Response to incidents is always based on a formal incident response plan, which is developed in accordance with security policies and organizational goals. In the capacity as the day-to-day executor of that plan, the IT security of operations professional participates in the development of the incident handling and reporting procedures. The IT security of operations professional also provides input to the development of measures, which are appropriate to evaluate the effectiveness of the plan and to support incident management. Moreover, since the IT security of operations professional also has a responsibility to investigate incidents once they occur, that role also helps create the operational procedures for collection of forensic evidence.

## Incident Response

Because the role is responsible for routine execution of security processes, one of the most critical duties of the IT security of operations professional is to design and carry out incident response and penetration testing exercises. The purpose of those exercises is to confirm the appropriateness of the planned response. In that respect, the IT security of operations professional is directly involved in assessing the efficiency and effectiveness of the incident response program.

Operationally, the IT security of operations professional is directly involved in the reporting of incidents. Therefore, the person in this position has to be trained to carry out the organization's response actions. The IT security of operations professional is responsible for the routine day-to-day operation of network and information systems intrusion detection systems. There might also be a need to execute penetration testing activities and incident response tests if the threat environment warrants them. From all of these testing activities, the IT security of operations professional ensures that all lessons learned from incidents are recorded, and that feedback is then incorporated into future planning.

Finally the IT security of operations professional has responsibility for maintaining the capability of routine organizational communications systems. Specifically, that role assesses the effectiveness of all communications between the incident response team and the related internal and external organizations and then implements any improvement actions or changes where appropriate.

## Systems Operations and Maintenance

Obviously, the IT security of operations professional will play a large part in the everyday maintenance, monitoring, control, and protection of the IT infrastructure. This requires the IT security of operations professional to develop and maintain communications between the security administration team and all security-related personnel. That communication specifically includes technical support and incident management. Therefore, the IT security of operations professional is normally involved in the process that defines the day-to-day details of the security administration and risk management program.

The IT security of operations professional is directly responsible for ensuring that the operation and maintenance of IT systems supports and enhances day-to-day business operations. In that respect, the IT security of operations professional also enforces routine security administration procedures in accordance with any relevant standard, policy, regulation, or law. The IT security of operations professional role also monitors and enforces all personnel, application, middleware, operating system, hardware, network, facility, and egress security controls. In particular, the IT security of operations professional assures the consistency of these controls through security testing.

Additionally, the IT security of operations professional administers the security aspects of the regular change management process and subsequently ensures that the change is made correctly. The role also develops a continuous monitoring process, which is based on standard IT security performance measures, to support the routine monitoring and enforcement process.

The IT security of operations professional's primary responsibility when it comes to the IT system and its operation is to design and maintain the daily/weekly/monthly process of backing up the data contained in those systems. In conjunction with that duty, the IT security of operations professional also arranges how those backups are stored and maintained both on and off-site.

The IT security of operations professional is also responsible for the ongoing measurement of the effectiveness of security controls, processes, policies, and procedures. Since a measurement program of this scope is always based on a plan, the IT security of operations professional is mainly responsible for the actual execution of whatever measurement process the organization chooses to adopt.

Finally, the IT security of operations professional is responsible for ensuring the consistency of the process. That includes making certain that all requisite procedures are carried out in accordance with all plans, policies, and regulations. This responsibility is mainly enforced by checking to see that all plans are properly implemented.

The problem with change is that it can cause an organization to lose control of its assets. That loss of control happens when a process or technology has been changed so many times that it is hard to tell what it really does. To counter that, a disciplined process of record keeping is absolutely required to keep track of all changes to the system. That record keeping is one of the important roles of the IT security of operations professional. In order to ensure consistent control over changes to the organization's technical assets, the IT security of operations professional has to label and track all of those assets and then ensure that any proposed change is analyzed for impact. Once that analysis is complete, the IT security of operations professional is responsible for ensuring that the approval to change the item is authorized by the appropriate decision maker. Following that authorization, the IT security of operations professional does regular testing to ensure that the change is persistent and that the system functions as required.

From the standpoint of security technologies, the IT security of operations professional is responsible for collaborating with all IT support, incident management, and security-engineering teams to ensure that any new additions to the automated security functionality of the system are properly implemented, controlled, and managed. This responsibility implies that the IT security of operations professional should perform routine, proactive security tests and execute surveillance operations aimed at establishing that the appropriate set of controls are in place and working properly.

The goal of the routine monitoring process is to ensure optimal system security performance at all times. Specifically, the process should be designed to demonstrate the ability of the organization's security controls to address system and network vulnerabilities. In that respect, the monitoring should demonstrate compliance with all relevant standards, policies, regulations, and laws. It should also identify any needed improvement actions.

## Network and Telecommunications

Because the bailiwick of the IT security of operations professional is routine operations, this role is responsible for monitoring and maintaining all perimeter defenses, defense-in-depth strategies, and data encryption processes for the network. This involves monitoring the performance of network and telecommunications security personnel and the effectiveness of the network and telecommunications security program. This is typically based on a performance measurement and monitoring program, which the IT security of operations professional establishes. The aim of such a program is to ensure the organization's compliance with all applicable network plans, policies, procedures, directives, and regulations. This is enforced through routine network-based audits and management reviews, the aim of which is to ensure compliance with network and host-based security policies.

Given the monitoring role of the IT security of operations professional, this function should also be involved in the development of the network security strategic plan. This plan is always aimed at installing and maintaining substantive network security controls. The IT security of operations professional is not responsible for developing the controls themselves, but is responsible for the subsequent monitoring to ensure that they are effective. The IT security of operations professional should always be involved in the development of routine security maintenance procedures.

Accordingly, the IT security of operations professional should be responsible for the development of the network audit and security performance reporting processes and the compilation of network data into measures for analysis and reporting. As discussed earlier, the aim of that process is to identify intrusions of the network and to protect against malware. That requires the IT security of operations professional to follow a disciplined and continuous audit tracking and reporting process, designed to ensure that network security controls are effective. The IT security of operations professional also tests strategic network security technologies for effectiveness and ensures real-time network **intrusion response**.

The IT security of operations professional also has the primary day-to-day responsibility to defend network communications from tampering and/or eavesdropping via utilities like sniffers. This obligation is a part of the same routine network security audit process and administration of security controls. The IT security of operations professional is responsible for arranging and overseeing tampering controls in the operational environment.

## Operational Aspects of Procurement

Because violations of operational procurement policy and procedure can be potentially harmful, an important duty of the IT security of operations professional is to monitor the routine procurement process for correct performance. In that respect, the IT security of operations professional focuses on whether the procurement function follows correct procurement procedure. The assessment of correctness involves ensuring that agreed on levels of IT security practice have been included in all procurements. That might include inspections, walk-throughs, or audits of any artifact that falls within the purview of the security function.

Correctness also involves proof that the procurement process has executed all of the required reviews of contract documents, such as statements of work or requests for proposals, in order to demonstrate that IT security considerations have been addressed. The criteria and process for doing that might actually be dictated by roles such as the CISO; however, the people who actually do the hands-on work to ensure that those criteria have been met are the IT security of operations people.

From an operational and managerial standpoint, the IT security of operations professional conducts detailed security analyses, and reviews all procurement procedures in order to ensure that security practices are followed correctly. That role also routinely evaluates the effectiveness of the vendor management program as it relates to policies and procedures of the organization.

The IT security of operations professional is also responsible for ensuring that due diligence is done with respect to the vetting of all third-party relationships. The IT security of operations professional is also particularly accountable for enforcing all formal controls that are employed to mitigate security risks in supply chain management.

## Security Risk Programs

Since operational failure of the security system represents a huge risk to the organization, somebody has to ensure the continuous correct functioning of the controls that have been established to ensure risk management. That is one additional duty of the IT security of operations professional. There are usually more risks than can be mitigated, so the IT security of operations professional is also responsible for conducting the routine threat and vulnerability assessments that are required to identify emerging security risks.

The role reviews performance of the specific risk management controls and provides recommendations for changes to the tools and techniques for risk management. Because this is an operational problem, the IT security of operations professional is also responsible for providing input to the development of future controls.

Finally, the IT security of operations professional identifies changes to risk management policies and processes which might have occurred due to changes in the business environment.

## System and Application Security

Many threats can emerge during the system and application lifecycle process. Thus, it is the IT security of operations professional's responsibility to monitor the application and system maintenance process to ensure that the day-to-day functioning of the IT systems and software lifecycles does not involve risk. This activity primarily comprises the evaluation of the performance of security controls throughout the system and software lifecycle to ensure that they comply with security policies and standards.

Operationally, the IT security of operations professional ensures the integration of security practices into the SDLC and verifies compliance with all identified IT system or application engineering standards and best practices. The IT security of operations professional also monitors engineering processes to ensure that vulnerabilities are not introduced during the coding process.

The IT security of operations professional is also primarily responsible for ensuring that configuration management practices are effective, and that security controls built into the process identify and mitigate any vulnerabilities induced during the lifecycle of the system.

# Doing the Actual Work of Security: The IT Security Professional

*It was evening. The CISO was sitting in his study, watching the rain fall on Manhasset Bay, outside his Port Washington house and smoking his nightly cigar. He was wondering whether he should give up that $125 a day habit when the solution to a problem that he had been wrestling with all week suddenly came to him. Since that sort of thing happened all of the time during his nightly cigar breaks, he decided the expense was probably justified.*

He had finished up the staffing for the security management teams the month before. The interview process had featured the customary set of fresh-out-of-college grads, all of whom were looking for their big chance. The CISO had waded through that enthusiastic group like a great white shark, picking off nothing but the best and brightest. Now that he finally had those newly minted IT security engineers and IT security of operations professionals in place, he had to do the rest of the staffing. It was that task that he had been mulling over while watching the spring rain come down.

The challenge was simply one of numbers. Because the IT security professional role did most of the hands-on work of security at each site, that role constituted the bulk of the organization's security personnel. The CISO had to come up with a reliable way to ensure a large number of competent people. That task would not be difficult if those people all worked in one place. Since the company's facilities were distributed across the globe, there was a simple matter of scope involved. In essence, the CISO would have to figure out a way to ensure that his management team at all of the sites would recruit the most capable people to fulfill the requirements of the IT security role.

One of those ubiquitous reality shows was playing in the background, the one where people competed to avoid being fired. That gave the CISO an idea. He decided that he would set up a little competition. The rules of the game would be simple. Each of the new IT security engineers would design the IT security professional role for their respective sites. Then the site's IT security of operations professionals would recruit the right people to fill that role. The CISO would make it clear that the management team that did the best job with those two tasks would be promoted and any losers would be shown the exit. That ensured two satisfactory outcomes, as far as the CISO was concerned. First, it meant that he would always have the most successful performers working for him, even if he had not personally chosen them. Second, and more important, it meant that any blame for failure would be assigned to the managers, rather than the CISO himself.

The CISO had always envisioned the IT security professional as the "boots on the ground" role from the standpoint of his staffing strategy, since that role was directly responsible for enforcing the detailed cybersecurity practices at each site. Likewise, the IT security professional was also responsible for ensuring that those practices remained viable over time. In essence, the IT security professional was the role that actually implemented the security, by tailoring the company's security strategy down to its specific application in practice and then maintaining the correctness of those practices. Consequently, the CISO considered that role to be a particularly critical function for his own career's sake.

The company classified the IT security professional role as "information security staff" rather than "information technology staff". That was because besides the technical elements of information security, the IT security professional role is also responsible for people-centered aspects, such as personnel security, training and education, and regulatory compliance. It was important to get the wide range of requirements for that role right. He began jotting his notes.

## On the Job with an IT Security Professional

The EBK requires that IT security professionals exhibit eight general capabilities. These are:

1. Manage, design, and evaluate data security
2. Evaluate enterprise continuity programs

3. Design and evaluate incident management programs
4. Design, implement, and evaluate IT security training and awareness programs
5. Design and evaluate personnel security programs
6. Design and evaluate physical and environmental security programs
7. Implement regulatory and standards compliance
8. Design, implement, and evaluate risk management programs

## Data Security

The IT security professional has an important role in ensuring the overall security of data, because that role is primarily responsible for evaluating and enforcing the specific IT security controls that regulate the non-technical aspects of the security system. The IT security professional also manages those control processes.

The IT security professional develops and documents the non-electronic policies and procedures that are used to ensure privacy, access, retention, disposal, incident management, disaster recovery, and configuration control. In conjunction with that duty, the IT security professional also develops the data and information classification, sensitivity, and need-to-know requirements. Additionally, the IT security professional assists in the development of authentication and authorization policies that dictate user privileges and permissions. Finally, the IT security professional is responsible for the classification of data and the development of the organization's acceptable use procedures.

From a design and evaluation standpoint, the IT security professional devises the information security controls for the non-electronic elements of the system. Of course, this is always based on the perceived risks. Therefore, the IT security professional develops the security testing procedures to assess how well those controls address known risks. In that respect, the IT security professional evaluates the effectiveness of information protection solutions in the light of measurement data, which characterizes the known security and privacy breaches. The IT security professional then recommends improvements to maintain the correct level of data protection.

## Enterprise Continuity Programs

The IT security professional role does not design or manage the continuity programs, but because it has general responsibility for **operational controls**, it has to stay on top of the performance of the continuity process. That mainly involves the use of data from reviews, tests, and training exercises to recommend areas in the continuity process that might need improvement. Those recommendations could be derived from crisis management tests, training, or exercises. The IT security professional also continuously validates the organizational response plan against any additional external laws, regulations, or directives that might become relevant.

## Incident Management Programs

The aim of incident management is to detect, contain, prevent, or recover from harmful incidents. Because the IT security professional is responsible for the non-electronic aspects of organizational controls, this role is intimately involved in that process. In order to ensure that those controls meet the policy and procedure needs of the organization, the IT security professional has to be involved in the development of the incident management plan, including specification of the services that the incident response team must provide.

The IT security professional is also involved in developing the substantive plans for incident response, including the development of the procedures for incident handling and reporting. Finally, the IT security professional is involved in the coordination of incident response exercises and penetration testing activities, and forensic evidence gathering in conjunction with the roles that are primarily responsible for performing those functions.

Because the aim of the IT security professional is to make the overall incident management process as effective as possible, this role has to measure and collect data about incidents. This is necessary in order to assess and improve the effectiveness of incident response activities. Such data typically involves assessments of the effectiveness of penetration testing and incident response tests, training, and exercises as well as the effectiveness of the lines of communication between the incident response team and related internal and external organizations.

## Security Training and Awareness Programs

In order to ensure proper security performance, the workforce has to be aware of the recommended practices and methods for information security. In addition, the people with specific roles in the information security process have to be properly trained to ensure that they have optimum knowledge, skills, and abilities. This is an important responsibility of the IT security professional, because that role has primary responsibility for the human element of information security.

The IT security professional is responsible for establishing and overseeing the security awareness and training program, including development of the policies that direct that program as well as the specific goals and objectives of the program. The IT security professional develops a workforce training and awareness program plan and then validates that plan with security subject matter experts (SMEs) to ensure completeness and accuracy. Once the plan is established, the IT security professional maintains changes to the plan in order to ensure the continuing currency and accuracy of all training and awareness materials. The IT security professional also provides routine reports about the IT effectiveness of the security training and awareness program to general management.

Because the IT security professional is responsible for maintaining the currency and effectiveness of the training and awareness program, the person in the role must find routine ways to communicate the importance of the program, and management's commitment, to the workforce. Operationally, the IT security professional conducts focused needs assessments to determine gaps in knowledge and skills, and then prioritizes the results of these assessments in order to form a ranked list of critical needs. As needs change, the IT security professional develops awareness and training materials that are appropriate and timely for the intended audience and delivers that training to intended audiences based on currently identified needs.

In order to assure compliance, the IT security professional has to assess the IT security awareness and training program for adherence to corporate policies and regulations. The IT security professional then ensures that information security personnel are receiving the appropriate level and type of training. The IT security professional also measures employee performance against corporate security objectives and assesses the awareness and training program for effectiveness and coverage of current IT security issues and legal requirements.

## Personnel Security Programs

Since the IT security professional is responsible for **non-electronic controls**, this role establishes and oversees the personnel security function. Personnel security involves all of the actions that are done to ensure that the human resources element of the organization is strictly under control. This is true both in the case of employee as well as in the case of the contractor. Controls for personnel security are intended to detect and prevent employee-caused breaches such as theft, fraud, misuse of information, and noncompliance. These controls implement such principles as separation of duties, job rotation, and job classification.

It is the responsibility of the IT security professional to establish the personnel security function and to define the security practices for each of the individual roles at each site. In order to assure this, the IT security professional defines and documents the rules and procedures for personnel security within the organization and then evaluates the effectiveness of the overall personnel security program in light of those rules. The IT security professional will then subsequently recommend any changes that will improve internal practices, or security organization-wide.

In order to ensure the continuous effectiveness of the personnel security program, the IT security professional also has to ensure that personnel security procedures are aligned with organizational security needs. Because much of personnel security rests on maintaining behavior that complies with all rules and regulations, the IT security professional also periodically reviews the personnel security program for adherence to the dictates of standards, policies, and laws.

## Physical and Environmental Security Programs

The IT security professional is responsible for establishing and overseeing the physical security process, which is the other function traditionally linked with personnel security. Physical and environmental security ensures access to equipment and physical information storage places. Physical security also involves all of the organization's controls that are designed to make sure that the organization is safe from man-made or natural disasters, as shown in Figure 5-3, including unauthorized physical intrusions, threats to physical facilities and buildings, and threats to the physical locations where IT equipment is kept.

The IT security professional is typically responsible for establishing the physical security program, which involves the steps to align the practices of the physical security program with the overall security goals of the organization. The IT security professional develops policies and procedures that are used to identify and mitigate physical and environmental threats to

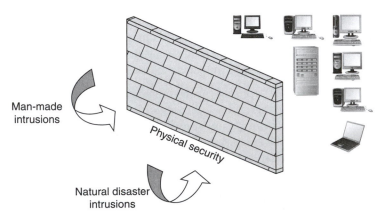

**Figure 5-3** Physical security

© *Cengage Learning 2012*

information, information processing personnel, facilities, and equipment. The IT security professional also develops a physical and environmental security plan that specifies all formal security tests and contingency plans. Physical security planning is always done in conjunction with the other security planning functions, such as personnel and continuity.

From these plans, the IT security professional develops and deploys the countermeasures that are needed to mitigate all identified risks and vulnerabilities. In order to ensure that this is done properly, the IT security professional continuously assesses the overall effectiveness of the physical and environmental security controls that have been deployed and makes recommendations for improvement. That assessment involves the review of data from incidents and the results of tests of the security controls. Besides routine planning and oversight, the IT security professional is also responsible for evaluating any acquisitions that might have implications for physical security. The findings from that evaluation are then reported to management.

## Regulatory and Standards Compliance Process

Given that the IT security professional is responsible for non-electronic controls, that role is also accountable for ensuring that the organization complies with all applicable information security laws, regulations, standards, and policies. The IT security professional is primarily responsible for the monitoring of the compliance process to ensure its continuing effectiveness. This involves assessing the organization's security compliance practices to guarantee that they comply with organizational policy and procedure. This typically requires extensive internal audits to determine if control objectives, controls, processes, and procedures are effectively applied and maintained. From these audits, the IT security professional then recommends any necessary remedial actions.

## Risk Management Programs

Risk management is another important aspect of the IT security professional's portfolio. Risk management involves those policies, processes, procedures, and technologies that might be used to identify all relevant risks to information assets, personnel, facilities, and equipment. This information is then used to develop mitigation strategies. The IT security professional is responsible for assessment of the effectiveness of the risk management program and the implementation of changes where required. That includes the direct evaluation of all individual security controls, tools, and techniques to ensure that they remain current with the emerging risk and threat environment.

The IT security professional creates the risk management practices that lie within the risk management process. That includes the development of targeted plans for risk containment and mitigation. Obviously, in a global company it is impossible to deal with local situations using a one-size-fits-all approach to risk. Therefore, one duty of the IT security professional is to tailor the concepts that guide the general risk management process down to the level of practical, day-to-day execution. That tailoring involves the development of processes and procedures for identifying, assessing, and mitigating risks. Since the decision to apply mitigation or risk acceptance strategies has financial implications, the IT security professional is also responsible for ensuring that the eventual risk management strategy meets the requirements of the business side of the operation.

The IT security professional maintains the site's security response in alignment with all company-wide, risk-based security policies, plans, and procedures. The maintenance of correct alignment requires each individual IT security professional to be able to map the organization's risk management practices down to the appropriate set of standards, policies, regulations, and laws. The IT security professional then develops and applies the necessary controls to establish the concrete risk management program for each setting.

Because this solution has to be cost-effective, the IT security professional performs the requisite operational assessments to evaluate the effectiveness of the present risk management approach. Where discrepancies are identified, the IT security professional is accountable to develop a solution that brings the practices back into line with general policy. These assessments are also used to update all applicable security controls.

## Chapter Summary

- The EBK functional roles perform the day-to-day security work.
- There are four roles within the functional category.
- Each functional role is important to security.
- The chapter explains the duties and competencies of the digital forensics professional and the rest of the cybersecurity team.
- The chapter explains the duties and competencies of the IT security engineer and the role's specific relationship with the electronic elements of the security solution.
- The chapter explains the duties, competencies, specialized role, and particular importance of the IT security of operations professional.
- The IT security professional plays a specialized role in ensuring security and is responsible for a wide range of duties and competencies.
- The IT security professional is a critical role because it involves the actual implementation of security practices.

## Key Terms

**Chain of custody** Formal assurance that evidence has passed from agency to agency without tampering.

**Civil litigation** Court proceedings related to non-criminal legal action.

**Computer forensics** The analysis of computer equipment to obtain evidence for civil or criminal proceedings.

**Digital forensics professional** A person who practices digital forensics; implies specialized knowledge and training.

**Electronic evidence** Evidence that exists in electronic form in a computer or other digital media.

**Functional role** The roles in cybersecurity work that are most directly involved in designing, implementing, and sustaining the mechanisms to ensure information.

**Incidents** Undesirable events associated with attacks or violations of information.

**Intrusion response** A targeted response to a violation of secure space; a countermeasure targeted to mitigate a particular type of event.

**IT security engineer** Cybersecurity role specifically devoted to development and maintenance of enterprise information security architectures (EISA).

**IT security operations and maintenance professional** Cybersecurity role devoted to monitoring and control of functioning of the day-to-day cybersecurity process.

**IT security professional** Cybersecurity role specifically oriented toward development and maintenance of the non-electronic aspects of the cybersecurity process.

**Non-electronic controls** Controls typically associated with ensuring continuity, compliance, physical, personnel, and secure software development in a cybersecurity solution.

**Operational controls** The control processes associated with day-to-day business operation.

**Operational security** The sustainment part of the cybersecurity process; ensures 24/7 protection of the assurance target.

**Penetration testing** Testing that takes place with specific knowledge of the targeted environment; often used to test a specific defense.

**Privileges** The level of access authorization granted to a given individual.

**Professional certification** A formally recognized documentation of competency in an area of professional work.

**System development lifecycle (SDLC)** The well-defined set of steps that a system developer follows in the development and maintenance of an information system.

# Questions from the CIO

The CIO requires you to brief her on the current status of your investigation. This will be an important part of your continuing work on this project, since it is essential to be able to describe all of the ramifications of the functions of the key security personnel. Consequently, the CIO would like you to answer the following questions for her:

1. What differentiates the forensic specialist from all of the other functional categories?

2. Besides investigating crimes, how else does the forensic specialist contribute to security?

3. What is the relationship between forensics and risk management?

4. What is the IT security engineer specifically responsible for, and why is that important?

5. What is the primary capability required for the IT security engineer, and why is it essential?

6. How do the IT security engineer's duties impact the security of applications?

7. What is the difference between the IT security engineer and the IT security of operations professional?

8. What is the specific focus of the IT security of operations, and why does it have to be continuous?

9. What differentiates the IT security of operations from other monitoring functions?

10. What is the difference between the IT security professional and the IT security engineer?

11. Why are IT security professionals particularly useful in the human factors areas?

12. What is the difference between the IT security professional and the IT security engineer when it comes to risk management?

# Hands-On Projects

HANDS-ON PROJECTS

Using the Case in Appendix 1, develop a detailed set of role definitions for the roles in the case. Ensure that the following requirements are satisfied:

- The digital forensics process is well-defined and implemented within the architecture.

- Security of operations is continuous and effective.

- There is a process to ensure that all necessary non-electronic controls are in place and functioning as required.

# chapter 6

# Defining the Corollary Roles for Security

## Including Security Functions from Other Areas

*The CIO was satisfied with the CISO's two tiered strategy. His idea about distributing the functional roles clearly got around the problem of ensuring custom security at each of the company's global sites. Meanwhile, his three executive roles neatly centralized policy control at the top. In fact, she was confident that the CISO's new strategy was solid enough that it would get unanimous approval from the board. That approval was critical, since she would need the board's strong support to enforce the changes that she would have to make. She had called a meeting of the leadership team for 9:00 a.m. that morning in order to clear the way forward.*

*The acceptance of the proposal was going to afford a huge boost to her status at the company because, no matter how up-and-coming the CISO might appear, the overall responsibility for running the IT operation still rested in her hands. She had weathered the storm after the initial disaster mainly because the board saw her as the sole person capable of keeping the company's systems running at their maximum potential. But questions still continued to be raised about her ability to protect those same systems.*

*That was a particularly vexing problem for her, since arraying company defenses against targeted attacks was an entirely new challenge. In fact, as she thought about it, the diverse range of problems facing her was almost too much to bear. As she looked out over a rainy New York harbor that Friday, she thought about how radically things had changed since she had started her career back in the 1980s. It was hard enough back then just to keep the computers running. Now, she not only had to ensure their optimum performance, she also had to worry about the whole operation being compromised by some third world hacker. Worse, as she found out the last time, she didn't have to just worry about hackers breaking down her firewalls. She also had to deal with every other hazard from disgruntled employees to the locks on the doors.*

*As an example, her 7:00 a.m. meeting had been to discuss the merits of solid core versus polymer technology for the doors on the server rooms. Listening to the **physical security** types argue about door frames was an excruciating experience for somebody who was a programmer at heart. What was worse, she recalled that she was having too many of those conversations lately. Thanks to those discussions, though, the CIO was becoming aware that there were ancillary functions that were integral to assuring the security of her operation. Because those functions performed tasks that were not strictly speaking "electronic," they were a part of the conventional business operation. More important, since they were over on the business side, she didn't actually control them. That lack of control for operational purposes caused some serious hurdles.*

*The CIO knew from previous dire experience that each one of the ancillary roles brought aspects of protection to the overall scheme that were essential to ensuring the reliable execution of the process. She also knew that a failure to integrate the contributions of those roles could leave potentially serious holes in her information security strategy. So as she was watching the rain sweep down from the direction of Long Island Sound, it suddenly hit her that the process she was about to sponsor to the board was not complete; she still had to make sure that the security competencies associated with functions such as physical security and procurement were factored into the general definition of roles.*

*That realization led her to do two things. First, she had her administrative assistant cancel the meeting planned for that morning. Second, she picked up the phone and ordered up the CISO, who was not happy to be hauled down to the CIO's office a half hour before what he thought was going to be the start of the most important meeting of his life. He was even less happy when he found out that the CIO had decided that the meeting wasn't going to happen at all. The final thorn in his paw was when he found out what the CIO had in mind for him to do.*

*Upon hearing the explanation of the CIO's logic, he found to his total chagrin that he absolutely agreed with her. Obviously, in order to be considered complete, the security strategy had to include all of the competencies that would be required to execute the security process. Likewise, if there were missing functions and somebody found that hole, there could be untold damage to the company, not to mention his career. More as a result of the latter than the former argument, he made the commitment to identify those parts of the business operation that could potentially involve or impact the security process and then document the required competencies. As it turned out, that commitment would take the CISO and his team another three months to fulfill.*

*The guiding principle for the CISO during that period was that any area in the company that could potentially be exploited by any type of adversary had to be identified and dealt with. That identification process would require people who knew the territory, and he felt that he was not one of them. Therefore, the CISO dipped into the company's coffers to hire an all-star team of experts in the non-electronic areas of security. That group identified two functions that they felt were the most likely targets for exploitation.*

*The first area was, not surprisingly, the physical security part of the operation. Physical security was a vast area of traditional security work in the CISO's company, as it usually is in most large*

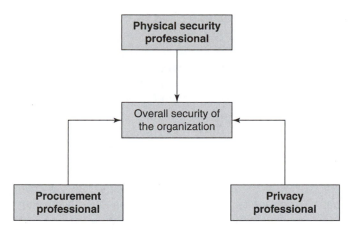

**Figure 6-1** Overall information security scheme

© Cengage Learning 2012

firms. The second area was a whole lot more interesting to the CISO because it was already beginning to see some significant regulation. It involved a number of components, both electronic and procedural, which posed coordination problems. That was the area of **personally identifiable information (PII).** Protection of PII was just an emerging concern for the company, since there were no actual laws governing it. But since unauthorized access to an individual's PII violated most **privacy** rights, it was an important issue. Finally, the CISO, on his own authority, decided to add procurement to the list. There had already been several highly visible security problems caused by defects in acquired products, and all of his bosses wanted to ensure against any more repeats.

The problem that the CISO faced was that both physical security and procurement were long-standing company functions. They were co-equal to the information security operation in their reporting lines to the CEO, and neither of those functions viewed information security as a priority. The other area, privacy, clearly had connections to the information security function. That was because confidentiality, which is one of the three cornerstones of information security, was plainly involved. Because the general requirement for confidentiality cut across most of the company's operation, it was hard to decide where the specific role fit.

The EBK was a useful guide in that respect, since it contained standardized definitions of competencies that would incorporate these three areas into the overall information security scheme. The roles that those competencies fit into were given the uncreative labels of **"physical security professional," "privacy professional,"** and **"procurement professional,"** as shown in Figure 6-1.

## Ensuring the Physical Protection of Information

The CISO and his team spent considerable time thinking through the specific competencies that would be required for the physical protection of information. It was absolutely essential to differentiate between the set of activities that was required to just protect information, versus the entire set of practices in the larger domain of physical security. Essentially, this requirement was a more of a politics and turf distinction, since the company already had an extensive and well resourced physical security operation.

*The director of that operation left nothing to chance when it came to conventional physical security practice. His unit fielded the most advanced electronic surveillance and intrusion detection systems available on the market. Besides electronic monitoring, he also employed more than 15 security personnel for each individual facility, who provided human monitoring and foot patrols to back up the passive and active monitoring functions. In addition to protection, he also ran a worldwide business intelligence gathering and analysis operation that would be the envy of the CIA, many of whose former agents he employed. All of that intelligence gathering and interpretation was in service of anticipating and preventing attacks on the company and its employees both domestically and abroad.*

*The only problem was that the director of physical security and all of his executive staff saw information security as a minor part of their overall mission of protecting the company's assets. That attitude was understandable, given the fact that physical security had been a formal part of the organization since 1928 and the director himself had been in charge of the operation since the late 1970s, whereas the company's entire interest in information security was less than three years old. In fact, in the beginning of organizing the information security function, there had been talk of placing that operation directly under the director of physical security.*

*The saving grace from information security's standpoint was the fact that the director of physical security had been an old Marine gunnery sergeant and he didn't want to have anything to do with computer types. His comment was that "computer geeks make me nervous." Moreover, he really didn't view information as an organizational asset, since as far as he was concerned, artifacts like computer files were pretty "abstract." So he strongly suggested that the information security function ought to be organized and run as a separate unit from the physical security operation. The CEO had been watching the organization process from the sidelines and he tended to agree with that assessment, but for a different set of reasons.*

*First and foremost, the CEO thought that there was not a single person in the physical security operation who had the slightest idea about how to secure an intangible asset like information. That was mainly due to the fact that everybody in that function had either been in law enforcement or the more hands-on branches of the military. Furthermore, none of the 1,100 people who worked in the physical security operation had had any formal education or professional background in the cyber aspects of security, and none of them had ever expressed any interest in getting any. In short, the staff of the physical security function was no more qualified by experience or training to ensure information than any of the other employees in any other function in the company.*

*Second, the physical security operation was set up to secure tangible assets; it did not have the right equipment to protect virtual space. For instance, physical security might have been able to monitor access to the tangible places where those information assets were stored, but it was not equipped to manage what happened within those places, since those assets all existed in virtual space and the protection was aimed at tangible access control. The specific evidence of that lack of control, which the CEO cited during his arguments with the director of physical security, was the way the intrusion sensors and video cameras were placed. Those sensors and cameras were all set to monitor the doors of the computer facilities, rather than the internal activities of the computer staff. Thus, anybody who had legitimate access to the space was by definition not monitored or controlled. That was the reason why it had been so easy to pull off the first attack on the company.*

*The CEO was committed to not having that happen again. So it was his preference to put the management and planning for the physical security aspect of the information security operation into the hands of the people who were in the best position to benefit from good security, which was the information security staff itself. The information security staff, from the CISO down, drew a huge sigh of relief at that pronouncement. However, that relief proved to be fleeting once the CISO began to think about such new areas of responsibility as the acres of* **perimeter** *fence around his data processing facilities, not to mention the need to secure every conventional and unconventional route of access in and out of those areas.*

*A protection problem like that led the CISO to conclude that some sort of specialist would be required. That specialist would have to be able to think through all of the physical security protection needs for each of the company's information processing sites and devise the appropriate defenses.*

# Physical Security Professional

In our preceding story, a new specialized role would have to be created that would be competent in the design and implementation of physical protection for information. The EBK lists six general requirements for that role:

1. Design and implement enterprise continuity
2. Implement incident management
3. Evaluate personnel security
4. Manage, design, implement, and evaluate physical and environmental security
5. Evaluate procurement
6. Implement risk management

## The Physical Security Specialist and the Design and Implementation of Enterprise Continuity Programs

The purpose of the continuity function is to ensure the long-term survival of the organization's information assets. Given that goal, the physical destruction of the equipment and space where that information is stored and processed would represent a serious threat to the organization. Of course, off-site backups are usually available should such a disaster occur. But any information recorded after the last backup would be totally lost; therefore, business survival depends to some extent on having a good continuity plan in place, one that factors physical disasters into the response. An effective continuity plan requires the planner to specify steps to ensure all aspects of enterprise continuity, including business recovery, disaster recovery, and incident handling.

The planning for all of this takes place as part of the strategic planning function for continuity of operations. Plans for ensuring survival of the information security function are designed and documented as part of that overall process, implemented, and then continuously tested. That development, implementation, and oversight is the responsibility of the physical security professional, who is in charge of all long-range and operational security survival plans for the information processing function. The aim is to ensure that that function survives in the event of a natural or human-caused disaster.

Because it involves physical phenomena, the physical security professional is also the role that is directly responsible for designing, maintaining, and improving the disaster response plan. Disaster response is primarily supported by day-to-day operational testing, targeted training, and the occasional organization-wide disaster exercise. The role of the physical security professional is to ensure that each of these functions is carried out on a routine and continuous basis. The general aim is to ensure that the organizational continuity of the operations plan and its associated procedures function as intended.

## The Physical Security Specialist and the Implementation of Physical Security Incident Management Controls

Incident management has both an electronic and a physical focus to it. The primary role of the physical security professional is to plan, implement, and oversee the most effective way to respond to physical incidents and disasters as they occur. In the particular case of incident management, the physical security professional is responsible for installing, testing, and updating the **physical security controls**. That process includes identifying the sources of physical threat, putting controls in place to contain and recover from threats, and planning and coordinating the pre-designed incident management response to physical security incidents. The physical security professional also collects, analyzes, and reports data generated from physical security incidents.

It is also the role of the physical security professional to ensure that the organization learns from all incidents that occur in the physical universe. This is done by collecting and analyzing any relevant data pertaining to the functioning of physical security controls and then ensuring that that information supports operational planning. In addition to their monitoring duties, physical security professionals also help proactively thwart physical attacks by identifying vulnerabilities in the physical protection scheme. The identification is usually done through penetration tests as well as incident response exercises. The physical security professional is also responsible for coordinating, integrating, and leading all physical security responders during an incident event.

## The Physical Security Specialist and the Design and Evaluation of Physical Security Aspects of Personnel Security

The physical security professional is responsible for ensuring all of the physical aspects that involve people. In that respect, the role is responsible for establishing and overseeing the controls that ensure the protected space against violations and harm that originate from any human source. To fulfill that responsibility, the physical security professional designs and implements the tangible controls to ensure physical monitoring of all protected space. That includes physical controls to detect unauthorized employee activity such as unauthorized access, employee theft, misuse of equipment, or noncompliance with organizational policy.

It is also the responsibility of the physical security professional to establish the physical security requirements for the personnel security function. That includes the definition of the physical security procedures for all personnel categories. In that respect, the physical security professional is accountable for the definition and documentation of the rules and procedures for regulation of worker access to physical space. The physical security professional also evaluates the ability of the physical protection scheme to properly enforce those policies and procedures. If an enforcement problem is identified, the physical security professional will then recommend any changes required to correct the practice.

When it comes to personnel, the physical security professional has to ensure that the physical security procedures that everybody is expected to follow stay aligned with the organization's security requirements. Proof of that alignment centers on the ability to document that those personnel policies are aligned with all relevant external and internal directives. Therefore, the physical security professional periodically reviews the physical security plan to make certain that it continues to comply with all applicable policies, standards, guidelines, policies, regulations, or laws.

## The Physical Security Specialist and the Design and Evaluation of the Physical and Environmental Security Program

Since the physical security program is by definition the domain of the physical security professional, this specific competency area is the one that involves the most extensive set of tasks. The physical security professional is the person responsible for designing and maintaining the effectiveness of those tasks. That includes the definition and deployment of all defense strategies, defense-in-depth schemes, and authorization functions for the protected, physical space. Those duties also involve management of the performance of the physical security system and assessment of the effectiveness of all physical security controls. In order to meet this requirement, the physical security professional undertakes a physical security planning process and then implements the appropriate set of approved controls based on the outcomes of that planning.

The physical security professional also sets up the performance measurement and monitoring program, which ensures the proper functioning of the controls that are established to ensure the integrity of the physical space. The aim of this monitoring program is to ensure the organization's compliance with all of the elements of the physical security plan, along with the plan's policies and procedures. Compliance is enforced by routine audits of the functioning of the physical security controls, as well as management reviews designed to ensure that those controls enforce security policies as intended.

Operationally, the physical security professional should participate in the definition of the overall security plan for the organization, as well as the specific development of the security of operations procedures that will underlie that plan. In that respect, the physical security professional plans all physical security control requirements, develops an action plan and associated mitigation strategies for the physical space, and creates a remediation strategy designed to address any identified control deficiencies. These various factors are all incorporated into the physical security portion of the overall cybersecurity plan.

The physical security portion of the plan should be an integral part of the overall strategic plan for security and is always composed of security controls that can be objectively evaluated. Each of those controls is deployed in accordance with the appropriate organizational security policy. The physical security professional is responsible for developing the physical security controls and monitoring the physical security process in order to ensure that those controls remain effective.

Because of this latter responsibility, the physical security professional should also be the individual most responsible for the conduct of the review, audit, and performance reporting processes for physical security. Likewise, the physical security professional should handle the subsequent compilation of reporting data, whose aim is to maintain a record of intrusions and violations of the physical space in order to learn how to better respond to them. That level of knowledge requires the physical security professional to institute and oversee evaluation mechanisms for the gathering of assessment data about the existing security situation. Those mechanisms should be designed to ensure that all physical security controls function effectively. The actual evaluation process is supported by ongoing analysis of the results of scheduled physical security audits. In support of this latter responsibility, the physical security professional also establishes and maintains a routine process by which the performance of physical security controls is confirmed by tangible observation.

Finally, with respect to the technologies that underlie and enforce physical security, the physical security professional also routinely evaluates, selects, implements, and tests those technologies for effectiveness. That assessment process is implemented through routine reviews and evaluations of the state of the physical security perimeter, as well as assessments of the defense-in-depth scheme. The analysis of any relevant data that is obtained from those evaluations is then used to recommend further remediation activities. Physical security audits can often also be supplemented through independent penetration testing to verify and validate the performance of the physical security controls. The physical security professional is responsible for overseeing all of those evaluation activities.

## The Physical Security Specialist and the Design, Implementation, and Evaluation of Risk Management Programs

Because mitigating the physical side of risk is the primary duty of the physical security professional, that role is particularly involved in the overall risk management process. That mitigation process starts at the top of the business. So, one role of the physical security professional is to develop the organization's physical security strategies, policies, plans, and procedures. Because those procedures have to comply with any externally imposed directives, the physical security professional also has to ensure that these plans conform to any relevant standard, regulation, or law involving risk management.

When it comes to the specific management of risk, the risk management plan has to establish a set of tangible physical security controls to detect any pertinent threats as well as mitigate them. This detection and mitigation process is done in order to ensure continuous protection from physical security threats. In conjunction with that larger purpose, though, the physical security professional also has the responsibility to monitor and report on the performance of all of the physical and electronic controls that are used to identify and respond to risk. The outcome of that monitoring, analysis, and reporting process ought to be an understanding of how well physical risks are being identified and controlled, as well as the ability to proactively identify risks as they manifest themselves. Knowledge of current risks, as well as early identification of any new risks, allows the organization to rationally manage its responses and ensures an agile reaction to any new problems that might arise.

In order to ensure continuous knowledge of the risk situation, the physical security professional also assesses the physical components of the risk management process and maintains ongoing and effective records with respect to its effectiveness. That knowledge is then communicated to key stakeholders where appropriate. To satisfy reporting requirements, the physical security professional conducts regular process assessments in order to ascertain whether the requirements of the physical security plan are being met. Obviously, these assessments have to reference the plan and its specific purposes in order to maintain alignment between general physical security strategies and the actual performance of the physical security work. Where it is necessary to take steps to maintain that alignment, detailed outcomes of the process assessments might be passed to the appropriate decision maker for further action.

# Keeping the Company Liability-Free

*The CISO was generally aware of the need to protect the personal privacy of customers and suppliers. The company's lawyers had made sure of that; however, the CISO hadn't really understood the actual, iron-clad obligation to protect the personal information of individuals whose records were stored in the company's many databases until the summons to appear showed up in the company's legal offices. Unfortunately, the exploit that had caused all of the trouble in the first place had now come back to haunt it in the form of a massive class-action lawsuit. The case was predicated on the harm that was done as a result of the identity thefts leveraged off of the stolen data.*

*The arrival of the bill of particulars from the plaintiffs' lawyers included a nightmare listing of malfeasance when it came to protecting the personally identifiable information (PII) entrusted to the company. That included such negligent acts as the failure to encrypt **personal data** like social security numbers and birthdates. It also contained a litany of instances where reasonable practices to protect that data simply didn't exist. So, after consulting with the company's legal team, the CEO, CIO, and CISO decided that the best defense would be to prove that the company had done everything that a reasonable person ought to do to ensure the safety of the stolen information. That concept was known in the legal community as "due diligence." The chief outcome of their decision was to make the definition of a specialist role in the protection of individual privacy essential to the company's continued well-being. Thus, the role of the privacy specialist was born.*

*The CISO was handed the responsibility for defining that role. He knew from the fallout over the lawsuit that the specification of the precise capabilities required for a privacy specialist was going to be an extremely important task. In his mind, this role would be an oversight position, whose primary duty would be to ensure that individual privacy was not violated by any specific act of the company. The way the CISO viewed it, the privacy specialist would be in charge of enforcing the privacy rights of the people whose data the organization kept.*

*In service of that aim, the CISO believed that the particular responsibility of the privacy specialist was to devise a tangible system of specialized policies and controls that would ensure that the information of every individual that the company dealt with was protected. That protection had to provably involve every reasonable means possible. In the CISO's mind, the privacy professional's primary duty was to devise and then maintain those controls, along with their associated technologies, to ensure that the organization did not disclose PII to any person who was not authorized to view it. That rule applied to both internal and external agents.*

*The CISO did not need the court case to underline the importance of privacy protection. The consequences of the loss of personally identifiable data, which was valued by the plaintiffs' lawyers at $187.2 million, put a certain amount of urgency in his efforts to establish that position. The CISO knew from the beginning that it would take comprehensive understanding of the ways that the organization was obligated to maintain the confidentiality of personal data, in order to properly define the role of the privacy specialist. Therefore, he believed that it was* *important to state the exact set of competencies that would be required to design and coordinate the controls to ensure that every reasonable effort had been taken to ensure privacy.*

*Privacy protection gets most of its influence from the fact that loss of personal data has critical consequences in the legal domain, as well as impacts on company reputation. The problem, however, was that privacy protection is not an information security function in the classic sense. Instead, it is more of a highly focused legal and ethical obligation that applies across the organization.*

*For instance, it is possible for anybody with the proper authorizations to violate the confidentiality of any person's PII simply by looking it up. In fact, many people in the company need to have access to confidential information in order to do their job. That can include such diverse and unrelated positions as ordering clerk, human resources professional, financial staff, administrative assistants, and some secretaries. As a result, the privacy specialist role has to create a specific set of actions that can be integrated into conventional business practice so that they will ensure comprehensive protection of personal data, while not interfering with day-to-day work.*

*The CISO and his entire team felt that in order to ensure that personal information was protected from malicious acts, personnel errors, or accidental harm, it would be necessary for every operational function to perform common due diligence functions. Accordingly, they believed that the steps that were required to ensure that due diligence should involve everything from electronic to the most human-centered functions.*

# Privacy Professional

All safeguards, from the most virtual to the most concrete personnel and physical security procedures, have to be properly designed and monitored in order to ensure correct practice. Due to the comprehensiveness of that requirement, the definition itself is going to need input from everybody. That was because all of the organization's functions would eventually be required to carry out the actions that the privacy specialist role was responsible for. The EBK was a help in this because it lists six high-level competencies:

1. Design and evaluate data security for privacy considerations

2. Manage, design, implement, and evaluate incident management programs for privacy considerations

3. Design and evaluate IT security training and **awareness** to ensure privacy considerations

4. Design and implement personnel security protections to ensure privacy

5. Manage, design, implement, and evaluate regulatory and standards compliance programs to ensure privacy

6. Manage, design, implement, and evaluate privacy risk management programs

## The Privacy Specialist and the Design and Evaluation of Data Security for Privacy Considerations

The privacy specialist is the principal designer and overseer of the controls to protect PII. Therefore, the privacy specialist also has to have input into, if not specific control over, the process by which the company's actions to ensure the confidentiality and privacy of personal data are designed and implemented. The condition for oversight and control extends throughout the lifecycle of any given information item and it applies to personal data that is represented in any form of media.

Thus, the chief competency for this position has to include the ability to create large-scale privacy protection schemes. The privacy specialist has to be directly involved in the setting of information privacy policies at the corporate level. Ideally, participation at the corporate level will also ensure that all relevant standards, guidelines, requirements, directives, or laws for the protection of personal information are incorporated into the privacy protection process. There are serious legal consequences involved if the organization is not provably capable of responding to violations of privacy. Specific procedures for protection of personal information should ensure due diligence when it comes to effective incident management, secure access, retention, and disposal of personal data.

Ensuring that personal information is properly protected requires the privacy specialist to identify, document, and label all personally identifiable data held by the organization, along with each item's required level of protection. The next step, once the relevant data has been identified, is to assess all risks to that data and then specify the specific steps that will be taken to protect it. Those steps are then turned into concrete procedure by an appropriate set of privacy controls, which ought to be based directly on the perceived risk of compromise to the data. These controls implement the organization's data security policies and acceptable use procedures, which naturally should reflect all relevant standards, regulations, or laws.

The privacy specialist then routinely audits and tests that control set. From the results of these audits and tests, the privacy specialist is able to certify the effectiveness of the organization's data security policies, processes, and procedures. If deficiencies are subsequently identified by those audits and tests, the privacy specialist then suggests changes based on the results. Since those tests will also reveal actual violations and privacy **breaches**, the privacy specialist must also ensure that any necessary changes or improvements are done to maintain the appropriate level of data protection.

## The Privacy Specialist and the Design and Evaluation of Incident Management Programs

The aim of incident management is to detect, contain, prevent, or recover from harmful incidents. Because the privacy specialist is responsible for ensuring against incidents that affect personally identifiable data, that role is involved in the incident response process. Specifically, the privacy specialist develops incident management policies and procedures as they impact personal information. That includes specifying the actions of the incident management team where personal information is involved.

The privacy specialist is responsible for the development of plans for responses where incidents affecting personally identifiable data are involved. That includes design of the specific procedures for incident handling and reporting, as well as the development of practices for forensic evidence gathering. In order to test the effectiveness of incident response procedures, the privacy specialist is also involved in the coordination of incident response exercises and penetration testing activities. This is always done in conjunction with the roles that are primarily responsible for carrying out those functions, such as the CISO role.

The aim of the privacy specialist is to make the incident response process effective where personal data is involved. In that respect, the privacy specialist establishes, measures, and collects data about all incidents in order to assess and improve the effectiveness of incident response in the case of privacy. Those evaluation activities include the steps to assess the effectiveness of penetration testing and incident response tests. In addition, the privacy specialist works to ensure the most effective lines of communication between the actual incident response team and the privacy function.

## The Privacy Specialist and the Design, Implementation, and Evaluation of IT Security Training and Awareness Programs

PII is an essential part of the business function, because it is handled by most of the people in the organization. That scope of involvement requires every worker to be aware of the critical importance of privacy in their day-to-day work. In order to ensure the proper level of awareness among the organization's workers, all of the issues involved in ensuring the protection of personal data have to be reinforced through training and awareness programs.

Moreover, besides the conventional workforce, people with specific roles in ensuring privacy have to be properly trained in the methods, practices, and technologies of privacy protection. Because the privacy specialist has the primary responsibility for protection of personal information, it is an absolute requirement for that role to ensure that all of the training steps necessary to ensure optimum capability have been taken by everybody involved in privacy protection.

In that respect, the privacy specialist role is responsible for establishing and overseeing awareness and training for personal information protection. That includes development of the actual training program's goals, as well as the specific teaching objectives of the privacy awareness and training process. In order to do that effectively, the privacy specialist has to develop and validate a training and awareness program plan. Since the requirements for privacy reach across the organization, the privacy specialist works with appropriate subject matter experts (SMEs) to ensure that the plan is complete and accurate.

Once the awareness and training plan is established, the privacy specialist maintains that scheme under strict change management. The reason why change management is required is that the dictates of due diligence require the training plan to be provably current and correct. The requirement for currency and correctness also applies to all training and awareness materials.

In order to enforce the requirement for currency and correctness, the privacy specialist conducts focused audits and reviews to determine where gaps in workforce knowledge and skills might be present. The privacy specialist prioritizes the outcomes of those assessments in order to formulate a priority list of awareness and training needs. As those needs change, the privacy specialist develops new awareness and training programs and materials which are appropriate and timely for the intended audience. The privacy specialist then ensures that these new programs are delivered to the intended audiences in an appropriate and timely fashion.

The privacy specialist ought to assess the privacy awareness and training program for compliance with corporate policies and regulations. Additionally, the privacy specialist must always ensure that information security personnel, in particular, are receiving the proper level and type of training. Because of that requirement, the privacy specialist is responsible for measuring information security workers' performance against corporate privacy goals.

## The Privacy Specialist and the Design and Evaluation of Personnel Security Programs to Ensure Privacy

The privacy specialist is responsible for ensuring that PII is protected. Since the people who have the best access to that information are the organization's own trusted personnel, the privacy specialist has to establish controls sufficient to ensure that the people who have been trusted to access personal information are strictly monitored. That requirement applies to both employees and contractors.

General controls for personnel security are intended to prevent and detect security breaches such as theft, fraud, misuse of information, and noncompliance. These controls implement such classic cybersecurity principles as separation of duties, job rotation, and **classification**. All of these principles also apply to privacy protection. Therefore, it is the responsibility of the privacy specialist to design a privacy protection scheme that ensures that all individuals who have access to personal data are managed and controlled.

In order to achieve the proper level of monitoring and control, the privacy specialist defines and documents personnel security rules and procedures for privacy protection. The privacy specialist then evaluates the overall personnel security program's effectiveness in enforcing those rules. That evaluation enables the privacy specialist to subsequently recommend any changes that will improve internal practices for privacy protection.

To assure the continuous effectiveness of privacy controls, the privacy specialist has to ensure that those controls remain in alignment with organizational security goals. That requires the privacy specialist to review the privacy protection program to ensure that it complies with all organizational standards, procedures, directives, policies, and procedures. Also, because much of the general security process relies on ensuring acceptable behavior, the privacy specialist also ensures that the privacy controls are continuously monitored.

## The Privacy Specialist and the Management, Design, Implementation, and Evaluation of Legal, Regulatory, and Standards Compliance

The privacy specialist is specifically responsible for ensuring that the organization's privacy policies and practices comply with all applicable standards, regulations, and laws. This is a critical task, since the privacy of personal information is strictly regulated in some industries and the general attitude of the law toward privacy protection is increasingly stringent.

The privacy specialist has to make certain that an organization-wide compliance program has been established in order to ensure across-the-board compliance with privacy requirements. This is primarily a coordination function, in that it requires the privacy specialist to work with and coordinate every person who might be involved in the process of ensuring privacy. To fulfill that obligation, the privacy specialist aids in the development of specific organization-wide compliance strategies, policies, plans, and procedures. This is always done in reference to any existing privacy standards, regulations, or laws.

Legally, the organization is obligated to document that it has kept careful track of all sensitive and confidential data at all times. In order to ensure that the necessary oversight and control over sensitive data has been implemented and enforced, the privacy specialist has to design processes and control requirements that can in essence prove that the organization has complied with any applicable law, within the jurisdiction where the company does business.

Once all sensitive data items are identified and properly secured, the privacy specialist develops a plan of action and associated mitigation strategies, designed to make sure that any program deficiencies are identified and corrected. The effectiveness of the plan is demonstrated through focused audits of the privacy process. The privacy specialist uses the results of these audits to recommend any necessary remedial actions and also establishes compliance record keeping and reporting processes to support these recommendations. These processes ensure that the evidence exists of the presence of control processes for privacy.

The privacy specialist also monitors, assesses, and evaluates how effectively each of the organization's individual personnel and IT systems perform with respect to privacy. This evaluation is carried out by compiling, analyzing, and reporting the outcomes of the regular performance measurement process. The aim of this measurement process is to demonstrate that the organization's privacy controls satisfy all applicable standards, policies, procedures, guidelines, directives, regulations, and laws.

For **compliance** reporting purposes, the privacy specialist is also accountable to maintain ongoing and effective communications with key stakeholders. The aim is to be able to obtain field reports on the effectiveness of the privacy protection process. To fulfill this part of the role, the privacy specialist conducts internal audits to determine if privacy control objectives, controls, processes, and procedures have been performed as expected and then routinely reports the results to the involved parties.

## The Privacy Specialist and the Management, Design, Implementation and Evaluation of Risk Management Programs for Privacy

The privacy specialist develops and deploys programs to identify threats to privacy, evaluates the likelihood and impact of each threat, and devises an effective strategy for mitigating risk. The aim of that process is to devise a strategy that will mitigate any risk to privacy that the organization considers meaningful. This must be done at an affordable cost.

The privacy specialist is responsible for establishing a risk management program for privacy-related risks only. Because risk management is always driven by the impacts of the event in the real world, the aim of the general risk assessment process is to help decision makers understand what the priority threats are. The privacy specialist is responsible for the privacy part of that assessment. To fulfill this responsibility, the privacy specialist devises effective mitigation strategies and implements the necessary changes to the risk management process in order to address all emerging threats to personal data.

The privacy specialist's role is to ensure that the appropriate policies, processes, procedures, and technologies are in place to manage all relevant risks originating from people, facilities, or the equipment. Since management involves having a mitigation strategy, the privacy specialist is responsible for developing the practices that support that strategy. The decision to apply mitigation, or risk acceptance, strategies has financial implications, so the privacy specialist is also responsible for ensuring that the eventual risk management approach is cost effective.

The privacy specialist documents and maintains records of all risk-based practices used to protect personal data. This is a record keeping function. Since the aim is to protect the organization from claims of malfeasance, that record keeping is based on the appropriate set of standards, directives, regulations, and laws.

The privacy specialist develops the necessary control set to ensure that risks to personal data are controlled. In support of that purpose, the privacy specialist performs ongoing threat and vulnerability assessments to identify any emerging security risks. These assessments are also used to update the applicable security controls. Finally, the privacy specialist is responsible for the implementation of changes to the risk management program for personal data, including the direct evaluation of all individual security controls, tools, and techniques.

**6**

# Ensuring the Security of the Things That the Organization Buys

*The CISO had worked his way through the two positions identified by his outside experts. Now he turned to the one function he had the most interest in: procurement. He was particularly interested in procurement because he knew that the company was much more vulnerable than anybody suspected. Isolated incidents had been happening on the company systems, which indicated the presence of application layer attacks. But nobody had been able to pin down the source until the prior week.*

*That was when one of the CISO's top code analysts had discovered an open trap door inviting unknown raiders into the company's information resources. It was buried in a piece of commercial software. Given the reputation of the supplier, that vulnerability should never have been there in the first place. That got the CISO to thinking about what other purchased products might actually have malicious surprises buried in them. The upshot of that thinking was that he decided to create a procurement role for his security staff. The chief responsibility of that role would be to ensure that the company purchased products in a secure way.*

*Procurement is a process, after all, so it seemed logical for the CISO to assume that it would be a simple matter of outlining good security practices for the procurement people and then have the new role ensure that they followed them. That assumption held up for about a week, which was how long it took the CISO to get his arms around the incredible range and diversity of the things that the company bought. He found that everything fell into the domain of procurement, from services, raw material, and hard goods to legal advice, new products, and maintenance contracts. Likewise, those purchases were made from everybody from local vendors to worldwide, multi-tiered supplier networks. Moreover, because the company's operational needs were always changing, the CISO could see no way to create a rigid set of rules for the procurement process, since the process itself changed as the acquisition of new products changed.*

*When it comes to procurement, the role of the security specialist is to create and maintain a specialized process that will ensure that purchased products are sufficiently free of security vulnerabilities when acquired. Specifically, a security specialist would ensure that all relevant controls for acquiring products, goods, and services, which were in any way related to the company's information processing function, are implemented and functioning properly. The problem is that the controls that are needed to ensure the security of a physical product, like a computer or a router, are different from the controls that are needed to ensure that the software that those devices are running is secure.*

*To complicate the matter further, purchases in most large corporations involve a supply chain. Accordingly, in order to ensure the security of any of the products emerging from that supply chain, it is essential to guarantee that every link in that chain is secure. The CISO wrestled with the diversity problem for some time before he came up with an approach that he thought would be workable. The idea was built along the same lines as the approach he had used to deal with diversity in the implementation of the company's general security procedures. Rather than dictating specific company-wide practices that everybody who was doing procurement would follow, he would simply require that the various procurement processes establish security features that are relevant to their areas of responsibility. Those features would, of course, be customized to the specific type of procurement that was being undertaken by the new procurement specialist role.*

# Procurement Professional

The processes that are followed by each organizational unit amount to standard operating procedure. The requirement to ensure that each unit followed secure procurement practice would be satisfied by the presence of a specialist on the staff whose specific duty would be to design, implement, and subsequently maintain a secure procurement process tailored to that particular unit's needs. Thus, a specialist position would be embedded in every major procurement function in the company. From the standpoint of the EBK, the activities of that role encompassed all four perspectives: manage, design, implement, and evaluate secure procurement processes, as shown in Figure 6-2.

## The Procurement Specialist and the Management, Design, Implementation, and Evaluation of Secure Procurement Processes

The procurement specialist is responsible for ensuring that the organization's acquisition processes are conducted in a secure fashion. This role is primarily responsible for defining and enforcing a coherent process for procurement. Since all processes originate from policy, the procurement specialist must first ensure that general policies and procedures for secure procurement are defined, documented, and included in the overall procedure manual.

Specifically, the procurement specialist is obligated to create and then maintain a formal set of technical and behavioral controls over the procurement process. These controls have to ensure that that standard procurement process is monitored for acceptable performance and that risks are identified and mitigated. In order to meet that responsibility, the procurement specialist focuses on whether the controls for the procurement process adequately address the information security needs of the organization; where risks are identified, the procurement specialist mitigates them through new controls.

This role is also responsible for establishing and routinely evaluating the effectiveness of the vendor management program. Thus, the procurement specialist is the role that is most

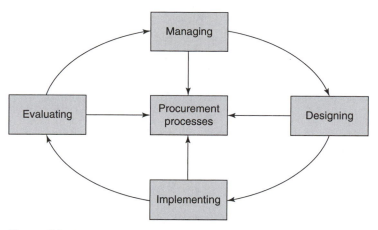

**Figure 6-2** Securing procurement processes

© *Cengage Learning 2012*

responsible for ensuring that due diligence is done with respect to ensuring secure third party relationships. In that respect, the procurement specialist ensures that all security procedures are followed correctly up and down the supply chain. This normally involves making certain that adequate levels of security practice are maintained between all suppliers and that all meaningful risks have been identified and mitigated in the supply chain. It also involves ensuring that all contract documents, such as statements of work or requests for proposals, have been analyzed to ensure that they include all of the requisite security considerations.

## Procurement as a Major Organizational Function

Procurement is a major organizational function, and so the security activities that are embedded and maintained by the security specialist have to be formally planned as well as executed. From an operational standpoint, the procurement specialist devises and then assists in detailed security analyses. The procurement specialist also routinely reviews procurement procedures to ensure that all necessary security requirements are included and followed correctly.

The procurement specialist role is more oriented toward security than it is toward purchasing. Therefore, it is important that the lines of communication between the procurement specialist and the people responsible for general security management are open and effective. Because purchasing affects the entire organization, effective communication is particularly important between this role and the people responsible for identifying and analyzing overall risk. The lines of communication between procurement and risk management have to be formally defined in any security plan.

# Chapter Summary

- The corollary role consists of three component functions.
- Each component function of the corollary role is vital to security.
- Specific environmental factors make ensuring physical security difficult.
- There is a relationship between the physical security professional and the rest of the information assurance (IA) team.

- The privacy professional has a specialized focus.

- There is an important relationship between the privacy professional and information security.

- The loss of personally identifiable data has serious impacts and consequences.

- There is an unusual relationship between the procurement professional and general acquisition.

- The acquisition professional plays a central role in ensuring security.

## Key Terms

**Awareness** Lowest level of training aimed at imparting general knowledge to the entire organization.

**Breaches** Specific incidents of intrusion, unauthorized access, or misuse of information.

**Classification** The process of defining the level of sensitivity of information as a means of defining privileges to access it.

**Compliance** Proven conformance with policy, procedure, standard, regulation, directive, or law.

**Perimeter** The area drawn around the protected space. Anything within the perimeter is protected, and anything outside is not protected.

**Personal data** Data about a single individual.

**Personally identifiable information (PII)** Data that can be used to identify a single individual.

**Physical security** The area of security devoted to protection of the physical space and the physical entities within it.

**Physical security controls** Physical countermeasures put in place to secure physical space. Guards, gates, and locks are examples of physical controls.

**Physical security professional** A specialist in physical security.

**Privacy** Ensuring that all personal information about an individual is protected.

**Privacy professional** A specialist in protecting personal information.

**Procurement professional** A specialist in acquisition.

## Questions from the CIO

The CIO requires you to brief her on the current status of your investigation. This will be an important part of your continuing work on this project, since it is essential to be able to describe all of the ramifications of the functions of the key corollary security personnel. Consequently, the CIO would like you to answer the following questions for her:

1. Why are the roles in this chapter called corollary roles? What differentiates them from the functional roles in the last chapter?

2. Why is the task of the physical security professional particularly difficult? What is it about diversity that makes it so?

3. Specifically, how is risk management in the physical space conducted? What differentiates it from the same process in virtual space?

4. What is the privacy professional role focused on, and why is this important?

5. Why is legal and regulatory compliance a particular focus for the privacy professional?

6. Are privacy professionals responsible for all risks, or are they limited to a specific set of risks? If they are limited, why is risk management particularly important in that area?

7. Why is there a relationship between procurement and security? What would be the consequence of not considering security in the procurement process?

8. Security in the procurement process can be overlooked because of a couple of factors. What are they, and how might they influence how an organization approaches security?

9. One important role of the security professional in the procurement process is to provide input to the development of procurement policy. Why is that important, and what would be the outcome if the security professional was not involved?

# Hands-On Projects

Using the case in Appendix 1, develop a detailed plan for ensuring physical security, privacy protection, and secure procurement processes for ACME. Ensure that the following requirements are satisfied:

- Consolidation of protected items into a protected perimeter, or perimeters
- Control of internal physical access
- Protection of customer data, particularly credit information, from violations by internal personnel
- Protection of customer data from intrusions
- Protection of outsourced and insourced products from malicious entities
- Assurance of secure acceptance procedures

# chapter 7

# The Data Security Competency

## Rewinding the Story Back to the Start: Defining the Required Competencies

*During the reorganization, the executive team, which was composed of the CEO, the CIO, and the CISO, had taken to calling the first year after the Chapter 11 "Year one". It was partly a statement about the company's new attitude toward security, and partly an accurate representation of the timeline they were going to follow to get the company back on its feet. That timeline was built around two projects that would be conducted in parallel over the first two and a half years.*

*First, the company needed a clear statement of standard operating procedure to guide every aspect of its security operation. The goal of the first project was to formalize and then document a set of security practices that would fit effectively into the company's overall management framework. Second, the company needed to specify who would be responsible for carrying out each of those practices. The executive team felt that this latter goal would be achieved by defining a comprehensive set of roles and then assigning an appropriate set of security practices to each role.*

*The CISO had solidified his leadership position in the company during the first year by actually going from site to site building awareness and soliciting feedback. Due to his efforts and the air miles that he had put on his company credit card, it now seemed that the company had a practical commitment to security. As the CISO was trudging around the globe, the rest of the team was back in New York working on an even tougher assignment: getting agreement on a complete and logically consistent set of security functions for the company as a whole.*

*The executive team was well aware that it would be both time-consuming and politically diffi-cult to embed an effective set of security requirements in the company's conventional day-to-day operation. Nevertheless, everybody from the CEO down felt that they were going to need an explicit definition of competencies to dictate how the security work should be done. Otherwise they would not have any benchmarks to manage it, and it made no sense whatso-ever to the executive team to stand up a major function like security without also providing an explicit means to judge its subsequent performance.*

*Since the CISO was busy traipsing around the globe, somebody else had to head up the effort to actually define those competencies. So, the CEO decided to put together a task team com-posed of security engineers from six of the company's key sites. He wanted to take the team approach to get a wide range of insight about the problem. It seemed like the best way to ensure buy-in would be to involve the people who were most responsible for ensuring the security for each site.*

*Fortuitously, the CISO reappeared from one of his red-eye trips just as the members of the task team were being briefed about their new assignment. The CISO had caught enough flak from the site managers on his last round of visits to conclude that the only way to document standard competencies would be to focus the descriptions of required activities at a "universal" level of application. That turned out to be a wise decision, since during his subsequent trip, which was to Singapore, he began to work out a highly effective process for customizing each standard competency to the explicit environment of each individual workplace.*

*Because the competencies that are associated with ensuring the security of the data itself were a critical concern. The CEO asked the team of security engineers to define those first. The team members were not happy about that assignment, since there are many activities that might logically be a part of a data security competency. The team would rather have started with a better-defined area like continuity management, whose elements were well known and accepted across the company. Nonetheless, because the organization's data was unquestionably one of its most important assets, the CEO felt that it was particularly important to get the data security in place. So the team was stuck with establishing compe-tencies for a topic that was essentially broad in scope, but whose components were not commonly agreed on.*

*The team members knew that data security in the most general sense entailed any principle, policy, or procedure that would ensure the confidentiality, integrity, availability, and privacy of any form of data. That included any type of storage. They also knew that the competen-cies associated with data security would underlie the development and implementation of all of the electronic and behavioral controls required to ensure those three principles. Therefore, in practical terms, the team envisioned the data security process as a primarily managerial function, whose chief purpose was to incorporate the various areas of elec-tronic, physical, and personnel security into a single, comprehensive system for ensuring the organization's information.*

*Given its understanding of the general aims of the data security competency, the team felt that the primary focus should be on ensuring a state of security for every meaningful unit of com-pany data. Achieving such a state would involve a broad range of controls, both electronic and behavioral. Therefore, team members decided that the practices associated with data security would clearly involve such areas as cryptographic, network and application, and system level security. It also decided that all of the practices necessary to ensure the right set of managerial and behavioral controls should also be included in the data security competency. Because the team felt that the process areas would require the most time and study, it decided to approach the definition of the competencies for the management areas first.*

# Data Security: The Manage Function

The EBK specifies four basic competencies for the management of data security. These are all policy-based activities that must be implemented at a high level across the organization. The effect of these four competencies is to ensure that data security is properly managed:

1. Ensure that **data classification** and data management policies and guidance are issued and updated

2. Specify policy and coordinate review and approval

3. Ensure compliance with data security policies and relevant legal and regulatory requirements

4. Ensure appropriate changes and improvement actions are implemented as required

# Data Security and Policy Assurance

Policies are the foundation for all types of organizational control. They state the desired behavior, or specific outcome, that the control must ensure. For that reason, the data security manage function is geared around policy creation and enforcement. Accordingly, that function states the organization's precise obligations to ensure the confidentiality, integrity, and availability of its data.

Policies themselves can be divided into two types: general and specific. General policies provide directional guidance in broad terms. They are given tangible effect through human-centered or technical controls. Because they are intended to be applied universally, the concrete implementation of a policy requires interpretation. A common security policy, such as acceptable use, is an example of a general policy that requires interpretation. The resulting controls that ensure acceptable use in day-to-day practice will depend on the situation or technology in question. On the other hand, specific policies, such as **firewall** criteria, apply to a particular situation or technology. Thus, a specific policy is narrowly constrained to a particular issue, and the implementation of the associated controls requires little interpretation.

The objective of the data security manage function is to ensure that the appropriate policies are developed and deployed across the enterprise. Examples of common security-related policies that have data security implications are:

- *Computer security policy*—Policies that guide data security work; these are the principles that dictate the conduct of the computer security operation.

- *Data retention policy*—Policies that guide how data will be retained and backed up; these are the guidelines for archiving and disposing data.

- *Acceptable use policy*—Policies that guide individual access and employment of data; these policies draw the line for employees when it comes to their personal use of data.

- *Remote access policy*—Policies that guide access to data from remote locations; these principles dictate the rules for when and how data can be accessed from remote devices.

- *E-mail policy*—Policies that guide the use of e-mail by the organization's employees; these policies lay down the rules for the use of the company e-mail service.

- *Removable storage policy*—Policies that guide access and use of removable data devices such as thumb drives and portable hard drives, as well as who can remove what from a site.

- *VPN policy*—Policies that guide and define the use of the VPN; includes all **access control** practices as well as what can go over the VPN.

# Designing an Effective Approach to Assuring Trusted Access

In conventional practice, the security of data is established through a deliberate set of electronic and managerial controls. The generic purpose of those controls is to underwrite trust by regulating access to the organization's data. The controls themselves are designed, implemented, and maintained as part of a formal data security management function. The effect of that set of controls is to ensure that only those people who are trusted by the organization are given access to its data. The process that establishes and maintains a trust relationship between the organization and any subject seeking access is generically termed "access control."

The access control process assures the rights of access of any person or process that seeks to gain entry to any physical space or electronic system. The access control process is built around four fundamental principles, which work together to ensure that only trusted subjects have access to secured data. These are:

1. *Identification*—Establishes that the subject is trusted

2. **Authentication**—*Establishes that subjects are who they say they are*

3. **Authorization**—Ensures that the subject is assigned appropriate access privileges

4. *Accountability*—Ensures that those privileges are monitored and enforced

## The Identification Principle and Data Security

Operationally, the identity function ensures that subjects requesting access to a given item of data are known and trustworthy. The people responsible for securing that data are responsible for assigning unique labels to all valid users and processes that certify that trust. That assignment of identities is typically determined by organizational security policies, which are established as part of the overall policy setting process. For data that have been classified, that assignment process might include the requirement for background checks. In the case of unclassified data, the assignment of a valid access identity might require nothing more than a confirmation that the subject is an employee.

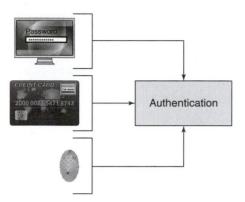

**Figure 7-1** Authentication principle

© *Cengage Learning 2012*

## The Authentication Principle and Data Security

Once an identity has been assigned, management has to authenticate the subject every time it requires access. This process typically involves use of an authentication token. Three classic tokens are normally used to authenticate identity. These are "something you know" (e.g., a password), something you have (e.g., a credit card), and something that you are (e.g., a unique physical attribute like a fingerprint), as shown in Figure 7-1.

**Proving Who You Are Through Something You Know** Passwords are the most common way to ensure trusted access. Because they are so frequently used, most of conventional data security is founded on them. If it is not necessary to maintain strict access control, a password-based system can be a simple and effective way of protecting data. A password-based authentication system requires authorized users to present a unique combination of letters and numbers at the time they are authenticated. The fact that only the authorized users should know what their combinations are, provides an efficient and straightforward way to tell whether people are who they say they are.

**Proving Who You Are Through Something You Have** Another way to establish trusted access is to ask subjects to produce a valid identification token. The most common example of this approach is a key, which serves as de-facto proof of identity; a key should only be carried by an authorized user. Thus, holders of a particular key should only be able to open locks that they have the authority to open. But because people can lose their keys, physical access tokens such as swipe cards or RFIDs are typically combined with passwords to increase the strength of the protection. This is called two-factor authentication.

**Proving Who You Are Through Something You Are** Authentication using the actual physical characteristics of a subject is typically known as biometrics. Biometric authentication is highly secure because physical characteristics such as fingerprints are unique to the individual and hard to duplicate. They are also impossible to lose. On the other hand, the technology that underlies biometric identification is still in its infancy; the process can produce false negatives and, even worse, false positives. As the technology improves, it is expected that biometric authentication methods will become the authentication method of choice.

## Ensuring Tighter Security Through Multifactor Authentication

Each of the previous types of authentication methods has advantages and disadvantages, both from a usability perspective and also from a security perspective. Thus, in order to increase the overall effectiveness of an authentication system, more than one of these factors might be required. The combination of more than one means of authentication strengthens the degree of control. A common everyday example of the multifactor approach to access is in the bank card and PIN combination. The card represents something you have and the PIN represents something you know. Because both the PIN and the card are required, it is easier to trust that the subjects seeking access are who they say they are. Biometric access control systems will provide an additional factor to common access control situations as they become more common, which will enhance the security of most situations.

**The Authorization Principle and Data Security** Once a subject's identity is confirmed, specific rights to access data have to be assigned. This step is necessary because modern computer systems contain many types of data, from trivial to top-secret. People who have gained access to the system still have to be allowed to only access data that they have a right to see. The principle of authorization delineates those rights, which are normally called "privileges." Privileges are typically assigned by the owners of the system, and are based on the recognized level of trustworthiness of each subject.

Assigning privileges implements the organization's specific security policy. That assignment is based on data classification. Classification involves a four-step continuum: unimportant, sensitive, secret, and top secret. Data is classed into categories of trust based on its value and sensitivity. Decisions about what data falls into each category are normally based on the business case and reflect the general importance of an item of data. As an operating principle, classifications limit access to the minimum data that a subject needs to do a job properly. People who need to have a high degree of access because of their job responsibilities are then subjected to a much greater degree of scrutiny in order to prove their trustworthiness.

The process for determining a subject's level of trustworthiness is typically based in human resources. The process can involve various levels of background checks and might even require a polygraph where trust has to be absolutely assured. Depending on the importance of the data and the level of assigned privilege, it might also be necessary to re-visit that question of trustworthiness for each subject on a regularly scheduled basis.

**The Accountability Principle and Data Security** The accountability principle ensures that inappropriate accesses are identified and reported. Accountability enforces the policies, rules, and criteria for access control. Top-level managers establish accountability policies. IT management typically has the responsibility for embedding those policies into the system's automated functioning and then maintaining their applicability. The system then monitors users' actions to ensure that none of those criteria have been violated. Along with enforcement, accountability is also responsible for ensuring that the system evolves with its environment. As a result, accountability is often tied to other EBK functions such as risk and incident management. Operationally, accountability maintains a continuous understanding of the threat environment through routine security functions like incident reporting and risk analysis. As that understanding evolves, accountability essentially closes the loop with the policy makers who dictate how the organization's data security function will evolve.

# Designing Data Security into the Operation

*The CISO blew back into town on a major high from his Singapore experience. Given what he had found out about local customization of general policy, he was rather pleased by the way the team had laid out the management process for the data security function. The four principles for ensuring and enforcing controlled access were represented in a tangible policy framework that would allow the company to exercise across-the-board control of access. At the same time, the approach also retained the necessary flexibility to support customization of those policies to specific situations. The CISO felt confident that the implementation process at each site would be a relatively easy step. That was, until the company's various units began to tackle the job of customizing data security policies into specific procedures.*

*The problem lay in the diversity and scope of the data security operation. The CISO knew from his experiences in Singapore that if those competencies were going to be implemented, they would have to be customized to the situation. That was why the team had chosen to focus its definition of each competency at the highest level possible. The assumption was that a high-level definition of outcome would let the individual site manager tailor a set of behaviors that would specifically achieve that particular result.*

*Each site then had to actually address the problem of putting those principles into practice. Logically, it seemed like the most reliable way to convert a general concept into a set of concrete, day-to-day practices would be to formulate and adopt a routine, company-wide methodology. That methodology would then dictate the process for tailoring concepts into practice at every site. The CISO had proven that that tailoring could be done, in what for a New Yorker was one of the most alien environments among the company's holdings. Now it was time to roll out what he had found to the rest of the company.*

*The CISO turned to the compliance officer to carry out that task. At first glance, the compliance officer seemed like a bad choice, since everybody in the company knew that she had the people skills of a marine drill sergeant. Nonetheless, she also had an uncanny eye for detail and an unchallenged ability to connect the relationship dots between the disparate elements of the organization. The data security requirements of the company involved what seemed to be an endless array of dependencies, and it seemed like she would be the only person capable of keeping a workable picture of the actual interrelationships among the various elements in her head. So she was given the unenviable task of turning general policy into unbreakable practice for all of the company's widespread holdings. The CISO saw the fact that she actually wanted that job as an additional bonus.*

*As planned, the compliance officer used the general competency areas of the EBK as a guide for developing the elements of that process. These recommendations provide a coherent direction for anybody who is trying to approach the creation of procedures for any of the competency areas. There are eight of these for data security. The recommendations are a mix of management and technical activities, whose general purpose is to ensure an effective state of data security:*

1. *Develop data security policies using data security standards, guidelines, and requirements that include privacy, access, retention, disposal, incident management, disaster recovery, and configuration*

2. *Identify and document the appropriate level of protection for each item of data*

3. *Specify data and information classification, sensitivity, and need-to-know requirements by information type*

4.  *Create authentication and authorization system for users to gain access to data by assigned privileges and permissions*

5.  *Develop acceptable use procedures in support of the data security policy*

6.  *Develop sensitive data collection and management procedures in accordance with standards, procedures, directives, policies, regulations, and laws (statutes)*

7.  *Identify an appropriate set of information security controls based on the perceived risk of compromise to the data*

8.  *Develop security-testing procedures*

# Turning Policy into Concrete Practice

Policies are general statements about intent; they chart the course that the organization intends to follow for a substantive period of time. They are normally published to the organization as a set of rational guidelines. A well-defined set of underlying procedures is needed to ensure that the people in the company actually follow that course. Those procedures and their accompanying practices are typically created through a deliberate design process. In the case of data security, the aim of the design is to establish the behavioral and electronic controls that are required to guarantee the most effective data security process possible. Accordingly, the resultant data security process should satisfy three universal criteria in order to be correct:

1.  The data security process should incorporate an integrated set of behavioral, physical, and technological controls.

2.  The data security process should be strategic in direction and apply organization wide.

3.  The data security process should continuously execute the routine practices that need to be performed by the normal business operation.

The data security process itself is operationalized through a set of real-world security controls, which have to be tailored to fit the specific threat environment for the given situation. In the case of data security, these controls support five common purposes:

1.  *Prevention*—Ensures that all requisite measures are in place to prevent harm

2.  *Detection*—Ensures that all intrusions and violations are detected

3.  *Deterrence*—Ensures that all intrusions and violations are punished

4.  *Containment*—Limits any damage that might occur from an intrusion or violation

5.  *Recovery*—Ensures restoration of the data to a prior state in case of disaster

## Factoring Risk into the Development of Policy

Data security policies are the foundation for defining, deploying, and maintaining the necessary security controls. However, there is a step that has to take place before those policies can be developed. That step involves asset identification and risk analysis. There is no point in developing policies if you don't know what you are protecting or what threatens it. So, prior to defining the policies to protect the information base, it is critical to explicitly characterize its form both in terms of its contents and also how those contents relate to each other. Once all of the items of information that will fall within the protection scheme have been identified, it is then possible to prioritize the specific risks to each individual asset and think about how those risks will be mitigated.

## Asset Baseline Formulation—Identifying What Has to Be Protected

Data can exist in three dissimilar states: digital representation, documentary representation, and personal knowledge. In many instances, the same item of information is recorded electronically, as well as on paper, or perhaps in both media. It is a waste of resources to protect something in its electronic form if the documentary representation of that same item is not secured. In order to make intelligent decisions about data security, the organization has to know what data it has, and specifically the many forms it might be represented in. That is the function of the asset identification and baselining process.

This process identifies, classifies, and labels every item of data that is valuable to the organization. The aggregate set of data assets is then documented and recorded as a baseline, which is a tangible, hierarchical, formally defined, and documented structure. The decisions that establish baselines are business decisions that involve all stakeholders. Each item placed in a baseline is given a unique and meaningful label associated with its placement in the baseline structure. The baseline map of data assets is then maintained as an operational resource, in the same way that the accounting ledger is maintained to keep track of financial assets.

## Understanding Priorities Through Risk Analysis

Once the asset baseline is known, the risks associated with each item of data have to be identified and assessed. Risk assessment is a critical step in the process because it systematically analyzes and then identifies all of the potential threats to the baseline. Risk assessments evaluate the damage associated with each threat and point to all acceptable options. This enables the business to prioritize the risks it faces. This is a business process, in the sense that there are never enough resources to secure all of the data; however, if priorities are established, it will allow the organization to deploy its resources in the most cost efficient and effective way. Since there are never enough resources to address all potential threats, the next step in the process involves a tradeoff; the organization has to decide about the value and criticality of each individual data item and then estimate the specific degree of resource commitment necessary to assure it. The aim is to identify the most valuable data items and then dictate the sequence for securing them, as well as the degree of protection that is required.

## Aligning Policy to Priority and Implementing Controls

An appropriate set of policies is then formulated once the organization's protection priorities are established. The outcome of this phase of the process is a practical policy framework that will guide the deployment of the controls to secure every item in the protection scheme. That framework is then used to justify each control that is placed in the scheme. Ensuring exact alignment between the company's priorities, the policies that underwrite those priorities, and the controls that implement each policy is the surest way to also ensure that the organization's data security dollars are well spent.

The actual deployment of the underlying control set is dictated by an implementation plan. That plan should specify a precise schedule for installing each control and an estimate of the cost of maintaining it. Each control is then subject to routine operational testing, in order to ensure that it is performing correctly and that it continues to satisfy the policy that it is aligned with. The aim is to be able to say over time that the performance of the aggregate set of controls in the protection scheme is sufficient to satisfy all security goals.

# Ensuring Optimum Resource Allocation

The general aim of the data security function is to make certain that any attempt to access the organization's data is properly controlled. The purpose of that control is to protect items of value from unauthorized access. The key to ensuring that that protection uses resources efficiently lies with the concept of classification. As stated earlier, there are never enough resources to secure every item of data. Consequently, the organization has to be able to guarantee that, at a minimum, its priority items of data are kept safe. The ability to factor all of the data into manageable groups, with common security properties, allows the organization to make decisions about the resources that have to be committed to protect each group.

## Classification

The process of sorting data into groups based on value, or sensitivity, is called "classification." In essence, a classification contains all data at a particular level of criticality, or importance. Classifications allow the organization to make rational decisions about the value of data of a certain type. It can then assign an appropriate degree of control for each type based on business value. That assignment creates layered groups of data items at different levels of priority. The items in the group of highest priority are fully protected, while items of lesser value will still be given some protection appropriate to their relative status in the priority queue. The term that is commonly used to describe the outcome of a classification process is "defense in depth."

Classification levels are implemented hierarchically; each successive layer describes an increasingly rigorous degree of control, which is required to ensure trust. Every level implements a well-defined set of rules that ensures that access is restricted only to those individuals who have been proven trustworthy. Establishing classification levels within an organization makes the resource allocation process a lot easier and more cost efficient. It allows the organization to make intelligent choices about how to protect four simple groupings of data rather than an uncounted number of individual items. In conventional practice, these four groupings are labeled "unclassified" (any item of data that has not received a classification), "confidential," "secret," and "top secret."

## Privilege

All people with access rights have to be assigned some degree of privilege, the level of which is based on the degree of trust. For instance, people given a low level of trust would have restricted privileges, whereas people who are trusted would be given much less restrictive privileges. Since the level of privilege defines what an individual can and cannot do, an individual's assigned level of privilege is the basis for enforcing access rights, as shown in Figure 7-2.

In organizations that require a high degree of trust, privileges are assigned based on the clearance level. A clearance is nothing more than a pre-determined amount of trust that is

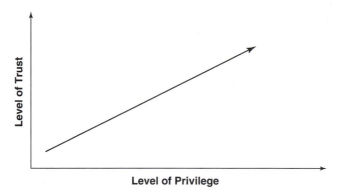

**Figure 7-2** Privilege

© Cengage Learning 2012

assigned to each subject. Like classifications, clearances cluster individual people and processes into groups that share common security properties. The problem with clearances is that they are resource intensive; the organization has to make a considerable investment in backgrounding each individual before a level of trust can be assigned. In the case of the highest clearances, this can be a huge expense. In popular media, the concept of clearances is almost strictly in the province of the military and spy agencies; however, clearances are also useful in many other types of organizations where an elevated degree of security is important.

# Managing the Automated Data Security Process—Account Management

Data security is frequently automated. Automation is useful, because of the size of most data repositories and the number of people seeking access. Based on the prearranged assignment of privilege, automated access control systems are the only means capable of handling that kind of volume. Like any other automated system, access control systems have to be managed. In this case, management essentially amounts to the determination and assignment of access rights to each subject.

Automated access control systems require all users to have an established identity prior to seeking access. The specific role of management is to link user identities to the applications, databases, and services they are permitted to access. The identities have to be created and assigned. This is called "account management." To implement this assignment, management determines each person's, or process's, level of privilege and records the appropriate access rights in the system. Users or processes authenticate that assigned identity each time they attempt access. The automated part of the system then enforces the assigned rights.

"Account management" describes the actual management process that assigns and monitors **user privileges**. It is not possible to institute proper access control without account management. This process ensures that the identity of all authorized users is continuously maintained in the system. It also routinely ensures that all valid associations between user identities and the applications, data, and services are correct. Account management creates, maintains, and deletes user accounts, as well as manages changes in access rights. In addition, user authentication procedures and access tokens, such as user name and password, are assigned and administered by the account manager. Because each individual user has to come through the account management process in order to obtain an identity, that function becomes the public face of data security.

Operationally, because of the volume of data and the complexity of most business operations, automation is the only realistic means of ensuring controlled access to an electronic system. That automation is typically implemented using an access control model as a template. The actual authorization process is enabled by a feature of the operating system that permits or denies access based on the subject's known level of trust. This feature is known as a reference monitor. System management programs the reference monitor to ensure that only the proper set of access privileges is granted to each subject.

The reference monitor is built around an authorization database. The authorization database stores the criteria that drive the decisions about access permissions as well as every trusted subject's information. In complex organizations, development and ongoing sustainment of that database is likely to be a resource-intensive activity. In order to ensure secure access, it is necessary to keep an up-to-date reference monitor. Otherwise, untrusted or even malicious people might inadvertently slip past the automated controls.

# Standard Models for Securing Data

It is hard to create a coordinated access control operation within a large, complex organization. The availability of a commonly accepted model for defining how the process should be structured can be invaluable. Over time, organizations that have had a special stake in data security, primarily governmental entities like the Department of Defense, have developed standardized models for structuring an access control system. Each of these models has a different focus and application based on its uses.

## Criterion-Based Access Control

As the name implies, criterion-based access control systems are built around a set of pre-defined access control policies, or rules. The administrator implements a set of system-controlled security policies for each protected object that the reference monitor uses as a point of reference to guide decisions about access. Once the administrator defines the criterion, it is always invoked whenever access to the attached data object is requested. That allows all security policy criteria to be established and enforced by a single automated process, which greatly simplifies the overall access control function.

Criterion-based access control is typically implemented by means of a pre-programmed access control list (ACL). An ACL specifies the authorized users of the system, their access rights, and the specific permissions they have for each object on the system. In a typical ACL, each entry in the list specifies a subject or a process as well as the specific access rights that that subject has for each particular object. Those permissions are usually attached to the object. The list specifies which use, or process may access the object and the operations that can be performed on it.

The list is automatically referenced each time a service is requested. Although ACLs provide the most popular means to protect information stored in a computer, they are not limited to computer resources. A physical security example of an ACL is the checklist that the guard uses to control the physical access of individuals to the facility. The advantage of an ACL is that it allows the administrator to designate access rights separately for every individual, since access is based on the permissions that are granted to that subject.

## Policy-Based Access Control

A centralized, policy-based approach is a very efficient way to control access to electronic data. There are three different ways that those policies can be focused, structured, and applied: mandatory access control, **discretionary access control (DAC)**, and **role-based access control (RBAC)**. Mandatory access control is enforced based on classifications. DAC is enforced based on criteria set by the owner of the data. RBAC is enforced by the system based on the organizational role of the individual seeking access.

These three different models are not mutually exclusive; in fact, the newer types of access control are built on the foundation of older approaches. For instance, a foundational relationship exists between DAC and the RBAC approach, in the sense that permissions in both cases are granted to groups rather than individuals. Notwithstanding how each of these approaches is implemented, all of the underlying models have a particular function and purpose and are applicable in different real-world situations. Therefore, a grasp of the principles and practices embodied in all of them will serve as the basis for understanding how to design a functional access control system for any type of organizational setting.

## Strict Control—the Mandatory Access Control Model

Mandatory access control follows a strict set of rules to define access rights. These rules are derived directly from the security policies of the organization. Mandatory access control then allocates a subject's access rights based on a known set of predetermined security attributes. In operational terms, this allows the security administrator to define policies that will be enforced for all users of a given type, in all instances.

Mandatory access control is enforced centrally. In systems where mandatory access control has been implemented, the administrator of the system establishes organization-wide security policies that no other user of the system can override or change. In that respect, mandatory access control is a particularly strict way to ensure access rights. Because of the complexity of assigning those rights, it has not been widely used outside of the federal government and the military.

In a mandatory access control system, the subject's access permissions are assigned based on the security attributes that they possess and the rules that have been established for those attributes. In application, mandatory rules cannot be overridden without special authorizations. Access is controlled automatically by the system using embedded, preset criteria. In addition to controlling access rights, the system also actively controls what can be done to a protected object based on the same established criteria. For example, even if a subject were permitted to access a document that was classified top secret, the system might not allow that same subject to share the document with any other person.

That raises the issue of "least privilege," which is an important concept in any form of access control, but particularly important for mandatory access control systems. A good illustration of the restrictions of least privilege is where people with the appropriate level of clearance might still not be allowed to view a top secret object if they did not need that information to do their jobs.

Least privilege is also called "need to know," which can be implemented to determine who is allowed to access a given piece of information at a specified time. This decision is based on the level of clearance of the user and the sensitivity of the object that is being accessed, as well as other variables such as time and place of attempted access. For instance, a user might have access rights to a document from a cubicle in a secured building but not be able to access the same document from a home computer.

## Controlling Access Through Assignment—Discretionary Access Control

In the world of business, the most common model for access control is DAC. As the name implies, under this system user rights are assigned by the owner or manager of each protected object. Thus, DAC allows the owner of a file or object to selectively grant or deny access to it. The owner of the protected object decides which users get access, and what access rights they can have. DAC uses the identity of every subject, process, or group to make decisions about the type and level of privilege that each will receive.

DAC systems use three general criteria (role, content, and time) in order to make their decisions about rights. These criteria are not mutually exclusive; in actual application, they can be combined to support an extremely efficient and highly secure specification of the privileges that will be granted to users in the organization. For instance, depending on the situation, the CEO might fulfill at least two roles: boss and outsider. If the CEO is at work, that person might have the access rights that would be assigned to a boss; however, if that person is at home, those rights might be only those of an outsider. A DAC system can implement that distinction based on whatever criteria are established in its programming. For instance, it might grant the CEO access to all company information at 3:00 p.m., while denying access to anybody logging in under the CEO's credentials at 3:00 a.m. The ability to discriminate based on an established set of criteria is a handy feature for companies who want to exercise precise, policy-based control over access rights.

The controls themselves are discretionary, in the sense that a subject with a certain level of permission can pass that permission on to any other subject, unless otherwise constrained. Because this supports the common business requirement for efficient communication, DAC is popular in conventional organizations. Since privileges are granted based on characteristics, the assignment of access rights might not necessarily be direct. For example, members of a group with similar trust characteristics might require similar access rights. In the case of that group, every member would assume the access rights that the group has been assigned.

The owner of a protected data object assigns permissions for that object to each group seeking access. That assignment process gives the owner explicit control over the access rights of groups that might be transitory. A good example of a transitory group is outside contractors. The organization can extend access rights to subcontractors who might be working on the same project. That assumes that these managers have the same security characteristics as the prime contractor's project management staff. Authentication in that case would be membership in the project management group as well as the assigned project's open status. Once the project has been closed out, those permissions can be revoked using the same process.

## Controlling Access by Type—Role-Based Access Control

RBAC is a common form of DAC that involves the assignment of specific access permissions to protected objects based on an individual's role. Because of its simplicity and flexibility, RBAC is a particularly effective means to secure access in large or complex networks.

In the case of RBAC, workplace roles are given privileges to carry out assorted job functions. Employees then acquire the permissions needed to execute system functions, which have been assigned to each role. In that case, the actual management of access rights requires the simple assignment of the role to the user. This simplifies the business process, because the only staffing issue would be to select the person with the right security attributes to fill a given role.

The guiding principle behind an RBAC system is that access permissions can only be assigned based on the specific roles that each user fulfills. In practice, users are associated with a set of roles they may perform. Those roles are given the specific access permissions necessary to perform the duties associated with them. Thus, the subject's access rights to objects are based strictly on the role he or she fulfills at a particular point in time.

RBAC could be difficult to differentiate from DAC. Where the two differ is in the fact that RBAC assigns rights to the business function, rather than to the objects and data that the people in the function interact with. In essence, RBAC assigns privileges based on the properties of the function itself rather than on the people and objects that comprise it, as DAC would do.

Users and programs (subjects) are granted permission to access system objects based on the duties that they perform, not by their security classification, which makes the process of assigning authorizations more straightforward. In addition, RBAC allows for greater flexibility in the day-to-day management and enforcement of security policies. Individual workers can be assigned to roles and easily reassigned from one role to another without modifying the fundamental security control structure of the system. Those roles can be changed and permissions can be granted or revoked centrally in response to the changes in technology and processes of the organization, as shown in Figure 7-3.

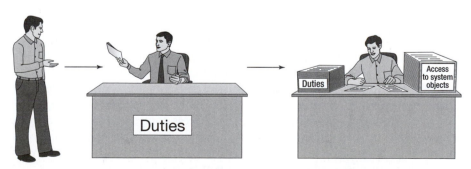

**Figure 7-3**  Role-based access control

© Cengage Learning 2012

# Data Security: The Implement Function

*Everyone on the executive team felt that they had established a sound concept for rolling out the data security function as an operational process. The range of models for assigning and controlling access privileges had been identified and customized to company needs, as had the actual tailoring process for data security. What remained to be seen was whether all of that work could be translated into a practical, everyday data security function. That job of translation was handed to the compliance officer.*

*In doing that, the CISO also had another agenda up his sleeve. He was convinced that most of the actual day-to-day execution of the data security process just depended on ensuring routine compliance with the specific controls that had been set to regulate authorized access. The CISO believed that the key to success was going to lie in enforcing those controls. Since the compliance officer's forte was ensuring that people toed the line, it just seemed right to have her implement the process.*

*He directed the compliance officer to make absolutely certain that the data security management process include a robust set of management and technical controls to ensure that all specified data security practices were followed to the letter. He also suggested that in any case where those practices were not followed correctly, the compliance officer could have her way with the offender. Knowing the compliance officer's preference for scorched earth, he sat back in his expensive leather office chair, clasped his hands behind his head, and chuckled as he pictured what would happen to the first person she caught violating any required procedures. He knew that it would not be pretty and, more importantly, he was also sure it would not happen again. For direction, the EBK provides a top-level view of the competencies required to ensure compliance with a process. As a group, the steps involved include:*

1. *Develop and verify data security access controls*
2. *Maintain privileges and associated profiles*
3. *Execute the access management process according to established procedures*
4. *Implement media control procedures and continuously monitor for compliance*
5. *Implement and verify data security access controls, and assign privileges*
6. *Address alleged violations of data security and privacy breaches*
7. *Apply and maintain confidentiality controls and processes in accordance with standards, procedures, directives, policies, regulations, and laws (statutes)*

## Establishing Effective, Operational Intrusion Detection

Detecting intrusions and other violations of the integrity of the system is one of the primary operational duties of anybody managing the data security process. Most harm to data comes from unauthorized access. In that respect, intrusion detection and access control are two sides of the same coin. Even so, intrusion detection has to be implemented as a separate function from access control because its aims are different. Access control ensures that only authorized users are permitted access, while intrusion detection ensures that any attempts to gain unauthorized access are detected. The precise role of intrusion detection is to identify and isolate attacks, violations, or misuse of data on the system before harm can occur.

In general practice, there are two different ways that intrusions can be detected. The most recognizable way might be through electronic utilities such as firewalls. There are four basic approaches to automated intrusion detection: pattern matching, which looks for malicious byte sequences; state matching, which looks for known patterns of behavior; and the analysis engine and traffic anomaly approaches, which are anomaly-based and heuristic.

The most rudimentary automated mechanisms are the pattern matching and state matching approaches. These scan network traffic for attack signatures, which are stored in their database. They are easy to use, but since they rely on known patterns of attack, they require frequent updates in order to be effective and they are always fooled by a novel exploit. The anomaly-based approaches, analysis engine and traffic anomaly, utilize suspicious behavior as the basis for decision-making. Both of these approaches get around the limitations of fixed, signature files because they are heuristic; they develop baselines of normal traffic and then make decisions about unauthorized access from these baselines. Because uncharacteristic behavior is the basis for detection, these systems can identify novel attacks. Both of these approaches have their advantages and disadvantages. Software utilities like firewalls monitor network traffic and can respond in real time without human intervention. However, automated processes cannot detect or respond to novel events, which are the preferred method of attack of sophisticated intruders. Human intervention is also required.

Human-based audit processes use event logs, critical system files, and other evidence-based means to identify exploits that an automated system cannot recognize. Essentially, a human-based audit monitors audit trails. An audit trail is a record of system activities. The audit itself utilizes data generated by system, network, application, or user activity. This approach is much more effective than an electronic one, since it utilizes human intelligence to detect intrusions. Nevertheless, people are limited in how much data they can process; any attack, violation, or misuse that is detected through an audit has invariably already taken place.

## Incident Reporting and Operational Response

A system for detecting incidents is useless if it is not accompanied by an effective operational response. Consequently, intrusion detection and operational response should be tied to a formal incident reporting function. When a violation of system integrity is identified, the incident reporting function kicks in. Incident reporting should be able to describe both the type and estimated impact of the incident for response analysis. That description is given to the operational response team for coordination and action. The operational response team then acts to contain any harm and prevent reoccurrence.

In practice, incidents can be either potential or active. Potential incidents include such things as pre-attack probes, unauthorized access attempts, or structural vulnerabilities. Active incidents always require an operational response. If it is possible to confirm that an unauthorized access or exploitation has occurred, then corrective actions have to be undertaken. Depending on the type of incident, corrective action can comprise a range of potential activities. In all respects, the purpose of the corrective action is to contain and minimize any harm.

# Cryptography—Another Part of the Data Security Puzzle

**Cryptography** is an essential part of data security. It is almost impossible to ensure the confidentiality and integrity of data in today's world without employing some means of making it unreadable, except to authorized people. In conventional practice, data is stored or transmitted in a form called "plaintext." It is possible to read plaintext, and so it is easy to compromise data that is recorded in that form. Because it hides the meaning of plaintext, mathematical mechanisms are typically used to record and transmit data that must be secured. These mechanisms fall into the general category of a process called cryptography.

Cryptography is based on the science of mathematics and has two aims. The first is to protect the confidentiality of data by scrambling it in such a way that it is unreadable by anyone but authorized people. The second aim is to provide a scientific basis for authenticating message integrity. As a result, cryptography has become the commonly accepted mechanism to ensure the confidentiality and integrity of data in the electronic universe. Since the assurance of confidentiality and integrity is the cornerstone of trust, cryptography has become an important practical function in today's business world.

## Keys and Algorithms

In simple terms, cryptography involves an **encryption** algorithm and a key to decipher it. The cryptographer employs a mathematical process, called an algorithm, to scramble a message. Then the same algorithm is followed to decipher the message. Consequently, the details of the mathematical operation have to be agreed on in advance between the sender and the receiver.

Nevertheless, in the case of encryption/**decryption**, only a limited set of fairly well-known algorithms are used. That is a weakness, since it would be easy for an adversary to duplicate the algorithm by trying out a few common mathematical approaches. Therefore, one more component must be combined with the algorithm in order to produce a secure message, and that is the key. The key can be infinitely variable and it disguises the meaning of the message. Although an adversary might know the algorithm, it is almost impossible to guess the key. The algorithm and key relationship can be illustrated using a building alarm system. There are a limited number of companies that manufacture building alarms. So it should be easy for a prospective burglar to figure out how to defeat any alarm system simply by studying all of them. However, every alarm uses a unique code to activate or deactivate it. That code is known only to the person who is using the alarm and is the essential ingredient in the protection scheme. The algorithm is the equivalent of the alarm system and the encryption key is the equivalent of the alarm code. Thus, the encryption key is the thing that makes the encryption process truly secure and useful.

There are two basic types of cryptographic keys: secret key (symmetric), and public key (asymmetric). In secret key cryptography, the same key is used for both encryption and decryption. In essence, the use of the key is symmetric. In public key cryptography, the encryption and decryption operations are the same, but they use different keys. In other words, the use of the keys is asymmetric. Both types of systems provide a reasonable degree of privacy, but public key systems are the method of choice for secure communication in business.

## Cryptography for the Masses—Public Key Infrastructures

**Public key infrastructures** (PKIs) evolved to facilitate asymmetric transactions. The term PKI describes the collection of technologies, protocols, and policies that maintain, distribute, create, and validate public keys and their associated information. PKIs serve as the trusted third party in a secure transaction and involve a certificate authority (CA), a key directory, and all of the associated management rules. Other components such as key recovery, and registration procedures, may also be included in a PKI.

The function of a PKI is to provide a digital certification through a CA, which is then verifiable through a Registration Authority (RA). A digital certificate is a public document that contains information which identifies a user, the user's public key, the time during which the certificate is valid, and other information. The digital certificate is unique to the individual user.

# Data Security: The Evaluate Function

*With the establishment of a template for the incident response process, as well as the implementation of an effective set of cryptographic controls, the CISO felt that the requirements of the data security function had been properly defined. All that remained was getting a process in place that would ensure that the data security process was maintained over time. Since the compliance officer had been on a long winning streak, he turned to her again to deliver this project. He had one other motive as well; the compliance officer was an expert in evaluating organizational performance. It seemed clear to the CISO that she was the right person to establish the review process that would keep the organization up to speed in data security.*

*Because the aim of data security is to ensure the continuing confidentiality, availability, and integrity of data assets, regular evaluation is an important function. The compliance officer told the CISO that the best way to certify continuous correct performance was to inspect the controls that had been put in place for data security. If these inspections were done on a regular basis, it should be possible to ensure the continuing integrity of the data security controls themselves, and by implication the baselines they were set to protect. In the compliance officer's view, those evaluations should be done on a routinely scheduled basis. Therefore, it was important to maintain a regular and disciplined inspection process.*

*The EBK provides advice about how to conduct those inspections in the form of four high-level recommendations. These are managerial activities, whose main purpose is to assess the continuing conformance of each data item and its associated controls with policies, standards, regulations, and laws. The functions that the EBK specifies for evaluation are:*

1.  *Assess the effectiveness of enterprise data security policies, processes, and procedures against established standards, guidelines, and requirements and suggest changes where appropriate*

2.  *Evaluate the effectiveness of solutions implemented to provide the required protection of data*

3.  *Review alleged violations of data security and privacy breaches*

4.  *Identify improvement actions required to maintain the appropriate level of data protection*

# Data Security and the Maintenance of Continuous Effectiveness

A data security solution has to satisfy two logical requirements. First, the protection has to be complete, in the sense that everything that requires assurance is secured. Otherwise attackers could just waltz through the holes in the defense without detection. Second, the assurance safeguards themselves have to be provably correct and effective. A non-working or ineffective countermeasure control is useless. The first principle implies the need for a comprehensive, top-down approach to ensure that all logical bases have been touched in developing the security scheme. The second requires the organization to adopt a process that ensures that the personnel and technical controls employed to ensure data security are, and continue to remain, effective.

The problem with these requirements is that the actual steps that have to be taken to assure continuous effectiveness are time-consuming and require the investment of precious resources. There are serious consequences if the organization's data security defenses have holes in them or are ineffective. For example, a secure network without policies to control the people who operate it can be breached by the people who operate it no matter how sophisticated the technology is. That also underscores the idea that, no matter how robust the firewall, there are no practical safeguards unless all of the necessary measures to ensure security are in place and functioning properly.

High-level security frameworks like the EBK employ three principles. The first principle really just represents good business practice and states that the collective body of knowledge within the profession can be tapped for expert advice about the best way to deal with a practical concern. The practice recommendations of the EBK embody that type of advice. The second principle is governance, which simply describes the generic organizing and control function that underwrites any form of good management. The governance function integrates every aspect of security practice into a single substantive, continuously evolving control-based model. The final principle, continuous assurance, implies the need for an explicitly documented organization-wide audit and review strategy.

A formal, organization-wide evaluation strategy verifies that the controls put in place to ensure data security stay effective. In many respects, the evaluation process amounts to nothing more than the assurance of proper execution through routine audits and reviews of the controls that comprise the system. These audits and reviews are performed to validate that the overall security requirements of the business continue to be satisfied. The strategy that underwrites that assurance can be based on existing information security auditing models such as the Information Systems Audit and Control Association's COBIT Guideline, or it can be proprietary to the particular business. Regardless, the strategy must be comprehensive and ensure continuous oversight.

## The Data Security Evaluation Plan

Because the actions involved in ensuring data security are complex, particularly within a large organization, the routine evaluation process should be defined and implemented by a plan that dictates how the operational evaluation of the data security function will be carried out. The plan should define the criteria for evaluation as well as the required roles and responsibilities of all participants in the evaluation process. In addition, the plan should dictate all aspects of timing and participation. Since it sets the strategic direction and states the procedures for evaluating whether the data security function meets organizational policy, it must be kept up-to-date with respect to those goals. Moreover, the organization's commitment to evaluation must be sustained through continuous monitoring of the process as well as annual reviews by top-level managers.

The evaluation plan should specify how the asset baselining, access control, status accounting, and data integrity functions will be carried out. The rules for the administration of the routine inspections or audit processes must also be expressly itemized and documented. Finally, the plan must specify the decision makers who will be responsible for ensuring that the evaluation process itself remains current and effective, along with their authority, scope, and responsibility.

## Maintaining a Record Through Status Accounting

The aim of a well-managed data security function is to continuously ensure the integrity of the organization's data assets. The ideal situation then is to know the precise status of all data and associated controls at all times. Maintaining that up-to-date knowledge also means that it will be possible to restore any lost data to a specified recovery point if a disaster occurs.

In order to implement the status accounting function, the current state of the data asset has to be explicitly known. The day-one status of the data asset base is established through the baseline status evaluation, which was discussed in the section on baselining. That evaluation precisely describes where and in what medium all instances of the data are stored, as well as the method of backup and storage, including the timing and the policies, standards, regulations, and laws that govern data retention and use.

The status accounting function then ensures that the data and its associated controls are fully maintained in that day-one state. In its operational form, the status accounting function is a highly specific type of internal accounting. Accordingly, many of the concepts that are used to track the flow of financial funds through accounts are also employed to track and record asset information. As in financial accounting, separate accounts, which represent the asset baselines, are established. The detailed contents and controls of each asset baseline, as well as each individual transaction on that baseline, are then recorded in a ledger. In order to establish the status accounting function, the following data should be kept for each baselined item:

- The label and description of the information item
- The level of sensitivity and classifications needed to access it (if any)
- A description of the controls
- Specific evaluation measures that will be used to monitor the ongoing integrity of the item

The baseline's controls are then continuously verified to assure the integrity of the information asset it describes.

## Status Accounting and the Assessment of Control Performance

The control set for each asset baseline also has to be evaluated by the status accounting function and takes place every time the integrity of the baseline itself is examined. The purpose of the evaluation of the control set is to assure its effectiveness as well as to confirm the completeness of the coverage. From a timing standpoint, this assessment of the effectiveness of the control set can only take place after the entire baseline of information assets and the associated controls is in operation in the target environment.

In that respect, the assessment of control performance is a formal operational-testing process, in that the evaluation of controls is planned, implemented, and monitored in the same way as any other IT testing activity. The evaluation should routinely characterize control performance compared to organizational expectations. Nevertheless, ad-hoc business considerations can also be added to any specific evaluation. In actual execution, the testing must take place according to a schedule within a specified timeframe that fits real-world business considerations.

Specifically, the evaluation assesses the degree of correctness of the baseline. It tests the accuracy of each item of data in the baseline, as well as its placement and labeling within the baseline hierarchy. In conjunction with that assessment, the evaluation also evaluates the appropriateness and effectiveness of the specific safeguards for each item as well as its continuing conformance with policies, standards, regulations, and laws. The evaluation criteria are the objective means of confirming the ongoing integrity of the data as well as the effectiveness of the controls. Therefore, those criteria must be assessable by direct observation.

## Chapter Summary

- Data security involves any principle, policy, or procedure that ensures the confidentiality, integrity, availability, and privacy of any form of an organization's data.

- The EBK specifies four basic competencies for the management of data security. The access control process assures the rights of access of any person or process that seeks to gain entry to any physical space or electronic system.

- Authentication, **identity management**, and authorization are among the fundamental principles of access control.

- Access control can include criterion-based or policy-based models.

- Encryption is critical to data security because it ensures the confidentiality and integrity of data in the electronic universe.

- Methods of key control include secret keys and public keys. The PKI is a collection of technologies, protocols, and policies that maintain, distribute, create, and validate public keys and their associated information.

- The data security evaluation plan sets the strategic direction and states the procedures for evaluating whether the data security function meets organizational policy.

## Key Terms

**Access control** All standardized controls utilized to ensure that only authorized individuals have access to protected data.

**Authentication** The process of establishing the identity and trust status of a person or process attempting to gain access.

**Authorization** The process of determining and assigning access privileges to all authenticated users and processes.

**Cryptography** Literally means hidden writing; a method of hiding information in another item such as a webpage.

**Data classification** The process of determining the sensitivity requirements of data—also the process of assigning a trust status to an individual (part of privilege setting).

**Decryption** The process of translating an encrypted message back to plaintext.

**Digital signatures** A hash value calculated from the plaintext of a message used to authenticate the sender by means of their public key information.

**Discretionary access control (DAC)** A method of access control wherein the owner of the rights to the data can transfer or assign access privileges to other individuals.

**Encryption** The process of converting a plaintext message into ciphertext readable only by the sender and the holder of a valid decryption key.

**Firewall** Firmware designed to ensure electronic access across a network; can be both reactive and proactive.

**Identity management** The unique identifying data assigned to each individual who has been validated for access by system management; also the recording of maintenance of that data on the system.

**Public key infrastructure (PKI)** A public management authority who issues and certifies the validity of private and public keys; essential for public key encryption.

**Role-based access control (RBAC)** Access control model where rights to access are granted to individual organizational roles rather than people; particularly efficient for access control in large complex organizations.

**User privileges** The specific rights of access of a given user assigned by system management.

# Questions from the CIO

The CIO requires you to brief her on the current status of your investigation. This will be an important part of your continuing work on this project, since it is essential to be able to describe all of the ramifications of the functions of the key functional security personnel. Consequently, the CIO would like you to answer the following questions for her:

1. Access control is an important function in data security. Specifically, tell me why access control is important to preserving confidentiality and integrity and what would be the result if access were not controlled.

2. The simplest and most economical way of identifying an individual is through a password. What are the conditions that are required to establish password protection, and what are some of the reasons why passwords might not be the best approach to security?

3. Classifications are hierarchical and enforce confidentiality. Specifically, tell me how classifications protect confidential data. Then tell me what the limitations of a classification system are. What is an alternative approach?

4. Policy-based access control is the foundation for the other access control methods. Tell me what those methods are and then tell me specifically how policy underwrites the execution of each of them.

5. DAC differs from RBAC in one particular aspect. What is that aspect and how is it implemented?

6. The access control process is automated using a particular software mechanism. What is it and how does it operate?

7. Cryptography is a mathematical process. How can mathematics be used to determine whether a message is authentic or not?

8. Keys are used in cryptography. Specifically, tell me what a key is and why it is necessary in order to encrypt a message. Then tell me what the difference is between secret key and public key approaches.

9. A PKI is a type of management structure. Specifically, tell me what the purpose of a PKI is and why it is useful in practical business applications.

10. Status accounting has two targets. Specifically, what does status accounting look at and why is it necessary to look at both things? What would be the consequence if both evaluations were not done?

# Hands-On Projects

HANDS-ON PROJECTS

Using the case in Appendix 1, outline a set of data security (access) controls and how they would be implemented for that facility. Then, develop an audit plan to assess data security measures. Ensure that the following requirements are satisfied:

- The access control model is justifiable by the business case.
- There is an explicit organizational plan for implementing the access control model.
- The personnel security process is synchronized with the access control model.
- There are measures in place to protect the organization against incorrect or repudiated electronic business transactions.

Extra credit will be granted if the student can devise a process for issuing **digital signatures** to all employees.

# chapter 8

# The Digital Forensics Competency

## The CIO Gets a Monday Morning Surprise

*Monday morning always brought some sort of surprise to the CIO's inbox. Over the years, the appearance of those unanticipated little problems had perversely become a comfortable part of her weekly routine. Comfortable is one thing; however, this week's surprise was something else. It was more like opening a door expecting to find a Chihuahua and finding a pit bull instead.*

*The message was from the office of general counsel, and it notified her that the company had just been served with an **e-discovery** subpoena. The CIO was a self-admitted mainframe dinosaur. She understood both of those words, but she didn't have the slightest idea what "e-discovery" was, or what it implied for her work week. With a big sigh, she rang up the general counsel's office and told him to send up one of his bright-eyed and bushy-tailed litigators to explain it to her post-haste.*

*Of course the person they sent was probably all of 28 years old, which made the CIO feel even more like a fugitive from the Jurassic Period. The lawyer explained that the company was litigating over a matter that amounted to a major copyright infringement case involving former employees. The documentary evidence supporting the company's position was both unbelievably extensive and super-complex.*

*The lawyer assured her that although the incident itself had taken place on her watch, her only involvement came as custodian of the electronic records. The problem was that those records included such things as texts, e-mails, and chats as well as posts on anonymous message*

servers that had supported the entire gambit. Moreover, as the CIO knew, the basic electronically stored documents themselves had their own meta-data markings, which meticulously
recorded all of the actions taken against that record from the time of its creation to the
present.

According to the lawyer, untangling that mess was the simplest part of the problem. Besides
ensuring the veracity of the data as well as its storage and handling, there was also the matter
of having to maintain strict rules of evidence and other unbreakable requirements of court civil
procedure. In addition, the lawyer pointed out that any failure to adhere to legal **chain of custody** requirements and the integrity of the original file formats, which he called the "native"
formats, would likely lead to the case being thrown out of court. And since the total price tag
on the litigation itself was in the neighborhood of $230 million, everybody from the chairman
of the board all the way down to the lawyer himself did not want to see that happen. The ball
was definitely now well into the CIO's court.

The CIO was not pleased by the prospect of getting thrown into the deep end of the information age before she had even had her morning espresso. She quickly got rid of the lawyer, who
was making her nervous anyway. Then she rang up the head of her digital forensics team and
told him to drop everything and get up to her office immediately. In reality, she had to admit
to herself that she only had a hazy idea about what the digital forensics professionals were
actually doing down there in the bowels of the company. So she was not exactly sure what
that particular individual would have to drop. But she was absolutely certain that whatever he
was up to was less important than what she was going to hand him when he arrived.

The problem that the digital forensics team leader, who was on the other end of the phone,
had was that he was in the middle of a delicate process of reconstructing the exact steps of
an electronic exploit that had rocked the company the prior week. Since that reconstruction
involved building up a chain of evidence based on events that had occurred only microseconds
apart, that was delicate work indeed. So the summons from the 44th floor was not exactly
welcome. What is more, the digital forensics professional was not exactly a top floor sort of fellow. He was more of a head-down, nuts and bolts kind of guy. So he anticipated that his presence up there with the "suits" was not exactly going to further good employee relations. The
mismatch between the suits and the nerds had been a major source of dissonance in past projects, and he did not expect the situation to be any different in this case.

Nevertheless, he did know his stuff. So he dug around under his desk, found his best pair of
Birkenstocks, and punched the button for the executive floor. As far as he was concerned, the
elevator could have dropped him in the Emerald City of Oz and the surroundings would have
seemed less alien than the 44th floor. He started to get back on the elevator when it hit him
that, for the sake of his team if not for his own sake, he was going to have to find the courage
to make his way down to the corner office, where the CIO herself held court. He pushed open
the 12-foot-high frosted glass doors of the outer office, which led into a huge anteroom car-
peted in that blue Mohawk plush with little star designs in it. He noted that his arrival must
have been anticipated, because the receptionist was standing there with a cup of coffee that
was not made out of paper for a change.

The CIO herself was actually charming in a spider-and-fly sort of way. Of course, that was
because she needed his exotic expertise in the worst sort of way. So she was on her best
behavior, even though he looked to her like a "hippie" if anybody still used that 1960s term.
For his part, the CIO scared him to death. He hated policy types and he particularly hated

*old-fashioned DP administrators, since they clearly did not "get" the new technology like he did. Nevertheless, once she began to lay out the problem, he actually felt himself getting interested, since it was going to let him gather the forensics for a really important civil case. He had investigated everything in his short professional career from incidents and exploits to disciplinary actions against employees, but these were minor compared to evidence-gathering for something as big and complex as the kind of business espionage he was looking at here.*

*With the CIO's blessings, the forensics team leader made his way back to his own comfortable, subterranean domain and began to think about the way to structure and run an ideal forensics discovery operation.*

## Ensuring the Integrity of the Process

In its simplest form, the digital forensics competency involves reconstructing events that have already occurred for the purpose of documenting what happened through evidence. The whole point of the forensics process is to generate proof that cannot be disputed, because it is based on empirical observation and the recording of fact. In that respect, the aim of the digital forensics process is to ensure that the procedures that are used to gather those facts are explicitly trustworthy. Assurance of trust is important because the integrity of the evidence in a legal process should not be a subject of dispute. Thus, forensics procedures have to be executed in a way that ensures the absolute integrity of the evidence obtained from them. This uncompromising requirement for consistency is a critical element of the forensics process because it assures that the outcomes of that process are as factually correct as possible.

The aspect that distinguishes digital forensics from the general forensics investigative process is the nature of the evidence. Evidence arising out of the electronic discovery process is not part of the physical universe. It typically exists in the form of binary representation, in some sort of mass storage device like a hard drive or a flash memory stick. The evidence itself can be anything from an executable code artifact or the contents of a system table all the way down to electronic text or pictures hidden by mathematical processes such as steganography. Because of the ubiquitous use of computers in modern life, the electronic evidence that is produced can legitimately be an element of every conceivable type of civil or criminal action, from simple Internet scams through theft and even industrial espionage.

In its raw, electronic form, none of that evidence is easy to read or understand, so the task of forensic discovery in the cyber universe is both a difficult and highly involved process. The main problem is that virtual space creates illogical conditions that conventional physical evidence-gathering practices cannot accommodate. Thus, new methods for evidence gathering have to be employed. For instance, one of the wonders of cyberspace is that it is possible to commit a crime that could be described in no other terms as a "bank robbery" from the safety of a location 6,000 miles from the actual scene of the crime, as illustrated in Figure 8-1. Consequently, a lot of the actual evidence of that crime would be on a hard drive on a computer that is located in another part of the world. The virtuality of cyberspace permits this sort of "uninvolved criminality" and it also imposes unique complications of access and timing on the gathering and recording of forensic evidence.

A lot of forensic evidence exists as binary information within a computer system. Because of the dynamic nature of the internal representation process for such information, it is easy for

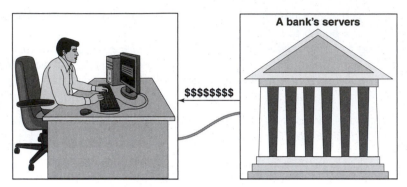

**Figure 8-1** What constitutes a bank robbery?

© *Cengage Learning 2012*

the forensic investigator to take actions during the data gathering process that can irreversibly damage the evidence or violate legal rules of procedure. Therefore, proper management and planning for the process itself helps ensure that the organization will not unintentionally violate the integrity of the forensic process. The EBK specifies six common work functions for the management of digital forensics. These are all policy-based activities that must be implemented at a high level across the organization in order to be effective. The effect of these six activities is to ensure that the digital forensics process is properly resourced and managed:

1. Acquire the necessary contractual vehicle and resources—including financial resources—to run forensic labs and programs

2. Coordinate and build internal and external consensus for developing and managing an organizational digital forensic program

3. Establish a digital forensic team—usually composed of investigators, IT professionals, and incident handlers—to perform digital and **network forensics** activities

4. Provide adequate work spaces that at a minimum take into account the electrical, thermal, acoustic, and privacy concerns (e.g., intellectual properties, classification, and contraband) and security requirements (including access control and accountability) of equipment and personnel, and provide adequate report writing/administrative areas

5. Ensure appropriate changes and improvement actions are implemented as required

6. Maintain current knowledge of forensic tools and processes

## Creating a Trustworthy and Sustainable Forensics Function

Three elements are required in order to ensure that the forensics process is both trustworthy and sustainable. First, a mechanism has to be in place to assure that the personnel who do forensics work have been properly trained. Forensics work requires a broad range of capabilities, many of which are typically not found in conjunction with each other.

Specifically, good forensics investigators have technical capabilities that allow them to work comfortably at the level of binary representation and transmission for a wide range of technical media and processes. In addition, forensics investigators also need a good working knowledge of the rules of criminal and civil procedure as they apply to the gathering and preservation of legal evidence. Finally, forensic investigators need the kind of investigative skills that are normally found in people like police detectives.

It is hard for an organization to assure that its forensic investigators will have all of these capabilities without the presence of a formal training process that has been carefully planned and developed to produce a well-defined skill set. Those skills have to be trained into each forensics investigator, so the essential first step in creating a sustainable forensics process is to document the policies necessary to ensure an acceptable level of capability.

The second element that ensures trustworthy and sustainable forensics activities concerns specialized tools and equipment. These are required to ensure that every aspect of the collection and handling of virtual evidence is documented in such a way that the absolute integrity of the chain of custody is maintained. Because of the nature of digital evidence, it is almost impossible to collect and preserve it without tool support. Thus, the second requirement in the establishment of a digital forensics process is to define the specific tool set that the organization chooses to adopt to support its forensics processes. Because of the wide range of commercial tools and their potential applications, this is not a simple matter of opening up a catalog and placing an order. The assurance of a properly resourced array of forensics tools requires a well-designed, policy level planning process. The outcome of that process should be a defined set of criteria that establishes the exact nature and depth of the work that the tool set is expected to support. That planning process also requires ensuring the precise resource levels to guarantee that the correct tools are available to the right people as needed.

The third element concerns the establishment of the interface between the forensic process and the overall IT operation. In essence, the condition has to be assured where conventional IT processes will enable all necessary activities of the digital forensic process. There are two types of policies required to ensure alignment between normal IT and digital forensic work. The first type of policy dictates the procedures to ensure that forensics work is properly synchronized with the activities of the overall IT operation. For instance, existing data classification policies that define data types and access to data based on position, data sensitivity, and need to know may have to be modified to permit forensic personnel to access the data in the course of their assigned duties. The impact and reach of digital forensics can be widespread, and this may result in a lot of systems being examined for forensic implication. Since that is the case, it is highly likely that policies and procedures will need to be created in advance or modified to ensure that forensic workers get the access necessary to do their jobs.

The other place where new policies are likely to be required is in the area of change control. Since the typical system environment and the data that reside within it usually change independently of the forensics process, there have to be policies in place that will ensure that any changes that do occur in the conventional operation will not change or destroy information that might be relevant to a later forensic investigation process. Many operational procedures overwrite or in other ways alter past records, so specific measures have to be put in place to ensure that all potentially meaningful digital evidence is protected from inadvertent change or destruction. These procedures are not typically instituted as part of the digital forensics process. Rather, they are adaptations of the standard operating procedures of the normal IT process.

## Sustainability and the Specific Case of Data Retention Policies The one single aspect of the conventional data processing operation that is certain to require definition from a forensic perspective is the **data retention policy**, which is the required retention period for all kinds of data. This policy sets a specific period of time to retain each record

type, after which that particular record is erased from the system or archived in places that are difficult to access.

The range of types of data that an organization would typically collect is large and potentially unwieldy. From a forensics standpoint, those records can range from data that is associated with the business through system log files and historical copies of files. It can even include e-mails, texts, chats, and system and network transactions. Therefore, for economic reasons, not all data should be retained. For instance, spam is more than a nuisance; it clogs user inboxes and can adversely affect the performance of the system if it is not removed in a timely fashion. The data retention policy would dictate how and in what timeframe spam is removed.

**Planning and the Question of Whether to Outsource** In today's litigious environment, it is prudent for most large organizations to maintain a forensics capability. Creating that capability requires defining the exact operational responsibilities for leading and managing the digital forensics process, including practical considerations such as work space, tools, personnel, and reporting chains. The planning that underlies the creation of the digital forensics process typically goes as far as the determination of a standard set of correction, remediation, and mitigation actions to control and limit adverse effects. These reactions can range from the simple rebuilding of a single machine to shifting to a backup site while a large portion of the enterprise is rebuilt.

Forensics work can be time-consuming and expensive. Depending upon the size of the firm, it may be advantageous to maintain a group of in-house trained forensic personnel, along with tools and a workspace. On the other hand, depending on the situation it may also make sense to outsource the forensic work to a third-party contractor. Determining the best approach and then organizing and communicating the strategy to the rest of the firm is part of the overall digital forensics strategic management process.

# Meanwhile, Back at the Bat Cave, the Forensics People Start the Ball Rolling

*Since the forensics operation was located in the basement of the building, it did not take long for its eight denizens, all of whom were more-or-less devoted to comic books, to start calling their place the "Bat Cave." The ding of the elevator heralded the arrival of the team leader, and all of them gathered expectantly in front of the doors as the elevator opened. It was not common for anybody on the 44th floor to even recognize that the forensics operation existed, let alone summon one of their own up to that sacrosanct place for a meeting. The forensics professionals all knew that something was up.*

*What they found was that they had a lot of work to do. Essentially, forensics is a process that is similar to putting together a puzzle. It requires collecting, and then carefully assembling, the pieces of the puzzle into a coherent picture of the event in question. That assembly is relatively easy to do when the pieces can all be found in the same box. But with digital forensics, the pieces can be scattered through an endless array of boxes with perhaps only one or two relevant pieces mixed in with a bunch of irrelevant pieces in each box. Then to make matters worse all of those pieces are usually intangible, a formal process of identification, cataloging, and recording is necessary in order to start the process of assembly.*

*The forensics crew all knew this, but they were not prepared for the amount of digging that was going to be required in order to simply start the reconstruction work. Terabytes of corporate documents, numerous databases, and CAD/CAM files were involved. In addition, there was a ubiquitous set of e-mails, texts and web postings to sort through. In fact, the initial scan of the terrain took a full week to complete.*

*After he had read the preliminary reports, the team leader decided that he and his people would have to ramp up the entire forensics function in order to get the job done within the ridiculously short timeframe that the CIO had set for him. He dug out his one and only tie from the bottom of his desk drawer, half-tied it, and then got back on the elevator for his second trip up to the 44th floor.*

*Needless to say, his request to more than double the budget for the forensics operation did not sit well with the CIO. On the other hand, given the critical importance of the project, she knew that she was going to have to give the team leader everything he wanted if she was going to protect her own precious backside. Nevertheless, she did manage to attach one prudent condition: she insisted that the team leader come up with a detailed and viable plan for ensuring that the new resources would be used in the most cost-efficient and cost-effective manner possible. That request was actually long overdue, and the team leader knew it.*

*Up to that point, the management reporting lines for the forensics process had been basically flat. That is, forensics was a back room operation with little actual supervision in terms of both process and quality control; all of the members of the team knew each other and understood how the work was structured and run. On the other hand, they were also constantly stepping on each other's toes in doing that work and there was no assurance that what they were doing was even adequate. The team leader knew that that situation was not going to be made more efficient by the addition of another dozen new analysts and a bunch of new equipment. So he accepted the CIO's general premise that he had to come up with a way to better organize and control the management and technical activities of his newly expanded function.*

*He decided to base that organization around the development of a formal set of recommendations to ensure that the activities that constitute the forensics process remained correct. In essence his aim was to develop a set of standard operating procedures that would ensure that the forensics process was doing what it was supposed to do. He had heard through the grapevine about the work that the CISO was doing with the EBK, and he knew that that document specified the basic design requirements for the digital forensics competency. So he borrowed a copy from a friend in the CISO's office and sat down to organize his function based on best practice advice. Basically, the EBK focuses on seven things:*

1. *Develop policies for the preservation of electronic evidence; data recovery and analysis; and the reporting and archival requirements of examined material in accordance with standards, procedures, directives, policies, regulations, and laws (statutes)*

2. *Establish policies and procedures for the imaging (bit-for-bit copying) of electronic media*

3. *Specify hardware and software requirements to support the digital forensic program*

4. *Establish the hardware and software requirements (configuration management) of the forensic laboratory and mobile toolkit*

5. *Develop procedures for the preservation of electronic evidence; data recovery and analysis; and the reporting and archival requirements of examined material in accordance with standards, procedures, directives, policies, regulations, and laws (statutes)*

6. *Establish examiner requirements that include an ongoing mentorship program, competency testing prior to assuming individual case responsibilities, periodic proficiency testing, and participation in a nationally recognized certification program that encompasses a continuing education requirement*

7. *Adopt or create chain of custody procedures that include disposal procedures—and, when required, the return of media to its original owner in accordance with standards, procedures, directives, policies, regulations, and laws (statutes)*

## Creating a Digital Forensics Process

At its core, the actual practice of digital forensics requires a mix of skills. On the surface, these skills do not intuitively relate to each other. Intimate knowledge of how electronic data is represented and manipulated is required; however, it is also essential to have a lawyer's command of legal procedure and the investigative skills of a trained police detective. Moreover, strict deterministic rules do not apply to the collection of evidence, because that evidence resides in a diverse and highly dynamic virtual environment. In most cases, the individual skills of the practitioner and the appropriate use of tools typically determine the success of a forensic exercise.

Nevertheless, there are some basic principles that can be universally expected. These define the elements and sequence of a digital forensics process and they can also be used to both structure and run a digital forensics operation. In order to implement a digital forensic function, three sequential activities have to be performed: data collection; data recovery and analysis; and reporting.

**Creating a Data Collection Capability** The process of data collection typically involves the generation of a forensically sound copy of the evidence for the purpose of analysis. Since that evidence usually resides in a number of diverse places, the collection process always originates with the identification of all of the locations where instances of relevant data exist. This is basically a tool-supported inventory process. Nonetheless, it is critically important to implement a formal protocol to ensure that the collecting agents have looked in all of the places that they need to look. Besides being kept in diverse places, that information can be stored in a number of ways. That includes archived and existing active files, files that are protected either by encryption or passwords, or even in latent files such as deleted or partially overwritten sectors. There are also files that are only used by the system and hidden files. In most cases, none of that information is viewable, so the skills and tools have to be specified and put in place to allow the organization to obtain whatever forensic evidence is required for its purposes.

Because that evidence is usually electronic, the forensic collection process has to be ensured to be technically and empirically sound. That assurance is necessary to guarantee beyond a shadow of a doubt that all of the evidence collected will be a true and accurate reflection of fact at a given point in time. Ensuring legally correct evidence is a tricky proposition, because it relies on the proper use of tools. These tools, and their accompanying methods, are necessary to ensure that all relevant evidence has been obtained. Appropriate use of tools implies the definition of a fundamental set of technical capabilities. In essence, these capabilities represent the required skill set for the forensics professional in each organization. Likewise, as tools and methods change over time, it is also important that the organization ensure that its forensics professionals keep abreast of those changes.

The organization also has to ensure that its forensics professionals have a good working knowledge of all relevant rules of civil and criminal procedure. Most importantly, the organization has to have mechanisms in place to guarantee the integrity of the chain of custody. In its simplest form, chain of custody requires the documentation of each step of the process as it occurred. Because the forensics professional is typically working at the level of internal representation of electronic data, the forensic process needs to use a set of dedicated tools to record as well as continuously authenticate the precise status of the evidence at any point in the process. Electronic evidence is basically intangible. In the case of litigation that relies on electronic evidence, it is critical that the organization is able to certify that that evidence has been obtained in a proper way and has not been tampered with. A formal protocol to ensure integrity has to be spelled out in any plan to establish a forensics process.

At its root, that plan should establish strict control over access during the collection and analysis phases. It also should ensure that the integrity of the data can be confirmed both before and after each access. This level of governance is particularly essential in a court of law due to the unique volatility of electronic data and its ease of alteration. If the protocols that underlie the organization's chain of custody arrangements cannot be documented, then the data might be legally suspect. The fear of having an iron-clad case thrown out of court because the chain of custody has been broken is the reason why the unqualified assurance of its authenticity is such an important aspect in establishing the overall forensics process.

**8**

### Chain of Custody and Policy

Chain of custody is highly detail-oriented and requires a roadmap of policies and procedures that is designed to ensure maximum compliance with a wide range of rules and regulations. One universal requirement for a forensics process plan is the creation of unambiguous policies and procedures. These have to be designed and then tested in advance to ensure that they support critical forensic functions such as data collection in criminal matters, data collection in response to civil proceedings, and data collection in response to internal investigations.

Each of these policies has an attendant set of procedures that are important to successful implementation. In order to be effective, these need to be planned and tested, and the staff has to be trained to execute them properly. This level of detail work is essential as part of the design function in the forensics competency. Finally, because of the highly technical nature of forensic investigations, the work is often outsourced to specialty firms. Even in the case of outsourced work, policies are required to address the role of contract personnel before, during, and after the outsourced work.

### Establishing the Recovery and Analysis Function

The second principle involves the protocols for the analysis of data once it has been collected. It is difficult to stipulate standard operating procedures for an analytic process simply because the process itself involves so many variables, most of which are situational. For instance, the analysis activity will be different depending on whether it is in support of litigation in civil or criminal matters. It is also going to be different if it is part of a post-incident analysis, since the aim there is to determine the nature of an attack and how to better defend against it, rather than to support litigation. **Forensic analysis** methodologies and tools even apply to the recovery of data after a hardware or software failure.

However, some general organizational requirements always apply in the analysis process. First, the analysis approach has to be repeatable, because it is critical for opposing experts

**Figure 8-2** Taken, but not gone

© Cengage Learning 2012

to be able to validate a given set of findings by duplicating the process. Otherwise, the evidence would likely be inadmissible in court. Second, the forensic analysis process should be structured to address four basic conditions. The first and most obvious condition is that sufficient evidence has to be obtained to support legal action. There are two related questions involved with the evidence gathering process. The first is whether all existing evidence has been identified and collected. The second is whether that collection process satisfies all of the requirements of the legal rules of procedure.

Outside of the considerations related to evidence there are two procedural ones. The first has to do with whether the forensic analysis is being used to reconstruct an electronic crime. The reasons for differentiating between an analysis done to investigate a crime versus one done to investigate non-criminal issues is that the aim of the former is criminal prosecution, while the other is oriented more toward learning about a specific event that has occurred.

Finally, forensic analysis can be used to determine what was accessed, taken, or harmed. This final application is a particularly unique condition of electronic information, since it is one of the few things that can be taken or tampered with without any physical sign that anything has happened, as shown in Figure 8-2. Things would clearly be missing after a robbery in the physical world, but information can be stolen without any obvious sign that it has ever been accessed. Since it is hard to even tell which items have been affected, the exact focus of the investigation has to be specified in advance in order to narrow down the items that have to be considered. This rule is primarily intended to ensure that resources are used efficiently.

## Writing a Forensic Recovery and Analysis Plan
There are two primary targets for the forensic recovery and analysis process. First and most obvious is the computer itself. The network that the computer is attached to is also subject to the same kind of analysis. In the case of the computer, the forensics professional has to be able to assemble all of the evidence that was obtained in the collection process. That can include everything from the date and time that the evidence was gathered, through notes about the techniques that were used to collect the evidence as well as any tool use. These findings are typically summarized in the working notes that the analyst will later turn into the final report. The method for doing this should be repeatable, so the forensics plan should specify the precise protocol that the organization intends to follow.

For instance, analysts will generally work from the outside in, meaning they first process any external media like thumb drives or CDs. Then they move on to the internal circuitry for the purpose of mapping all relevant sources of evidence. Once that is done, analysts use the appropriate tool to identify, obtain, catalog, and analyze evidence from both external media and internal circuitry. The details of both the method and the tool support have to be specified in the forensics plan.

The forensic analysis of network traffic, using the right reconstructive methods and tools, can also provide considerable supporting evidence about breaches and violations. Analysis of a network can be conducted from a retrospective point of view, as a means of preventing the reoccurrence of an event, but it can also take a prospective approach, in the sense that the determination that an event has occurred can lead to a much broader analysis of the circumstances and context surrounding that event. Network analyses are also tool-supported. Because networks have different requirements and conditions than computers, the scope of the forensic examination process as it applies to networks has to be stated in the plan.

The specification of the precise scope of application is particularly important in the case of network-oriented forensics, because those tools have to be in place prior to the event. That is due to the fact that the forensic analysis is typically based on the logging of traffic over the network; that information can only be obtained if a sensor is in place. Because of the use of similar traffic monitoring tools for incident detection systems (IDS) there is some debate about where to draw the line between monitoring for forensics purposes versus incident response. That is why, no matter what tool is used, the extent of network monitoring for forensics purposes has to be spelled out in detail.

**Setting Up an Effective Communication Process** There are several critical elements for ensuring successful communication. The first of these is planning. Done right, the plan will reduce the risk of errors or omission in reporting the results of a forensics investigation. Additionally, the plan should ensure that the reproducible actions taken to obtain the results are clear and understandable. Reproducibility simply means that the same actions taken by different people would still produce the same results. It also ensures the acceptability of the evidence in all legal proceedings.

The plan must include the formal provisions for communicating the results of the recovery and analysis phase to decision makers as well as any attorneys. In operational terms, this means that any procedures for communication have to ensure that all parties can understand and work with each other. Equally important to the specification of those procedures is the requirement that any findings involved in any form of litigation adhere to all court rules of procedure for forensic evidence. That includes the findings that support affidavits and expert testimony. Finally, it must be ensured that all communications in a legal proceeding are expressed in a way that can be easily understood and acted on by jurors. Given the legal implications of most forensic evidence, the communication process and the method of documenting outcomes has to be both well defined in the plan and then rigorously adhered to.

Additionally, the communications plan has to ensure that the findings contained in the report document any expert conclusions drawn from the evidence. In general, these conclusions should only be statements of fact about questions that have been raised by decision-makers or participants in the litigation. For instance, the report could state that the evidence supports the contention that a certain event occurred at a certain time. If there are specific laws, policies, or standards involved in guiding the analysis, then the plan should ensure that these are clearly stated. In addition, the protocol must be unambiguous, ensuring that the evidence is directly mapped to the requirements of those regulations.

From a process standpoint, because the report is meant to support decision-making, it should generally be reviewed and discussed by the client prior to its publication. The forensic examiner who has been assigned to the case is normally responsible for preparing the actual report. The examiner sends the report to the client, and the client is then responsible for distributing it to the opposing attorneys or other interested parties. The client is solely accountable for taking whatever actions are implied by the findings, based on best judgment. That might include ordering additional analysis based on new questions or concerns about the initial findings. The plan should always ensure that proper procedure is followed in these areas.

# Putting Forensics on an Operational Footing

*It was a beautiful late-summer sunrise in New York City. The team leader and his golden Lab, Buster, were doing their 6:00 a.m. circuit of the Reservoir in Central Park. The team leader liked to have a run at the start of the day, just to get the blood flowing to his brain. Buster's motives were unclear, beyond taking care of the business that he was not going to be able to do while cooped up in the team leader's apartment. As they both ran the circuit, the team leader was thinking that very soon he was going to have to substitute action for planning. He had concluded that it was time to draw up a procedure manual that would guide the entire forensics operation.*

*Fortunately, the CIO had loved his initial design work, and she felt that the management structure that he had laid out was more than adequate to launch an enhanced forensics process. Now that he had the CIO's full support, he decided that it was time to get the gang at the Bat Cave back together to flesh out a set of protocols for the new hires to follow. He was also aware of the fact that by thinking through the process, they were going to also organize the core team of analysts a whole lot better.*

*As soon as he turned on his system, he began to put together a general set of implementation guidelines that he and his cronies could flesh out over the rest of the day. The EBK had been useful to him in the planning and design stage, so he turned to it one more time to see what it said about implementation. The EBK specifies 13 items for the implementation function. Like design, these activities are a mix of management and technical requirements. As a group, their role is to ensure that the digital forensics function is smoothly embedded into the ongoing operation:*

1. *Assist in collecting and preserving evidence in accordance with established procedures, plans, policies, and best practices*
2. *Perform forensic analysis on networks and computer systems, and make recommendations for remediation*
3. *Apply and maintain intrusion detection systems; intrusion prevention systems; network mapping software; and monitoring and logging systems; and analyze results to protect, detect, and correct information security-related vulnerabilities and events*
4. *Follow proper chain of custody best practices in accordance with standards, procedures, directives, policies, regulations, and laws (statutes)*
5. *Collect and retain audit data to support technical analysis relating to misuse, penetration, reconstruction, or other investigations*
6. *Provide audit data to appropriate law enforcement or other investigating agencies, to include corporate security elements*
7. *Assess and extract relevant pieces of information from collected data*
8. *Report complete and accurate findings, and result of the analysis of digital evidence, to appropriate resources*
9. *Coordinate dissemination of forensic analysis findings to appropriate resources*
10. *Provide training as appropriate on using forensic analysis equipment, technologies, and procedures, such as the installation of forensic hardware and software components*
11. *Advise on the suitability of standard operating environment's (SOE) baseline standard for forensic analysis*
12. *Coordinate applicable legal and regulatory compliance requirements*
13. *Coordinate, interface, and work under the direction of appropriate corporate entities (e.g., corporate legal, corporate investigations) regarding investigations or other legal requirements, including investigations that involve external governmental entities (e.g., international, national, state, local)*

## Reconstructing Events

The simplest requirement for forensic evidence is that it is believable in court, so the forensics process has to produce objective evidence that is empirically obtained. Because credibility is such an important factor in the forensics process, it is necessary to have a reliable set of policies and procedures to ensure that the discovery and processing of that evidence is always done correctly.

Specifically, these policies and procedures have to ensure that forensics professionals adhere to a trusted protocol in performing their investigation. That protocol covers everything from procedures for identifying what data to collect to the identification of the sources that it will be obtained from. Data collection is an important element in the forensics process because that data comprises the evidence. Thus, the policies and procedures have to guarantee that the data is acquired and preserved in accordance with all of the requirements of a given case.

**Characterizing the Incident** Since the actual requirements for each forensics project are derived from the type of incident being investigated, the next step in the process is to understand the precise nature of the incident. This, in turn, will define the scope of the analysis. It will also dictate how the actual investigation will be conducted. For instance, there would be considerable difference in the actions that are taken to collect and analyze a simple criminal trespass versus an industrial espionage episode or a bank robbery.

The first necessity in any forensic discovery effort is to characterize all of the implications and potential outcomes of the incident under study. That determination is not as easy as it might sound; most of the impacts of a cyber event are in the virtual world and cannot be observed or characterized in physical terms. For example, if a hurricane blows into town, it is easy to survey the damage it causes. But an all-out cyber attack that could conceivably cause equivalent damage would leave no observable results.

Thus, the first step in the process involves identifying and surveying any known areas of impact in order to characterize the underlying harm that occurred. This first step is not a whole lot different from the crime scene surveys that detectives in the physical world do, in order to define what happened and who the victims were. Since an understanding of the exact nature of the event will point to the places that have to be investigated, this step ought to narrow the sources of evidence down to a workable set.

**Identifying the Sources of the Data** The next stage is the identification of the precise sources of data to support the investigation. This step is not a simple process, since there are always bewildering arrays of potential data sources in the electronic universe. Any one of these sources could be tapped to reconstruct a misuse, penetration, reconstruction, or other investigative event. Consequently, the first step in establishing the investigation is to identify only those sources that are likely to be relevant to the incident at hand. In general, that data can be found in two places.

**System Logs** The first source is electronic logs. The electronic log information that most computer systems generate as part of their normal operation can be one of the likeliest sources for investigative data. Those logs continuously document what happened in various parts of the system. For instance, firewall logs, intrusion detection/prevention **system logs**, and access control logs all contain entries that provide step-by-step descriptions of the events that took place during a computer incident. In essence, the logs contain the detailed record of what transpired.

But those logs are not created and configured by chance; they require careful and detailed human intervention in order to be set up and maintained. One important early aspect of the implementation process for forensic discovery is to ensure that all of the electronic record keeping logs that record system activity exist and are collecting reliable data about system events.

**Physical Media** The other source of evidence is the actual media on which the digital record is kept. This can include all internal storage sources such as static memory as well as disks and other forms of storage. There are also external media on which a record of system events might be kept, including thumb drives, CDs, and other forms of external storage such as tape. Any one of these artifacts could provide meaningful evidence to support the investigation.

Because that evidence exists in digital form, it has to be obtained through the use of supporting tools such as unerase and undelete software as well as tools designed to read data represented at the binary level. All of these tools do their work at the system level, which means they are designed to allow the analyst to both see and subsequently evaluate the evidence at hand. However, the actual interpretation of what evidence is meaningful versus data that is irrelevant in a court of law has to be done by a human being.

**Evidence Handling Protocols** Evidence handling protocols are generally dictated by what that evidence will subsequently be used for. For instance, if the evidence has to be available for use in court, strict chain of custody procedures must be adopted from the outset in order to ensure trust. Trusted procedure is critical in the case of chain of custody, because any perceived deviation from the specified protocols for the process will generally lead to the evidence being rendered inadmissible in court. Furthermore, because of the legal concept of "the fruit of the poisoned tree," it is possible that one questionable item of evidence can also eliminate other forms of evidence that might be derived from that item.

Since that principle applies in both criminal and civil cases, the assurance of the integrity of the chain of custody is a critical part of setting up and executing the discovery process. It is essential that chain of custody protocols exist and comply with all relevant standards, procedures, directives, policies, regulations, and laws. It is also equally critical that these protocols are documented and enforced.

**The Analysis and Reporting Phases** After collecting all of the relevant evidence, investigators analyze the data in order to establish the constituent events. Based on the results of the analysis process, conclusions can be drawn about the actions that are needed to correct, remediate, or report a happening. If the decision involves reporting the incident to law enforcement, or engaging law enforcement in the subsequent investigation, then procedures will also have to be present to allow the evidence to be shared with the appropriate authorities.

Operationally, this sharing will require the organization to provide the appropriate pieces of evidence and to respond to requests from law enforcement or other investigating agencies. A similar situation occurs in legal discovery events that are brought in the form of a subpoena. Pre-planning and preparation is essential to success here, as time is usually a factor when evidence sharing is done under a court order.

The final element of the forensics process is the dissemination of the findings, as shown in Figure 8-3. Dissemination is typically done in the form of a report that distributes the results

**Figure 8-3** What happened?

© Cengage Learning 2012

of the forensic analysis to the appropriate authorities and acts as a historical record. The principal feature of the final report is always the recommendation about the root cause of the incident. Where the root cause is known, the necessary steps to prevent a reoccurrence of the event at a future point in time are also provided.

**Ensuring a Capable Workforce** Even if the forensics process is properly defined and the tool set is correct, the workforce still has to be capable of performing all of the requisite forensic tasks. The forensics process requires its own set of formal training procedures to ensure that the workforce is capable of performing all necessary duties. An important aspect of that requirement is that most forensics examinations are done by a third party. These third-party requirements are likely to have conditions built into them that might not be familiar to the forensics staff.

Consequently, there have to be provisions built into any workforce capability development plan to ensure that the particular workers on a given project are sufficiently trained and knowledgeable to meet the specific requirements of that project.

Moreover, as forensics investigations progress, it is frequently necessary to coordinate, interface with, or work under the direction of other appropriate organizational entities, such as corporate legal counsel or even the physical security operation. That requirement for cooperation can also include external governmental entities at the local, state, national, and even international level. Therefore, it is important to build situational awareness and the ability to facilitate inter-group work into the skill set for forensics professionals. These abilities can be ensured by targeted training and awareness programs.

## Managing the Forensics Process Through Evaluation

*The Bat Cave was humming; with the addition and training of the new staff and the installation of the new equipment, the actual forensics work was progressing at an unprecedented pace. The reports coming out of the Bat Cave were all being routed up to the CIO and then distributed to the appropriate investigative and legal entities. In fact, the CIO was so pleased by the output of that group that she had even taken the unprecedented step of coming down to actually see the operation in progress. And she was reminded one more time that technology had passed her by.*

*That made her nervous. She was still the putative head of the forensics function, even though her responsibilities as corporate CIO and the various responsibilities of the basement gremlins that currently surrounded her couldn't be more different. Unfortunately, though, the CIO was also well aware of the fact that if any of these low-paid techies made a mistake that got the company's big case thrown out of court, the axe was going to fall on her neck and not theirs. She had not gotten where she was without a healthy instinct for self-preservation, so she immediately began to think about the best way of ensuring that every step that the forensics process took was both visible to her managers and also under their strict control.*

*The only way she could establish management control was through regular evaluations of the process as well as its products. Those reviews had to produce information that could be used to determine the exact status of the operation as well as ensure its continuing capability. In her mind, that assurance would require regular inspection of the forensic process.*

*At a minimum, those inspections had to demonstrate that the forensics work complied with all requisite policies and regulations, including assurance of the chain of custody. It would also entail inspections and tests that were oriented toward certifying the correctness and integrity of the evidence as well as the processes that were used to obtain and interpret the data.*

*The compliance officer was assigned to structure and oversee those inspections. The aim was to conduct regular reviews of forensics work on a routinely scheduled basis, with a special emphasis on monitoring the work that underlay the company's big case. Knowing the special personality of the compliance officer, the CIO was certain that all of the necessary rigor and discipline would be imposed on each of those inspections. But the CIO still needed to ensure that the review process itself was conducted in the most effective manner possible.*

*Since the EBK had gotten to be something of a bible in the establishment of the forensics process, the compliance officer turned to it one more time to see what was required for a proper evaluation program. What she found were nine high-level functions, which were primarily management in orientation:*

1. *Ensure the effectiveness of forensic processes and accuracy of forensic tools used by digital forensic examiners, and implement changes as required*

2. *Review all documentation associated with forensic processes or results for accuracy, applicability, and completeness*

3. *Assess the effectiveness, accuracy, and appropriateness of testing processes and procedures followed by the **forensic laboratories** and teams, and suggest changes where appropriate*

4. *Assess the digital forensic staff to ensure they have the appropriate knowledge, skills, and abilities to perform forensic activities*

5. *Validate the effectiveness of the analysis and reporting process, and implement changes where appropriate*

6. *Review and recommend standard validated forensic tools*

7. *Assess the digital forensic laboratory quality assurance program, peer review process, and audit proficiency testing procedures, and implement changes where appropriate*

8. *Examine penetration testing and vulnerability analysis results to identify risks and implement patch management*

9. *Identify improvement actions based on the results of validation, assessment, and review*

# Ensuring Correctness Through Routine Evaluations

The aim of the evaluation function is to make certain that the controls that are instituted to ensure the quality and disciplined performance of the forensics process do not erode over time. As new systems are brought on line and older systems are changed or retired, the organization can lose track of its information assets. Without constant oversight, the performance of the forensic process can become slipshod and undisciplined. This erosion produces potentially serious vulnerabilities in operations such as the forensics process. Therefore, it is essential that the processes and their performance are regularly assessed, tested, and verified as being accurate, appropriate, and up to date. This review process also produces timely information that managers can use to fine-tune the forensics operation so that it is always functioning at optimum capability.

There are several strategies to maintaining up-to-date understanding of the capability of the forensics process. One is based on routine reviews. At regular intervals, such as quarterly or semi-annually, all relevant forensics procedures, protocols, and technologies are reviewed to ensure their effectiveness against corporate goals. A second method is to institute rigorous change management control into the forensic process itself. In that respect, the reviews and tests that are done as part of the evaluation of the correctness of the change ensure that the components of the forensics process always remain up to date and valid. This latter approach eliminates any time lag that might take place between significant system changes and updates to the forensic process and its technologies.

Both of these approaches validate the correctness of the forensics process; however, the practical solution is usually a combination of the two. Some elements, particularly those that are part of the technology, are best included into the change process itself. This ensures that the technology that underlies the forensic capability is always in step with the enterprise as it changes. Since policy and procedure and other high-level functions are not usually subject to change management, they need a more rigorous review process involving inspections and audits.

Inspections, audits, and other types of human-powered reviews are much more resource-intensive, so they are normally done on a routine, periodic basis. The target of these kinds of inspections is usually the forensics policy, protocols, procedures, and other activities that are not subject to empirical tests. The overall plan that establishes the forensics operation should be used to plan and schedule these types of evaluations. The aim is to ensure that all aspects of the program receive periodic review, whether change is a factor or not. The evaluation of policies, procedures, protocols, and training creates a series of baselines that can be used to actually understand the organization's forensic capability. Moreover, as the various requirements for the process change, these baselines can be adjusted to meet the new situation. That is why evaluation is a necessary and important aspect of the forensic process.

# Chapter Summary

- The digital forensics process involves reconstructing events.
- The thing that differentiates digital forensics from other forensics is the nature of the evidence, which is virtual.
- Forensics is always supported by tools because of the virtual nature of the evidence.
- Good forensics investigators need to have technical skills and also understand court rules of procedure.

- The conventional data processing policies related to data retention have to be shaped with the needs of the forensics process in mind.
- Outsourcing of the work impacts forensics planning.
- The practice of digital forensics is essentially individualistic because there are so many variables involved.
- The first step in any forensics process is data collection.
- The second step in any forensics process involves analysis.
- The third step in any forensics process involves reporting of the results.
- The simplest requirement for forensic evidence is that it is believable in court.
- The requirements for a forensic project are dictated by the nature of the investigation.
- System logs and the media itself are the typical sources of forensics data.
- The aim of inspections and reviews is to ensure that the forensics process meets all legal and regulatory requirements and is functioning properly.
- One method of ensuring proper performance is through regularly scheduled inspections.
- Another method of ensuring proper performance is through change control of technology and processes.

**8**

## Key Terms

**Chain of custody** A legal concept involving assurance that evidence is correct and has not been tampered with while being handled.

**Data retention policy** This policy sets a specific period of time to retain each record type, after which that particular record is erased from the system or archived in places that are difficult to access.

**E-discovery** Request for and supplying of electronic evidence.

**Forensic analysis** Protocols for the analysis of data.

**Forensic laboratories** Used to conduct testing processes and procedures.

**Network forensics** Analysis of physical components of a network.

**System logs** Electronic files that provide step-by-step descriptions of the events that took place during a computer incident.

## Questions from the CIO

The CIO requires you to brief her on the current status of your investigation. This will be an important part of your continuing work on this project, since it is essential to be able to describe all of the ramifications of the functions of the key digital forensics personnel. Consequently, the CIO would like you to answer the following questions for her:

1. Planning seems to be a more important factor than one would assume in an exercise as technical as digital forensics. What are the five benefits of good planning for digital forensics operations?

2. Trustworthiness seems to be a particularly important issue when it comes to forensics data. Why is trust so important, and how can it be both established and also violated?

3. Specifically, why might digital forensics work be outsourced? What are some of the unique pitfalls of outsourcing for forensics work?

4. The identification of data sources is a critical exercise for forensics work. There are two important reasons for this. What are the reasons, and what is the benefit of doing the identification correctly?

5. Chain of custody is clearly important. Cite four ways that chain of custody can be broken or violated and explain the consequences for each of these.

6. Forensics is like putting together a puzzle where the pieces are in multiple boxes. Relate that statement to the way that forensics data might be stored and retrieved for analysis.

7. One of the functions of the forensics process is disaster/incident recovery. Explain how forensics is involved in that process and why it is a unique asset to it.

8. Why is it important to have clear-cut, well-defined, and robust interfaces between the forensics function and regular data processing activity?

9. What is the specific relationship between the forensics process and the legal process? What are three ways that forensics can support legal activity?

10. Maintaining the integrity of tools and processes through change management is an intriguing way of assuring the status of the forensics operation. Explain how change management can ensure that the forensics process is conducted as capably as possible.

# Hands-On Projects

1. Using the case in Appendix 1, create the following security-related policies:

   a. Forensic data collection policy

   b. Forensic capability assurance policy

2. Using the case in Appendix 1, identify and document the appropriate rules and regulations for the three different types of data collection: law enforcement driven, civil action driven, and internal investigation driven.

3. Using the case in Appendix 1, outline the minimum set of forensic capabilities that would be required for that case. Describe what training is needed to achieve that capability.

# chapter 9

# The Enterprise Continuity Competency

## 1500 Hrs. on a Wednesday Afternoon

*It was a bright blue day in the Hamptons and the CEO was relaxing at his place way out on the tip of Montauk Point. He was sitting on his stone back patio in a deck chair enjoying the mid-afternoon sun, sipping a cold glass of Riesling, and listening to the peaceful sounds of seagulls hovering over the waves. It had been a tough year rebuilding the company, and he felt like he deserved the one-month break that he was taking in his ocean front rental, even if it was costing him a cool 120 grand for the privilege. The weather was great, the wife and kids were enjoying the exclusive beach, the golf with his pals was revitalizing and, best of all, he had left strict orders back in the city not to disturb him. That situation was about to change—drastically.*

*At that precise moment, a huge tropical depression swept off the Sahara. In the great mixing bowl of the earth's weather, these disturbances almost always presaged serious Atlantic storms. This particular front featured the lowest barometer readings that the National Oceanic and Atmospheric Administration (NOAA) meteorologists monitoring the GOAS satellite for that sector had ever seen. The front moved past Dakar and made its way out into the South Atlantic, sucking up enormous amounts of heat and moisture as it headed for the Cape Verde Islands. By the time it had passed over the island of Santiago at 2015 local time, it had already escalated into a major Atlantic storm. The Cape Verde Islanders, who during that part of the season lived with storms, had their capital of Praia buttoned up tight. But even they were amazed by the force and power of the wind.*

*By 2300, the National Hurricane Center issued its first tropical storm warning. Then, around 0230, the storm got a name, "Tamara." The fact that NOAA had almost run through the alphabet showed what kind of year it had been for Atlantic hurricanes. As they attempted to get a fix on the storm's track, the scientists at NOAA were also seeing a rare drop in the westerly steering winds that normally guided storms of this type into the Gulf of Mexico. Without those winds, the tendency of cyclonic storms to drift toward the earth's Poles was accelerating the track northward. The initial tracking data indicated that the target might be anywhere from Bermuda to the U.S. east coast.*

*The weather had been exceptionally warm that year. As Tamara churned her way across the Atlantic, it was going up the scale toward force 3. Finally, around 0430, one of NOAA's hurricane hunting P-3 Orions got a definite fix on the storm and its track. The data was not good; Tamara was a Force 4 killer and it was headed directly at the east coast of the United States. As hurricanes approach land, they typically recurve to the north. Tamara, on the other hand, was on a straight track toward the largest populated area on the east coast: New York City.*

*At 0530, the night shift at the company's security op center decided to deploy the company's Bell 206B3 to pick up the CEO and his family. He might have left orders not to be disturbed, but based on the tracking data, all of Long Island looked like it was going to be re-sculptured. And at the rate that Tamara was increasing in force, it was likely that nothing on Montauk Point was going to be part of the remaining landscape. At the same time, the op center activated the company's disaster plan.*

*At the CEO's personal request, the Bell dropped him in the parking lot next to the op center and then proceeded on to Westchester to drop off his family. The disaster plan was one of his personal contributions to the security capabilities of the company, and he wanted to be there to supervise its implementation. Disaster planning was a subset of the continuity plan that the CEO had been sold on when he took over the company. The continuity plan laid out the entire range of principles, policies, and procedures that he and his highly paid consultants felt were necessary to ensure that the organization would continue to function should a situation like the one that was about to happen ever occur.*

*The CEO had not been thinking specifically about a hurricane when the plan was finalized. In fact, only 12 hours earlier, he had been primarily thinking about his golf swing; however, he was certainly happy that he had had the foresight to get a continuity process in place before Tamara showed up on his doorstep. As he saw it, the entire continuity process was all about strategy. The whole point of the process was to have a well-designed and disciplined response in place to deal with every foreseeable contingency. Fortunately for the CEO and his company, one of those contingencies included Tamara.*

*Since the EBK had been generally accepted as the basis for structuring security activities within the company, the CEO had turned to it to organize the continuity process. Thus, the* **continuity strategy** *that the CEO and his consultants had adopted involved 11 required activities. These activities were all policy-based, and as a result it was possible to implement them across the entire operation. The effect of these 11 activities was to ensure that the enterprise continuity process would be properly planned and managed.*

# Continuity Management: Ensuring Effective Recovery from an Adverse Event

The goal of enterprise continuity management is to develop and then oversee a process to ensure that the critical elements of the organization's information and information processing function survive in the event of a disaster or other adverse event. From the manager's perspective, the enterprise continuity function is primarily a planning and monitoring activity. Planning and monitoring are also basic elements of conventional management. Nevertheless, where continuity differs from the routine management process is in its orientation; most organizational planning and monitoring processes are focused on *prevention*, while enterprise continuity is focused on *recovery*.

The role of enterprise continuity is to assure the re-establishment of the company's information processing capabilities, along with its data assets. In essence, the aim of continuity is to ensure that systems and data are restored as quickly as possible. The enterprise continuity function is built around a pre-defined set of activities that are meant to bring the physical system back to a pre-determined level of performance. Enterprise continuity also has to follow the same type of formal process to ensure that the data in those systems will be restored to a specified level of trustworthiness. All of this reconstruction has to take place within an optimum timeframe.

In order to underwrite those assurances, the enterprise continuity function adopts policies and procedures that are specifically tailored to ensure a well-defined and disciplined response to all foreseeable events. In that respect, the enterprise continuity management process employs three sequential activities to assure the enterprise continuity response. The first of these activities is strategic planning. Strategic planning itemizes and describes all foreseeable contingencies that might impact the organization. The second activity is a logical extension of the first. It deploys an optimum set of disciplined actions, which are designed to prevent or minimize the impact of every one of the contingencies identified in the initial strategic planning process. The final activity is disaster planning. Disaster planning is meant to ensure a disciplined recovery from a specific disaster. The disaster planning process is different from general continuity in that it is much more focused on responses to well-defined and highly specific occurrences. It delineates and then maintains a detailed set of steps to follow if a specifically foreseen contingency occurs.

Since the adverse events that an information operation might encounter typically involve the storage and transmission of data, much of the enterprise continuity process is built around developing secure backup and storage strategies. In conjunction with assuring optimum and cost-efficient data protection, enterprise security also ensures that the people who are responsible for executing the continuity and disaster recovery plans are properly prepared. In effect, continuity management ensures that all of the people involved in the continuity process understand their assigned roles. In conjunction with designating and assigning roles and responsibilities, the continuity process also makes certain that the people assigned to those roles are adequately trained and available when needed.

9

# Friday—0900

*The NOAA C-130 had plowed its way through the leading edge of the hurricane and was now in the eye. It was a beautiful day down there, right in the middle of the giant hurricane. The pilot always thought that that was one of the oddest phenomena of a cyclonic storm. The four Allison T56A 15 turboprops had practically come off the wing getting them there, and the pilot was in no mood for the return trip. But he had found out what he needed to know.*

*As it began to push up against the northern New Jersey shore, Tamara had finally begun to recurve north toward Manhattan and Long Island. It was now packing 120 mile an hour winds, which downgraded it to Category Three on the Simpson scale. But that still meant that New York City could expect a storm surge of between 12 and 25 feet. Since elevations in Manhattan average about 33 feet above sea level, that meant that a lot of downtown and midtown was going to be under water.*

*That was bad news for the Port Authority of NYC, of course. But that wasn't the CEO's specific problem; his problem lay in the Port Authority's beautiful old art deco building on 8th Avenue, which lay well within that flood plain. Since that particular building housed the main beachfront landing stations for several of the major transatlantic cable providers, and since those cables accounted for about 98 percent of the data transmission capability between the northern United States and Europe, he was about to lose all voice and data connectivity to the rest of the world. Notwithstanding the fact that the company's headquarters was sure to suffer a lot of wind and flood damage, he knew that they also had to find an alternative route across the Atlantic. Otherwise, the company would be back in the same mess it had been in the last time the computers stopped working.*

*They set up the war room in the cafeteria off of the op center. That location was selected because it was the only room large enough to hold all of the participants. Everyone on the crisis team had their binders with them and the tables were marked for various operational units. The mood in the room was quiet and professional; everybody was prepared. The CEO opened the meeting with some simple words, reminding everyone that they had practiced this, and that the plan would work. He wished everyone and their families well, and reminded the team members that if they needed help, they should feel free to speak up early. More motivational than substantive in nature, the goal was to provide a positive start for the upcoming test. The CEO also reminded everyone that unlike some disasters, the slow approach of the hurricane had given everybody time to coordinate the response. He then turned the meeting over to the CIO, who was going to walk the entire team through the timeline of upcoming events. She was perfectly in command of the situation and it showed; she knew that she and her team had done all of the homework necessary to ensure success.*

## Successful Preparation Is No Accident

The enterprise continuity function encompasses those principles, policies, and procedures which ensure essential business functions in the event of a disaster. In that respect, the focus of enterprise continuity is not on preventing the disaster from occurring. Rather, enterprise continuity encompasses all of the actions needed to ensure business survival after the fact.

The key to success in continuity is preparation. That is the reason why strategy and planning are such essential elements of the continuity process. Since strategies are implemented by people, the focus of most of the preparation is on developing the precise plans that will dictate what to do in the face of an anticipated contingency. That includes the designation of key positions, the roles and responsibilities of those positions, the order of succession, and the communication plans that establish the chain of command. Since strategies have to be kept current, part of the planning process has to be devoted to ensuring that the drills and rehearsals that are necessary to maintain the continuity process at the desired state of readiness are routinely carried out.

## Identifying Contingencies to Address

An essential component of the **continuity planning** process is the identification of contingencies to address. Every foreseeable contingency has to be recognized and characterized. Then management has to develop a strategy and attendant action to ensure that each of those contingencies is addressed by an effective response.

The development of contingency plans is based on a threat assessment, which identifies only those contingencies that require a formal response. Every one of these formal responses is documented in a **preparedness plan**; the actions outlined in the preparedness plan represent the steps that the organization plans to take to address every contingency of significance.

## Preparedness Planning

Operationally, the specific steps involved in ensuring that each threat is properly addressed are detailed in the preparedness plan. The purpose of the plan is to document the strategy that the organization will follow in the case of each of its priority contingencies. The aim of the plan is to ensure a substantive across-the-board response that will offer the best tradeoff between the harm that a given threat might cause and the cost of putting the actions in place to mitigate it.

One of the key principles involved in preparedness planning is the issue of foreseeability. In simple terms, foreseeability means that a threat is sufficiently understood to allow the organization to make specific planning assumptions about it. Those assumptions are detailed in a threat scenario. The goal is to come up with an overall set of plans that will cover every reasonable threat scenario. Each scenario is updated as additional knowledge is gained about the nature of the threat itself. Scenarios are then prioritized; **prioritization** is based on the assumed likelihood and impact of each threat.

## The Role of Estimation Methods and Tools in Planning

Various estimation methodologies and tools are used to support the response planning process. They might include such common practices as threat models, or probability of occurrence and net-present-value estimates of economic impact. Once the organization fully understands the implications of each of its chosen priorities, it prepares and then maintains a substantive continuity response.

## Preparing and Maintaining an Effective Response

The organization is responsible for maintaining a strategic perspective in the development of its continuity plans, which should be developed through a formal strategic planning process. The continuity plan dictates, in precise terms, the exact procedures required to restore operation of the information processing function. Each procedure has the specific assignment of staff and resources associated with it, as well as timing and cost information for every resource. These procedures are documented down to the level of the specific steps that will be taken to prevent or minimize damage.

One of the broad aims of the continuity plan is to ensure operational resilience and timely recoverability of the IT platform itself. In that respect, the continuity plan must demonstrate that the organization is positioned to address all likely threats to the information processing function. Practically, the preparedness plan lays out the critical path that the organization must follow to ensure timely **restoration** of damaged information processing equipment. It also must specify the criteria for evaluating the integrity of that equipment's constituent data.

This kind of detailed preparedness planning is driven by the same threat modeling, risk assessment, and **threat analysis** processes that underlie the data security function. Many of the activities that support data security management also support the formulation and maintenance of the enterprise's preparedness plan. Nonetheless, the preparedness strategy should be developed independent from the development of the data security process, since the inherent aims of the two functions are different.

The preparedness plan should also continue to evolve with the threat environment and the realities of the business climate. Preparedness planning must always be aware of the status of three basic components of the overall information processing function: the data—including all protected information baselines; the physical facilities and equipment; and the information processing function's personnel. That final category includes all operational staff, not just critical personnel.

## Risk Assessment and Preparedness Planning

The information needed to support the planning for a response in each of these areas is obtained by means of a conventional risk analysis process. The role that risk assessment plays in continuity planning is to help develop priorities. It is important to be able to prioritize risks, since that is the way that decision-makers assign resources.

No organization has the resources to address every potential threat because there are so many threats to deal with. Therefore, it is important to limit the preparedness plan to just those events that represent the highest likelihood of occurrence and greatest potential harm. Because each threat response will be resource-intensive, this part of the planning process requires planners to make intelligent choices about consequences and resources.

Those decisions usually require a little bit of fortune telling. By definition, the threats have not yet happened, and indeed might never occur. Consequently, the preparedness plan typically prioritizes responses by category, or type of harmful event. The aim is to address any potential eventuality that might fall within a given class of event with a single response. For instance, whether the equipment is damaged by a major hurricane, a leaking pipe, or somebody accidentally spilling a drink in it, the outcome of getting a piece of electronic equipment wet can be anticipated. The preparedness plan can then specify the steps to react to any form of water damage, including maintenance of spare equipment and how and when backups will be taken and deployed.

# Successful Recovery Is No Walk in the Park

Although they focus in the same general area, there is a huge difference between preparedness planning and disaster planning. Preparedness plans seek to ensure that the enterprise will continue to function in the face of a wide range of potential occurrences. Disaster plans apply in the instance of a specific disaster. In that respect, disaster plans are drawn up for a particular type of event only. Moreover, disaster plans only address events that are likely to cause enormous harm to the organization, such as hurricanes, earthquakes, terrorist events, or other kinds of human mischief. The sole aim of the disaster plan is to ensure that as much of the organization's assets as possible are recovered should that specific event occur. Since disaster planning only applies to crises, it is also sometimes known as **crisis management**.

The tangible outcome of the disaster planning process is a **disaster recovery plan,** or DRP. The DRP specifies the explicit set of steps that will be followed in order to ensure optimum recovery from a specific occurrence. Because the impacts of a specific disaster can generally be characterized in advance, this allows the organization to have an optimized response in place prior to the event. Since there are a number of potential disasters that *could* occur, the likelihood of that occurrence is an important consideration with DRPs.

The goal of a DRP is to minimize loss of information and the interruption of business should a disaster occur. The types of disaster that must be planned for will vary based on the specific requirements of the situation and even things like geographic location. Thus, one of the initial practical requirements in doing disaster planning is to itemize all of the events that might require a response. DRPs only address major events, like earthquakes or floods; they can be extremely resource-intensive. Consequently, DRPs are only drawn up for the most likely scenarios. For instance, it would be a waste of resources to develop DRPs for hurricanes in Michigan, since no hurricane has ever occurred there. But since tornados are a regular event in that state, it would be good DRP practice to have a plan in place to respond to one of those.

Because there are never enough resources to respond adequately to every event, that list has to be prioritized. Most of the disasters that organizations plan for are the physical type, such as human-caused and natural catastrophes. For that reason, DRPs are inclined to only encompass the tangible elements of the information processing function, primarily the technology. A DRP will typically contain detailed instructions for restoring the physical components of critical systems, as well as how to move staff from the damaged site to an alternative site away from the disaster zone. Disasters can be broken down into three categories: natural, site, and civil. Site disasters head the priority list, because they are more likely to happen than the occasional natural or civil disaster, and they can be destructive. Natural disasters are next on the list because of their potential impact; even though the occurrence of a hurricane might be rare, when a hurricane does rolls ashore it always causes damage. The last item on the list is the possibility of civil disturbance. In the United States, a civil disturbance is less likely to occur than a fire. And even though it might cause widespread damage, a civil disturbance is not as potentially destructive as a hurricane is. Generally, the more likely and destructive events tend to get higher priority.

Timing plays a large part in shaping the organization's overall recovery strategy. The length of time that the system and its information will be unavailable dictates such things as when there will need to be a staff migration to an alternative site. The DRP typically applies only if the disruption will be for an extended period. That decision is made strictly on the business case. Thus, a DRP requires adequate understanding of the impact that the downtime will have on business processes. If it is estimated that the period to return the primary site to normal operation will be appreciably longer than the period to migrate the information processing function to the alternative site, then the DRP kicks in.

# Anticipating Disasters

Disaster planning has to be approached on both a long-term and a short-term basis. In the long term, there has to be a well thought-out plan in place, which will ensure successful recovery from all disasters that fall within its scope. In order to guarantee that disaster plans remain effective, it is important in the short term to continue to classify threats and assess their potential danger. Accordingly, the process also has to incorporate a way to sustain a balanced and realistic assessment of only those disasters that could cause a loss of business value. In order to do that, the organization should perform a regularly scheduled update of the **disaster scenarios** that drive the disaster planning process.

In the short term, crisis managers must have in their hands a precise set of steps, which they will follow to respond to a particular class of disaster. These are called disaster scenarios. The contingencies that drive each disaster scenario have to be precisely specified and then cross-referenced to the procedures that will be followed in the event that that eventuality should occur. The specification is always embodied in an explicit plan that contains clear and unambiguous instructions for each individual circumstance.

Because disaster planning is built around procedures that are aimed primarily at the human resources element, planners must itemize the precise roles and responsibilities of each of the participants in the disaster response. This is a behavior-centered process that requires the development of highly focused motivation and education programs. Those programs have to ensure that the managers and other stakeholders responsible for implementing and maintaining the plan are properly trained.

Finally, disaster plans have to be tested. This is an absolute requirement for the implementation of the disaster recovery process. It requires the planners to both refine and operationally test their assumptions on an ongoing basis, with the aim of proving that the specific strategies embodied in the plan effectively address the requirements of each specific circumstance.

## Documenting a Recovery Plan

Although the list of potential disasters might be long, the plans that address them always encompass the same three elements: disaster impact description and classification; response deployment and communication processes; and escalation and re-assessment procedures. **Disaster impact classification** entails the understanding and description of the practical implications of the threat. For instance, knowing that a hurricane is coming does not really address the consequences that might result. What must be determined are the outcomes of having a hurricane come ashore. Once all contingencies have been classified and their likelihood assessed, a formal response can then be prepared.

Because a disaster never occurs the same way each time it happens, the planned response is generally based on assigned roles rather than fixed procedures. That is, the response designates the right people to react in the case of a disaster, rather than a specific set of steps they should follow. For instance, since it is impossible to dictate in advance how to fight a building fire, it is sufficient to know that the local fire department is the proper agency to call. A proper plan will designate which fire station to call, along with the station's detailed contact information.

Finally, because disasters involve a considerable helping of the unknown, there have to be a defined set of escalation and re-evaluation procedures. A well-defined set of **escalation procedures** ensures a proper response should events continue to escalate or not meet the planning assumptions. Thus, the plan has to include a specific and well-defined mechanism for re-evaluating and re-classifying the threat picture and then re-deploying the appropriate response.

# Friday 0950: The CIO Discovers the Advantages of a Solid Plan

*The cafeteria off of the op center was an extremely active place as the assorted task teams went about their business. In the meantime, much like the eye of the approaching storm itself, the CIO sat calmly in the middle of all of that carefully choreographed action sipping a cup of tea and basking in the glow of knowing that she had just covered herself with glory. The source of her profound sense of self-satisfaction was the fact that, even though the CEO liked to think of himself as the godfather of the process, the entire continuity concept had been her idea. She had sold the idea of continuity planning to the CEO shortly after he took over the reins of the company. It was not a hard sell, since the reason why the CEO had been hired in the first place was to pick up the pieces from the prior disaster. And there was no more appropriate function to underwrite that goal than a fully developed and comprehensive enterprise continuity process.*

*Over the succeeding year and a half, the CIO had overseen the development of the disaster scenarios, the risk analysis, and then the documentation of all of the policies and plans to ensure continuity. In fact, she had written most of those policies and plans herself. Consequently, she knew that the company was going to literally be able to weather the approaching storm. She also knew that that capability was good news for her status at the company. The even more satisfying aspect of the current disaster was the knowledge that the CEO owed her big-time.*

*The secret of her success lay in the set of detailed planning assumptions she had developed, along with the exacting design of the continuity process that was now rolling out around her. In fact, from her point of view, the whole essence of good continuity management was sweating the details of the design process. She had labored long and late into the night to ensure that the actual process that had turned the best practice principles for continuity management into concrete action was both coherent and complete. So she was sure that the response to the upcoming challenge of the hurricane was going to be the best that could be developed.*

*She had based the particular design process she had adopted on the four common work functions for enterprise continuity design. These represent a mix of management and technical activities that as a group are intended to ensure an effective enterprise continuity response:*

1. *Develop an enterprise continuity of operations plan and related procedures*

2. *Develop and maintain enterprise continuity of operations documentation, such as contingency, business continuity, business recovery, disaster recovery, and incident handling plans*

3. *Develop a comprehensive test, training, and exercise program to evaluate and validate the readiness of enterprise continuity of operations plans, procedures, and execution*

4. *Prepare internal and external continuity of operations communications procedures and guidelines*

## Drawing the Right Set of Assumptions

The enterprise security design process operationalizes a formal set of disaster prevention and recovery assumptions. The tangible outcome of that process is a detailed prescription of the set of operational steps that will be taken in response to any event that falls under those assumptions. Continuity plans always involve two things. The first is a set of specific statements that document and justify why particular contingencies have been selected, while other foreseen contingencies were not selected. The second is a complete and detailed specification of the strategies that will be used to maintain continuity in the case of each contingency.

The rationale behind the first item is that there will always be more threats than can be feasibly mitigated; however, threats are always time-sensitive, since new ones can arise at any time and old threats can become more dangerous. The assumptions that guided the assignment of priorities have to be made explicit in order to steer the future evolution of the response. These assumptions are always based strictly on the organization's threat picture at the current point in time. Assumptions have to be periodically updated, because that picture is constantly changing. One important side benefit of maintaining the assumptions in alignment with the known threat picture is that it documents the organization's due diligence in maintaining its continuity response should a disaster occur.

As a new threat is identified, a set of assumptions has to be developed about its impact on critical business functions. The assumptions will normally be based on the likelihood and impact of the threat as well as the areas of the business that might be subject to harm. Given the uncertain nature of most threats, there is always guesswork in the process. Nonetheless, the outcome of the process of thinking through and documenting priorities is always the same. All of the assumptions that underlie the organization's continuity strategy have to be maintained current and as relevant to the threat situation as possible.

The second element of the design process is much more directly focused. That is the development of the actual continuity strategy. Organizations devise continuity strategies out of their own particular business philosophy. Given the relationship between business goals and the strategy that is adopted, there is no such thing as a uniform method for development; every organization approaches the challenges of ensuring enterprise continuity in its own unique way. The only given in the process is that the strategy that is eventually implemented, as well as the philosophy that drives it, must be uniformly understood and commonly accepted throughout the entire organization.

The latter condition, that there must be a well understood and commonly accepted specification of strategy, is an absolute necessity because there cannot be uncertainty about how to respond to an adverse event if it occurs. It is important that the organization both implement and then fully communicate a universal continuity strategy. Moreover, in order to make it acceptable to all of the employees, this strategy must be fully sponsored by executive management with concrete accountabilities for performance built into the process.

Because adverse events do not usually arrive in neat packages, it is also important to embed a set of unambiguous criteria into the overall continuity plan that, dictate precisely when the plan will be activated and when it will terminate. The exact criteria for activating the continuity plan have to be understood by every essential person in the continuity process. Regular drills ensure that those people understand exactly when, where, and how their roles are involved.

## Two Essential Factors in the Development of the Continuity Plan

The aim of continuity is to ensure the preservation of the enterprise's information assets. In that respect, the approach that is taken to the process of preservation is dictated by two fundamental factors. The first is the timing of the recovery, and the second is the level of reliability that has to be guaranteed for the recovered data. Given those two factors, the design process requires the organization to establish two fundamental objectives: the **recovery time objective (RTO)** and the **recovery point objective (RPO)**.

**Recovery Time Objective** In simple terms, RTO specifies the maximum acceptable downtime for the information processing operation, while RPO specifies the minimum level of trustworthiness that is required for the restored data. Ensuring the timely access to, and reliability of, the organization's data is the whole point of the continuity process; these two fundamental building blocks will define the precise shape of any particular organization's continuity process.

RTOs are business decisions; the choice about where to set the RTO is based on the information processing demands of the business. In terms of the three fundamental principles of cybersecurity (confidentiality, integrity, and availability), RTO represents the availability principle. The recovery period defined by each RTO is an exact measure of time. It defines the maximum operationally acceptable interval that a specific information system or information processing function can be unavailable before unacceptable harm occurs.

**Recovery Point Objective** RPO is a different concept altogether, because it represents the integrity principle. Since integrity is an essential element of cybersecurity, every enterprise continuity plan has to specify a minimum acceptable level of trustworthiness for the recovered data. The data recovery process generally depends on identifying the last point where the data was known to be correct, so trustworthiness is usually defined by the last backup point. Because any data entered on the system after the last backup cannot be trusted, RPO is typically set at the shortest feasible interval. Data that is created or modified outside of that interval has to be considered lost or in need of painstaking restoration procedures to ensure its validity.

The RPO indicates how much data loss the organization is willing to accept in the light of its business goals. Obviously, business considerations like value and investment have a lot to do with setting the RPO in each particular instance. There is a direct tradeoff between the value of data and the cost of backing it up. Thus, the desired RPO and the investment to ensure that that objective is met are generally traded off against each other. The aim is to arrive at an optimum balance between the investment in assurance and the value of each item of data. The practical case might be made for investing whatever it takes in real-time backups to ensure the reliability of the data that is vital to the organization's survival. On the other hand, the value of data that is non-essential might not justify a backup of more than once a week.

**Trading Off the Two Factors** RPO and RTO are two separate concepts which are in some respects mutually exclusive of each other. To get the system back to running in the shortest possible time, it is usually hard to ensure the integrity of the data; therefore, the optimum RPO versus RTO also has to be decided. Organizations where computers are needed to drive the business, such as automated manufacturing plants, generally favor the shortest possible RTO. On the other hand, in an institution where the credibility of the data is more critical to the organization, like a brokerage house or a research laboratory for instance, the integrity of every byte of data has to be ensured. As a result, in designing a continuity solution, an **optimum tradeoff** point has to be decided between how soon the system is restored versus how trustworthy the data will be.

It is that need to find this balance that drives the practical decisions about whether to adopt a hotsite, warmsite, or coldsite approach. Ideally, the RPO would be positioned exactly at the point of system failure, meaning there would be no data lost. But in order to maintain such a high level of assurance, it would be necessary to run a continuous mirror backup operation. Since that would entail the cost of maintaining duplicate equipment at an alternative location, this approach would probably be economically infeasible for most organizations.

Because businesses perform a wide range of functions, some more critical than others, there is both a general and a specific aspect to setting the RTO and RPO points. From the management standpoint, in order to implement a practical continuity response, it is essential to have a single RTO and RPO for the business. Such a single fixed point of restoration is necessary in order to allow managers to make strategic decisions about bridge financing and even publicity in the wake of a disaster.

Because most business operations comprise diverse functions, it would be unrealistic to think that every aspect of the business can be brought back into operation at the exact same RTO and RPO. However, it is possible to determine RTOs and RPOs for each of the individual, critical processes of the business. Once these are known, it should be possible to aggregate the average of these into a practicable RTO and RPO for the overall business. In that respect, the overall RTO and RPO would actually become a realistic composite of the RTOs and RPOs for each of the processes governed by the enterprise continuity planning process.

# Creating a Practical Enterprise Continuity Process

The goal of enterprise continuity is to mitigate the impact of a disaster as close to the event as is feasible. But the continuity process also has to fit within the specific operating parameters of the business. That practical requirement implies the necessity to do a comprehensive and detailed analysis, in order to ensure that the enterprise continuity function and the day-to-day operation of the business are properly aligned.

The design of the continuity process must ensure that the RTO and RPO that are eventually selected are compatible with the needs of the business and its underlying information processing operation. In order to ensure that compatibility, the design process has to make sure that five practical requirements have been met. First, the design process has to make certain that all of the essential business functions are identified. Second, the design process has to ensure that the relative contribution of each of these functions to the overall operation is known. Third, the specific hazards that threaten each function and their likelihood of occurrence and impact have to be described. Fourth, the practical RTO and RPO settings for each function can be determined from this analysis. Finally, an aggregate average RTO and RPO for the business is set.

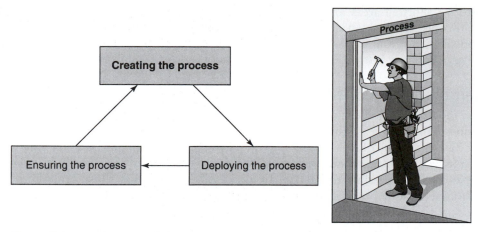

**Figure 9-1** Enterprise continuity process: creating
© Cengage Learning 2012

Creating the process is just one step of the enterprise continuity process, as shown in Figure 9-1.

## Identification and Prioritization of Protected Functions

The logical first step in creating a specific continuity plan is to identify and characterize all of the things that will fall under that plan. The business first identifies and then prioritizes the functions that are essential to ensuring its continued operation. The criticality of the function is designated based on how central that process is to fulfilling the general business purpose. The common sense question to guide that identification process is whether a failure of the function would either significantly impact the overall business operation, or whether it might lead to an irrecoverable loss of data or significant financial losses.

Once the value of each process has been understood and characterized, a priority is assigned to it. That priority is based on the process's assumed criticality to the overall business purpose. Continuity planning requires a priority listing of all functions, because the next step in the process will develop a continuity solution for each function. Each one of those functions will require a commitment of resources, so the pragmatic aim of this step in the design process is to ensure that the functions with the highest priority receive the resources that they need, with the most essential activity receiving the highest priority.

Once a list of requirements is prepared, the actual source of the resources must be designated. The organization first identifies the internal resources that will be called on. Then it identifies the external resource contributions, such as those of alternative sites or third-party services. A specification at this level of detail will help the organization to identify potential shortfalls in resources or capabilities. Shortfalls indicate where the organization does not have the resources or the capability to meet a given recovery objective. These shortfall areas should be itemized and then justified to the recovery objectives. That justification can lead to a more realistic set of priorities.

It is very important to identify the shortfall areas, because those are the potential points of failure in the recovery plan. Accordingly, the process of adjusting the plan to fit within available resources is an extremely critical element of the continuity planning process. Knowing where the shortfall areas are is a benefit to long-term management of the process, because that knowledge tells managers where adjustments to the plan are necessary. It should then be possible to create a feasible design once all of continuity's resource requirements have been appropriately justified to the business priorities of the organization.

## Designing the Continuity Solution

Next, the organization ensures that the continuity plan is feasible. There is no standard rule for how to ensure feasibility, but there is one absolute requirement: all critical functions must have a specified RTO and RPO. The RTO and RPO for each function must also have a customized set of incident response and recovery procedures associated with them. Moreover, it must be possible to validate by direct observation that those procedures exist. In addition, it must be possible to demonstrate that those procedures are operating properly.

### Specification of RTOs and RPOs
The RTO is assigned based on the criticality of the component in the overall business process, whereas the RPO is assigned based on the level of integrity required for the restored data. Because of resource constraints, these typically trade off against each other on a sliding scale. Where greater integrity is required, a longer recovery time is also necessary. Whatever the relationship between RTO and RPO, it is a rule of good planning that every important function must have a RTO and RPO associated with it.

Because the practical concern lies with the ability to provide sufficient resources to achieve a stated RTO and RPO, it is essential to establish an exact estimate of the resources required to accomplish both of those objectives. Typically, that statement entails an estimation of the number and types of personnel who will be required to do the work, along with each person's duties, where they will be housed, and any training requirements. Accompanying the personnel resource plan should also be a detailed estimate of the physical space requirements and the equipment and services that will be needed to do the work. That detailed resource estimate accompanies each RTO and RPO in the plan.

### Specification of Incident Response and Recovery Actions
Operationally, the incident response procedures have to be specified down to the level of the personnel who will be involved in carrying out each action, the technologies that will be used in that process, and how alternative sites will be accessed and utilized if needed. The specification of procedures has to address all of the potentially significant operational and environmental factors, including technology, personnel limitations, and geographic factors. It should also incorporate any specific plans for migration of the process to another site, or the utilization of contracted or outsourced services during the time the function is unavailable. Finally, because organizations change constantly, there is the implicit requirement to update the continuity plans on a regular, if not continuous, basis.

### Identification and Documentation of the Solution
All of the actions needed to satisfy the RTO and RPO requirements for each critical function addressed by the continuity plan are recorded on an individualized statement of work (SOW). This is a specification of standard operating procedure. It should describe all of the requisite procedures and the accompanying resource needs for each critical function. The SOW itemizes those procedures down to the level of prescribed behaviors for each individual, or process, that is part of the continuity response for that particular function. The SOW includes the identification

of requisite personnel, work area, equipment, and supply or service capability, along with any shortfalls that have been identified. By rule, all shortfalls for critical functions must be addressed, or an organizational justification for not addressing the shortfall must be provided in the SOW.

The SOW documents all of the organization's assumptions about continuity and has to be based on a careful analysis of the various business circumstances and environmental conditions for a given organization. The SOW is meant to provide the clearest possible guidance on the process that will be followed to address every contingency that can be foreseen. To ensure the continuing applicability of the recommendations in the SOW, it is important to perform regular audits of the steps specified in the plan.

## Ensuring that Everybody Knows What to Do

The documentation of the continuity plan effectively completes the process; the set of recommendations that constitute the continuity plan express the organization's continuity strategy. Detailed procedures are specified for each RTO and RPO. Assuming that they have been correctly prepared, these procedures should assure the continuity of the organization's critical functions and services. The people who are responsible for implementing and managing the plan have to be fully aware of what is required of them. But one final step still remains.

The business has to be able to ensure, with certainty, that all of the participants in the process clearly understand their specific roles and responsibilities. Operationally, that assurance amounts to making certain that the people who are responsible for performing the actions detailed in the plan are capable of carrying out their assignments. The actual assignment of the people who will participate in the plan should have taken place at the time that the critical functions were identified. Normally, the managers who are responsible for implementing and overseeing the continuity function are given a list of the key people who have been designated for each function. These lists serve as the basis for the assignment of tasks, as well as the estimation of the need for any other types of resources.

Once the assignment of roles and responsibilities is complete, the organization needs to plan and execute a focused, top-to-bottom awareness, training, and education program. The goal of that program is to bring everybody in the organization up to the proper level of capability. The outcome of the training and education process is that everybody who is essential to the success of the continuity plan is fully capable and aware of their duties.

From a human factors perspective, it is critical that all of the levels of management, from senior managers down to team and project leaders, actively support the process. Continuity is a resource-intensive process which, like car insurance, only really makes its value evident after the fact. Without strong endorsement and support from the top, it is hard to maintain the necessary degree of management discipline to ensure that the process remains effective.

# Friday 14:00: The Plan Gets Implemented

*Tamara spent a little time beating up New Jersey before she turned her full attention to New York City. Fortunately, from the perspective of the people on Manhattan, the storm's track took it just east of the Lower Bay, so the barrier islands east of Islip absorbed most of her initial fury. Nonetheless, the massive amount of water pushed along by the storm surge rushed through the*

Verrazano Narrows like a freight train and smacked Jersey City and the southern tip of Manhattan. Lady Liberty was abruptly ankle deep in water, and the Holland and then the Lincoln tunnels flooded successively, along with most of the West Side, up to midtown. Lower Manhattan was sitting under 10 feet of water. The effect of the surge was mainly limited to the West Side and downtown. But, that didn't really make much difference since the subway system, which had almost immediately flooded, promptly carried the water all the way up to 135th Street.

The company headquarters were right on the East River in the East 50s, and that worked to its advantage; the storm surge didn't go in that direction and the East Side was tucked up behind the shoulder of Brooklyn and Queens. Plus, the effort of moving inland across Long Island had to some extent pulled Tamara's fangs. The windows in the building had all been carefully shielded by a clever set of automatic louvers that banged shut as soon as the wind approached the breaking point of the glass. Aside from wiping the satellite communication equipment off of the roof, the wind damage was minimal. But, there was no electricity, no phone service, and the primary beachfront routers over on the West Side were a thing of the past. There was not going to be any Internet connection between Manhattan and the outside world for the foreseeable future.

That situation would have been a total disaster for the company if it had not been so well positioned to deal with it. The emergency generators, which had been carefully protected from any potential flood damage, kicked in. There was minimal flooding, which the pumps that had been installed in the building's sub-basements quickly disposed of. Within five minutes, the company and its physical infrastructure was back in operation.

Of course, that didn't do much for the information processing function, since connectivity was still an issue. But the company had even planned for that eventuality as the first of its hotsites came on line. In fact, as a result of the careful arrangement of hotsites and warmsites, which were arrayed all the way from the hills of Pennsylvania up to Albany, the company had not missed a beat in the conduct of its worldwide business operations. The company had done two things to ensure its success:

1. Executed continuity of operations and related contingency plans and procedures
2. Controlled access to information assets during an incident in accordance with organizational policy

# Deploying the Enterprise Continuity Process

When a catastrophic event occurs, with or without much advanced notice, the objective of the enterprise continuity process is to ensure that critical business functionality continues uninterrupted. In that respect, the execution of the enterprise continuity plans is a specific plan in itself. The execution plan dictates how the organization will shift from normal operations to continuity operations. There are two basic ways that transition can happen: planned and unplanned. Planned transitions work well when the disruptive event can be foreseen, such as an approaching storm. Planned transitions also allow an organization to make last-minute adjustments to staffing and can provide for a more orderly, lower stress change. Unfortunately, a lot of transitions are unplanned; thus, there is no advance notice of the event that activates the continuity response. For instance, the electric grid seldom gives customers advanced warning before shutting down, nor do telecommunication cables give notice when interrupted by a backhoe.

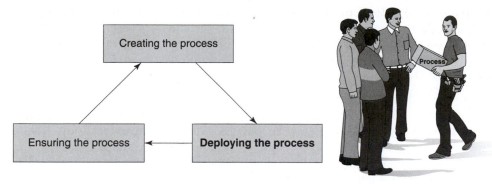

**Figure 9-2** Enterprise continuity process: deploying
© *Cengage Learning 2012*

The transition to enterprise continuity operations should be as automated as possible to prevent loss of computer functions, connections, data, and on-line transactions. The shift to an alternative source should be instantaneous. What cannot be easily automated is the shift of personnel from normal operations to continuity operations. Whether the shift is accommodated automatically, or as a result of advanced planning and meetings, the same approach is used to change systems and human resources over from normal operations to continuity operations.

This is the second stage of the enterprise continuity process, as shown in Figure 9-2.

## Ensuring Continuous Availability Through Redundancy

At its core, the aim of enterprise continuity is to ensure that the information processing capability of the organization is continuously available and that the integrity of the data is always maintained. Because both availability and data integrity require the electronic elements of the system to operate in an uninterrupted fashion, this implies a need for system redundancy. The rule involved here is as old as data processing itself, which is that the only way to ensure the integrity of electronic data is to back it up.

Given that rule, a lot of the actual implementation process depends on simply ensuring the most effective backup mechanism possible. In operational terms, this requires the organization to create and then maintain the ability to switch its information processing function from a primary site to an alternative site in the event of a disaster. The ideal achievement of this principle would be redundant information processing functions sufficient to ensure the absolute availability of the system without loss of data. However, except in rare cases, the value of the system and its data would not justify the resources that would have to be committed to reach that level of assurance. Consequently, the simple rule of thumb is that the level of redundancy is a function of the value of the data. The idea that the perceived value or criticality of the data determines the level of redundancy introduces the notion of alternative data recovery sites.

## Total Redundancy: Data Recovery Hotsites

There are instances where the information processing capability and its data are so critical to the survival of the organization that continuous capability has to be preserved no matter the cost. Examples of this type of information processing operation would be national security or national defense systems, or the critical components of our infrastructure, such as power. Systems such as those are assured by building total redundancy into their operation, but the ability to achieve that level of redundancy literally requires the operation of a second, or mirror, site. The term that is used to describe such a rigorous approach to continuity is a data recovery, or DR, hotsite.

Hotsites provide near instantaneous recovery and total data integrity protection. They literally mirror the real-time processing activity at the primary site and provide instant backup, in the sense that they are operating in parallel with the primary function. They have the same hardware, data communication, and environmentally controlled space that the primary site has, which assures the ability to maintain the exact same level of capability if operation at the primary site is interrupted.

However, because the organization is essentially running redundant information processing operations, hotsites double the cost of the IT function. This is prohibitively costly for most normal businesses. A lot of businesses also have information processing functions that must be kept in continuous operation in order to ensure survival, such as the transaction or order processing functions of most commercial establishments. The movement within the industry has been for third parties to offer shared hotsite arrangements as a specialized service. That allows a business to distribute the cost of maintaining a fully redundant processing function among a number of partners, which makes providing that capability more cost-effective.

## Partial Redundancy: Data Recovery Warmsites

The next step down from total redundancy is the Data Recovery Warmsite (DRW). This provides the equipment and communications interfaces that will allow the system to perform automatic backups in the most efficient timeframe possible. Depending on the criticality of the data and the information processing capabilities of the primary and secondary sites, those timeframes can be set to be nothing more than milliseconds, or they can be set to be minutes or even hours. In all cases however, the processing at the secondary site does not mirror the actual real-time processing at the target site, which means that a gap in time always separates the data that is entered at the primary site from the data that resides on the backup system.

By definition, the data at the warmsite cannot be assured to be the same as the data at the primary site, so it has to be restored in the event of a disaster. Thus, the RPO that is set for the data becomes a critical decision factor. As explained earlier, the RPO defines the backup interval, which is established as part of the overall continuity plan. The parameters for that are matters of business judgment and they can change based on changes to the threat picture as well as changes to the criticality of the data. The restore point might be nothing more than a momentary gap that would occur as the information processing capability at the primary site automatically prepares a batch of transactions for transmission to the backup site. Or, the restore point could represent a significant gap in time. For example, in the case of noncritical data, the restore point might be the time it would take to do a full system backup, which in most operations is only done at the end of each day.

Restore point parameters are typically established based on a "best economic estimate" of the cost of achieving a given RPO, which is always a function of the value or criticality of potential missing data. Restore points are meant to optimize the cost/risk factors for information that would be lost. Because the actual restore point can be tailored to the exact circumstances and then changed if the situation warrants, warmsites are generally considered the most practical approach to ensuring enterprise continuity. Furthermore, because they allow the organization to fine-tune its continuity strategy to the resources it has available, warmsite services are also becoming increasingly popular in the commercial world.

## Simple Operational Redundancy: Data Recovery Coldsites

When it comes to ensuring continuity, data recovery coldsites are at the bottom of the assurance ladder. That is because they are nothing more than a secure storage facility for routine backups done at the primary site. Nevertheless, until network communication capabilities became more cost efficient in the 1990's, coldsites were almost the only option available to the typical large data processing operations of most conventional businesses. They still have considerable utility as a cost-efficient solution to continuity where longer RTOs and RPOs can be tolerated.

Data recovery coldsites provide a hardware and software environment that is compatible with the conditions of the primary site, as well as the most recent backup of the data. It is possible to move staff from the primary site to the coldsite and quickly start up operation if the primary site becomes unavailable. But since a coldsite provides nothing more than the equipment and communications links to accommodate that migration, there will be considerable lost time in a coldsite approach. Data will also be lost, since the coldsite will only have a copy of the most recent backups.

Because it is normal practice in most information processing operations to perform backups on a routine daily schedule, there will always be a significant gap between the data on the backup versus its actual state when the primary site was lost. Consequently, any data that was entered between the point where the backup was taken and the point where the primary site went down will either be lost, or it will have to be rebuilt. The cost to rebuild lost data is always factored into the calculations of the most economically feasible restoration point.

On the other hand, coldsites have a considerable economic advantage over the other two approaches, because they do not require any form of parallel operation; it is possible to resume business operations as soon as the staff is moved. The obvious disadvantage lies in the fact that there will be a significant gap in the data, since the operation will have to roll back to the point of the last backup.

Coldsites are effective for functions that have a time lag built into them. Payroll is an example: paychecks are only issued in week or month increments, and the amounts don't change, so a weekly backup is sufficient to keep the data current. Timeliness and lost data are also why coldsites don't work well for operations based around high transaction processing volumes.

# Monday 0900: The Lights Come Back On

*By Monday, what was left of Tamara was in the process of dumping unprecedented amounts of rain on the residents of Prince Edward Island. At the same time, New York City was beginning to shake off the effects of the massive storm. There was a lot of lowland flooding, and the wind damage on the eastern face of Long Island had been disastrous. But in general, the storm passed like all other storms, leaving the residents of the area to clean up the mess.*

*The most important result from the company's standpoint was that there had been little loss of business functionality in the hours during and after the storm. The primary hotsite, which was located an hour away in Stroudsburg, Pennsylvania, had picked up the processing load immediately, using leased access on the Atlantica-1 and BDNSi undersea links out of Boca Raton, Florida. Almost immediately, the transmission load got a little uncomfortable, since the link to the landing stations in Florida was a little on the distant side. So, the mirror network operations center in Pennsylvania routed some of the northern traffic over leased space on the Canadian CANTAT-3 in order to take the processing load off of the Florida connections. All of the westbound traffic was re-routed out of Redondo Beach over the CSC2-Pacific ring, and that took any of the remaining traffic pressure off of the eastbound links. All of this had been anticipated and the necessary contractual arrangements had been made in advance.*

*As soon as the hotsite took over the processing, all but the essential New York staff was put on a special train to Albany to wait out the storm in the company's own warmsite facility. That move ensured that the entire New York City–based information processing function was fully operational through the duration of the storm. The company's continuity plan was a total success, but there was still work to be done.*

*Before everyone put the event behind them, the CIO wanted to do a comprehensive postmortem in order to learn from the experience. Mainly, she was looking for areas of improvement and suggestions for different ways of dealing with the event that had just occurred. The meeting continued for another half hour as she went over a list of specific procedures that she wanted to look at, making certain that the people who were assigned to look at them would use appropriate levels of detail in their analysis. She reminded them that what had just taken place was more than a drill, and that future successes depended upon how well they learned from this one.*

*The CIO was pushing evaluation because she knew that the sustainment of the process was one of her most important responsibilities. She wanted to ensure that the continuity process would continue to function as it just had, and she didn't just want a routine review. She wanted to ensure optimum preparedness. So she looked to the EBK to see what it said about ensuring that the measures that were put in place to guarantee recovery and restoration were effective. Specifically, she wanted to assess the ongoing effectiveness of the plan and its assumptions, as well as the overall capability of the organization to planned responses at the proper level of diligence.*

# Ensuring the Continuing Effectiveness of Enterprise Continuity Process

Regular evaluation of the effectiveness of the continuity process ensures that that process can be sustained over time. The evaluation of the effectiveness of any organizational process establishes the necessary accountabilities and discipline to ensure its sustainment. In the case of continuity, the evaluations are aimed at assessing the effectiveness of the procedures specified in both the preparedness and disaster recovery plans. The main purpose of such an assessment is to identify any operational situation where a procedure is either missing or ineffective. If problems are identified, the role of the evaluation process is to notify the decision-makers who are responsible for bringing that process back into alignment.

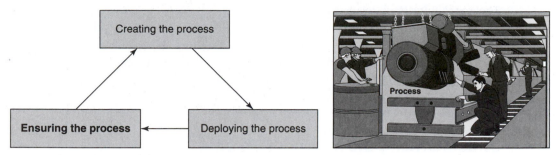

**Figure 9-3** Enterprise continuity process: ensuring
© Cengage Learning 2012

In the day-to-day business world, the continuity evaluation process is used to verify the continuing effectiveness of the approach adopted to ensure preparedness or timely recovery. Occasionally, the evaluation processes might be called out by third parties in order to verify compliance with some aspect of a contract or regulation. For instance, a third party could request an evaluation of the preparedness plan in order to determine whether the organization has complied with a specific regulatory requirement.

In practice, the evaluation process tests the performance of continuity procedures in the light of a set of specific assumptions about a potential threat. The aim of the evaluation process in that respect is to certify the ability of that procedure to satisfy the planning assumptions. The evaluation always assesses three things: the correctness of the policies or assumptions that underlie the process, the ability of the participants to carry out requisite procedures, and the capability of management to oversee the overall process.

In all three instances, the outcome of the evaluation process ought to be explicit evidence that the right set of policies are in place and that the correspondingly correct set of practices are being followed to achieve the stated objectives of a given plan. In addition to assuring the continuing effectiveness of each of the requisite activities in the plan, the operational evaluation process also helps the organization refine its response over time. At a minimum, the evaluation process involves routinely assessing the two dominant focuses of the continuity process: business impact and threat response.

Ensuring is the third step of the enterprise continuity process, as shown in Figure 9-3.

## Looking at the Consequences

**Business impact analysis** determines what the consequences are for some particular aspect of the business operation. These analyses normally involve the use of threat scenarios to drive the actual assessment. The scenarios can range as far as the imagination of the planners and the limitations of the business case, but they have to focus on a set of likely threats, since their role is to shape the subsequent consideration of the impact of each of those potential disasters on business events.

For instance, planners might consider such pedestrian issues as whether the organization could sustain operations in the face of a shortage of properly trained staff. They can also consider significant disasters like hurricanes and terrorist events. Additionally, business impact analysis can consider background concerns in the company's business environment, such as the loss of stock price if the company has a major security breach.

Given the wide range of potential considerations, the actual assessment criteria that drive the consideration are rarely strictly technical. For instance, it is perfectly appropriate in a business impact analysis to consider the effect of such events as a reduction of the funds to support preparedness, or an unanticipated increase in the cost of maintaining the response at a given level of desirability. It is also appropriate to consider legal and regulatory hazards, such as the potential for fines or other kinds of penalties if critical data were not available to support a Sarbanes-Oxley audit.

## Understanding the Impact of Threats

Threat analysis is an operational process that is carried out to ensure the continuing effectiveness of continuity plans. A continuous approach is required, because new threats are constantly emerging. Threat assessments test the likelihood that a given threat could occur, and they evaluate the degree of potential loss or harm that would result if it did. All threat assessments ask four common sense questions:

1. What could go wrong?

2. How likely is it to occur?

3. What are the consequences if it does?

4. What do I need to do to counter the threat?

Given the result of that inquiry, the threat analysis should be able to tell the organization what all of the specific threats to each asset are and how each identified threat could exploit that asset. Because of dependencies between the various parts of the organization, the threat analysis should also be able to tell how the impacts on a given asset will influence any other part of the asset base. In order to keep the threat picture up to date, threat analyses are routinely done to identify the threats that each asset faces. Given those goals, threat analyses test specific scenarios within the preparedness plan. Typically, that entails assessing the performance of the electronic and human resource elements that ensure the continuity of critical assets, rather than examining the general threats to the entire asset base.

The aim of a threat analysis is to characterize the specific harm or disruption that a given event will cause and then evaluate the ability of the associated procedure to protect against that harm. The outcome of that assessment either validates the ability of the procedure or identifies areas of improvement. Because the threat picture is constantly changing, it is important for an organization to regularly assess the critical assets in the preparedness plan in order to ensure that they are properly protected. This is an ongoing commitment on the part of the organization, since without a continuously functioning operational threat analysis process in place, it is impossible to ensure the continuing effectiveness of the preparedness plan.

# Chapter Summary

- The role of continuity is to restore functioning to pre-disaster status.
- Continuity primarily ensures the security of data and processing in the event of a disaster.
- Continuity is a strategic function.
- The purpose of contingency planning is to anticipate disasters with a formal response.

- The role of contingencies in ensuring preparedness is to provide planning targets.

- Disaster planning focuses on a small set of specific events rather than general continuity.

- Policies are required in order to develop continuity designs.

- The recovery time objective specifies the maximum acceptable downtime for the information processing operation.

- The recovery point objective specifies the minimum level of trustworthiness that is required for the restored data.

- A data recovery hotsite provides near instantaneous recovery and total data integrity protection by mirroring the real-time processing activity at the primary site.

- A data recovery warmsite is the next step down from total redundancy; it provides the equipment and communications interfaces that allow the system to perform automatic backups in the most efficient timeframe possible.

- A data recovery coldsite is a secure storage facility for routine backups done at the primary site; it is a cost-efficient solution to continuity where longer RTOs and RPOs can be tolerated.

- Regular operational evaluations of the continuity process ensure that the process can be sustained over time.

- A business impact analysis uses threat scenarios to determine what the consequences are for some particular aspect of the business operation.

- Threat analysis is a continuous operational process that tells an organization what all of the specific threats to each asset are and how each identified threat could exploit that asset.

# Key Terms

**Business impact analysis** Routine evaluation of the business environment in order to ensure continuing relevance of the continuity plan.

**Continuity planning** Planning to ensure that critical functions and data of the organization are sustained in the event of disaster.

**Continuity strategy** Specific strategy to ensure continuity.

**Crisis management** Another term for disaster planning.

**Data recovery coldsites** Alternative site that would allow migration of staff to ensure recovery with some loss of data.

**Data recovery hotsites** Alternative site that mirrors processing of a primary site in real time.

**Data recovery warmsites** Alternative site that provides the same capabilities of the primary site. However, data is backed up to the secondary site on a schedule so there will be losses based on optimum economic value calculations.

**Disaster impact classification** Prioritization of a disaster based on the harm it would cause.

**Disaster recovery plan** The specific steps the organization will take to recover its information processing function and data following a foreseen disaster.

**Disaster scenario** Assumptions about the course of a disaster embedded in the disaster recovery plan.

**Escalation procedures** Procedures that allow the organization to respond in a disciplined fashion to an unforeseen event.

**Optimum tradeoff** Finding an optimum relationship between recovery time and recovery point based on economic factors.

**Preparedness plan** The organization's specific strategy to respond to foreseen disasters.

**Prioritization** Planning the order in which a threat will be addressed based on the potential harm it will cause.

**Recovery point objective (RPO)** The specific level of integrity that data will be restored following a disaster.

**Recovery time objective (RTO)** The specific time that the organization estimates will be required to achieve restoration of the system and its data.

**Redundancy** The approach of utilizing alternative sites as a means of ensuring against loss of data and functionality.

**Restoration** The process of ensuring that data is restored to a desired level of integrity following a disaster.

**Threat analysis** Continuous operational analysis of the threat environment in order to identify any changes that will have to be planned for.

# Questions from the CIO

The CIO requires you to brief her on the current status of your investigation. This will be an important part of your continuing work on this project, since it is essential to be able to describe all of the ramifications of the continuity process. Consequently, the CIO would like you to answer the following questions for her:

1. The overall enterprise continuity response is organization-wide and strategic. Why does that have to be the case? What would be the outcome if it were limited to just some units?

2. The enterprise continuity process is based around defined contingency scenarios. Why is this necessary? How should those contingencies be developed and what should they be based on?

3. The continuity planning process involves specific steps to protect data, equipment, and personnel. There are also other factors that might be addressed in a continuity plan. Name one other aspect of a continuity plan and explain why it is important.

4. Classification of events into types allows for cost-effective responses. Explain that statement and tell me what the consequences would be if types were not used.

5. Policy is the basis for every aspect of the continuity design process. Why are policies and designs so closely linked in the development of continuity responses?

6. DR hotsites are effective solutions, but they have a number of side effects that might not be so desirable. Name three problems with DR hotsites and explain why they might

prevent implementing that kind of approach. Also, tell me one standard way of getting around one of those problems.

7. The primary question that has to be answered for a warmsite is the timing of the backup. What other things need to be considered when contemplating a warmsite solution?

8. Coldsites are useful as low-cost solutions to the continuity problem, but they have several drawbacks that make them unattractive. Itemize those drawbacks and explain why they are considerations.

9. Business impact evaluations in the operational environment concentrate on answering four questions. What are those questions and why are they meaningful to the continuity process?

10. An ongoing threat analysis is necessary because the threat picture changes constantly. Name three areas of threat that always have to be considered, and itemize three general risks that might be likely to undergo frequent change in each of those areas.

# Hands-On Projects

Using the case in Appendix 1, develop a detailed plan to protect the company from equipment failure at its primary site. Ensure that the following requirements are satisfied:

- The integrity of the data will be preserved as economically as possible.
- There will be minimal interruption in the order entry and shipping functions.
- The plan will be sustainable.
- All disasters that might be encountered in the upper Midwest will be mitigated by a plan.

Extra credit will be granted if the student can demonstrate an economic justification for the RTO and RPO that is selected.

# chapter 10

# The Incident Management Competency

## Ensuring That the Company Dodges the Bullet

*It was Friday evening, and the CISO was pulling the curtains of the floor-to-ceiling windows that formed the outer wall of his office in preparation for closing up for the weekend. He stood there for a minute with his hands clasped behind his back and looked out over the East River. From his perch 44 stories up, he could see down past Roosevelt Island and Hunters Point to the traffic crawling through the freezing drizzle across the Long Island Expressway Bridge. More often than not, he would already have been on the train headed in that direction, since he lived in Manhasset. But today, he had spent the news hour monitoring the 62-inch plasma TV in his office.*

*A couple of months ago, he had had that TV hooked to multiple tuners so that he would be able to watch six channels at the same time, in separate windows. Normally, he just used that feature to follow his favorite football and basketball teams. But today he had another, more personal, motive; he was watching CNN, CNBC, and Fox as well as WNBC4, WABC7, and Fox5 waiting for one particular story to appear. He had monitored every one of those news channels throughout the early evening, but the report he was looking for had either missed the news cycle or had been contained. Instead, the airwaves were full of stories featuring puppies, small children, and Santa Claus.*

*The CISO snapped off the TV in disgust and headed for the executive elevator. He had been hoping for a tidbit that was a little meatier than those cheerful tales about holiday shopping. The source of his displeasure lay in the fact that he knew that his company's main competitor in global retail had just lost most of its customer information to some faceless hacker out there in* cyberspace. His spy network in the other company, which he had carefully built up with free Knicks and Yankees tickets, told him that perhaps 50 million consumer credit records had been stolen. If that was true, then that day's theft topped the prior record of 46 million, which was set back in 2007. In the midst of the holiday season, that kind of record-setting performance was not something that their chief competitor wanted to be known for. He made a mental note to check with his network over there in the other company to find out how they had managed to steer clear of that dubious distinction.

As the CISO entered the elevator, he held the door for the CEO, who was coming down the short flight of wide marble stairs from what the other company executives drolly called "the Penthouse." The CEO, who was a true power player in the company, made the CISO nervous. As the doors closed, the CISO said with an uneasy grin, "Glad it was them, not us." That just irritated the CEO, who had always thought that the CISO was way too pleased with himself. Announcing the theft of 50 million credit cards in the middle of the Christmas buying season was not an event that the CEO wanted to even think about. So the CEO said to the CISO, with just the slightest hint of menace in his voice, "Why don't you drop by my office bright and early on Monday morning and bring me up to speed on your plans for ensuring that the same thing doesn't happen to us." With those words still hanging in the Christmas air, they both headed in opposite directions, the CEO to his limousine and the CISO back to his office. It was going to be a long weekend.

Back on the 44th floor, the CISO flipped his custom executive office lighting system back on and gazed out the window in the direction of LaGuardia Airport. It was full night across the river now, and all he could see were the lights of Queens. As he stood there looking out the window at the snow that was beginning to fall, he thought about how he was going to approach the challenge that the CEO had just dropped in his lap. Since he was a strategist at heart, the CISO always ran down a mental checklist of the steps that had already taken to counter the problem.

First, he was able to check off the creation of an incident management policy and all of its related activities. Developing that policy and the associated procedure manual had been a side project during the time they had been doing the role definitions for the company. He was glad that he had had the foresight to get such a manual written, even though it meant that he had not seen much of the wife and kids during that period. He was also happy that he had had the good sense to formally publicize that procedure manual throughout the company, since it established the fact that he was not a late-comer to the party. Finally, he was especially thankful that he had already selected and then put in place what he considered to be a crack team of **incident response** professionals.

The CISO pulled out a pad of paper and began to make a list of items to cover with the CEO on Monday. The list had seven action areas outlined on it. Those areas represented the general steps that the CISO planned to take to formalize the incident response process. Additionally, the CISO felt it would be a good idea to cross-reference the items on that notepad to the standard set of activities that the EBK specifies for incident management. What he found were the same seven activities. These were all policy-based, in that each activity was meant to be implemented across the organization as a whole:

1.  Coordinate with stakeholders to establish the incident management program.

2.  Establish relationships between the incident response team (IRT) and other groups, both internal (e.g., legal department) and external (e.g., law enforcement agencies, vendors, and public relations professionals).

3.  Acquire and manage resources, including financial resources, for incident management functions.

4. *Ensure coordination between the IRT and the security administration and technical support teams.*

5. *Apply lessons learned from information* **security incidents** *to improve incident management processes and procedures.*

6. *Ensure that appropriate changes and improvement actions are implemented as required.*

7. *Establish an incident management measurement program.*

# Considerations in the Incident Management Process

An incident is any event that disrupts normal operating conditions. Incidents can range from user errors and power disruptions to malicious activity. The role of incident management is to maintain the incident response capability of the organization over time. The general incident response process encompasses a set of logical monitoring, analysis, and response activities. The incident response management function integrates these activities into a substantive and appropriate response to each adverse event as it happens. Incident response management ensures that any potentially harmful occurrence is first identified and then reported and that the response is fully managed.

## Foreseen and Unforeseen Events

The incident response management process applies whether the organization is reacting to an event that was foreseen or unforeseen. The only difference in the execution of the process is in whether the actual steps to mitigate the incident were planned in advance. For example, most organizations have a set of specific responses in place to respond to common types of network **intrusions**. The actual substantive response is deployed based on the type of network incident. The organization itself is likely to have automated incident response utilities built into its networks. Because there are only so many ways that a network can be penetrated, those automated responses will counter most classic types of network attacks. So the presence of a pre-defined automated response on a network will ensure a timely and generally appropriate response to a large number of common incidents.

However, many incidents are unforeseen. In that case, the aim of incident response management is to ensure that the nature of the incident is understood in as timely a fashion as possible, and that the best possible response is deployed. The key to ensuring that timeliness is a well-defined and efficient incident reporting process. Proper practice requires the actual report of any new occurrence to be submitted to a single central coordinating entity for action. Central coordination is necessary because new attacks do not usually present themselves in a single neat package. Usually, a series of suspicious occurrences represents the signature of an impending attack. A single entity for analysis has to be established to ensure that all of the information, from every diverse source, is properly assembled and analyzed. Once the nature of the incident is understood, the coordinator ensures that that understanding is sent to the right people for a decision about the response.

## Keeping Watch: Monitoring and Incident Identification

An incident response is initiated by the detection of an event that the organization deems harmful. The incident response procedure is then set in motion through a formal incident reporting process. Incident reporting ensures that every potentially harmful event gets an organizationally sanctioned response. Effective incident reporting relies on the presence of a well-established monitoring function. That function monitors the overall operation and it is designed to provide the most timely incident identification possible. The goal of incident identification is to distinguish the presence of a security violation, an attempt to exploit a security flaw, or even the existence of an inadvertent breakdown in security functioning. The aim is to make that identification in as timely a fashion as possible. The monitoring techniques that are used to ensure that timeliness can range from audits of system logs all the way through to the use of automated intrusion detection systems (IDS) or simple malware and virus checking scans.

## Getting the Incident Report to the Right People

The incident reporting function is set in motion when an incident is identified. Just like a crime in the physical universe, once the occurrence of an incident can be confirmed and its nature understood, an incident report is filed. The incident report documents both the type and estimated impact of the event. The incidents that are reported should not be just limited to major events. They can include everything from routine security breakdowns in the system all the way through intentional, or inadvertent, violations of policy. If the incident has been foreseen, then the response would typically follow the agreed-on resolution specified in the incident response plan. This recommendation would be used by the IRT.

Whatever the nature of the breakdown or violation, the incident reporting process must directly and reliably lead to an appropriate response. That response is normally provided by a formally designated and properly trained IRT. IRTs operate like the police; they are called as soon as practicable after the event and they follow a disciplined process to ensure the best possible result. The IRT is given specialized training and equipment that is designed to ensure that optimum resolution. The fact that the IRT has been given that training and equipment to achieve that purpose also justifies why the IRT should deal with the event, rather than the people who might have reported it, as shown in Figure 10-1.

## Potential Incidents and Active Incidents

In practice, incidents are either potential or active. Potential incidents include things like pre-attack probes, unauthorized access attempts, denial of service attempts, or flaws in the organization's security architecture that are identified by the staff. One other source could be the formal notification of the existence of a potential security vulnerability by an outside organization, such as Microsoft or US-CERT. Potential incident reports can also result from internal analyses done by the users of the software. For instance, IT management can send out a notice that vulnerability has been identified during the use of the product.

The advantage that potential incidents have over active incidents is the time that is normally available to craft a proper response. That thinking-through process is typically supported by a comprehensive analysis of all of the technical and business factors associated with any potentially harmful outcomes. Once the likelihood and impact of exploitation is known, a deliberate response can be developed and implemented that most appropriately fits the precise nature of the incident.

The organization does not have that luxury of time in the case of active incidents. If it is possible to confirm that an unauthorized access, denial of service, or successful vulnerability exploitation has occurred, then the appropriate corrective actions must be undertaken immediately. Those actions are dictated by the circumstance. They can range from applying a

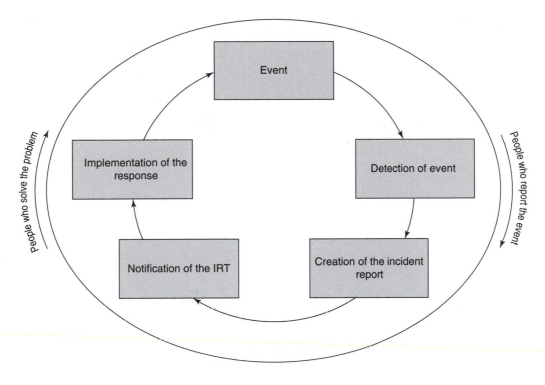

**Figure 10-1** The role of the IRT

© Cengage Learning 2012

technical patch, reconfiguration, or reinstallation of the system all the way up to a change in policy and procedure or the implementation of new enforcement mechanisms for the entire organization.

The IRT is responsible for responding to an active incident. The goal is to contain any immediate harm from the incident and to study the circumstance of the occurrence in order to prevent its happening again. Where a technical process is involved, the incident response function supervises the implementation of the change to the target system. Where a change to organizational policy or procedure is necessary, the IRT facilitates the coordination and documentation activities that have been prescribed.

# Establishing a Structured Response

It is a given that incidents will occur. How well those incidents are responded to is dictated to a great extent by the level of preparation of the organization. The role of the incident management function is to ensure that adequate preparation has been done to underwrite that success. Given that proper preparation is a key requirement, it is essential to develop commonly accepted and properly understood statements about the steps that have to be taken to respond to incidents. Accordingly, a detailed set of formal policies and practices is needed to establish that structure of the organization's incident response capability.

Depending on the organization and its business requirements, the structure of the incident response process can be varied. Therefore, the best way to decide what should be in a structured incident response process might be to think about what specific guidance and expectations senior management should have about how incidents should be handled. Broad guidance, such as "the incident response team is authorized to take appropriate steps deemed necessary to contain, mitigate, and resolve a security incident" provides a governing framework. Specific guidance, such as who is authorized, how much authority they have, and under which circumstance, helps to direct the process in the case of specific events. These itemized practices are formalized in an organizational procedure manual that describes the specific behaviors required to satisfy the aims of each **incident response policy**.

Along with a prescription of organizationally standard practices, the incident response manual provides a sanctioned definition of concepts such as "incident" and "incident response." The manual also specifies the role of the IRT, since a clear definition of those specific responsibilities ensures that everyone will be on the same page during the process.

## Arraying Resources to Ensure the Right Level of Response

One of the first tasks of incident response management is to deploy the right resources to address the incident. In that respect, a balance has to be maintained between responding appropriately and over-reacting. The incident response manager gathers initial facts, analyzes them, and determines the level of response. The investigator on the scene can then decide the right level of involvement for escalating the incident.

That decision is based on the details of the initial investigation and guidance provided in the incident management policy. There are many factors that go into making the decision to respond to an incident. Not responding can result in losses and interruptions to business. So can improper responses. Errors in response mechanisms can lead to issues that will impede legal and/or civil actions against malicious parties. Well-designed directions can assist incident response management in answering those questions and improve the odds of a successful response.

## Formulating the IRT

The centerpiece of the incident response process is the IRT. This group of technicians, managers, and support personnel, as shown in Figure 10-2, has to be able to perform the tasks required to investigate and recover from incidents. The team is staffed by people with the skills and experience needed to address a given type of occurrence. Ideally, that team will comprise subject matter experts who have sufficient practical knowledge of the area that is being impacted by the event, as well as the training needed to implement the incident response plan. Because most incidents in cyberspace require specialized tools, it is important to also ensure that the appropriate technology is provided to do the information gathering and perform the analyses as well as to implement the desired response.

Since the right personnel and equipment have to be designated to properly address the incident, a specific IRT has to be assigned to each incident. Because many incidents are similar, these teams are likely to be able to address a range of possible eventualities. For instance, it doesn't matter what type of fire breaks out: the logical response would be to organize a group of people into a team that has the training and expertise to be able to

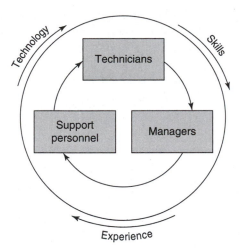

**Figure 10-2** The building of the IRT

*© Cengage Learning 2012*

fight fires. As a result, it is possible to address most types of fires with a single group of specialized personnel.

On the other hand, the incident types that a given team is assigned to also have to be formally documented. It would make no sense for management to send the fire department to deal with a law enforcement issue, or the police to deal with a fire. Therefore, it is important to ensure that the types of incidents that each formally constituted IRT has been designed to address are well defined, appropriate to the skills and training of the team, and that the assignment is commonly understood across the organization.

## Managing the IRT

Organizational strategy and expectations for incident response defines the structure of the IRT, its members, and their responsibilities. An important element in creating the team is getting its composition right. Usually, the IRT is composed of a team manager, computer specialists, network specialists, computer crime investigators, corporate legal, public affairs, and security personnel.

For each incident, the team manager examines the initial information in order to determine which elements of the full team are needed for the investigation. Factors that the team manager might consider include the number and type of hosts, networks, and operating systems involved; the assets that were attacked and the sophistication of the attack; and the business impact, publicity, internal political issues, and any corporate liability.

# The Right Strategy Emerges

*The CISO liked to stay at the Waldorf when he was working over the weekends; part of the attraction was in the amenities, of course. But mainly, he just liked the idea that important people had been staying there for more than a century. Plus, it was just a short walk down*

*East 50th to the company's headquarters, so he didn't need a cab. The snow the night before had already turned to grey slush, but it was a bright and sunny day with temperatures somewhere in the 40s. As the room service guy was laying out his breakfast, the CISO was looking down on Park Avenue and watching the traffic whizz by. He was thinking two things. First, he was thinking about the difference between weekend and weekday morning traffic. Second, he was thinking that he needed a plan, and he needed it fast.*

*The CISO suspected that Monday's meeting with the CEO was not going to be the usual "big-picture" session. So he was going to have to bring along with him, in sufficient descriptive detail, conclusive proof that the company could identify and respond to incidents in a timely and highly effective manner. In the CISO's mind, that was going to require him to prepare an itemized plan for the incident management function. That plan would have to undoubtedly embody the principles of good incident management, and it would also need to clearly illustrate to the CEO and whoever else was at that meeting the precise means that the CISO proposed to employ to satisfy those principles.*

*That meant that at a minimum this weekend, he would have to produce a comprehensive statement of the coordinated and systematic activities that the organization planned to take to respond to likely types of incidents, as well as the mechanism that would be used to respond to incidents that were unplanned for. He knew that in order to prepare this plan, he would also put together a standard definition of what the likely incidents were and what the criteria were that would trigger a response. In addition, he would also have to specify the composition and role of the IRT. The problem was that he didn't know all of the details himself. That led him to call the manager of network operations at his home in Jersey City and ask him to meet him at the CISO's office in an hour.*

*The CISO made it clear that the request was not a suggestion: it was an order. On the other hand, the CISO didn't consider his demand to be much of an imposition, since the network manager could just hop on a PATH train at Journal Square and be at the CISO's office in an hour. Given the network manager's carefully nurtured Grizzly Adams persona, the guy would probably want to walk over from 33rd Street. Considering the fact that the CISO was going to be holed up all weekend in his office working on the incident response plan, that seemed like a fair trade. Since the Giants were out of the playoff race one more year, he knew he wouldn't have much to do that Sunday anyhow. So the CISO finished breakfast, dressed, and then walked the five blocks to his office.*

*The reason why the CISO particularly wanted the manager of network operations was that that person also doubled as the primary team manager for all of the company's IRTs. The network manager was also the IT person with the most experience in the company. He arrived as promised, all six foot six and two hundred and fifty pounds of him, complete with bushy beard. The CISO tried and failed to imagine the network manager in his domain, which was the network operations center. Instead, all he could imagine when he saw the network manager was tall trees and chain saws. Nevertheless, he had had long-standing proof that the guy really knew his stuff. They both were aware of the fact that the primary responsibility of the IRTs was to respond to security incidents with a formal investigative process. The goal of that investigation was to produce a bias-free account of the facts associated with an incident and then deploy an appropriate response.*

*The network manager explained that the incident response process followed five standard steps. The first step represented simple common sense: the investigator had to determine whether an incident had, in fact, occurred. If that was the case, then the investigator tried to get an accurate estimate of the harm that the incident represented. Once the potential impact of the incident was determined, the incident response manager would decide on the level of response that was required and which team members should be involved. The incident manager and the team then took the steps to control and contain the incident. Once the incident was brought under control, its characteristics were documented for further study. This final step was, in effect, a forensics exercise, so the formal responsibilities of the team ended there. But the incident manager still had to ensure that the chain of custody of the evidence was maintained.*

*Based on what the network manager had just told him, the CISO could see a substantive strategy emerging. He was well aware of the fact that the chief problem with getting any kind of hard and fast approach implemented for incident response was that each incident is different in its particulars. It would be nearly impossible to put together a single cookie-cutter plan to dictate the right set of responses for a large, complex organization. However, the opening was clearly there to deploy an appropriate response from a collection of pre-planned responses. Thus, a suitable response could be implemented as soon as the incident was characterized.*

*For instance, the network manager told the CISO that he had a detailed plan for incident response associated with the company's web servers. He had a separate one for its e-mail servers, another for its business records in the databases, and so on. Each of these plans worked like a landing checklist: the people responding to the incident simply ran down the items on the list in a sequence to ensure the safe interruption and recovery of those services.*

*Keeping that advice in mind, the CISO could see that all he needed to do was to get all of the company's other functional managers to develop the same type of contingency plans for the likely incidents in their areas. Those plans could then be validated for effectiveness and the team could be trained to ensure a disciplined and appropriate response. In the CISO's mind, having an optimized response already in place for each likely incident would eliminate the confusion or errors that might otherwise occur in the middle of dealing with an event. All that would be required would be a customized set of pre-approved checklists, and the protocols for deploying and implementing the steps specified in each list.*

*The CISO was elated. Customizing security actions based on the specifics of the situation was the underlying basis of his entire approach to organizing the security operation. He knew that the EBK's recommendations for the planning process centered on the same type of strategy. As a result, he was certain that he could use the authority that the EBK had gained around the company to sell his plan in the Monday meeting.*

## Creating a Systematic Response

There are several steps that should be taken to prepare an enterprise to respond to incidents in a systematic way. First, there needs to be a current inventory of each of the elements of the organization that have been placed under the incident management function. That inventory requires the organization to identify all of the specific organizational processes and activities under incident management control.

Once all of the affected parts of the organization are identified, the impact of any prospective response has to be fully characterized. That includes a description of the impact on existing policies, procedures, and systems, along with any cascading or ripple effects that might take place as a result of a specific response. Besides the obvious technical or procedural implications that are involved in this characterization, this description could also touch on such diverse things as legal, regulatory, and forensic responsibilities.

That inventory should include all of the information assets that the organization chooses to protect as well as the equipment and systems that process it. It is also important to have an exact idea of the status of the software on those systems. Obviously, it would be hard to deploy an effective response if the security status of the software and equipment, which are part of that response, is unknown. For example, prior to instituting a response to a network intrusion, the current status and configuration of the network devices, servers, and clients has to be known. Having systems patched and up to date not only eliminates many potential vulnerabilities, but it also assists in ensuring that the people who are responding to the incident know where to start. When patching is ad-hoc, IRT members will not know whether the system they are trying to address was protected against the specific vulnerability that caused the incident.

## Developing Baseline Metrics

The effectiveness of the incident management process is hard to assess, because there are few metrics that can be used to characterize an ad-hoc event like an incident. Because incidents take place outside of day-to-day, routine operations, they often do not fit into the standard measures that an organization uses to judge performance. As a result, the only metric that can be reliably used to characterize the performance of the incident management process is the benchmark. In order to use benchmarks, it is first necessary to document the current state of the items under incident management control. That state has to be known because current status is used to assess whether variations have occurred in the execution and outcome of the process. Accordingly, any tests and reviews that are done in order to assess the performance of the incident management process must be measured against past benchmarks.

An incident management benchmark is typically taken at the point in time where the organization was last known to be secure. In order to establish an assessment process for incident management, the organization must be able to confirm that it is in a secure state. For that reason, the first step in creating a metrics program is to confirm that all of the elements under control of the incident management function are understood and documented and can be confirmed to be correct. At a minimum, this documentation should include an overall statement of the standard assessment process for each element under incident management control and a generic operational testing and review plan to ensure that those procedures retain their effectiveness. There should also be a mechanism to ensure that all relevant staff members are adequately trained in their incident response role and that all staff are capable of utilizing the tools that have been provided to address a given incident.

# The CISO Steps up to the Plate

*Monday rolled around and the CISO was sitting in the board room with his carefully prepared incident management plan. The plan had taken two long days to develop, but the CISO thought it would provide all of the assurance the CEO was asking for. He was dressed as usual in one of* his $4,000 Armani suits and he was freshly shaved, showered, and looking as chipper as ever. The fact that he had only had about four hours of sleep in the past 48 hours was immaterial, since his only aim that morning was to make sure the CEO didn't see him sweat.

He was actually looking forward to this meeting, since the plan he had under his arm outlined a simple but effective process. It was based on the initial idea that he and the network manager had discussed about 40 hours earlier, which at that point seemed like an eternity. The fundamental strategy involved a grass-roots process for first identifying, then characterizing, and finally prioritizing potential incidents. It also included a mechanism that would allow all major stakeholders in the company to customize a planned response to the incidents that they saw as most pressing.

The CEO walked into the room with his primary supporters from the board following in his wake. He sat down at the end of the long conference table and quickly dispensed with the usual niceties. Then he turned to the CISO and said, "Well let's hear it." The CISO finally had the opportunity to step up to the plate in front of the people who were his boss's boss, and he was planning on swinging for the fences. The fact that the news had finally broken that morning that the other company had been hit for 50 million records particularly aided his cause. The fallout for the other company on Wall Street was an ugly spectacle indeed. The CISO knew that everybody in the room was looking at him to provide the answers, and they were ready to spend whatever it took to make sure that they never had to face the shareholders with the same sad story as their peers across town.

The presentation featured the usual handouts and PowerPoint show. What the CISO outlined was an across-the-board process. It was aimed at identifying all of the priority areas of threat and preparing customized responses based on local knowledge about the best approach to take to handle any incident should it occur.

The CISO's plan called for an immediate marshalling of the heads of the company's functional business units and then the subsequent delegation of the incident identification and response planning down to the local level in each unit. He explained that that assignment would give the company a boots-on-the-ground picture of what had to be done that would ensure that the responses fit the exact circumstances of the situation. Obviously, the time and expense of doing that would be a cost. But he pointed across the room to the NASDAQ ticker on the TV screen in the corner as simple evidence as to why that cost was justified. Nobody in the room wanted to be responsible for losing 40 percent of the company's stock value in a mere three hours. The approval to go ahead with the implementation process was automatic. As usual, the CISO turned to his old friend the EBK to validate his implementation plans.

# Planning for Incident Management

The goal of incident management is to maintain a proper and timely response to all potential, logical threats. Each of those individual responses embodies the most appropriate and capable set of measures to address the specific threat. Incident management oversees and coordinates the deployment of those measures in a way that is designed to best ensure that the most effective possible actions have been taken to counter that threat. In order to ensure that effective coordination and control is exercised over the standard incident response process at all times, the incident management function itself has to be properly planned.

## Making Incident Management Routine

In order to ensure consistent execution, the incident response process should be founded on a standard set of policies, procedures, and techniques. The role of incident management is to ensure that the conduct of the incident response process is properly aligned with the dictates of those relevant policies, procedures, and techniques. Because they involve the entire organization, incident management has to be established by formal plan.

The goal of the incident management plan is to ensure that the incident management process is established as part of the routine, day-to-day functioning of the entire organization. The incident management process then routinely coordinates the activities outlined in that plan. The plan itself specifies the standard practices that will be employed during the response to a given class of incidents. It also itemizes the schedule or timetable that will be followed for the actual response process. Because it is the sanctioned statement of how the incident response process will be conducted, the formal incident management plan is also an important baseline document for the organization as a whole: it serves as a point of reference for the day-to-day decision making about the incident response process.

In addition, the plan guides the allocation of resources for the overall conduct of the incident response process. This is particularly useful with respect to the allocation of financial resources, because it allows decision makers to make the tradeoffs between their protection needs and available resources. The incident management plan organizes and focuses the deployment of those resources in a way that allows them to be used most effectively.

The incident management plan makes explicit the organization's strategy for responding to incidents. That strategy serves as the basis for the deployment of the overall set of planned responses. It is an excellent way to gauge ongoing performance, since it makes the steps in the process explicit. Because the incident management plan details the exact actions that will be taken in the event of an incident, it also serves as an ideal mechanism for assessing whether the contractual and regulatory obligations of the organization are being met.

Finally, the incident management plan provides the basis for ensuring that the right technical and procedural response is in place to address a specific class of incidents. Because it will serve as a guidepost for a number of different constituencies, the incident management plan should be simple and easy to understand. It should leave all of the members of the organization knowing precisely what activities will be carried out in the event of an incident and the timing for performing them.

## Incident Response and Data

Because of the need to choose the right pre-planned responses, the incident management process has to collect as much information as possible about its immediate environment. It also has to ensure that the shape of the environment continues to be understood over time. Accurate knowledge of the environment is essential to the structuring and long-term maintenance of the incident management process.

Therefore, it is critical to gather data to provide the most in-depth understanding of the nature of the incidents taking place in the organization. Knowing the "who, what, why, when, and where" of an incident can lead to more accurate decision about the best course to follow in the event of the next occurrence of that incident. That is why the information that is collected as part of the initial incident detection is so essential to the rest of the process.

The first step in implementing an incident management process is to develop a formal means to record data about events in the organization's immediate environment. That includes recording everything from political and weather data, right down to threats to the hardware, software, and network elements. The information recorded through that data-gathering mechanism will then provide useful insight as to threats that might occur. That knowledge can then be used to develop and fine-tune the response. Without such a record, the organization might be fated to repeat history.

The information that is gathered should be as quantitative as possible, since measurement-based data can be analyzed for such things as inferential and descriptive trends. The availability of analyses based on a rich and comprehensive pool of incident data will help decision makers handle immediate incidents, as well as to chart the course for the long-term deployment and coordination of the incident response process.

## Containment Considerations—the Problem of Dependencies

Once the event is understood, the IRT will attempt to isolate and contain all systems that might be affected. The aim is to prevent the spread of the problem. Decisions about the systems that will fall within that containment perimeter have to balance the risk of a contaminated system spreading the problem against the need to keep as many systems running as possible. The aim of this part of the process is to obtain enough information for management to make an informed decision about the potential risks involved in establishing the containment perimeter.

Because of dependencies between systems, this is not a simple matter of just identifying all of the currently affected systems. The team also has to be able to perform a comprehensive scan of all of the affected systems, in as much depth as is necessary, in order to underwrite confidence that the problem has been identified and contained. In particular, simply restoring the affected systems without isolating and repairing the vulnerability that caused the incident in the first place would merely be asking for it to occur again.

## Automating the Incident Management Process

Much of the work that is involved in gathering information about an incident is done through the use of automated tools. Automation saves time and reduces the risk of error in the data gathering process. As events are unfolding during an incident, automation can enhance the reliability of the data gathering, as well as the overall execution of the response.

For example, in the middle of an incident, human error can exacerbate the problem of reliability, whereas a tool running a pre-tested script will consistently ensure that the right actions are taken. In addition, automated scripts can make certain that data is preserved correctly for later analysis. Furthermore, automated tool sets make painstaking and time-sensitive tasks like forensic duplication and recovery of digital information much easier and more dependable.

Automation can also leverage staff capabilities with a minimal investment in training. Teaching people how to do accurate and detailed investigative data gathering is time-consuming. The necessity to get the investigation 100 percent correct places a burden on workers during a crisis. Having basic incident response tasks pre-loaded as scripts allows workers to perform complicated tasks without making overly complex demands.

# Ensuring Consistent Execution

*The weekend of Easter, the CEO invited the CISO over to Peter Luger's in Great Neck for a porterhouse. It was one of those days in April that made the CISO think more about baseball than hockey, so he drove the SLK all the way over from Manhasset with the top down. Normally, any conversation with the CEO was a source of some anxiety for the CISO, but today he knew what the topic was and he was looking forward to the chat.*

*The CEO was sipping a nice Pinot Noir at his private table next to the window. It didn't take the CEO long to cut to the chase, since he had a golf date near his place in Sagaponack way out on the other end of the island. The CEO had a concern that he wanted to kick around with the CISO off the record: even though they had spent a lot of money setting up a robust incident management function, nothing had actually happened to justify the expense. The CEO was no dummy, and he realized that the lack of show-stopping incidents to point to was actually a good thing. But his board was not quite as knowledgeable. He asked the CISO for any suggestions about how he could justify the expense of maintaining robust incident protection.*

*The CISO had actually been waiting for that subject to come up for several months, so he had an answer right at his fingertips. The problem was that there was no actual proof of performance for the incident management function, which either he or the CEO could use as evidence that the process was working. He pointed out that any contingency management process like incident management works a lot like car insurance: the people paying for that insurance only think that the cost is justified after they have had an accident. But since the whole idea is not to have accident, people who buy accident insurance have to do so without any real deep-seated appreciation for its usefulness.*

*Even so, the CISO had worked out a solution that he thought would satisfy the most cynical member of the board. His answer was to approach the justifications from an incident perspective. In simple terms, he wanted to justify the system by assessing all of the threats that it was meant to counter and then documenting the effectiveness of the response that was provided. He felt that if incident response management could prove that it could protect the company from the things that it was designed to address, that proof would serve as de-facto evidence that the investment was paying off. In addition, conducting a focused set of evaluations aimed at characterizing the effectiveness of the incident management process would also serve as a realistic demonstration of the things that could go wrong if that process did not exist. Finally, the CISO pointed out that a program of targeted audits and penetration tests fit well with the overall concepts of the EBK evaluate function.*

# Auditing and the Incident Management Process

Even though the responses that incident management coordinates are by definition not part of day-to-day routine, the incident management process itself is a systematic management function. It conducts prescribed incident management activities just like any other management function. What is more, those prescribed activities can be evaluated for such things as reliability and effectiveness. Therefore, a formal organizational review process such as audit can be used to confirm that the incident management process is operating as intended as well as to identify opportunities for future improvement. Periodic audits should be used to ensure that the incident management process continues to operate as planned.

For each intended response, the audit should examine the planned steps, the actual response, and the activities that took place during the occurrence. Based on the results of that examination, a recommendation can be made to senior management about ways that the incident management process can be improved. Among other things, the reports should summarize the effectiveness of the planned actions, how well all parties communicated with each other during the event, how effective the tools and techniques were in producing the desired outcome, and conclusions about how satisfactorily the team was prepared and trained.

The audit process has many applications beyond incident management. It establishes a level of in-depth understanding that will allow managers to judge the performance of the incident response process with some confidence. Within conventional business settings, audit lets managers confirm that the practices they have adopted are achieving their desired results. Audit also ensures accountability in the workforce by documenting the actions of individual workers. Finally, audits apply at any level in the incident management process, from low-level technical activities to high-level management issues. Given all of these advantages, a periodic audit of the performance of the incident response management function can make an important contribution to its overall health.

## The Audit Function and Assessment of Performance

The purpose of audit is to assess the execution of a specified set of activities, which take place within a given setting. The goal of the audit is to verify the correctness of those activities. Audits typically confirm three specific things. The first item is the continuing applicability and relevance of the policies that guide the process. The second item is whether the procedures that have been created to execute the process remain correct and complete. The third item is whether the management of the process is capably overseeing its execution.

Audit involves a number of related processes that all serve the same general purpose, which is to confirm correct practice. Accordingly, in the case of incident management, the items that might be addressed by an audit could include such questions as whether incident management procedures are appropriate, whether the toolsets that are employed in incident management are effective, whether the response and recovery time goals for each incident are achieved, and whether the staff displayed a sufficient degree of capability.

## Conducting an Audit

The audit process maintains accountability by accumulating evidence to support conclusions about the audit target. For that reason, the audit process has to be able to objectively describe every relevant aspect of the operation of the entity being audited. Audit gathers sufficient objective evidence by observing and documenting the specific behavior of the operation under examination. The aim is to gather sufficient evidence to be able to characterize the performance of the function over time, with some degree of assurance.

Since the audit process has to guarantee consistent interpretation, substantive steps have to be taken to ensure that, when faced with the same evidence, all auditors will make the same observations and draw the same conclusions. Those requirements imply the need for a highly specific set of audit criteria. For that reason, audits are always performed using such concrete criteria. The parties in the audit process have to agree in advance what those criteria are. This agreement is necessary because people and organizations typically do not enjoy being audited. Therefore, the exact terms of the examination have to be nailed down.

Audits are scheduled by plan. The auditing personnel have to be given the freedom and independence to perform the audit in that plan. Likewise, the resources necessary to conduct the audits should also be specified and cross-referenced to the audit objectives. An audit manager is typically designated to oversee the audit itself. The role of this manager is to supervise, monitor, and evaluate the activities of the audit team. The audit manager selects the auditors, assigns the various audit roles and responsibilities, plans and schedules audit activities, and assumes responsibility for overseeing the audit reporting. The auditors themselves must have the technical and professional know-how to perform a proper audit.

The audit process is likely to involve a number of related steps, many of which are documentation intensive. Therefore, prior to conducting the audit, the auditors typically prepare working documents for use during the process. These documents are tailored to the circumstance that is being audited. They include the checklists that auditors will use to evaluate the audit target and the forms that will be used to gather evidence. These checklists and forms are critical documentation artifacts; they guide the execution of the process and, to some extent, shape the form of the conclusions.

When it comes to technology, it is important when planning the audit to keep two rules in mind. First, electronic records have to be audited using the same methodology and level of rigor that is applied to the more traditional body of audit evidence. Second, the outcomes and conclusions of the review of electronic records have to be recorded in the exact same fashion as the traditional audit evidence. Checklists are particularly important in ensuring proper coverage in both respects, because they direct the auditor's attention to items of interest that they might not otherwise consider. In applied terms, if a technical item is not on a checklist it is unlikely to be reviewed. Typically, the checklist ensures that meaningful aspects of technical items, like the operating system and network utilities, are always examined. In addition, the checklist will identify and call out system records such as event logs, which are automatically maintained by the system and which are essentially invisible to auditors.

## Ensuring the Correctness of Audit Evidence

After the collection phase, the evidence that is obtained during the audit must be authenticated. Since much of audit is a matter of expert opinion, auditors must make every effort to ensure their perspective is correct. This can only be accomplished by testing their inferences. The goal of the audit process is to gather sufficient reliable, pertinent, and practical evidence to demonstrate that a specified function is being carried out as intended. At the point where the audit is deemed complete, all objective data and conclusions must be authenticated by means of a suitable analysis.

## Penetration Testing: A Different Type of Audit

Penetration testing has come into vogue over the past decade. It is a particularly effective way to evaluate the capability of an organization's security processes, because the penetration tester is taking on the role of the adversary. The tester aims to identify any security vulnerabilities by attempting to penetrate the organization's existing security defenses. Since each of those penetrations would be considered an incident if it were being performed by an actual attacker, penetration testing is a particularly instructive way to evaluate the capability of the incident responses of the organization.

Penetration testing is often referred to as "ethical hacking," because the tester attempts to attack the system at the request of the owner. To be ethical, however, penetration testers need to follow clearly defined rules which are established at the beginning of the process. Since the testers normally employ the same methods or techniques that an adversary would use, penetration tests produce especially meaningful insights into state of the organization's security situation.

The purpose of penetration testing is to evaluate the effectiveness of a given security function. There are a number of different ways that penetration testing is done. All tests can be conducted from the perspective of both external and internal attackers. A penetration test that is initiated from the outside will typically attack the network. Internally focused penetration tests aim to assess the effectiveness of the defenses in the IT environment.

The first is the zero-knowledge test, which is conducted using only publicly available information about the target. The most rigorous form of zero-knowledge test is the double-blind exploit, where the tester has little or no knowledge about the target, and the security staff is not notified that a test will be conducted. Since that situation is the closest to mimicking real life, double-blind testing is a particularly effective method to test the incident identification and response procedures of a target function.

The partial-knowledge exploit involves some information about the target. In this case, the penetration tester is more likely to be mimicking the actions of somebody who is either local, or who has some knowledge of the target.

The full-knowledge exploit is more characteristic of an attacker who has insider knowledge, or who might be an actual insider. Full-knowledge attacks are difficult to defend against, since the attacker already knows where the holes in the system are. Such attacks can be an excellent way to demonstrate the subsequent capability of the incident management process.

Finally, there are targeted tests, which are carried out to examine a pre-defined issue. In many cases, the penetration testing team works with the target's internal IT staff to identify or resolve some sort of specific problem.

Penetration testing generally involves four standard activities, as shown in Figure 10-3. The first of these is exploration, which is where the target is identified and characterized. The second step is examination, which is where different probes are used to gather data that will support the attack. These are typically tool-based. A map of the avenues of attack is then drawn from those probes. Once the target is fully understood, the tester will attempt the exploit that was planned. The final phase in the process is the documentation of findings, typically in the form of a report to the management of the organization sponsoring the penetration test. The results of this report can help an organization evaluate the effectiveness of its defenses as well as its ability to respond to incidents. That understanding can lead to better means of responding to incidents involving applications, networks, and behavioral or physical exploits.

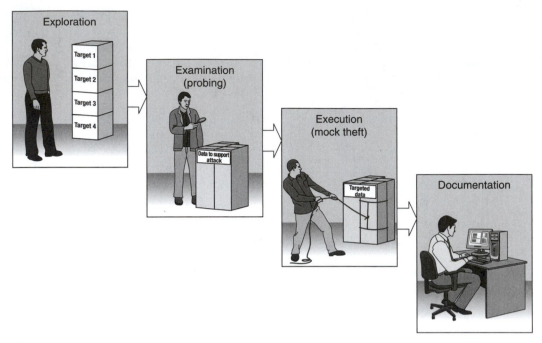

**Figure 10-3** Penetration testing

© *Cengage Learning 2012*

# Chapter Summary

- An incident is any happening that disrupts normal operation.
- The incident response process applies to both foreseen and unforeseen events.
- Incidents can be either potential or active.
- Pre-planned responses can be prepared for potential incidents.
- Pre-planned responses are based on assumptions about various contingencies.
- The incident response team is the key organizational mechanism for responding to incidents.
- The incident response process is coordinated by the incident management function.
- It is necessary to identify priority threats in order to ensure proper use of resources.
- Baseline metrics are important for assessing variations in the incident management process.
- Incident response relies on automation because the process is so complex and time is short.
- Staff capability is important, both in terms of tool use and knowledge of the process.
- Gathering as much data as possible from events will lead to better incident responses.
- Penetration testing is an effective way to assess the performance of incident management.
- Audits provide information that can be used to improve the incident management process.

# Key Terms

**Incident response** The pre-planned set of steps defined in the incident response plan.

**Incident response policy** The general organizational guidelines for how to respond to incidents; meant to help dictate specific procedures.

**Intrusion** An event involving unauthorized access, or a violation of the rules for information retrieval and use.

**Security incidents** Any happenings that could represent harm to information placed under the protection of the incident response function.

# Questions from the CIO

The CIO requires you to brief her on the current status of your investigation. This will be an important part of your continuing work on this project, since it is essential to be able to describe all of the ramifications of the functions of the incident management process. Consequently, the CIO would like you to answer the following questions for her:

1. An incident is any activity that disrupts the normal operation of a computer system. Name four types of potentially disruptive events. Only one of those events can be electronic.

2. Potential incidents represent threats that have yet to happen. Why is the identification of a potential incident a particularly useful thing to incident management, and what is the role of scenarios in the process?

3. What are the primary goals of the recovery function? What are three considerations that have be kept in mind to ensure proper recovery?

4. Incident reports can originate from a number of sources. Name three different types of general sources for an incident report.

5. The IRT is composed of different types of members. Name four potential types of players on an IRT.

6. The best way to restore electronic elements is from a clean backup. What are three considerations that have to be kept in mind when creating the backup?

7. Lessons learned from incidents are important parts of the process. Specifically, why are lessons learned so important, and in what ways do they contribute to improving the process?

8. The IRT can be different for different incidents. Why is that the case? Why is it necessary to have a good understanding of the nature of the incident before forming the team?

9. Penetration testing is a particularly important contributor to the incident management process. Explain why that is the case, and provide examples of how penetration test results can be used to improve the incident response process.

10. Audits gather evidence that can be used to ensure that the process is functioning correctly. Name one other major contribution that an audit can provide to incident management.

# Hands-On Projects

1. Using the case in Appendix 1, outline the contents of the following security-related policies:

   - Incident response policy
   - CIRT membership
   - Incident response checklists

2. Using the case in Appendix 1, outline and document the steps to collect incident response data for three different types of systems:

   - Production
   - Banking
   - Customer service

3. Using the case in Appendix 1, outline the information needed in the incident responder's toolkit for the systems associated with the enterprise.

4. Using the case in Appendix 1, develop an audit plan to assess incident response measures.

5. Using the case in Appendix 1, develop a detailed plan for restoring critical services after an incident. Include all levels of information, operating systems, applications, OS data, and application data.

# chapter 11

# IT Security Training and Awareness

## The Human Factor Is Always a Problem

*It was late spring in New York City, and the CISO was perched at his customary spot on the arm of the massive chair in front of the CIO's desk. He particularly liked sitting that way in meetings because it made him look informal, an image that he carefully cultivated. The compliance officer was also at the meeting, along with the heads of human resources (HR) and IT operations. They were all arrayed in extravagant leather chairs along the window wall to the CIO's right. The CIO's office reeked of executive privilege, which reminded the CISO that someday he would like to have a corner office just like the one he was sitting in now.*

*The topic of the meeting was the company's new generic role definitions. Two months ago, the implementation of those new roles had seemed like a no-brainer. The requirements for each role had been well defined. Likewise, the general duties for each role had been captured in a company-wide **procedure manual**. The CISO had proven in Singapore that the manual could be customized to the specific requirements and culture of each site. Fortunately, the CIO had decided that it would still be good idea to prototype the entire implementation process at a single site.*

*She picked one of the company's more advanced research facilities in Corvallis, which was located 80 miles south of Portland, Oregon. Both the CIO and the CISO had agreed that the Corvallis advanced manufacturing plant was an ideal place to put the standard role definitions into practice. The facility at Corvallis was relatively small, with fewer than 300 employees, but the staff was also diverse enough that the executive team could get a good read on how well the implementation process would work in one of the company's facilities. Moreover, the lines of business in Corvallis were representative of the entire company, and the close proximity of that facility to the Oregon State campus guaranteed a well-educated workforce. Given all of these factors, both the CIO and the CISO were pretty sure that implementing the roles at the Corvallis facility would be an easy early win for them to build on.*

*The succeeding two months had proven just how wrong that assumption was. The CISO had to grudgingly admit that the CIO had been wise to prototype the implementation process rather than just roll it out. The problem with implementing those roles was not with the individualized work practices, which continued to remain provably correct. Instead, the problem lay in the disciplined performance of the day-to-day tasks that were required for each role. Simply put, even though most of the staff had advanced degrees in everything from economics to electrical engineering, the routine execution of their assigned security duties was inconsistent at best.*

*There would be days when an outsider looking at the Corvallis facility could not find a single instance of incorrect practice. But there would also be days when it seemed like the entire staff had forgotten that standard security practice even existed, let alone how to implement it. As a result, in the prior two months, several of the audits and penetration tests, which were being done as validation checks, had shown that it was possible to simply walk through the company's defenses.*

*The result of the Corvallis "disaster," as it was referred to by the members of the company who thought that the CISO was not quite the genius that he thought he was, was a new-found interest in resolving the human factor problem. That was the reason why the CIO, the CISO, the compliance officer, and the heads of HR and IT operations were all meeting in the CIO's office that morning. And it was the reason why the item that was foremost on their agenda was a dependable IT security training and **awareness** program.*

*The CISO was feeling a little "shown up" by the events at Corvallis, so he was scrambling to get back on the high ground. He pointed out that the EBK provided recommendations about the standard approach that a company could take to manage workforce training and awareness.*

# Ensuring Secure Behavior

The goal of the training and awareness function is to ensure a reliable level of secure practice across the entire organization. The awareness part is responsible for communicating the fundamental concepts of information security to everybody in the organization. Those basic concepts are meant to assure a floor level of general knowledge for the overall workforce. On the other hand, a minimum level of basic awareness does not ensure the effectiveness of individual members of the security staff. That kind of assurance can only be provided by focused training. The training function is responsible for making certain that the individuals who perform specific information security tasks have all of the requisite knowledge, skills, and abilities to carry out their designated duties.

In essence, training and awareness involve two separate focuses. Awareness is wide-ranging and general in its aims, whereas training is targeted and involves the delivery of specific knowledge to a defined group. That is why those two functions have to be approached differently in the development of a comprehensive awareness and **training program**.

Training and awareness both help the organization to respond appropriately to security threats. Since there are different types and degrees of threat, organizations will deploy their training and awareness functions differently based on their own specific threat situation. Because of that difference in purpose and application, the design of training and awareness programs has to be approached differently.

For example, it would be acceptable to conduct a simple awareness campaign to ensure against ubiquitous attacks like phishing scams. On the other hand, targeted attacks on the network are likely to require highly specific knowledge about firewall configuration, which the organization would only provide to a few key employees. That knowledge would be supplied to those employees through an intensively targeted program of instruction.

To further illustrate, consider that training and awareness are different activities with some similarities. Each has a distinct purpose and each is part of a progressively more rigorous and extensive learning process. Awareness is the lowest rung on the ladder. Effective awareness programs ensure that all employees at every level in the organization appreciate the need for, and are capable of, disciplined security practice. Security discipline requires every participant to be engaged in coordinated security activities. The fundamental aims of security are then achieved by that coordinated group effort; however, the actual requirements and form of that effort vary across the organization. For example, employees at the highest levels of the company, such as the CIO, CFO, and CIO, are focused on strategic issues. Nevertheless, in order to support the security effort, they have to be aware of all of the issues that have to do with costs, benefits, and overall impact of security failures. Otherwise, they will not be able to make informed decisions about strategic directions. Consequently, building comprehensive understanding at the C-level might actually be one of the most important jobs of the awareness function. Yet awareness is also critical at all of the other levels of the organization; every one of those levels has to be made aware of the security requirements that apply specifically to them.

The relationship between awareness, training, and **motivation** is shown in Figure 11-1.

## The Broad Focus of Awareness

Every organization requires some basic form of awareness in order to ensure that its employees are conscious of and can perform their general security duties. Awareness targets the general user community; a proper awareness function should inform users about their general security duties as well as motivate them to execute those duties on a disciplined basis. Awareness topics might range from steps to ensure the general awareness of security issues to more formal things, such as learning about specific technical functions like the installation of security patches.

Awareness                Training                Motivation

**Figure 11-1** Awareness, training, and motivation

## The Narrower Focus of Training

Training, on the other hand, affects the performance of specific tasks. It is much more evident in the overall effort to maintain workforce competency. Ideally, training should happen when a person is hired. Without adequate training, it is not possible to ensure that employees will know their security duties. Accordingly, the training program should be focused on ensuring that all employees are provided all of the technical and procedural knowledge that they need to perform their jobs correctly.

Training should always be done on a continuous basis. It is human nature for people's attention to wane over time, particularly if tasks involve the same repetitive activities. Also, the drumbeat pace of technological change ensures that any set of procedures or rules will evolve over time. All of the company's employees should receive scheduled, periodic updates to their security knowledge in order to ensure that they continue to understand their specific assurance tasks and all of the applicable conditions of their jobs.

In addition to the general training for all staff positions, specialized training should be required for the members of the staff who are expressly responsible for performing the information security function. Such training should include targeted programs centered on how each individual's responsibilities should be carried out and how those responsibilities should then relate to the general conditions for security. Focused training of key individuals guarantees that those people are both competent as well as generally aware of the terms and conditions of their particular responsibilities.

## Motivating Consistent Performance

The goal of training and awareness is to ensure that people make consistently correct choices about security in their day-to-day work. This requires the ability to identify a potential security issue and the knowledge to act appropriately. Workers must be able to recognize the security concerns that exist for them and know how to respond correctly in each situation. Moreover, those people have to be motivated to take the right actions no matter how personally inconvenient those actions might be for them; security practices can be downright inconvenient at times.

The best way to motivate workers to do the right thing is through training and awareness programs, which are designed to reinforce the importance of disciplined security practice. In order to be effective, the information security process itself has to be performed in a disciplined fashion. That means that all of the employees in the organization have to execute their security duties in a way that will ensure the reliable performance of all required practices. Inconsistent execution of assigned security duties is a serious problem, because any inattention or unsecure practices could potentially open up holes in the organization's defenses that an attacker could exploit.

That requirement for **consistent practice** implies that attention ought to be paid to ensuring the **disciplined behavior** of the workforce at all times. Motivation requires awareness, and nobody can be fully motivated without being given the necessary knowledge to understand the reasons for the behavior that is required of them. Thus, the importance of performing day-to-day security-related tasks in a disciplined manner has to be reinforced for everybody in the company. That is especially true in the case of any practice that adds to the workload of the employee, and unfortunately, information security practices are often viewed as that kind of burden. People must understand both the reason for what they are doing and its importance. That kind of insight is necessary in order to motivate people to do something that they might otherwise consider to be unnecessary work.

An individual's behavior is often based on what has worked in the past. Because people tend to adopt practices based on prior experience, successful experiences form the basis for a person's understanding of correct practice. In an organizational context, the perception of correct practice is often formally embodied in a standard set of principles and procedures, which serves as the practical reference point for defining **acceptable behavior** and unacceptable behavior for the group. In the information security world, these principles and procedures are typically documented in an organization-wide procedure manual, which serves as the basis for structuring and running the training and awareness function.

Training and awareness are essential elements in the information security process because they ensure that all employees understand their security duties. But along with that knowledge, training and awareness should always provide the explicit motivation for carrying out those duties. Motivation is an important concept in assuring secure behavior, because it initiates, directs, and sustains all forms of human activity. It is motivation that underwrites consistent performance of security tasks and ensures a person's willingness to perform their assigned tasks time after time, even if the performance of those tasks becomes tiresome. Motivation also dictates the level and persistence of a person's commitment to the larger aims of security.

Motivation is typically reinforced by **accountability**, which ensures consistent performance and enforces individual responsibility. That is, the things that an individual is asked to do are monitored to ensure that they are done right. That monitoring is part of the organization's overall accountability scheme, which rewards appropriate actions and discourages inappropriate ones. It is impossible to enforce accountability if employees do not know or understand what the organization requires them to do. Therefore, the organization also has to ensure that all of its employees know what is expected of them, as well as the consequences of non-compliance.

Accountability is based on the assignment of individual responsibility for a given set of security tasks, followed by regular monitoring of the execution of those tasks. Along with the explicit assignment of tasks to each of its workers, the organization is also obligated to then make certain that all workers are trained and knowledgeable in all aspects of their particular security duties. That includes keeping workers up to date in all of their assigned practices as they change over time. Being able to ensure that everybody in the organization takes responsibility for personal security duties is a critical condition for ensuring that the business remains protected. No matter how potentially correct the security practices might be, if the people who are responsible for carrying them out do not do so on a disciplined basis, then security breaches are inevitably going to occur. Every organization has to undertake a deliberate, planned effort to maintain every worker's commitment and current knowledge.

# Building a Knowledgeable Workforce

*The upshot of the meeting was that the CISO was designated to fly out to Corvallis and see what he could do about developing a new approach for the training and awareness function— one that would actually work this time. In his view, and the view of the other people in the room, the same model that had been so successful in planning and implementing the overall cybersecurity function would probably work with awareness and training. The actual activities of the program would have to be tailored from the general procedure manual based on the specific situation on the ground in Corvallis.*

*The CISO stepped onto the plane for the six-hour flight to Corvallis with the procedure manual in his briefcase. Business had been good since the unfortunate events of two years prior, so rather than flying into Portland and driving the scenic 80 miles to Corvallis, he flew directly into Corvallis Muni A on the Gulfstream IV that the company had recently purchased at a fire-sale price from a failed brokerage firm. Since he was the only passenger, he had plenty of room to spread out his documentation and go directly to work. His express intention during the flight was to come up with the same type of grass-roots tailoring approach for the training and awareness process as the one that had worked so well in Singapore.*

*The first thing he noticed when he got off the plane was the large number of trees and the small number of buildings. From his city-boy perspective, all of that wildlife made him faintly nervous, so he was glad to see the local security engineer and a couple of his security professionals waiting for him with a brand new SUV. On the way in to the facility, the CISO couldn't take his eyes off of the countryside, which in its own way was as alien to him as Singapore had been. The security engineer was a talkative sort of fellow; as they chatted their way up Route 99, the CISO discovered to his surprise that the security engineer was on the exact same page as the CISO was when it came to what had to be done about the training and awareness function.*

*The security engineer told the CISO that he had been closely involved with the initial attempt to put the role definitions into play and he felt that, although everybody understood what was required of them, it was unrealistic to expect them to carry out all of the little security-oriented tasks without giving them constant reinforcement. In order to ensure that the employees at the Corvallis facility got the message, the generic training and awareness program that was in use across the company would have to be customized to the constituencies at each site.*

*It was an article of faith among the company's security staff that one size definitely did not fit all. Customization of the work functions was not the issue; that had already been done. In fact, all of the work functions for the Corvallis facility had been defined well before the first attempt at instituting secure practice there. But nobody had thought about the need to do the same thing for the training and awareness function itself.*

*The problem was a motivation issue. The staff at that facility, and for that matter at all of the company's other facilities, were accustomed to routine training. Even though the people in Corvallis were professionals, it was impossible to guarantee that they would actually pay much attention to what they were likely to view as one more obligatory training exercise. In the security engineer's view, it was clear that the process of delivering the content had to be carefully customized to ensure that employees would actually internalize what they had learned.*

*As the security engineer continued to talk, the CISO was coming around to the conclusion that motivation might be the single key factor in the successful implementation of any security scheme. The problem always seemed to lie in inspiring people to do things that were not visibly productive. Places like the military enforced the necessary discipline to do unpleasant things by imposing a rigid top-down chain of command. But this was the Corvallis facility, which was full of graduate engineers and MBAs. The CISO knew that those people would not take well to being lined up and told to march in formation. He had to come up with a better plan.*

*That was where the security engineer and his staff of security professionals came into the picture. Based on the security engineer's assumptions about the problem, they had been working on a tailoring process for their site. This had the advantage of both facilitating the security training and awareness at their site as well as providing the basis for customizing the training and awareness process at all of the other sites in the company. This framework was inspired by the EBK design function for training and awareness.*

## Designing the Training and Awareness Program

The training and awareness program ensures the suitable execution of three types of standard organizational activities: routine tasks, **operational duties**, and management responsibilities, as shown in Figure 11-2. The execution of these activities is dictated by policy and implemented by plan. The aim is to build an explicit policy and procedure framework that will contain all of the understanding and motivation needed to ensure secure practice. Much of the design of

**Figure 11-2** Standard organizational activities

the training and awareness program revolves around the development and delivery of content that will ensure optimum routine practice.

## Routine Tasks

Routine tasks are the actions that an individual takes to ensure security during a normal workday. These might entail such things as following secure housekeeping procedures or establishing rigorous individual password protection. Motivation is an important concept with routine tasks, due to their boring and repetitive nature. Even though a long and complex password might ensure against password theft, it is still going to take a certain amount of convincing to get users to adopt one. That persuasion is necessary, because users will know that they will have to enter that password many times a day.

## Operational Duties

As the name implies, operational duties are the activities that ensure the overall security of the system during normal operation. The consistent execution of an individual's operational duties is not just a matter of maintaining the security features of the system. Operational duties include such things as regularly monitoring network use, in order to ensure that prescribed policies and procedures are being followed. Operational duties are often drilled into each employee as part of the overall training process; however, just as with routine tasks, those duties can become so habitual that the individual will not give them the required attention. That lack of focus can lead to serious errors and breakdowns in overall security.

## Management Practice

The category that represents the highest level of **security behavior** is the consistent execution of good management practice. Information security operation has to be properly managed in order to be effective. If proper management is a requirement, then a broader set of considerations than simple routine and operational issues applies. Those considerations can range from ensuring that the security strategy is properly implemented, all the way down to such fundamental activities as doing the supervision necessary to ensure that all of the organization's individual employees are following required security procedures.

In all of these instances, however, the essence of good management lies in ensuring the know-how and motivation for workers to properly do their jobs. Knowledge and motivation do not happen by chance. The final role of the security training and awareness function is to ensure that the organization's managers are capable of doing their jobs right. The training and awareness function also has to ensure that those managers are properly motivated to consistently carry out their assigned duties.

# Training and Awareness: A Constant Evolution

The training and awareness function must guarantee a minimum level of correct and disciplined behavior by all personnel. That level is subjective, so the behaviors that underlie it have to be defined by plan. Decision makers make deliberate judgments about the threats that the organization is likely to face, and then they prepare concrete awareness and training strategies to mitigate those threats. The strategies must ensure that all aspects of knowledge and required behavior are anticipated and then factored into the learning process. For instance, if there is a potential for social engineering exploits, there might be a need to develop a specific awareness campaign to inform the staff about how to counter those attempts.

## Who Receives Training?

In large corporations, this analysis and planning to determine what the necessary learning factors are might amount to a major HR initiative that involves the formal assessment of the educational background of every employee in the organization. With smaller organizations, the decision about what to provide in the way of additional training might require nothing more than listing the specific threats that have been foreseen and the steps to counter them. Whether it is an expensive project or a simple investigation, the aim is to ensure that all necessary learning is provided as required.

## The Role of Discipline

Because people in an organization must be motivated to execute their security duties in a disciplined fashion, a good awareness program also has to ensure that all users will follow good security practice. Since there is a lot of potential material that might be included in an awareness program, one of the responsibilities is to ensure that only material and topics relevant to the target learners is presented. Learners must see and understand how their interests are affected by their actions. The presentation must also be interesting, or it will not ensure the proper level of attention.

## The Role of Knowledge and Capability

Awareness alone does not assure reliable security. It is also necessary to ensure that individuals responsible for performing all specific assurance functions are knowledgeable about the precise requirements of their roles. That implies the need for a greater degree of knowledge and **capability** than is typically provided by an awareness function. That enhanced level of knowledge is typically underwritten by formal training. The purpose of training is to make sure that organizational functions, which are required to ensure safety and security, are performed correctly. Training ensures that all participants have the specific skills necessary to carry out their assignments and that the level of organizational capability is continuously maintained. Training can be expensive, but it is an effective way to guarantee capable, long-term execution of security processes.

A properly designed training program will produce optimally skilled and knowledgeable employees who are ready to execute their day-to-day jobs in a secure fashion. In addition to ensuring a capable staff, a properly functioning training program should also ensure that new hires have the requisite set of identified skills and behavior when they start work.

Moreover, training programs should ensure a continuous increase in the performance of all of the company's personnel. Training programs are established by a plan that defines the precise training requirements for each staff category. The training plan itemizes the schedule and the resource requirements for each identified training need. Because the plan specifies the actions that the company will take to ensure staff capability, it is likely to be complex and hard to maintain. All the same, because of the importance of security to the overall functioning of the company, the security plan must be assured to be as correct as possible. The evolution of the plan should be placed under strict management control at the time it is formulated, and then the contents of the plan should be evaluated on a regular basis to ensure currency.

The plan leads to the actual program, which is developed by the training staff. The training itself is delivered as part of the program. The staff develops a tailored approach, which is designed to meet the security requirements and achieve the required competencies for the various managerial, operational, and technical roles. Planning in this instance is usually based on the current and desired capabilities of the incumbents. The approach employs targeted training materials, manuals, and presentation media. It also defines a method of continuous assessment and performance rating to evaluate the learning needs of each individual. The actual training process is iterative. To ensure currency, each individual in the training program undergoes an annual performance review in order to identify and consider any supplemental educational needs.

The training is guided by a formally documented set of training requirements, which are developed for the organization as a whole. Along with those requirements there should also be customized learning content that ensures the training needs of each individual role. The specific requirements for this content are typically derived from data that is collected as part of the ongoing performance reviews for those roles. The people responsible for administering the training review the feedback obtained from the day-to-day operation. These results are factored into the refinement of the competency requirements and are subsequently reflected in the programmed response. The actual training activities take place in a scheduled fashion. The key to ensuring the continuing effectiveness of this activity lies in the constant formal evaluation and review process that occurs as people are trained and then put that training into day-to-day practice.

## Data and Feedback

The data generated by the assessments can be used to fine-tune the training process. It can also provide feedback to the organization about the progress that is being made toward ensuring that the proper array of trained resources is in place. The data provides an objective overview of the capability of the organization's human resources. Managers can use that data to coordinate strategies and plans for security as well as match the organization's personnel to specific needs and tasks.

For example, it would be pointless to embark on a rigorous software testing program if nobody trained in the discipline of software quality assurance was available at the time. The skills inventory that a properly documented training program would create would identify exactly who the people were in the organization who had the necessary skills. That would allow the organization to deploy its resources more efficiently. If software quality assurance was considered essential to the business case, then the people necessary to perform that function could either be moved from other jobs or hired.

## Ensuring Disciplined Practice

Training is organized, skill-based instruction that is intended to produce an explicit outcome. Consequently, all training programs provide job-specific skills. Training prepares individual workers to execute a series of steps without concern for the context, or the reasons why those steps might be necessary. Done right, training can ensure a highly effective and disciplined process. In that respect, training provides a quick and satisfactory outcome if the threats to the organization never change or if adaptation to new threats is not required. If change does occur, then the managers who administer the training function have to evolve the training content to address the new context.

Training is an ongoing commitment for any organization that wants to ensure the continuing evolution of its staff capability. The managers of the training operation have to constantly monitor and control the development of the content and delivery for each training program. That evolution has to be supported by a formal assessment and review process. The maturation of the training program flows from the ability to refine security requirements. That ability, along with the knowledge that is gained by the assessment of the routine performance of security activities, should keep the training program relevant. Because it is a resource-intensive and often time-consuming activity, the training program requires a commitment by the whole organization, particularly the top-level people, to maintaining a timely and complete understanding of security requirements and staff capabilities.

# Moving the Training Function up the Ladder of Success

*It was three weeks later, and the Corvallis experiment had gotten off the ground in spectacular fashion. The initial analysis of the threat environment was complete, and the risk assessments had targeted some initial areas that clearly had to be addressed. The security professionals at the site were busily collecting best practices and incorporating them into learning modules that could be delivered to the appropriate elements of the workforce. Best of all, the local incident response team had already begun to feed incident data into the process, and that was making the fine-tuning of the content look even more promising.*

*The whole strategy was beginning to look promising indeed. The CISO was about to step back on the G4 when somebody asked the simple question, "What's the plan for implementing the training and awareness program here?" The CISO literally took a step back. It dawned on him that nobody involved in the development of the training and awareness content had thought about simple things like scheduling and delivery. In fact, nobody had even thought about the order that the content should be delivered in. So he picked up his cell phone and told his office that he would be staying in Corvallis a while longer. The rain that had made the surrounding countryside so green started to fall.*

*From the standpoint of developing the actual training process, it seemed like all that was needed was to define the right procedures and content. The people on the security team, including the CISO, had just assumed that the actual implementation of the training function itself would be more of a HR issue. That idea was nice in theory, but it didn't hold up in reality, mainly because the HR people had no idea whatsoever of what was required to ensure a property as abstract as "security." That led the local head of the HR function to point out sarcastically that his staff was better at keeping records and filling out forms than they were at addressing emerging threats.*

*It was going to be necessary to put a program in place that would ensure that the right content was delivered at the right place, at the right time. In the CISO's mind, that ability seemed to hinge on whether the people at Corvallis could identify the specific security needs of each unit and then prioritize those needs into a schedule. Those priorities would provide the basis for deciding who needed to be trained first.*

*The need to make decisions about priorities implied the need for someone to think through and then direct the day-to-day delivery of content. The only people capable of doing that were the members of the local security team. To their credit, team members had already looked at the EBK for guidance and found four functions they needed to think about.*

## Determining the Actual Training Needs

A formal process ensures that the organizational training and awareness function addresses existing threats. The first step in that process establishes a precise picture of what each member of the organization does. That means that each employee's work function and the attendant security needs have to be understood and documented. At a minimum, a thorough **job task analysis** of the **employee work functions** has to be done. This initial understanding is an essential requirement for then deploying the relevant training and awareness content. Likewise, the training itself must be driven by an ongoing process to identify the threats that each work function might address.

The amount of analytic work that is required to achieve the proper level of understanding can be costly. Nevertheless, it is a required pre-condition to establishing properly targeted training and awareness. The knowledge that is conveyed in the training, along with the associated motivational approach, has to be provably aligned with the situational requirements. That alignment also has to be maintained continuously correct. Otherwise, the training will not serve the purpose it was intended to serve and the organization would simply be wasting time and money. The decisions that underlie the maintenance of that alignment are supported by measurable performance criteria. These criteria are necessary in order to decide how to fine-tune the delivery as well as to ensure that the process itself is generally living up to requirements.

For information security, the most common measure of performance is incidents and their associated losses, typically expressed as a dollar cost. This measure can be directly tied to the work functions that are involved in each incident, such as the security professional, or physical security specialist. Most day-to-day aspects of security work for any role or function can be evaluated based on incident reporting and costs. That measurement data can also support decision making about the effectiveness of the associated training for that role. Consequently, it is possible to control how the training and awareness function evolves based on data that is routinely collected as part of the assessment of the overall security process. The management control that enables can then ensure that the training continues to address the concerns of the company. Quantitative understanding is an advantage when it comes to ensuring the correctness of any process, but the assurance works best if that quantitative feedback is designed into the training process at the beginning.

# Implementing a Capability Maturity Process

The outcome of a properly administered training and awareness program is an increased level of organizational capability. This is a strategic goal, which is based on the achievement of four progressively, better-organized states of security:

1. *Recognition*—The organization recognizes the need for security.
2. *Informal practice*—The organization understands informal security practices.
3. *Security management*—The security practices are planned and monitored.
4. *Deliberate control*—Decisions about security practices are based on data.

## Recognition

These levels of competence are achieved by implementing more and more capable training and awareness processes. The affect of each increase is summative, in the sense that in order to reach the next level of maturity, additional processes are added to the set of processes that were established in the prior level. The first step is recognition. To achieve the recognition level, an organization must meet two conditions. The first condition is that security issues have to be publicized through simple mechanisms such as posters, handouts, or reference cards. The aim is to ensure that all of the members of the organization are aware of topics related to security. This awareness does not involve formal presentations of security topics; it simply involves publicity of important security issues to the organization as a whole.

Recognition has been achieved if the level of the organization's community understanding and discourse is raised. This second condition is met if members of the organization are aware of the existence of security threats and the need to address them. Recognition fosters minimal understanding of proper assurance practice, which should not go beyond employees thinking about simple precautions. Ideally, all employees should be able to associate the existence of common threats with the steps that must be taken to prevent or avoid them.

The recognition level provides little substantive protection, but some adverse events can be headed off, as shown in Figure 11-3. For example, until employees recognize that social engineering exploits exist, they will continue to be susceptible to them. Once that recognition is achieved, whether through a posted reminder or by discussions around the coffee pot, employees are more likely to think twice if approached for sensitive information.

**Figure 11-3** Recognition of issues

© Cengage Learning 2012

## Informal Practice

The informal practice level is characterized by conscious awareness of security practice. Organizational awareness programs should consistently reach everybody, and they should alert the membership to hazards that are peculiar to the organizational environment. Two conditions must be met to achieve this level of security.

First, analytic work should be done to understand and characterize the risks that are resident in the day-to-day workplace. Since awareness programs have to be planned, and the effective level of awareness will vary depending on the line of business, the organization must plan carefully to ensure that the requirements of the specific situation are addressed. For example, the awareness program at a "mom and pop" Internet business has different requirements and addresses different concerns than the one at NASA. The measure for success is that the awareness function is focused on the problems in that environment.

The second requirement of a proper informal security practices program is "common knowledge and acceptance." There has to be an intuitive understanding of the need for uniform practice by everyone in the organization. The achievement of this level of understanding does not require a rulebook or a rigid, uniform adherence to detailed requirements; it simply requires consistent execution.

Since members of most organizations have a range of perceptions of the threat level, varying from none to outright paranoia, they will approach the practice of security differently. If the individual members of an organization understand the security goals differently, none of those goals will be achieved. That is because the performance of the required practices will not be uniform or coordinated, which is necessary to have reasonable assurance. Therefore, the informal practice level of awareness has to ensure a floor-level of understanding of security goals.

The learning that supports understanding is tailored to the needs of the individual situation and learner. For that reason, procedural awareness programs are learner-centric and situational. The program is deliberately resourced, planned, and deployed from those needs. There should be a formally organized effort to develop and publicize best practices. These are typically promoted in the form of adages, like "always check for viruses," rather than explained in depth. Commonly accepted correct practices should be embedded in the workplace.

Although informal practice programs begin to concentrate and direct the organizational response, they are minimally effective in preventing adverse events. Their value lies in the fact that the organization is able to establish a basic level of assurance with a small resource commitment. In that respect, they may be more cost-effective than more formal response programs because they ensure a fundamental level of preparedness without placing much of a burden on the organization's resources. This level will not guarantee that costly exploits will not occur, but a good awareness program is valuable and will raise the overall level of security of the organization. Informal practice programs also build the critical mass of group consciousness necessary to move to the next level.

## Security Management

The next stage is the first institutionalized response. It is the security management level. This level is frequently underwritten by training programs, which are designed to instill the right set of skills. There are two conditions associated with training at this level. The first is that the practices and security requirements of the organization are clearly understood. Everybody in the organization knows its precise security requirements and everyone has access to material that explains in detail how they operate. The second condition is that security practices are standardized based on formally acknowledged and commonly accepted best practices implemented with clear procedures.

In order to achieve this level, an explicit understanding of organizational context is necessary. That understanding is needed to underwrite the design of the training program. The knowledge needed to support that understanding is derived from an inventory of past security incidents. The outcome of that inventory is an identified set of threats that can be targeted by individually coordinated training exercises.

At this level of teaching and learning, an in-house staff may not necessarily deliver this content. One of the primary differences between this level and the deliberate control level is the fact that training is not institutionalized as a process. Instead, training is often left up to the initiative of individual managers and process owners within the organization. Although some training goals are achieved, others go unmet because they were not recognized as necessary or the functional area was busy doing something else.

The security management level represents a quantum advance over the informal practice level, because it establishes security training as a continuous process. It allows an organization to target its most persistent needs, and it delivers solutions to basic security problems. The lack of uniformity in addressing all of the threats is a continuing concern. Nonetheless, if one follows the old adage that 20 percent of the vulnerabilities produce 80 percent of the problems, this level provides considerable benefit.

These programs fail to provide consistent security, because they are not part of the routine organizational planning function. They are also not normally overseen or coordinated, and they are not able to adapt to new threats quickly enough to provide really reliable assurance. This creates the potential for unanticipated events causing problems. For instance, most of the recent highly publicized breakdowns in security have resulted from changes in the technology or the culture that surrounds it. Training programs at the managed level do not adequately adapt to such change because they are purely reactive; the necessary training might be deployed only after the building is already burning. The ideal outcome for any type of security function is to anticipate problems in advance. Consequently, dependable oversight and repeatable outcomes are a much more attractive alternative.

## Deliberate Control

The deliberate control level is fully managed. It conveys a set of commonly understood best practices, which effectively address the current security needs of the organization. The deliberate control level ensures a broad, coherent, and institutionalized security function, which is embedded in the overall organizational planning and decision-making process. Better organizational control is achieved by using a formal planning and deployment process, which begins with an organizational risk assessment and subsequent planning activity. Risk assessment and planning are complex activities that are driven by circumstance rather than rules. The only way to ensure the level of critical thinking that is needed to successfully adapt to circumstances is through tailored training programs, which are designed to enable effective decision making based on accountability. In fact, the controlled level is enforced by accountability.

Proper accountability requires three conditions. The first condition is that the various roles necessary to ensure security are assigned and understood among all staff and management and that the overall responsibilities are assigned for each role and then placed within an accountability system. The second condition requires a complete and correct set of best practices and control objectives, which are implemented by a clear-cut set of procedures. These procedures must be clearly and unambiguously defined, documented, and tailored to fit the entire range of known security needs of the organization. The third condition requires that the practices that have been selected as "best practices" are accompanied by an objective and valid set of metrics. These quantitative measures have to characterize the ongoing performance of the security function.

The deliberate control level is based on a systematic risk assessment, the outcome of which is an explicitly identified set of threats that are targeted by organizationally sanctioned practices. The appropriateness and effectiveness of that targeting is continuously monitored and assessed. The substantive security response itself is a mix of selected procedures, technologies and methods, which are integrated by design into a complete organizational system. The requirements for executing that system are then delivered through a comprehensive training program.

The delivery process is programmatic, in that the training is an established process within the organization's operating structure. The suitability of the training must be supported by all relevant managers. Third-party suppliers may also be involved in the training, but an institutional stakeholder will always coordinate the training of third-party personnel from inside the contracting organization. Accountability for the success or failure of the training process is vested with the stakeholder. The organization must demonstrate a commitment and ability to perform the entire training function by ensuring that the staff is empowered and resourced to perform it properly.

The advantage gained by an effective, organization-wide training program of this type cannot be overstated. Security is a complex and multidisciplinary challenge, which is rooted more in individual behavior than technology. Most security problems arise from the failure of individuals to follow correct procedures, or from an individual's inability or unwillingness to comply with security requirements. A properly functioning training program will provide workers with the knowledge necessary to do their jobs correctly. In addition, it will reinforce the cultural and behavioral norms associated with the security operation. Then, if an individual employee subsequently breaches those norms, the organization will be able to enforce accountability. That combination of knowledge and motivation allows the overall cybersecurity goals of the organization to be assured and maintained with confidence.

The deliberate control stage represents a major advance over the prior levels because it establishes information security training as a systematic process. It places the security operation on a day-to-day footing and directly addresses known information security issues. In addition, it facilitates timely incident response and ensures that any threat that is identified will be contained with minimal damage. The deliberate control stage also produces data that can be used by managers to identify trends and problems as they appear and initiate much timelier remediation or problem resolution actions.

# Ensuring Continuous Effectiveness

*The CISO had one final concern that he wanted to address before flying back, and that was the issue of sustainment. He had a firm belief that the training program developed at the Corvallis facility would ensure the disciplined execution of security duties by all staff at the site. But he wanted to back that belief up with a little fact, and that is where the security engineer for the Corvallis facility came in. The engineer was a graduate of Oregon State's business school rather than an actual licensed engineer, so he had a background in process development. He was something of an expert in operations research, which fit the undertaking that the CISO had in mind.*

*The CISO called the security engineer into his temporary office and outlined an aggressive set of goals for the continuous assessment and improvement of the newly instituted training process. His intent was to always know the status of each individual worker with respect to whether that person had sufficient knowledge to do his or her job properly. What he wanted to institute was a comprehensive assessment process that would be able to both characterize the current effectiveness of the training program as well as point out the directions that the organization would have to take in order to ensure a continuing high level of capability. He knew that the engineer would want to take on that challenge, because that is where his education and interests lay. More personally, the CISO could tell that the engineer was as ambitious as he was; this was a golden opportunity to show the people in New York just how good he was at his job.*

*The CISO was confident that the evaluation process was in good hands. He officially handed off the aegis for the continuing development of the company's entire training program to the Corvallis engineer and stepped into the G-4 for the flight back. Since the CISO was not exactly an outdoorsy type, and since beer and getting close to the wildlife seemed to be the main pastime for the folks in that town, he was not exactly sorry to be leaving. In the meantime, the engineer took up the challenge of coming up with an effective evaluation process. The EBK specifies these five standard work functions for the training and awareness evaluation perspective:*

1. *Assess and evaluate the IT security training and awareness program for compliance with corporate policies, regulations, and laws (statutes), and measure program and employee performance against objectives*

2. *Review IT security training and awareness program materials and recommend improvements*

3. *Assess the training and awareness program to ensure that it meets not only the organization's stakeholder needs, but that it is effective and covers current IT security issues and legal requirements*

4. *Ensure that information security personnel are receiving the appropriate level and type of training*

5. *Collect, analyze, and report performance measures*

# Establishing an Effective Review Process

The training and awareness function requires a commitment by the whole organization, particularly the top-level people, to continuously evaluate security practice in order to ensure a trustworthy state. Those reviews are needed in order to develop the specific programs that are required to achieve and then sustain that state. In order to maintain the continuing relevance of the content in those programs, the training and awareness function has to be kept up to date regarding evolving security requirements. Likewise, the materials employed in the training and awareness program also have to evolve with the changing state of security and technology in order to convey the message correctly. In practice, the evolution of both the training and awareness program and the materials that support it is implemented by a formal assessment and review process.

Assessments and reviews ensure better management control over the training and awareness function. A baseline of requisite actions allows managers to judge the current appropriateness of individual training and awareness programs as well as decide on future directions for them to go. In order to perform those assessments, the organization has to have a point of reference, which is usually a description of desired behaviors for every job classification that forms the basis for the training and awareness process. The description of desired actions characterizes the actual response and should itemize the specific security actions that each role in the organization is meant to carry out.

It is the duty of the organization to take the proactive steps necessary to ensure that everyone has a proper and complete understanding of the actions they are supposed to take to ensure security. The ability to determine the current status of each individual, with respect to those required actions, allows the organization to design the right training program. For example, an individual worker might have a different understanding than what might actually be required, about the amount of housekeeping it takes to secure personal computers. If that is the case, once the behavior of each employee is assessed against the requirements for securing mobile devices, any individual deviations from those requirements can be targeted and brought into alignment.

## Defining and Enforcing Proper Procedure

In order for an organization to be reliably secure, the entire workforce has to understand what constitutes proper procedure in each individual case. Workers also have to understand the consequences of a failure to do what is required, and those consequences should be communicated. The communication of required actions and the subsequent **enforcement** process requires two factors to be made explicit. First, the required actions for each person have to be defined and communicated to that individual. Second, the consequences of a failure to perform those specific actions have to be stated.

The statement of actions and accountabilities should clearly delineate the responsibilities and expectations for each and every individual worker. Operationally, these actions and accountabilities are usually expressed in some type of formal organizational document like a procedure manual. The contents of that manual serve as the tangible basis for structuring and running the training and awareness process and then assessing individual performance. The actions and accountabilities in that manual should be consistent with the general security requirements and security policies of the organization for each individual employee group. The aim is to assure that all requisite behaviors for each group align with the overall security aims of the company as a whole.

The statement of required behaviors has to be sufficiently rigorous to ensure adequate security, while giving workers flexibility to do their jobs. The rigor of the security actions that are specified in the procedure manual should be directly related to the type and degree of overall security required by the organization as a whole. Highly secure operations will use a different rulebook than organizations where less security is required. In all cases though, both the required action and the reason for instituting such a rule must be made clear, particularly where technical constraints are involved.

# Ensuring that the Training Process Is Sustainable

Training developed using continuous reviews is more likely to produce optimally skilled and knowledgeable personnel, because the results of this review process are incorporated into the ongoing hiring process. The aim of that process ought to be to ensure that new hires "hit the ground running" with all of the requisite skills and behavior. On the other hand, in order to keep the people who are already in the organization up to speed with organizational requirements, the training program needs to be iterative.

The need for repetitive training is partly due to the fact that the people who are receiving the training have to be updated on new technological advancements. Repetition is also important because the people who populate those roles are likely to change over time; it should be assumed that the person fulfilling the role at any given time is not the one who was originally trained.

## Improving the Process Through Assessment

Evaluation also leverages the current capabilities of the organization to higher levels. That improvement is either accomplished through focused training or targeted hiring. Evaluation results go into continuously revising the training program for each individual employee group in order to ensure the increased capability of that group. In that respect, the review process feeds directly into the development of a formal training program for the organization as a whole, which is designed to increase the general level of capability of the organization's human resources.

In that respect, the reviews also underwrite the production of the actual content that is employed by the training staff. The training program customizes a training approach that is designed to satisfy the security requirements and achieve the necessary competencies for managerial, operational, and technical roles. That training content is based on the current and desired capabilities of the incumbents. The key to refining training content lies in the assessment of the specific performance of the people entering and exiting the process. That sort of pre- and post-evaluation approach can be used to assess the effectiveness of training materials, manuals, and presentation media. In order to keep training materials consistent with organizational requirements, the review of these materials should also be iterative. Materials should evolve to make them responsive to change in the security environment. Finally, reviews serve as the basis for continuous assessment of the learning needs of each individual worker. Because individual worker performance should be assessed, organizations should be able to determine and then reinforce each worker's supplemental learning needs.

The steps that are taken in the training process itself are prescribed in the training plan. The development of those plans is also iterative, where feedback is provided to the day-to-day training operation. The results of the reviews are factored into the refinement of the competency requirements and are reflected in a revised response.

### Review Data as an Organizational Resource

The actual assessment should take place in a scheduled and programmatic fashion. Since the assessment of the performance of security duties serves as the basis for directing and refining the process, the individualized performance data that the evaluation process generates should be maintained as a HR asset. That information can then be analyzed to ensure that the individuals who are being trained meet all of the necessary criteria for sufficiency.

The data generated by these analyses can be used to fine-tune the training process as well as to provide management feedback to the organization about the progress being made toward achieving the right mix of trained resources. Data obtained from regular and systematic assessments can be used to coordinate the deployment of the right people to meet a specific organizational challenge. For example, it would be pointless to embark on a rigorous testing program if workers knowledgeable in testing were not available at the time. Nonetheless, sufficient review data would let the organization either hire the necessary people or move them from other jobs. In that respect, review data can help assure overall organizational security performance because it gives managers the kind of insight into the actual performance of the process that they will need to develop a capable workforce.

# Chapter Summary

- Human factors are an issue in assuring secure performance.
- Training and awareness are the two ways to ensure secure behavior.
- Motivation is an important element of consistent performance.
- Discipline is an important outcome of proper motivation.
- Training and awareness ensures the correct performance of routine tasks, operational duties, and management responsibilities.
- Accountability and oversight are reinforced by training.
- Training and awareness programs are deployed by formal plans.
- Training and awareness programs can be advanced up a capability ladder.
- Effective training and awareness is ensured by reviews of both programmatic and individual performance.

# Key Terms

**Acceptable behavior** Behavior that falls within the common norms of a group.

**Accountability** Assignment of specific responsibility to carry out a particular task or perform a specified behavior.

**Awareness** (security) General or company-wide recognition of the existence of a security requirement or concept.

**Capability** The ability to perform a given set of tasks or execute a given behavior.

**Consistent practice** Confidence that a given task or behavior will be executed for a specified period of time within a specific context.

**Deliberate control** A level of security practice where all organizational decisions about security practice are based on data.

**Disciplined behavior** Ensuring a reliable response by an individual or group to a given event or situation.

**Employee work functions** Activities specified for a given employee as part of their work assignment.

**Enforcement** The specific measures that will be taken to ensure compliance with a given requirement.

**Informal practice** A level of security practice in which the organization informally acknowledges a set of defined practices for security.

**Job task analysis** A characterization of the specific functions that a given corporate role must carry out in order to fulfill the requirements of the position.

**Motivation** The internal condition that activates or drives behavior.

**Operational duties** The activities that ensure the overall security of the system during routine operation.

**Procedure manual** A formal statement of the recommended approach to a given task or job requirement.

**Recognition** A level of security practice in which the organization generally recognizes the need for security.

**Security behavior** Behaviors designed to ensure the security of the individual and the organization.

**Security management** Levels of security practice where security behaviors are planned and specified for all employees and then monitored for performance.

**Training program** A formal skill development process aimed at increasing or ensuring the capability of a given group of people.

# Questions from the CIO

The CIO requires you to brief her on the current status of your investigation. This will be an important part of your continuing work on this project, since it is essential to be able to describe all of the ramifications of a properly developed training and awareness process. Consequently, the CIO would like you to answer the following questions for her:

1. Differentiate awareness from training. Why are both approaches necessary?

2. What is the role of workforce training and awareness? What specific advantage does it provide a company?

3. Why should security training ideally happen at the time a person is hired? What are the potential pitfalls if this is not done?

4. What is motivation? Why is it essential to security? How is motivation ensured?

5. What is the function of oversight? What essential ingredient is required in order to make oversight work? How is it assigned?

6. Training provides situation-specific skills. What is the potential problem associated with that and how can it be overcome?

7. How is training linked to capability? What are the stages for increasing capability in an organization?

8. What is the role of accountability in enforcing disciplined practice? What are the consequences of not documenting accountabilities?

9. Why are group norms essential to enforcing accountability? What has to be specified as part of accountability in order to ensure acceptable behavior?

10. What is the function of the training review/evaluation process in the assurance of organizational security? What would happen if training programs were not evaluated on a regular basis?

# Hands-On Projects

HANDS-ON PROJECTS

Prepare a detailed procedure specification for one of the EBK work functions, which is suitable to support training. Specify the skill requirements for that function and how those requirements will be ensured. Along with that plan, specify an evaluation process to ensure that the recommended practices will be understood and performed properly.

# chapter 12

# Securing the IT Systems Operations and Maintenance Function

## Getting the Concept into Practice

*The CISO hauled himself off the Gulfstream at the LaGuardia Executive Terminal. He had worked into the night the day before in Corvallis, finalizing the training program and he thought he was going to die from the jet lag. Even so, he was happy to be back in the city. As he stepped onto the metal stairs leading down to the tarmac he felt re-energized, although it was still not quite 6:30 in the morning. The noise and bustle of the city around him was a lot more familiar than the sound of wind whistling through the pines, which was all he had heard at 6:30 a.m. in Corvallis. He was feeling relaxed because he was looking forward to a period with no surprises.*

*The CISO was reasonably sure at this point that the initial implementation steps had been successful and that the more exotic problems of the implementation process were behind him. It was time to turn his attention to establishing the company's day-to-day operational security posture. That didn't exactly mean that his task would be easy, even though most of the security categories that he planned to concentrate on involved functions that the organization already did on a routine basis.*

*For example, he knew that all of the company's employees had had experience with some aspect of network, physical, and personnel security, as well as software assurance. Even though those functions were being done in four different parts of the company, they had been in place prior to the overhaul. Moreover, because those functions had been embedded in the day-to-day operating environment of the company, their necessity was accepted by everybody involved.*

*The first of the more conventional processes that the CISO decided to tackle was the IT systems operations and maintenance function. That was because routine system operations and maintenance activities played such an important role in ensuring the routine execution of the overall security process. The aim of the operations and maintenance function, as the CISO saw it, was to guarantee that the rest of the company's security processes worked in concert with each other to produce a dependable state of security.*

*The CISO was aware that ensuring the secure interaction of all of the components in the company's far-flung IT operation was going to pose a complex coordination problem. Potentially unwieldy organizational processes would have to be coordinated to work with each other to achieve the right level of security. The CISO knew that breakdowns in that interaction could create potential gaps in the security system. He remembered that it was just such a gap, between the physical security and the personnel security functions that had let the fox so fatally into the henhouse the last time. To make the problem worse, an optimum balance had to be struck between the organization's productivity goals and security.*

*Balance was an issue because, in reality, the company's cybersecurity function was a serious drag on productivity. The executive team, from the chairman down to the CISO, recognized that fact. The problem was that the extra procedures required to ensure the right state of security also added extra time to the performance of day-to-day tasks. And as the old saying goes, "Time is money." Everybody in upper management wanted to make certain that the assurance activities that were required for day-to-day work provided a sufficient level of security, while still ensuring that workers would be able to carry out their assigned duties in a productive way.*

*The first task for the CISO and his security team was to design a company-wide management process that would ensure that a diverse set of security practices, ranging from physical security all the way to electronic and personnel security, were blended into a smoothly running everyday process that did not get in the way of the company's bottom line. This implied that the IT security operations and maintenance function was going to be more of a coordination and management challenge than a technical one.*

*Management discipline is typically enforced in an organization by audit and control, which meant that the IT security compliance officer and her minions would play a significant part in overseeing the routine security of operations process. Therefore, the CISO planned to directly involve the compliance officer in the development of the substantive security of operations practices. The aim in involving the compliance people early in the planning process was to ensure that the necessary oversight capabilities and supporting controls were built directly into the basic security of operations function, rather than strapped on later.*

*Even so, since the fundamental goal of effective management is to ensure that the company's work is performed as efficiently as possible, that also suggested the need to involve the security engineering and general management teams at the various sites in the development. Consequently, the CISO called the representatives of those three roles—security, internal audit, and executive management—together for a weekend retreat at the company's new meeting facility in Montauk, way out in Suffolk County.*

*The meeting facility was the same place the CEO had rented the summer of the hurricane. After the storm, the CEO had simply bought what was left of the place. Thanks to hurricane*

*Tamara, it was remarkably cheap. With the smell of old money soaking into everything from the furniture to the shrubbery, the CISO laid out his ambitious vision of the approach to developing a sustainable IT systems operation and maintenance process. That approach involved the following 11 common work functions associated with managing the IT systems operations and maintenance process:*

1. *Establish security administration program goals and objectives*

2. *Monitor the security administration program budget*

3. *Direct security administration personnel*

4. *Address security administration program risks*

5. *Define the scope of the security administration program*

6. *Establish communications between the security administration team and other security-related personnel (e.g., technical support, incident management)*

7. *Integrate security administration team activities with other security-related team activities (e.g., technical support, incident management, security engineering)*

8. *Acquire necessary resources, including financial resources, to execute the security administration program*

9. *Ensure operational compliance with applicable standards, procedures, directives, policies, regulations, and laws (statutes)*

10. *Ensure that IT systems operations and maintenance enables day-to-day business functions*

11. *Ensure that appropriate changes and improvement actions are implemented as required*

# Establishing a Coherent Process: Strategic Planning

The assurance functions that the security of operations process touches span the whole company. They include such diverse activities as the information technology operation as well as the personnel function. Given the number of possible participants in the operations and maintenance process, the logical way to establish a formal security of operations function is through an organization-wide strategic planning activity.

For that reason, the IT operations and maintenance process should be deployed as part of the overall corporate strategic planning effort. The plan delineates the procedures that will be used to ensure the security of the organization's day-to-day operation. The formal procedures in that plan then become the official mechanism to coordinate the often complex interactions of the functions that make up the organization's everyday security scheme. The term that is used to characterize such a coordination process is **strategic governance**.

Strategic governance takes place within an organization-wide control infrastructure, which is established by the plan. The aim of strategic governance is to first establish and then maintain the optimum level of overall management control needed to realize the company's goals. The tangible strategic governance infrastructure for security is a rational and explicit set of management procedures. Taken as a whole, those procedures represent the organization's specific means to establish management control over the organization's major security functions.

The imposition of substantive management discipline across the entire organization implies the need to commit a considerable amount of capital to perform the work. Thus, the strategic plan for operational security should also enumerate how the company will assign resources to ensure the level of control that is desired. Because the maintenance of uninterrupted security across the operation is good practice, it is important to lay out those resource commitments on an explicit schedule or timeline. This should be done in such a way that each resource that is committed is directly associated with, and fully traceable to, the security policies and goals it is meant to implement.

## Implementing the Process: The Operational Security Plan

The detailed, day-to-day description of the operational security process is documented in the operational security plan, which provides an unambiguous statement of how the company will coordinate and control its information security practice. Since the operational security plan is the blueprint for implementing and managing a reliable operational security function, it should contain a detailed description of each practice and its relationship with every other related practice in the scheme. This formal description of operational practices and their various associations will then be used to manage the operational security function on a routine basis. Because the plan communicates the company's fundamental course of action to ensure everyday security, it is an important **baseline** document.

The purpose of the operational security plan is to organize and coordinate the company's security resources, in order to ensure reliable, day-to-day operational assurance of the business. The goal of the operational security plan is to ensure proper routine execution of all required security practices. It is assumed that the suitable performance of those practices will ensure the long-term sustainability of the overall IT operations and maintenance function. Nonetheless, in order to ensure proper coordination, the appropriate set of controls has to be established and then monitored as the security scheme evolves.

In addition to specifying required practice, the operational security plan is also a useful contributor to the maintenance of a cost-effective security scheme over time; the plan provides managers with a tangible description of existing security controls. That documented baseline of controls can then be used as a point of reference to understand and prioritize new threats and risk requirements as they appear. In that prioritization process, the costs of implementing each practice in the security scheme can be weighed against the estimated cost and potential likelihood and impact of each threat that the company faces.

In application, the operational security plan has to ensure a detailed understanding of the security activities that each person in the company is expected to undertake, as well as the time frame for performing those actions. In that respect, because it embodies a documented set of specific security activities, the operational plan is also an excellent way to gauge the ongoing performance of the overall information security function and judge the individual effectiveness of the people who are part of that process.

In addition to specifying personnel resource commitments, the plan should also specify and assign the requisite job responsibilities and accountabilities to each of the stakeholders assigned to the process. Because real-world sustainability implies the availability of the right set of human resources, the plan should also itemize the number and capabilities of people who will be allocated to the operational security function.

**Creating the Operational Security Plan** The operational security plan is a formal statement of the practices that the organization plans to undertake to ensure everyday security for the company. This plan provides the guidance necessary to ensure the long-term, routine security needs of the organization. In simple terms, the operational plan specifies only those practices that the organization feels it will need to assure that its immediate security goals are met. Consequently, there is always the implicit understanding that, should the environment change, the operational security plan will have to change correspondingly.

Operational security plans have to be agile, because of the constantly changing threat picture. Accordingly, operational security plans are drawn up to address the security situation for a limited period, typically less than a year. The reason for adopting a shorter time frame is to ensure that an effective approach is always available to address the realities and demands of the current situation. For that reason, the ability to manage change intelligently and rationally is an essential quality of good operational security planning.

**Developing the Operational Security Plan** The first stage in the operational planning process is a status **assessment**, since the aim of the plan is to fit the operational security response to the precise threat picture. A rigorous evaluation of the status of the current security situation and the likely threat environment for the extent of the planning period is necessary in order to decide where to go next.

The goal of the status assessment is to understand the organization's state of affairs with respect to the things that threaten it. The status assessment should provide a detailed understanding of the organization's security approach and its effectiveness in addressing meaningful threats. The assessment should itemize all known security threats along with their likelihood, impact, and their ensuing priority. It should also describe the controls that are currently being employed to counter those threats. Finally, it should provide recommendations about how effectively the most urgent threats are being addressed by the existing security response. The **threat assessment** then spells out the specific steps that need to be taken to ensure that the organization can continue to meet its security goals.

The actual planning for the response takes place once the threat situation is thoroughly understood. The plan should specify a coherent framework of tangible policies, procedures, and practices for operational assurance. These practices are then documented. The documentation should describe and justify the practices that will be deployed to implement the operational security response for that year. The goal of the plan is to balance the feasibility of those practices against the needs identified in the risk analysis. Where a framework model like the EBK was used, the plan should also provide a map between the practices and the recommendations of the model. Finally, because technology is important, the plan should detail every aspect of the array of electronic tools that will be employed as well as the exact process that will be used to install and operate those tools. The combination of practices and associated technology will then constitute the explicit security operating environment for that particular year.

# Designing the Operational Security Function

*The CISO's security team members had kicked the topic of security operations around long enough to be pretty certain that they had gotten their arms around the planning issues. The primary concern during those discussions had been the relatively unique focal point of the* operations process versus all of the other processes. In the team's opinion, the distinguishing aspect of the security of operations process was the diversity, rather than the depth, of its responsibilities. Rather than focusing on deploying a set of focused activities to secure some specific area of concern, the security of operations process was aimed at ensuring that the practices that currently existed in all of those areas were carried out in a disciplined and coordinated fashion, at all times, across the entire company.

That presented an interesting new challenge to the compliance officer, who up to that point had been mainly interested in ensuring that the company met all legal and regulatory requirements. Because those requirements were well documented and generally well accepted, her only real challenge had been ferreting out any intentional, or unintentional, violations of the rules. This was done via the audit process. However, with ensuring the integrity of the security of operations process, the compliance space became a lot more extensive to say the least. In effect, the task of the compliance function would now be to review every aspect of the day-to-day operation in order to identify any non-conformances.

The compliance officer was aggressive, but she wasn't reckless. So she told the group, in the colorful terms that she had picked up in her 20 years in the army, that enforcing the requisite discipline to ensure the security of operations plan would take a lot more resources than she had at her disposal. She added that she should probably not have to point out to the group that the company's security scheme encompassed a multitude of practices, ranging from the highly technical to totally people-centered. All of those would have to be audited for conformance in order to ensure that they were operating correctly. That implied a continuous oversight mission that the compliance officer was not ready to accept.

She was well aware of the fact that the actual process of monitoring the company's routine functions would amount to nothing more than a simple internal auditing task. Assuming she had enough staff, that would be easy to do. But the condition had to be that the steps that comprised those functions were well defined. If the steps were not well defined, her operation could never guarantee compliance. To reinforce that statement, she cited the cardinal rule of auditing, which was that in order to certify anything, there had to be concrete evidence to base the audit determinations on.

The compliance officer insisted that she would never take on the task of monitoring unless the security controls were documented in such a way that it would make them auditable. She also pointed out that she would need a whole lot more security professionals to do the actual audit work at each site. The CISO didn't have a problem with that latter request, since he knew that adding to the compliance staff would only serve to expand his own empire. But he did have some concerns about the former, since it was unclear what it would take to make the security controls concrete. He eventually decided that the best way to approach the problem of creating auditable controls was to shift the responsibility for their definition to the security engineers at each site. His rationale was that since each engineer had been the architect of the site's customized controls, each engineer would be in the best position to ensure that those controls were properly documented.

For her part, the compliance officer said that she would make it her personal crusade to ensure that a precise architecture of tangible and objectively observable controls was embodied in the operational plan for each site. Moreover, because she absolutely did not tolerate failure in her own operation, she was going to be particularly merciless to any poor security engineer who created a control that did not produce the hard documentary *evidence that her people would need to audit it properly. She assured the group, with what they felt was a disturbing amount of relish, that she thought that it would probably only take her metaphorically staking a few such unfortunate victims out over an anthill, for everybody to get the message that the only acceptable security control was one that was unambiguous.*

*That approach also pleased the CIO and the CISO, since it meant that the organization as a whole would have a tangible architecture of security controls that line managers could then use as a proxy to evaluate and enforce security discipline. The problem was that somebody at one of the sites had to actually step-up to be the first to develop a customized and auditable control set. It was clear that that effort was going to be a difficult and time-consuming task. Moreover, nobody was quite sure that the compliance officer's threats about anthills weren't just her attempt at humor.*

*The company-wide search for volunteers among the security engineers created the opening for the IT security engineer at the Corvallis site. He had always been a risk-taker and he had a flair for detailed design work; the opportunity to design a framework of concrete operational controls, which would allow management to monitor the security behavior of the entire company, was too tempting a chance to pass up. He had also not missed the fact that this would further increase his stock with executive management.*

*The incident that had first brought the Corvallis security engineer to the attention of the powers-that-be had been his innovative approach to implementing the training and awareness process for his own site. That program had subsequently become the prototype for training and awareness in the entire company. So in the mind of the Corvallis security engineer, the challenge of also designing the standardized process for implementing the IT security of operations function for the entire company would give him another chance to showcase his talents. Of course, the fact that he also had a trick up his sleeve helped.*

*In developing the template for the training and awareness program for the organization, he had used his in-depth knowledge of the workings of the EBK to create a standard process that was correct and coherent. The resulting training and awareness process constituted a complete set of standard practices. He was certain that he could use that same approach to define a process that would let each site develop a customized* **control framework**. *The EBK specifies the following 10 standard activities for the IT operations and maintenance design function:*

1. *Develop security administration processes and procedures in accordance with standards, procedures, directives, policies, regulations, and laws (statutes)*

2. *Develop personnel, application, middleware, operating system, hardware, network, facility, and egress security controls*

3. *Develop* **security monitoring**, *test scripts, test criteria, and testing procedures*

4. *Develop security administration change management procedures to ensure that security policies and controls remain effective following a change*

5. *Recommend appropriate forensics-sensitive policies for inclusion in the enterprise security plan*

6. *Define IT security performance measures*

7. *Develop a continuous monitoring process*

8. *Develop role-based access, based on the concept of least privilege*

9. *Maintain the daily/weekly/monthly process of backing up IT systems to be stored both on- and off-site in the event that a restoration should become necessary*

10. *Develop a plan to measure the effectiveness of security controls, processes, policies, and procedures*

## Designing a Controls Framework

In the case of every one of the EBK security functions, the design stage creates a framework of concrete security procedures and practices, which then serve as the basis for executing the process in the real world. The aim of the design stage for the security of operations function is to define and document a correct and comprehensive architecture of explicit control behaviors, which can then be monitored on a day-to-day basis to ensure the secure operation of every aspect of the company's everyday business process. The architecture is composed of a finite set of defined security controls. The controls specify the behaviors that are meant to secure that particular element of the operation, along with their associated technologies. To be correct, the entire architecture of controls must ensure a continuously functioning security system.

The design documents a tangible set of security controls, which can be objectively assessed for performance. The purpose of those controls is to ensure the desired level of security functioning for all of the company's operational assurance processes. The success of the company's security operation will depend on management's ability to then make certain that the company's security controls continue to address all of the current and relevant security threats. This capacity relies on the existence of timely and accurate information about threats, as well as knowledge about how well the security practices that have already been deployed are performing. That information is obtained by means of routine internal auditing activities, which are designed to generate up-to-the-minute data about the effectiveness of each practice.

In order to ensure that the appropriate **decision maker** makes the right decision, that data has to be captured, analyzed, and then distributed to the person in the organization who is responsible for acting on it. The designation of the appropriate person to receive and then act on specific feedback from the monitoring process has to be formalized in the design. Potential targets to get that monitoring information might include the top- and mid-level managers, who are responsible for overseeing the execution of the company's routine operational processes. Other potential targets might include the technical managers and staff who have to ensure that the technology that supports those processes is functioning properly.

Even though it might seem like a bureaucratic exercise, the need to define the exact lines of communication is a critical element of the overall operational security process. When lines of communication are not clearly drawn, miscommunication can occur, as illustrated in Figure 12-1. That is because all of the activities that go into the security process have to be properly coordinated. Security managers have to get the information that will let them effectively manage the interaction of the various functions within the security operation. Clear reporting lines as well as established accountabilities are essential elements in maintaining effective lines of communication. Those lines of communication also have to be updated as the structure of the operational security function changes.

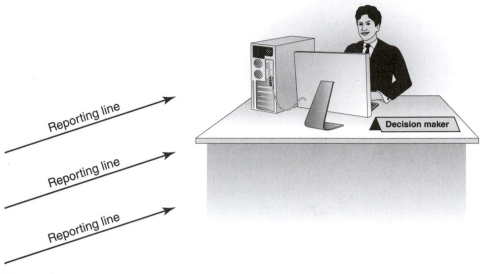

**Figure 12-1** Clear reporting lines

© *Cengage Learning 2012*

The design also has to specify the steps to ensure timely and effective corrective action in the face of inevitable change. Thus, the design has to provide a mechanism for bringing the operational security process back into line with any new realities in the security environment. In order to ensure continuing proper alignment, the design should establish the standard operating procedure that managers, technical staff, and end users will follow to report any new security circumstances, or to respond to any unforeseen security events. This procedure is called **incident reporting** and it is an essential feature in all security operations. Finally, the design has to specify the method that will be employed to ensure that the requisite corrective actions have been implemented and are effective.

## Human Factors: Ensuring Proper Performance

In order to ensure proper performance, the design has to unambiguously dictate the performance criteria for each participant. Moreover, the accountability for performing all required security tasks has to be assigned as clearly and directly as possible in the design. Personal accountability is a critical requirement in ensuring reliable performance. In order to ensure a disciplined security operation, the organization has to document and assign explicit responsibility for the management and execution of all assigned security responsibilities. Without a formal assignment of responsibility, it is hard to guarantee that security assignments will be carried out correctly, or even at all. Therefore, in order to ensure routine, day-to-day success, each employee category has to be assigned explicit, everyday security behaviors. That assignment has to be documented and delegated to workers, in a clear and unambiguous fashion. Then, the appropriate enforcement mechanisms have to be established. Enforcement is necessary in order to ensure that personal commitments to security are lived up to by all of the people in the organization.

Additionally, the tangible security controls have to be "socialized" into the company. In essence, the people who make up the organization have to be motivated to execute the requisite security behaviors satisfactorily. For that reason, the means that will be employed to ensure understanding and acceptance of the security process must be specified in the design.

The standard mechanism for ensuring the right level of capability is the training and awareness function. Training and awareness is an important component of operational security because it ensures that a continuing level of competence and discipline is always maintained. It is not enough to have a set of defined procedures in place if the people in the organization are either unable or unwilling to carry them out properly. Ensuring the existence of a training and awareness function is an essential element in the design of an operational security process.

## Technology: Ensuring Proper Support

In addition to specifying the concrete steps that must be taken to ensure the capability of people, it is also necessary to specify the specific technologies and products that will be used in the operational security process. This specification has to be complete, and it has to be explicit down to things like the version and model numbers of the equipment and software. A highly detailed specification of technology is essential, because that technology typically dictates how the tasks that underlie the process will be performed. As a result, the placement and the planned interrelationships between all operational security tasks and the products that support them must be specified in the design.

Besides specifying security functions, the relationship between security technology and any features of the company's conventional technological products and processes also has to be defined. Because security technologies are extremely varied, the application of those technologies must be made unambiguously clear and their ongoing operation and maintenance has to be equated to the parts of the conventional IT operation that they are intended to support. In addition, the design must describe the method that will be employed to ensure that all relevant technologies are updated, or maintained on a secure basis.

# Establishing Reliable Day-to-Day Security

*The Corvallis security engineer and his team had produced a top-level design that was, to say the least, detailed. It documented a complete and logically correct architecture of controls that appeared to address every possible routine contingency. The CISO was pleased with the complexity of the relationships in the design and the level of detail of each of the controls, since that would let him produce the kind of charts and graphs that were guaranteed to impress the CIO and the CEO. The problem was that, because the design was so complex, most of the security team felt that it was not going to be implementable.*

*The concern was with the number of controls. The Corvallis security team had essentially solved the problem of specificity by dictating a control for every possible contingency. That approach guaranteed that all of the bases would be covered; however, in doing so, it would be necessary to install security practices and technologies that would be way out of line with the company's financial goals, as well as a serious drag on corporate productivity. Because of the business requirement for a good ratio of security to cost, it was obvious that there had to be a middle ground somewhere between the all-or-nothing proposition of the current security control structure and the company's obligation to maintain a well balanced and financially feasible operational security response.*

*Although the Corvallis security engineer was well versed in security, he was a lot less at ease with corporate politics. He could feel his career slipping through his fingers as the executive team continued to debate his solution. Nobody on the security side wanted to compromise on what they saw as necessary security. Nevertheless, the business side of the company, including the CEO himself, had other ideas. They were aiming to keep the company as profitable as possible, and they felt that spending money protecting things that were either trivial or unnecessary was not the way to guarantee generous executive bonuses. They were well aware of the fact that the company had been hit before, and none of them wanted to repeat that disaster. Even so, they were not convinced that every piece of information in the company had to get the maximum level of protection.*

*The problem seemed to center on finding the best way to ensure the minimum level of acceptable day-to-day security for the maximum amount of information, given the shifting realities of funding and business constraints. Finding the right balance required the ability to commit resources to security incidents based on their likely impact, which is a lot like deciding how to deploy the resources to fight fires. In most cities, the fire department has a specific strength; however, the actual allocation of fire resources at any given point in time is dependent on the number and type of fires and the firefighters available. Consequently, it is important to be able to make good decisions about what to deploy based on the impact of any particular fire and the current resources available. The assumption is that if the people making the assignment of resources have the best and timeliest information at their disposal, they will be able to assign the right resources to any situation that might arise.*

*That is also the way it is with security. A minimum level of security is always required for every organization. This fundamental level typically comprises essential security technologies like firewalls and virus checkers and simple procedural rules, like passwords. Above the basic level however, the relentlessly shifting demands of the threat environment require the ability to analyze, prioritize, and assign security resources to threats as they appear. The question was how to turn the idea of coordination of resources based on risk into a reality. The security engineer recognized that in order to make effective choices about resource assignments, decision makers would need access to the best possible data about the current risk situation. He also recognized that in order to satisfy that aim, two large organizational processes would have to be synchronized to work in tandem.*

*Since deployment would rely on being able to identify and prioritize threats as they arose, one of those processes was risk analysis. Clearly, the organization had to be able to identify threats and assess their impacts as well as stay on top of the current risk picture in order to make good decisions about deployment. However, deciding on the actual form of the response was also an operational task, so the other process had to involve some form of incident response management. In essence, the organization had to be able to ensure that the deployment of a response to a new threat was correct, properly executed, and effective. Fortunately, the EBK, which had served as the security engineer's practical guidebook throughout the process, contained recommendations for implementing and then ensuring just such a series of actions. Those recommendations were:*

1. *Perform security administration processes and procedures in accordance with standards, procedures, directives, policies, regulations, and laws (statutes)*

2. *Establish a secure computing environment by applying, monitoring, controlling, and managing unauthorized changes in system configuration, software, and hardware*

3. *Ensure that information systems are assessed regularly for vulnerabilities, and that appropriate solutions to eliminate or otherwise mitigate identified vulnerabilities are implemented*

4. *Perform security performance testing and reporting, and recommend security solutions in accordance with standards, procedures, directives, policies, regulations, and laws (statutes)*

5. *Perform security administration changes and validation testing*

6. *Identify, control, and track all IT configuration items through the continuous monitoring process*

7. *Collaborate with technical support, incident management, and security engineering teams to develop, implement, control, and manage new security administration technologies*

8. *Monitor vendor agreements and service level agreements to ensure that contract and performance measures are achieved*

9. *Establish and maintain controls and surveillance routines to monitor and control conformance to all applicable information security laws (statutes) and regulations*

10. *Perform proactive security testing*

## Turning Operational Security into a Process

The maintenance of a secure operational security response is built around a systematic and rational information gathering and decision making function that leads to appropriate adjustments in the system as the security situation evolves. That process is part of the company's overall organizational resource management scheme. The only goal of that process is to maintain the security capability of the organization within optimum levels of investment. The approach itself should be both proactive and reactive.

The approach's proactive activities would include such things as formal identification of threats and vulnerabilities and the creation, assessment, and deployment of optimized security solutions from that knowledge. The reactive activities include such things as the maintenance of an effective reaction to external or internal security events. The response that is eventually authorized in both cases is based on the degree of acceptable risk.

Some type of risk analysis typically underwrites the organization's ability to deploy **proactive response** and **reactive responses**. Normal risk identification activities involve such things as the day-to-day monitoring of operation, along with operational testing. Analysis seeks to then understand the degree of risk and impact of any threat that is identified. Typical analysis activities include the assessment of the root causes of incidents as they occur, along with the investigation of potential weaknesses in the existing infrastructure that might be identified through the incident reporting process. Once those impacts are understood, the decision maker has to select and authorize a formal remediation. The specific changes required are monitored and assured to confirm that they were done right and were properly integrated into the security system.

The operational security function ensures that everyday business activity is secure by making the necessary changes to address threats as they appear. Changes that are corrective in nature typically involve the identification and removal of security vulnerabilities and fixing actual errors in execution. An example of the latter type of change would be taking the steps to properly install features that were not implemented properly in the first place. Once the required corrective action has been taken, the operational security function is also responsible for confirming that the adjusted response is both correct and appropriate.

Preventive change involves the management of vulnerabilities that are known to exist, but that have not yet led to a security incident. Those types of vulnerabilities can be addressed before they cause harm, or they can be monitored for later corrective action.

## Implementing the Security of Operations Process

Like all large organizational functions, the security of operations process is established by plan. That plan incorporates all relevant security principles, criteria, assumptions, prerequisites, and requirements into a substantive organization-wide program. The plan's aim is to install a consistent, day-to-day set of security activities. The operational security plan details the existing security situation. It also lays out the specific steps that the organization will take to maintain a desired security status given those conditions.

Because the goal of the security of operations plan is to maintain a prescribed level of assurance, it is based on information from a regular audit of the security status of the organization. This assessment is done on a routine, scheduled basis, in order to determine the organization's exact status at any given point in time. The assessment describes the organization's current state of security. It then identifies and categorizes any emerging threats that need to be addressed. The assessment documents the concerns that are expected to have a meaningful impact on the organization and assigns each concern a priority based on its likelihood and impact as well as the resources that will be required to address it.

Information about threats lets the organization develop an explicit infrastructure of policies, procedures, and technologies. The aim of the operational policy and procedure development process is to define the right set of processes and activities to ensure every aspect of routine security functioning. Since modern security is highly dependent on technology, it is critical to define the right set of associated security technologies. From a planning standpoint these technologies must be specifically itemized and related to the security policies and procedures that they support.

## Identifying and Reporting Incidents

Although it is often a separate organizational function, the process for identifying and reporting incidents is in reality inseparable from the operational security process. That is because operational security is founded on the ability to always align security to the existing threat picture. Incident reporting provides the necessary eyes and ears to underwrite that ability. In order to ensure a disciplined and coordinated incident reporting process, the means of reporting each incident has to be standardized. All of the procedures to report threats have to be well understood and followed by all of the members of the organization. That understanding requires a commonly accepted, well-defined reporting process. In order to ensure that proper understanding is maintained, the steps involved in the problem reporting process should be reinforced by the training and awareness function.

The sources of incident reports can be both formal and informal. Formal reports are tied directly to the operational tests and reviews that are part of the regularly scheduled security assessment plan. The informal reporting element involves all of the members of the organization. Even though they are not formally a part of the security of operations function, end users are excellent sources of feedback about security problems, since they are the people who are on the front lines. A correctly structured security of operations process will make it convenient and easy for everybody in the organization to report any security issues they come across.

Because security breakdowns are as likely to involve such non-technical things as malicious insiders or failures in physical protection, the reporting of incidents should not be limited to the technology alone. A comprehensive security of operations process will extend into the business environment. In that respect, the operational tests and reviews that comprise the security of operations process should also be aimed at identifying problems in any part of the operation that might impact the security of the organization.

For example, if proper security procedure requires an individual to always sign out when leaving the premises, any variation from that prescribed behavior would then be recorded and reported to management. That variation would then be analyzed and a decision would be made about the resolution of the problem. This part of the process is driven by the assessment of risk, in that decision makers would authorize the required response based on an understanding of the risk that might be represented by a particular individual's behavior.

## Performing an Effective Analysis

Effective security of operations requires managers to make an informed decision about any problem that might be identified by the routine monitoring function. The monitoring elements of the security of operations process should also be able to evaluate the impact of threats or problems and then recommend a rational decision about what has to be done next. The role of the management part of the process is to ensure that the selected approach represents the most effective security response, as well as the greatest cost benefit for the organization as a whole.

Analysis supports that type of good decision making because it helps the decision maker understand the consequences of a particular action. Most corporate decision makers are not well versed in the nuances of security, nor do they have time to think about security in the way a security professional would. Nevertheless, in order for an executive to make the right decision, the outcomes of that decision have to be fully understood. So, it is important that security professionals provide decision makers with all of the relevant and necessary information to make good decisions.

In order to make an informed decision, the decision maker needs to know the implications of taking a particular step, versus the implications of all other alternatives. That means the analyst must look at a number of standard aspects of threat. First, the analyst needs to understand the scope, or boundary, of the threat. In simple terms, the analyst must decide about the scale of the problem. He or she must also determine whether the threat has critical or non-critical implications. This prevents the organization from wasting resources resolving trivial or unimportant issues.

Next, the analyst catalogs all feasible impacts of the threat on the organization's security and control architecture, policies and procedures, and any associated strategies or plans, such as the continuity plan. Because the results of the analysis support accurate decision making, it is essential to communicate the basic reliability of the evidence that was used in the analysis phase to the designated decision maker. Because decision makers are normally too busy to digest minutia such as this, the communication must be done in such a way that the reliability of the evidence supporting the recommendation can be understood by them.

Once the impacts of the threat are fully understood, the analyst should also provide an estimate of the cost-benefit implications for each option, including factors like the total cost of ownership, or the marginal loss percentage. Finally, the analyst ought to perform a feasibility analysis for each remediation option. This final step is necessary in order to ensure that the decision that is recommended is technologically and financially feasible.

From an implementation standpoint, the analysis process itself should evaluate all affected elements of the security system as well as any inherent dependencies among those elements. The elements that are affected are then studied to determine the impacts of any proposed change. Then the findings from that study are communicated to the appropriate manager for authorization of the proposed change.

The results of the analysis also provide the formal incident documentation, since they are recorded and maintained by the organization. This is done in order to ensure a continuous detailed record of the performance of the security system, as well as to support any additional causal analysis that might be carried out to better understand the security and control issues that might be associated with a given incident.

All requisite information about the incident being studied is gathered on a standard form. The analyst then attempts to replicate or verify the existence of the reported problem, as shown in Figure 12-2. This step is important for the sake of efficient use of resources. Even though an incident report has been submitted, it does not necessarily mean that the problem actually exists. So, the shape of the problem has to be confirmed by independent testing. That confirmation process ensures cost-effectiveness because it prevents the organization from expending any additional resources chasing after phantom incidents.

### Developing a Response Strategy from the Analysis

Once the security vulnerability or violation of procedure has been confirmed, the analyst sets out to understand its character and implications. That understanding is then used to develop a response strategy. The analyst makes a list of the technologies and processes in the existing security system that will be modified by the response and the specific components within those elements that will be changed as a result. Then the analyst develops a change strategy for each element. Along with the overall strategy, the analyst also itemizes the resultant impacts on any dependent elements and interfaces that might be affected by the modification.

The next step in the process is to make the necessary changes to ensure a better and more effective response; however, in order to maintain chain of command, it is important to obtain the appropriate authorization from the right manager. Ensuring that the change is authorized by the right individual is a critical step, because security is a complex field with many issues that a lot of executive-level decision makers do not understand. Consequently, upper-level managers either intentionally, or by default, delegate important decisions with significant resource implications to people who are not authorized to make them.

An example of an improper assignment of authority would be where a technical worker would make a decision about investment in technology for a project that should more appropriately be made by a CFO. Because of the potential for inappropriate decision making, a process has

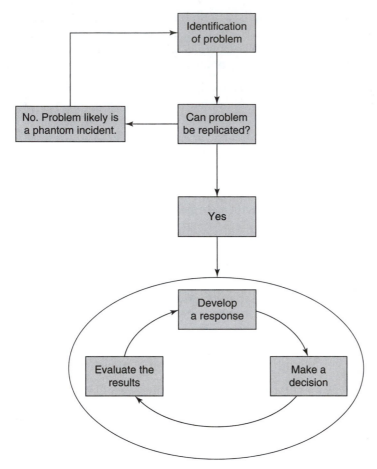

**Figure 12-2** Effective problem analysis

© Cengage Learning 2012

to be followed to ensure that the authorized decision maker makes an informed decision about issues that are part of his or her area of responsibility. The role of the security analyst is to prepare all of the information necessary to help the appropriate manager make the right decision and then ensure that that information gets to the responsible individual.

Since there might be a number of people authorized to make resource decisions, the appropriate decision maker has to be identified and designated as part of the analysis. If the change is important enough, or formal configuration management procedures are used, the decision making entity might actually be a pre-selected executive board, which is composed of all potential decision makers.

The results of the analysis, with a full explanation of the implementation requirements for each remediation option, are reported to that decision maker, or decision making body. The report must clearly outline the impacts of each option and it must be understandable to lay decision makers. In addition, each option recommended must be fully and demonstrably traceable to the business case. Once an option for change has been authorized, it is turned over to the response management function for implementation in the operational environment.

**Evaluating the Results of the Decision** Although the response management function is responsible for ensuring corrective action, the security of operations process establishes and sustains that corrective action. The role of security of operations in the process of implementing corrective action encompasses those activities that establish and then validate a selected remediation.

The security of operations process ensures that the response that has been authorized is correctly implemented. Security of operations is responsible for coordinating the development and implementation of all technical, human resource, and procedural requirements associated with the response. Those requirements have to be unambiguously communicated to the appropriate change agent. The security of operations function then works with the change agent to ensure that the remediation has been made correctly and is effective.

In order to ensure proper tracking and management, the activities required to execute the change should be documented in a detailed **statement of work (SOW)**, which should be communicated to the change agent in the form of a contract. The SOW also includes the criteria that will be used to determine whether the change was successful.

Changing anything in a security system for a large organization typically involves a complex set of technological and human-centered processes. Maintaining proper coordination for all of those is a difficult task. A simple change can sometimes cause greater problems because a dependent item was not identified, or was inadvertently affected. Thus, the boundaries for the change have to be precisely specified, as well as the criteria for assuring that only the items that should be changed are actually affected. This must all be communicated to the change agent prior to beginning the change process. The change itself is typically done by people outside of the operational security function. For instance, the manager of the information technology operation would institute the actual change to a technological item. Nevertheless, it is the role of the operational security process to ensure that the change is made according to the established criteria. Oversight is a continuous process when it comes to ensuring the integrity of the security system.

That oversight normally involves monitoring the change through reviews as specified in the SOW. Security of operations ensures that all reviews specified by the statement of work are conducted at their appropriate checkpoints and that all action items that issue out of every review are addressed by **rework**. The aim is to ensure that the eventual end product of the change satisfies all closure criteria. The assurance of satisfactory performance of rework should be based on explicit test and evaluation criteria. Finally, security of operations conducts a verification and validation exercise to ensure that the change is correct and that there is traceability between the change and the change authorization.

# Maintaining Operational Capability

*The newly redesigned operational security process was being field-tested in three locations. These three sites were the ones that the Corvallis security engineer felt would be most representative of the company's general business environment. They included a plant outside of Detroit that specialized in heavy metal manufacturing, an electronics facility in Gaithersburg, Maryland, and the company's main supply depot in Anniston, Alabama. The outcome that the*

*Corvallis security engineer was trying to confirm was that the company would be able to deploy and maintain a consistent and stable operational security process in practice. He was certain that he had gotten the design right this time, but there were too many people, with too much at stake, to take any assumptions on face value.*

*That was especially true for the managers of the line operations at the selected test facilities. Those managers were definitely not thrilled by the fact that they could not simply adjust their operation as they saw fit, without going through a complicated authorization process. In fact, the whole emphasis on ensuring a coordinated, rational, and authorized response had led to a mutiny among the plant managers. Several of them went directly to the CEO to complain that the security function was dragging down productivity.*

*So the Corvallis security engineer was dispatched to each of his test facilities to find out whether operational security discipline could be maintained in a manner that didn't get in the way of normal company operations. Since the whole concern involved nothing more than various people's opinions at this point, he knew that he needed solid performance data in order to get a final approval from the CEO. The CEO liked data-based decision making so much that he had been pushing that principle from the top. So there was plenty of support for the security engineer's evaluation plans.*

*The security engineer wanted to get into each facility and gather data directly from the various processes that were running there. That meant that he would need a baseline to measure from, so he planned on establishing a recurrent monitoring process at each site that would gather a standard set of measurements from a coordinated review process. The only issue was deciding what would be included in the baseline. He knew that the whole operational security plan was based around people, processes, and technology, so his intention was to develop a measurement system for each site that would encompass all of the integral parts of the security function. The security engineer was turning that around in his head as he was getting his bags at Detroit Metro Airport when it suddenly came to him that the executive team was actually trying to find the right balance between investing too much versus the consequences of not investing enough. And that decision was driven primarily by risk.*

*Using risk as the index, he reasoned that it ought to be possible to create a sliding scale of value that would help the organization's executive decision makers determine precisely how much to invest in controls for each pertinent piece of the operation based on an assessment of risks to each piece. Since he had already provided what most people considered an exhaustive list of controls, it should be possible to decide which of the relevant controls were appropriate for each operational circumstance based on the degree of risk. So he turned to the EBK, which specifies the following seven activities as part of the measurement perspective for security of operations:*

1. *Review strategic security technologies*

2. *Review performance and correctness of applied security controls in accordance with standards, procedures, directives, policies, regulations, and laws (statutes), and apply corrections as required*

3. *Assess the performance of security administration measurement technologies*

4. *Assess system and network vulnerabilities*

5. *Assess compliance with standards, procedures, directives, policies, regulations, and laws (statutes)*

6. *Identify improvement actions based on reviews, assessments, and other data sources*

7. *Collect IT security performance measures to ensure optimal system performance*

## Evaluating Everyday Risk

A successful operational response requires continuous awareness of the state of normal functioning. The aim of that awareness is to ensure that the operational security process remains appropriate and free of risk. The monitoring process that supports that awareness entails the routine detection and cataloging of likely threats, along with the description of all of the potentially adverse impacts that each threat represents. In order to ensure proper operational security, the effectiveness of the controls that have been deployed to ensure everyday security has to be documented.

Where operational security gets involved with risk management is in the obligation to maintain a continuous flow of information about how effectively threats are being addressed. The security of operations monitoring process establishes the means to provide the continuous assessment of threat. It is the responsibility of security of operations to ensure a continuous understanding of the company's threat and risk situation, as shown in Figure 12-3. Accurate and up-to-date information is necessary in order to ensure that decision makers have the

**Figure 12-3** Continuous scanning of the environment

most accurate picture of how and where to invest their security resources. In practical terms, the specific role of security of operations is to detect and then document each potential threat in order to ensure that a rational management decision is made about what to do about it.

In its operational form, the responsibility of the security monitoring function is to identify and characterize emerging threats. The outcome of that monitoring should then allow the right managers to make the right decision about whether a response is justified. In most settings, this type of decision making is actually a business function, rather than a security one. For that reason, all threats have to be identified, understood, and prioritized so that a practical business decision can be made about which threats actually justify the investment in controls and which threats do not.

This decision making takes place without regard to whether a given threat deserves an immediate response. Threats are often identified before their actual impact is fully understood. The analysis that ensures the right level of understanding is actually carried out by the risk management function, but risk management depends on the operational security function to describe the current, existing threat environment. The interdependence between these two functions also illustrates how the various other elements of the information security domain interact to ensure a fully integrated and systematic **security architecture**.

## Ensuring a Secure Architecture

Because the overall purpose of security of operations is to ensure a continuously effective security process in day-to-day operation, the security of operations function has to ensure the continuing correctness of the organization's security architecture. In its practical form, the process that underlies this capability has a high-level focus and it applies organization-wide. Thus, the operational security evaluation function essentially involves a systematic, organization-wide assessment process.

The aim of that assessment process is to maintain a dynamic and effective security and controls environment. The assessment function monitors the security operation in order to ensure that the most appropriate and capable set of security policies, processes, and technologies are deployed. The actual evaluations themselves focus on the processes, procedures, and technologies that comprise the organization's security system. The assessment ensures that those processes, procedures, and technologies all continue to be optimally correct and effective. In addition to ensuring the effectiveness of the overall security function, the operational security assessment function also ensures that all of the interrelationships between the organization's processes and technologies are correct.

Consequently, the security architecture should be assessed and evaluated on a regular basis, in order to determine two things. First, it must be assured that the organization's security policies, procedures, and technologies continue to remain effective. Second, any emerging trends in security should be identified and a strategy developed to address the relevant ones. Ideally, the assessment process is supported by a robust set of security **metrics**. These metrics should be standard and they should characterize the state of the organization's security processes, procedures, and technologies.

It is important to maintain the continuing correctness of the security architecture because the policies, processes, and technologies that comprise it essentially decide how secure the organization will be. Likewise, because the security situation is constantly changing, it is important that this architecture of policies, processes, and technologies is able to evolve correspondingly. That is the reason why assessments of the performance of the security of operations function and all of its associated controls should be done on a regular basis. Therefore, a defined and continuous operational testing process is essential.

It is also crucial to monitor the ongoing performance of the threat environment. Operational threats frequently originate from external sources, so in order to ensure comprehensive understanding of emerging threats, it is necessary for the organization to actively monitor all interfaces with all external actors. This monitoring process ensures comprehensive identification and reporting of threats from any source as they appear on the organization's security perimeter. The aim is to identify security threats and control failures, or violations of procedure. The most common examples of this kind of operational testing are active attempts to break the security system, such as pen-tests or ethical hacks; however, any method that tests and ensures the effectiveness of the people, processes, and technology of the security solution would be considered acceptable.

## Management Data and the Security of Operations Function

Because the overall security of operations function supports good management decision making, steps need to be taken to ensure that hard data about organizational functioning is collected and then distributed to the right decision makers. This is a critical part of the operational security planning process, since it takes accurate and up-to-date management data to support intelligent decisions about how to allocate security resources. Moreover, because it is so important to stay on top of the operational security situation, part of the security of operations process should be devoted to ensuring that the data gathering function stays as optimally effective as possible.

Effective management of any long-term security situation depends on the ability to recognize and evaluate developing threats, while judiciously managing the adjustments that have to occur in order to respond effectively to changing circumstances. As a result, the security of operations function has to embody specific mechanisms for responding to change. In particular, a formal capacity has to be built into the operation, which will allow the organization's decision makers to authorize change in the most rational way possible.

# Chapter Summary

- Security of operations is established by a formal planning process.
- The operational security plan is a subset of the overall strategic plan.
- The operational security plan specifies practices that sustain the security process.
- The design for operational security is built around a persistent set of controls.
- The purpose of the design is to create a monitoring and control capability.
- Two generic types of controls are those for people and those for technology.
- Continuing assessment is an important part of the security of operations function.
- There are two types of operational security responses—proactive and reactive.
- Most responses are the result of incident reporting.

- In order to make a rational decision about a change, all relevant information has to be gathered and analyzed.
- Changes have to be authorized by designated decision makers, who are supported by analysis.
- Secure processes require regular and systematic evaluation.

# Key Terms

**Assessment** The process of determining the status of a target environment.

**Baseline** The present status of the elements of the operating environment.

**Control framework** A collection of explicit controls designed to accomplish a purpose.

**Decision maker** The person in the organization authorized to make a specific decision.

**Incident reporting** Process to alert organizations to potentially harmful security events.

**Metrics** A measurement process which produces discrete objective data.

**Proactive response** A response in advance of a potential incident.

**Reactive response** A response that takes place after an incident has occurred.

**Rework** Additional work required to finalize a solution; usually results from a review.

**Security architecture** The specific framework of controls used by the organization.

**Security monitoring** Reviews or tests undertaken recurrently to ensure a given situation.

**Statement of work (SOW)** The specification of work to be done to accomplish a given mission.

**Strategic governance** Large-scale process designed to ensure management control.

**Threat assessment** Formal process used to identify and characterize threats.

# Questions from the CIO

The CIO requires you to brief her on the current status of your investigation. This will be an important part of your continuing work on this project, since it is essential to be able to describe all of the ramifications of a properly developed security of operations process. Consequently, the CIO would like you to answer the following questions for her:

1. What is the purpose and importance of routine security of operations?

2. What are the control principles that are part of security of operations?

3. How do you implement and enforce operational controls?

4. What is the purpose and application of process architectures?

5. What differentiates the operational strategic plan from the strategic plan? What specific things does an operational plan need to ensure that a strategic plan doesn't?

6. What is the purpose of the status baseline in operational planning? What would be the consequences if one of these did not exist?

7. Why is the assignment of accountability for implementation and execution a critical step in operational planning? What would be the consequence if this were not done?

8. How does incident reporting support operational response? What would be lacking if that function were not done?

9. What is the difference between a potential and an active incident? How are these two determined?

10. What is the point of the operational response? What benefits does that provide for the overall security process?

# Hands-On Projects

**HANDS-ON PROJECTS**

Establish an incident reporting and analysis process by creating all of the documentation that would be required by such a process. Define the lines of communication for reporting incidents at the engineering facility in the case in the Appendix. Then:

1. Define three explicit analyses that might be run for any incident

2. Provide a standard form for reporting the results of those analyses

3. Establish reporting lines based on the case

12

# chapter 13

# Network and Telecommunications Security

## Back in Familiar Territory

*The CISO was sitting on a stool in the Golden Cicada on Grand Street in Jersey City. He had walked there from the nearby PATH Station. It was one of those nice, clear fall evenings that made the nearby lights from the skyscrapers in Manhattan look like you could walk over there. Somebody somewhere was burning leaves; that smell brought back memories from when he was a kid in Ohio. He still had enough of the small town in him to recognize that the Cicada was quite a joint, even if he himself would have preferred the marina a little further up Marin Boulevard. Ten years ago, the surrounding neighborhood was mainly old abandoned factories, which made the Cicada seem more like a good place to get killed in. Now, the urban renewal had improved the atmosphere a lot, even though it had only really amounted to creating vacant lots where the factories used to stand.*

*The time had finally come to drill down to the network security part of the process, and he wanted to talk with the guy who was the master of the company's far-flung networks. The Cicada appeared to be rough on the outside, but as the CISO looked around the place, he actually appreciated the down-home atmosphere. Of course, he also knew that he was going to be sitting there with Paul Bunyan himself. The CISO was waiting for the network operations manager, who did his off-hours business out of his local haunts. The guy was doing him a favor, so the CISO decided to lose the Gucci loafers for an evening and come over to Jersey for a legendary dumpling at the Cicada, even if there were still tight creases pressed into his Rock & Republic jeans.*

*The CISO had worked with a lot of nerds, but he had never worked with one quite like the network operations manager. The guy was as righteous a geek as any he had ever encountered. But he was probably six foot, six inches tall and 250 pounds of muscle, and he had played linebacker at Iowa for four years. Admittedly, the lumberjack shirts and the red bushy beard were an affectation. But the fact remained that the network operations manager was an exceedingly knowledgeable guy. So when the little door at the front of the place opened and the network operations manager wedged his industrial size frame into the place, the CISO knew he was about to get some extremely useful advice. The thing the CISO couldn't stop marveling over was the fact that the network operations manager still hulked several inches over him, even though the CISO was sitting on a tall stool at the bar.*

*After a little small talk, they settled at a table with a couple of Buds. The CISO actually never drank mass-market beer, especially from a long-neck bottle, but he needed the guy's insight on the network security issues, so he made the exception just to fit in. The network operations manager told him that there were no known problems with the company's telecommunications infrastructure. Like most organizations, the company had gone the* **virtual private network (VPN)** *route back in the late 1990s, when the advent of tunneling technologies and strong encryption made the scalability and cost advantages of the Internet far preferable to the old wide area intranet that the company had been running. The standardized, site-to-site VPN that had evolved over the subsequent decade carried both data and voice and was a model of up-to-date internetworking.*

*The local area networks at each of the installations that populated the company's VPN sat behind robust and well-maintained firewalls that ensured that the private networks at each of those sites would be secured from the general Internet. Likewise IPSec tunneling protocols and Cisco concentrators with built-in, scalable encryption processing (SEP) ensured that nobody on the outside could read the company's mail. Remote access requests at each site were handled through AAA (authorization, authentication, and accounting) remote access servers attached to VPN optimized* **routers** *and Cisco secure, private, Internet exchange (PIX) firewalls.*

*The bottom line was that from a security standpoint, the actual network infrastructure was as robust and capable as it could be. Nonetheless, the network operations manager could see one major flaw in the scheme: the lack of any kind of unified or coherent approach for the management of the overall network operation. That missing strategy posed a serious operational problem for managers like him. Without uniform guidance, it was hard to make any kind of change to the network as a whole without a lot of negotiation between the various stakeholders. In fact, the network operations manager said that rather than researching and implementing new, more responsive technologies, he spent most of his time just making sure that everybody in the network operation was on the same page. As a result, a lot of staff time and money got wasted just checking signals in the huddle.*

*Since the technology never stopped evolving, that time-lag was creating a serious response gap between the installation of new equipment and the implementation of the steps necessary to ensure that that equipment did not create security problems. For example, the operations manager told the CISO about an instance where, while migrating a database from one server to another, the maintenance staff had forgotten to turn off the old server. Since the new server and the old server were still linked, and the old server had had its firewall taken down, that meant that the entire database had been inadvertently left wide open to the Internet. That particular exposure was there for a couple of days until somebody caught the problem while doing routine port scans. The operations manager told the CISO that that sort of potentially catastrophic situation happened all of the time, mainly because the guys in the network opera-tion had a tendency to swing too soon at the pitch, at least whenever hot new technology was involved.*

*For his part, the CISO noted that the network operations manager used a lot of sports meta-phors. That was understandable given his background. What was not understandable was the role of the CIO over the past 10 years. In his mind the only thing the CIO should have been doing during that time was fostering effective and cost-efficient communication between her various telecommunications managers. Instead, her lack of attention to that obvious manage-ment detail had left it up to the individual heads of the different network functions to keep a coherent security response. Fortunately, the company had had individual managers, like the network operations manager, who were extremely capable. Nonetheless, it would be a lot safer and simpler to just have an effective organization-wide management process in place to guide the decisions about keeping the network secure.*

*Without putting too fine a point on the matter, the CISO decided that he would undertake that development process himself. He was aware that the CIO would probably not think that a coherent set of company-wide management policies were important to the day-to-day oper-ation of the system, since she was very much involved with the technology itself. On the other hand, the CISO was sure that the CEO would recognize the importance of management con-trol of the network security process. Better yet, the CEO would be likely to make the favorable comparison between the CISO's enterprise-wide vision and the CIO's lack of focus when he started thinking about her successor.*

*In order to put the policy creation process on a standard basis, the CISO turned to the EBK. He was aware that that document specified the following nine common work functions for the management of network and telecommunication security:*

1. *Establish a network and telecommunications security program in line with enterprise goals and policies*

2. *Manage the necessary resources, including financial resources, to establish and maintain an effective network and telecommunications security program*

3. *Direct network and telecommunications security personnel*

4. *Define the scope of the network and telecommunications security program*

5. *Establish communications between the network and telecommunications security team and related security teams (e.g., technical support, security administration, and incident response)*

6. *Establish a network and telecommunications performance measurement and monitoring program*

7. *Ensure enterprise compliance with applicable network-based standards, procedures, directives, policies, regulations, and laws (statutes)*

8. *Ensure that network-based audits and management reviews are conducted to implement process improvement*

9. *Ensure that appropriate changes and improvement actions are implemented as required*

*These work functions are policy-based. The aim is to establish an effective infrastructure of high-level policies across the organization.*

# Creating a Managed Network

Good security management starts with the creation of a coherent set of policies. The purpose of those policies is to define the basic mode of operation for a given network, in order to ensure the confidentiality, integrity, and availability of the information that flows across it. The list of policies can be long, and will vary based on situations unique to an organization, but a generic set of policies should cover the areas described in the following sections. Because they guide use and establish general accountability, the policies that define the rules for how the network should be used are perhaps the most far-reaching of the general policies for security.

## Acceptable Use Policies

The network exists for specific business purposes, which have to be kept in strict alignment with the network security policy. Business users in particular have responsibilities with respect to the use of networking resources. Therefore, acceptable use policies have to be created to outline the proper use of the network for different types of users. These types are typically factored into three categories: end-users, administrators, and outsiders. A standard acceptable use policy is fine for the end-users of the system who are employees and guests. Administrators, however, need a different set of policies because of their enhanced authority. These people will have more rules defined as part of their terms of acceptable use. Finally, third parties like business partners and other outside agencies have to be able to access the business's networks in order to work with the organization. These separate entities have to be treated as untrusted unless they can be authenticated and authorized, since their behavior is outside the organization's range of control.

The standard acceptable use policy begins with a statement of business goals and objectives. After defining the business purposes of the physical network, the importance of the information that is transmitted along that network also has to be emphasized. Ownership and secondary use rights, as well as security rules have to be clarified. Specific definitions of acceptable use and examples of prohibited use also have to be provided. Examples of typical acceptable use criteria include authorized business purposes, minor personal use, and work-related education. Typical prohibited uses include conducting any personal outside business, harassment, pornography, spamming, trafficking in passwords, fraudulent or other criminal activity, and any anti-company blogging, e-mails, and Web sites.

## Remote Access Policies

Remote access allows users who are outside the physical boundaries of the network to access the network and its resources. Because remote access can be facilitated through a variety of mechanisms, the organization needs to select the appropriate ones for its circumstances. The remote access policy includes several types of definitions. The most important one defines what constitutes remote access for that particular business and who in the business will be allowed to use it. Another important aspect of remote access is the need to establish the proper expectations for users of the network. For example, it might be made clear that the security rules are the same with remote access as they are when an individual is connected to a local machine.

Rules to control authentication tokens are important because remote access brings with it the issue of logins and passwords. The first stop is a credential check via a remote access server. If the proper credentials are presented, then the user is granted access to the system. For this reason, the remote access policy needs to stress the importance of not divulging the tokens or information associated with one's account for remote access. Because physical safeguards are not in place, protection becomes more problematic If unseen individuals who are seeking access have the right credentials, they will not be otherwise supervised or controlled.

Another issue with remote access is the use of resources that may not be under the control of the organization, specifically mobile computing devices. The ability of those devices to hook to a network raises the prospect of viruses and other forms of malware coming from a machine that may not be protected. Addressing this issue in the remote access policy can be as simple as only allowing access to a certain set of approved devices, or it can include a number of lesser restrictions.

In addition to the various policies associated with remote access, there are normally several technical requirements that are specified as part of acceptable use policies. One of the most common elements of a remote access policy is the method of transmitting encrypted communications over the Internet. Because of the need to carefully control the technical environment, encryption is typically supported through the use of VPNs. These are generally the most reliable and cost-efficient ways to ensure a stable and well-defined **network architecture**. If a VPN approach is selected, several technical specifications have to be provided. Those specifications entail connection points and VPN methods. Since the details of the VPN connection may change over time, it is best not to state those in the policy directly.

## Network Security Control Policies

Although the design and implementation of network security controls is site-specific, there are several elements of network security policy that are common across all areas. The first of those is the need to specify the physical security controls. Physical security of network components is a foundational element of network security; if an attacker obtains physical access to network components, then the ability to secure the network is significantly impaired.

A crucial element of a network security policy is the description of a set of tangible controls to address physical security. Elements of physical location, physical access, and environment are crucial aspects of securing a network. For instance, sample elements of a network security control policy include such specifications as, "all network equipment closets and cable runs should be built according to appropriate codes and standards," or "all network equipment should be kept under lock and key," or even "only authorized personnel will be granted physical access to network equipment."

Along with the physical security controls, there is also the requirement for controls for logical security. This is nothing more than the rational practices that the organization chooses to adopt to ensure the proper execution of the network. Logical access controls ensure control of the electronic elements of the network. Logical security controls create boundaries between network segments and are also used to control the flow of traffic across those segments. Routing boundaries, VLAN boundaries, and subnet boundaries are all common methods of controlling traffic flows. Sample elements of a network security control policy might include, "subnets will be used to separate the network into logical elements," or "VLANs will be used to control access to different segments of a network," or even "all activity on infrastructure devices will be logged."

The third set of network security control policies are those that are designed to ensure the everyday integrity of the networks themselves. These are the operational practices that will be followed to make certain that the system always functions within acceptable levels of performance and that any intrusions or undesirable actions against the system are detected and addressed in the shortest time possible. The first of these is the need to maintain the integrity of the network infrastructure. Those policies include the maintenance of a correct logical infrastructure design. One of the goals of an attack against a network is to change the network's behavior, which would enable an attacker to capture or alter traffic across the network in a virtually undetectable manner. For this reason, protecting the integrity of the network is of prime importance.

Along with the integrity controls for the system, there should also be controls that ensure the fundamental conditions of information security. The ultimate goal of infrastructure/network security is to provide the appropriate level of control as required by the information needs that are being transported across the network. In order to ensure fundamental control, the network administrator should always monitor and log review network activities in order to verify that the appropriate levels of confidentiality, integrity, and availability are being provided. Those reviews should be aimed at ensuring compliance with the policies and procedures established for the network. Because the controls have to work properly, a mechanism to monitor and verify their performance has to be specified. This specification is necessary in order to ensure the functioning of the control set over time.

# Culture Always Comes First

*The CISO decided to spend a little time down in the network operations center. He had been thinking about what the network manager had told him about how the lack of a coherent management framework caused serious problems with coordination and control. He was pretty sure that he knew what to do, but he wanted to confirm his decision with a little observation. What the CISO had in mind was the development of a comprehensive, top-down design of a network security management process. He knew that implementing that design was going to be a problem unless he had the entire network staff on board. Unfortunately, network operations were about as far from his comfort zone as he could possibly get. A little soak time with the nerds in the op-center would help him get acclimated to the culture.*

*The op-center was a couple of floors down from the CISO's office on the 44th floor. All of the company's critical functions were on the top three floors and were only accessible by an elevator that required a key. The network operations center certainly qualified as a critical function, so it was up there in the lofty space with the executive staff and their support personnel. As he went through the biometric exercise that let him in, the CISO was struck by the fact that the op-center lived up to Hollywood's expectations of what a high-tech command and control center ought to look like. The desks of the operators were arrayed in a* concentric semicircle around a "big board" video wall that displayed the schematic details of the network operation in real time. A board just above the video wall was showing a mosaic of up-to-the-minute news events. That was the "ready board." The point of that device was to keep the techs in the op-center aware of what was happening in the outside world. Should any incident occur on the network anywhere in the world, the ready board would slide down over to the left side of the room and begin active monitoring read-outs of the incident.

The techs were sitting at individual desks which represented the area of specific network technology they were supposed to monitor. In general, each tech had three monitors arrayed on the desk to support his or her specific area of responsibility. The lighting was subdued and the conversation was primarily through headsets, so there was constant chatter in the background.

The network operations manager got the CISO a seat in the "war room," which was a glassed-in area at the back of the op-center that served as a meeting room in case of emergencies and as a lunch room for the techs in all other cases. The op-center manager seemed to be channeling Custer, or maybe Buffalo Bill that day, since he had lost the checkered shirt and red suspenders and opted for a buckskin coat instead. From their seats at the table closest to the window wall, he pointed out the intricate array of devices and interconnections that constituted the U.S. and Canadian network of the company. The entire array was all controlled from this op-center. Although there were mirror sites for Europe and the Pacific Rim in Amsterdam and Singapore, overall command and control originated from this site in New York.

As the CISO had suspected, each site operated independently. That was good for close coordination of operations, but it was not so good from the standpoint of uniformity of action across an interconnected network. At times, there were some serious glitches at the artificial network boundaries that were caused by misunderstandings about **configurations** and even simple operating procedures. These problems had been kept off the radar of the company's executive staff simply because the network operations crew had quickly and competently handled them as they arose. Luckily, none of the issues so far had involved security breaches.

Nonetheless, both the network operations manager and the CISO recognized that those problems never should have happened and that the potential for a serious network security incident was definitely on the table. As the CISO laid out his ideas about designing a uniform operating procedure for the network, the op-center manager was more than enthusiastically on board, so much so that the CISO endured an extremely painful handshake of gratitude from the guy. The CISO then let himself out of the op-center using the same biometric access control process that he had followed on the way in. He noted with relief how important the logging of access was down there.

In the CISO's mind, the next step was to get somebody to head a design project. The Corvallis security engineer was good at operational planning but was really not a hardcore technical type. So the CISO began to think about how he could get the maximum insight while still keeping the big-picture perspective on security that had served him so well. Then it hit him: the perfect candidate to help with the design was right there in his own op-center. He dashed up to his office to get the wheels turning to transfer the Corvallis *security engineer to New York to head up the planning effort, with the op-center manager seconded to him.*

*The CISO expected the Corvallis security engineer to be overjoyed at the prospect of coming to the big city; he didn't expect the guy to act like he was being transferred to the gulag instead. The problem was that the Corvallis security engineer clearly liked trees better than nightlife. On the other hand, the CISO was pretty sure that the op-center manager knew where all of the trees in the area were. Between the two of them, they could probably enjoy nature while putting together an iron-clad design for managing the network. So he did the necessary approvals to put them together. The design that the CISO was looking for had to be the right mix of management and technical activities. He also knew that the EBK had the following recommendations about activities that would ensure that the network security process was correct:*

1. *Develop network- and host-based security policies in accordance with standards, procedures, directives, policies, regulations, and laws (statutes)*

2. *Specify strategic security plans for network telecommunications in accordance with established policy, to meet organizational security goals*

3. *Develop standard operating procedures for network and telecommunications security operations and maintenance*

4. *Develop effective network domain security controls in accordance with enterprise, network, and host-based policies*

5. *Develop network security performance reports*

6. *Develop network security and telecommunication audit processes, guidelines, and procedures*

# Defining the Boundaries of Trust

Rules that define the boundaries of **trust** are an essential factor in the establishment of a network security function. Trusted parties are the networks that are known; they can be authenticated and their rights assigned. Known networks fall within the boundaries of trust. Untrusted networks, however are the networks that are either not known or cannot be identified. As a result, those types of networks fall outside the boundaries of trust. Their security status is either unknown or known to be unreliable. Although elements of an organization's trusted network might still communicate with an untrusted one, that network needs to be protected from any harm that might originate from the untrusted source.

## Policy Development for Network Components

The primary distinction between network equipment and computer equipment is that network equipment has the specialized job of communicating data, rather than processing it. Networks embody the computer elements that are dedicated to channeling data from sender to receiver. The physical components that are typically unique to networks are switches, **hubs**, routers, and cables. Switches and hubs are the physical components that interconnect the computers within a network, and routers connect that network to a common resource such as the Internet. Cables provide the direct physical link between all of these elements.

The underlying software that enables the physical components' ability to interconnect with each other establishes two types of control: connection control and transmission control. Connection control ensures the connection between any type of relevant electronic device and a network. It sets up a temporary transmission link between the various devices that are involved in an exchange of data. Software drivers that are embedded in those devices as well as the related network access protocols establish and then facilitate that link. Those drivers and their operating protocols have to be properly configured in order to ensure suitable control over the connection, which has to be maintained and updated over time.

The other software-enabled function in a network is transmission control. As the name implies, transmission control regulates the transmission process and ensures that the communication between devices is flowing properly across the connections that were established by the connection control function. Transmission control is regulated through software drivers that are built into the communications devices, as well as the operating systems of the interconnected computers. Machine-level processes encode the data for transmission between the devices and also detect and recover from any breakdown in the transmission process. The primary aim of the security aspect of transmission control is to ensure that the components of the system that are doing the actual encoding and transmitting are correctly arranged and that the software required to assure a secure transmission process is installed and working properly.

## Policy Development and the Secure Network Design

Networks have to fulfill the business purposes of the organization. For that reason, several pieces of business information are required to design a secure network. First, the criticality of the information on the network has to be known. In order to develop an "informed" design, the designer needs to know the sensitivity of the data that is processed by the components of the network. To get *that* knowledge, the designer has to inventory the types of information that flows through all of the relevant devices on the network.

Next, the designer has to determine how that information is communicated between devices. Essentially, the designer needs to find out what information is passed around the network and how the components of the network are used to communicate it. Once the sensitivity and means of transmitting the data is understood, the designer ought to be able to develop an effective protection scheme for network transmissions.

The collective knowledge of who will be transmitting information and what kind of information will be transmitted should dictate the form of the network security scheme. Most network security schemes are based around the formulation of enclaves. An enclave is nothing more than protected space. Designated enclaves are put behind firewalls with the most secure enclave being firewalled behind the most rigorous defenses. This concept is the basis for **defense-in-depth** designs for networks.

The advantage of a defense-in-depth approach is that the architecture of the network will block access to critical elements of the company's data. For instance, the router in front of the company's critical file servers can restrict access to the critical file segment to those devices located in other segments, such as the senior executive suite. This will prevent the CEO from checking his reports from a different machine than those that have been authorized. It also makes it significantly harder for an attacker to do the same thing, as shown in Figure 13-1.

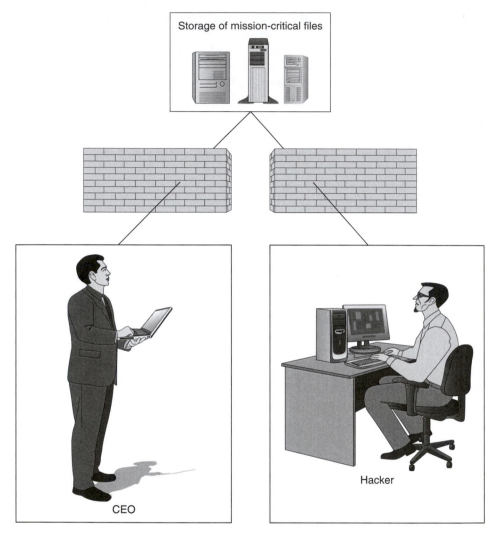

**Figure 13-1**  Blocked access

# Putting the Pieces Together

*The design project for the network security function was complete, and the Corvallis security engineer couldn't wait to get out of New York and back to the more leisurely pace of Oregon. He and the network manager had formed a bond of sorts over the two months that the Corvallis engineer had had to spend in Jersey City. The Corvallis engineer, whose impressions of New Jersey had mainly been formed by the television series* The Sopranos, *had not expected to find such a variety of coastal flora and fauna and so much open space. It was not an impossibly long drive down to the wildlife and nature areas north of Fort Dix. Plus, as the CISO had suspected, the network manager certainly knew his way around a forest. In fact, the Corvallis security engineer thought that the opportunity to explore the areas in the stretch between*

*Jersey City and Atlantic City with the network manager was one of the best parts of his time on the east coast.*

*The design was finished, and it was as comprehensive and detailed as it was practical. It had a complete set of policies, and the underlying procedures provided sufficient direction to theoretically allow anybody working on the network to have uniform protection. The engineer and the network manager were waiting anxiously in the wide hall outside the CISO's office to do the unveiling. Their anxiety was for two different but highly related reasons. The Corvallis engineer just wanted the CISO to bless the design so he could hop on the next commercial flight back to Oregon, while the network manager just wanted to get back to what he really liked to do, which was managing the network. They both knew that if the CISO didn't like what he saw, they would be stuck back in the little office the company had provided for them. So they were both anxious to make the sale.*

*The CISO breezed up the hall with the entire executive staff in his wake. That was a good sign as far as the network manager was concerned. He knew that the CISO never rolled out anything that he didn't already know would add to his legend. The presentation itself was not as easy as either the security engineer or the network manager would have liked. That was because nobody in the room, with the possible exception of the CIO, understood the constraints that the underlying technology put on the security process. So both of the presenters stuck to the same message, which was that the actual technology didn't matter as long as there was a robust management control process in place to ensure that all of the actions involving the implementation and practical use of that technology were proper. The security devices and applications just had to be intelligently selected, properly configured, well-controlled, and clearly understood.*

*The CEO liked the concept of policy-based control, which both the security engineer and the network manager knew would mean that the CISO would love it. In fact, the CISO loved it so much that he decided to take over the implementation process himself. The security engineer and the network manager knew better than to actually breathe an unqualified sigh of relief right in front of the company executives. Nevertheless, they were both planning their official "retirement from the project" celebration. The next day, the security engineer was indeed making his way down the jet way at LaGuardia with the avowed purpose of never seeing New Jersey again.*

*On the other hand, the CISO knew he would need the network manager for one more little task: planning the technical details of the actual implementation process. Since the whole point of the design was to enforce top-down uniformity, that was not as difficult as the CISO might have imagined. The network manager was more than happy to take up that challenge as long as there was something in it for him. The CISO, who was not particularly technical, understood what that meant; the network manager had him over a barrel. The following week, the company announced that the manager of the network operation center had just been promoted to director of network security for the entire company.*

*As far as the new director of network security was concerned, that promotion and the raise that was attached to it made the implementation process a lot easier. He also had the EBK to turn to, and that document provided some useful practical advice. The EBK specifies the following 10 steps for the implementation function for network and telecommunications security:*

1. *Prevent and detect intrusions, and protect against malware*
2. *Perform audit tracking and reporting*

3. *Apply and manage effective network domain security controls in accordance with enterprise, network, and host-based policies*

4. *Test strategic network security technologies for effectiveness*

5. *Monitor and assess network security vulnerabilities and threats using various technical and non-technical data*

6. *Mitigate network security vulnerabilities in response to problems identified in vulnerability reports*

7. *Provide real-time network intrusion response*

8. *Ensure that messages are confidential and free from tampering and repudiation*

9. *Defend network communications from tampering and/or eavesdropping*

10. *Compile data into measures for analysis and reporting*

*Like the design function, these are a mix of management and technical activities. As a group, their role is to ensure that the network and telecommunications security function is embedded as part of the ongoing operation of the organization.*

# Implementing the Network Security Function

The process of implementing network security starts with architecture. A network can have an open architecture like the Internet, where everything is connected to everything, or it can have a partitioned architecture where access to each partition is based on a defined set of access rights. The open architecture is most common because it is easy to implement, but it offers no network level protection against intruders or malicious code. The segmented approach is more difficult to design and implement, but that approach offers significant improvements in security and traffic management, and it typically provides that without additional hardware for the same levels of functionality.

The segmented approach to network security entails a partitioned or subdivided topology. The goal of that partitioning is to prevent any successful intruder from getting into other parts of the system. Effective segmentation is based on establishing a number of concentric security perimeters. The physical components of a segmented network, which typically create those virtual partitions, are the routers and firewalls that secure the boundaries of each layer. From a network topology standpoint, the outermost perimeter constitutes the dividing point between the assets that the organization wishes to control and the ones that it does not seek to protect. The perimeters, which define the boundaries of each succeeding layer, signify ever-increasing levels of security.

In practical terms, segmentation takes place at the point where a trusted network component has to be distinguished from a less trusted one. As a result, the outermost perimeter of the network is by definition the most insecure part. Since the outer perimeter of the network is the area that is the easiest to access, it is the point that is most frequently attacked. For that reason, sensitive information should always sit behind the maximum practical number of layers, secured by firewalls and filtering routers. That arrangement creates the defense-in-depth scheme, as shown in Figure 13-2.

In addition to the proper architecture, specific network security functions can improve network security efforts. Firewalls can be configured to control traffic across various segments,

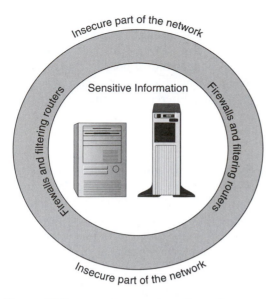

**Figure 13-2** Protecting sensitive information

© *Cengage Learning 2012*

limiting access to predefined traffic by function. **Intrusion Detection System (IDS)** devices act as monitors of those segments, examining network or host traffic and reporting on traffic that appears to be improper. Devices such as VPN endpoints can act as portals to a secure network connection inside the organization's network, allowing secure communication channels to authorized devices outside the network.

## Network Security Devices: The Firewall

Firewalls and IDS devices are two of the most common network security devices. The component that is most closely associated with the enforcement of access rights is the firewall. Firewalls can be implemented in hardware, software, or both. These high-level software utilities sit on the router end of a physical network and protect it from access by other networks. Typically, firewalls ensure that only trusted networks can gain access, and they are also used to monitor and regulate network traffic across the network. Firewalls come in many sizes and levels of complexity. Having numerous firewalls, with each one set up to protect its own segment, is generally considered to be good practice because it creates a defense-in-depth. Network security policies that are embedded in the software of the firewall dictate access at each level of security. The ability to ensure that an effective set of policies for access control is configured into the firewall is an important part of the overall network security process.

Firewalls regulate the flow of network traffic according to a set of rules. The development of the rules to embed in firewalls will ensure that those devices limit traffic on a network to only those enclaves that are specified in their rules. For instance, in the database server portion of the network, the only traffic that might be allowed across the network boundary would be the data transmitted between the various database servers. Those transmissions would only obey the established communication protocols; other traffic to and from the machines would be blocked. Segmentation into enclaves would also allow the network to act as a security mechanism for data, because it would create the basis for a defense-in-depth scheme.

The details behind firewall settings at each location will obviously be subject to change as new applications impose new access criteria in the firewall protection scheme. The only important point from a security standpoint is that any firewall rule changes have to be approved by a designated authority such as a change control board or a configuration manager. The approved change is then implemented via the configuration management process. In that respect, changes in firewall settings are no different than the changes that are made to software and other controlled entities.

## Software-Based IDSs

The other common network security device is the IDS, which functions as an early warning sensor on the perimeter of the system. An IDS analyzes network traffic. Its primary function is to identify and isolate attacks. It does that by monitoring activity on the system boundary, or by assessing performance data during the actual operation of the network. There are two main types of IDSs. The software-based version is embedded in the network software itself. The hardware versions are micro-coded into the physical equipment of the network.

IDSs are designed to analyze network traffic for packets that match patterns of malicious behavior. They alert an operator that potentially malicious behavior is occurring on the network. An IDS is a valuable warning system if it is combined with a network design that segregates traffic using firewalls.

Because software-based IDSs are embedded in the network itself, they are typically called network intrusion detection systems (NIDS). These systems analyze the network packet information as it flows across its boundaries. NIDSs do their work in real time; they monitor the streaming of network packets through the various transmission links of the network, then analyze packet information for trouble. If threats are identified, NIDSs will usually sound an alarm, or they might even shut down the link. There are four ordinary approaches to network-based intrusion detection: pattern matching, state matching, analysis engine, and traffic anomaly-based software systems. The first two methods rely on identifying patterns within the data. The other two do their work by identifying suspicious behaviors in the routine functioning of the network.

The simplest method by far is the pattern matching NIDS, which checks inward-bound packets to see if they match specific signatures that are stored in the NIDS itself. Those signatures represent a known set of attacks. In that respect, NIDSs function in the same way that a virus checker does. They identify and respond to pre-identified patterns in the network traffic that are known to be malicious. For that reason, attackers only have to use unique patterns in their code in order to avoid detection.

State matching NIDSs are more reliable than the pattern matching approach because the NIDS bases its judgments on behaviors rather than pre-programmed patterns. As a result, state matching NIDSs can identify an impending attack that might have an unknown code pattern, based on its uncharacteristic behavior. Nonetheless, because that particular NIDS uses a pre-defined set of characteristic behaviors as a point of comparison it requires frequent updates of its behavioral signature database in order to be effective.

At their heart, analysis engine methods use anomalous activities that are known to be suspicious, such as starts and restarts, or logins at strange hours, as the point of reference for their response. In many ways the analysis engine approach just represents practical, common sense security. For instance a person trying to unlock a door in the middle of the afternoon would probably not raise suspicion, while the same person would be suspicious if they were doing the same thing at 3:00 a.m. Statistical anomaly-based systems get around the limitations of pattern matching because they can make decisions based on deviations from "predictable" behavior. Statistical anomaly-based NIDS build baselines of normal traffic over time, in order to identify deviations from those baselines. Because variations in behavior are the basis for the identification, these systems can spot previously unknown attacks. The problem with these systems is their complexity; because they are reliant on their baselines to judge responses, NIDSs must also have a good picture of what the "normal" traffic environment looks like in order to function properly.

Traffic anomaly-based systems monitor the network for out-of-the-ordinary traffic activities, such as a sudden flood of TCP packets or the unexpected appearance of a new node on the network. As a result, traffic anomaly-based IDSs can recognize formerly uncharacterized attacks. But these systems suffer from the same problem as the statistical anomaly-based approaches; they have to know what "ordinary" traffic looks like in order to be able to make decisions about anomalous behaviors.

**Audit-Based Intrusion Detection Approaches** Audit-based intrusion detection approaches are really just special applications of the audit function. Audit-based intrusion detection depends on data in system logs. Events that take place within the system are recorded in those logs. That data is then analyzed by means of a conventional audit function. The aim is to spot changes that are not permitted or patterns of use that are suspicious.

The audit examines standard, machine-based logs, which can be adapted for security purposes. A system log is a record of the processing activities for a particular area of the system. Although that data is typically generated automatically and kept in static files by the system, it can also be kept in paper logs maintained external to the system, such as visitor logs.

Audits are done to evaluate operating data that is contained in the system, network, application, and user activity logs. The audit trails captured in those logs can alert the human staff to suspicious activity. The outcome of this kind of evaluation is typically additional investigation. The aim is to obtain all of the evidence that is needed to understand intruder activity and then provide information for proceeding with remedial action. Types of events that can be captured in an audit trail include such things as network connection events, a system-level event, or an application-level event. Specialized logs can be created to record use and even keystroke data.

The main problem with the audit-based approach is the sheer volume of data that the system logs produce. This makes it hard to formulate audit trails, automated auditing tools which can be set to look for specific patterns in the data. Whatever approach is used, it is important to ensure that the logs contain data that can be trusted, since many attacks are aimed at disabling or even wiping out the logging data.

It is normal practice for operators to examine the logs in order to understand the meaning of automated alerts, such as those from firewalls and IDSs. The use of an integrated intrusion detection approach, which combines automated monitoring with audit-based analysis, helps the managers of the network ensure that network traffic remains appropriate to the purposes of the business.

**The Change Control Function** The network is an essential part of the operating environment of any organization. Just as changes to the system's software should be placed under configuration management control, so too should network changes. Thus, changes to firewall rule sets should undergo the same scrutiny as changes to the operating system or other critical applications. Network devices, such as routers and switches, are programmable. It should be standard policy for all network security components, including applications such as IDSs and firewalls, to be kept under tight change control. The use of a change control board to approve changes over network configurations will offer the same level of protection to the network components as it does to operating systems and applications.

## Staying on Top of Change

*Both the CISO and the new network security manager were pleased with the level of control that they had just implemented. The management of the network was now fully integrated into an organization-wide policy and procedure scheme that ensured close coordination between the various operational areas. The implementation of a control board for network configuration management had eliminated the firewall and IDS configuration problems, which had plagued the network operation since the 1990s.*

*Moreover, because most of the functioning of the network was now under audit scrutiny, it was theoretically possible to provide audit trails that would allow the CISO and the network security manager to document their success. The evidence required to prove that their process was working was already sitting in the many logs that were maintained by the system. The only thing that had to be done was to ensure that the scheme that they had so carefully crafted would not degrade over time.*

*Both the CISO and the network security manager knew that the rapid and sometimes radical change in the threat picture was going to be a problem. Those changes were basically due to the emergence of new threats or the evolution of the technology. The CISO and the network security manager also knew that simple mismanagement was probably the single point of failure for their system. So their aim was to get a monitoring and assessment process in place that would ensure that the network security manager would always be on top of the network as it evolved over time.*

*The CISO was ready to hand the responsibility for that over to the network security manager for a couple of reasons. First and foremost, the CISO simply didn't have the time to monitor the network. The CISO had also grown to like and trust the network security manager. The guy obviously had the kind of good judgment and common sense that was needed to run an operation as complex as the network security function. More importantly from the CISO's standpoint, the network security manager had exhibited the kind of personal loyalty that the CISO liked to see from close subordinates. That loyalty boded well for the future of their relationship in the company, since it meant that the CISO could count on the network security manager in his ongoing efforts to scramble to the top of the executive pyramid.*

*The CISO went back to his lair on the 44th floor and left the network security manager to handle the definition and implementation of the evaluation process for the network security function. The network security manager was planning those evaluations on a routinely scheduled basis because he felt that it was important to maintain a regular and disciplined understanding of the status of the system. He had played football long enough to develop a profound under-standing of the need for discipline.*

*Just like the CISO, the network security manager used the recommendations of the EBK as the starting point for his thinking. The EBK specifies these six high-level functions for evaluating the network and telecommunication security competency:*

1. *Perform a network security evaluation, calculate risks to the enterprise, and recommend remediation activities*

2. *Ensure that appropriate solutions to eliminate or otherwise mitigate identified vulnerabilities are implemented effectively*

3. *Assess fulfillment of functional requirements by arranging independent verification and validation of the network*

4. *Analyze data and report results*

5. *Ensure that anti-malware systems are operating correctly*

6. *Compile data into measures for analysis and reporting*

*Their aim is to assess the continuing conformance of the network and its associated equipment and security controls with policies, standards, regulations, and laws. Those functions are mana-gerial activities, whose main purpose is to keep the network security function in a secure state.*

## Ensuring the Security Is Always Up to Date

Consistency is always a threat to the operation of networks. If an organization's approach to security remains constant over time, then the inevitable change to the technology and the threat environment will gradually make the network less secure. Even with a good design, a strong set of controls, and professional operators, the network will develop holes with the passing of time that can be exploited by adversaries. Those holes might be caused by a failure to update obsolete technologies, or they might be the result of implementing new technologies in an unsuitable manner. Either way, if it is not dealt with directly, change will create vulnerabilities.

One of the best ways to stay on top of change is knowing the current state of the security system at all times. That knowledge is gained through a series of regularly scheduled network security evaluations, formal exercises that verify designs, configurations, and operations. Hands-on penetration tests and ethical hacks can also be done to test the network resiliency against known attack vectors. In addition, a regular set of penetration tests can be used to certify the state of the network for both upper management and organizational stakeholders. The results of those tests would also be reported to the board of directors and shareholders.

## Attacking Your Own Network

In order to test for specific vulnerabilities, test protocols are run at the chosen points in the network. These tests are almost always real-time tests, in that that they are conducted under live, operational circumstances. They are designed to verify the assumptions that are embed-ded in the test cases. The results will at a minimum verify that the network is capable of detecting the target test events. If the intention is for the function being tested to respond to, or block, the test exploit, then there have to be outcomes available that will either validate that assumption or prove it to be false.

**Figure 13-3** Compliance auditing

© *Cengage Learning 2012*

Because it is usually one of the testing requirements for active tests such as penetration tests, it is also necessary that those tests should be conducted in a way that does not tip off the network's operators that they are about to occur. That is because one of the primary aims of testing is to corroborate that the people who are operating the network are able to respond correctly in a given situation. The ability to provide that independent validation is useful information about the overall state of network security.

## Read Your Security Audit Reports

In addition to the periodic active tests, like penetration tests, there are other ways to evaluate the performance of the various mechanisms that underwrite the security of the network. Like all other IT functions, the network should be subjected to standard internal audit-based compliance auditing. These audits are meant to verify that the specified controls are in place, operating as intended and doing the job that is expected, as shown in Figure 13-3.

These periodic audits can verify the effectiveness of everything from the simple, such as password rules, to the complex, such as firewall and IDS performance. Periodic external audits provide feedback about the status of the systems as configured. Internal audits can also verify that internal business processes, which have been designed to enhance or enable the functioning of the network security function, are operating as designed and as desired.

# Chapter Summary

- The role of network security is to ensure that all of the components of the network continue to satisfy their intended purpose.

- Networks are managed through coherent policies and their attendant procedures.

- A critical element of network security is designing the right set of coherent controls.

- Comprehensive controls over the process constitute an essential element of security.

- Defining the boundaries of trust is the first step in establishing security enclaves.

- Enclaves define the segments of the network that have to be secured.

- Network devices are set on the perimeter of network segments to control traffic through each segment.

- Segmentation into increasing levels of security is how defense-in-depth is realized on a network.

- Two general types of control on a network are connection control and transmission control.

- Network devices have to be configured to ensure optimum connection control and transmission control.

- There are four kinds of automated network security devices called network intrusion detection systems (NIDS): pattern matching, state matching, analysis engine, and traffic anomaly detection systems.

- Audit-based intrusion detection uses systems logs. It can be very effective, but is often too slow to react.

- The essence of network security management is ongoing evaluation, because of the continuous changes in technology and the threat environment.

# Key Terms

**Configuration** The specific array of software or hardware items that make up a component or system.

**Defense-in-depth** The arrangement of protection into increasingly stronger layers of security.

**Hub** A component of a network that interconnects two components with each other.

**Intrusion Detection System (IDS)** An automated system that identifies unauthorized attempts to access the system and responds according to preprogrammed instructions.

**Network architecture** The specific arrangement of the components of a network.

**Router** A software and hardware item that is directly responsible for directing the flow of packets from one device to another over a network.

**Switch** A low-level network device that determines the specific direction of a network packet from one segment to another.

**Trust** The ability to authenticate a given individual or process as trustworthy.

**Virtual private network (VPN)** A dedicated communication network that uses a public transmission system like the Internet.

# Questions from the CIO

The CIO requires you to brief her on the current status of your investigation. This will be an important part of your continuing work on this project, since it is essential to be able to describe all of the ramifications of a properly developed network security function. Consequently, the CIO would like you to answer the following questions for her:

1. Firewalls are used in network security to control access to network segments. There are a number of potential applications for that control function. Please name three of them.

2. An IDS will typically sound an alarm when an unauthorized access is detected. What would that alarm look like, who would receive it, and what are the potential responses?

3. A security event management system is a type of IDS. What differentiates an IDS from a security event management system, and where are security event management systems useful?

4. Network architecture depends on information criticality. Explain how the criticality of information will affect the form of the architecture of a network.

5. Policy-based network security control is the foundation for a secure network operation. Why is this true? What is it about networks that make policy so important?

6. Remote access policies are particularly essential for a given type of technology. What is that technology, and why is remote access policy so important?

7. The network security function is automated using two types of appliances. What are they, and how do they work together to create a secure network?

8. Change to network configuration is operationally controlled through a particular management process. What is that process, and how does it operate? What does it provide?

9. The change control board is part of the process mentioned above. What is the function of such a board, and how does it work with the other process to ensure continuous network security?

10. A VPN is a specialized type of network. Why are VPNs popular, and what does it take to create one? Would it be possible to obtain the same effect as a VPN using other approaches?

# Hands-On Projects

Using the Humongous Holdings case in Appendix 1, outline the design of a network that implements a set of general enclaves for the different business functions. Then:

- Outline the network security criteria for each enclave
- Identify and document the appropriate locations of firewalls and IDSs on that network
- Develop an audit plan to assess network security

# chapter 14

# Personnel Security

## The People Problem

*Nobody on the security team wanted to tackle the people problem, even though the attack that had brought the company to bankruptcy court had basically been due to a breakdown in personnel security. The team members knew that the challenge of securing the behavior of thousands of individual employees was well beyond their capabilities, so they kept putting the issue on the back burner until the CEO decided to force the issue. The CEO knew that personnel security was not a back burner issue; in fact, he felt that prior experience alone should have made that fact clear to his security team.*

*Therefore, he made a command decision that the human resources challenge had to be taken up sooner rather than later. He had also decided that solving the people problem was going to take a different skill set than his present executive team possessed. The CEO had known for a long time that the CIO was a stone geek. If he needed any further proof, he had to look no further than the fact that she was still hiring based strictly on technical virtuosity. That was especially disturbing, since it was that exact same philosophy that had caused the meltdown three years ago. At the same time, the CEO was absolutely certain that the CISO was fully aware of the issues that the human element brought to the table, and he also knew that the CISO had no interest in navigating those potentially career-ending waters unless he had a scapegoat handy, should the ship hit a rock. Furthermore, the CEO had decided that the CISO's candidate for that honor was the compliance officer, who had absolutely no problem with the concept of keeping the employees in line.*

*As a matter of fact, the compliance officer had just told the CEO that all she would need was enough auditing resources and she would guarantee that everybody followed the rules. But the CEO didn't think that having an auditor looking over everybody's shoulder would boost company morale. And even if he did think that totalitarianism was a good idea, he knew he couldn't afford it. Nevertheless, the CEO did think that the compliance officer had a valid point. All of his high-paid consultants had told him that the personnel security function could only be founded on commonly accepted rules of behavior enforced by oversight. The assumption was that if well defined policies and procedures were established, everybody in the company could then be held accountable for executing the security activities that applied to them.*

*Of course, the CEO also realized that the single point of failure was the assumption that the company could tell whether or not an employee was actually following the rules. Obviously, the company's managers had to be able to monitor the behavior of their employees in order to judge whether it was correct or not. In order to be effective, that monitoring also had to be across the board and continuous, since it is impossible to predict when a given employee might decide to start behaving badly.*

*The criminal gang that had taken down the company the first time around was a perfect example of why it was important to be able to ensure the trustworthy behavior of the workforce at all times. The members of the gang had all gotten sterling performance reviews during their short time with the company, and they were never suspected of plotting anything dire; the whole point in a criminal exploit being to ensure that one is not being suspected of anything. Of course, the fact that the entire gang had immediately been handed a full set of **access privileges** didn't help, since those privileges by definition got the gang members past the company's security controls.*

*In hindsight, that assumption of trustworthiness looked like an outrageous breach of good practice. But, cybersecurity is founded on the assumption that once an individual has been granted access to the system, he or she can be trusted within the scope of those privileges. The problem is that humans are notoriously erratic; it only takes one malicious employee with the right set of privileges to bring down the entire organization. That was the case three years ago, and the CEO sincerely believed that that problem had to be dealt with, or the same thing could crop up again.*

*The CEO had considered a technological solution, since there were plenty of vendors out there who were willing to peddle him one. The technology would let the company automate its rules for electronic access and enforce those rules on a systematic basis. Unfortunately, the CEO knew that policy management systems are only as good as the criteria that are built into them. So if a security factor were left out, it would never be enforced or even recognized as missing. He also knew that in order to be effective, automated policy managers have to be almost continuously updated, which makes them extremely resource-intensive. Worse, the people responsible for doing that updating would be just the people the CEO wanted to keep his eye on. Therefore, although he accepted that policy management software might be part of the eventual solution, he also knew that something additional was required.*

*What the CEO was looking for was a feasible and cost-effective way to assure the secure behavior of all employees and **contractors** within the corporation. The level of control would have to be precise enough to ensure a minimum level of required behavior, while encompassing every point of failure involving people. The need to address the wide variety of human* *performance issues across the company opened the door for the one member of the security engineering team who had a background in both technology and behavior.*

*The security engineer at the Detroit manufacturing plant might have been overseeing security in a heavy metal facility, but she had an MBA from the Ross School at the University of Michigan. There she had gotten an in-depth grounding in all aspects of human performance management. She had worked with the Corvallis security engineer on the training and education part of the overall security process, and during that time she had learned that her area of expertise could be guided by the EBK.*

*Thus, she put together a proposal for developing comprehensive management and technical controls for the human resources function, which was based on the top-level functions specified in the EBK. That proposal caught the CEO's eye right away, since it mirrored the following steps that he thought were necessary to ensure long-term personnel security:*

1. *Coordinate with IT security, physical security, operations security, and other organizational managers to ensure a coherent, coordinated, and holistic approach to security across the organization*

2. *Ensure personnel security compliance with standards, procedures, directives, policies, regulations, and laws (statutes)*

3. *Acquire and manage the necessary resources, including financial resources, to maintain the personnel security program*

4. *Establish objectives for the personnel security program in alignment with overall security goals for the enterprise*

5. *Ensure compliance through periodic audits of methods and controls*

6. *Ensure that personnel security is a component of enterprise continuity of operations*

7. *Direct ongoing operations of the personnel security program*

8. *Ensure that appropriate changes and improvement actions are implemented as required*

9. *Ensure personnel security compliance with standards, procedures, directives, policies, regulations, and laws (statutes)*

# Planning for Personnel Security

Personnel security is meant to address insider threats. Outsider threats are the ones that most people think of when they think of attacks, since that is the domain of hackers and other popular media types. Nevertheless, the threats that originate from the people who are already inside the organization are by far the most common source of harm, and they cause the greatest damage. They are also the hardest to stop. Consequently, in order for a company to be secure, it has to set up a mechanism to ensure that its workforce is, and remains, trustworthy. Like many organizational processes, establishing that mechanism involves a plan.

The personnel security plan should lay out a comprehensive strategy that will guard against the malicious actions of human beings in the workforce. The plan should encompass regular employees as well as people who work for contracting organizations. It should also provide a means to assure the secure behavior of visitors and other people who might temporarily be within the company's security perimeter. Because that perimeter marks the divide between trusted and untrusted space, the first step in ensuring a permanent trust is to delineate the company's **security boundaries**.

## Defining the Boundaries of Control

The personnel security boundaries demarcate the physical space that the organization intends to control. It is important to set a realistic perimeter, because people constantly come and go across the virtual and physical security boundaries of the organization and it would be economically unfeasible to attempt to control the behavior of those people beyond a reasonable point. As a result, the security perimeter is normally set at a place that offers an optimum level of assurance for the resources that the organization intends to commit.

The tradeoff between the degree of control desired, and the resources that are available, plays an important part in determining the type of protected space that is incorporated in that perimeter. There are two types of perimeters, as shown in Figure 14-1. One is the electronic perimeter, which is essentially the extent to which virtual assets like information are controlled. The other is the physical perimeter, which is a geographic point that constitutes the boundary between controlled and uncontrolled physical space. Both of these perimeters are defined based on two criteria. The first criterion is available resources. The second criterion is desired level of security, which is an estimate of how rigorously the organization wants to assure the space.

The perimeter expands and contracts depending on available resources and the level of security required. Given the same level of resources, a facility that demands a high degree of control (e.g., a defense installation) will have a much smaller perimeter than one where little

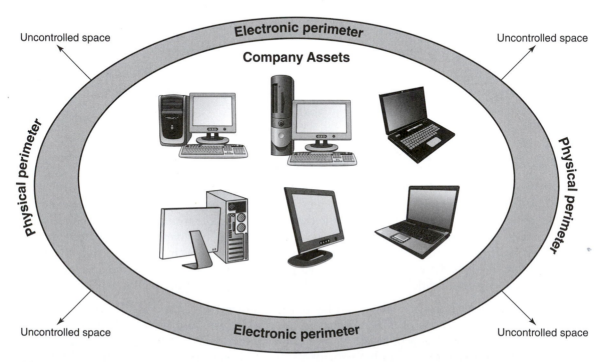

**Figure 14-1** Two types of perimeters

© Cengage Learning 2012

control is required. If the perimeter of the defense installation has to be expanded, then a greater level of resource commitment is required.

## Identifying Personnel Security Functions Based on Risk

The elements of personnel security are varied, because the process could logically entail any activity that involves the people in the workforce. Because of that variety, each of the elements that could potentially influence the personnel security process has to be identified. Then an approach has to be defined that will allow the organization to coordinate those elements in a way that will reliably ensure the secure behavior of the human resources that fall within its boundaries. The diverse elements that might be included include such things as the control functions that regulate how everyday work is done, as well as the many virtual components that assure proper electronic access. Because these activities are so wide-ranging and there are no clear-cut rules for what should be included, every organization has to make a conscious decision about which individual elements it wants to incorporate into its **personnel security strategy**.

Unfortunately, in most organizations it is hard to get agreement about what elements to include and what elements to leave out. The only practical way to underwrite the decision-making is to undertake a threat identification process, the aim of which is to identify and categorize all factors that constitute risk in the human resources realm. Knowing what those factors are is critical to ensuring a coherent security response. For instance, if there are employee thefts, then there might be a need to install cameras in a certain area. Or if e-mails are being sent that could reveal confidential information, then automated controls for the e-mail system might be required. Since controls cost money, a tradeoff between investment and resultant harm has to be factored into any strategy.

## Ensuring Reliable Behavior

Every personnel security strategy has to specify the process and procedures that will be used to ensure the disciplined behavior of all participants in the process. In simple terms, this means that the plan has to spell out the steps needed to make certain that the human resources of the company consistently follow required security procedures. The need to enforce the reliable execution of each worker's assigned security responsibilities is an essential part of personnel security, because all of the measures that constitute the personnel security process have been placed there for a reason.

The requirement for disciplined practice also means that some attention has to be paid to the notion of motivation in the process, since it plays such a crucial role in assuring disciplined execution. Because security activities usually add to the workload of the people in the company, it is necessary to ensure that those people understand the reason for their required security duties. Continuous reiteration and reinforcement of the reasons for security helps to enforce consistent and predictable security behavior.

## Managing Change to the Workforce

New members are continually being added to the workforce, while others are being deleted from it. As a result, the assignment or removal of the access privileges of each of those individuals has to be underwritten by a formal process. Normally, the human resources function is responsible for establishing and maintaining the privileges of all of the members of the organization, and then IT enables the access rights to the system. Accordingly, it is important that the human resource function that determines and assigns privileges has an established communication channel with the technical side of the operation.

The traditional divide between human resources and IT is one of the likeliest spots for the personnel security process to fail. Consequently, it is important for human resources to ensure that each individual worker's access privileges have been accurately conveyed to the IT function and that any subsequent change to those privileges is updated in a timely fashion. Effective lines of communication have to be maintained between the two functions in order to ensure that users' access rights always reflect their employment status. Otherwise, the potential exists for employees to gain access to things that they are not justified to see, because their current status does not match their assigned level of privilege.

## Documenting the Personnel Security Function

The aim of the personnel security function is to ensure against malicious or inadvertent harm due to the actions of trusted individuals. Two factors make this a difficult task. First, since all employees are by definition trusted to some extent, they have free right of entry to everything that they have been authorized to access. Second, and more important, the actions of people are notoriously hard to control. People are creative, so they are capable of finding imaginative ways to get around any static defense, and their motivations are as varied as the individuals who have them. Consequently a statement of what people *need to do* is an important way of managing their performance.

Typically, the things that the company expects each individual to do is documented in a company procedure manual. The practices contained in that manual then become the behaviors that the organization will use to judge employee behavior. The procedure manual also serves to remind workers what their security duties are. Since people's actions are dictated by how they understand their assigned duties, it is also essential to ensure that everyone in the organization correctly understands how the practices in the manual apply to them. That understanding must be sufficient to ensure that everyone will correctly and consistently perform the routine security practices required of them.

Procedure manuals state the rules for everybody in the organization, which means that the dictates of the procedure manual apply to all of the workers in the company, from the CEO down to the humblest worker. Because they must be embedded in the culture, those rules have to be derived from the organization's norms. Likewise, since no two places have exactly the same set of norms, it can be assumed that every organization will adopt a slightly different set of rules. Nevertheless, those rules should accurately reflect the existing culture of the workplace.

In practice, a formal procedure manual ensures the ability to judge whether a person is behaving within established rules. A comparison of the behaviors dictated by the manual and the actual behavior of each employee provides a legitimate basis for judging whether those actions are appropriate. The ability to objectively evaluate the actions of an employee is a critical part of the security control process, because it allows managers to assess and make decisions about employee activities at a given point in time. For example, if an employee works past business hours, that might be a sign of diligence. It might also be a sign that the employee is up to something. That is where a rule such as, "in order to ensure **separation of duties**, employees may not work after hours without another person present," is an extremely helpful way to quickly judge whether the employee is diligent or suspicious.

Whether the rules in the procedure manual are correct is not the issue, although all standard rules of conduct should promote effective behavior. The important point is that a documented set of rules creates an observable point of reference, which managers can use to judge the suitability of everyday behavior of all of their employees. If workers understand the rules for after-hours behavior and are then discovered working after hours, managers have the basis to enforce appropriate discipline. Thus, in conjunction with the rules of behavior, there should also be a specification of the disciplinary measures if violations take place.

Procedure manuals function at two levels; they can be general, but they can also be tailored to specific situations. Most procedure manuals document a universal code of conduct that describes a small set of general rules for all employees. These rules tend to be normative—they establish ordinary right and wrong. Behaviors can also be tailored to fit particular circumstances, in which case they tend to be prescriptive. Prescriptive rules of conduct define a given set of behaviors for a given situation. In both cases, the purpose of those rules is to shape the everyday actions of the people in the organization.

## The Special Situation of Contractors

Because a lot of IT work is **outsourced**, the personnel security process has to state explicit rules to ensure the security of contracted work. These policies and procedures have to guarantee that contractors are following the same security procedure that is required for all employees of the organization. In most cases, contract employees require the same access to information as regular employees doing the same type of work; however, contractors present a special problem in that they are not as well controlled as regular employees. That is because they work for somebody else. Worse, because they work for another organization, it cannot be assumed that contract employees have gone through the same screening and orientation processes as regular employees have. Consequently, access rights for contractors have to be precisely defined and then rigorously enforced. That oversight includes formal and informal reviews for contract employees and other explicit forms of control, such as policy management software, to ensure proper use and accountability.

# Making Personnel Security Real

*The Detroit security engineer had developed what she thought was a realistic security plan. It was built around an extensive communication process between the managers of the various key security functions, and it enforced a set of solid personnel policies. However, although it appeared to be resource-efficient and it had a well defined evaluation scheme, it didn't have much detail. It was clear to the security engineer that it would be impossible to implement any of the plan's features without giving the people who were doing the actual human resources management work more explicit guidelines about how to hire and assign personnel.*

*That was where the engineer's background in organizational development came in handy. She knew that it was going to take input from across the organization in order to capture the necessary detail, so she assembled a team of stakeholders from the various organizational functions. These people represented a range of levels and job types, not just corporate executives. The aim of the group was to undertake a comprehensive job-task analysis while building consensus and gaining buy-in across the entire company. Since the company had a lot of different lines of business, the team was too large to meet as a single body, so the engineer subdivided the meetings into geographic areas and met with each local group separately. That meant she spent a month on an airplane, moving from one site to another. She felt this was necessary in order to get the wide-ranging give and take needed to get a complete listing of jobs and the associated security requirements.*

*The outcome of the job-task analysis was an intimidating pile of reports that represented the roles and responsibilities for every unit in the entire company. The next step in the process required the engineer and her support team to begin the arduous task of sorting that list into a single, unduplicated dictionary of security requirements, which would characterize all of the company roles and responsibilities. That activity took weeks. In the end, the engineer had a solid foundation of common duties that she and her team could use to document the personnel security process. The first and most useful thing that dictionary provided was an identification of where the gaps existed in the security responsibilities for each job category. The dictionary also provided the basis for testing whether the security activities in each category satisfied the basic principles of security.*

*With the course of action now established, the security professionals on the engineer's support team went through the list of jobs, one job at a time, for the entire company and asked two questions. The first question was, "are the security requirements for each of these jobs complete?" If the answer was "no," then the security professional did all of the research necessary to fill in any of the perceived gaps with explicit job-tasks. Then the security professional checked to see whether each of the new roles met the relevant requirements for secure practice that were dictated by the EBK.*

*In that respect, the competency requirements for each general role in the EBK provided a point of reference that allowed the security engineer to validate her own plans. Using those competency requirements, she looked to see whether adequate separation of duties, **least privilege**, and psychological acceptability conditions had been established for each job. That comparison provided an authoritative confirmation of the tailored security requirements she had assigned to each role. The actual implementation of those requirements would be guided by the following steps dictated in the EBK:*

1. *Establish the personnel security processes and procedures for individual job roles*

2. *Establish procedures for coordinating with other organizations to ensure that common processes are aligned*

3. *Establish personnel security rules and procedures to which external suppliers (e.g., vendors, contractors) must conform*

# Screening and Hiring Personnel

In most organizations, the responsibility for implementing and sustaining the personnel security functions falls to human resources (HR). In concept, that assignment makes sense, since the HR function is traditionally responsible for documenting and managing a company's job categories, as well as hiring and orienting new employees. Moreover, since HR is the unit that is normally responsible for overall management of the job assignment process, it would be logical to have HR take the lead in the creation, implementation, and oversight of the personnel security function.

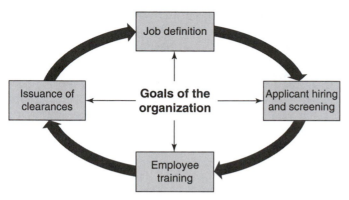

**Figure 14-2** Conventional personnel security practice
© *Cengage Learning 2012*

The personnel security process involves four large-scale activities: job definition; applicant hiring and screening; employee training; and the issuance of clearances, where required, as shown in Figure 14-2. In most companies, these practices are all done by the HR function. The additional features that ensure secure employment practice ought to be added to these routine HR employment activities at the appropriate point in the process.

## Job Definition: Building Security In

Logically, the entry point into the process of assigning privileges to company roles is the job definition process. Since job definitions are normally written for all of the positions in a company, the commonsense place to embed security requirements is at the point where all of the other relevant requirements of the job are dictated. Traditionally, job definition involves determining who supervises the position, the lines of authority and reporting lines, and the requisite activities and responsibilities associated with the work. In addition to customary functions, job definition is also the place where the level of privilege and sensitivity requirements can be determined and assigned.

That determination is usually generic; electronic and physical access privileges will apply to anybody holding that particular position. The primary aim of the documentation of privilege is to ensure that the requirements associated with the principle of separation of duties have been satisfied. The principle of separation of duties partitions any work assignment in such a way that no one individual person performs a process without the involvement of another person. That separation is enforced by segmenting the standard task requirements of a process in order to ensure that more than one person is involved in executing it.

On the other hand, individual employees should only be granted the access privileges that they need to do their work. For instance, if analysts analyze data, they would need access to that data but they would not need to change it. As a result, they would not be granted that right. Since rights are assigned to the job, not the individual, the definition of a fundamental set of privileges for each job category ensures that all employees who are authorized within that category can work interchangeably and still satisfy the requirements of least privilege.

If least privilege rights were not generically assigned, employees would need their rights re-assigned every time they moved to a different job in the company. Assigning a generic set of privileges to each role allows employees to carry those privileges with them as long as the work they are doing meets the criteria that have been used to determine the privileges for the job category they are working in. The assignment of that privilege begins with the background screening and hiring process.

## Background Screening and Hiring

Background screening helps the organization confirm that the prospective employee fits the security requirements for a given position. The security criteria adopted by the organization are the driving force behind the screening process. These criteria should be appropriate to the situation, and the rigor of the screening ought to reflect the sensitivity of the work. For instance, an employer is not likely to conduct an extensive background check for a secretary's position, unless that position is located within a highly secure site, in which case extensive security checks might be justified.

Background checks can involve tangible investigations done by professional investigators. Those kinds of checks are normally only done for sensitive positions. In most cases applicant screening and hiring amounts to an automated records check to confirm the basics of the individual's credentials. Typical background checks look at such things as criminal history. Other factors might include such things as work and educational history.

With sensitive positions, background checks could include an examination of the prospective employee's legal history, financial and/or credit history, medical history, immigration and/or IRS records, and anecdotal observations about the candidate's public behavior. This level of examination is necessary because employees who have a personal vulnerability from their past are easy to compromise.

## The Special Circumstance of Clearance Levels

If the situation requires clearances, it might be necessary to assign a **clearance level** to each job definition. The clearance level delineates the security restrictions associated with the job category as well as the officially authorized access rights. The specification of the levels of clearance required for each position is based on factors such as the type and sensitivity of the information accessed by that position.

The clearances and the associated controls are assigned to each position based on the potential risks and injuries that might ensue should a security breakdown occur. The assignment of clearances is always something of a balancing act between too much control, which will make the worker unproductive, and too little control, which can create an unacceptable risk of compromise.

## Managing the Personnel Security Process

The personnel security process ensures three fundamental security properties. First, personnel security guarantees that each worker can be trusted, within whatever security criteria are established for the specific job. The aim is to make certain that each new hire satisfies basic, company-wide security criteria for that position.

The second quality ensures that individuals know how to execute the requisite security behaviors for their given level of privilege. Logically, it would be both self-defeating and counterproductive to require a behavior but then not take steps to ensure that people knew how to perform it. Therefore, the personnel security function has to undertake systematic and targeted training and awareness activities to make certain that all of the employees in the organization understand their security duties.

The third property is alignment. The personnel security function has to ensure that each individual employee's level of privilege is always maintained appropriate to the person's job function. The aim is to avoid a situation where an employee gets a higher level of privilege than can be justified by his or her level of recognized trustworthiness. This condition is usually termed "authorization creep," and it can occur if an employee changes jobs frequently, if there are substantive changes to a system or application, or if outside contractors are used, as shown in Figure 14-3.

If there is a potential for authorization creep, then the organization has to institute a tracking process to make sure that the proper level of privilege is maintained for the degree of employee trustworthiness. The purpose of this third condition is to establish whether there is a need to revisit that employee's background to assign a new level of authorization, or whether a change in assignment is required to ensure that the employee only does work appropriate to his or her level of trust. If there *is* a change in authorization, then there might also be a need to train or retrain the staff member.

## Defining the Principles of Control

An individual who is authorized to use the system, but who then chooses to commit a malicious act is perhaps the most dangerous threat among the entire set of potential threats to a company. Because that individual is already inside the normal boundaries of the security system, there are rarely formal mechanisms to detect and mitigate malicious behavior. Even so, some managerial controls *can* be deployed to detect and prevent harm from malicious insiders. The principles behind these controls were first laid out by Jerome Saltzer and Michael

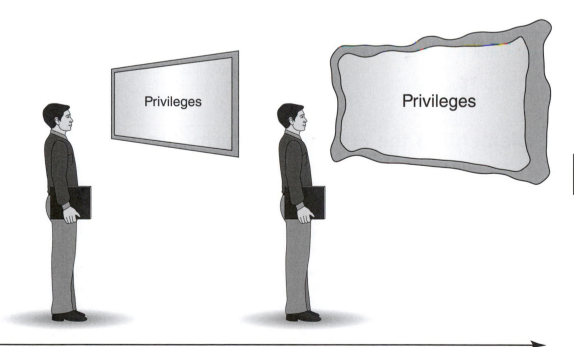

**Figure 14-3** Authorization creep
© *Cengage Learning 2012*

Schroeder in the early 1970s, and they are just as appropriate today. Saltzer and Schroeder provide eight security principles, of which four are arguably relevant to personnel security.

The first of these is the principle of open mechanism. Under this principle, the mechanisms that an organization employs to protect itself should not assume that the people who are doing the attacking are ignorant of the details of the defense. Since insiders are usually familiar with the mechanisms that are used to protect the organization, they would generally know their way around all of its defenses. The idea is to build unique features into the protection scheme at points in the access process that a person with knowledge of the general shape of the defense would not know. That includes such things as using restricted passwords, which an individual would need to progress further, or cipher keys that are needed to decrypt a message. The second principle is that of separation of Privilege. This principle requires that the access control mechanism should be based on more than one token. Multi-factor authentication is an example of this principle in application. The third principle, that of least privilege, has already been mentioned earlier. Least privilege is a fairly well known control principle in all forms of security, and not just for information. It states that workers should only be granted the minimum privileges that they need to carry out their specific job functions. In the old-fashioned spy world, this principle would be known as "need to know." The final principle is psychological acceptability, which dictates the requirement for ease of use. It stipulates that the protection mechanism should be easy to operate.

There is one other concept that is not part of Saltzman and Schroeder, and that is individual accountability. This concept is a condition, not a design principle. It is a universal requirement needed to make the enforcement of security possible. The condition of individual accountability simply requires that each individual has to be held responsible for his or her actions. A state of accountability is created for all users by the identification and authentication process and the subsequent monitoring of their activities within the protected space, which is technically part of the principle of open design. This state is necessary so that adverse actions can be traced back to the user who initiated them and appropriate corrective action can be administered to ensure subsequent proper use.

# Implementing the Personnel Security Process

*The security engineer had developed a design that she thought captured all of the principles of good personnel security management. It ensured that every job category in the company would be given privileges commensurate with the type of work involved. It also ensured that the necessary checks and balances were in place when it came to the process itself. Implementing the process companywide, however, was going to represent a new kind of political challenge, since the CEO insisted that that implementation had to be done by HR.*

*The engineer hated that idea. She was no control freak, and in the past, she had had no difficulty handing off her work to be implemented. But in this case, she had a big problem with the idea of HR being involved in any aspect of implementing the cybersecurity personnel security process since she had genuine concerns about HR's ability to understand, let alone correctly and properly manage, a design aimed at controlling virtual space.*

*Her main problem was with the staff capabilities in the HR unit. The members of the staff, who were not clerical, had a background in everything from education to social work, so they were good at the minutia of paper work and worker problems. But none of them had the technical foundations to understand the unique demands that cyberspace placed on the security management process. In the engineer's mind, the inability to understand the underlying conditions for controlling access to something as abstract as the information resource had the makings of a disaster.*

*The CEO conceded that the HR staff might be a little light in the hardball process area, but he also pointed out that since they were responsible for overseeing the company's people, they could not be left out. He suggested that the engineer might also involve IT on the implementation team in order to add a little technical savvy. Then, the engineer could coordinate the overall project from the top using a team concept. He also added that since he understood that that represented a level of responsibility way beyond the call of duty, he would be willing to move her out of Detroit to the company's Jacksonville test facility once the project was finished.*

*The engineer didn't have to think about that offer too long. Although she was a loyal Wolverine, the prospect of escaping the miserable Michigan winters and the Detroit area in general had her assembling her new joint task force before the end of the week. She knew that the EBK had five recommendations when it came to implementing the personnel security process, and she intended to use those as her roadmap for the project. The recommendations were:*

1. *Coordinate within the personnel security office, or with HR, to ensure that position sensitivity is established prior to the interview process, and that appropriate background screening and suitability requirements are identified for each position*

2. *Coordinate within the personnel security office, or with HR, to ensure background investigations are processed based on level of trust and position sensitivity*

3. *Review, analyze, and adjudicate reports of investigations, personnel files, and other records to determine whether to grant, deny, revoke, suspend, or restrict clearances consistent with organizational requirements, national security, and/or suitability issues*

4. *Coordinate with physical security and IT security operations personnel to ensure that employee access to physical facilities, media, and IT systems/networks is modified or terminated upon reassignment, change of duties, resignation, or termination*

5. *Exercise oversight of personnel security program appeals procedures to verify that the rights of individuals are being protected according to law*

## Practical Considerations for Implementing Security

The aim of the personnel security process is to restrict user access to the minimum amount of information necessary do the job. The idea behind this goal is to prevent users from gaining access to information that they are not specifically authorized to see. This is done by limiting the individual to only those particular items of information that are necessary to do the work.

The goal of the personnel security process is to make certain that measures are in place to ensure that all access to information is highly controlled. Access privileges are typically assigned to user categories as part of policy setting. The policy for access privileges has to be based on careful study of the information requirements of each job type.

Because situations exist where users need elevated access in order to perform a special task, there also has to be an exception function built into the assignment of access rights for a given class of user. Elevated rights can be granted to individual workers by means of that exception process.

In other words, the user who requires elevated privilege can only be granted one access to information items that they need to perform a specified task. If that access is granted, it might still be necessary to ensure additional trustworthiness through background screening. This screening is critical in cases where there is a high risk of harm if elevated privileges are granted.

Ease of use is also an important aspect of the implementation process, because security adds to everybody's workload. Whatever security measures are employed must be easy enough to follow that the people who have to perform them will not consider them a burden.

In some respects, this is a design issue as much as it is one of implementation. Nevertheless, the implementation process has to ensure that the mechanism that is eventually employed will be easy to use.

## Implementing Trust Through the Screening Process

**Personnel screening** is the process that is used to assign trust. It assures that the individuals who have been granted privileges are trustworthy and that they can continue to be trusted. The personnel security screening process is the practical mechanism for ensuring that trust. Screening defines the requirements that will underlie how separation of duties and least privilege will be assigned, and it underwrites the enforcement of individual accountability.

Because they will, by definition, be "trusted," everybody in the organization who is granted access privileges should be given a minimum level of screening prior to the authorization of access to the system. The screening of end-users obviously does not have to be as rigorous as it would for system staff, but there should always be routine procedures to ensure that everybody who accesses the system meets the company's guidelines for the assignment of trust. This is typically part of the user identity management function, and it might not involve anything more difficult than requiring that the prospective user present a valid employee ID.

The level of screening that takes place will obviously be much greater where there is sensitive information, or where a high level of privilege is required. If that is the case, active background checks and other mechanisms might be employed, up to and including polygraph examinations. Depending on the level of trust, re-certifications might also be required. If that is the case, the screening process might take place every year, or even twice each year. Because it is extremely resource-intensive, this screening should be done proportionate with the risk and magnitude of harm that might be attached to a given user category.

## Workforce Training and Education

Once an individual has been hired, it is essential to provide sufficient security training to help the employee comply with the stated policies and practices that apply to the position involved. For that reason, training requirements are frequently embedded in the position description. Ensuring workforce capability is a traditional responsibility of the HR function, because inadequate knowledge of required security practice is one of the primary causes of breakdowns in the overall security process.

In addition to ensuring capable performance of security tasks, the awareness, training, and education function also underwrites enforcement. Accountability requires clear knowledge of the consequences of inappropriate behavior. While a lack of understanding of the rules can be viewed as human error, it is in fact a failure on the part of the organization to ensure that employees are informed and competent to perform their security duties.

## Keeping Identities Up to Date

When it comes to user access, one of the more important personnel security issues is the need to keep user access authorizations up to date. As mentioned previously, the level of privilege can change, sometimes permanently and sometimes only temporarily, based on employee movement in the organization. Accordingly, access privileges can change based on two types of conditions: a change in job, or a termination.

Change in job can be temporary (e.g., an employee covering for an absent colleague) or permanent (e.g., a transfer or promotion). In the first instance, users often need to perform duties outside their previously defined scope. Although this could require some sort of change to their privileges, those privileges should also be promptly removed when they are no longer needed to perform the new job.

When an employee moves to another position their privileges might have to be adjusted. If the individual is moving within the organization, the process of background screening and granting privileges is followed as if that individual was a new employee. In the case of a permanent move, however, it is important for the company's managers to also remember to remove the access privileges of the prior position. The failure to remove prior privileges is another critical point of failure in the personnel security process; there have been many instances where employees have continued to maintain access rights for previously held positions within the organization after separation, and that can lead to all sorts of mischief, since it essentially surrenders control over access for that particular individual.

Finally, there is the issue of maintaining appropriate authorizations in the case of changes to the system itself. In day-to-day business operation, applications are always being added, upgraded, or removed, which might radically alter the way that the application processes authorizations. For this reason, it is important to keep the identities and associated privileges for the authorized users of a given application under strict control within the IT function. The aim is to ensure that there is no alteration in privileges for any account based on a change to the system.

## Personnel Changes

Turnover in employment is a natural part of the business process, but it can create serious vulnerabilities. People who leave the business might intentionally or unintentionally take valuable knowledge with them. Moreover, every employee's access privileges are aligned to a specific job function. So when an employee changes positions, or leaves the company entirely, there has to be a timely and reliable way to ensure that the accompanying privileges are either re-aligned with the new status, or revoked entirely.

In these cases, the role of the personnel security function is to make certain that any change in rights associated with any change in employment status is processed in a way that preserves the integrity of the organization's security processes, specifically access control. If the steps to ensure up-to-date privileges are not part of the personnel security process, the organization will open up holes in its access control scheme over time. Moreover, if people who are no longer part of the organization continue to retain access to company systems, they will have insider access to organization information. That condition is clearly not acceptable under anybody's definition of security.

The solution is a procedure that will ensure that *all* of the privileges associated with any person who has left the company are revoked as soon as possible. In almost every case, the total revocation of access privileges is part of the process for terminating an individual's employment. There are two different scenarios for termination: **friendly termination** and **unfriendly termination**. Because the situation is different in these cases, the security response is also different. No matter what the cause, however, a carefully planned response is essential to assure the security of all company information in the case of termination.

With a friendly termination, the employee is normally leaving the company under mutually agreeable terms. These types of terminations are common, but a disciplined process still has to be followed to ensure that the employee transitions out of the company in a secure fashion, no matter how friendly the conditions of separation might be. That process is built around a set of routine operational procedures that ensures the secure separation of outgoing or transferring employees. These procedures are usually established and supervised by the HR function.

In the case of a friendly termination, the purpose of the secure separation procedure is to ensure that user account privileges are removed from the system. This must be done in a timely manner. The procedure associated with friendly termination is composed of several steps. The user's access privileges are removed first. This is typically done by re-acquiring, or changing, the authentication tokens associated with each account.

Along with the access tokens, any physical property that might contain company data have to be secured. Physical property might range from computers to memory sticks and CDs. Next, every account associated with that user should be inspected to ensure that the data stored there has retained its integrity. This might seem like an unnecessary step in the case of a friendly termination, but even friendly terminations can lead to inadvertent errors. Finally, if the person separating from the company has had access to sensitive data, it might be necessary to obtain formal non-disclosure agreements as well as secure all cryptographic material. The integrity of the encryption system should also be verified.

When an employee leaves the organization under unfriendly circumstances, a different set of procedures applies. Unfriendly terminations are not rare, but because they are usually for some specific cause and involve a unilateral decision on the part of one of the parties, they will occur less frequently than friendly terminations. Since there is likely to be ill feelings, there is a much greater potential for mischief. Consequently, in these circumstances, the company has to pay greater attention to the security implications.

The procedures associated with unfriendly terminations are generally no different from those associated with friendly ones, but with an unfriendly termination, each step has to be more carefully executed. Along with the functions that are normally associated with removing an individual from the system, several additional actions should be considered.

First, the employee's access to the system must be immediately ended if there is reason to suspect that the termination will take place on unfriendly terms. The termination of access privileges should occur as close as possible to the point where the individual is separated from the company. Ideally, access privileges should be removed at the precise time that the decision is made to fire an employee. Under no circumstances should the employee be allowed to access the system after having been fired. If, for some reason, the employee continues to work after the notification takes place, then any duties assigned should not require system access.

It is especially important to ensure that the access privileges of the IT staff are revoked as soon as it appears that an unfriendly termination might be in the offing. If IT workers are allowed to retain access privileges after dismissal, they are ideally situated to get whatever personal paybacks they want. Therefore careful attention has to be paid to removing that access.

Even employees with general user accounts can create problems. For instance, data can be "lost," files can be damaged and other "accidental" errors such as the destruction of media, can occur. Finally, and more importantly, if the employee retains access privileges, they can copy data prior to termination and then walk out the door with it. Finally, where terminations are extremely unfriendly, or where employees have access to critical functions or information, it is advisable to immediately and physically remove them from the area.

# Evaluating the Success of the Process

*The Detroit security engineer was not exactly thrilled by the outcome of the implementation process. She had expected that the final product would be a relatively easy-to-administer document that would communicate all of the requisite security rules in a simple and understandable way. What HR gave her instead was 150 pages of regulations.*

*The engineer had already anticipated that kind of result, given HR's penchant for rules and complexity, and she was certainly willing to live with HR being responsible for maintaining and enforcing all of them. But since her aim was to prove to the CEO that the personnel security process was a living, breathing entity, she didn't know how she would be able to do that by dropping on his desk the stack of paper she was holding in her hand.*

*So she called a meeting of her security team, the HR people, and the manager who was the liaison from the IT function. She told them that her aim was to get a management process in place that would make it easy to ensure that the personnel security function was effective. Moreover, she wanted to be able to prove that it was going to continue to function properly through whatever changes the circumstances might require. Since there were work rule specifications in the procedure manual for 187 different job titles, she knew that she couldn't rely on job description as the basis for judging the general effectiveness of the personnel security function. What she needed instead was some key aspect of individual performance that would generate the data to let her prove the effectiveness of the overall process.*

*The team wrestled with a number of potential indicators of performance, but all of them suffered from a lack of collective relevance. Finally, the member of the team who, oddly enough, happened to have a background in philosophy and ethics suggested that what was needed was a set of common rules of conduct. Her thought was that if the company were to adopt those rules as the overall foundation for assessing security performance, they could be used as a baseline to evaluate the individual performance of each employee. All that would be required was agreement across the organization on what those rules were, as well as a standard assessment process to evaluate how close everybody in the company was to complying with those baseline requirements.*

*Common rules of conduct would accomplish two valuable things. First, they would provide an easy-to-understand and practical reference to guide each employee in day-to-day behavior. Second, the company could monitor the security performance of its employees using those rules as a basis for enforcement. The obvious problem was getting agreement on the rules themselves. In order to be effective, they had to be comprehensive yet simple enough for everybody to understand and turn into action.*

*The process of developing those rules touched off a bruising, three-week firefight among the various stakeholders, since everybody had their own ideas about what was proper and correct. Fortunately, the CEO understood the need to have that baseline so he oversaw the process from beginning to end. It took a while, but under his benevolent dictatorship, a sensible baseline of practices began to emerge. It was limited in its complexity but robust when it came to enforcing the principles of personnel security. Once he had gotten the signoffs from all of the stakeholders, he turned that set over to the Detroit security engineer for proof of concept through the evaluation process.*

*The security engineer, in turn, was beginning to experience the miserable weather that marks November in Detroit. She was confident in the outcome, though, because she knew that she had the EBK's three high-level recommendations for evaluation covered:*

1. *Review effectiveness of the personnel security program, and recommend changes that will improve internal practices and/or security organization-wide*

2. *Assess the relationships between personnel security procedures and organization-wide security needs, and make recommendations for improvement*

3. *Periodically review the personnel security program for compliance with standards, procedures, directives, policies, regulations, and laws (statutes)*

*As the freezing rain continued to fall outside the security engineer's dirty office window, she started to browse the catalogues for winter beachwear in Jacksonville.*

## Evaluating Formal Codes of Conduct

At its core, the purpose of the personnel security function is to monitor the actions of trusted individuals. This is a difficult task, because people are unpredictable. It is especially difficult to ensure the behavior of the members of any workforce. Since it is hard to anticipate what people will do, it is important to provide specific criteria that will be used as a yardstick to judge the appropriateness of their actions. These criteria are normally expressed as a "code of conduct."

In simple terms, a code of conduct is a basis for determining whether an individual employee's actions are appropriate. The code of conduct defines the suitable behaviors for the workforce as a whole. These behaviors should embody and reflect the company's own values and principles. The relationship between those behaviors and the corporate values that they are derived from provides a legitimate basis for ensuring that the actions of individuals are appropriate.

For this reason, the code of conduct provides a valid point of reference to explicitly ensure the acceptable behavior of each of the members of the workforce. Evaluation of the acceptability of individual actions can then underwrite the enforcement of accountability for all of the people in the organization. The specific means of evaluating and enforcing that accountability is through personnel reviews.

## Personnel Reviews

The overall success of the personnel security function depends on the organization's ability to ensure its long-term effectiveness. Consequently, the regular review of the workforce's performance of their security duties is an essential part of good personnel security practice. Regular reviews are necessary because the activities that are involved in the personnel security process are often complex. Accordingly, the accepted mechanism for determining whether the workforce process is performing its assigned duties is a formal inspection, or review of their work practices. Because people are individuals, the only feasible way to conduct those reviews is by the use of expert judgment.

That judgment should substantiate four practical things. First, it has to be confirmed that all employees maintain the level of privilege that is consistent with their own levels of certifiable trustworthiness, and that the authorizations for those privileges are up to date. Second, it has to be confirmed that all of the privileges that are assigned conform to the principles of least privilege and separation of duties. Third, it has to be confirmed that the privileges that have been assigned to each individual continue to be appropriate to the job function involved. Finally, it has to be confirmed that all of the required security training for each employee has been successfully completed.

The reviews of the personnel security process should be conducted on at least two levels. Large-scale reviews should be conducted on a company-wide basis in order to confirm the general effectiveness of the organization's personnel security operation. Focused reviews should also be conducted for each job category in order to confirm that all of the employees in that category conform to the requirements for that particular group. Since conditions can change over time, the assumptions behind the privileges as well as the process for assigning them should also be periodically reviewed for each category. The aim is to confirm that the specific privileges that have been assigned for a given job category continue to be valid and effective.

# Chapter Summary

- Personnel security entails the steps to control the activities of the individuals who work within an organization.
- It is important for each business to develop an explicit security strategy for itself.
- The boundaries of personnel security must be set.
- To be effective, security discipline has to be continuous, carefully planned, and executed.
- People have to know both the reason and importance of what they are doing in order to properly motivate them to perform security tasks in a reliable fashion.
- The purpose of security procedures is to define what has to be done by each individual in order to achieve satisfactory levels of cybersecurity.
- The only way that a business can establish and execute a repeatable set of actions is by documenting required behavior.
- Given the importance of critical systems, it is particularly essential that the business is able to ensure the effectiveness of security staff and technology.
- All users of a system should be made aware of what constitutes acceptable behavior.
- These rules should be in writing and be able to serve as a code of conduct.
- Least privilege is the practice of restricting a user's access type to the minimum necessary to perform his or her job.
- Separation of duties is the practice of dividing the steps in a critical function among different individuals.

- Personnel screening is a process that is employed to assure the security of the individuals who are involved in a security process.

- The clearance level delineates those requisite security behaviors as well as the officially authorized privileges for the position.

- Assurance is usually based on a defined set of behaviors that are formally evaluated for effectiveness.

# Key Terms

**Access privileges** The level of trust assigned an individual, expressed in terms of the types and levels of sensitivity of data the person has access to.

**Clearance level** An assigned level of trust determined after a standard, rigorous, and formal screening process.

**Contractor and outsourced** Work that has been assigned to individuals who are employees of an entity whose services have been hired by the contracting company.

**Friendly termination** Separation from the company under good terms, usually to move to another job.

**Least privilege** The assurance that privileges will only allow an employee to access information needed to do a job properly.

**Personnel screening** A standard process that is employed to confirm basic details of employee history, which is applicable to all employees as part of the hiring process.

**Personnel security strategy** The specific organizational approach to ensuring secure worker behavior.

**Security boundaries** The protected perimeter within which all individuals are assumed to be trusted—the separation between trusted and untrusted space.

**Separation of duties** The assurance that no one individual can control a process—primarily enforced by having different people carry out parts of the same function.

**Unfriendly termination** Separation from the company under circumstances where the party being terminated is likely to bear bad feelings.

# Questions from the CIO

The CIO requires you to brief her on the current status of your investigation. This will be an important part of your continuing work on this project, since it is essential to be able to describe all of the ramifications of a properly developed personnel security process. Consequently, the CIO would like you to answer the following questions for her:

1. Why is personnel security such an especially critical element of overall security?

2. What special factors make personnel security hard to implement?

3. What is the concept of least privilege?

4. What does the concept of separation of duties accomplish?

5. What is the purpose of giving a clearance?

6. Why is it particularly important to secure the systems staff?

7. Why are codes of conduct and rules of behavior important?

8. What is personnel screening and why is it important? How does it differ from the clearance process?

9. Why is the assignment of individual responsibility for security duties an essential part of personnel security?

10. Why are contractor considerations important elements of personnel security in today's industry?

# Hands-On Projects

Complete the following case exercise as directed by your instructor.

Refer to the case in Appendix (A). You have been assigned the responsibility for planning the HR control policies for the entire company. Prepare a complete code of conduct to secure the personnel who work there. Here is some background that might help you do this:

- There are no rules of behavior.

- Accountability is not assigned.

- There is no personnel planning process.

- The password system is not monitored. Expired passwords are allowed to remain on the system.

- There are no provisions for least privilege or separation of duties.

- There is no formal clearance structure to define and control diverse levels of security.

# chapter 15

# Physical Security

## Bridging the Great Divide

*The CEO had a problem. His director of physical security didn't want anything to do with the CISO, and there was no way the CEO was going to convince him otherwise. That wouldn't be much of a concern in most instances, since the CEO outranked him. But in this case, the director of physical security controlled a vast and rich empire, and the size of that domain made him an influential player in the company, particularly when it came to security.*

*The director of physical security oversaw more than 300 full-time employees who were housed in a security operations command center that was state of the art. From that center, his operation ran non-stop monitoring services for every one of the company's facilities no matter how small or isolated they might be. What is more, those monitoring services were not just TV surveillance; they also included proximity-based motion **sensors** and laser tripwires at each critical **location**. The entire array was hooked into the security center by real-time IP-based feeds.*

*Along with facilities, the employee protection service was able to guarantee the safety of company employees, no matter how far-flung the assignment. That was because every employee on overseas duty was guarded 24/7, either indirectly through electronic monitoring, or directly through armed escort. The operations center also housed a sophisticated strategic intelligence-gathering and threat analysis unit that kept managers apprised of all situations that might represent a potential risk to personnel or facilities. Fifty-five employees tracked the course of events in every place where the company did business worldwide, using satellite imagery and feeds from every major news network. Their daily situation reports and intelligence briefings let the company deploy around-the-clock strategic responses wherever they were needed.*

*It was hard to argue with the success of the physical security operation, since the savings from the theft and loss prevention program alone paid back the budget for the entire physical security operation within the first three months of each year. That return on investment made the director of physical security a force in corporate politics. The board of directors had not missed the fact that for nine months a year, the physical security operation was contributing directly to the bottom line of the company. The CEO trod very lightly indeed around the director of physical security.*

*He still had the problem that nobody in the entire physical security operation wanted anything to do with information protection. He felt that that attitude might have been acceptable back in the days when the company could secure all of its proprietary knowledge just by locking up the mainframe. But it no longer made sense now that the company ran a global electronic empire in a halfdozen different countries and cultures, some of whom were decidedly unfriendly to U.S. interests. It was the CEO's considered opinion that the company was going to repeat the events of three years ago without a coordinated effort between the physical security function and cybersecurity. Thus, it was time to force the issue.*

*At the next major shareholders' dinner, which was held at the Grill Room of the Four Seasons, the CEO mentioned that the actual point of attack in the first incident was a physical exploit. He explained that the attackers had simply accessed the target devices and run routines directly on them. Since that equipment was far inside the defensive perimeter, even the defensein-depth architecture of the information protection scheme couldn't prevent the attack from being successful.*

*That little gambit brought a wave of silence around the room. Some of the more important shareholders even put down the forks that they had been stuffing their faces with just the minute before, and focused their attention on the director of physical security, who, not liking to be put on the spot, shot back that a breakdown in the personnel security process was what had actually let the fox into the henhouse. The CEO pointed out that the fact remained that the damage had all been done through proximity. The cause was a failure of the functions responsible for ensuring that strangers did not get the kind of **physical access** that they needed to do their fatal mischief.*

*To reinforce the importance of coordinating physical security with information security, the CEO also pointed out that notwithstanding the damage an attacker could do, the harm from a major physical disaster, like a serious fire or hurricane, at a critical information processing facility would likely close the company's doors permanently. That new idea shut up the director of physical security for a couple of minutes. He thought he might be able to pawn the blame for another attack off on some other function, like HR. But he knew that the responsibility for earthquakes, tidal waves, fires, and floods was going to be all on him. So he sat at the far end of the table staring out over the Hudson River, sipping the last of his Montrachet and thinking about the coincidence that the site of the old World Trade Center was directly across the street behind him. That sad fact alone settled the matter, so he said the three little words that the CEO had been waiting to hear: "Let's fix this."*

*Getting the director of physical security on board meant that there weren't going to be any more roadblocks to integrating physical protections into the information security scheme. The CEO quickly formed a high-level corporate task team to do the planning. Because of the importance of getting a solution in place as fast as possible, that planning group was made up of an all-star list of company executives. They included the CISO, the compliance officer, the Corvallis security engineer (whose stock had been rising fast), and the manager who directed the physical security operations center.*

*The physical security operations center director was designated for the team because he had a background in strategic management from the CEO's old alma mater, Purdue. As a result, the CEO hoped that the op-center director would have the necessary vision to help plan the strategic integration of two very divergent functions. Likewise, the physical security director had nominated him because the op-center was the one that was the most dependent on data; the op-center director was the person who seemed to have the best handle on the issues of threat in cyberspace.*

*The op-center director was also the one person in the physical security function that the director of physical security trusted the most. That trust was important, because the physical security director was still extremely uncomfortable when it came to dealing with the assurance concerns of computerized information. Frankly, that old dog had no desire to learn any new tricks. The fact that his right-hand man was a member of the planning team meant that the planning process could be undertaken with the full authority of both of the key functions involved in the process.*

*The CEO didn't want the CISO to chair the planning group. It wasn't that he doubted the CISO's ability to deliver a competent solution. It was just that, for acceptance's sake, he did not want the eventual response to look like an information security production. Given the compliance officer's well-known personality issues, he felt that she would not be the right person to lead the group either. So he appointed co-chairs: the Corvallis security engineer and the director of the op-center.*

*These two were an excellent fit personality-wise. They were young, smart, and aggressive, and they both knew their respective areas front-to-back. That increased the CEO's confidence that he would be able to establish an effective integration of these two diverse areas. The Corvallis security engineer also had one other advantage, and that was his ability to use the EBK as a framework to create workable, real-world solutions. The EBK specifies the following five top-level functions for the physical security management process:*

1. *Coordinate with personnel managing IT security, personnel security, operations security, and other security functional areas to provide an integrated, holistic, and coherent security effort*

2. *Acquire necessary resources, including financial resources, to support an effective physical security program*

3. *Establish a physical security performance measurement system*

4. *Establish a program to determine the value of physical assets and the impact if unavailable*

5. *Ensure that appropriate changes and improvement actions are implemented as required*

# The Physical Security Plan

Physical security protection is implemented by a formal, organization-wide physical security plan. This plan should be aligned with the business purposes of the company because the actions that the plan dictates should be directly traceable to the organizational assets that the plan is designed to protect. The problem is that most physical security plans are developed separately from the planning that defines the activities of the information security process.

This division is caused by the fact that physical protection involves concrete things, while information assets are intangible. The people who are responsible for the overall security of the organization do not always view information assets in the same way as physical assets. As a result, the steps that are taken to ensure physical protection of information processing facilities and equipment can be badly coordinated with the things that are done to protect the information itself. Worse yet, because information can be viewed as "different," the responsibility to protect the equipment that it resides on might be left to the information technology function rather than physical security. Since information technology managers are not oriented toward protecting tangible assets, that assumption can result in no physical security at all.

Therefore, physical security planning has to establish a physical security process that is fully integrated with the processes that ensure the company's information assets. At a minimum, there should be deliberate procedural controls to ensure against physical intrusions into any protected space. There should also be controls to ensure that sensitive materials are always stored in a safe and secure location. Ultimately, the physical security plan has to make sure that only the people who have a legitimate right can physically access the information resource.

The physical security should also ensure that the organization will respond with logical and effective actions, which will minimize loss of information in the event of a physical disaster. Therefore, there should be a calculated response in place to react to all priority threats. Moreover, because the exact circumstances of a physical security exploit can be hard to anticipate, the plan must also include a standard mechanism for re-evaluating the status of a known threat in order to deploy the most appropriate response.

## Defining Protected Space

The first step in the planning process is a comprehensive inventory of all of the physical assets that fall within the protected space. This space is the area that the organization aims to secure. As it is with personnel security, the size of the protected space is typically dictated by the security resources that are available and the required level of security. If there are few resources, then the area of the protected space is, by necessity, small. If there are abundant resources, the protected space can be larger at the same level of security.

Documenting and accounting for the inventory in the protected space is done in the same way that it would be for any other physical inventory process. Physical items are catalogued, counted, and sorted into groups. Those groups form a baseline of known physical inventory items. Baselines are typically composed of all of the physical items that might need to be factored into the protection scheme, including all equipment and other physical property, as well as access points and aspects of the facilities that contribute to the overall security of information.

The baseline is then regularly inspected in order to ensure that it continues to retain its basic integrity and security properties. As items are added to, or deleted from, each baseline group the form of the protection scheme is evaluated for effectiveness. Controls are then changed, added, or even deleted in order to continue to ensure the security of the protected space. In that respect, it is essential to maintain a continuous understanding of the status of the items in the protection scheme.

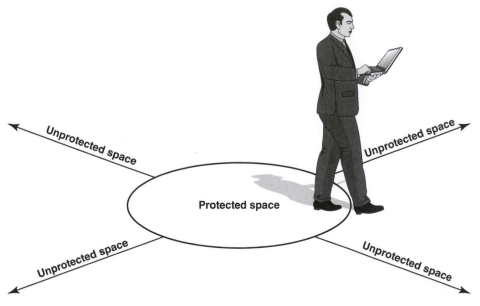

**Figure 15-1** Leaving protected space
© *Cengage Learning 2012*

Physical security involves concrete things, and they are not as susceptible to change as virtual ones. Nonetheless, the value and importance of items of physical property is directly related to the information they contain or can access, and therefore the contents of a physical device and its inter-connections has to be known and continuously evaluated. Otherwise, protected information can fall through the cracks. For example, a laptop is a piece of physical property whose value is dictated by the information it currently contains. New information, or information that changes the value of the laptop, can easily be transferred to it. Likewise, since laptops are extremely portable, they can easily be taken outside of the protected space (see Figure 15-1). Thus, it is very important to keep track of what information each laptop has on it and who is accountable for the security of the laptop itself.

Because of the need to assign accountability, it is also important to provide a specific statement of responsibility for all protected property. That responsibility is established by the organization through the specific assignment of security tasks to individuals, who are then accountable. Those accountabilities are always explicitly assigned in the physical security plan, which establishes unambiguous security responsibilities for each task item in the physical security baseline.

Subsequently, the performance of those assigned security duties is monitored and enforced by a standard auditing function. That audit function is also installed by the security plan. The primary aim of audit is to monitor all assigned security tasks in order to document their precise level of performance. The information that is subsequently derived from those audits can also be used to improve the physical security scheme. The whole aim of audit is to determine that the physical security process is being done in a coordinated fashion and that physical security is fully integrated with the other processes that ensure information.

## The Physical Security Process

The role of the physical security process is to guarantee that the organization's information is protected from all harm that originates in the physical universe. That harm can include instances of unauthorized physical access as well as natural or manmade disaster. In each of those respects, physical security ensures that meaningful, potential threats have been identified and that the required measures are in place to respond to those threats effectively. Like almost every other aspect of cybersecurity, the physical security process is monitored and enforced through a regular management function.

The first step in establishing a physical security management process requires the tangible items that have to be protected to be factored into a baseline. There are normally three classes of items in each of those baselines: equipment, people, and the environment. Each of these categories requires different types of safeguards and different techniques to ensure them. The first category is made up of those tangible things that are associated with the computer itself. Typical items in that category are hardware, power supply, and network connections.

The second class involves threats from the people who use the computer. Control of the human resources is really the duty of the personnel security function. Nevertheless, access to the equipment and other essential elements of the information system has to be restricted through physical access controls that are implemented and administered by physical security. In that respect, personnel security decides who should be trusted while physical security maintains the **gates, guards, doors, and locks** that ensure that only those people who are trusted gain access.

The final group comprises those things that are part of the environment. This category is probably the most confusing, because the environment includes all of the hazards that are associated with natural events, like hurricanes and floods. The environment also encompasses all of the safety concerns of the physical space, and because the threats in this group are so wide-ranging, they are also continually changing. This means that much of the environmental security planning process involves anticipating threats that might not ever occur. For instance, if you are based in hurricane country, it is important to have an effective plan in place even if a major hurricane has not hit a city in a while.

## Physical Security Threat Assessments

Getting a practical response in place to counter a physical security threat relies on the ability to prioritize just those things that will threaten the organization. Those priorities are defined by the level of the threat and the availability of personnel and financial resources. That prioritization becomes the front end for a formal organizational planning process that dictates the physical security response. Because circumstances are always changing, the only way to ensure the continuing effectiveness of physical security plans is to perform an ongoing evaluation of the physical security threat environment. This requires that the organization track and prioritize the likely hazards in the surrounding physical environment and their probability of occurrence.

For example, even though they happen frequently, problems with the configuration of the system do not cause the same level of damage that a hurricane might. If a choice has to be made about which threat to respond to first, that decision should be based on the amount of actual harm that could reasonably be expected to occur from each. If it were probable that a hurricane would occur within a finite period, then there would have to be a lot of probable instances of application failures within the same period to justify making the latter a higher priority. If a hurricane was considered unlikely, then the organization should invest the majority of its resources in keeping the system properly configured.

This kind of decision-making is a balancing act that should always be supported by substantive analysis. Since harm and probability are equal factors in formulating a physical security plan, the estimates of probability of occurrence and degree of impact have to be based on timely data, which is gathered from the relevant parts of the physical environment. Using that data, the threat assessment process can identify and prioritize a list of harmful events. That list would be based on those events that have both a high degree of potential for injury, as well as a high likelihood of occurrence. The outcome of that assessment process would then produce a ranked set of physical security threats that need to be addressed in the physical security plan.

# Designing for Physical Protection

*The physical security plan seemed to integrate the newer information security measures with the classic practices of physical security. The items that had value were all identified, and the responsible parties were assigned for each item. The two team leaders knew that the next step in the process was to get a workable design to secure the items within a particular protected space; however, that was the point where they both parted company.*

*The information security side of the argument was represented by the Corvallis security engineer. He had been through his own personal struggles of setting up the information security scheme at his shop, and he had some distinct ideas about the physical assets that needed protection. The problem lay in the fact that the assets that the security engineer considered important were only partially covered by the current physical security scheme. As an example of why that situation was dangerous, the security engineer pointed out that without visitor escort, the potential existed for unauthorized people to just stroll into sensitive areas. In fact, in his own opinion that was exactly how the attack three years ago had been carried out.*

*The idea of the company having to realign its physical security processes to encompass a bunch of new procedures gave the op-center director a major case of heartburn. It meant that somebody in the physical security operation would have to expend a lot of time and money to do the realigning, and the funds to underwrite that were not in his budget.*

*Moreover, he felt that there had to be a way to protect information on some sliding scale that was not going to drag the company into another bankruptcy from sheer inefficiency of operation. It just seemed like a simple matter of common sense to avoid trying to protect all of the information in the company all of the time. To him, the investment that that effort would require was simply not justified. He had considerable military background, and he was familiar with the concept of defense-in-depth, so he put together a design that summarized his ideas and ran them past the CEO.*

*The op-center director's idea made use of the fact that the company had already prioritized its information assets based on their perceived value and had identified the risks to each. So the company had a priority ranking of all of its information items arranged from high value, high risk to low value, low risk. Using that list, he factored the company's entire set of information items into four groups. Those were "protect at all costs," "protect," "protect if funds are available," and "no need to protect – either no value or no present risk." Then he set about looking at what it would take to ensure those conditions for each category.*

*What he came up with was a set of categories based on an increasingly more rigorous series of electronic and behavioral controls. The top group was protected by all of the policies, procedures, and technologies the company could bring to bear, whereas the last group was not controlled at all. The two middle groups received progressively less control as the priority of the items declined.*

*The CEO loved the idea, since it did two things. It ensured maximum protection for the items that he considered critical, and it made the best possible use of the company's security resources. As soon as the security engineer saw it, he bought into the obvious logic of the design. He and the op-center director then set out to create a system that would provide maximum defense-in-depth protection at a minimum cost. The security engineer knew that the design part of the EBK contained the following five items for physical security:*

1. *Identify the physical security program requirements and specifications in relationship to enterprise security goals*

2. *Develop policies and procedures for identifying and mitigating physical and environmental threats to information assets, personnel, facilities, and equipment*

3. *Develop a physical security and environmental security plan, including security test plans and contingency plans, in coordination with other security planning functions*

4. *Develop countermeasures against identified risks and vulnerabilities*

5. *Develop criteria for inclusion in the acquisition of facilities, equipment, and services that impact physical security*

*These items provided an ideal process for creating a defense-in-depth approach.*

# Incorporating Physical Security into the Information Protection Scheme

The design of an information security scheme that incorporates physical security into the overall process is much more involved than the design of strictly electronic protection. That is because there are so many sources of breach in the physical universe. For instance, although it is easy to monitor the comings and goings of users through a firewall, it is a different matter entirely to ensure the perimeter integrity of every door and window in a large building. The design of a physical security protection scheme is based around the concept of establishing **secure spaces**, which are the physical areas that the organization has chosen to certify as secure. By inference, all secure spaces within the physical boundaries of the enterprise itself are trustworthy.

The goal of the design is to ensure that access to secure physical spaces is controlled and that the organization is able to react effectively to intrusions into that space. Secure spaces are cost-efficient because the measures to ensure their security are generally only deployed at the perimeter of the space. This creates an effective borderline between controlled and uncontrolled locations, which can then be ensured by physical access controls such as fences, gates, and guards. Since the area within that perimeter is considered secure by definition, the controls that protect that space can be less rigorous than they are at the boundary. For instance, internal controls are generally limited to passive monitoring devices like cameras and door sensors.

Since some items within the security boundary are more important than others, secure spaces are generally nested within each other in a defense-in-depth arrangement. Individuals who are seeking to access the most important items have to pass through successively more rigorous access control mechanisms as they move into successively more secure spaces. The concept of control of physical access at the perimeter still applies; however, since those perimeters are arranged within each other, the physical access controls can be made increasingly more powerful at each boundary. Each level of control will provide progressively more rigorous protection to whatever is within that space.

Because the protected space itself is increasingly more limited, a higher level of protection can be achieved with fewer countermeasures. For instance, it takes a lot of fences, gates, and guards to ensure the outer perimeter of an army base. On the other hand, the single door to a highly secure room within that base can be protected with sophisticated electronic and physical access control measures. These measures might provide a much higher degree of assurance than any point on the outer perimeter, but they would still probably cost less than it would to install and maintain the outer fence system. As a result, a defense-in-depth approach allows the organization to layer its defenses in a way that ensures the highest degree of security for its most important assets at the lowest possible cost.

## Threat Identification and Strategy

While it is difficult to protect against every physical threat, there are basic steps that can be taken to defend against the ones that are the most likely to occur. The first principle in designing a security scheme is that all practical points of weakness have to be identified and then explicit controls have to be developed to address the threats that might possibly exploit those points of weakness. Since physical security protection is built around creating secure perimeters, the controls have to be concentrated on the most likely places where that perimeter might be breached.

Secure space should always be accessed through secure perimeters. Defense-in-depth dictates that those access points should represent increasingly rigorous levels of control. Accordingly, an appropriate set of controls have to be placed at the access points to ensure the integrity of each of the designated boundaries in the physical security design. Those controls typically require tailoring policies, procedures, and technologies to ensure the three fundamental characteristics of a secure perimeter: location, access, and control.

Location is the primary factor in a physical security plan because it dictates the form of physical access control. For instance, a facility located at the top of a mountain would use much different access controls than one that was located in a busy city. That rule also applies when it comes to developing the policies and procedures to ensure protected space. For instance, policies that ensure the physical security of highly sensitive equipment would be entirely different if that equipment was already located in a secure facility versus being more accessible to the public.

The operating principle in all of these cases is that the physical location serves as a de-facto control technique; therefore, the controls that ensure security have to be tailored around the conditions of the location. For that reason, the location and level of desired security have to be factored into the planning process when it comes to the development of a physical security scheme. Where possible, it is also important to tailor each control to ensure that it represents an optimum fit with the enterprise's security strategy. For instance, if the company were planning to construct a building that contained its most critical information, the general policy would be to locate it in the center of the protected space, not close to the fence line.

## Maintaining Secure Access

Security information in the physical universe depends on the security of the equipment that it resides on. The primary responsibility of physical security is to ensure that all of the enterprise's information processing equipment is properly safeguarded against unauthorized access. For the first 30 years of the computer business, this was not a major problem, since mainframe CPUs and peripheral devices were not even remotely portable. Measures to protect that equipment could amount to nothing more than making sure that the computer center was locked up at night. That situation has entirely changed with the advent of all sorts of mobile computing devices.

Because information processing equipment is now highly mobile, organizational control has to be enforced through a set of sometimes intricate control procedures. These procedures are aimed at regulating the physical movement of information processing equipment in and out of controlled space. In practice, those procedures specify and enforce the assigned rights of each individual seeking to cross the boundary between secure and unsecure space. As far as the actual control points are concerned, they are set up to limit the number of access points and strictly control entry into secure space through each point. Access in and out of secure space is only granted to people who can be authenticated; people without proper authorization have to be denied. Access control enforces the same general criteria in both the virtual and physical worlds. For that reason, the access control process for physical space is implemented through the same identity, authentication, and authorization functions that are used to control electronic space.

Practically speaking, the active element of that control is monitoring. In the physical universe, monitoring depends on being able to observe the behavior of people and processes within the secure space. The aim of that monitoring is to ensure that that behavior will always comply with security requirements. There are simple, people-centered control mechanisms that ensure behavior within the controlled space, such as gates and guards. In the case of more sensitive settings, there are also various electronic access control mechanisms such as RFID monitoring, closed-circuit TV (CCTV), and access control biometrics.

All of these technical features are identified in the physical security planning process for the information security function. The physical security plan implements the design. It specifies all of the specific policies, procedures, and technological countermeasures that will be deployed by that particular organization to counter a given threat. The plan also provides the criteria that will be used to decide whether those countermeasures are effective. Logically, much of the success of a security plan rests with its ability to evolve as the threat picture changes. Consequently, the criteria that provide the basis for that judgment are an especially important part of the plan.

Those criteria serve as the tangible points of reference that can be used to evaluate how close each policy, procedure, and countermeasure comes to satisfying its security purposes. As a result, all of the necessary criteria for evaluation have to be spelled out along with the objective means of determining whether the requirements of that criterion were satisfied. The policies, procedures, and relevant countermeasures, along with the pertinent criteria, are specified in the design and then documented in the physical security plan.

## Establishing the Right Internal Countermeasures

Because equipment is tangible, it can be protected by ensuring the integrity and security of the space that it resides in. The approaches that are used to create that secure physical space typically involve the same kinds of controls that are used in conventional physical security situations. That includes such long-established control methods as gates and guards, locks, passcard and swipecard readers, video cameras, and safes, as well as simple administrative procedures such as ensuring visitor accompaniment. There are some exceptions that are brought on by the special circumstances of information processing equipment.

## Ensuring Against Malicious Actions in the Secure Space

The security of the protected space is based on controlling any malicious human action within the space itself. Ensuring human behavior within the protected space is important because most of the serious material damage to computers comes from intentional or deliberate acts of people. The most common examples of this are criminal acts such as theft of computer equipment or documents and outright **vandalism**. Specific access control mechanisms have to be put in place to ensure that only trustworthy people have access to the facility, equipment, and data and that during the period of access, each individual within the secure space is monitored and controlled.

**Ensuring Network Equipment** Network devices are tempting targets because they are dispersed; some of the physical parts of a network, such as cables, are located outside protected space. In particular, because network cables extend out of the normal sphere of protection, they are more vulnerable than most parts of the system. With networks, there are two kinds of security failures that can ensue. An untrusted party can physically access a server or a network transmission device. That access would potentially violate the confidentiality, or integrity, principle. On the other hand, a network would not be able to perform its basic transmission functions if it were vandalized.

The only practical way to ensure security in dispersed network equipment is through electronic countermeasures such as transmission monitoring and emanations security. These measures are normally part of the network security process. Nonetheless, where physical security *can* be involved in the protection of networks is in the prevention of unauthorized access to the network equipment that resides within the protected space. This is done by establishing and protecting secure perimeters.

**Protecting Portable Devices** Mobile computing causes an entirely new set of problems for physical security, because the outright theft of the equipment will negate any other kind of countermeasure, including encryption. The requirement for the protection of portable devices is a relatively new addition to the field of computer security; ten years ago, it was almost physically impossible for a person to walk out the door with a desktop CPU and not be noticed. Now it is a simple matter of popping a small memory stick, a removable hard drive, a notebook computer, or a PDA into a pocket or briefcase and disappearing. Moreover, since people use portable devices in odd places, it is hard to even think about physical security when an employee might be doing a little extra company work at a Starbucks. Rigorous physical control measures are required for any mobile equipment that contains sensitive data, which normally means that sensitive files on portable devices have to be encrypted.

Three interlocking security conditions apply to portable devices. The first condition is that there have to be explicit countermeasures installed on the device itself. The second condition is that there have to be countermeasures in place to protect the data on the device. The third condition is that whatever security controls might be installed, they have to be easy for the user to operate. That is Saltzer and Schroeder's "psychological acceptability" principle in action.

Physical protection of portable equipment typically involves the installation of monitoring functions like GPS trackers. These functions are often built into the device and simply have to be activated. They are usually invisible to the user, and they create the capability for the owner of the device to track its whereabouts no matter where it is taken. Security of portable devices is further augmented by simple procedural safeguards, such as storing them in a secure space when they are not in use.

Measures like GPS tracking and secure storage protect the device, but it is also prudent to secure the data on the device. That typically involves software-based access control mechanisms such as passwords. There are also software controls to hide files within the computer itself. In something as easily lost as a portable device, strong encryption is the only really effective measure to ensure data security.

Finally, since the effectiveness of these techniques depends on systematic and disciplined user practice, security measures for a mobile device must be easy to use. The idea is to make the security process transparent to its user by automating it. This is why automated countermeasures such as pre-installed GPS tracking devices are built into most portable products.

# Understanding the Variables in Physical Access Control

*As far as the security engineer was concerned, the design part of the process was the hard part; however, the op-center director begged to differ. That was because the op-center director had been through the process of implementing physical controls before. He knew from experience that the actual installation of any kind of physical control system was going to suffer from Murphy's classic dictate that "if anything can go wrong it will." The problem stemmed from the fact that the security engineer had only installed countermeasures in the virtual universe, where the computer did a lot of the distribution and set-up work. The sheer scale of identifying secure space and then establishing the countermeasures to make those perimeters secure demanded much more creativity and flexibility than the security engineer was used to exercising.*

*The security engineer learned his lesson the hard way when he went out to the pilot installation, which was in his own plant in Corvallis. He knew that the essence of good security was ensuring that the location aided in the protection of the installation. As he drove up to the facility, which was located in a scenic forest, he could see that those big old Oregon trees came right up to the side of the building. Several of the larger ones overhung the roof. Since that did not give an adequate field of vision to monitor prospective intruders, the first task he proposed was to cut out a secure perimeter of several hundred yards. The idea of slaughtering a bunch of trees in order to provide an adequate perimeter was vetoed right away by the CEO, which also probably saved the security engineer from being lynched by the several hundred tree-huggers who worked in the Corvallis facility.*

*But the problem remained: the tree situation made the facility extremely vulnerable to any approach through the forest. As an alternative, the engineer decided to install a fence and electronic tripwire system. He would have used television monitoring, but the forest was too thick to allow for that. It took time and money, but the initial installation of the fence was extremely successful. Notwithstanding all of the trees that were still inside the perimeter, the fence provided an adequate physical boundary, and the laser tripwires would detect any movement six feet on either side of the fence.*

*In his office that night, the security engineer broke open a cold beer to celebrate his achievement. Unfortunately, he never got a chance to taste it as the first intruder alert went off. He rushed to the monitoring center only to discover that a squirrel had hit one of the tripwires. In fact, he was to make that same discovery 28 times that night, before the security staff finally disabled the system for good. In that time, which his staff later referred to as "the night with no sleep," his system had accounted for 13 squirrels, five possums, four owls, three raccoons, two bats, and a bobcat.*

*The security engineer learned two things from that debacle. First, he now knew that most of the denizens of the surrounding forest were nocturnal. Second, he had finally figured out that there are many more factors and avenues of attack in physical space than there are in virtual space. The security engineer was used to being attacked through an established electronic access point, like a firewall. He was not used to physical security's wide-open, three-hundred-and-sixty degree attack space, particularly when that space was both vertical and horizontal.*

*The security engineer now had to think about how to prevent people from getting into his secure spaces through the many doors and windows of the building. At the same time, he also had to think about how to prevent them from climbing in from the overhanging trees or burrowing in from somewhere in the surrounding landscape. That didn't even include the **natural disasters** that occasionally hit the area, like a good old-fashioned Pacific Northwest forest fire, which was a real concern for the engineer, since his facility was indeed embedded in a forest.*

*The solution obviously required everybody's input. The security engineer and the op-center director pooled their collective experience in an attempt to come up with a solution that would incorporate the necessary security measures from both of their fields. The op-center director pointed out that even without the tripwires, the fence did provide some security, in that it kept accidental intruders out of the initial perimeter. Because it was topped by razor wire, the fence made certain that the people who did breach that perimeter were motivated. Since the next perimeter could not go any further than the walls of the building, the op-center director pointed out that there would need to be a layering of the automated monitoring capabilities from the outer walls inward. That was the problem that both of them were wrestling with.*

*Because of the many issues that they were going to have to deal with inside the building, the rest of the solution would have to incorporate the basic principles of physical security in a novel fashion. That is, the defense-in-depth part of the solution would have to be based on concentric perimeters within the building that could be secured by technology. Fortunately, the EBK provided a basic way to structure that process. Because security situations change over time, much of the following six items specified for implementing physical security revolved around the continuing identification and mitigation of risks:*

1. *Apply physical and environmental controls in support of physical and environmental security plans*

2. *Control access to information assets in accordance with standards, procedures, directives, policies, regulations, and laws (statutes)*

3. *Integrate physical security concepts into test plans, procedures, and exercises*

4.  *Conduct threat and vulnerability assessments to identify physical and environmental risks and vulnerabilities, and update applicable controls as necessary*

5.  *Review construction projects to ensure that appropriate physical security and protective design features are incorporated into their design*

6.  *Compile, analyze, and report performance measures*

## Meshing the Controls with the Plan

Physical security is not a simple matter of selecting the right gates and guards. It also involves the steps that the organization takes to build physical protection directly into the protected space itself. It is important to include security into the physical planning, because every facility is susceptible to natural and manmade disasters. The planning for the construction and long-term maintenance of the facility should involve contingency plans to protect the secure space. These safeguards must be developed as part of the overall strategic planning process. The process of creating an effective array of controls involves a number of different factors. For instance, the potential for theft can be reduced by establishing a high degree of visual control. But in order to create that capability, there has to be careful architectural planning in advance for the placement of walls. Access points can be reduced, which enhances access control; however, the location of doors has to be planned to ensure that the control points do not restrict the free flow of business.

Plans for physical access control should incorporate both the normal means of access, such as gates and building doors, with controls for other secondary access points such as fire escapes and service and delivery docks. The planning process involves the identification and evaluation of the likelihood and potential impact of each unauthorized access through each potential point of entry. Because intruders can use any of those places in the building, the vulnerabilities that have to be considered are not just in the horizontal plane. Along with normal potential points of building access, like doors, the vulnerability assessment has to account for roofs, basements, fire escapes, and upper windows.

Access points like service entries and loading docks represent a special control problem, because in order to ensure timely delivery of goods and services, outsiders have to be able to come and go through those points as efficiently as possible. That implies a minimum amount of restriction. Since untrusted people are crossing the organizational boundary, there still has to be sufficient control at the perimeter to ensure the requisite level of security. In conventional business operations, this problem is normally solved by treating service points as if they are outside the perimeter, even if they are actually within the building. Thus the **perimeter controls** are placed behind the service point rather than the outer walls of the building, and the service point becomes untrusted space.

## Implementing the Measures to Control Access

The overall protection requirements for secure space have to be specified in order to build an effective physical access control system. Practically, that specification should clearly describe the depth, height, and width of the physical space that will be secured. Once the form of the

**Figure 15-2** Will the guard see everything?
© *Cengage Learning 2012*

secure space is defined, the physical access control measures can be added. These measures are typically traditional control mechanisms, including such conventional things as natural **barriers, fence systems,** walls and mechanical barriers, and human surveillance.

Perimeter controls are the first line of defense. They are usually passive things such as high ornamental shrubs, decorative streams, and even long, grassy lawns. Perimeter controls can also be active things like electronic tripwires and motion sensors. Structural barriers such as fences, gates, **bollards,** and facility walls and doors are also passive devices. Fences enclose secure areas and designate property boundaries. Gates and bollards secure the entrance and/ or exit points from a secured area; gates define the actual entry and exit positions whereas bollards, which are posts or barriers, control traffic by funneling it into the access point.

Human-based control methods, such as guards and foot **patrols,** are a low-tech, labor-intensive way to secure space. Guards are an effective control mechanism if they are adequately trained and disciplined. The advantage of guards over the other approaches is that they bring human judgment to each situation; however, they are also subject to inattention and boredom, and they can often miss key indicators of intrusion, as shown in Figure 15-2. For these reasons, effective human-centered security has to be regulated by well-defined procedure and constant discipline.

## Perimeter Controls: Barriers

Perimeter controls establish defense-in-depth. They should be specifically designed to ensure the space they are set to protect. Their main function is to control access and then monitor behavior within the space. Perimeter controls come in various types, the simplest of which are the passive barriers, such as doors and windows. Since they are the likeliest point of access, all doors and accessible windows must be controlled in order for a defense-in-depth security scheme to work properly.

Barrier devices entail simple physical issues. For instance, the robustness of the door might seem like a simple concern, but if the perimeter can be breached by a well-aimed kick, then the space itself should not be considered secure. Other factors have to be thought about for the same reason, such as ensuring the robustness of hinges and doorframes. Windows are as important as doors in perimeter defense, since they also serve as points of access. Because they are never used to enter or leave a building, they also make a logical choice for somebody who is looking to breach a physical perimeter. The choice of window technology, therefore, makes a difference in the level of security.

The final barriers are the walls themselves, which are vulnerable to violent attacks, such as explosives, or more subtle attacks, such as hammers and chisels. Because an exterior wall can be breached through both of those means, it is important to ensure that the walls of the information processing facility are not easily accessible from outside of the building.

## Perimeter Controls: Locks

Locks are the most commonly used mechanical controls, and every type of lock can be breached. There are four types of locks: cipher, combination, deadbolt, and smart. With a cipher lock, the right sequence of buttons is required in order to gain entry. Combination locks also require a sequence of numbers in a specific order. Deadbolt locks are typically built into the door, providing a much more robust level of security. Finally, the new generation of smart locks embodies some form of electronic intelligence, which regulates access through biometrics.

Once the lock is installed, the aim of the physical security function should be to protect the **key**. Much of the physical security process for locks involves key control procedures to issue, sign out, inventory, and manage lost keys. Biometric access control techniques will make key control less of an issue because they use physical characteristics as the key. Fingerprints, retina scans, signature dynamics, voice recognition, and even hand geometry are hard to duplicate and impossible to lose.

Unfortunately, biometrics is still an expensive and unwieldy method of access control, since individuals seeking access must already have their physiological characteristics registered in the system. Another electronic, state-of-the-art method for access control is the **smart card**, a credit card–sized plastic token that has a special machine-readable key embedded in its surface. The most common example of a smart card is the plastic card that is in almost universal use as a hotel room key.

## Intrusion Detection in the Physical Space

**Intrusion detection** methods and technologies are not just used in the electronic universe. They are also used to ensure the integrity of the physical space. Intrusion detection methods include people-based solutions such as foot patrols and closed-circuit TV surveillance. Physical intrusion detection can also involve electronic measures like ultrasonic, microwave, infrared and pressure sensors.

Intrusion detection in the physical space is as important as electronic intrusion detection, since damage from physical intrusions such as vandalism and theft can be as harmful as damage from any electronic exploit. The goal of the physical intrusion detection function is to identify and then provide real-time response to violations of the protected space. The method for detecting intruders is often based on electronic measures. Physical intrusion detection sensors can be based on alterations of electrical circuits and light beams as well as sound, vibration, and motion detection. Electronic sensors are typically installed on access points such as windows, doors, ceilings, and walls. Sensors can also be installed in less obvious points such as ventilation openings.

# Evaluating the Physical Security Process

*The planning was done and the countermeasures were in place. It was now time to confirm that the physical security process for the Corvallis facility worked. Because of the spectacular failure of the initial pilot test, the team members decided that one more incident like that would be a career-ender. So they did the evaluation of their new physical security approach under highly controlled conditions at the Corvallis site only.*

*Limiting the test to Corvallis also made sense because, like all of the rest of the EBK functions, the physical security process was tailored specifically to that site. What the team wanted to know was whether the planning and deployment methodology was transportable, since the implementation process for the EBK recommendations was meant to be standard across the company. In effect, what was being tested was the method for laying out the physical security scheme, not the specific solution itself.*

*What the team members wanted to ensure was that the steps they had followed to design and deploy the physical security controls for the Corvallis site were effective. Accordingly, their testing was aimed at validating the process that was used to implement the physical security controls at the Corvallis site. The testing included such traditional approaches as audits, which sought to confirm that everybody was properly following procedure, as well as operational tests of the system to confirm that problems were caught and corrected in as timely a fashion as possible.*

*In addition, the testing included creative approaches like penetration tests, which required the team to organize a group of testers who were both knowledgeable in security procedures as well as the ins and outs of protecting information. Most important of all, the testers had to have a good eye for the nonconventional flaw. In practical terms, that meant that they had to find the hole in the defense that nobody else would think of. That took as much creativity as it did computer skills. Fortunately, Corvallis was the sort of place where the unconventional liked to gather, so it was a matter of scouting around town until the security team found the right group of out-of-the-box thinkers.*

*The evaluation process was a two-pronged affair. The security team did the evaluation in the conventional way by collecting all of the event logs and culling out the relevant testing data. The hacking group began a zero knowledge exploit that was designed once and for all to tell whether the physical security system worked. The security engineer and the op-center director knew that they had to collect enough information to satisfy the following six high-level evaluation criteria specified in the EBK:*

1. *Assess and evaluate the overall effectiveness of physical and environmental security policy and controls, and make recommendations for improvement*

2. *Review incident data and make process improvement recommendations*

3. *Assess effectiveness of physical and environmental security control testing*

4.  *Evaluate acquisitions that have physical security implications and report findings to management*

5.  *Assess the accuracy and effectiveness of the physical security performance measurement system, and make recommendations for improvement where applicable*

6.  *Compile, analyze, and report performance measures*

# How to Measure Success – Conventionally and Otherwise

An evaluation of the effectiveness of a security solution typically involves some form of audit, which is a process of standardized interviews, observations of both human behavior and system documentation, and other steps to gather relevant evidence. The aim of the audit process is to develop a full and accurate picture of the entity that is under scrutiny. It takes a comprehensive, organization-wide process like audit to collect the evidence necessary to get that complete picture.

The audit process is always managed separately from and entirely independent of the management team of the place that is being audited. An independent audit manager has to be appointed to ensure that autonomy. The role of the audit manager is to supervise, monitor, and evaluate the performance of the audit. Specifically, the audit manager plans and schedules audit activities, assumes responsibility for the audit reporting process, and controls the follow-up procedures.

Since audits are conducted using concrete criteria, the people performing the audit have to be aware of all relevant criteria for their audit. The auditors themselves must have the technical and professional know-how to perform a proper audit. They must understand the system being audited as well as the requirements of proper physical security practice. Auditors must also be knowledgeable about how the audit target operates, and they must have a working knowledge about the laws and regulations that govern and shape the environment of the audited organization. The overall aim of the audit team is to guarantee consistent conclusions; all auditors should make the same observations and draw the same conclusions from the same evidence.

The audit process involves a number of related steps, most of which are documentation-intensive. In practical terms, this means that the audit activity at each stage revolves around either preparing or reviewing audit documentation. Because it drives the rest of the process, the most important substantive activity in audit is always the preparation, validation, and distribution of the audit forms and checklists. Checklists are particularly important in the case of physical security audits, because the auditors are not likely to have complete expertise in all of the areas being audited.

The first step in the audit process is to specify the precise scope of the audit. Then it is necessary to prioritize the audit targets that fall within that scope in such a way that the ones that are most critical to understanding the problem are the ones that are examined first. The goal of the prioritization is to be able to ensure the correctness of those elements with the greatest influence on the physical security process as early as possible.

The audit is aimed at gaining an understanding of three critical and highly related requirements. The first requirement is that the inter-relationships between all of the components of the physical security scheme are known. The second requirement is that specific threats are identified, evaluated, and documented. The third requirement is that all vulnerabilities that could be exploited by those threats are documented and associated with a control.

The audit examines data generated by logs of system, network, and application and user activity. Audit trails obtained from those logs provide details about violations and attacks and the resulting response. Because log data is so important, it is important to ensure that logs were not tampered with during the event under investigation.

Audits are a commonly accepted means of confirming the proper functioning of a given entity; however, since audits are evidence-based, they are limited to observations about existing events. Penetration testing, on the other hand, is a creative act that seeks to exploit security vulnerabilities. It simulates an attack on the system at the request of the owner. To be ethical, penetration testers must have clearly defined goals, which are assigned by the organization that is being tested. To be effective, the testers must use the same methods or techniques that an adversary would.

The purpose of penetration testing is to evaluate system security by attacking it. Testing methods are based around four activities. The first of these is discovery, which is where the target is identified and documented. This is followed by enumeration, where the tester attempts to gain more knowledge about the target through various kinds of intrusions. Once the knowledge is obtained, vulnerability mapping takes place. This is where the tester maps what is known about the test environment to recognized vulnerabilities. Finally, once the vulnerabilities have been mapped into the target environment, the tester attempts to gain access. The results of the exploits that are run can help an organization identify vulnerabilities, gaps, intrusion response capability, monitoring and logging capability, and reporting.

# Chapter Summary

- Physical security centers on the definition of coherent measures to safeguard against direct physical attacks.

- The classic purpose of physical security is to account for and control tangible information and IT assets.

- Physical security can only be assured by explicit procedures.

- Assets should always be protected with several perimeters. This is called a layered defense.

- Location is the primary determinant for physical security because it dictates the requirements of the access control system.

- Access has to be granted and monitored.

- Authorization needs to be continuously monitored.

- The basic mechanisms that are used to underwrite physical security are designed to control access and detect intrusion.

- The process is normally instituted through a strategic planning activity that is monitored and enforced by a consistent and ongoing security management function.

- The only sure way to protect facilities is to define a finite physical space and an effective set of countermeasures to realistically assure the integrity of the area.

- Secure workspaces evolve from a comprehensive threat analysis and subsequent prioritization process, which leads to a carefully arrayed physical security plan.

- The process of establishing physical security rests on the ability to distinguish the threats and vulnerabilities that apply to a given situation.

- Controls are an essential part of physical security.

- Most highly secure facilities make use of more than one form of authentication to control access.

- **Perimeter intrusion detection** can be used to ensure the integrity of a facility.

# Key Terms

**Barriers** Physical impediments to access.

**Bollards** Physical structures, usually made of cement or steel, that are designed to impede the progress of a vehicle or other large entity, like a tank.

**Doors and locks** Structural and mechanical barrier devices designed to control access.

**Fence systems** Barrier devices designed to prevent access to a physical space.

**Gates** Barrier devices that are part of fence systems that can be used to regulate traffic flow.

**Guards and patrols** Human-centered, physical security countermeasure.

**Intrusion detection** Process employed to detect a penetration of secure space.

**Key** Authentication token for lock mechanism.

**Layered defense** Concentric defenses of increasing strength designed to put the most valuable assets behind the maximum degree of protection.

**Location** A countermeasure in physical security based around optimum placement of protected space in the general environment.

**Natural disasters** Events that are beyond human control, such as a flood or an earthquake.

**Perimeter controls** The countermeasures placed on the boundary between secure and unsecured space.

**Perimeter intrusion detection** Boundary countermeasures designed to identify penetrations of secure space.

**Physical access** Access to the tangible elements of the system, such as servers.

**Secure spaces** Specifically designated physical areas ensured by access controls.

**Sensors** A form of access control, frequently electronic, that is designed to detect the presence of intruders.

**Smart card** A token with computer-readable information inscribed on it that grants access to secure space.

**Vandalism** The act of committing willful damage to an asset.

# Questions from the CIO

The CIO requires you to brief her on the current status of your investigation. This will be an important part of your continuing work on this project, since it is essential to be able to describe all of the ramifications of a properly developed physical security process. Consequently, the CIO would like you to answer the following questions for her:

1. Why are natural disasters important physical security concerns? How can they be safeguarded?

2. Why is it important to keep architecture in mind when designing information-processing facilities?

3. What is the relationship between access control and protection from harm from malicious human actions? How do the various categories of access control ensure that?

4. Why is physical security one of the most critical elements of overall security?

5. What two factors make physical security so hard to implement?

6. What three factors must you consider in establishing a secure area?

7. What three categories of things can go wrong in the physical universe?

8. Contingency plans have three generic procedural components. What are they?

9. Authentication is based on three broad categories. What are they?

10. There are four types of physical security controls. What are they?

11. There are three primary objectives when it comes to fire. What are they?

12. There are three types of physical storage media. What are they, and what are the common threats?

13. What is the goal of perimeter intrusion detection?

14. Why is it particularly dysfunctional if the responsibility for physical security is assigned separately from the overall cybersecurity function?

15. What typical business functions might power problems impact?

16. Why are multifactor authentication techniques more effective than single authentication measures?

17. What is the purpose of sensors in perimeter and building security?

# Hands-On Projects

You have been assigned the responsibility for planning a defense-in-depth for the administrative offices shown in Figure 15-3. What are five physical vulnerabilities that you see in the layout? What are some of the controls that you would deploy to address these? In particular, ensure a defense-in-depth for the Operational IT space.

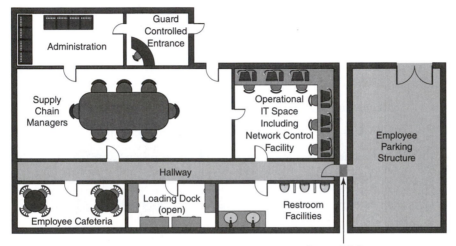

**Figure 15-3** Defense-in-depth diagram

© Cengage Learning 2012

# chapter 16

# Procurement

## Surviving the Supply Chain

*The CISO decided that he had dealt with his final problem when he got the word from his army of auditors and field testers that the company's security system was working as planned. In fact, the reams of flattering reports from the company's facilities had him thinking elevated thoughts. Specifically, that elevation involved exactly one floor, and it led to the CEO's penthouse. The CISO had coveted the CEO's office, and now that he had learned that the CEO was first in line for the vacant position of company president, that office seemed like a viable possibility. The CISO had felt for a long time that he was the right person to be sitting in that office whenever the CEO vacated it. So, in anticipation of his next big move the CISO was thumbing through the stack of executive office furniture catalogues that he had been accumulating. That was why he was especially displeased to have his thoughts interrupted by a call from the network manager.*

*The network manager told him that the company had just been hit by another denial-of-service attack. This attack had the same signature as the one from three years ago, and servers had started to topple globally. However, this time the company's special hot server solution had saved the day. Although those servers had not been able to fend off the attack the first time around, this most recent attack was a little less powerful and the extra horsepower had ensured that processing, although slow, did not cease entirely. More important, there were no associated physical or insider attacks. All those events had taken place while the CISO was reading an article about ergonomic office chairs in one of his fancy catalogues, so the network manager was already able to report that the company was back on an even keel and doing business as usual.*

*The CISO had gotten most of the subsequent credit for that success. Even so, he still wanted to find a culprit, especially since this new event had put a serious crimp in his career plans. That's why he launched an inquisition with the system staff that would have done credit to Torquemada. Given the incentive that the CISO's various creative threats provided, it didn't take long for the system staff to identify the source of the problem. The whole exploit had originated from a single line of C++ code, which was embedded in the company's monumental customer relations management system. That little defect had opened the door for some faceless hacker to cause the stack overflow that the company had just dealt with.*

*If the CISO was mad at his information technology (IT) people earlier, he was figuratively foaming at the mouth when the system manager explained the problem by telling him that the company probably had thousands of little land-mines like that in its code base. The system manager told the CISO that he couldn't estimate exactly how many problems there were, since most of the software that the company was running was purchased from third party **suppliers**. Thus, nobody on the IT staff had the slightest idea what was actually in the programs that the company was running. Although the CISO had a decent background in technology, he was more of a manager than a developer. Nonetheless, he had not missed the point that the system manager had just made: that he could not guarantee the security of anything in the company that involved software.*

*The CISO was an ambitious fellow, and he knew that any serious security glitch, no matter how far removed it was from his conventional areas of responsibility, would be laid directly at his feet. And since the current problem clearly stemmed from a fault in the way the company procured its software products, the CISO launched an all-out effort to get the entire procurement situation under control. The task team was headed by the CISO himself. He brought the compliance officer along because he was sure that the problem was going to have a compliance element. He also knew that the compliance officer was willing to deal without mercy with any unfortunate procurement officer who failed to follow correct procedure. Along with the relevant executives, the CISO included the former security engineer at the Detroit manufacturing facility, who was now residing in Jacksonville. That was because she was an experienced hand in testing. He also had the feeling that her expertise in organizational development would come in handy. Finally, the CISO added a security engineer from the company's Gaithersburg facility. The security engineer there had a master's degree in software engineering from Carnegie Mellon University with additional background work at US-CERT.*

*The team quickly isolated the problem, which could be summed up in three words: lack of control. In a nutshell, nothing in the company's procurement system was even close to properly controlled. Because organizational control is enforced through coordinated actions, the lack of coordinated action meant that the people, processes, and technologies that comprised the company's supply chains were essentially unmanaged. To illustrate the situation, the team pointed out that although the suppliers that the company dealt with were major companies, their products, especially software, contained components that were integrated from numerous unvetted sources worldwide. Any one of those sources could either intentionally or unintentionally embed a killer flaw in the final result. Furthermore, for competitive reasons, none of the companies in any of those supply chains was willing to share their detailed product information with anybody else. The team didn't have to explain to the CISO why not knowing who actually made the product, or what it contained, represented a serious security problem.*

*As far as the CISO was concerned, the solution lay in developing a systematic and repeatable control process to ensure that what was being brought into the company met the basic criteria for security. Obviously, not knowing what was in the product, or who actually made it, was an especially glaring example of how bad the current situation was. However there were many other instances to reinforce that, including the semi-notorious fact that orders for goods and services were placed without an accompanying purchase authorization, in order to speed up the delivery process. That breakdown in procedure created the potential for outsiders to slip all sorts of malicious things past the company's security system.*

*The obvious lack of a systematic, company-wide process gave the CISO a place to start. Given the total absence of control up and down the **supply chain**, the first thing that the CISO and his team wanted to develop was a practical means to ensure that the company always knew exactly what it was getting from its various suppliers. So the CISO set out to devise a reliable way to ascertain the contents of each product. Once the contents were known, the CISO wanted to put a routine process in place to assess the risks that those contents represented. With the risks identified, a well-defined set of standard organization controls would then be instituted to ensure that any identified risks were fully managed.*

*The requirement to establish the precise state of the product's contents implied the need to build a front-end monitoring and control capability into the procurement process. The function would ensure that suppliers met basic requirements for supply chain transparency and product integrity across the company. At the same time, the compliance officer began to work on defining the audit and control process to tighten up the actual contracting function. Her goal was to ensure that no supplier could ever outsource work without the company's written consent. This would target the suppliers who had been passing contract work to unspecified or unknown companies in the Pacific Rim and India.*

*Because tightening control across the company would require the participation of all of its purchasing managers, the procurement people had to be included in the strategic planning process. Both the Jacksonville security engineer and the security engineer from Gaithersburg had extensive experience in the area of planning and managing technical procurements, so they were appointed co-leads in the development of a standard management process that would ensure the security and integrity of the company's supply chain and the reliability of its products. Because of her experiences in Detroit, the Jacksonville security engineer turned to the EBK as a guide for setting up a practical management framework for a secure procurement process. The two team leads looked at the following nine recommendations and started to develop a better managed procurement process:*

1. *Collaborate with various stakeholders (which may include internal client, lawyers, CIOs, CISOs, IT security professionals, privacy professionals, security engineers, suppliers, and others) on the procurement of IT security products and services*

2. *Ensure the inclusion of risk-based IT security requirements in acquisition plans, cost estimates, statements of work, contracts, and evaluation factors for award, service level agreements, and other pertinent procurement documents*

3. *Ensure that suppliers understand the importance of IT security*

4. *Ensure that investments are aligned with enterprise architecture and security requirements*

5. *Conduct detailed IT investment reviews and security analyses, and review IT investment business cases for security requirements*

6. *Ensure that the organization's IT contracts do not violate laws and regulations, and require compliance with standards when applicable*

7. *Specify policies for use of third party information by vendors/partners, and connection requirements/acceptable use policies for vendors that connect to networks*

8. *Ensure that appropriate changes and improvement actions are implemented as required*

9. *Whenever applicable, calculate return on investment (ROI) of key purchases related to IT infrastructure and security*

# Making the Business and Assurance Case

Procurement involves those activities that constitute the **customer** role. Since there are suppliers for every customer, the companion process to the customer role in every procurement activity is the supplier role. These roles are two sides of the same coin, but they involve different assumptions and they operate differently. In order for the procurement process to be secure, the activities of both sides of that transaction have to be properly coordinated.

In general, a procurement is a request for goods or services that comes from any point in an organization. Those requests can originate from any level in the company. Consequently, it is hard to ensure that every request is cost-justified or even needed, let alone secure. For that reason, the first step in imposing order on the procurement process is to require a fully documented justification for each procurement request. Documenting why an item should be purchased typically involves providing a specific statement of the additional value that that product or service will add to the organization.

The formal justification for the purchase marks the start of the secure procurement process. The need itself might arise out of a formal business analysis, or it might amount to nothing more than an executive decision made by an individual decision-maker. Whatever the basis, the need is typically documented on an organizationally standard procurement request, which is then inserted into the procurement process. The practical goal of the procurement process is to allow everybody who is going to be involved with the purchase, or use of the product, from managers to technical support and security professionals, to have their say in the process. That ensures the buy-in of all prospective participants, and it also ensures that a wide range of expertise will be available to think-through the business and assurance case.

The pragmatic world of business demands an open process because all purchases are a matter of tradeoffs. Because expenditures are involved, the successful product or service will usually have to satisfy the needs of competing groups, as well as each group's personal agenda for what's required. Making certain that every one of those groups participates in thinking-through the form of that purchase ensures the right product functionality and security requirements. The eventual outcome should be a better balanced set of functions that maximizes the value for all of the stakeholders, within the resources that are available for the purchase.

## Factoring Risk into the Process

Purchased products have a considerable business advantage over products developed in-house. That is because purchased products are less costly and immediately available. Nevertheless, if it is hard to guarantee defect-free products when the development is done in-house, think about the odds against getting defect-free products from people who work for somebody else and are located on the other side of the world. That is why the establishment of a risk identification and management process is an essential part of ensuring the security of the procurement process. Risk management involves assessing risks, designing mitigations, monitoring risks throughout the development process, and adjusting the risk mitigation activities based on the results of the monitoring activity.

An effective risk assessment at the beginning of the process will ensure that the specific features that are needed to address risk can be built into the product from the start. Moreover, from a business standpoint, the proper understanding of risks allows the purchaser to buy only those security functions that address the threats that are known to exist. The ensuing specification of the requirements for a product or service always involves a much wider range of features than the things that are strictly devoted to security.

Nevertheless, for the sake of future inter-operability all required features, both general and security-related, have to be integrated into the overall specification of required functions. Therefore, a preliminary risk assessment is important to the development of the specification of the **functional** and **non-functional requirements** of the product. The understanding of threat at that level is usually driven by a standard risk assessment process, such as architectural risk analysis, abuse and misuse cases, and attack patterns.

## Developing the Request for Proposals

Once the risks are sufficiently understood, the next logical step is to document the functional and non-functional requirements that will be needed to address them. Ideally, these requirements should flow directly from the understanding of each risk. Requirements are communicated to the suppliers through a **request for proposal (RFP)**. RFPs are well known in the industry because they serve as the most generally recognized means for communicating product requirements. The specific purpose of the RFP is to clarify the exact set of functions required for the product.

The RFP is a notice that is sent to all logical sources to provide a solution for a price quoted. That solution must address the problem specified in the requirements. The RFP is usually responded to by a certain deadline and is a formal business artifact. Its aim is to provide an understandable and unambiguous description of the requirements of the particular product, including all of the functional and non-functional security requirements.

A good RFP will increase **competitive pressure**, which is a vital element in the procurement process because it allows the organization to encourage the highest possible level of performance from its suppliers. Essentially, the wide-spread publication of an RFP will force a larger group of potential suppliers to compete with each other to get the organization's business. This is likely to drive down the eventual price as well as put the suppliers on notice that they must give the requirements stated in the RFP their "best shot."

The best way of ensuring competitive pressure is through a supplier's conference, where the RFP is sent to a number of suppliers. After a specified period, all of the suppliers who received the RFP are called together for a meeting, where the functional requirements are explained and clarified in the presence of all competitors. That conference ensures the best possible understanding of what the product should look like. It also allows the suppliers to view their competition and make judgments about what they are going to have to do in order to win the business.

The RFP is normally accompanied by a document that is commonly known as a specification of requirements, or a "spec." The spec spells out in explicit legal terms and the precise contractual behaviors that are required for the product, including all of the requisite security requirements. The behaviors stated in the spec describe all of the meaningful aspects of the product being acquired, including the business, organizational, and user requirements as well as safety, security, and other criticality features. In addition to the functional requirements, the spec should also document the assumptions that went into their development, including an itemization of the risks that have been identified as well as the recommended mitigation strategies.

Because it defines the form of the product, the spec also serves as the basis for its development or purchase. For this reason, the spec must provide a full itemization of the requisite behaviors and capabilities of the product, including a valid set of functional and non-functional requirements. Similarly, all required behaviors across internal and external interfaces have to be specified. Because products exhibit many other qualities beside simple behavior, the spec must also communicate the non-functional business and assurance requirements.

It is in the specification of non-functional requirements that all applicable safety, security, human factors, interface, operations and maintenances, design **constraints**, and qualification features of the product are stated. By convention, all functional and non-functional requirements must be directly traceable to the needs expressed in the statement to acquire. They must be kept consistent with those needs throughout the procurement process to ensure that the final product is correctly aligned to business goals.

## Selecting the Right Supplier

It is the responsibility of the acquiring organization to specify how the supplier will be selected. The selection approach usually incorporates such things as a methodology to evaluate the proposal and evaluation criteria that will guide the assessment. In addition, details like the process that will be employed to assess project risk might also be included in the statement of approach. The actual assessment and selection of the winning bidder will be based on each supplier's ability to prove that it can deliver the product as specified and with the minimum amount of potential risk.

The process for evaluating each supplier's proposal centers on determining whether all of the requirements described in the spec are documented, traceable, testable, feasible, and consistent with the needs of the acquirer. Moreover, to ensure that the requirements of the spec are adhered to, the acquirer should also specify exactly which reviews and audits will be undertaken to confirm compliance.

## Developing the Procurement Plan

The procurement plan is the essential artifact in the actual management of each procurement project. Good procurement program management depends on the creation and execution of a proper procurement plan. At a minimum, this plan should ensure that the contract will guide the actual procurement process. It must spell out all of the respective responsibilities of the organizations involved in the process, including how continuing product support for the eventual purchase will be provided.

Once the project is begun, the acquiring organization monitors the activities of the supplier throughout the contractual lifecycle of the project. This is done through some combination of joint reviews and third-party auditing. In addition, if the product is being developed from scratch, the acquiring organization is usually responsible for authorizing and then verifying the effectiveness of all changes to the product. Those modifications are the inevitable consequence of the developer's ongoing refinement of their understanding of product requirements, and they are a normal part of the product development process. Nonetheless, any actual changes to the product have to be negotiated between the acquirer and the supplier. All proposed changes are analyzed in order to determine their potential impact on project plans, costs, benefits, security quality, and schedule; a decision maker designated in the contract provides an authorization.

Eventually, the supplier will be ready to deliver the completed product or service to the acquiring organization. When that time comes, the acquiring organization must be prepared to conduct a formal acceptance process. This process and its associated criteria are usually itemized in detail in the contract, or project plan, which defines the expected form of the final product as well as the methods that will be employed to assure it. Most procurement plans specify the test cases, test data, test procedures, and test environment that will be used for product testing, as shown in Figure 16-1. At a minimum, the organization will use the acceptance procedures specified in the contract, or plan to conduct acceptance reviews and tests of the deliverable. The product will be considered accepted when all acceptance conditions specified in the procurement plan are satisfied. Finally, after acceptance, the acquiring organization has to arrange how the supplier will deliver the product. That process also has to be specifically stated in the procurement plan.

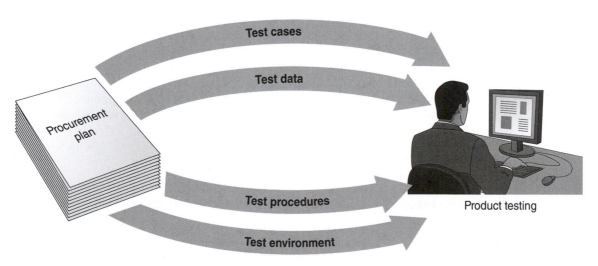

**Figure 16-1** Product testing

# Designing an Effective Procurement System

*The definition of the management approach for the procurement process appeared to be making some progress, but everybody on the team knew that the proof was going to be in the actual procedures themselves. Because procurement essentially involved the whole business operation, the team was faced with a difficult balancing act. Obviously, standard practices were going to be required to ensure that the procurement process was controlled and systematic. However, if the procurement procedures were made too detailed and rigid, the company would run the risk of limiting its options when it came to bidding and negotiating contracts with suppliers. Even worse, there was the concern among the security staff that they would not have sufficient input if the process were run strictly by purchasing and that lack of input could lead to important security concerns being missed.*

*The primary issue lay in the fact that the supplier was really in control of the development of the product, since the supplier did the actual work needed to create the deliverable. The company's suppliers were understandably unwilling to provide a lot of insight into their production processes, since the practices that made up those processes were proprietary and in many cases involved trade secrets. Consequently, the team was faced with trying to control activities that the other party in the agreement wanted to keep hidden. The lack of transparency was a particular problem when it came to the use of sub-contractors. A supplier's proprietary processes made sub-contractors essentially invisible to the acquirer, who then, as a result, might be dealing with companies that the acquiring organization would never deal with if their presence was known.*

*This lack of visibility into the process was intolerable if the aim was to ensure that all of the company's products were as secure as possible. The members of the team could envision situations where critical products and services might be developed by their closest competitor. In that case, the competitor would have the advantage of knowing who was using the product, while the company itself would not know who was involved in developing it.*

*The solution seemed to lie in creating a procurement process that allowed for the greatest degree of business flexibility for the contractor, while ensuring the maximum amount of visibility and control over the entities in the supply chain. That implied the need to adopt a standardized and well-defined review process for the supplier base. The Jacksonville security engineer had a long history of developing strategic management processes, both professionally and academically. She was particularly expert at evaluation practices. To her, this particular challenge looked like another organizational development problem, so she volunteered to define a standard process to enforce substantive supply chain visibility. That process was risk-based and it was meant to allow the company to monitor contractor performance up and down the supply chain. From her prior experience, the security engineer knew that the EBK defined the following four high-level management activities for procurement:*

1. *Develop contracting language that mandates the incorporation of IT security requirements in information services, IT integration services, IT products, and information security product purchases*

2. *Develop contract administration policies that direct the evaluation and acceptance of delivered IT security products and services under a contract, as well as the security evaluation of IT and software being procured*

3. *Develop measures and reporting standards to measure and report on key objectives in procurements aligned with IT security policies and procedures*

4. *Develop a vendor management policy and associated program that implements policy with regard to use of third party information and connection requirements, and acceptable use policies for vendors who connect to corporate networks. Include due diligence activities to ensure that vendors are operationally and technically competent to receive and evaluate third party information, and to connect and communicate with corporate networks.*

# Incorporating Security into the Process

The acquiring organization is responsible for defining and subsequently following a set of operating procedures for each procurement project. These procedures are developed directly from the acquisition plan and they describe the specific steps that will be taken to ensure the security of the procurement project. Among those procedures are steps to ensure that basic security is built into the project itself. The design of that security process should also ensure that all of the activities within the supply chain for that particular procurement are secure and that the final product can be certified as secure when accepted.

In service to the aim of building security into the product, each design itemizes a comprehensive set of relevant processes, activities, and tasks which the designers feel will achieve the assurance goals of that specific procurement effort. In order to ensure the right level of security, designers have to embed activities into the project that will provide reliable measures of assurance. Typically, many of those activities will involve tests and joint reviews, so the participants, execution, timing, and location of all of those assurance activities have to be specified.

In addition to the specification of the way reviews and tests will be done, the design should also describe the means by which all of those testing and review processes will be coordinated. That includes providing a comprehensive description of the various roles and responsibilities of the individuals who will be performing each security test or review. Because two entities are always involved in the development of the product, the explicit assignment of responsibility for each planned assurance activity is an essential component of the design process. Accordingly, it has to be ensured that the staff of the group building the product is in absolute alignment with the staff of the people purchasing the product when it comes to the security of the product itself. Otherwise, critical security procedures or concerns might fall through the cracks. Finally, the design should also define the milestones at which the supplier's progress will be assessed. The actual oversight function that these milestones will underwrite provides the basis for overall monitoring of the security aspects of the project.

The security process itself is essentially a project management function. Strictly speaking, the procurement process does not involve any of the traditional lifecycle development tasks, except testing and acceptance. That is because from the customer perspective the products that are acquired through the procurement process have already been developed. Instead, the generic form of the procurement process for the customer involves carrying-out various planning and control functions.

## Understanding the Constraints

The procurement process should always be undertaken based on detailed and precise knowledge of all of the constraints that might affect the delivery of the product. The aim of the constraint identification process is to optimally fit risk within constraints. Knowledge of constraints is gained through consideration and analysis of all of the potential influences on the product delivery process. The goal is to structure the delivery process in such a way that each meaningful risk will be satisfactorily addressed within existing constraints.

In that respect, there will probably be a range of constraints involved for each risk. Each constraint will have different characteristics and each will affect risk differently. Sources of constraints vary. In the case of procurements, they generally fall into five categories. First, there is the user, who is likely to favor "easy to use" over "secure." Then there is the manager, who will tend to stress financial factors over security functionality. There is also the problem of technical feasibility, particularly where the solution requires leading the target. Additionally, there are potential laws and regulations which, if violated, might create legal and regulatory compliance risks. Finally, there are standards which, if violated, could produce unacceptable solutions.

In actuality, the outcome of constraint analysis will typically be something that is called **"negative problem space."** Negative problem space, as shown in Figure 16-2, is created when the satisfaction of one constraint causes problems with another. For example, the optimum security technology (technological feasibility) might cost too much (management) or be too hard to use (user). The real task in constraint identification is to perform all of the necessary tradeoffs to ensure the optimal solution to address all known factors. In applied terms, constraints would be relaxed against one another in order to achieve the best practical resolution. That resolution is then translated into a contract between purchaser and supplier.

## Formulating the Contract

Typically, a good **procurement contract** will satisfy two simple rules. First, it will describe the entire set of product or service functions in enough detail that their requirement will be

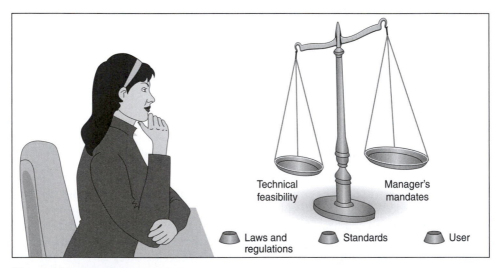

**Figure 16-2** Negative problem space

unambiguous. Second, the contract will provide a clear means of determining whether a specified function or service has been provided. The contract, which is the central document in the procurement process, substantiates both of these in the form of an official agreement between parties. In that respect, the contract must legally define all of the requirements of the acquisition for all parties, including cost and schedule. In addition, the contract addresses such legal issues as usage, ownership, warranty, and licensing rights associated with the product or service.

The contract expresses the behavior of each of the product's required functions, which should be described ways that can be observed and documented. Along with the behavior, the contract should specify a process and an accompanying set of objective criteria that will be used to judge whether the requirements have been correctly implemented in the deliverable. Because any kind of modern technology is complex, the performance of the desired functionality can usually only be evaluated in terms of some proxy. Consequently, there have to be objective, behavioral criteria placed in the contract, which can be specifically associated with the proper performance of the desired functions that they represent. These criteria provide the mechanism for evaluating an essentially invisible and complex product.

From a business standpoint, the contract should focus on the three Ps: performance, price, and protection. From a security standpoint, the most important of these is protection. That protection should always represent a deliverable. To enforce all requirements, the contract should be a legal document that is expressed in legally acceptable contractual language. Organizations don't need to use a contract for everything they buy, but a formally executed contract offers a number of benefits from a security perspective. It forces the organization's security, legal, and business staff to consider all of the risks associated with the purchase. Better yet, if the **criteria for evaluation** are clearly stated, a contract puts the acquiring organization squarely in the driver's seat during the actual procurement and installation process. That is, the acquirer will have a concrete basis for ensuring proper performance of all deliverables in the procurement process, no matter how esoteric they might actually be.

## Administering the Contract

Once the planning and management framework has been established, the supplier will undertake the work that was specified in the contract. If the procurement process involves any form of development, the supplying organization almost always oversees and controls the actual work in progress. This includes planning and deploying all of the stipulated security elements of the plan. Security is practiced as a discipline throughout the process; therefore, the oversight and control elements, which are specified in the contract, have to be enforced throughout the life of the contract. Thus, project managers for the acquiring organization must be able to oversee the progress of the technical work. They must also be able to review costs, schedules, and project status and resolve any relevant problems that might be identified in the performance of the work.

Normally, the supplier is responsible for oversight and control over all subcontractors. This is always done in accordance with the stipulations for subcontractor management that have been placed in the contract. In practical terms, this means that the supplying organization is responsible for ensuring that all applicable contract requirements and conditions are clearly understood by any sub-contractors. That responsibility involves assuring that all aspects of the product, including physical elements, systems, software, or service requirements, which are prepared by subcontractors, fully comply with the specifications of the contract.

In order to make certain that this happens, the supplier must conduct all contractually required verifications, validations, or tests of subcontractor work. Finally, the supplier has to deliver the product or service to the acquiring organization. In order to provide a smooth transition between the two organizations, the supplier should be contracted provide routine technical support or installation service to the acquiring organization during the changeover.

# Implementing Effective Supply Chains

*The design of the new procurement process had the potential to enforce the necessary visibility into each contractor's work, but the problem was that the supply chain that the company routinely operated through was still essentially uncontrolled. In almost every case, the primary contracting organization stood between the company and any sub-contractors that might be used on the project. The company's real concern was with subcontractor trustworthiness. The fact that a supplier used subcontractors without the direct involvement, or even knowledge, of the company's purchasing managers made the entire team nervous.*

*The aim of procurement was to ensure that the company's products were supplied by the most capable organizations; however, the team recognized that the marketplace was essentially anonymous. In order to ensure some element of continuity, the company's procurement professionals had no option but to deal with the usual set of suppliers. The problem was that all of the regular suppliers knew that every one of the company's top executives was unwilling to stray far from its trusted base of contractors. That knowledge took competitive pressure out of the bidding process, which meant that the company's supplier community could demand higher prices for their products and services because they knew that the company would eventually have to come to them to get what they wanted.*

*The CISO knew that spreading the net as wide as possible would maximize competitive pressure. But the catch was that, in order to ensure a responsible process, the company would have to know precisely how trustworthy each prospective new supplier was. Otherwise, the company could be purchasing its technical products from unreliable sources. The CEO didn't need to be told that that approach was dangerous. But the problem was that, given the global nature of the technology business, it is impossible to know how trustworthy every potential supplier is.*

*The CISO had his team look into developing a systematic way to determine whether a new supplier could be trusted to deliver a secure product. For the first time in the process, the Gaithersburg engineer took over the leadership of the group. Because he had worked for a long time in the defense industry, the Gaithersburg security engineer knew that there were internationally recognized certifications of the trustworthiness of manufacturing systems. He said that those certifications had been around for years in the quality assurance universe, which explained all of the Six-Sigma and ISO 9000-2000 public registries that the company used for its manufacturing facilities. As a result, he explained that there was no reason why audited third party registrations of trusted security capability could not be instituted up and down the company's supply chain. He pointed out that a **third party certification** registry for software security was already available under a scheme that was known as the **Common Criteria**.*

*On the surface, it seemed like a good idea to mandate that all information technology purchases should have Common Criteria certification, since that was an easy way to get objective, third party assurance that it was secure. That approach looked workable in theory.*

*Unfortunately, as soon as the team dug into the problem, it discovered that Common Criteria certifications were only for individual products, and the cost of obtaining those certifications was high. Furthermore, no supplier who wanted to stay in business for long would be willing to spend the money to get a single instance of its product certified, unless they were mass-market places like Microsoft or Oracle.*

*Even though the idea of requiring Common Criteria certificates for software wasn't feasible, the team still liked the concept of audited third party certification. The thought that it could obtain the necessary assurance of trustworthiness by simply asking the supplier to produce an audited certification of its level of security capability was attractive from both a security and a cost perspective. The team also recognized that a financially justifiable and generally accepted certification would serve a valuable purpose from a business standpoint. That is, a certification process would let a company provide objective, independent assurance that it was trustworthy, even if it was located in another culture 3,000 miles away.*

*That business advantage would also reduce uncertainties about security in the procurement process, because a regular audit would identify the risks associated with a given contractor. Moreover, by identifying the inherent risks, a standard certification of capability would also provide an objective basis for trading off business requirements and project cost against each vendor's areas of weakness. That tradeoff capability would be useful when it came time to negotiate the contract. Finally, given the inter-dependence between the capability of the process and the overall security of the product, certification would also represent the best means of putting appropriate risk controls in place for whichever vendor was eventually selected.*

*The CISO, who was always looking for new ways to enhance his standing in the company, felt that the opportunity to address risks while increasing competitive pressure was too good an opportunity to pass up. So, he made a strong case to the board of directors that it was essential for the company to require certification of supplier process capability. The board, which could also see the business advantage, had no problem accepting that proposal, so the first order of business for the CISO was to define a reasonable approach for ensuring trust based on the certification of process capability.*

*The CISO turned to the Jacksonville security engineer, rather than the engineer from Gaithersburg, to spearhead the task team. The CISO felt that she had the requisite understanding of organizational processes; moreover he always had the threat of shipping her back to Detroit to hold over her head as leverage. He was certain that she would give it her best shot. The Jacksonville security engineer felt that the main problem with separate product certifications was that the auditing process for each certificate was too involved. That made the auditing of each company financially infeasible. Nonetheless, she also had the CISO's mandate in front of her, which was that audited, third party certifications were the best way to establish a trust relationship with anonymous suppliers in a global marketplace. The question she faced was, "What would be the most effective basis for implementing a worldwide certification process?"*

**16**

*In the Common Criteria, the required engineering and supporting processes are specified in a detailed profile of functions called a protection profile (PP). This PP is then written into the contract. The approach she began to see emerging was similar to that; however, while Common Criteria ratings were based on technical evaluations that were performed for each specific piece of software, her approach would be to make the supplier's security processes themselves be the actual target of evaluation. The business advantage in that approach would be that the focus of the certification would be on the overall production process, rather than on each* individual product. That would allow supplier organizations to certify the competency of their processes with a single external audit. This, in turn, would be a much less costly and cumbersome situation than having to certify each individual product separately.

As with the Common Criteria, the Jacksonville security engineer's approach would allow the capability of a given supplier's supply process to be evaluated against a requisite security capability profile that the company's security team could prepare in advance. The assessment would determine a set of standard process ratings for each individual supplier that could be aggregated into a general supplier capability rating. The rating for each supplier could then be used to determine who could provide the most secure product. This could be done by using the target capability, which was specified for each given project, as the comparison point to judge just those suppliers who were capable of delivering a trustworthy product.

The Jacksonville security engineer knew that the process of implementing certificates of trustworthiness would require a complete revamping of the policies and procedures for procurement across the company's entire supply chain. She was ready to begin the negotiation, or renegotiation as the case might be, of contracts in order to ensure that the process of certifying trustworthiness was instituted and working in an organized fashion. The EBK supported her with the following five high-level stipulations built into the procurement implementation process:

1. Include IT security considerations as directed by policies and procedures in procurement and acquisition activities

2. Negotiate final deals (e.g., contracts, contract changes, grants, and agreements) to include IT security requirements that minimize risk to the organization

3. Ensure that physical security concerns are integrated into acquisition strategies

4. Maintain ongoing and effective communications with suppliers and providers

5. Perform compliance reviews of delivered products and services to assess the delivery of IA requirements against stated contract requirements and measures

# Developing the Assurance Framework

Unless it is otherwise stipulated in the contract, the supplier organization is usually responsible for the development of the assurance plan for any development work. This plan is generally evolved directly from the requirements specified in the contract. The aim of this step is to allow the supplier to define the specific procedures that will be employed to ensure that the product is developed in a safe and secure environment. Based on that understanding, the supplying organization normally defines the resources that will be committed to execute the work as well as the scope and extent of acquirer involvement at each stage. This assurance approach puts the responsibility for the implementation of the security elements of the proposed acquisition squarely in the hands of the supplier.

In the specific case of ensuring product security, the supplying organization is responsible for specifying an explicit process to assure the security outcomes stated in the contract. This assurance is implemented by conducting the threat assessment activities that are needed to satisfy the contract and then evaluating all of the resultant risks for likelihood and impact. Once this assessment is complete and decisions have been made about what risks will be mitigated, and how that mitigation will take place, the supplying organization creates the actual plan for assuring that particular project.

The first thing that has to be defined is the organizational structure, authority, and responsibility of each participant in the process. That definition of authority and responsibility has to include all external organizations such as subcontractors. The definition of the assurance requirements is the critical first step in the planning process, since the steps to develop the product will always take place within those requirements. Assurance requirements have to exist before any kind of meaningful decisions can be made about practical aspects of production, like the environment and the standards, procedures, tools, facilities, equipment, and tests that will be employed.

Once the assurance requirements have been defined, the next step in the process is to define how the work will be done. In practical, project-management terms, that usually amounts to creating a work breakdown structure (WBS), and referencing the resource commitments, such as budgets, staffing, physical resources, and schedules, to each task in the WBS. Explicit tasks designated in the WBS ensure the proper management of security, safety, and other critical requirements of the software. Finally, there is the matter of ensuring proper management of subcontractors. Where subcontractors are used, the method that will be employed to select them must be specified. In addition, all involvement between the subcontractor, the supplier, and the acquirer must also be defined. That specification includes all security assurance, verification, and validation activities. It also includes the approach that will be used to utilize any third party verification or validation agent.

Since the supplier organization is the one that draws up the assurance plan, there also has to be some consideration of how the acquiring organization will be involved in the actual assurance process. Although this involvement is generally through scheduled joint reviews, there are other options for increasing acquirer visibility into the process, such as audits. Since audits are expensive, these are usually only called out in the contract. Other process considerations that have to be settled include deciding whether informal meetings will be allowed between the acquirer and the various supplier types, such as primary contractor and the subcontractors. Management control also has to be established over any changes to the form of the deliverable.

The one area of assurance that is likely to get the most attention is risk management, which entails the identification of all potential process, technical, and resourcing risks. There has to be a specific strategy for managing existing risks, as well as addressing any new or emerging risks. That strategy is based on a clear statement of the organization's policies with respect to risk mitigation, as well as procedures for reporting and addressing emerging risks. In order to ensure uniform management, the strategic approach to risk has to be standardized across all procurement projects, up and down the supply chain.

**16**

Much of modern technical work is done through a chain of suppliers rather than by a sole developer. There are, frequently, levels of subcontract work, from individual units all the way to integrated modules of units, which are prepared by organizations other than the primary contractor. An unvetted supply chain introduces a number of potential risks into the subcontracting process, because undesirable or even malicious elements can be inserted at the subcontractor level at any point in the supply chain. Consequently, it is important in the management of any acquisition project to have a mechanism for rigorously monitoring and controlling the production of the software at all levels in the supply chain.

## Using Standard Assessment to Identify Trusted Suppliers

Without the ability to know the people you are dealing with, there can be no trust. Any acquisitions using a supply chain have to be supported by an evaluation process that will ensure in-depth understanding among the various participants. This is where a profile of standard security requirements comes in handy. Any procurement process that involves competing suppliers has to carry out some sort of objective assessment in order to compare the capability of each supplier to deliver the product. Independent auditing of individual capability further supports that goal in the sense that audited, standard certificates of capability ensure that any company that wishes to acquire a product can find a trustworthy supplier anywhere in the world.

That profile of security requirements accomplishes two different, but useful, things. A standard profile lets the customer determine whether an individual supplier is carrying out the practices that the customer considers necessary to ensure security. The capability of the performance of the practices arrayed in that profile can then be confirmed by third party audit. Since it could be possible for a practice to exist, but to be executed poorly, proof of the capability of those processes is as important to the assessment of supplier trustworthiness as proof of their existence.

## Evaluating Capability: Identifying Best Practices

Processes incorporate practices that can be associated with a given level of performance. In essence, the assumption is that the product can be trusted if a certain set of fundamental practices are involved in its preparation. The link between the capability of the supplier's process and the quality of the product has been known for a long time; therefore, the idea of employing a process-based capability assessment to certify the relative security of the product is not a radical new concept.

Capability assessments determine whether a specified set of base practices exist. These practices represent the measurable elements of a capable process. In essence, those practices comprise the complete and correct set of activities that must be performed over the entire production cycle of a trusted product or secure system.

Each base practice is differentiated through a goal statement, which specifies its unique purpose and describes the exact behaviors that must be observed in order to ensure correct performance of that practice. Although the required practices can vary based on a given security situation, the aim of the assessment is to determine whether what is being done in that situation represents the desired level of security practice.

## Evaluating Performance: the Capability Dimension

The second dimension involved in the assessment of organizational processes is capability, which characterizes how effectively a given practice is being carried out. Capability is determined using a standard set of management attributes, which might be considered to be characteristic of a given level of management capability. The assessment is then based on the presence or absence of those attributes at a given level of capability.

Management attributes are used to differentiate capability levels. The intention is to provide a rational means to characterize current process capability. The presence or absence of required management practices can then be used to decide about the process's degree of trustworthiness. In order to increase trustworthiness, the activities at each new level must provide evidence that the requisite management attributes are present. An auditor or evaluator can develop the evidence to prove that a particular process purpose has been achieved.

# Evaluating the Procurement Process

*The CISO was particularly pleased by the outcome of the implementation process. Procurement seemed to be standardized along a set of simple but effective practices. The alignment between procurement policy and procedure and the actual execution of the procurement projects seemed to be functioning as intended. The procurement lifecycle process seemed to incorporate the necessary* **inspections** *and audits. More important, the novel security capability certification approach, which he was touting as having been developed under his leadership, had been instituted and the key suppliers up and down the supply chain were beginning to fall into line with the demands for assessment.*

*Because the company was one of the "900 pound gorillas" in the industry, it was able to induce its suppliers and their subcontractors to get third party certification of their base practices for security. That shifted the costs of security monitoring down to the suppliers, since they now had to bear the expense of doing the actual external audit to certify security capability. It also had the unanticipated bonus of making suppliers "get real" about their own process capability when it came time to bid on projects.*

*Suppliers were able to estimate the likelihood of being able to deliver a given product by simply comparing their assessed level of security capability against what the company was demanding, in terms of requirements for secure practice. In the instances where the supplier's practices were way out of line with the necessary requirements for security, suppliers were also able to make informed resource decisions about whether it would be worthwhile to pursue the business.*

*The omens all seemed to be pointing in the direction of a successful implementation; the only remaining hurdle was gathering the necessary proof. That assignment went to the Gaithersburg security engineer, since with his software engineering background he was the one with the experience in evaluating structured processes. He had worked for years in the federal space, and he knew all of the tricks of the trade for documenting the long-term performance of the activities required to satisfy a federal contract, including every form of review practice and audit technique on the books.*

*Because of his extensive experience in ensuring that project elements lined up with federal regulations, guidelines, and contract requirements, he knew that most conformance evaluations were based on review processes, many of which were unchanged since the Second World War. He was not in a mood to invent any new practices. Instead, he wanted to custom-fit those proven solutions to the current challenge, which was ensuring that the newly created procurement process functioned as specified.*

*The EBK was helpful in that respect, because it laid out a clear set of directions for what had to be considered in those reviews. The only task for the Gaithersburg security engineer was to ensure that all of the EBK directions were met. The EBK defines the following seven general areas of evaluation for procurement:*

1. *Review contracting documents, such as statements of work or requests for proposals, for inclusion of IT security considerations in accordance with information security requirements, policies, and procedures*

2. *Assess industry-applicable IT security trends, including practices for mitigating security risks associated with supply chain management*

3.  *Review memoranda of agreement, memoranda of understanding, and/or SLA for agreed levels of IT security responsibility*

4.  *Conduct detailed IT investment reviews and security analyses and review IT investment business cases for security requirements*

5.  *Assess and evaluate the effectiveness of the vendor management program in complying with internal policy with regard to use of third party information and connection requirements*

6.  *Conduct due diligence activities to ensure that vendors are operationally and technically competent to receive third party information, connect and communicate with networks, and deliver and support secure applications*

7.  *Evaluate the effectiveness of the procurement function in addressing information security requirements through procurement activities, and recommend improvements*

# Types of Reviews

Reviews are important in procurement operations, because they enforce oversight and control and they let the customer coordinate contract review activities, interfaces, and communication with the supplier organization. Although there is a range of possible reviews that might take place, they can generally be factored into two categories: formal and informal. The difference in review types lies in who controls the review. If the producer conducts the review, then the review is considered informal and is usually called a **walkthrough**. If the product or process is reviewed by anybody other than the producer, it is considered to be formal and is usually called an inspection or audit.

Walkthroughs are common in information processing operations. They can be as informal as a programmer demonstrating a segment of code, or they can be regularly scheduled sessions involving whole teams or groups. The advantage of a walkthrough is that relatively little time is consumed, so the resource commitment and cost is negligible. The disadvantage of a walkthrough is that it is not rigorous. The producer controls the presentation, which means walking a reviewer past holes in logic that neither side will be able to see, or do anything about.

Inspections and audits have rigor, but they require resources and have concomitant costs. The whole point of an inspection review is that the producer surrenders the artifact for analysis by a third party. That third party can be either external or internal, but the analysis is essentially performed outside of the production process. This means that there is a much higher error detection and correction rate. In addition, inspections always generate documentation in the form of reports and recommendations. Since inspections and audits are usually scheduled events, they are most often part of the fabric of the project plan and contract.

In most cases, usually by stipulation of the contract, the supplier performs these walkthroughs, inspections, and audits with representatives of the acquiring organization. This is a called a joint review. Joint reviews are verifications and validations that are performed with both the acquirer and supplier present. They are normally done to demonstrate that the purchased software product or service satisfies its respective requirements.

The outcome of the inspection process consists of reports that issue out of the reviews. In the case of these reports, the supplier should make the results of all evaluations, reviews, audits, tests, and **problem resolution** meetings available to the acquiring organization. The method for doing this is usually specified in the contract.

## The Security Review Process

The purpose of the security review process is to monitor the actions of the supplier organization and bring any deviations in required practice to the attention of the supplier and the acquiring organization's management. These kinds of reviews are particularly important in the procurement process, because the acquisition of secure products requires precise understanding of both the logical and physical details of the deliverable. Accordingly, a great deal of oversight is needed to help managers determine that the process is correct and the product meets requirements. That includes ensuring that an appropriate development methodology is in place, that standards are employed and being adhered to, and that any emerging trends in security are being considered. Reviews also ensure that the necessary documentation is available to correct any deviation from a contract or standard.

Since it isn't possible or realistic to evaluate every artifact in the process, progress can only be charted through regularized inspections of a defined set of deliverables. That inspection takes place at pre-planned and mutually agreed-on entry and exit points. There are several organizational givens built into the review process. First, it has to be stressed that reviews are monitoring and reporting tools; they are not responsible for fixing security problems. Nonetheless, they *are* responsible for reviewing all security and development plans for completeness.

Reviewers should participate in technical inspections as well as review all test plans and test results for compliance with standards and adherence to regulations. In that respect, reviewers are responsible for registering non-concurrence where any non-compliance is found. Because of the latter responsibility, the review process also needs an effective enforcement mechanism to back it up.

The problem with reviews is that they complicate the issue of group dynamics. Nobody likes to be evaluated; therefore, an organizational awareness has to be built that ensures that everybody in the process understands the importance of security reviews. Most of the problems encountered by reviewers revolve around staffing, authority, and control issues, which is why security reviewers must have an independent reporting line.

Finally, the security management team is usually not capable of dealing with traditional managers, who are more comfortable with production than inspection. These executives are more likely to back the production units over security if the issue is getting the product in the door. Ultimately, the organization must be responsive to security recommendations.

## Launching the Security Review Program

There are eight steps required to launch a security review program. Step one is initiation, which requires the organization to define the key security review leadership and operational roles and produce a formal organizational plan. The next step requires identification of the relevant security issues. This is usually done in conjunction with acquisition and line project managers. In this process, the security manager and staff must identify and prioritize the key security review issues.

The organization then creates a generic security review plan. Security audit and control activities are defined, required standards and practices are identified, and the security review plan is integrated with the project management plan. Once the security review plan has been developed, it is time for the organization to implement the standard procedures to guide the security review process. This normally involves training security review personnel in security review methods.

After the review personnel are prepared, the organization implements the actual security review process. That implementation process assigns roles and responsibilities, develops a schedule, defines and performs the monitoring activities, and reports and resolves problems. Finally, the security review program must be periodically evaluated to determine whether it is performing effectively and as intended.

**Security Reviews: Product Assurance** The security review process focuses on two different kinds of assurance: product assurance and process assurance. Since security reviews are primarily an oversight function, the first step is to confirm that all processes have been followed and are compliant with contractual requirements. The product must then be assured to have fully satisfied all functional and non-functional requirements specified in the contract.

**Security Reviews: Process Assurance** Process assurance is the other side of the security assurance coin. The acquirer has a contractual right, which is usually implemented in the project plan, to a certain amount of transparency between customer and supplier. This visibility must be ensured by the security assurance process. Given the process-oriented nature of security, process assurance is the element that is potentially most interesting to security professionals.

Development processes, which are part of the production of the product, must be proven to comply with all contracts, standards, and plans associated with the project. In addition, contractually defined performance assessment measures and evaluation criteria have to be specified and then used for both product and process evaluation. The security assurance must confirm that these are compliant with all relevant standards.

Confirmation requires rigorous oversight of the security practices that are part of the project. Every aspect of security practice for development of the product must be assured to comply with the requirements of the contract. This includes the review and test environment as well as all associated practices related to process assessment. Because subcontractors are often involved in production, the security assurance process also has to ensure that all applicable prime contract requirements are passed down to the subcontractor and that the subcontractor software products satisfy prime contract requirements.

The success of any project depends on the capability of the people who do the work. Security reviews do not have a mandate to make the company's personnel more capable, but they must determine whether workers possess the requisite knowledge and skills to meet project requirements. If that is not the case, the security reviews ensure that the right people are notified to provide sufficient training.

# Chapter Summary

- Procurement involves the customer and the supplier.
- The procurement process has to be standardized in terms of practices and documentation.

- Understanding risks prior to starting the procurement process is important.

- The means of communicating procurement requirements is called a "request for proposals."

- The specific functions required in the purchased product are itemized in a **software requirements specification (SRS)**.

- The SRS serves as the basis for defining the security requirements of the project.

- The acquiring organization must provide selection criteria for choosing a supplier.

- The acquisition plan guides the procurement process and specifies monitoring and control activities between customer and supplier.

- Procurement process design should start with precise knowledge of the constraints.

- Constraints have to be traded off against each other to achieve an ideal solution.

- The contract establishes two things: the functions required and the means that will be employed to determine whether they have been provided.

- Contracts are always kept under change control to ensure that the current version is correct.

- Procurement plans always specify the roles and functions of the participants.

- Procurement plans must have explicit rules for managing subcontractor work.

- The essence of secure supply chain management lies in always knowing who you are dealing with.

- The ability to certify security capability gives acquirers many options when it comes to supplier selection.

- Compliance with all of the stipulations of a procurement process is monitored by reviews.

- Reviews ensure two things: the security of the product and the security of the process in which the product was produced.

# Key Terms

**Competitive pressure** Ensuring the best deal by involving the maximum number of bidders.

**Common Criteria** An international standard for evaluating the security of a software product, e.g., ISO 15408.

**Constraints** Factors that might limit a solution.

**Criteria for evaluation** The basis specified by the acquirer for determining successful bidders.

**Customer** The acquirer role.

**Functional requirements** Behaviors that the product must exhibit or perform.

**Inspections** The least formal independent review process.

**Negative problem space** The situation created when the satisfaction of one constraint would prevent the attainment of another.

**Non-functional requirements** Qualitative conditions that the product must satisfy.

16

**Problem resolution** A formal agreement process by which identified faults in an acquisition are resolved.

**Process dimension** The presence or absence of base practices which have been specified as necessary or correct.

**Procurement contract** A legally enforceable agreement between a customer and a supplier to provide goods or services.

**Request for proposal (RFP)** A formal notice issued to a potential supplier to provide a product or service at a specified price and within a specified time period.

**Software requirements specification (SRS)** A statement of all functional behaviors and non-functional qualities that must be provided to satisfy a particular software proposal.

**Supplier** The role that provides a product or service.

**Supply chain** A hierarchical framework of entities that all work together to develop a product. Work at the bottom of the process is passed up to organizations that integrate those units into larger products.

**Third party certification** Official recognition by an uninvolved party in the acquisition process that an organization has met a specified set of requirements.

**Walkthrough** The most informal method of inspection, in which the producer takes the reviewers on a tour of the product. The primary value is educational; however, some insights might be obtained.

# Questions from the CIO

The CIO requires you to brief her on the current status of your investigation. This will be an important part of your continuing work on this project, since it is essential to be able to describe all of the ramifications of a properly secure procurement process. Consequently, the CIO would like you to answer the following questions for her:

1. What is the special problem with software purchases? Why are they more difficult than conventional product acquisitions?

2. Why is it important to involve stakeholders in the process? What can they contribute?

3. What are constraints, and how can they be related to each other to achieve an optimum solution?

4. What is the correct approach to ensuring that the product is delivered as specified, and how are these specifications produced?

5. What is the role of the RFP?

6. What two factors does the contract ensure?

7. What eight steps do you follow in reviewing the security of an acquisition?

8. What is the role of subcontractors and how can they be controlled?

9. What is the potential role of third party certification in supplier selection?

10. What types of reviews are there, and how do you tell the difference? Which type would likely be more effective?

11. Why is the definition of roles and responsibilities so important in the acquisition process?

12. What two things do security reviews ensure? What is the difference, and why is one more potentially important?

13. How is legal and regulatory compliance documented, and why is that important?

14. How does the security assurance plan work? What does it specify?

# Hands-On Projects

Refer to the case in Appendix A. You have been assigned the responsibility to put together a standard contract to acquire a new enterprise management system. You know that to start the process, you must first understand all of the constraints that this system might face. Using the scenario outlined in the case, do the following:

- Identify all of the potential regulations that might need to be observed
- Identify all other compliance areas, such as contracts
- List the specific requirements that will have to be undertaken to ensure the necessary compliance
- Ensure that there is a mechanism in place to audit the compliance with each specific requirement
- Devise a standard operating procedure for doing that

16

# chapter 17

# Legal and Regulatory Compliance

## The CEO Learns the Facts of Life

*The CEO's best friend ran a large financial firm in midtown Manhattan. They had gotten to be pals mainly because they were next-door neighbors, if having 20 acres of manicured lawn with extensive walls and shrubbery between residences could really be considered "next door." That summer, they had taken to spending weekends golfing at Shinnecock Hills, which was just 10 miles from their places in Sagaponack. After a round on a cloudy Sunday in September, the CEO and his buddy were sitting on the terrace at the Old Club House doing what CEOs did these days, which was complaining about the number of regulatory hoops their respective companies had to jump through.*

*Afterward, the sun came out of the clouds on the way up NY 27 and the temperature rose, which was a whole lot better than it had been out on the course that morning. It occurred to the CEO that that was always the way it was at Shinnecock. Maybe it was because the course was laid out back in the 1800s by a Scot who just brought Scottish weather along with him to add authenticity to the setting. The CEO felt like he needed to think. The conversation about regulation had raised his concern, mainly because he really didn't have the slightest idea what the company's actual situation was when it came to the IT function. The CEO was in the SLK that day, so he decided to drop the top and take a leisurely cruise up toward Montauk, just to do a little thinking on the beach.*

*As the big waves broke, the CEO began to think about all of the **regulations** that he knew the company had to comply with. Off the top of his head, he could think of Sarbanes Oxley* and the defense units in his enterprise, which complied with the National Industrial Security Program Operating Manual (NISPOM). He also thought that part of the company's financial services operation had to comply with Graham Leach Bliley (GLB) and the dictates of Basel II. Then there were the contracts, all of which had terms that were potentially a problem if they were violated.

Contemplating the many complexities of the legal and regulatory environment was beginning to make his head hurt, so the CEO decided right then and there that it was time to get the situation under control. In order to do that, he needed a formal program. That following Monday featured the executive staff meeting at 7:30 a.m. It was the usual silver coffee set, fruit, and bite-size quiche kind of informal meeting that he held with the chief operating officer and the chief financial officer. That meeting was when they all checked signals to make sure that the top-level policy parts of the organization were in harmony with each other. This time the CEO included the CISO and the compliance officer in the meeting. The reason why the CISO was there was obvious to everyone, but the presence of the compliance officer, who rarely ventured out of her domain, was a lot less clear.

The C-Level executives looked at the compliance officer with some interest. Her fearsome reputation was common knowledge around the company, even if the sightings of her outside of her native habitat were rare. She was known for the kind of iron discipline that would have made a Spartan jealous. Moreover, she had attitudes about anybody she considered to be a "slacker" that were downright medieval. She was at the meeting because the CEO thought that she was the right person to get the legal and regulatory situation under control. The CEO needed somebody who was aggressive enough to track down and inventory all of the legal and regulatory commitments that the organization was subject to. That person would also have to have the motivation to build a control system from scratch, which would ensure compliance with the terms of those commitments. The compliance officer had already proven that she had the iron will to do that.

The CEO laid out the scope and depth of the assignment to the compliance officer. He explained that in order to ensure a proper chain of command, she would be doing the project under the supervision of the CISO. Then, because it was only fair, he asked her whether she was willing to accept such a big assignment. The compliance officer had been getting bored just assuring the integrity of the security function. So, she gave the CEO the same sort of look that Attila the Hun must have given his bosses when they asked him if he wanted to go out and invade Europe, and answered with an immediate, "Yes."

After the meeting, the CISO took the elevator down to the 43rd floor with the compliance officer in order to discuss strategy. The compliance officer was located a floor below him along with the rest of the company's operational heads. He couldn't help but notice that the compliance officer's office had no decorations whatsoever, except an ornately framed picture of her cat. Her chairs were the typical grey, straight-backed models you would normally find in somebody's enlisted barracks. That was appropriate, since they reflected the compliance officer's former career as a command sergeant major in the Army.

The CISO suggested that the EBK could be a valuable asset in formulating a top-level structure for the project; however, there were probably some other high-level models that the compliance officer might want to consider. The compliance officer pointed out the she had a lot better sense of strategy than the CISO gave her credit for. She told him that she had already read the relevant parts of the EBK for the regulatory competency. In response to that, the CISO's *only thought was that the compliance officer was going to be a real handful to manage. The compliance officer said that the EBK specified 10 common work functions for the management of regulatory compliance. These are all policy-based activities, so they had to be implemented at a high level across the organization in order to be effective. The outcome of these following 10 activities is to ensure that the regulatory compliance process is properly managed:*

1. *Establish and administer a risk-based enterprise information security program that addresses applicable **standards**, **procedures**, directives, policies, regulations, and **laws** (statutes)*

2. *Define the enterprise information security compliance program*

3. *Coordinate and provide liaison with staffs that are responsible for information security compliance, licensing and registration, and data security surveillance*

4. *Identify and stay current on all external laws, regulations, standards, and best practices applicable to the organization*

5. *Identify major enterprise risk factors (product, compliance, and operational) and coordinate the application of information security strategies, plans, policies, and procedures to reduce regulatory risk*

6. *Maintain relationships with all regulatory information security organizations and appropriate industry groups, forums, and stakeholders*

7. *Keep informed on pending information security changes, trends, and best practices by participating in collaborative settings.*

8. *Acquire the necessary resources to support an effective information security compliance program*

9. *Establish an enterprise information security compliance performance measures program*

10. *Ensure that appropriate changes and improvement actions are implemented as required*

# Compliance and Coordination

Compliance simply designates a condition or state in which the organization can be assured to satisfy relevant legal and regulatory requirements. Those requirements might come from a variety of sources, including government, industry, and contractual. Compliance is an important consideration in the information security universe. That is because the failure to comply with a legal requirement or regulation can cause significant harm to the organization, not just financially but also in terms of loss of reputation and even criminal outcomes.

Compliance usually has extensive reporting requirements. As a result, the issue with compliance is not so much ensuring that controls are in place. Rather the aim is to ensure that management is always aware of how the legal and regulatory obligations of the organization are met. The challenge is to develop objective evidence that all necessary requirements have been satisfied and then preserve and report that evidence to the appropriate legal and regulatory entities. Those entities vary, and each of them might have overlapping and sometimes conflicting compliance requirements. As a result, it is normally considered correct practice to establish a single unified compliance process to coordinate the diverse number of compliance obligations that the organization will face.

17

## Building Management Control

The formal compliance effort should be systematic and well-organized, which is why the activities that ensure compliance are typically arrayed into a formal management infrastructure. Formal infrastructures of controls are the most effective means to ensure general assurance of the compliance process. The controls that are in the infrastructure comprise a related set of organizational activities, whose sole purpose is to ensure an overall state of compliance. Because those control structures are not naturally occurring, they have to be built.

In order to be effective, each control structure needs to embody a complete set of controls. The key concept here is "complete." All of the potential compliance issues have to be identified, evaluated, and addressed. Because of the general complexity of the compliance process, it would be impossible to achieve a reliable state of completeness without adopting a single, comprehensive policy framework to structure the process on. The aim of that comprehensive policy framework is to effectively ensure the coordinated implementation of all of the relevant compliance policies across the entire organization.

Coordination of any complex form of activity requires a coherent control framework that will allow managers to judge whether their day-to-day activities are consistent with applicable organizational policies. A comprehensive system of best practice controls, which have been tailored to ensure compliance, is an important asset for any organization. That system will allow the organization to confirm that the routine activities that it undertakes to ensure compliance are operating as intended. The ultimate requirement is to demonstrate practical, real-world control. That is the reason why it is advisable to use a formal model of correct practice to guide the process. Common models of correct practice, such as the Information System Audit and Control Association's (ISACA) Control Objectives for IT (COBIT), exist in the public domain and can be used to do that.

## The Need for a Comprehensive Approach

A comprehensive approach to management prevents the piecemeal execution of the compliance function. Piecemeal is bad from a compliance standpoint because it gets in the way of the coordinated generation of organization-wide proof of correctness. Every enterprise probably undertakes some kind of compliance activity. Nevertheless, what amounts to a compliance function in most organizations can, in fact, be a disconnected series of activities that have been implemented as the need arose. Those activities usually amount to nothing more than ad-hoc reviews and reports and they are generally done based on some manager's understanding of the right way to satisfy a particular requirement. Those informal practices tend to embed themselves in the organization over time; and they are likely to become even more ad-hoc as new reporting requirements are added. That can be extremely dysfunctional, simply because it does not enforce the coherent across the board control that a large organization needs to underwrite its compliance efforts and the end result would be that the actual compliance would neither be complete nor correct.

Lack of a coherent approach can lead to serious, material weaknesses in compliance and reporting that might have grave consequences later on. For instance, there are both state and federal regulations for financial reporting; however, the actual assurance of the integrity of those reports is usually distributed between two different organizational units, accounting and IT controls. In many cases a third unit, internal audit, is also involved. Those units are all likely to have different frames of reference when it comes to the timing and scope of the actual financial reporting. Thus, if the financial reporting process is not properly coordinated, there is a possibility for inaccurate, conflicting, or even false reports. Given the regulatory climate, reporting failures can have civil and even criminal penalties attached to them. It is possible to define an organization-wide program, whose sole purpose is to make the compliance function systematic. As with any complex deployment, such a comprehensive program can only be achieved through rational planning.

## Planning for Control

Control over any large organizational function is enabled by the creation of specific policies that are operationalized by accompanying practices. The practices are expressly designed to implement the policies that they are designed to support. Policies and practices are created and related to each other by means of a formal planning process. Planning for compliance entails the creation of explicit control elements to enforce the organization's stated policies. Those controls ensure that all forms of reasonable care are exercised in the management, use, design, development, maintenance, or operation of the organization's compliance process. In order to ensure effectiveness, the implementation of that control has to be both comprehensive and coherent across the entire organization.

The goal of the planning process is to define the specific activities that are needed to ensure that a required organizational function is carried out in a systematic fashion. The focus of the planning is on establishing control over the operational compliance function. The aim is to ensure that the activities the compliance function carries out meet a specific standard of performance. Typically, those activities also realize some sort of business purpose, so it is essential to make sure that the relationship between the controls and the business purposes that they support is explicit.

The management control process is enabled by control objectives, which can be standalone for a given purpose, or integrated with other controls to achieve a general state of accountability for a function. In order to be considered properly implemented, the outcome of the control objective has to be objectively observable. Control objectives serve a number of related functions, but they all accomplish one specific purpose. They define an operational activity that takes place within some sort of rational management framework. In that respect, control objectives represent a coherent set of procedures which are specifically related to each other by their purpose.

## Control Objectives and Procedures

In practice, control objectives are implemented by means of a tailored set of procedures. Because a procedure is needed to implement a control objective, there is at least one procedure written for every control objective. The purpose of a procedure is to communicate how a given function is to be performed. Each procedure specifies, at a minimum, the expected input and output criteria and the interrelationship of that procedure to all associated procedures. Along with the procedure's description, the qualifications and skills of the person performing it should also be described. If there are any associated tools, practices, methodologies, or conventions involved in the execution of the procedure, those should also be itemized.

The execution of each procedure has to be systematic and consistent. In order to ensure the necessary reliability, each procedure has to be accompanied by an explicit set of work instructions which describe how the work will be done. Typically, those instructions are documented in a work plan, which outlines all of the tasks that have to be done in order to achieve a given purpose. The work plan itemizes each task, the skills required, and the organizational resources needed to do the work. In addition to detailing how the work will be done, the plan lists the accompanying activities that will be undertaken to evaluate the effectiveness of that work.

The work plan is developed at the point where the overall compliance process is instituted. Since the plan is subject to change, it has to be associated with an organizational stakeholder who can serve as the decision-maker. Because unknowns are a given in any security process, this plan must be a living document; there have to be provisions in the work plan for updating it on a regular basis.

## Sorting Out Complexity in Compliance Management

One of the challenging aspects of regulatory compliance is the problem of complex, overlapping, and continually changing requirements. The compliance process does not deal with just one kind of thing. It could conceivably involve laws, regulations, contracts, torts, and even customs. Moreover, the stakeholders in all of those situations can be numerous and often overlapping, and the conditions can be constantly changing. It is important to have a single organizational management process in place, whose primary purpose is to ensure that all of the relevant expectations for compliance are met in all instances.

In order to establish the compliance management function, it is first necessary to identify the specific laws, regulations, standards, best practices, and contractual requirements that will fall within the compliance management process. To carry out that identification, everything that falls within the scope of the compliance management process has to be characterized and related with respect to its specific connection with the purposes of compliance management. That justification is necessary because the process of maintaining compliance is not a simple matter of enforcing a set of rules.

Because of the overlapping and sometimes contradictory nature of compliance requirements (e.g., federal versus state regulations), it is essential to be able to understand the nature and importance of each regulation. In many cases, the compliance requirements are unclear, or require interpretation in order to figure out how they apply to current business conditions. Finally, different compliance directives have different vocabularies, so it is important to ensure that the actual meaning of a regulatory term is understood by all of the parties involved.

## Developing Meaningful Metrics

At the end of the planning process, the organization should have a well-defined compliance function. The process isn't complete until the activities of that function are understood by the rest of the organization. That understanding must be in totally unambiguous terms. Clear communication is an important consideration for understanding, because ambiguity is another potential point of failure for the management process.

For instance, a planning concept like "threat" may have a different meaning for a manager versus a technical person, as shown in Figure 17-1. The people who are responsible for the operation of the system are likely to characterize a threat as intrusions into the system, or malicious code. Consequently, they would characterize threat by concepts like occurrence, or downtime. Managers, on the other hand, are more likely to see threats in terms that are meaningful to them, such as cost and lost production time. Those concepts would be measured in dollar value or cost. The problem of characterizing threat in ambiguous terms

**Figure 17-1** Interpretation is everything

© Cengage Learning 2012

can be a serious concern if it leads to misinterpretation of the execution or outcomes of the overall compliance process.

The requirement for clarity implies the need to develop a suitable set of standard metrics to underwrite the performance of the compliance process. From the standpoint of common understanding, metrics are generally a product of the organizational environment. The type and rigor of those measures will vary based on the overall context of the business process. For instance, a highly secure government facility is likely to require extensive and rigorous metrics based around objective measures of technology and process, while qualitative and even anecdotal data might be perfectly acceptable in a simple business organization.

Generally, the basis for any decision about metrics is rooted in the level of control that is required. Broad measures, such as number of incidents, are perfectly acceptable to judge performance where the required level of control is not particularly high. When a high degree of security *is* essential, it is necessary to employ a detailed set of quantitative measures. The process starts by defining what the organization wants to know about its operation. Those definitions are generally expressed as outcome statements such as, "the results of the audit process will be used to assess compliance." Then those statements are refined down to the proper level of detail by continuing to break each measure down into sub-factors. This happens until a proper level of understanding is reached. For instance, "the results of the audit process will be used to assess compliance" might be decomposed all the way down to focused statements like, "the reliability of the controls over financial reporting will be assessed based on a numeric compilation of the material weaknesses identified in the general ledger system."

17

By rule, the attributes embodied by each sub-factor must be directly traceable to the higher-level measures that they were derived from. For example, if audit of compliance is the accepted measure of success at the top, the acceptable measure might be "number of audits conducted." Once that measure is decomposed into its sub-factors, the outcome might be "number of material weaknesses identified" or "number of non-compliances" or even "number of prosecutions for non-compliance." Whatever the eventual outcome, all sub-factors should be directly traceable through the hierarchy of measures up to the top-level measures. This is a dynamic process because the sub-factors and their associated values are all constantly changing. Thus, the measures that are part of the metric process have to be continuously refined and updated.

# The Compliance Officer Goes for a Run

*The compliance officer had spent a long week trying to figure out how to operationalize the controls for the compliance function. Although she was not the sort of person who wandered off task, she still found herself going in circles trying to come up with a control set design that made sense. Her dilemma in this case was caused by the complexity of the compliance process and the extreme level of detail that was required in order to get an auditable set of controls in place. Usually, whenever she wanted to focus or was feeling frustrated, she liked to jog the 15 blocks over to Central Park and then do some serious running.*

*Given the mood she was in today though, she practically ripped up the asphalt on 59th Street getting there. She accepted the fact that she was probably the most competitive humanoid on the island of Manhattan, but today's overwhelming urge to beat the problem into submission by sheer physical exercise was rare even for her. The trouble was that the company was so big and the compliance process was so "squishy." There were an infinite number of contracts and regulations, so the static controls that she was so comfortable with creating and **auditing** were also going to be infinite. That complexity led her to conclude that simply itemizing controls was not going to work. Without the ability to generate evidence there was not going to be any reliable control over compliance.*

*She jumped on the path at 59th and East Drive and proceeded to pick up the pace. The thing about running was that you felt the pain for the first couple of minutes while your body shut down all of the nonessential services and started channeling blood to the heart and lungs. After that was done you felt like you could run forever, especially when the endorphins kicked in. The compliance officer didn't smoke or drink, but she knew that she was hooked on that natural high. Whether it was the additional oxygen to the brain, or those endorphins, it suddenly hit her as she swung past the zoo at a brisk 6-minute-per-mile pace. She had been focusing on auditing compliance, whereas she should have been focusing on a generic control process that could be tailored to any of the many compliance needs by the people who were the stakeholders and then audited based on that tailoring. She didn't slow her pace, but she began to think through what that would require.*

*She really hated to admit it, but the CISO was right. He was the one who had first come up with the tailoring idea to solve the diversity problem, and she was just adopting his same concept. In general terms, the issues associated with compliance were both common and relatively simple. You only had to define a generic set of applicable policies for each of the common regulatory areas, and then it was just a matter of tailoring out a specific set of controls to implement those policies. The best part was that the tailoring could be done by the stake-holders who the law or regulation applied to. In fact, those individuals were probably the only ones who were even capable of defining the right controls, since they were the people who lived with the outcomes.*

*She swung back down the 65th Street Transverse road and set a new personal best getting back to her office. One hot satisfying shower later, she sat back down at her desk to draw up the general tailoring plan. She knew that because of the dynamic nature of the legal and regulatory environment, the general compliance policy development process would have to be really high-level. Yet these policies would absolutely have to satisfy the actual overall compliance purpose. She began to lay out an iterative process, where the people who would eventually specify the policies and their associated controls would start from the only thing that she cared about: the protection of the company. Then they would circle down to the eventual definition of concrete, auditable behaviors. The beauty of that approach was that she would be able to oversee the process of developing the controls, rather than have to develop the controls themselves. The thing she particularly liked about her idea was the fact that the requirements for the design process in the EBK were similar to the approach that she had in mind. The EBK specifies the following four simple management activities:*

1. *Develop enterprise information security compliance strategies, policies, plans, and procedures in accordance with established standards, procedures, directives, policies, regulations, and laws (statutes)*
2. *Specify enterprise information security compliance program control requirements*
3. *Author information security compliance performance reports*
4. *Develop a plan of action and associated mitigation strategies to address program deficiencies*
5. *Develop a compliance reporting process in a manner that produces evidence that a process exists*

# Designing from Policy to Practice

In addition to spelling out the sequence and timing of the steps of the process, the compliance program design process should provide a detailed description of the actions that will be taken to achieve a particular end. For that reason, the design of a tangible set of compliance policies is the essential first step in creating a substantive compliance process. Managers and designers have the same general goal, which is to enable practical, real-world compliance. Where those two differ is in their focus. The aim of managers is to develop practical organization-wide strategies to achieve business goals. The focus of designers is to document the specific actions that will be undertaken to put those strategies into practice. Accordingly, the first critical success factor for the design process is the development of a detailed specification of the steps the organization will take to ensure adequate day-to-day compliance for a given business purpose. In order to ensure consistent and uniform practice, the design has to create a sustainable management infrastructure, which will be composed of practices that characterize the compliance function for the organization.

The overall aim of the design function is to institutionalize a comprehensive set of standardized and repeatable practices for the everyday execution of the compliance function. Thus, one of the essential steps in building a formal compliance system is to specify the requisite security policies, procedures, and work practices to ensure proper execution of the compliance function. That specification has to embrace both technical- and behavioral-level concerns, and its activities have to be embedded at all of the relevant levels in the organization. For that reason, the design has to characterize all required compliance actions in implementable terms. That characterization should be sufficiently detailed to ensure that the actions in the design are fully understood and can actually be put into practice by the people responsible for their implementation.

There should also be a tangible means of evaluating whether the resulting compliance infrastructure is effective. The need to ensure proper everyday performance of required practices is a different issue than the need to evaluate the performance of the controls themselves. In the case of the former, the focus is on judging the overall effectiveness of the process. In the case of the latter, the focus is on judging the appropriateness of a given set of activities. For that reason, the second critical requirement in the design process is the description of a formal mechanism to ensure that the process always stays focused on ensuring compliance. In order to guarantee its ongoing effectiveness, there has to be a way to determine whether the actions that were specified for the compliance function are consistently achieving the purposes that they were meant to satisfy. Thus, it is important to be able to judge how effective the activities of the compliance function are in their day-to-day execution.

## Tailoring Compliance

At a high level of generalization, every compliance function should operate like any other one, in the sense that they all ensure that the terms and conditions of laws, regulations, and contracts are adhered to. That assurance is based on evidence. Because environments are different, the actual steps of the compliance process have to align with the circumstances. Proper alignment requires that all relevant technology and operational factors are embodied in the design of the compliance process for that particular situation. This is called tailoring.

Tailoring is a coherent conceptual exercise that drills down hierarchically, from the organization's environment all the way to the definition of discrete practices. Approaching the design that way ensures that the resultant management infrastructure will be both comprehensive and complete. Nevertheless, since the eventual outcome of the development process is an unambiguous set of controls, this process involves a set of successively more focused tailoring passes over the same topic in order to ensure that the requisite work practices are specified in adequate detail. The final product of that refinement process is a coherent and unambiguous set of concrete policies, procedures, and work practices which are directly aligned with each other and which precisely fit the specific requirements of that particular security environment.

## Defining Concrete Policies

Because design essentially involves critical thinking, the process is typically carried out top-down. For that reason, the first step in the design process is the specification of the policies that will underwrite the compliance function. Policies are the organization's statement about the general outcomes it wishes to achieve from a given process. Since they shape the rest of the process, those policies should be both comprehensive and concrete. The complete set of policies will constitute the framework that will dictate the overall scope and application of the subsequent compliance function. Once a set of policies has been developed, procedures have to be established and referenced to operationalize those policies. Because those procedures define the steps that will be taken to enable the execution of the policy, every policy must be accompanied by the right set of procedures to enact it.

## Refining Control Statements

Given the requirement for an effective set of procedures to accompany each policy, the design process goes through a series of stages to achieve the right level of definition for each supporting procedure. The procedures that substantiate each policy are focused into increasingly explicit control statements. At the top, this hierarchy is composed of general statements about activity and intent. Those more general statements are successively broken down into clear and explicit descriptions of the practices to be performed. This iterative process is followed until the desired level of control is reached. The eventual outcome of following this sequential breakdown process is a logical collection of unambiguous activity statements that are directly traceable to the policies that they implement.

## An Example of the Functional Decomposition Process

Any process that is decomposed top-down will eventually produce a concrete array of electronic and management controls, which ought to ensure that all levels of the process contribute to the desired outcome. That successive breakdown into component parts produces a logically articulated set of control statements that are applicable at each level of organizational functioning.

Compliance is enforced by policies, their attendant management procedures, and the work instructions that implement those procedures. Policies are always required to guide the overall direction of the process. For example, the policy might state that the monitoring of a given regulation must produce auditable evidence. At the level of management procedure, a number of behavioral processes would have to be designed to assure that evidence was recorded and then subsequently audited. Finally, at the work instruction level, there would typically be a number of concrete work practices specified to ensure that each procedure was embedded into the day-to-day operation. For example, the form of the evidence collection document might be specified along with the auditing control procedures that would ensure proper chain of custody.

## Documenting Work Practices

The organization's formal work practices provide a detailed description of how compliance will be implemented and enforced. Work practices clearly explain how each procedure will be executed. The key to success is consistency; each work instruction must have a set of metrics and measurement methods associated with it to help managers judge whether the work has been satisfactorily performed.

Because specification at the level of work practices requires a good deal of description, the manual that specifies the work practices is typically a long document. These can be unwieldy in practice unless they are broken into more manageable specifications. There are typically three kinds of work practice specifications. These are not mutually exclusive. Instead, each document reinforces the other. The total set communicates the precise steps that the organization will follow to implement the compliance process. These are the specification of management practices, the specification of operational practices, and the specification of assurance and accountability practices.

**Management Work Practices** The specification of management work practices lays out the details of the management oversight for the compliance process. Performance of the practices contained in the management specification ensures that the compliance process will meet its stated goals. In other words, the specification of management work practices comprises the details of the management function for the compliance process. A management specification assigns explicit roles and responsibilities, and it defines the detailed accountability mechanisms. It also specifies in depth how performance of each compliance work practice will be monitored, measured, and assessed.

**Operational Work Practices** The operations specification is the roadmap for the execution and maintenance of the specific compliance process. It itemizes the practices that comprise the everyday performance of real-world compliance duties. Operations specifications describe the routine execution of each practice. Managers frequently refer to these documents when advice is required about how to perform the process correctly.

**Assurance Work Practices** The specification of assurance work practices documents how the organization will verify and validate that the execution of the compliance function is correct. These specifications are meant to ensure consistent and reliable execution of all compliance duties. The person who will be responsible for assessing that performance must be specified, as well as the measures that will be used to evaluate the performance of each practice.

---

# The Compliance Officer Gets Up Early

*The compliance officer was up early, even for her. The sun was just starting to make its way up over Long Island Sound, and although it looked like it was going to be a decent early spring day, it was still too dark to tell. The compliance officer never regretted living so far out in New Rochelle, especially since it was an easy 10 minutes down to the Number 6 train at Pelham Park. Her location here in Pelham gave her the best of two worlds: inexpensive green space and a relatively easy commute.*

*She was up early because she was planning to lay out the implementation plan for the CISO. The problem was that she still didn't feel like she had her arms around the process. Her forte was auditing, not process, and she was beginning to get the sense that the details of the implementation part were slipping through her fingers. Her overall design was well received by everybody, but although it touched all of the necessary bases, it was not a reasonable starting point for actually implementing the compliance process throughout the company's diverse worldwide holdings.*

*She thought maybe an early run would give her the inspiration she needed. Plus, she had to get her customary eight miles in before she dressed and took the train down to the city. She slipped out the door of her condo and headed downstairs. The dog on the floor below her began to bark. Since the dog knew her really well, she guessed that he probably just wanted to go out on the run with her. He was a big Lab who ran every day with his owner. She was not a big fan of dogs but they had their uses, and having a friendly old fellow like that as a running companion was definitely appealing since her big, lazy cat was not into any form of exercise whatsoever.*

*She ran a loop around Glen Island and, as she ran, she was thinking about what it would take to get a working set of controls in place. The sun was fully up by that point and the grey morning mist was starting to disappear from the low places on the island. She was watching things get lighter and listening to the rhythmic sound of her footfalls on her usual six-minute-per-mile pace when the solution to the implementation problem just suddenly came to her. She remembered that the exact same thing had happened with the design problem, and so she was beginning to think that the exercise itself had something to do with those sudden bursts of inspiration. Maybe it was the extra blood in her brain?*

*She had been spending too much time viewing implementation as a dissemination problem when it really was one of participation. Because compliance in the information security sense was a brand new concept, she had been assuming that the implementation would literally be from the ground up. But since she was an auditor by trade, she had always intuitively known that that wasn't the actual situation. In fact, there were tons of controls out there, many of them relevant to her specific needs. The problem was that there was no rhyme or reason to how they were organized and they basically did nothing more than ensure the few limited things that they were specifically designed to address.*

*She had to find out what she already had. Only then would she worry about what she needed to add to make it a consistent system. The rest of the process fell into place from that assumption. She could structure the implementation around an inventory of existing controls. That inventory could then be vetted based on whether it achieved the compliance control mission. Then she could decide what else she needed to have there. More important, all of the inventorying would be done by the functional unit heads, since they were the only people who knew their own operation. That would free her up to provide the high-level oversight that was needed to ensure a complete solution.*

*Once the controls and gaps were all identified, she could then work with the same managers to tailor out a coherent set of controls. Since the tailoring would be done by the managers themselves, there would be automatic buy-in to the process, and that would make it easy to get the sort of acceptance she would need if she wanted the process to be self-sustaining. She picked up the pace to a sprint and ran all the way back to her condo, where she was greeted by what had to be one of the world's fattest cats, who acknowledged her presence by stretching, rolling over on his other side, and falling back to sleep. She still had a couple of hours, so she grabbed a towel and her copy of the EBK to see what it had to say about implementation. She found that the EBK specified the following four, mostly management, functions for the implementation of a regulatory compliance process:*

1. *Monitor, assess, and report information security compliance practices of all personnel and the IT system in accordance with enterprise policies and procedures*

2. *Maintain ongoing and effective communications with key stakeholders for compliance reporting purposes*

3. *Conduct internal audits to determine if information security control objectives, controls, processes, and procedures are effectively applied and maintained, and perform as expected*

4. *Document information security audit results and recommend remedial action policies and procedures*

*As a group, their role seemed to be to make sure that the regulatory compliance function was embedded in the day-to-day operation of the organization.*

# Finding Out What You Need to Have

The first step in implementing any comprehensive and consistent function for practical use is to find out what you already have. The organization ought to know what it already does in order to decide about the direction that it ought to head. That is especially true with compliance, since in most cases there will already have been some type of formal reporting requirement for every form of company activity where compliance is required. Moreover, those processes have probably been in place since the inception of the organization. For instance, if the company is publically held, then there would be a year-end report requirement. Accordingly, a review of the existing controls and their documentation and reporting lines is an essential first step in implementing a company-wide compliance process.

Because of the extent of the existing controls and their generally ad-hoc nature, that review is likely to be time-consuming. Nonetheless, a summary of current status is essential, because it would be nearly impossible to implement a uniform compliance process without adequate knowledge of the current control situation. Without a sense of what the current control situation looks like, it would be more likely that the organization would implement unnecessary new controls. That would be a problem, because too much control would be a waste of resources and interfere with the day-to-day operation of the business.

Historically, some industries such as financial services and health care have stringent regulatory and compliance environments. However, most industries do not. In order to meet the requirements for satisfactory compliance monitoring and reporting, those organizations will have to change how they currently conduct their day-to-day business. For instance, the organization will probably have to modify or enhance the controls it has in place over the financial operation in order to enable greater visibility into its processes. That visibility is normally enforced through audits. Audits require the conventional business operation to produce evidence, which would mean that besides performing its normal functions, each business unit would have to generate and preserve auditable evidence to ensure proof of compliance. The generation of that proof can be a time-consuming task that could distract from the routine functioning of the unit. The requirement for greater transparency can also cause an efficiency problem for the business units themselves. One way to get around the problem of acceptance is to adopt a standard model for implementation, as discussed in the following subsections of this chapter.

## Step One: Control Environment

It is important to ensure that the compliance strategy is properly aligned with the overall strategies of the business. Otherwise, it is likely that compliance and conventional business processes will work together in an uncoordinated and dysfunctional fashion. That alignment is assured through strategic planning. Because of the scope of the consideration, the information that is needed to ensure proper alignment has to be obtained through any relevant source involved with the compliance process, either internal or external.

The people who implement the compliance process must obtain detailed feedback from business process owners and users. These stakeholders are most likely to know what the specific compliance needs are for their areas. The best way to guarantee high-quality guidance is to put together a formal organizational-level planning or steering committee of those stakeholders to oversee the conduct and activities of the compliance process. At a minimum, that committee should include representatives from senior management, conventional unit management, and the information security function.

The role of the committee is to ensure that information about compliance strategies and the compliance program's ongoing operation is communicated to senior management and the board of directors. The test of whether this requirement is being met is whether the CEO, CFO, and the board of directors are suitably aware of compliance program activities, challenges, and risks. At the same time, the committee should also ensure that all relevant compliance plans are effectively communicated to the correct business process owners and other appropriate parties across the organization. There should also be a mechanism in place to formally monitor how well the compliance operation is doing with regard to the strategic plan. If deviations from that plan are detected, there should be a strategic level means to return the organization to its established course.

**Assignment of Duties** Additionally, there should be a means of ensuring that all applicable managers have sufficient capability to fulfill their compliance responsibilities. Identifying and then training the right managers will require the organization to survey its key systems and data in order to determine the appropriate stakeholders. The roles and responsibilities of each of those stakeholders will have to be defined and documented so that they are understood by all of the parties involved in the process.

Finally, the people who actually execute the requisite compliance activities will have to be given sufficient authority to carry out their assigned roles and responsibilities. To ensure that those responsibilities are fully understood the people who are directly responsible for internal control should acknowledge their acceptance of their assigned duties. At the same time, the business process owners of the data should also be informed about their duties and provide the same type of acknowledgement. Once all of the requisite duties are assigned and fully understood, the specific items of information that are needed to ensure an effective compliance process should be defined. That definition will include how the information will flow between business process owners and the people responsible for internal control.

**Ensuring Capable Staffing** The people who are responsible for ensuring compliance have to be capable. The implementation process should include a mechanism to ensure staff capability. First, the separation of duties for all of the participants in the compliance process has to be ensured. All compliance responsibilities must be assigned in such a way that no one individual is solely responsible for the compliance duties of a critical process.

At the same time, the minimum amount of information needed to execute assigned tasks has to be defined for each person who performs compliance duties. This prevents people who are executing assigned compliance tasks from stepping on each other's assignment. Designating minimum information needs for each role also satisfies the personnel security requirement for least privilege.

Along with the definition of job responsibilities, controls have to be put in place to ensure an appropriate and timely response to job changes and terminations. The aim is to ensure that the ongoing performance of the compliance function is not hampered by normal staff turnover. In a related area, the organization also has to ensure continuous learning for all relevant compliance staff.

Continuous learning is leveraged by formal, ongoing training and skill development programs for the people who are doing compliance work. In order to ensure the proper execution of the compliance process, it is necessary to identify and document the training needs of all personnel who support compliance. That training should touch on every aspect of compliance for all staff, including ethical conduct, general security practices, confidentiality standards, integrity standards, and compliance and reporting responsibilities. Finally, because contract staff is a fact of life in modern corporations, a specific definition of the compliance role of those individual has to be defined. The aim of this final condition is to effectively control all of the various types of people who are associated with the compliance process.

**Compliance Process Architecture** It is important to ensure that everybody in the process has sufficient information to do their jobs properly. Management has to define that substantive information capture, processing, and reporting controls are in place to ensure that the information that is used for management decision making about compliance is complete, accurate, valid, and fully authorized. The aim is to ensure the quality and integrity of information used for any compliance process.

The first step in ensuring the currency and integrity of the data that is used for decision making is for management to periodically review its policies, procedures, and standards. The aim of that activity is to ensure that they reflect changing business conditions. Management must also have procedures in place to identify deviations from required practice. This is necessary in order to investigate and install remedial actions. Specifically, management has to ensure sufficient information to allow it to effectively assess the organization's ongoing state of compliance with all requisite policies, procedures, laws, regulations, or standards.

## Step Two: Assessment of Risks

Risk assessment is the second step in the process of implementing a formal compliance process. Proper risk assessment requires the organization to have a sufficiently focused, organization-wide process in place to conduct threat identification and risk **evaluations**. For that reason, the first requirement in establishing the risk assessment process is to adopt an entity- and activity-level assessment approach that can reliably be used to identify any existing threats to compliance. That approach should also be able to provide sufficient information to allow the organization to evaluate the probability and likelihood of any threats that are identified through that process.

The approach must be able to provide an objective assessment of the impact of threats. That estimate should be in the form of a business impact analysis on critical systems and on the overall business performance of the organization. That assessment must be based on qualitative and quantitative criteria. In order to ensure that the compliance process aligns with the business function, the development of those criteria should be done using the advice of stakeholders from the various functional areas of the business, which are participants in the compliance process.

## Step Three: Instituting the Proper Controls

The third stage of the compliance process institutes the controls that are appropriate to the risks that are known to exist. The implementation of controls is the counterpart to the assessment of risk. In that respect, the organization should use a formal process to determine whether the controls that are developed out of the risk assessment properly accept, mitigate, transfer, or avoid risks, as well as fall within technical and cost feasibility parameters.

The control set must be explicitly designed to address the specific requirements of the threat environment. Nevertheless, there are some general terms and conditions that must be met in order to ensure that whatever controls are adopted are effectively and properly embedded in the organization's day-to-day operation.

Because controls for compliance have to be instituted organization-wide, their implementation should be through a formal strategic planning activity. At a minimum, sufficient controls should be ensured to address the risk of non-compliance for critical systems and significant company locations. Criticality and significance of both the electronic and physical elements of the organization is determined based on the relative importance of the system or location to the overall operation.

It is also important to create and maintain sufficient documentation of the controls that have been established for all significant processes, controls, and activities. This documentation underwrites the organization's existing understanding of the actual controls that underwrite substantive compliance. Even in the case where risks are considered acceptable, formal documentation should be provided of the acceptance of each risk. If the risk is accepted rather than addressed, any offsets should also be specifically documented. That includes all insurance coverage, contractually negotiated liabilities, or self-insurance.

## Step Four: Assessing the Effectiveness of the Control Set

The next step in the process entails comprehensive assessment of control performance. Once the control set is implemented, the organization should be committed to active and continuous assessment of performance. The assessment is also a tool for ensuring the effectiveness of the design and implementation processes. Ongoing assessment should also be used to ensure the continuing correct performance of the control system over time. Since a continuous and comprehensive assessment program has to be dictated by plan, it is important to have a formal one in place to ensure the effectiveness of the control set.

As part of the assessment process, there should be a mechanism for routinely evaluating the performance of the controls for significant IT functions. That plan should provide a consistent approach to addressing both general and specific compliance issues, and it should prescribe the types of activities that will be used to carry out the assessments. That includes such activities as reviews, audits, and inspections. The timing of these activities, as well as their objectives, should be laid out in the assessment plan. In the end, the assessment plan should ensure that the controls adhere to all organizational policies, procedures, and standards as they relate to compliance.

Besides ensuring the capability of the internal response, the assessment process should monitor changes in the external legal or regulatory environment. Change has to be recognized and responded to as it relates to the compliance of the business. If material change has occurred in the external environment, then internal control activities have to be changed or adopted as fast as possible to ensure ongoing compliance. In that respect, it is essential to ensure that internal activities to support continuous legal and regulatory compliance are arrayed in a timely fashion.

## Step Five: Documenting the Finished Product

The final step in implementing the compliance process requires documenting the form of the process itself. This documentation will be used to manage the system and, in order for the compliance process to be considered effective, it has to be documented that management has monitored the effectiveness of all of its internal controls for compliance in the course of normal operation. The assessments of control effectiveness have to be documented periodically in order to demonstrate that management has met that requirement. Where any material deviations in the operation of internal controls are identified, those deviations also have to be documented and reported as a part of the ongoing record of compliance process activity.

Because it describes the system and its overall purpose and functioning, the documentation set represents the system to outsiders. Since the documentation provides the basis for judging system operation, it is important that all measures of performance for both internal and external sources are defined, and that data is being collected and documented. That documentation can come in the form of reports from management and supervisory activities, comparisons, and benchmarks.

Documentation requires the establishment of appropriate metrics, and that is particularly true for benchmarks. Because benchmarks allow managers to chart the organization's course over time, they can be useful in maintaining the effectiveness of any organizational system. For instance, changes to a benchmark can be used to make decisions about where the compliance function has to go next. Understanding why any shortfall occurred in achieving a benchmark can provide an actionable basis for plans to address the problem.

In the most rigorous case, management might obtain independent reviews of internal controls from third-party providers. Any documentation obtained from those reviews should be retained to provide independent, audited proof of compliance. The organization can also use documentation from internal audits of the compliance function. Those reviews are typically specified in the overall assessment plan for compliance risk. The aim is to ensure that internal audits cover the full range of compliance issues, and to then make certain that all control issues and issues of non-compliance are followed up in a timely manner.

# The Compliance Officer Gets a New Job

*The compliance officer had to concede that she was nervous. For somebody as physically tough as she was, that was a hard thing to fathom. She was nowhere near mentally prepared to face the board of directors, and she was about to do that very thing. It was rare for a woman to reach the rank of command sergeant major in her former career, but she had gotten to that exalted position in a mere ten years because she always delivered the mission. She told herself that it was no different in this case. The CISO had asked her to move way out of her comfort zone to develop the compliance process for the entire company, and she had gotten the job done on time and on budget.*

*The process was rolling out worldwide as she paced back and forth outside the board room. She smiled as she thought back to her old enlisted life and the huge responsibilities she shouldered for that little bit of pay. Thinking of that, she muttered under her breath, "I would love to have the CISO in my unit for a week," just as he appeared in the 15-foot-high mahogany door. The CISO was all smiles. The compliance officer thought, with not a little bit of irony, that the CISO must really be pleased because he only got that way when he had scored bigtime with the board.*

*He had been in there presenting her solution to the compliance problem, which was ironic, considering the fact that she had done all the work. Since she considered herself the world's best NCO, she was more than happy to let the CISO take all of the credit. It was obvious that this was going to be a short appearance on her part; as she accompanied the CISO into the room, she felt some of her tension ease. The actual meeting was a "love-in." The board was excited about the scope and depth of the process. For the first time, the CEO felt that he could trust the compliance status of his own day-to-day processes. In fact, the board and the CEO were so pleased with what she had done that they had decided to promote the compliance officer to a new title in the company: director of organizational controls. That meant she was moving up to the 44th floor, which was no big deal for her, because all she would have to pack was the picture of her cat. More important, though, it would give her the authority to turn the controls process she had developed for compliance into an organization-wide mechanism for ensuring alignment between control and business strategy.*

*As the meeting droned on, she tuned out of what was being said. Instead, she was thinking that the best part about organizational controls, at the level that they were now defined, was that they created real visibility into the operational processes of the organization. She planned on instituting a regular evaluation process for those controls that would give her all of the data she would need to support informed decision-making across the organization. Since the compliance controls were already in place, she decided to start with them first. She knew that the EBK specified the following three high-level functions for evaluation of regulatory compliance:*

1. *Assess the effectiveness of enterprise compliance program controls against applicable standards, policies, procedures, guidelines, directives, regulations, and laws (statutes)*

2. *Assess effectiveness of the information security compliance process and procedures for process improvement, and implement changes where appropriate*

3. *Compile, analyze, and report performance measures*

# Evaluation Programs and Compliance

Evaluation is a regulatory imperative. The laws and regulations that govern most organizations usually have some sort of evaluation requirement built into them. The process typically entails the regular inspection of the controls that have been established to ensure compliance. The effectiveness of those controls is usually judged based on their ability to ensure the continuing integrity and effectiveness of the compliance process. Evaluations are typically done on a routinely scheduled basis, because it is important to maintain standard and disciplined assurance of all of the controls that enforce compliance. An effective evaluation program provides consistent monitoring of the status of the compliance controls, and it has to ensure that the confidence in the strength of that compliance can be confirmed by evidence.

Assessments validate that the appropriate controls are in place and functioning properly. An effective assessment program ought to be factual; meaning the outcomes of the assessment must be directly apparent, rather than anecdotal. In addition, all of the measures that are used to perform the evaluation should be both meaningful and appropriate. In simple terms, the outcomes of the evaluation should be understandable to all stakeholders and they appropriately fit the circumstance.

Compliance is evaluated through two types of generic processes: reviews or audits. The main difference between these two is their focus and degree of rigor. With reviews, the aim is to learn something about the process. Audits are a different matter entirely. They are done to ensure trust. Audits are the method of choice for assuring compliance, because the compliance process is built around making certain that a specific activity has been performed as required.

## Audits and Enforcement

Due to their presumed impartiality, audits ensure a much greater degree of confidence in the eventual result of the evaluation. Given the aim of enforcing trust, audits usually require a common, authoritative point of reference or standard to serve as the basis for the examination. With laws or regulations, the point of reference is usually the terms and conditions of the directive. Audits use documentary evidence about processes, procedures, and even deliverables to support their findings. They might verify compliance with plans, regulations, and standards within their scope. Audits can also be required by customer organizations to verify compliance with a defined set of requirements.

Because of the need for indisputable assurance, third parties are frequently involved in the audit process. In that respect, the auditors do their work as disinterested third parties whose only aim is to generate evidence-based conclusions. The third party is usually a professional auditing firm. Audits are also conducted by the regulating body itself. By convention, a lead auditor is typically the person who is actually responsible for conducting the audit. The lead auditor directs an audit team that is composed of subject matter experts trained specifically in auditing techniques

Frequently, an external agency accredits the findings. Usually that accreditation is provided by the body that has promulgated the law or regulation, such as the U.S. Securities and Exchange Commission, The Department of Defense, or Health and Human Service, or the International Standards Organization (ISO). The outcome of an audit is a set of attestations as to the facts of the examination, as well as the evidence that supports those attestations. These conclusions are aimed at certifying compliance with the aims of the audit.

## Managing and Improving the Compliance Process

Senior management is responsible for developing and implementing long- and short-range plans, the purpose of which is to achieve the organization's goals. One important aspect of planning is to ensure that the business strategies of the organization are properly aligned with its compliance process. In order to make that assurance, senior management has to make certain that all compliance issues, as well as all opportunities for improvement of the compliance process, are considered in the formulation of long- and short-range plans for the organization.

The organization's plans should provide detailed guidance about the actions that the business will need to take to organize, implement, deliver, support, and monitor the compliance process. Detailed guidance of this type is particularly important in the world of business. Managers must weigh and balance the deployment of any type of security function against the likelihood and material consequences of each potential threat. A comprehensive evaluation based on the appropriate criteria ought to be able to allow decision makers to understand whether their existing and planned compliance approach will satisfy necessary business requirements.

Evaluation is useful in satisfying this responsibility because it addresses a number of issues that managers are concerned about. For example, evaluation helps the enterprise understand the overall needs and requirements of the compliance function, and it identifies the specific compliance issues in an organization. From that identification, evaluation can tell what the risks are. A properly structured evaluation can help the organization balance the cost of controlling risks against the likely impacts of each identified threat. That makes for more efficient financial management of the compliance process in general. For that reason, evaluations of compliance risk and the cost of remediation should be done regularly.

## Critical Success Factors

Critical success factors are the basis for determining whether the compliance process has achieved its goals. These factors can be strategic, technical, or organizational. They include such considerations as whether the process is properly defined and documented; has specific policies, clear accountabilities, strong support, and commitment from management; maintains effective lines of communication; and employs consistent and clear measurement practices.

Critical success factors are composed of key goal indicators, which can be used to tell whether the process is achieving its business purpose, and key performance indicators, which assess the specific performance of the compliance process, as shown in Figure 17-2.

**Key Goal Indicators**  Key goal indicators belong to the business. They represent the specific activities that the compliance function needs to perform in order to further a specific

**Figure 17-2**  Critical success factors

© *Cengage Learning 2012*

business goal. Key goal indicators provide a description of the outcome of each control activity, and each key goal must be measurable.

If the key goal indicators produce substantive data, the data can be used to determine whether a compliance activity is furthering the business goals that it is referenced to. Data can also be used to provide an indication of the impact of not achieving that goal. Since they are compliance-oriented, key goal indicators tend to concentrate on the legal and regulatory issues of the business. If they are focused on all of the factors that are important to business success, key goal indicators can provide a comprehensive picture of how well the organization is doing with respect to its overall business purposes.

**Key Performance Indicators** Key performance indicators measure how well the process is performing. If they are expressed at the right level of detail, they can even assess the performance of individual controls. For this reason, key performance indicators are an objective means of evaluating both success and risk.

Key performance indicators are process-oriented, but they can be measured. The measures themselves focus primarily on tangible factors like cost efficiency, productivity, non-compliances, time factors, stakeholder satisfaction, staff competency measures, and benchmark comparisons. These factors can be turned into objective measures of performance, like cost per control, work units produced per control, non-compliances per control, and so on.

# Chapter Summary

- The compliance process begins with an identification of the things that require compliance.
- Compliance controls are arrayed in a comprehensive infrastructure and must specify precise, observable behaviors.
- Compliance has to be systematic.
- Metrics are necessary to monitor the compliance process.
- Controls are developed through an iterative process of functional decomposition.
- The approach to compliance involves tailoring standard models.
- Workforce training is an important part of compliance, and workers must be aware of the importance of compliance.
- Compliance systems are built from existing controls; where those controls already exist, they must be inventoried.
- Stakeholders are the best source of information about control needs.
- Understanding the regulatory environment is the first step in instituting control.
- Controls are based on risk analysis.
- Controls must be evaluated for performance; the evaluation process can be used to improve the organization.
- Critical success factors can be defined and used to evaluate controls.
- Evaluation is necessary to balance costs.
- It is important to define clear, auditable metrics.

# Key Terms

**Auditing** The process of generating proof and drawing conclusions from the evidence that can be attested to.

**Evaluation** A process of gathering evidence and drawing conclusions about the correctness or quality of a given subject.

**Laws** Legal mandates dictated by a body with the authority to issue those mandates.

**Procedure** The specific activities that will be undertaken to satisfy some policy dictate.

**Regulations** Requirements dictated by an agency or other legally constituted unit, which must be complied with; typically expressed in the form of a contract.

**Standards** A formal statement of best practices promulgated by an agency with the formal authority to issue them.

# Questions from the CIO

The CIO requires you to brief her on the current status of your investigation. This will be an important part of your continuing work on this project, since it is essential to be able to describe all of the ramifications of the functions of the compliance process. Consequently, the CIO would like you to answer the following questions for her:

1. The compliance process requires that all compliance activities are organized and administered from a central authority. Why is that centralization needed? What does it promote?

2. The organization must deliberately and in a disciplined fashion perform the compliance function as a systematic and sustainable process. Why is that needed? What would be the consequences if it did not?

3. The organization must define and enforce a substantive set of procedures and work practices, as well as assign roles and job responsibilities, and enforce accountability for compliance. What is the purpose of each of those requirements (e.g., what do they add to the process)?

4. The five practical steps involved in building a compliance function force the operation to think through the detailed requirements of its particular circumstance. What other conditions does this requirement enforce? What would be the consequence of not following these five steps?

5. Policies require procedures and work instructions. What do the latter two things add to the policy? What would happen if these were not there?

6. The purpose of the control status assessment is to characterize all of the current controls for compliance. Why is an inventory of those controls necessary? Why is it necessary to do an inventory in the first place?

7. The successful development of a compliance system depends on the ability to tailor the right set of controls. What is the tailoring process? What is it based on (e.g., what does it tailor)?

**17**

8. The approach to tailoring is hierarchical. Higher-level items are decomposed into smaller and more precisely defined subfunctions. What is the aim of that activity? Why is decomposition necessary, and what is the eventual outcome?

9. The only way that an organization can conduct a sustainable process is if it has documented controls in place. Why are documented controls necessary? What do they produce or create? Why is uniformity so important?

10. Work instructions itemize the standard operating steps that will be taken to enforce compliance. Why are standard steps necessary? What condition does this produce in the organization? What are the outcomes of these steps (in terms of specific products)?

# Hands-On Projects

HANDS-ON PROJECTS

Refer to the Humongous Holdings case in Appendix A. You have been assigned the responsibility to itemize all existing compliance controls mentioned in that case. Once you have inventoried the compliance controls, list the compliance requirements. The eventual outcome will be:

1. An identification of all compliance controls

2. An identification of all compliance requirements

3. An identification of the gaps between controls and requirements

4. Suggested controls to fill the gap between existing and required, creating a uniform compliance system

# chapter 18

# The Risk Management Competency

## The CEO Gets Nervous

*The CEO had been hanging around with his other CEO buddies at a conference at the Willard-Intercontinental in Washington, D.C. He was sitting in that little outdoor area on 15th and E, slightly kitty-corner to the back of the White House, having a late breakfast and talking shop with a couple of the guys who ran the kind of companies whose only line of business was the Pentagon. Weather in DC is bearable most of the year, but this wasn't one of those times. The temperature matched the humidity, somewhere in the high 90s. So the CEO and his cronies decided to take the conversation back into the lobby. As he sat there in Peacock Alley, the CEO never failed to marvel at the fact that people like Lincoln and Grant had once checked into that hotel at that same ornate counter on the far side of the lobby.*

*The conversation was about the current **threat** situation in cyberspace. His buddies were a lot more plugged into the national **security** scene than he was and they couldn't stop telling the CEO about the various killer exploits that were running around out there on the Internet. Given what had happened three years ago, those stories were making the CEO very nervous. He was thinking to himself that there were so many different types of attacks from so many different new sources that it was hard to use "security" and "computers" in the same sentence.*

*The CEO for one of the big defense contractors summed up his own computer security strategy with a little story. "The situation in cyberspace is a lot like what you would run into if you were out hiking and you ran into a grizzly bear," he said. "For a short distance, those things are as fast as race horses, so you can't outrun them. But you'll always be safe from grizzlies as long as you can outrun whoever you're with." That provoked a round of wise chuckles from the CEO's pals, but it wasn't helping the CEO digest his breakfast any better. He got the man's point, which was just Saltzer and Schroeder's "Work factor" principle. In simple terms, it meant that as long as your company was a little more secure than the ones around it, the predators out there on the Net would feast on the other guys. The problem was that he didn't actually know what his own company's running ability looked like.*

*As soon as he finished breakfast, he summoned the CISO down to Washington, D.C. on the Acela to find out what kind of shape the company was in. The CEO met the CISO at Union Station and they walked across E Street to Bistro Bis. Over a really good French dinner, the CEO retold the CISO the stories his pals had been telling him and asked him what he thought. The CISO could hardly believe his ears, since he had been telling the CEO the same thing for the past two years, and most of what he had been saying had gone right over his head. Now, the guy sits around over breakfast with a few of his buddies, and suddenly the risks inherent in cyberspace dawn on him? Nevertheless, the CISO, whose job hinged on keeping the company out of the papers, saw this as his chance to finally make the point. So he lined up all of the potential categories for risk over a second bottle of expensive 2005 Bordeaux.*

*Basically, the CISO said, the company could count on risks that originated from three different generic sources: the technology, the company's standard operating procedures, and the people it employed. All of those categories were a source of various kinds of potential harm or loss. The technology was a constantly evolving monster, which posed so many security risks that it was impossible to even list them; however, gaps in the organization's operating procedures were also a source of theft, loss, and harm. The CISO reminded the CEO that he had to look no further than the exploit that had brought the company to its knees as evidence of that. Finally, statistically speaking the greatest threat of all was the employees. The CISO quoted some general figures he had on hand about how organizational insiders are responsible for more security violations and outright breaches than all of the other categories of harm combined. And electronic crime is the most profitable criminal enterprise there is, far exceeding the profits of the drug trade. So, the company was eventually going to get hit by somebody and it was likely to be a show-stopper.*

*Maybe it was the intimate atmosphere of Bistro Bis, with its cherry wood interior, but that little lecture caught the CEO's attention. As a result, he asked the obvious question, "What can we do about this?" The CISO said that the only way to build effective defenses against an infinite host of threats was to find out what specifically threatens the company at any point in time. That would take a robust risk identification and management process, which the company presently didn't have. The CISO proposed a broad process for risk control that would, in effect, be a collection of systematic management activities. The goal of those activities would be to identify all forms of meaningful risk, analyze each, and then deploy an effective response. Given what he had just heard from the CISO, the CEO authorized the CISO to get that capability off the ground on the spot.*

*The CISO was on the Acela back to New York City. It wasn't much of a bullet train, but at least it beat the hassle of flying out of Reagan and into LaGuardia. The Acela dropped him at Penn Station, so it was an easy subway over to the office on the E-Train. When he got up to his expensive nest on the 44th floor, he opened his well-worn copy of the EBK to see what it had to say about risk management. Fortunately, there was a management process for risk management that specified six common work functions. As they were with most of the other EBK functions, those were policy-based activities that needed to be implemented at a high level across the organization. The effect of those six activities was to ensure that the risk management process was properly planned and overseen:*

1. *Establish an IT security risk management program based on enterprise business goals and objectives*

2. *Establish the risk assessment process*

3. *Advise senior management on the impact during the decision-making process by helping them understand and evaluate the impact of IT security risks on business goals, objectives, plans, programs, and actions*

4. *Acquire and manage the resources, including financial resources, necessary to conduct an effective risk management program*

5. *Make determination on acceptance of **residual risk***

6. *Ensure that appropriate changes and improvement actions are implemented as required*

# Ensuring That Risk Management Supports Business Goals

It is somewhat ironic that information security risk management is driven by information. In effect, the risk management process gathers and uses information from all available sources in order to decrease the possibility of overall risks to information assets. That information-gathering activity is aided by a set of formal practices and technologies. A successful risk management function depends on the ability to make certain that the situational awareness that those practices and technologies underwrite directly guides the organization's substantive decision-making processes.

In addition to ensuring adequate awareness of future risk, the risk management process also makes certain that a commonly accepted and systematic set of policies and procedures is in place to handle existing risks. The primary purpose of risk management is to ensure a disciplined and systematic response to the risks that the organization considers a priority. That responsibility is operationalized through a standard set of everyday procedures. Those procedures ensure that the risk planning, analysis, response, and process management function is always directly aligned to the goals of the business operation.

## The Risk Management Plan

Risk response is organized and managed by a risk management plan, which is a high-level document that details the standard approach that will be employed to control the risks that the enterprise deems worth addressing. There might be any number of specific strategies embodied in that plan, but the plan itself is normally built around a sequence of six standard elements.

The first element is the requirement to categorize all of the organization's information systems in terms of the value they represent. This is essentially an inventorying and valuation process that should produce a priority list of systems and their contents for defense-in-depth purposes. The idea is to identify those systems that contain the most valuable data and that are at the highest degree of risk. Assigning a priority to the systems that need to be monitored for risk ensures greater protection for the important ones and maximizes the use of the organization's security resources.

18

The next step in the process is the development of an integrated set of substantive risk controls. The ideal would be to create an array of specific activities to manage existing risks to all important systems identified in the first step. These controls have to be both comprehensive in their application as well as appropriate to the situation. The controls are typically detailed in a design document, which the organization develops through a formal process. The architecture that is captured in that design document should embody a tangible set of routine electronic and process-based actions that can be evaluated for their effectiveness over time.

The third step involves the implementation of the controls, which are embodied in that architecture. In this step, the selected controls for risk management are customized to fit the specific situation they are meant to address. Those risk control activities are then embedded in day-to-day practice. The intention of the implementation step is to make the identification, analysis, and response to risk a routine part of the standard operating procedure of the business. Accordingly, risk management controls should be put into place as an integral part of the functions they support. There should also be provisions in the plan for maintaining and improving the effectiveness of risk controls over time.

The fourth step uses formal assessment methods to underwrite that requirement for continuous effectiveness over time. Prearranged tests and reviews are conducted to ensure that the risk management process as a whole is functioning as planned. In addition, targeted assessment approaches are employed to evaluate the effectiveness of individual risk control functions. These targeted assessments are typically aimed at determining whether controls are operating as intended. The ideal outcome would be the ability to confirm through observation that the steps the organization has taken to ensure proper risk management remain effective.

If it can be confirmed that the risk management process is effective, then the systems that fall under the risk management function can be certified as secure. Because the risk picture changes, that assurance is always subject to the restrictions of time and new priorities. Nevertheless, if all of the prior steps have been followed correctly and the monitoring of control functioning is sustained and accurate, then the organization can generally assume that it has an effective risk management process in place.

It should be noted that the successful execution of this process requires the involvement of senior management and technical managers, and it is also likely to be influenced by external drivers such as laws and regulations. If the organization takes the steps to ensure that the outcomes of the risk management process are properly aligned with the business goals and objectives of the organization, it is possible to have an institutionalized and systematic risk management process. With a formal function for risk management in place, senior management can then direct resources to ensure the proper level of risk management.

## Implementing a Managed Process

The steps to establish a risk management process involve five material considerations: planning, oversight, **risk analysis**, risk response, and continuous monitoring. The first consideration is implicit; all of the operational aspects of the risk management process have to be sufficiently planned. Operational planning is the essential ingredient in any kind of systematic organizational function; therefore, every step of the day-to-day practices that describe the organization's risk management approach have to be specified right down to the who, what, when, and where of execution.

A permanent oversight process is essential, once everyday risk management practices have been embedded in the organization's normal operation. The aim of that oversight process is to always stay on top of the organization's risk situation. Because it has to be continuous, the oversight process should be a standard management function that will always be able to characterize the present status of all identified risks. The oversight process should also be able to differentiate and then formally report new risks as they appear.

In order to maintain a sufficient understanding of risk, the organization has to institute a specialized risk analysis function that should be able to perform acceptable qualitative and quantitative analyses of any emerging risk event. The analysis function should also be able to carry out the analyses that are needed to ensure that currently existing risks are understood and contained. The ideal outcome of the execution of this function would be continuous assurance that risks to items that the organization considers priorities are properly understood and that any emerging risks will be identified and correctly described.

Once the analysis function has been defined and then properly staffed, it is necessary to specify the series of prescribed responses that the organization will make to the risks that currently exist. In addition to being substantive and correct, the responses should also be highly feasible and understandable. They should directly and provably target the known elements of an identified risk situation. These responses are then employed as dictated in the plan. It is important to have a pre-planned response in place for each known risk, simply because the problems associated with risk can happen quickly in cyberspace. Moreover, it is hard to decide what to do in the middle of an ongoing event. That is why a planned response, which has been tested for effectiveness and drilled into the staff, is so useful. The deployment of the response can be validated through assorted "live-fire" and hands-on drills and then updated as necessary.

The organization also has a duty to continuously monitor the operational risk environment. Constant vigilance is necessary because risks can appear at odd times and in unanticipated forms. Monitoring can be done through regular testing and reviews as well as day-to-day execution. A formal testing plan is necessary in the case of the former approach. In the case of the latter approach, front-line users are among the best sources of information about new or emerging risks. Because they use the technology in their day-to-day work, these users are often on the receiving end of the first probe or attack. It is good practice to establish a direct, easy-to-use, and clear reporting channel from the risk management function all the way down to the users in the organization. This channel can be maintained in many ways, but it is important that it be properly staffed and that the reports that come in are analyzed and acted on where appropriate.

## Risk-Handling Strategies

There are four options that can be employed in dealing with risk. The first is to accept the risk and consequent losses. The second is to avoid the loss by taking the necessary actions to eliminate the risk. A third choice is to mitigate or reduce the effect of the risk. The last option involves transferring the risk to another party through contracts, insurance, or a variety of similar mechanisms. No matter what approach is used, the organization has to adopt a formal strategy to address each of its priority risks. The decision about what to do about the risk is purely in the domain of the designated decision maker.

Accepting risk and the consequent losses is probably the most common approach, because many risks pass through the risk management function unidentified, or unacknowledged. It

**18**

is common practice to accept risks that occur rarely, or where there is little harm. In these cases, the cost of addressing the risk would not justify the potential cost of the harm. The decision to accept a risk can also change as the risk situation changes. Risks that have been accepted are sometimes called residual risks, because the potential for harm exists, even though the present harm from the risk has been judged to be acceptable. Residual risks are still identified and tracked through the risk analysis process.

Risk avoidance is aimed at preventing the risk from actually occurring. Information security has three standard components: prevention, detection, and response. The prevention element and all it involves are examples of risk avoidance. Training programs, which are designed to increase employee ability to recognize and respond to incidents, are good examples of this type of risk-handling approach. Because the least amount of harm will happen by having measures on hand to address the risk when it occurs, the formal information security process is heavily geared toward avoidance.

The last two components of the information security process, detection and response, are embodied in the **risk mitigation** and risk transference approaches. In the case of risk transference, the response requires an outside party to assume the consequences of the risk. Insurance is a prime example of this type of assumption. Obtaining insurance against specific risks does not prevent the risk from occurring, but it provides financial reimbursement to make up for a loss that will occur. Risk transfers work well when the risk is associated with a financial loss. They are less effective when the loss is associated with less tangible things, such as customer service/retention, organization reputation, or, in some cases, regulatory requirements.

Risk mitigation approaches are those steps that are taken to minimize the potential loss in the event of the occurrence of a risk. For instance, an intrusion detection system will not prevent someone from actually intruding on the network. Instead, these systems function as "burglar alarms" to limit the time that an intruder is allowed to roam undetected through a network. The limitation of time will not prevent damage, but it is meant to restrict the damage that might occur.

## Setting Up the Risk Management Planning Process

The risk management plan dictates the risk management process. The primary role of the risk management plan is to create the framework for the detailed policies and procedures that will comprise the risk management process for that particular organization. The top-level risk management plan provides the general guidance that is needed to ensure that the organization's overall business objectives and goals are understood and then factored correctly into the decisions that are made about risk.

The overall plan for risk management needs to be crafted in broad, organizational terms, with the specific details of the approaches to be adopted left to lower-level operational plans. It is important that this high-level document define the comprehensive processes and interrelationships needed to build a complete picture of the organizational risk situation. The ideal would be to create a roadmap that will let executive managers develop the strategies they will need to address existing risks.

First, the risk management plan should document the roles and responsibilities of the risk management team. The assignment of responsibility should be stated at a high enough level to allow the people on the risk management team to respond flexibly to situations covered in the plan. At the same time, the plan has to assign specific authority to the team to act on those situations that are the responsibility of the risk management process. The assignment of high-level roles and responsibilities also ensures that the routine supervisory and budgetary authority, which is needed to conduct the process as a normal part of doing business, is expressly assigned to the individual members of the team.

Finally, the concepts associated with risk management have to be defined in clear, organizational, specific terms. That definition is necessary in order to align the organization's overall security objectives with its business objectives. A comprehensive and detailed definition of key terms has to be provided as part of the planning set-up process. The purpose of those definitions is to ensure a common vocabulary. Definitions are important because most people's understanding of what constitutes risk is subjective. Consequently, the organization has to provide a precise specification of what constitutes a risk, the levels of **acceptable risk**, and the attendant approaches that will be used to address each risk. Specific directives for how to report risks and the thresholds for acting on risk reports also have to be pre-established for the various risk elements. Those reporting requirements will also apply to active, residual, and accepted risks.

The aim of risk management is to create a comprehensive catalog of all of the risks that are in the organization's particular risk environment. That catalog provides an all-inclusive record of the organization's assets, a statement of the acceptable levels of risk for each asset, and the constraints that will be placed on the protection of the asset by the technology or policies. The outcome of the risk cataloging process is an alignment of the policies that will be used for risk management with the business goals of the organization.

That alignment is needed to enable the tradeoff process. Tradeoffs will be used to decide the risk acceptance, risk avoidance, risk transference, or risk mitigation approach that will be used to ensure each asset against risk, as shown in Figure 18-1. Those tradeoffs have to appropriately reflect the organization's business objectives. An analysis of the priority of the information that enables those business objectives versus the risks that threaten that information is necessary in order to decide where to invest the organization's security resources. Defining **risk levels** needs to be done with respect to their impact on the confidentiality, integrity, and availability of the data in the organization's operational systems.

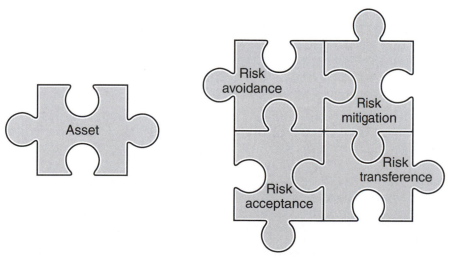

**Figure 18-1** The tradeoff

**18**

# The CISO Designs a Castle

*It was three weeks later, and the CISO could see that the risk management planning effort was going to be tougher than he had anticipated; there were far too many risks and there were way too few resources to adequately deal with them. Although that had seemed pretty obvious from the beginning, it was still a little discouraging to compare likely risks to the budget to manage them and come out with the balance so far overdrawn. The CISO decided to undertake a little expedition up to the CEO's office to see what the guy wanted to do about that situation. The CISO was formulating his strategy as he approached the huge glass wall of the CEO's outer office, which was at the top of the wide marble stairs. He was also wondering to himself whether the effect that created, which left anybody entering the CEO's domain with the impression that he was entering the pearly gates, was actually intended or not. The CISO was planning to transfer the monkey to the CEOs back: either fund more risk control or provide the CISO with a statement that the company did not choose to protect a specified set of items. Either way, the CISO knew he was covered.*

*The CISO had made it a point to cultivate the CEO's personal secretary with theater tickets for her grandson, since that gave him almost immediate access to the CEO whenever he needed it. In this particular case, she told him that the CEO was at lunch at Yasuda over on 43rd. That was a relatively short walk, and it gave him some more time to think through what he was going to tell the CEO. The CISO was well aware that it would be hazardous to his career if the CEO thought that he was trying to hold him for ransom. On the other hand, the CISO was painfully aware of just how exposed the company was without a lot more risk control. That would be a potential career-ender too. As he slid into a seat next to the CEO at the bamboo sushi bar, he had his speech memorized.*

*He told the CEO that they couldn't cover every risk, no matter how much money the company wanted to invest. They would have to prioritize their risk management process. He tried an analogy that he thought was nicely tuned to the Shogun atmosphere of the place. He explained that they were faced with a classic defense-in-depth problem that was going to demand some priorities. They could obviously ensure the emperor's safety if they locked him up in the castle, but the nobles were going to have a problem, since they would be left with fewer guards and lower walls. The residents of the town would have an even bigger problem, since all they could afford would be a few spears and a wooden wall. Finally, the peasants out there in the fields were going to be left to the mercy of the Mongols, since there were no resources available to defend them. The problem the CEO faced was deciding which one of the company's functions ended up in which group.*

*The CISO made a point of explaining why the company's executive leadership had to make that decision. They were the only people who could enforce it, and there were probably going to be a lot of functional managers who would not appreciate being "left for dead" out there in the fields. A strong hand would ensure that the prioritization process didn't turn into an outright civil war. The CEO could see the CISO's point; turf wars were a fact of life in any big company. But nobody in management would willingly let his area get kicked out of the protection scheme, since that would openly label it as unimportant. As a result, the CISO was going to need help implementing any scheme that would involve prioritization across functions.*

*The CEO was willing to make the commitment over his California rolls as long as the CISO gave him a workable plan. That sort of challenge was exactly what the CISO was looking for, since it would give him one more chance to show off his superior strategic planning skills. As he and the CEO parted company, he hustled back to his office to get the conceptualizing started. Fortunately, the EBK had a design perspective that specified the following five common work functions for risk management design:*

1. *Specify risk-based information security requirements and a security concept of operations*

2. *Develop policies, processes, and procedures for identifying, assessing, and mitigating risks to information assets, personnel, facilities, and equipment*

3. *Develop processes and procedures for determining the costs and benefits of risk mitigation strategies*

4. *Develop procedures for documenting the decision to apply mitigation strategies or acceptance of risk*

5. *Develop and maintain risk-based security policies, plans, and procedures based on security requirements and in accordance with standards, procedures, directives, policies, regulations, and laws (statutes)*

*These management and technical activities were mainly oriented toward the development of a coherent set of security controls.*

# The Coordinated Approach to Risk Management

Risk management juggles three generic factors: those risks associated with the information system, the business functions that are associated with the information in that system, and the extent of control necessary to manage those risks. The key to success lies in deploying the minimum number of controls to achieve a desired level of IT security, given the purposes of the affected business functions.

The risk management process can be carried out in two different ways. The most common way of doing risk management is ad-hoc, where **security controls** are created to fulfill specific security requirements as the need is identified. Many organizations use an ad-hoc approach to risk management simply because the deployment of a coordinated set of controls is a time-consuming undertaking. The ad-hoc approach is cost-efficient on a day-to-day basis, because it only creates controls that are needed at the time. Unfortunately, it is almost certain to result in flawed protection, because the organization is reacting to events rather than deploying a coherent defense.

The other approach to risk management is the coordinated approach. Because it is meant to provide comprehensive protection, this approach offers better security; it deploys a series of protection baselines in a defense-in-depth scheme. Those protection baselines are composed of a logical set of increasingly rigorous technical and behavioral controls. In most baselines the electronic controls are automated, while the behavioral controls entail a series of human-centered actions which are intended to produce a desired outcome. Each baseline is deployed to achieve specific security requirements, which are prioritized in terms of the criticality of the data.

Still, the creation, deployment, and on-going monitoring of the baselines is both time-consuming and costly. The degree of security justified under this scheme always has to be balanced against the level of effort and cost that is required to implement it. The aim of the coordinated approach is to identify the priority risks to the organization and then create and

18

maintain an effective array of controls to manage those risks. Because cost is a factor, a precise specification of the maximum degree of acceptable risk is necessary in order to ensure a realistic plan. Much of real-world planning typically involves deciding what level of risk the organization is willing to accept.

A decision about the degree of acceptable risk will lead to an assignment of priorities. Understanding the value of an item enables a decision about its priority, which, in turn, drives decisions about the practical form of the response. That value is typically expressed as the level of acceptability of the risk. Acceptability can be expressed in operational terms like, "Spend whatever it takes to ensure that this risk does not occur," all the way down to, "The harm the risk would cause does not justify the cost of addressing it." In order to decide about that level of risk, the decision maker must first know the value of the information the organization possesses.

Since decisions about the acceptability of risk lead directly to a coordinated security response, the risk management process always establishes a substantive, usually resource-based, link between each risk and the benefits of managing it. Operational factors that enter into that analysis of risk acceptance include such questions as, "What is the level of criticality of each particular information asset and what is the specific degree of resource involvement?" At a minimum, risk evaluations must answer one key question: "What is the tradeoff between accepting the risk and the harm it can cause?"

## Risk Management Planning and Risk Assessments

The overall purpose of the risk management function is to maintain an appropriate set of risk controls. Risk assessments are a particularly critical part of that overall purpose, because all control sets have to be periodically assessed to ensure that their protection is relevant and maintains its effectiveness.

Risk assessments are important because they identify the specific threats to the organization, how likely those threats are to occur, and the consequences of each threat should it happen. Because knowing where risks lie is a fundamental precondition for managing them, the term "risk assessment" is sometimes confused with "risk management." Knowing the likelihood and impact of each potential threat is an essential precondition; however, risk assessment is a tool that supports the larger risk management function, rather than an end in itself.

Risk assessments underwrite the strategy that is used to organize the risk management process, and they let managers deploy the specific reactive controls to respond to a risk. These assessments also monitor the effectiveness of those controls once they have been put in place. This ensures effective and up-to-date knowledge about the threat situation. Risk assessment precedes the implementation of the risk management function; a systematic risk assessment can direct the prioritization of the controls that the organization will then plan and install to do risk management. That targeted knowledge ensures the most efficient use of security resources. Risk assessment is an information-gathering activity that focuses on understanding the nature of all feasible risks. The risk assessment process identifies and evaluates each relevant risk, determines that risk's potential impact, and itemizes the controls that will be needed to respond properly.

Risk assessments should always answer two distinct but related questions. The first is, "What is the certainty of the risk?" The answer to that question is typically expressed as likelihood of occurrence. The second is, "What is the anticipated impact?" The answer to that question is normally expressed as an estimate of the loss, harm, failure, or danger. Ideally, both of these questions can be answered in easily understood terms. Understandability and credibility are key factors because the results of the risk assessment will guide the deployment and subsequent conduct of the risk management process.

## Conducting a Risk Assessment in Support of Planning

All risk assessments provide two specific pieces of knowledge: the probability of occurrence and the estimate of the consequences. There is a logical order to how these two issues should be approached. The first consideration has to be likelihood, since a highly unlikely event might not be worth the cost of further consideration; however, it is the estimate of the consequences that truly shapes the form of the response. There is never enough money to secure against every conceivable risk, so the potential harm that each risk represents always has to be balanced against the likelihood of its occurrence.

For this reason, the fundamental goal of the risk assessment process is to maximize the effectiveness of the operational deployment of security controls. It accomplishes that purpose by identifying those risks that have the greatest probability of occurrence and that will cause the greatest degree of harm. The options these represent are then arrayed in descending order of priority and addressed based on the resources that are available. Since all of the decisions about the tangible form of the risk management process will depend on getting the order of those priorities absolutely correct, it is easy to see why a rigorous and accurate risk assessment process is so critical to the overall success of any security system.

Risk assessments are always built around tangible evidence that is obtained by conducting interviews, documenting observations of both organizational and human behavior, auditing system logs, and examining any other form of relevant technical or managerial record. Because the sources of data about risk are diverse, the collection process has to be systematic and coordinated; every risk assessment should embody a commonly accepted and repeatable methodology which will produce concrete evidence that can be independently verified.

The gathering, compilation, analysis, and verification of data about risk can be time-consuming and resource-intensive. In order to ensure the effectiveness and accuracy of any particular risk assessment, the practical scope of the inquiry has to be precisely defined and should be limited to a particular problem.

Risk assessments typically target the various standard areas of threat: electronic, human, and physical. The insight gained from each assessment is then aggregated into a single, comprehensive understanding of the total threat picture, which serves as the basis for deciding how each threat will be addressed. It is perfectly acceptable to approach the understanding of risk in a highly focused and compartmentalized fashion, as long as the organization understands that the results of any particular risk assessment characterize only a part of the situation. The need to paint a detailed and accurate picture of all conceivable threats almost always implies a series of targeted, highly integrated risk assessments that take place over a defined period of time.

## Designing for Effective Risk Management

Every risk management process has to be designed to fit its particular environment and the overall operating circumstances of the organization. Accordingly, the design should describe

**18**

all technical and environmental factors that might impact the risk management process; the design has to ensure that the process is correctly aligned with the environmental, sensitivity, and security requirements of the context that the organization functions in. That is because organizational context will dictate the risk management model. For instance, there will be a different set of risk management procedures where the context demands rigorous approaches, versus one where the context is more relaxed. As a result, the context in which the process operates has to be clearly understood in order to design a proper risk management approach.

Once the context is understood, the scope or area of coverage of the actual assurance has to be defined. That definition should be the result of a formal planning exercise, because tangible organizational resources are involved. The failure to define an accurate and realistic scope for the risk management process could result in deficient protection and wasted resources, so distinctive and meaningful boundaries have to be established for the risk management process. In particular, logical interrelationships have to be understood between components, since the dependencies between the various elements that fall under the risk management process have to be factored into the assurance process. Scope is always tied to the actual resources available, so understanding which components will be a part of the risk management process and their actual interdependencies will allow the organization to be more realistic about what it will be able to protect.

**Definition of Roles and Responsibilities** The definition of roles and responsibilities is a critical step in designing the risk management function, since that definition ties personnel and financial resources to the activities that will be performed. It is also important to clarify the duties that are associated with each of those roles. Otherwise, participants are likely to bring to the party their own assumptions about what they are supposed to do, which could result in important activities falling through the cracks.

Roles and responsibilities are assigned by designating accountability for performance of each security activity as well as all of the organizational reporting lines that are associated with each role. If third parties or contractors are responsible for any aspect of risk management, the responsibilities and reporting lines of both the contractor and the organizational unit must be clearly defined.

**Definition of Priorities** In addition to identifying and relating the various resource elements, each of these elements has to be categorized in terms of general priority. Because priority is directly related to the criticality of the resource, it is essential to know the priority of each component in order to decide about the scope of resources to commit to its protection.

The determination of priority is based on a simple understanding of the purpose of each element. In addition to conveying the general importance of the element in the overall operating environment, the description of purpose satisfies two practical goals. First, it allows managers to make informed assignments of priorities for the protected components. Second, it allows managers to coordinate the implementation and subsequent execution of the cybersecurity functions that are assigned to each component.

**Sensitivity of the Information Versus Rigor of the Controls** It is essential to specify the sensitivity of each item of information within the system, because the sensitivity determines the levels of confidentiality, integrity, and availability required. This specification provides the necessary basis for determining the extent and rigor of the controls.

The specification also forms the basis for designing the controls that will be used to secure each component. Specification should not just be guided by a consideration of technical standards and protocols; at the very least, it should also consider the policies, laws, and any relevant constraints that might affect the confidentiality, integrity, or availability of information within the system.

The outcome of that specification should be a detailed statement about how the particular assurance requirement will be addressed by a particular control. In addition, the recommendation for each control should provide a justification for why that approach was taken. The aim of that justification is to explain the type and relative importance of the protection needed. Each type of data and information processed by the system should be classified based on the severity of potential negative impacts on the organization and the degree to which the ability of the organization to perform its mission would be affected, should the information be compromised.

The sensitivity of information should be characterized based on the risks a compromise would represent. The highest risk would be associated with compromises that would adversely impact critical information, or which might result in loss of life, significant financial loss, threats to national security, or the inability of the organization to perform its primary mission.

Moderate risks would be those risks that might not compromise critical information but where the losses would still have business impacts. Low risk items would be those risks where information might be lost but it would not be vital to organizational functioning.

## Risk Management Controls

The controls for risk management will always differ in their purpose and specificity. It is important to keep this difference in mind when designing and assigning control processes, because the people who will actually be executing each control have to know exactly how to perform all of the tasks that are required to make the control effective. Consequently, it is important to ensure that managers are not asked to perform highly technical tasks, just as it is equally critical that technical people are not asked to perform managerial duties. In both cases there is potential that the activities that underlie the control will either be misunderstood or misapplied.

It is also important to understand the operational status of the control. Knowing the present operational status of the control is important in the design process because many controls will already exist in the present scheme while others will not be in place. It is essential to have a complete understanding of where a procedure has already been implemented and where it has to be developed. This understanding is based on whether each necessary control item is operational and effective, or planned but not actually operational.

It is also common to have part of the control in place while other parts are still missing. If some parts of the control are implemented and others have been planned, there should be an explicit specification of the parts of the control that are in place and the parts that are not. Where there are planned measures, this description should also include a list of resources required to make them operational and the expected date.

Finally, situations will exist where controls would be desirable but it would neither be cost-effective nor feasible to implement them. If that is the case, then those controls should be noted for future planning as well as potential long-term monitoring of the risk that the measure was meant to manage.

**Control Types: Management Controls** Management controls are behavioral; they are based on policies and implement the organization's risk management procedures. They also manage risks through human-based actions rather than technology. These controls are typically designed based on a risk analysis, which should support a comparison between the costs of the applicable controls and the value of the information resource they are designed to protect. Management controls are always deployed based on the impact of the threats that they have been designed to address. It is important to design the appropriate administrative, physical, and personnel security controls into the risk management process from its inception. Because risks come in a number of forms, there can be an extensive range and variety of risk management controls.

Because these controls are primarily enforced by the testing and review process, the design must ensure that tests are performed during the development of the risk management process. The aim of the evaluations is to confirm that all of the necessary controls are an established part of the risk management process.

**Control Types: Technical Controls** Just as with the management process, the technical controls should also be well defined, understood, and followed. From a risk management standpoint, the most obvious technical controls are those that underlie the access control system. Technical controls are important and should be monitored closely.

The monitoring of technical controls is an essential aspect of management accountability as well as a technical issue. Consequently, the monitoring of technical controls from a managerial standpoint is often associated with audit procedures. A complete audit trail and a chronological record are evidence of adequate monitoring. The use of system log files is an example of this type of control.

# Implementing Risk Management

*The design process had proven something that the CISO had suspected about the information security process, but had never been able to confirm: the actual implementation of an effective set of security controls is at an organizational level that is far lower-level and more granular than most people thought. Thus his finished design was modular in the sense that it created small, well-defined, secure spaces with a high degree of boundary integrity. The design also enforced defense-in-depth, since those spaces were controlled in increasingly rigorous fashion. Finally, the security system that the design created was unmistakably cost-efficient because the priority areas that were identified by stakeholders were secured by security resources in a progressive fashion, from most vital to least important.*

*As a result, the CISO was eager to show off his handiwork to the CEO and the board. The architecture that the design entailed was a tangible thing, in the sense that the secure areas and their controls could be demonstrated in concrete terms right there on the smart-board in the conference room. The visuals that were produced on the company's organization chart* made the idea of implementation an easy sell. At the CISO's request, the board gave the mandate to implement the necessary change to the CEO, who was not exactly thrilled to have that particular ball handed to him. He was pretty sure that the implementation part of the process was going to create a knotty political problem indeed. Still, the CEO was the only person in the room with the clout to enforce the degree of change that was going to be required. He took on that responsibility with good grace while the board was in the room.

It was a different matter as soon as the board had filed out of the room. The CEO went over to the 15-foot-high mahogany door and made sure that it was shut. Then he turned to the CISO and made it plain in no uncertain terms that failure was not an option. To underscore that, he laid out a couple of carrots and one big, fat stick. First, the CEO was ready to spend whatever it took to ensure that the controls were implemented without a hitch. He added that the CISO had a free pass in terms of whatever authority he needed to enforce the change. Then the CEO, who was given to colorful language, made it abundantly clear that he did not want political problems from the functional managers across the company. More important, he did not want any complaints about the process to make it outside of the organization or to the board.

The CISO was well aware of what the second statement meant in terms of his continuing position with the business, so as soon as he got back to his office he began to form the implementation team. The first person he called was the Jacksonville security engineer, whose expertise in organizational process development was clearly needed. He also got in touch with the Corvallis security engineer, since he knew the guy understood customization. He had to promise the Corvallis security engineer that he could run the west coast operation from up there in the piney woods and never set foot in New York; once he did that, the guy was enthusiastically on board. Finally, he added the Singapore security engineer, who also understood the CISO's customization concepts. He could see from the design that the implementation process was going to take a lot of work at the local level, and he wanted the first rollouts to be in places where they had already successfully tailored the general security controls to their culture and operation.

The Jacksonville security engineer was the lead for that group, under the CISO's general supervision. She welcomed the challenge, since the implementation of the risk control set for any given facility was clearly going to be more of a management problem than it would be a technical one. That was what she was good at; she understood organizational development concepts. As usual, she also had the EBK to back her up, so she turned to it to lay out a general process. The EBK specifies the following four implementation functions for risk management:

1. Apply controls in support of the risk management program

2. Provide input to policies, plans, procedures, and technologies to balance the level of risk associated with benefits provided by mitigating controls

3. Implement threat and vulnerability assessments to identify security risks, and regularly update applicable security controls

4. Identify risk/functionality tradeoffs, and work with stakeholders to ensure that risk management implementation is consistent with desired organizational risk posture

These were the usual mix of management and technical activities, whose general aim was to ensure that the risk management function was embedded as part of the ongoing operation of the organization.

18

# Targeting the Security Controls

Risks represent a threat to some aspect of organizational functioning, and the management of risk is a complex process with lots of inherent detail. In order to implement the risk management process correctly, it is necessary to classify and understand the nature of the risks that are present in the organization's current operating environment. In general, risks can be classified into two categories: unknown and known. Unknown risks, also known as asymmetric risks, are not predictable and are not subject to management by standard risk management methods. Because of their unpredictability, they do not lend themselves to specific techniques for analysis. Known risks are those that should be logically expected to occur. Another name for known risk is intrinsic risks. In many cases, the probability of occurrence and subsequent impact of an intrinsic risk can be estimated. These risks can be managed and minimized by an effective risk management program.

The organization has to adopt and then follow some kind of structured process to identify, classify, and provide a meaningful response to the intrinsic risks that fall within the scope of the risk management process. Risk breakdown structures typically provide the needed organization and can be employed to systematize and coordinate the risk identification, analysis, and planning activities of a comprehensive risk management program. Risk breakdown structures classify areas of intrinsic risk into three standard categories: management, operational, and technical. Using these categories in some form of checklist, managers can systematically work their way through a practical risk management situation and evaluate the status of each of the standard risk items on the list.

The management category encompasses all of the potential risks to the organization's information assets or documentation. It also includes any of the risks that are associated with the assignment of roles and responsibilities and the risks represented by a failure to do proper contingency or configuration management planning. These are large areas of organizational functioning, so their analysis requires extensive coordination. Because of the sheer scope of each of these areas, the analysis process usually requires a large number of participants. Managers can use a risk breakdown checklist as a roadmap to guide the deployment of resources and evaluate the threat potential of each of the risks in each of these categories. In addition, managers can use the checklist to organize the raw data from each of these areas into logical categories for analysis once that data has been obtained.

The second category includes all of the operational risks, which are much more focused and detailed. Operational risks involve failures in the operational security activities that the organization carries out, such as: identifying management; identification and authentication processes; auditing; malicious code protection; and long-term system maintenance and communications security. These areas require the coordination of complex managerial and technical activities, so the analysis has to be detailed and closely controlled. A risk management checklist allows managers to both coordinate the data collection effort as well as aggregate the huge amount of data that is normally collected into a description of the risk to the operation of the organization.

Finally, there are the risks that are associated with the technical controls, including the predictable risks to electronic systems; however, they also include any electronic controls over media and the physical and personnel security environment. The technical risk category even includes risks that reside in the security education, training and awareness function. Because of their diversity and inherent complexity, every technical risk area has to be well defined in order to be properly analyzed. A checklist of categories for analysis provides the necessary structure. It ensures that the right data is captured for each category and that the eventual analysis is appropriate.

## Modeling Risks for Prioritization

The entities that comprise an organization, their relationships to each other, and the potential actions that could adversely impact them can be modeled using a formal modeling technique. An exact understanding can be derived from the application of such a method and will let the organization describe in graphic terms the things that threaten it, what those threats are likely to impact, and their likelihood of occurrence. That understanding can then facilitate the development of precisely targeted controls for each threat.

**Threat modeling** is a structured method that is used to analyze risk-related data. A successful threat modeling process requires a lot of creative thinking every conceivable threat should be put on the table and assessed. Threat modeling allows risk data to be modeled and subsequently communicated among team members. The major steps of threat modeling begin with a determination of the scope of protected space that the model corresponds to. The threats that might impact the components of that space are enumerated and specific details as to the potential likelihood and impact of the threat are collected.

In order to ensure that the analysis is comprehensive, data flow diagrams or similar information flow diagrams, such as UML-based use-case diagrams, are employed to help visualize and describe the target space. Those diagrams will help to ensure inclusive coverage. Descriptions of potential attack vectors and the impacts of each of those vectors on the protected space are used to think through and then describe the actual attack behavior. It should be possible to describe all potential attack vectors. Those should then be examined and understood from an adversary's point of view.

Once the threats are characterized, they are entered into a database that contains the detailed information about every attack depicted in the threat model. The implications of each threat then have to be analyzed and are typically based on assigning a criticality score. A standardized criticality score is an important part of the threat modeling process, because it allows analysts to classify each identified threat in terms of its likelihood and potential harm. Classification can then lead to a priority ordering of known threats from most dangerous to least dangerous. The ordering will allow management to concentrate resources on the threats that have the greatest potential for harm. It will also let managers assign fewer resources to lower priority threats. This classification process allows managers to build logical and substantive defense-in-depth schemes.

A focus on priority differs from the typical low-hanging fruit approach. Nevertheless, the implementation process has to be based on some kind of quantitative or rational method for assigning priorities. Without priorities to guide the implementation, it is likely that the easiest to understand or most obvious threats will be addressed first. That approach would disregard the business value of what was being protected. Given the requirement for thorough understanding in order to assign practical priorities, it is important to have a commonly agreed-on starting point to base the comparisons. That is the role of threat modeling, which goes a long way toward putting implementation on a quantitative and systematic footing.

## Measuring the Risk Management Process

Measurement is an important element of good management practice; it tells decision makers whether or not their objectives are being achieved, whether their results are in line with expectations, or even whether a process is under control. Risk management is no different than any other management program in that regard. Good risk management requires appropriate measures that reflect the security situation of the organization. Proper measurement relies on the availability of meaningful standard measures.

Qualitative and quantitative methods can both be used for risk analysis. Both allow the organization to prioritize its risks and responses, and both assume that risks can be analyzed and that that analysis can be used to manage risk. Qualitative methods do not attempt to produce actual metrics; instead, they focus on relative differences. Graphic scales are commonly used in qualitative analysis. Numbers may also be used, but they typically serve as proxies for comparison purposes, not actual representative quantities. The end result of a qualitative risk assessment is a matrix that differentiates between different relative levels of value.

In qualitative risk analysis, the measures that are used are typically a set of nominal values such as high, medium, and low. These categories are then given numbers so that the weights of relationships can be characterized. Using those nominal values, it is possible to distinguish between items receiving a score of high and those receiving a score of medium, for instance. Since it is not possible to truly rank different elements of the same class, the actual measurement itself is not precise. Nevertheless, since one of the main purposes of the risk analysis function is to determine priorities, qualitative analysis can be useful.

Quantitative analysis methods also exist if there is a need for more exact understanding of the problem. The value of quantitative methods depends on the quality of the data being used. For instance, in the case of an actuarial estimate, hard evidence, like the accuracy of records of birth and death, and the causes of injury and loss, coupled with other factors, can be used to build predictive mathematical models. These models can be studied by analysts, and the results from previous time periods can be compared to current results. In the case of risk management, accurate and reliable measures are difficult, if not impossible, to obtain. Furthermore, the changing nature of the IT environment will restrict the application of time studies. For this reason, a blend of both quantitative and qualitative measures is often used to arrive at the desired understanding.

Automated tools are frequently used to assist in the collection of risk measurement data because in most instances, risk management activities generate a lot of data. These automated tools can collect, filter, and condense large quantities of data into relevant data sets. They also ensure accuracy because they are not subject to fatigue or human error, and they can carry out activities such as pattern matching recognition in large data sets at machine speeds.

# The CISO and His Team Go All-In

*The CISO was sitting around with his task team leaders in the executive lounge on the 44th floor. He particularly liked to have meetings in that room because the wood paneling and regular floor lamps made the place a lot more relaxing than the rest of that floor's super-modern, new-money décor. Plus, it had the same kind of services as a Starbucks, so you could get a decent Café Misto from the nice white-coated old man who shuffled around the place waiting on people. The CISO was going over the process and the schematics of the risk controls that the task team had planned to implement, and he was extremely pleased. He could see that the process was guaranteed to get everybody's input, while at the same time it would produce a minimally intrusive set of controls that could be customized to slip as discreetly as possible into the standard operation at each site.*

*He went around the table, one at a time, to get each individual's thoughts about whether to take their presentation to the board that day, or wait until things had been refined. The Jacksonville security engineer spoke up first. She was by far the most experienced member of the group in the area of strategic organizational development. From her standpoint, she thought that the way that the general risk management process was localized to each setting, through the customization process, made the actual implementation of the process at each site as precisely focused on local problems as you could get.*

*The Corvallis security engineer agreed with her. In his mind, involving the people at each site in the design of the day-to-day controls ensured buy-in across the board from the conventional workforce. More important, his idea of having an entire local committee, including the blue-collar tech workers, evaluate and approve the design ensured that nothing would fall through the cracks.*

*Finally, the Singapore security engineer, who had just stepped off a bruising 20-hour flight from the Far East, added his input. Through all of his jet lag, the Singapore security engineer assured everybody that he had undertaken the entire process, from threat model to detailed control design, and he was certain that they had a workable routine risk management function established at his site, even if all of the risk management practices in the procedure manual were written in both English and Mandarin.*

*The CISO made up his mind to go "all-in" with the board that morning and roll out the plan. For a change, he was willing to share the credit with the entire team, mainly because they had earned it. He was also being generous because he still had one more little chore for them to do, which was to gather the substantive proof that they had a winning approach. The Jacksonville security engineer was put in charge of that process, mainly because she was the one who understood the EBK best from a business perspective. She knew that the EBK specified five high-level functions for the evaluation of the risk management process. She also knew that, like most of the rest of the EBK recommendations, these are managerial activities whose main purpose is to keep the risk management function sustainable.*

*One of security's most important principles is the rule that all processes will degrade over time. Threats change and adversaries improve in ability, with the result being greater risk challenges. In that respect, the evaluate function is designed to ensure that the risk management process also improves over time. The functions that the EBK specifies for evaluation are:*

1. *Assess effectiveness of the risk management program, and implement changes where required*

2. *Review the performance of, and provide recommendations for, risk management (e.g., security controls as well as policies/procedures that make up risk management program) tools and techniques*

3. *Assess residual risk in the information infrastructure used by the organization*

4.  *Assess the results of threat and vulnerability assessments to identify security risks, and regularly update applicable security controls*

5.  *Identify changes to risk management policies and processes that will enable them to remain current with the emerging risk and threat environment*

# Risk Management and Operational Evaluation of Change

Because the business environment is constantly changing, it is necessary to do continuing operational assessments of the risk situation in order to assure the validity of the risk management strategy. Operational risk assessments are established by a plan that has to be aligned with business goals and their accompanying strategies. The outcome of the planning process must be a relevant response to the current risk picture, within business constraints.

All plans for any form of risk management should be based on consistent, standard data, because management will use that data to make decisions about the degree of risk exposure, as well as the types of controls that will have to be deployed. Accordingly, all of the metrics included in the risk evaluation process must be unambiguously defined in the plan. Those definitions can then be used to ensure that the data from the assessment process is consistent.

Consistency is a critical factor; because stakeholders have to share a common understanding of the precise nature of the threats the organization faces in order to deploy an appropriate and trustworthy response. It is important to make certain that there is reliable understanding of what a given piece of information means. If the various people who are involved in the risk management process interpret the information differently, there is a potential for uncoordinated and ineffective operational responses. There is also the issue of credibility when it comes to the data itself: if there is no clear definition provided to function as the basis for measurement, then it is hard for decision makers to rely on the data.

The activities that are involved in operational assessment are planned and implemented in the same way as other types of organizational assessment activities. The operational risk assessment process employs risk evaluations to decide about the nature of emerging threats.

Rather than producing an overall risk management strategy, the goal of the operational risk assessment is to say with certainty that the currently deployed set of controls properly addresses the right threats. The assessment also seeks to prove that those controls continue to be effective given the overall aims of the business.

If the controls that are currently deployed do not address the aims of the business, then the operational risk assessment should provide the information necessary to allow decision makers to implement changes that achieve the desired state. Any review report that contains recommendations for change is typically passed along to the people who are responsible for maintaining the risk management process, instead of the top-level planners who initially formulated the response. The aim of that report is to provide explicit advice about changes that must be made to the current risk management process.

Planning for operational risk assessments involves the establishment of a standard schedule for each evaluation, as well as a defined process for problem reporting and corrective action. The routine nature of these reviews means that the organization should treat operational risk assessment exactly as it would any other continuous organizational process. It should be resourced and staffed to ensure that it functions as a part of the everyday business operation. Operational risk assessment does not typically entail the sort of strategic focus that was involved in the formulation of the security strategy. Instead, it makes use of a defined set of performance criteria to evaluate the performance of the routine operation of the risk management function.

Those criteria are typically laid down during the formulation of the initial risk management strategy. Every risk control that is deployed should have an explicit set of standard criteria built into its specification. These criteria should be both measurable and capable of being recorded in some meaningful fashion. In addition, the assumptions about cost and occurrence that were part of the original decision to deploy each control should also be stated as a means of maintaining perspective on the operational intent of that control. Standard performance criteria allow decision makers to judge whether that control is performing as desired and whether it is continuing to achieve its intended purpose. The organization will use the data produced by the operational assessment process to ensure the effectiveness of its risk management scheme.

## Evaluating the Overall Guidance

The real proof of a risk management program's success lies in the execution of the policies and procedures for risk. The test is whether those policies and procedures have achieved the desired business outcomes. Security assessments and evaluations can be used to verify that policies and procedures are functioning as designed, and assessments can produce evidence that those policies and procedures are effectively controlling risk. Actual operational assessment of risk management plans is done in a multi-phase process involving assessments, evaluations, and red team exercises.

The assessment process is mainly a "paper drill" designed to verify through interviews and records checks that policies and procedures have successfully covered the essential elements of risk management. There is no hands-on testing in an assessment, since it focuses at the policy/procedural level. An assessment is an examination of a set of policies and procedures, along with records associated with the operation of those policies and procedures over time, which evaluates whether the organization is actually operating as planned. The assessment also attempts to characterize the effectiveness of each procedure based on the historical data that is recorded about its execution.

An evaluation is similar to an assessment in that it too seeks to comprehensively examine the effectiveness of a risk management system; however, evaluations add a series of planned tests of the actual functioning of the process in order to confirm that features are functioning as they were designed to so. Both assessments and evaluations are designed to cover the entire breadth of the business.

Assessments and evaluations are general in focus and comprehensive; they do not go into sufficient depth to be able to address a particular focused target. As the scope of an evaluation narrows, it is possible to deepen the specific analysis at strategic points, which is the basis for a final technique known as a red team approach. This is often used to perform deeper dives into a particular aspect of risk management. A red team approach, which is sometimes also known as pen-testing, assesses the actual performance of a security control in the operational environment. Although it is narrow in scope, it is designed to probe deeply enough to assess the actual effectiveness of a control against a specific type of attack. The aim of a red team approach is to accurately judge the effectiveness of a particular control. These are time-consuming, resource-intensive exercises, because they rely heavily on skilled operators who attempt to violate the security in such a manner as to mimic real-world attacks.

## Program Management Review

Periodic reviews are necessary for any program, because they ensure that it is still meeting the objectives established by management. Risk management programs are no different. One of the important elements of the risk management process is to perform a series of reviews which are designed to assess the overall performance of the program. Two types of review are commonly used: a time-based review and an event-based review. It is generally a good idea to use both types of reviews in practice, in order to ensure complete coverage.

A time-based review is one that occurs at regular intervals, ranging typically from one to three years between reviews. These are top-down, comprehensive reviews that examine all aspects of the risk management program against the business objectives that are currently in place. The purpose of these time-based reviews is to ensure that the risk management program stays current with respect to both the controls that implement it and the ever-changing business objectives of the enterprise.

An event-based review is less comprehensive, but much more focused on a particular aspect of the risk management process. Like lessons-learned and after-action reviews, event-based reviews are meant to capture and record information about a particular element of the risk management program. For instance, if a business unit is reorganized, then business objectives may change. Because that change would represent a significant modification of the operating environment, it would be a good idea to make sure that the risk management program continues to support the goals of the business. For the same reason, it is also important to evaluate the risk management situation after an actual incident has occurred in order to ensure that the outcomes of the incident reflect the desired results.

The objective of both of these kinds of reviews is to ensure that the risk management program stays in step with changes in the business environment, as shown in Figure 18-2. Regardless of the type of review conducted, there are some common elements that should be looked at as a part of each review. The first of these elements are the security controls themselves. The review should determine how effective these controls were in responding to the occurrence that they were designed to prevent. In addition, the review should confirm that there was not a need for additional controls for that particular incident.

In conjunction with the assessment of the actual control set, the reviews should also examine the effectiveness of the policies and procedures that guide the implementation and routine operation of those controls. Those policies and procedures should be proven to align with the residual risk levels within the environment, as well as to address all of the known threats and vulnerabilities. If the need to add controls, policies, and procedures, or modify existing ones is identified, then the review report should itemize what those changes should be.

In addition to operational reviews, a standard operating procedure should be defined for conducting audits. Since most organizations have an internal audit function, the audit of risk management processes and procedures should be built into their regular internal audit

**Business environment**

**Risk management program**

**Figure 18-2** Keep the risk management program up-to-date

© *Cengage Learning 2012*

function. Conducting an audit of the risk management process as part of regular internal audit activity is an appropriate way to address the need for periodic audits of the risk management process. Rolling the assessment of the risk management function into regular internal audit activities is yet another way to institutionalize reviews of the risk management process.

## Chapter Summary

- Risk management is built around formal processes to provide information about risk to decision makers.
- The organization has a duty to continuously monitor the risk environment.
- The risk management plan is designed to address priority risks, not *all* risks.
- Prioritization of risk is built on likelihood of occurrence and resultant impacts.
- Priorities have to include feasibility and cost of implementation.
- Risk management plans have to be easily understandable to the organization as a whole.
- Risk management coordinates three generic factors: risks, business goals, and impacts.

- The overall purpose of risk management is to maintain an effective set of risk controls.

- Controls should be arrayed in baselines in a defense-in-depth scheme.

- Every risk process has to be designed to fit its specific environment.

- Unknown risks cannot be accounted for, but known risks can be addressed by planned controls.

- There are two types of risks: active and intrinsic.

- Intrinsic risks have to be monitored even if a response is not required at the time.

- It is important to know the operational status of every control.

- Operational assessments are needed because the business and threat environment change.

- Assessments are either time-driven or event-driven.

- Audits of the risk management process should be built into the routine internal audit function.

## Key Terms

**Acceptable risk** A situation where either the likelihood or impact of an occurrence can be justified.

**Residual risk** An intrinsic weakness that is currently not exploited by a threat.

**Risk analysis** The assessment of the overall likelihood and impact of a threat.

**Risk level** The degree of likelihood and impact that is considered acceptable before a response is required.

**Risk mitigation** A set of formal organizational processes that is designed to slow down or minimize the impact of an adverse event.

**Security** Confidence that a given approach will produce dependable and intended outcomes.

**Security controls** Electronic or behavioral actions designed to prevent or mitigate an adverse event.

**Threat** Adversarial action that could cause harm or an undesirable outcome.

**Threat modeling** Representation of the risk environment using a commonly accepted graphic modeling approach such as data flow or UML.

## Questions from the CIO

The CIO requires you to brief her on the current status of your investigation. This will be an important part of your continuing work on this project, since it is essential to be able to describe all of the ramifications of a properly developed risk management function. Consequently, the CIO would like you to answer the following questions for her:

1. Risk avoidance is one of four ways to deal with risk. What are the other three approaches?

2. Risks might not necessarily be addressed by a risk management plan. Why? What would be the conditions that might cause a risk to not be addressed?

3. Why is it important for the risk management process to align with business goals? What might happen if it were not properly aligned?

4. What do priorities do for risk management? Why are they necessary and what would happen if risks were not prioritized?

5. What is the outcome of the operational status assessment for controls? What does the organization learn? What does that assessment let the organization do?

6. What is the significance of a risk level? What does it dictate? Why is it necessary?

7. How are risk assessments and risk management plans related? What would happen if risk assessments were not done? Would it be acceptable to only do a risk assessment at the beginning?

8. What is the difference between a qualitative and a quantitative risk assessment? What is the role of each in the risk management process? Can the two approaches be combined? If so, how?

9. What is the difference between a time-based and an event-based review? Why are the two approaches needed?

10. What are the five material considerations of the risk management process? Why are these five considerations important? What would be the consequence of leaving out a consideration?

# Hands-On Projects

1. Using the case in Appendix A, prepare a model set of the following risk management policies:

   a. Risk acceptance, mitigation, avoidance policy

   b. Security control policy

2. Using the case in Appendix A, outline a set of 10 security controls and how they would be implemented for a risk that you identify.

3. Using the case in Appendix A, develop an audit plan to assess risk management measures.

4. You have just received data from a qualitative threat assessment of the computer security of your organization, with the impacts and probabilities of occurrence listed in Table 18-1. Properly place the threats in a list by priority. Assign High = 5, Medium = 3 and Low = 1. Which of the threats should you take action on, which should you monitor, and which ones may not need your immediate attention?

**18**

| Threat | Impact | Probability of Occurrence | Priority |
|--------|--------|---------------------------|----------|
| Malware attack | High | High | |
| Internet hack | Medium | High | |
| Keylogger attack | High | Low | |
| Disgruntled employee hack | High | Medium | |
| Weak incidence response mechanisms | Medium | Medium | |
| Theft of information by a trusted third-party contractor | Medium | Medium | |
| Competitor hack | High | Low | |
| Poor risk management planning | Medium | Low | |
| Inadvertent release of noncritical information | Low | Low | |

**Table 18-1**  **Probability of occurrence**

# chapter 19

# Strategic Management

## Looking at the Long Term

*The company had come a long way from its demise three years ago. It now had a well-organized information security function to protect its known problem areas. The CEO and the board of directors all agreed with that assessment. A lot of the credit went to the CISO, who had done most of the heavy lifting during that entire period. However, as far as the CISO was concerned, accolades from the board didn't contribute much toward supporting his lifestyle. He wanted more than just praise; he wanted the CIO's job, since in his mind, he felt like he was better qualified to sit in her pricey leather chair.*

*He had originally set his sights on the CEO's job, but it was obvious that the things that the CEO did were a career bridge too far at present. On the other hand, the CIO had essentially sat in her office during the entire security makeover. In the CISO's opinion, her over-attention to the technology made her low-hanging fruit. However, if he wanted to stage a coup, the CISO knew that he had to come up with concrete evidence that would convince the CEO and the board that he was a better choice. He thought he had found that proof in one word: alignment.*

*He had spent considerable time studying the company's overall security situation. At present, there were well-defined processes that met all of the requirements for comprehensive security. Nevertheless, there was little evidence that those processes could be counted on to continue to satisfy the organization's future security goals. That was because there was no standard mechanism to evolve the company's security processes as the threat situation changed.*

*During his travels, the CISO had noticed that the company had a planning process in place to ensure alignment of all of its other business functions with its strategic goals. That planning process always ensured that the operation of the business effectively realized the company's aims, addressed the needs of its customer base, and fit marketplace requirements as well as the general trends in the business climate. The product of that planning effort was a formal process that controlled the direction that the business would take in the next five-year cycle. It also ensured that the supporting functions would evolve accordingly.*

*Notwithstanding the aim of business alignment, the CISO's concern was that there was no specific provision in the strategic planning process to maintain proper alignment between business goals and information security's policies, procedures, and practices. The CISO thought he could make the case that the company's security resources could be wasted and that there might even be the potential for actual harm, if it did not ensure that the activities of the information security function were also kept in alignment with the organization's business goals.*

*The CISO was prepared to make the case to the board that the company's information security processes should be directly traceable to specific business aims, but he needed to boil that concept down into a distinctive catch phrase. He decided to call that process "security alignment." In his terms, maintaining the security alignment meant that security resources would be justified only in direct support of an associated business goal. The CISO was more than certain he could sell that concept to the board members, since they were already getting self-conscious about the amount of money they were pouring into the information security operation.*

*The CISO's aim was to demonstrate to the board that every IT security process should be tied to the security requirements of an identifiable aspect of the organization's business operation. If he could make that tangible connection, he felt that he could literally provide a cost justification for each individual security activity based on the value of what it protected. That justification would give the board a quantitative basis for making decisions about the activities that it absolutely had to fund, as well as those things that could be eliminated with little or no repercussions. Better yet, the CISO knew that the board would see that kind of decision-making capability as something that any responsible CIO should have provided in the first place.*

*He also knew that it would not be possible to generate the kind of company-wide information that was needed for quantitative decision making without adopting some sort of systematic process to gather the necessary data. The process would have to identify and maintain the linkages between all of the various security functions and the business goals they were intended to support. Once the linkages were established, the CISO knew that the activities to ensure that data gathering would have to be implemented and then maintained.*

*Instituting a function that stretched across the entire organization was going to take top-level support, but that had some hazards associated with it. Getting involved with strategic planning at the board of directors level would bring the kind of notoriety that the CISO didn't want. He particularly didn't want to be visible at this point, because he was afraid that the CIO would figure out what he was up to if she saw him consorting with the board.*

*Before he started the process of securing the necessary backing of the members of the board, he set up an ad hoc team whose aim was to prepare a white paper that would detail a comprehensive approach to the strategic management of IT security. He knew he was being particularly Machiavellian; since he was sure that once the ideas in the document were accepted by the board, the CIO couldn't derail the process without looking like she was being obstructive.*

*The team was headed up by the Jacksonville security engineer, who was becoming his go-to person when it came to organizational development work. In fact, he was thinking that once he got his well-deserved corner office, she might be a good candidate to replace him as CISO. As usual, the security engineer turned to the EBK to get her directions. What she found were the following nine competencies that are needed to manage the IT strategic management function:*

1. *Establish an IT security program to provide security for all systems, networks, and data that support the operations and business/mission needs of the organization*

2. *Integrate and align IT security, physical security, personnel security, and other security components into a systematic process to ensure that information protection goals and objectives are reached*

3. *Align IT security priorities with the organization's mission and vision, and communicate the value of IT security within the organization*

4. *Acquire and manage the necessary resources, including financial resources, to support IT security goals and objectives and reduce overall organizational risk*

5. *Establish overall enterprise information security architecture (EISA) by aligning business processes, IT software and hardware, local and wide area networks, people, operations, and projects with the organization's overall security strategy*

6. *Acquire and manage the necessary resources, including financial resources, for instituting security policy elements in the operational environment*

7. *Establish organizational goals that are in accordance with standards, procedures, directives, policies, regulations, and laws (statutes)*

8. *Balance the IT security investment portfolio based on EISA considerations and enterprise security priorities*

9. *Ensure that appropriate changes and improvement actions are implemented as required*

# Keeping the Process Coherent

Most information security functions operate under the dark star of **process entropy,** the principle that without continuous upkeep, a well-organized process will tend to fall apart over time. In the case of information security, process entropy is caused by the unremitting pressure of business competition combined with continuous evolution in the technology. Because it has to follow a coordinated set of activities to be effective, an information security function that suffers from process entropy can produce some very nasty surprises. That is why it is critical to ensure that all of the components in the overall information security scheme are properly coordinated and tightly coherent. The role of strategic management is to establish and maintain that coordination and coherence.

The aim of strategic management in the case of information security is to ensure that all of the people, processes, and technologies that make up the organization's overall security response are working together to satisfy the business purpose. The assumption is that the security function is justified and correct if it directly supports what the business is trying to do. In order to ensure that effectiveness, the business has to undertake a formal, organization-wide effort to define, integrate, and maintain proper alignment between its business purposes and its security function.

The executives at the top of the organization have to champion this effort, because they are the only ones with the authority to implement and enforce coordination of functions across the organization. Since much of security strategy involves specific methods and technologies, technical managers in the information security function also have to be involved in the process of maintaining proper alignment. That is because a majority of the security functions are built around lower level security technologies and technical practices. This means that both high-level executives *and* security managers at the next level down are essential participants in the process of ensuring alignment between strategy and implementation.

## Ensuring Cooperation Across Functions

The problem with strategic management is that a lot of key information security functions, such as information technology, as well as the personnel security and physical security functions operate divorced from each other. In many cases, these are separately managed units, which in some instances will even reside in disconnected parts of the organization. The role of strategic management is to ensure that these various functions work together in the most harmonious and effective manner.

In order to ensure proper real-world integration of these large organizational functions, strategic management has to create and then coordinate a top-level process to combine and ensure all of the security functions are working properly. In addition to its coordination role, strategic management has to ensure that that information security function continues to support those strategic goals. Thus, the overall information security process embodies a defined set of inherent security activities which are documented so that individual managers can tailor out a uniform set of best practices for their units.

Tailoring applies at any desired level of detail. The tailoring is accomplished by identifying the unique issues, problems, and criteria associated with each of the activities in the process. The necessary adjustments are then made to standard recommendations for correct practice. The aim of the tailoring is to ensure that the practical technologies and behaviors that are deployed achieve the established goals of the security function. The outcome of the tailoring process is an explicit set of practices that represents the organization's current approach to security.

## Creating a Strategic Management Model

The strategic security management process has to be planned. The plans that create that process are part of the overall corporate strategic planning operation. Those plans dictate all requisite actions for the organization's information security function, as well as how those actions will be carried out. The **strategic management plan** specifies the ingredients that will comprise the information security function as well as their associated resource requirements. In that respect, the plan provides a definition of each major component in the information security function, as well as a statement of the resource commitments that will be made to that function. In addition to resources, the plan specifies the administrative model that will be used to ensure proper management oversight.

The strategic management plan is the first step in the strategic management process, and the plan is successively refined over time as situations change. The plan defines the security actions of the organization in concrete terms. In order to ensure that the plan is composed of tangible activities, it is documented using a top-down process that starts at the level of general concept and is refined down to explicit action. Each general security requirement is broken down into specific procedures which are given explicit task descriptions. The aim is to provide a detailed description of the actions to be taken within the overall infrastructure of processes. That detail is necessary in order to ensure that each process is consistently executed. At the same time, the plan should also communicate an explicit understanding of how the various large components of the process interact with each other to achieve the goals of the general information security function. That interaction includes all of the relevant relationships between components.

Once the general framework is established, each of the inherent actions contained in that framework is documented, assessed, and improved over time. Although that definition and documentation process is labor-intensive, it will lead to repeatable security processes which produce predictable outcomes.

## Organizing for Proper Alignment

Strategic security management maintains an integrated set of organization-wide security controls along with associated technical countermeasures. In order to be effective, this complex and diverse set of things has to be synchronized, and that normally requires some sort of company-wide process. The synchronization process itself has to ensure a continuously appropriate relationship between the operational elements of the IT security function and the general vision, mission, philosophy, and cultural values of the organization.

The common justification for organization-wide coordination of a process like information security is that it ensures the optimum use of resources. If all of the organization's information security processes are perfectly aligned with its business goals, then none of the resources that are allocated to information security will be wasted. For that reason alone, establishing and maintaining good **strategic alignment** represents good competitive advantage.

In order for information security to work properly, it has to be implemented company-wide. Since the only people with the authority to enforce company-wide decisions of that type are the policy makers of the organization, the responsibility for ensuring overall implementation of the information security function has to be vested with the company's top-level leaders. Additionally, because the CIO and the CISO represent the leadership of the technology function, one or both of them have to be accountable for evolving the formal linkages between IT and the conventional business operation. The goal is for the technical leadership, as well as conventional general business leaders, to collaborate in the development of a suitable long-term coordination approach.

## Thinking Through What to Protect

Effective coordination of the information security function starts with the creation of an enterprise-wide process whose sole purpose is to integrate the domains of business and information technology into a single, unified management concept. Three big-picture questions have to be answered to get that process off the ground: What is the organizational mission? What specific organizational competencies do we have? What is the exact status of the business environment?

Organizational mission requires the organization to document all of its common business purposes and goals. That statement might require a little soul-searching across the company, because there can be a range of priorities. The outcome should be a clear statement of strategic priorities along with the business case that supports it. The second question is related to the first. The discovery of precisely what the organization's competencies are is another prioritization process. In identifying its key competencies, the business will identify the parts of the organization that are most important to it. The rule of thumb is to focus on only those parts of the business that represent a distinct competitive advantage.

The final factor, business environment, is outward facing. Business environment differentiates and then evaluates all external influences that might affect the competitive position of the business. The assumption is that if the company does all the homework necessary to understand where it fits on each of these three factors, it is in a position to prioritize and align the key components of its business processes with the processes that are needed to ensure them.

## Integrating Cultures as Well as Process

A critical element in ensuring the success of the strategic management function is the ability to ensure the most effective coordination between the people who are involved in the process. Information is a prime enabler of competitive advantage because it lets companies translate the knowledge they generate into business value. Leveraging corporate information into competitive advantage means involving people in the process who have traditionally not participated in planning long-term corporate strategy. Because there are diverse perspectives involved in the actual planning, it is important to use a formal process to ensure input from all of the people who are needed to define and maintain an effective alignment. The need for an actual process to ensure cooperation among all of the relevant parties stems from the fact that technology is something of a black box to conventional, executive-level decision makers.

In most organizations, information-processing managers have had a long history of isolation from the corporate strategy level. Since the members of each of those two groups are different from each other, the members of the board of directors are going to view technology's purpose, uses, and directions differently from IT's technical staff and managers. An important aspect of establishing an effective strategic management process is just getting the various important players into the same conversation. If a conscious effort is not made to incorporate everybody who should logically be involved into the process, then the special talents and insights of the information processing managers are likely to be left out of the corporate strategic plan for security.

As a result, one important aspect of the strategic management process is ensuring that the points of view of *all* constituents are represented. It does not seem logical to exclude the people who are expert in the operation of the actual function from the strategic management process, yet most strategic planning is done at the policy level, which is far above IT management. The challenge is to find a way to incorporate the unique vision and capabilities of information security and information processing managers into the overall long-term planning to secure the organization.

The overall people problem is that business executives usually do not want to have anything to do with their own information technology people. That antipathy can be an artifact of individual background, but it is most often due to the fact that IT is technology-centered. The focus on technology makes it different from the conventional management processes for the rest of the business. The consequences of the lack of understanding between business stakeholders and technical managers can lead to minor skirmishes between security and the various business process owners over implementation concerns, as shown in Figure 19-1. Whatever the actual situation, if understanding and cooperation concerns exist between the IT security function and the rest of the business, those differences have to be identified and resolved before the strategic alignment process can go forward.

**Figure 19-1** Conflicts can occur

© *Cengage Learning 2012*

# Designing for Governance

*The team members had been at work on their white paper for over a month, and the CISO was getting a little impatient. It didn't seem to him like it should take so long to come up with a simple process for ensuring that the business goals of the organization were properly referenced to the security to protect them. Worse, he was beginning to lose the interest of those members of the board whom he had secretly lined up to support him once the new alignment scheme was rolled out.*

*He started bugging the team with daily e-mails asking about developments. Finally, the Jacksonville security engineer told him to stop asking about progress unless he wanted a mutiny. She pointed out that although the eventual objective was clear, the problem was in how to get to that particular point. Rather than putting together a white paper with a bunch of obvious holes in the process, the team was trying to develop a consistent approach that would assure continuous alignment of the organization's security process to its business goals.*

*The team had encountered two practical concerns with the design of the strategic planning function. The first concern had to do with how change was managed. The technology that underlies information security is constantly changing. Moreover, because that underlying technology is also an essential part of some business process, continuous change in technology for security purposes also has to lead to commensurate changes in the business. This meant that the strategic management process involved a lot more than just charting and maintaining a proper strategic direction. It also involved coordinating change to business processes across the organization as a whole.*

*That need for strict coordination of information security and conventional business functions implied that the entire activity was best managed through a single corporate framework. That overarching management framework would integrate the management of all of the relevant security functions in the organization into a single coordinated process. Because of the pervasiveness of technology, the framework had to ensure that technical managers were involved as an* integral part in the strategic management of the organization as a whole. It seemed logical to the team that the information security management would play a role in overall business decision making. The Jacksonville security engineer was an expert in organizational process development; it was her opinion that the only way to ensure that the technology perspective was embodied in the strategic plans for the company would be to focus the responsibility for security at the level of executive management, not with the information security function itself.

That opinion set off a major firefight at the corporate level, since nobody among the top executives wanted to have anything to do with information security. The CEO, CFO, and COO were all captains of industry and they had not gotten to that lofty status by venturing into unknown waters, which is what the information security function represented to them. Moreover, the radical change in orientation was going to necessitate the development of a completely new set of large-scale practices for coordination of the security function, which might be costly. The planning would now have to be comprehensive, in the sense that corporate security plans would have to integrate information and corporate strategic planning into a single, organizational planning approach. It was clear to anybody who looked at the problem rationally that the only way to achieve a coordinated state of security across the organization would be to implement a single, uniform strategic management framework.

The obvious need for uniformity of control was the selling point that the Jacksonville security engineer used to calm the CISO down. The CISO had heard from the members of the board that the Jacksonville security engineer was planning something radical. That potentially career-ending piece of news sent him hastening down to the cluttered office on the 32nd floor, where the team had set up shop. The Jacksonville security engineer met him at the door, mainly because the sound of his anguished footsteps coming up the hall sounded like a buffalo stampede. She explained that a single control framework implemented his principle of a comprehensive, top-down system of security management practices.

Given that top-down control was the only way to coordinate the diverse functions necessary to ensure information security, it wasn't hard to convince him that a single coordinated control framework was the best answer. He also realized that in order to ensure that that control was universal across the organization, it had to be sponsored at the top, meaning the board. Of course, the CISO didn't miss the fact that somebody would have to actually manage that control function, since the members of the board were certainly not going to do that. The more he thought about it, the more he could see that he was the right person.

Clearly, the development of a new strategic governance model, which embraced such a diverse variety of large strategic functions, was not as simple as the original assignment. As the Jacksonville security engineer explained the actual situation, the CISO began to see that, rather than being the end of his career, this new direction offered a bonanza of possibilities. It would place him in an enviable position in the new corporate structure vis-à-vis the CIO. Moreover, it was apparent to him that the person who actually designed and implemented that governance system would be in a position to control the entire strategic management mechanism for the company. It all depended on what was included in the plan.

The CISO decided that he should take over running the work of the team. He was smart enough to know that the Jacksonville security engineer was the person who should actually develop the design for this new direction in corporate thinking. Nonetheless, he wanted to keep the credit for the eventual outcome all to himself. In order to ensure the Jacksonville security engineer's cooperation in his little case of deception, he promised her that once he had *eased the CIO out, the Jacksonville security engineer would be the anointed one; the CISO could appreciate a devious mind.*

*That satisfied the Jacksonville security engineer, since she had decided a long time ago that she could do the CISO's job a lot better than he could. Even so, there was still the problem of actually designing the new governance approach. She knew that the EBK only listed the following four competencies associated with the design of a strategic management function:*

1. *Establish a performance management program that will measure the efficiency, effectiveness, and maturity of the IT security program in support of the organization's business/mission needs*

2. *Develop IT security program components and associated strategy to support the organization's IT security program*

3. *Develop information security management strategic plans*

4. *Integrate applicable laws and regulations into enterprise information security strategy, plans, policies, and procedures*

*The Jacksonville security engineer decided that a lot of the development of the model would be up to her creative thinking.*

# Establishing Control

The term "governance" denotes the generic organizing and control principles that any organization will employ to manage its various functions. Where the governance concept applies directly to the security of information, it is called "**information governance**". The information governance process is the function that builds and oversees the coherent set of controls needed to assure information.

The outcome of the information governance process is a single, rational and continuously evolving management structure. The organization establishes information governance by specifying an integrated set of organization-wide policies and their attendant control behaviors. The creation of such a detailed high-level framework requires a comprehensive long-range plan, which is different in focus from the typical activities of the information security function.

The information governance process operates within the larger policy and procedure framework of the overall strategic governance process of the organization. Although information governance is a subset of the organization's overall governance responsibility, it is specifically focused on establishing the most effective set of control activities to ensure information security.

In order to ensure uniform performance, the rules for information governance must be explicitly understood and accepted throughout the organization. It is always important to document and then disseminate a set of specific information governance policies and accompanying management practices. These policies and procedures must be detailed enough to allow the company's management to engage in the strategic planning necessary to ensure a coherent solution.

A properly designed information governance function will ensure that there is a standardized management system in place for information security. That system will enable the organization to reliably achieve its security goals no matter what short-term changes might affect the process. Ideally, the information governance function will ensure the optimum integration of all of the organization's large-scale security processes into a single management system, which will assure consistent control of the information asset base.

## Governance Structures

The requirement for management control implies the need for a formal structure of organization-wide control behaviors that are specifically targeted on securing the company's information resources. That structure should be strategic in focus and be aimed at enabling the optimum inter-relationship between all relevant processes. The controls that are established within that structure represent the specific governance actions for that particular organization. The structure of the controls themselves should flow naturally from the overall goals of the businesses strategic governance process; control activities are always thoroughly thought through as part of the strategic management process.

The control structure spells out the specific activities that the organization will undertake to ensure a given long-term intention. Because the controls are tangible mechanisms for enforcing the requisite behavior, they reflect the ideas that the people who are doing the strategic planning have about security. The overall form of the control structure is normally established as part of conventional, top-level strategic planning. Since every business is different, it is likely to realize the form of its control process in different ways. Although the substantive form of the governance model will vary among organizations, the same rule always applies; all governance activities have to achieve a documented organizational purpose.

## Developing a Governance Process

As with all organizational management systems, the governance process is composed of a distinctive set of rationally derived and logically interacting control behaviors, which are deliberately designed to achieve a specific outcome. These components are called "controls" because they enforce specific outcomes. In their real-world incarnation, controls are specifically designed policies, procedures, and/or work practices. In their practical form, controls create a set of coherent behaviors that the organization then carries out in a systematic fashion.

Since the activities that are inherent in a control system interact to achieve a deliberate goal, the aim of any well-defined governance control system is to provide a detailed specification of the actions that are needed to achieve a particular strategic intent. In conjunction with the chief aim of regulating behavior, the outcomes of those controls should be specified at a level sufficient to support the specific measurement purposes of **quantitative management**. This means that all outcomes have to be explicitly observable and quantifiable.

A specification at that level is typically developed through a comprehensive, organization-wide strategic process. Because it is hard to capture all of the requirements of a complex system in one pass, it is a generally accepted principle that the design and implementation of a large-scale organizational governance system have to be undertaken hierarchically. The process starts with a set of top-level organizational goals. It then proceeds through an intermediate focusing level, down to the specification of the exact controls or behaviors that the organization deems necessary to achieve its general purposes.

Executed properly, the development process for a governance system will produce a single, comprehensive, and coherent set of integrated practices in real-life. Those practices provide specific benchmarks to guide managers in their day-to-day decision making. Ideally, those benchmarks will then ensure the desired control over every aspect of day-to-day operation. The resulting substantive management process will make certain that each of these benchmarks is being achieved through regular performance assessments.

In theory, a properly defined, organization-wide information governance system should be the mechanism for integrating information security strategies into the overall strategic management process. As previously discussed though, one of the chief reasons why the information security function has not been involved in corporate strategic planning is that the management of information technology operations has traditionally been focused downward into the technology itself, rather than outward and strategically. For this reason, one goal of a properly designed information governance system should be to ensure that information security management also focuses on the overall strategic management goals of the organization. The result of that focus ought to be a strategic management approach that will ensure that all long-term directions of the company, both strategic and operational, incorporate all of the behaviors necessary to secure the organization's information.

## Planning for Governance

A large-scale governance system, such as the one being discussed here, has to be implemented by a formal, organization-wide planning effort. The goal of such an effort is to merge all potentially useful organizational processes, including information security, into a single, unified strategic management approach. That task is not simply a matter of opening up better lines of communication between the various participants. It also involves ensuring that all of the various management perspectives are practically aligned and coordinated to achieve a defined set of overall organizational objectives.

Where information security is concerned, the problem with achieving that coordination is that the focus of security's management has to be on the difficult task of ensuring optimum performance of the company's technology resources. It is not easy keeping a large technology organization functioning on a 24/7 basis. It requires a concentrated focus on the complex details of computer operations. Technology managers, which include the people who run the computer security function, can never afford to take their eye off the ball. That required perspective does not convert well to formulating long-range information security strategies. This difference in focus is particularly inconvenient when it comes to maintaining alignment between security strategies and the evolving business case.

Given that two divergent perspectives are required, the strategic management process has to be structured in such a way that it will allow information security managers to carry out their traditional technology management functions. At the same time, the process has to ensure that the information security function is able to contribute to the decisions that shape the organization's long-term directions. Since both a strategic and an operational focus are required, the governance process has to ensure that the practical knowledge that is gained in undertaking routine operations feeds directly into the creation of long-range plans.

To achieve an effective operational focus, the governance process should document the requisite day-to-day actions of the everyday information security function down to whatever level of detail is necessary to ensure consistent performance. The process of documenting operational practices should build a common understanding about how to carry out the actions that are necessary to ensure acceptable security.

Additionally, the documentation process should ensure that lines of communication are established that will enable effective cooperation of the various disparate elements of the process, such as the electronic and physical security. The outcome of the definition of routine information security practice is a standard set of behaviors that the organization feels will satisfy the general goals of the information security operation. In most cases, this is the point in the process where the actual planning process stops.

In order to create a strategic **management capability**, the governance process also has to ensure that information security management and the various players in long-range corporate planning are formally linked. The aim of that linkage is to ensure the necessary strategic alignment between the goals of the organization and the activities of the security function. That coordination is established by creating a framework of formal planning activities at the corporate policy level, which are aimed at ensuring that the information security function contributes directly to strategic management.

## A Framework for Strategic Management

The behaviors that create the linkage between the information security operation and strategic planning constitute the strategic management approach to information security. That framework becomes the organization's specific information governance system and it dictates the steps that will be taken to ensure that information security managers are engaged in overall corporate strategic planning. In addition, the framework will tell all of the participants in the strategic planning and management processes exactly what actions are required of them.

The aim is to foster coordination and communication between all of the participants, thus making the overall process more efficient. The framework will also increase the visibility of the information security function with both internal and external stakeholders. Moreover, because the performance of activities specified in the framework can be observed, it will help to ensure that regulatory and contractual requirements are met.

**Better Return on Investment** From a resource standpoint, the objective evaluation of the performance of specific security activities also helps to ensure better return on investment, both in the short and long term. The ability to determine the financial benefit is important because there are always costs and risks associated with setting up a strategic function like information security governance. A well-established framework of required activities that can be objectively evaluated will help the organization to better evaluate the allocation of its resources. It will accomplish that by allowing the organization to base its resource allocation decisions on quantitative performance indicators. That quantitative basis, in turn, ensures better risk management and maximizes the value of the security processes over time.

**Enhanced Ownership and Accountability** A strategic governance approach also ensures enhanced ownership and accountability because it assigns clear responsibility for the execution of each function to specific owners. This leverages the ability to assess and control the performance of information security work, which provides the potential to optimize the costs and benefits of the overall security process even further. Notwithstanding the obvious payoffs in better coordination and control, the establishment of an IT security strategic management process also offers the potential to increase the corporation's overall, long-term profitability.

# Ensuring the Strategic Perspective

*With the development of the detailed governance framework, the CISO felt like he had finally gotten his arms around strategic security management. The model provided all of the control features that he had felt were lacking in all of the other instances in his career. It gave him the potential to develop and enforce long-term strategies to improve the organization's overall security posture, while still letting him manage routine operational security concerns. Better yet, it had the potential to provide an understanding of the information security process at the strategy level that had been sadly lacking in the past. Now all he had to do was implement the process.*

*That was not as simple as it sounded, because the organization would have to follow a top-down series of steps to define the necessary controls. The problem was that this level of definition had never been achieved before. If the process was going to be successful, the CISO knew that he would have to do three things. First, he would need to characterize all of the company's data assets and describe what threatens each. Then he would have to document a set of actions for each threat at a degree of specificity that would allow each response to be quantitatively evaluated. Finally, he would have to convince his superiors to underwrite the across-the-board implementation of the whole process, which might be the most difficult task of all.*

*Fortunately, he was at the end of a three-year period that was generally designed to accomplish the first two tasks. Thanks to the work that his teams had done to implement the other security functions, he had a decent idea what the shape of the data asset looked like. He had also spent a lot of time on controls for all of the other 13 areas in the EBK, so he had a complete collection of practices for every conceivable area of cybersecurity at his disposal. What he didn't have was an accurate map of how all of these controls fit together at the top. Nor did he have any sense of how to justify their worth in a business sense to upper management.*

*What he did know, though, was that this particular initiative was the key to his ambitions; all he had to do was fill in a well-defined set of blanks and he would look like the leader the company needed for its information functions. He knew that what he had to do was work through each control, one at a time, and specify the linkages that would produce outcomes that could be evaluated in objective terms. Then he had to array those controls into a practical management system. The benefit of the products of that system, in terms of enhanced management control and quantitative management data, was obvious. He knew that once it was drawn up in concept, there would be no question that the board would see it as the answer to its developing concerns about the cost and feasibility of information security.*

*The process itself was not rocket science, just hard work. The CISO knew that he had just the person available to deliver that kind of project in the Jacksonville security engineer. He gave her one last set of marching orders: "Build me a system of controls that I can sell to the board on its quantitative management merits." The Jacksonville security engineer was actually quite interested in doing this part of the project, since she could see that it would be groundbreaking as far as management theory for information security was concerned. She knew from the EBK that the following five general areas of competency might be part of the process, so she put all of them in her game plan:*

1. *Provide feedback to management on the effectiveness and performance of security strategic plans in accomplishing business/mission needs*

2.  *Perform internal and external enterprise analyses to ensure the organization's IT security principles and practices are in line with the organizational mission*

3.  *Integrate business goals with information security program policies, plans, processes, and procedures*

4.  *Collect, analyze, and report performance measures*

5.  *Use performance measures to inform strategic decision making*

# Control Objectives and Business Goals

Information security strategic management ensures the long-term security directions of the business by making sure that security's short-term operational activities specifically underwrite the organization's long-term intents. In order to establish the linkage between day-to-day execution and long-range strategy, all of the organization's security technologies, processes, and human resources have to be arrayed to support the organization's specific business purposes.

The information security function is operationalized by a set of designed behaviors that are then documented by a tangible set of controls. The documentation provides a formal description of the intended outcome of a given set of specific actions. The **control objectives** are an explicit statement of the expected outcome of each information security activity. Each outcome should be directly linked to a specific business purpose, based on what that objective is meant to accomplish. This means that the specific outcomes of the control objectives can be measurably linked to the company's individual business goals.

## Defining Control Objectives

Control objectives are defined in an action-oriented way and should always directly support some aspect of the overall business case. Security control objectives specify a precise assurance outcome. Since that outcome is always associated with a specific business purpose, a logically interrelated set of control objectives can provide a concrete description of what the company is trying to accomplish. For that reason, each security control objective should be directly traceable to the overall corporate goal that it is intended to implement. Because they describe explicit behaviors, control objectives can be quantitatively measured. That data can then be used to determine whether the control is effective.

## Steps to Evaluate Control

Strategic control can be ensured by the right framework of control objectives. The organization follows a deliberate organization-wide process in order to establish that control. The first stage in that process involves gathering all of the information necessary to define the organization's general requirements for information security. That information-gathering process involves identifying, labeling, and valuating all of the assets that might be placed within the **boundaries** of the company's protection scheme.

The next step in the process involves a risk assessment to determine the exact protection requirements for each of the individual items that the organization thinks that it might want to ensure. The risk assessment process identifies all of the vulnerabilities in the information base as well as the actions or events that might pose a threat. That assessment should be comprehensive, in that it should not be focused strictly on the electronic elements of security. It should also include any of the contextual factors that might impact security, such as legal and contractual requirements as well as any current and projected business requirements.

Once all of the threats have been identified, the organization makes a decision about priorities. The strategic decisions that are made here must ensure, at a minimum, that the organization's critical functions are protected. Since critical functions don't come with labels on them, executive managers have to decide about the business value of all of the organization's various functions. When the management team feels like it has gotten a handle on all of the information items of value, it creates a suitable set of control objectives to ensure that each threat is mitigated. The cost of that set of control objectives should be justifiable based on the estimated value of the information items it is set to protect.

Formal control procedures require an appropriately detailed specification of all of the behaviors needed to implement them. This specification of the actions to be undertaken documents the rationale for why that particular set of behaviors was chosen. The rationale details each behavior and its expected outcome. Additionally, it explicitly states the measures that will be employed to determine whether those actions have achieved the expected outcomes. Once that entire set of behaviors has been laid out, decision makers can undertake a rational tradeoff process. That tradeoff weighs the potential impact of each threat against the resources that will be required to mitigate it.

By specifying explicit behaviors, managers can evaluate whether the actions required by those behaviors are feasible. Since there are cost implications in implementing any control, the financial feasibility of the required actions should be evaluated. Because of the requirement to evaluate feasibility, each control objective must be stated in precise, measurement-driven terms. Those measures should be able to tell management whether a specific control has achieved its assurance objectives. The data that those measures will produce should allow managers to evaluate the relative performance of the control in relation to the associated costs of maintaining it. That evaluation will help decision makers maintain the most cost-efficient control set.

Cost-efficiency is important because there are never enough resources available to implement all of the potential controls. It should be possible to assess the general usefulness of each control in quantitative terms. A standard set of seven desirable characteristics is typically used to evaluate the general effectiveness of a given control, as follows:

- The first of these is effectiveness. To be effective, each security objective must provably underwrite a business goal. The control can be shown to support the purposes of a business process. Support must be timely, correct, consistent, and user-friendly.

- The second criterion is efficiency. Efficiency is important because each of the security controls has to operate in the most productive and cost-efficient manner possible. Saltzer and Schroeder call this "security of mechanism."

- The third criterion is confidentiality. Confidentiality is a fundamental condition of security. The control must ensure that sensitive information is protected from unauthorized disclosure or access.

- The fourth criterion, integrity, is also a basic security condition. The control must be shown to underwrite the accuracy and correctness of information in accordance with the values and expectations of its business purpose.

- The fifth criterion is availability. Availability is the last of the essential conditions of security. Availability controls must ensure that information is accessible when needed by the business process.

- The sixth criterion is compliance. Compliance assures that all information and information-processing activity complies with laws, regulations, or contractual arrangements associated with the business process.

- Finally there is reliability. Reliability ensures that the control will continue to address specified protection needs.

## The Details of Implementation

Once all of the controls are defined, they can be structured into a coherent system for information security management. This strategic concept involves the implementation of a fully integrated set of organization-wide security activities. Because of the prospective scope of the process, implementing those behaviors is hierarchical; it starts with the formulation of a limited set of security policies at the top and it ranges down to the specification of a large number of precise security actions at the day-to-day, operational level. In a top-down approach like this, the organization follows an explicit series of steps, which are designed to address the security concerns as they arise, at whatever level of focus. The practical outcome of this implementation process is a tangible strategic security management system.

The actual steps that are taken to implement a system such as this typically fall into four phases, as shown in Figure 19-2.

The first phase involves the establishment of the overall security requirements for the organization. In the second phase, the process establishes the scope of control for the eventual security system. Factors that might enter into decisions about scope include matters such as the level of criticality for each of the information items within the boundaries of the system and the commensurate degree of assurance required. Other scoping considerations might include how any new strategic initiatives will be incorporated into the actual security system, as well as how changes to market or regulatory factors might be handled. Accurate boundary setting

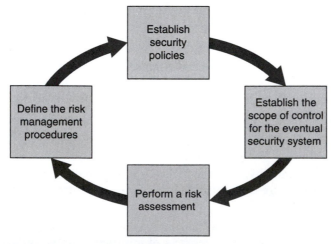

**Figure 19-2** Phases of implementation
© Cengage Learning 2012

is a particularly important aspect of the process, since there is an obvious direct relationship between the resources that will be required to establish the desired level of security and the extent of the territory that must be covered by the protection scheme.

In the third phase, the organization does a risk assessment. This is potentially the most important element in the entire strategic planning process, because it captures and categorizes the actual threats that the organization faces. Once all of those threats are identified, they are assessed to isolate only those that would create specific and undesirable outcomes. That leads to the final phase, which is the definition of an explicit set of risk management procedures.

These procedures are expressed as explicit behaviors that are referenced to the findings from the risk assessment and are normally captured in a set of control statements. The implementation of the control statements is normally done in priority order. Over time, the organization implements, evaluates, and fine-tunes the control set. Alterations to the control set are based on ongoing evaluations of the performance of each individual control.

# Making Strategy Quantitative

*The Jacksonville security engineer could see that she was in the homestretch. She had a control objective-based **information security management system** in place and she had begun to use the performance data that was pouring out of the process to do the fine-tuning that was required to optimize it. What she thought she had left to do was to make that data-gathering into a systematic process.*

*She didn't need her MBA to understand that the company's executives were dangerously divorced from the realities of the situation at the operational level. She was using the term "dangerous" because the people who were doing the strategic planning for the corporation had absolutely no idea what was actually going on down in the trenches. As a result, it was an artifact of pure chance whether the information security aspects of any strategic decision were even considered at all. Her aim was to drive situational awareness up through the various corporate levels by providing tailored evaluation results to the people who needed them.*

*Doing that was going to rest on the organization's willingness and ability to use standardized indicators of performance. Now that the control objectives had been installed, the next step in the process would be to capture the outcome data that they were producing and massage it into a form that top-level decision makers could understand. She made an appointment with the CEO to try to identify problems and issues he needed the system to address. Her aim was to build a direct pipeline between the monitoring of control performance, which was part of conventional operation, and the strategic needs of the upper-level management team.*

*The CEO was more than happy to discuss that with her, since his chief concern was justifying the investment in security to the board. There had been considerable impatience with start-up costs, which was followed shortly thereafter by questions about what security was doing for the company. He viewed the ability to address those questions by a substantive set of charts and graphs derived directly from current field data as a real boost to his own position as CEO. It was not hard for him to authorize a top-priority commitment to a project to link evaluation data to strategic decision making. He also added that he would like to see whether that data could be used to ensure the continuing effectiveness of the information security function itself.*

*The Jacksonville security engineer cemented her candidacy for next CISO with that little meeting. Because getting the right result was that important to her career, she wanted to do the job as well as possible, so she turned to the EBK for the usual guidance. There she found the following six required competencies that reinforced what she already had planned to do in the first place:*

1. *Determine if security controls and processes are adequately integrated into the investment planning process based on IT portfolio and security reporting*

2. *Review security funding within the IT portfolio to determine if funding accurately aligns with security goals and objectives, and make funding recommendations accordingly*

3. *Assess the integration of security with business/mission, and recommend improvements*

4. *Review cost goals of each major investment*

5. *Assess performance and overall effectiveness of the security program with respect to security goals and objectives*

6. *Assess and refresh the performance measurement program to ensure currency with organization's goals and priorities*

# Making Informed Decisions

Tangible observation and quantitative assessments of performance are critical to making intelligent management decisions. In order for management to make any kind of informed, long-range choice, managers have to be able to objectively evaluate the effectiveness of each of their planned actions.

For instance, the corporation knows to the penny how its financial assets are doing. Because there are quantitative measures to judge the performance of investments, it is relatively easy to make informed judgments about how to maximize their use in the future. That is not the case with security, which is why objective indicators of performance, which are easy for all participants to understand, are key to the strategic management of the information security function.

Because they are both technological as well as complex, the effectiveness of security activities can be hard for decision makers to assess. As a result, it is almost impossible for managers to get a true feeling for what an investment in security technology, applications, processes, or practices might mean in the long run. Those security technologies and processes typically produce intangible or indirect benefits, which are hard to judge against corporate goals. Objective data about the performance of those security processes and technologies can give managers all of the guidance they need to make informed decisions about how to steer the course. For that reason, any concrete data that characterizes the actual performance of the security function against stable and reliable corporate benchmarks is valuable.

Likewise, quantitative management data allows corporations to better judge security risks. IT risks are abstractions for the average corporate decision maker because they are usually the consequence of a technology process. An objective and understandable portrait of how IT security processes are performing can allow decision makers to both identify emerging problems as well as judge the potential risks and rewards of any proposed changes.

Given the number and complexity of the procedures that could be embodied in an information security management system, top-level executives are still not likely to be able to determine whether these are effective. The fact that a process has been defined and documented does not mean that it can be relied on. A mechanism to rate the actual effectiveness of each process that is involved in securing information is a useful tool both for assurance and for the purpose of ensuring continuous improvement of the security function.

## Ensuring Performance

Every organization needs to understand and improve the status of its own security response. That requires the ability to characterize the precise security status of its own information base as well as the effectiveness of the functions that regulate it. Neither aspect of that requirement is straightforward; the actual form of the information base is hard to get a handle on because it is abstract. Moreover, because the form of the information base is abstract, it is hard to estimate the required level of substantive control that is needed. As a result, it is important to build an understanding of the items that should be assessed and how to assess them.

Evaluation is an important element of any overall information security process. It is particularly important when it comes to strategic management because of the serious resource ramifications that are involved. Theoretically, any problem can be solved if you have enough time and money to throw at it; however, in the dog-eat-dog world of modern business, that approach isn't feasible. Ensuring that the organization develops, deploys, and maintains the most appropriate and capable set of security processes, tools, and technologies is essential to effective long-term decision making. That understanding can only come through regular and systematic assessment. Organization-wide, systematic assessments are done to ensure the continuous appropriateness and cost-effectiveness of all of the elements of the security response, from data security and forensics to the network security and the physical security process. Focused evaluations can ensure that the money that is invested in security provides the maximum benefit for the outlay.

Because assessments help the organization evaluate its strategies for long-term investment in the overall security architecture, those assessments should also look into future security trends. The actual identification of those trends might require various forms of professional opinion and involve legions of consultants. Whatever the approach, it is essential to ensure the identification of new trends as they relate to the evolution of the security system. Then, rational decisions about the most effective way to grow the security response can be made and evaluated as the situation progresses.

**Security metrics** have to be developed and collected to underwrite this process of assessment. Those security metrics must be standard, because they should be used for causal analysis and comparative purposes across the organization. In conjunction with that requirement, the metrics should also be used to improve process efficiency and resource utilization.

A variety of items of evidence might be required by various decision makers in order to get a substantive understanding of how to conduct the information security strategic management function. That includes documenting information security's specific role in formulating strategic security requirements as well as documenting how information security will participate in the strategic management process. That documentation is revised and updated as the security situation changes.

19

# Evolving the Organization

Evaluation also can be used to evolve the organization's security capabilities. This is an organizational development concept that constitutes the most proactive approach to long-term strategic management of the information security process. From a strategic management perspective, the assumption is that increased levels of security capability are best achieved by engaging in activities that have been proven to be effective over time. Here, organizational capability is judged based on the presence or absence of those distinctive key practices.

The degree of capability of an organization's information security process can be judged on the basis of how effectively the organization performs the requisite key practices. The evaluation process characterizes whether those practices are present as well as how well they are being performed. The assessment of performance is based on whether the appropriate resources have been provided to carry out each practice, as well as the general capability of the people who are performing the practice. If objective measures are used to judge the performance of each practice, then the organization is judged to be more capable than if no measures are used.

# Assessing Organizational Capability

As any organization refines the way it does business, it progresses through various levels of increasing capability. Each of these levels represents continuous progress toward an ideal state. The formal assessment of the level of performance of the practices used to protect information can provide a standard yardstick to measure the security capability of a given organization. That assessment also gives the organization a mechanism to evaluate and then improve its own security performance.

Capable performance is always judged based on assessment of the performance of a defined set of security practices. Each practice should have a purpose and consist of a set of base activities that are considered essential to achieve its purpose. That purpose is the reason for undertaking the practice in the first place. The practices that characterize each security process represent the unique, functional attributes of that process. These practices have to be present, even if their performance is not systematic.

Defined practices can also be used by the organization to do long-term, organization-wide security planning. Since these practices have to be deployed by the organization, they can be used to establish process development goals. The assumption is that the adoption of a standard set of security best practices can enhance any organization's ability to achieve and maintain optimal security performance as well as a cost-efficient response. An organization with a well-defined and mature set of best practices is likely to be more secure than one that is functioning without any formal security procedures at all. Each deployed security practice adds one more capability, the eventual goal being to create a complete security process based on the dictates of best practice.

The deployment of those practices is often done in a staged, logical fashion, in order to satisfy the practical realities of organizational development. Foundational practices, like risk management and data security, are added first. These are followed by practices like forensics and regulatory compliance that increasingly refine the security process. Likewise, the addition of each area of practice means that the overall security process has moved to a higher level of proficiency. Those proficiency levels can also be used to judge whether an organization is becoming more proficient in security practice.

The deployment of practices is supported by evaluation; practices are deployed and then assessed to ensure that they are functioning as intended. The security practices that are selected might be based on lessons learned from prior conduct of the security function, or they might be based on a standard such as ISO 2700, or a guideline like the EBK. Nevertheless, the organization still needs to ensure that the level of their performance meets the basic requirements for secure practice.

That need for assurance requires a formal evaluation, which attempts to describe two things. First, it seeks to confirm that the required practice is being carried out. Then it seeks to describe the level of performance of each practice. It is possible to characterize a given level of performance based on the level of management or organization of the practice. The performance of a given practice can be rated based on the extent to which it satisfies the security requirement of the business process it is tied to. The tie to the business aspect helps strategic planners determine whether the current set of practices adequately satisfies security goals.

## Chapter Summary

- Strategic management ensures coordination of security processes and requires top-level support.

- Strategic management operates within a large-scale framework of processes.

- Strategic management aligns security processes with business goals.

- Strategic management integrates a range of management perspectives and can be difficult because of the cultural differences between participants.

- Information governance is a strategic concept that coordinates and controls all of the functions related to information processing and information security.

- The information governance process must be aligned with the organization's overall governance process.

- Information governance frameworks are composed of a logically related set of control objectives that define an explicit behavior and an expected outcome.

- Control objectives should exhibit seven universally desirable characteristics.

- Because they are outcome- and criteria-based, controls can produce quantitative data that can be used to make judgments about the effectiveness of the security system.

- Assessment data supports good decisions; however, it is important to know how to get the right data in front of the right people.

- Organizations can progress along a **capability maturity** path by instituting a defined set of security best practices in a phased approach.

- Organizational capability can be assessed based on the presence of required practices.

- The other factor in capability determination is the level of management capability.

- There are five levels of management capability that can be used to create a strategic roadmap to a more capable organization.

# Key Terms

**Boundaries** A perimeter that incorporates all items that will be secured.

**Capability maturity** An increasing level of organizational competence.

**Control objectives** Explicit behaviors implemented to achieve a desired outcome.

**Information governance** The generic organizing and control principles that an organization uses to underwrite the management of its information function.

**Information security management system** A logical collection of controls assembled to ensure the confidentiality, integrity, and availability of organizational assets.

**Management capability** The level of assessed competence of the management process

**Process entropy** The tendency for organizational activities to become disorganized over time due to competitive pressure and technological change.

**Quantitative management** Decision making that is supported by empirically derived data.

**Security metrics** Quantitative measures of security performance.

**Strategic alignment** Assurance that the security actions of the organization directly support its goals.

**Strategic management plan** The prescribed activities to achieve the long-range intentions of the organization.

# Questions from the CIO

The CIO would like you to answer the following questions as part of your ongoing assignment. The CIO believes that these answers are necessary to determine whether you have properly defined the strategic management function for this company:

1. Explain process entropy. What is it? What causes it and what are the consequences?

2. Why should the strategic management plan be refined over time? What would happen if it wasn't?

3. Why is alignment important? What are the benefits to the organization as a whole?

4. What is a control structure? Why is one necessary to ensure strategic management?

5. Explain control objectives. Why is a control objective-based approach potentially valuable to strategic management?

6. What two factors underwrite capability maturity? How can they be used to evaluate an organization's security?

7. Why is evaluation important to strategic management? What does the organization get by collecting quantitative data?

8. Why does strategic management have to be approached top-to-bottom? Is there an alternative? What are the pros and cons of taking a different direction?

9. How do organizational cultural differences impact strategic management? Provide two examples of diverse perspectives.

10. Why is linkage important between processes in the security function? Is that a problem now? What are the potential solutions?

11. Why is control objective formulation a strategic concept? What is the long-range outcome of a coherent set of controls?

# Hands-On Projects

Refer to the case in Appendix A. You have been assigned the responsibility of assembling a coherent set of control statements for the administrative function of your choice. Based on the function you choose, complete the following tasks:

- Identify all of the requisite behaviors
- Identify all reasonably expected outcomes
- Relate the outcomes to the overall company goal of product development
- Provide a mechanism to ensure that these are always properly aligned
- Devise a standard operating procedure for doing that

# chapter 20

# System and Application Security

## Conflicts Happen

*The CISO really hated to deal with the company's information technology personnel. He couldn't get anybody in IT to talk strategy beyond next week, and those people never met a "silver bullet" technology that they didn't like. In the past, he had always let the CIO interface with the IT managers, since she was basically one of them anyhow. On the other hand he also knew that if he wanted the CIO's job, he was going to have to learn how to motivate IT to be a little more proactive in their thinking. The problem was that he had no idea where to start. He got up from his desk and walked over to the big windows that looked out across the East River toward the Bronx. Yankee Stadium was out there somewhere in the hazy distance, and he wished that he were sitting in his suite there, instead of wrestling with the software security problem here in midtown.*

*This time it wasn't a major hit that had inspired him. Instead, it was the constant flow of security problems that originated in IT, especially in the configuration and use of application and system software. It didn't take a technical guru to see that with just the exposures he knew about, some sort of crisis was right around the corner. As he was coming in on the Long Island Rail Road that morning, he had read in the Times that cybercrime in America had topped one trillion dollars this year. That fact alone was persuasive enough for him, since he knew who would be blamed for any losses, even if the information technology function was the actual culprit.*

*In the CISO's mind, it all boiled down to process. More specifically, the company needed to have a standard, organization-wide approach to managing the information technology function. That lack of organizational control was no surprise to the CISO, since he knew that information technology had always been a corporate side-show as far as the rest of company's managers were concerned. The CISO would have thought that the presence of a CIO in the corporate organization chart would have established the central role of information technology in corporate strategy. But all of the people in upper management had backgrounds in business, not technology. And none of them were conversant, or even interested in, technology issues. As a result, the CIO was never viewed as a peer by the CEO, the CFO, or the COO. Moreover, because the company's top executives saw the IT function as different, and perhaps even a little bit extraneous to the process of making money, the CIO was never included in any meetings where long-term business directions were being discussed.*

*That exclusionary attitude was to some extent encouraged by the CIO. She made it clear that she was far too focused on the details of her own operation to spend any time thinking about strategy. Her unwillingness to participate in the development of corporate business strategy was understandable, since it was an undeniably hard problem keeping the IT function operating to everybody's satisfaction. At the same time, the CIO had come up through the ranks in IT and she could never stop herself from diving into the technology when broader vision was required. That was also understandable, since a head-down approach to solving practical problems in computing was built into technology workers from day one and the CIO had done technology work since the Pleistocene. Unfortunately, that mind set also made it difficult for her to understand and address the large-scale corporate concerns that the information age had handed her.*

*The CISO was also well aware that the real cause of the problem was that the company's information technology management infrastructure had been developing since the first IBM 700 series was installed back in the 1950s. Over the next 60 years, that infrastructure had grown with the twists and turns of the technology. At this point in its evolution, the term "jungle" was probably an understatement when it came to the shape of its organization. Likewise, that convoluted and in some cases totally missing infrastructure had led to serious problems with quality and security across the corporation. Those security problems occurred in both applications and systems.*

*The root cause of the problem was that the management of IT projects was still being done as it had always been done. Project management was still backroom and off the cuff, and each project was strictly focused on implementing the application or system that was at its heart. Consequently, the development and maintenance activities for those projects took place without any control over project requirements. At the same time, those requirements were developed without any reference to the strategic aims and directions of the business. That was an artifact of the fact that senior management avoided information technology managers like they had a communicable disease. All in all then, there was no formal, strategic direction for the information technology function as a whole. That lack of overall organization and direction pretty much ensured that the IT's people, equipment, and financial resources were deployed like the weeds in a vacant lot. Worse, it created huge, exploitable vulnerabilities in information technology's day-to-day deliverables.*

*The failure of technical managers in a subjective area like security made perfect sense to the CISO. Information technology work is detailed and complex. More important it involves the production of an invisible product. Thus, the CISO knew that most of the real knowledge about what was actually going on in each project was concentrated with the people who were actually doing the work, namely the programmers and technical staff. The CISO also recognized that the divide between those workers and the supervisory function created an untenable situation for information technology managers. That is, managers never know as much about what is going on in their own operation as the workers they were supposed to supervise. Yet it was the information technology managers who are held accountable for any breakdowns, not the workers themselves.*

*Because in its particulars, application and system software development is such an individualistic exercise, the company had to provide a fixed point of reference to guide the process. The CISO's aim was to create a universal monitoring and control framework which was built around standard activities and relationships. That framework could be used as the common point of reference to manage the information technology operation as a coordinated entity. The CISO felt that an organization-wide, policy-based security framework could be put together in three steps.*

*First, all comprehensive models of standard best practice started with a framework of commonly understood processes, along with their associated practices. Those processes and practices then provide a foundation for tailoring. In essence, once the processes and practices are defined, the company can establish standard specifications for the execution of each task. When that is done, those specifications can be tailored into an explicit set of work instructions for each instance within the overall, top-down framework created by those standard processes, procedures, and practices. The standardized practices are adapted to fit the needs of each individual project through the creation of those work instructions and they should then organize project activities into the most ideal approach to security possible.*

*In the CISO's opinion, a standard, company-wide framework of policies and procedures, tailored into explicit work instructions, had a lot of advantages. First of all, a framework of practices would give information technology managers a basic point of reference that would let them gauge the performance of IT's various development and maintenance processes. The ability to judge performance would ensure more precise control. Moreover, formal definition and documentation of the requisite processes would make them repeatable, and that would ensure more consistent security and quality outcomes.*

*Standard activities and relationships are necessary to help project managers tailor out the actual substantive work practices for every project. Since the EBK provides advice for how to construct a management framework like that, the CISO was reasonably sure that he could find the advice he needed to let him structure such a process. He closed the curtains, walked back to his desk, and called up the electronic copy that he kept accessible at all times. Clicking on the section for securing applications and systems, he found the following eight common work functions:*

1. *Establish the IT system and application security engineering program*
2. *Acquire the necessary resources, including financial resources, to support integration of security in the **system development lifecycle** (SDLC)*
3. *Guide IT security personnel through the SDLC phases*
4. *Provide feedback to developers on security issues through the SDLC*
5. *Define the scope of the IT security program as it applies to application of the SDLC*
6. *Plan the IT security program components into the SDLC*

7. *Collaborate with IT project management to integrate security functions into the project management process*

8. *Ensure that appropriate changes and improvement actions are implemented as required*

*These were all policy-based activities that had to be implemented at a high level across the organization in order to be effective.*

# Security in the Lifecycle

In conventional practice, applications and systems pass through five general stages of development that constitute a "lifecycle." The conventional stages of the lifecycle are specification, design, coding, testing, and acceptance and use.

The first stage, specification, provides the definition of the product. There are various ways of providing that definition, including classic specification, prototyping, or even extreme programming. Whatever the method used however, the outcome of this stage is always an in-depth, documented understanding of the functions the software will be required to perform. That understanding should include both the functional requirements for security as well as the security properties that the applications and systems should possess.

The lifecycle then moves on to the design stage, where the product's actual plans are drawn up and the organization decides how to build it. Although there are many ways to do a design, the only purpose of this stage is to conceptualize and communicate the precise structure of the product. It is in the design stage that the actual security functionality and properties are realized in some tangible form.

Whether a project is a single component, or a series of components comprising a larger system, building security in from the beginning is essential in today's enterprise. Many aspects of a system and its security characteristics are established during the conception and design phase of a project, so the need to address them at the beginning of the cycle is essential. To ensure that systems and applications have the desired security characteristics, it is necessary to make the inclusion of these aspects a part of the firm's processes and procedures.

The design is communicated to the people who will actually build it. These people are normally called "programmers." Their function is to translate the design into a computer program. The only acceptable outcome of the programming stage is a correctly functioning code component. Defects typically result from incorrect practice, human error, or malicious intent, and the entire discipline of secure coding has been established to address this specific part of the process. In most cases, the programming stage is the place where security defects are created. These defects can be accidental, like buffer overflows, or intentional, like the installation of back doors and Trojan horses.

The best place to assure against security defects is the point at which they are actually created, which is at the programming stage; however, the actual programming work is so difficult that it tends to consume all of the programmer's time. Some kind of testing is always done during the programming stage to confirm proper functioning; if those tests are done by the programmer this is incorrect practice, since they violate the principle of separation of duties. It is essential for a designated group of testers to perform all assurance work, even while the actual programming is still going on.

Programming and testing are always done in parallel during the programming stage in order to confirm that the code is defect-free and functioning properly. Since that sort of conventional testing is primarily a quality control function, it has a slightly different orientation than the responsibility to identify defects that would represent sources of vulnerability.

The next stage in the process is the point where it is most logical to directly identify and fix defects. That stage is generically termed testing. Because of its purpose, the testing stage is the appropriate place for cybersecurity professionals to be involved in **software assurance**. Defects in code are not necessarily vulnerabilities, but from an application and system security standpoint, all vulnerabilities are defects. Thus, any vulnerability that might cause a loss of confidentiality, integrity, or availability must be found and fixed.

# Adopting a Top-Down Perspective

The aim of the application and system security function is to identify and eliminate exploitable defects in code. Those defects happen because of faulty practice in the development and operation of an organization's applications and systems. In conventional practice, application and system software security ensures that all instances of a given piece of software or a system are developed, configured, and maintained in a trustworthy fashion. In that case, trustworthy simply means that there are no exploitable vulnerabilities present in the everyday execution of code.

The other goal of application and system security is to ensure that each of the organization's applications and systems security functions perform as they are meant to. That assurance has to be reliable over time. A tangible set of well-defined, highly structured, and extremely dependable assurance practices for application and system security is essential to that reliability. Those practices must provide sufficient oversight and control to ensure that the development of software processes and products meets all of the organization's security goals throughout the lifecycle of those processes and products.

As with all organizational systems, the management approach to application and system security is based on a discrete set of rationally derived and logically interacting components. Those components and relationships have to be deliberately packaged into a coherent process in order to achieve that particular aim. A reasonably detailed level of planning is required to implement the broad integration of those components. That level of detail is normally reached through a top-down and inclusive strategic planning function.

The planning usually begins with policies and works itself all the way down to an associated set of real-world practices. In order to maintain the focus on the business direction, those policies should always be derived from strategic organizational goals. Policies should drive the execution of the security function throughout the conventional lifecycle of the development and maintenance process. Done right, the development process will produce a single, coherent, organization-wide system of integrated practices that will give managers highly specific benchmarks for success. The oversight is enabled by regular assessment of the performance of the project against each individual benchmark. Those benchmarks will let managers exercise a suitable level of control over their operations because they will be able to gauge progress of the technical work against measurable criteria.

## Measurement against Benchmarks

Tangible observation and quantitative assessment of performance is critical to the success of a comprehensive process control system. In order for management to ensure that a given process is functioning as required, it must be possible to independently evaluate the effectiveness of the individual activities that the process performs.

That is the reason why objective and easy-to-understand performance data is important to the application and system security function. It is almost impossible for managers to get a feel for whether an investment in equipment, applications, information, or infrastructure has paid off. Those kinds of investment typically produce indirect benefits, which are hard to gauge against corporate goals.

The existence of concrete information that characterizes the actual performance of the elements of the application and system security function against stable and reliable corporate benchmarks can give managers all of the guidance they need to steer a proper course. Likewise, quantitative management data also allows corporations to better judge application and system security risks.

## Identifying and Judging Risks

The software that comprises an application or a system is invisible and abstract to most corporate decision makers. A detailed picture of how applications and systems are performing can allow decision makers to both identify emerging problems as well as judge the potential risks and rewards of any proposed changes. Testing and reviews are the activities that make the product and its production processes visible.

Because much of testing is operational and oriented toward confirming that the software will behave as intended within its environment, the ability to also verify the presence of required functions provides important support for the testing phase. Testing must also have a reliable point of reference to confirm that the functionality that is present in the finished product properly aligns with the specification of the functions that should be there. That is the role of the project documentation. Testing makes use of documentation that is generated during prior stages in the software development process. Because that documentation provides direction to guide the subsequent testing work, its role has to be understood.

The documentation item that is most necessary to the tester is a detailed description of what the software is meant to do. That description should include a definition of the system boundaries, as well as the behaviors that the software is meant to exhibit. The latter description is necessary because it is essential to be able to say with some certainty that the software contains only the right set of functions. Otherwise, unintentional defects or malicious code segments might be introduced and will never be tested or inspected because their existence is unknown.

## Eliminating Hidden Problems

Two categories of unintended functionality have to be considered when testing to eliminate problems. The first is the presence of inadvertent software defects, which are currently the most common source of vulnerability in software. It should be recognized that although vulnerabilities always result from defects, defects don't always create a vulnerability; the presence of a threat is what makes a defect a vulnerability.

The second area of functionality always represents a threat. That is the presence of extra functionality, particularly in unused or hidden parts of the program. Hidden functionality is almost always put in the code that way for a malicious reason. That is why it is particularly important to identify and eliminate hidden functions in software. Because they are usually malicious, hidden functions are probably the most serious threat to the security of code. A testing process that focuses only on confirming the existence of required functions is inadequate.

The most frequently used method to identify hidden vulnerabilities is a code inspection, which is a resource-intensive process that could involve reading the entire program. Since modern programs can easily range between 100,000 and 500,000 lines of code, such inspections are infeasible unless a specific overall approach is adopted to focus the area of inquiry.

## Aligning Processes

Without detailed guidance, the design and implementation of a comprehensive organizational control system for application and system software security involves far too many variables to expect success. Therefore, it is an absolute necessity that a well-defined structure of already proven practices is available to guide the structuring of the process. The use of the model should produce a well-defined framework containing concrete activities that will satisfy the precise aims of the organization.

In the case of application and system security, the presence of a well-defined set of practices, arrayed into a model, ensures that the overall security function and its important features are fully incorporated into and aligned with the overall management structure of the organization. That incorporation should be based on defined and commonly understood policies and practices for both security and overall strategic management of the organization. The presence of a concrete and fully traceable model of best practices will then ensure that the application and system security process and the overall strategic management of the organization are always properly aligned.

A common framework will also enable all stakeholders to know what is expected of them. This makes the process more efficient and increases confidence both internally and externally in the organization. It also helps ensure that all regulatory and contractual requirements are met. Proper alignment will ensure better coordinated overall management of the organization. The maintenance of that alignment, in turn, will help ensure a better short-term and long-term return on IT investment.

## Ensuring Better Resource Allocation

There are always costs and risks associated with large strategic management projects; however, a well-established framework of defined processes allows the organization to better control the management of its resources by basing the monitoring process on quantitative factors. In return, enhanced control ensures better risk management, as well as optimum value. A defined framework of best practice also enables accountability, because responsibility and accountability have to be clearly assigned as part of the specific definition of the process.

Enhanced visibility and accountability leverage return on corporate investment. Visibility allows the company to better manage its functions to optimize their costs and attendant benefits, including better coordination and the creation of a comprehensive IT control structure. Additionally, that structure offers the potential to increase the long-term profitability of any company that is willing to make the initial investment.

## The CISO Plans an Attack

*The CISO's plan hit a stone wall with everybody at the executive level, especially the CIO, mainly because nobody thought that something as ambitious as restructuring the IT function was worth the cost. For that reason, the CEO, the CIO, and the CISO were all sitting in the library of the CEO's penthouse suite of offices trying to hash out their differences. The room was designed to reflect the reassuring atmosphere of an English club. The CISO noted that there was enough leather on the couches and chairs to make an entire herd of longhorns. The pile on the muted blue carpeting came up over the soles of his shoes, and the oak and stained glass cabinets must have cost as much as his new Aston-Martin.*

*In blunt terms, the CISO was hot. The main target of his ire was the CIO, but the CEO was not far behind. The CISO had worked a long time coming up with the concept that the other two had just shot down so cavalierly and he wanted to be heard. Above all, he wanted to leave the meeting with the understanding that the proverbial monkey would land squarely on the back of the CIO when the inevitable IT disaster took place. He then paused and added the caveat, "again." The CIO, who seemed to be totally without a clue as to why the CISO was so mad, spoke first, because she had the seniority.*

*The CIO's argument against the proposed effort was that the whole undertaking was too big and costly for whatever benefit it might produce. She pointed out to the CEO that if the process the CISO was proposing worked the way he intended it to, there would be no measurable return on the huge investment that was required to restructure the IT function. She also pointed out that the only possible return would be in the prevention of some sort of speculative catastrophe that originated in the application or system software realm. And she said that she had it on absolute authority from her IT management staff that they had the company's software assets well under control. The CIO simply could not see any reason to waste the company's money to address a non existent problem.*

*As the CIO laid out her case, the CISO was pacing around the 400-year-old Persian rug in the middle of the CEO's library. Given the fact that the rug was easily ten by fifteen feet and that he was making a circuit every 10 seconds, the extent of his agitation was obvious. Both the CEO and the CIO turned to him to see what he had to say. There were a number of things he would have loved to have said at that point, but none of them seemed like they would enhance his employment prospects, so he settled for a ploy he had been contemplating for some time. Since the CEO was a devotee of Texas hold-em, he knew that it was a gambit that the CEO would especially like. "I am responsible for security," he said, "So I would like to propose a little bet." The CEO was intrigued; he and his pals sat around the green baize enough for him to recognize a throwdown when he saw one.*

*The terms of the bet were simple. The CISO would hire a penetration tester who would do a zero knowledge pen-test of the company's systems. If the pen-tester didn't find anything, the CISO would tender his resignation on the spot. If the penetration test did come back with a report of significant exploitable vulnerabilities, then the CIO had to promise to throw herself on her sword instead. The CIO recognized a sucker bet when she saw one, so she refused to pick up that challenge. Since the CEO considered both of them valuable employees, he proposed a simple compromise which he hoped would settle the matter once and for all. If the pen-tester didn't find any significant problems, the CISO would stop pestering about restructuring; however, if the pen-tester could demonstrate that the company's systems were vulnerable, the CEO would throw the whole weight of the company's executive team behind the restructuring, as well as reward the CISO with a new corner office.*

*That discussion had taken place the day before. Today, the CISO was back at the Golden Cicada with his buddy the network security manager. The CISO was meeting one of the strangest people he had ever encountered. The guy was about 5 foot 4 inches tall and weighed about 100 pounds, with a hairdo that was startlingly similar to that of Prince Valiant from the Sunday comics. That is, if Prince Valiant was suffering from male pattern baldness. He had seven rings piercing the lobe of his right ear, a gold stud in the middle of his lip, and probably piercings God only knew where else. The little guy was meeting with the CISO, who he frankly considered to be a suit, at the personal request of the network security manager. Since the little man deemed the network security manager "a righteous nerd," which in his universe was high tribute indeed, he had consented to meet with the CISO, but only on his turf and only after midnight.*

*The network security manager seemed to be channeling Davie Crockett today, right down to fringed deerskin coat and pants and what appeared to be buffalo leather moccasins. The CISO couldn't help wondering where the network security manager got size-17 buffalo hide shoes in a place like New Jersey. The introductions were short, since the little man refused to talk directly to the CISO. The network security manager started the discussion by pointing out that the little man was the best there was when it came to zero-knowledge exploits. Furthermore, he was willing to do the hack without compensation simply to "send a message to the man." All the CISO had to do was authorize it.*

*The CISO was a little hesitant turning a freak like that loose on the company's systems. Just on appearance alone, the CISO was sold on the idea that the guy could do what he needed to have done. But a person with that unique skill set was also as potentially dangerous as a pit bull at a cat show, and the CISO didn't want to give him any ideas. On the other hand, he also remembered the look on the CIO's face as she said that the CISO was being "alarmist" when it came to the IT operation. He decided that wiping that condescending look off the CIO's face was a risk worth taking. So, the CISO made a deal with the network security manager: he would authorize the hack if the network security manager would be present during the exploit. The CISO figured that at a foot and a half taller, the network security manager would provide an intimidating enough presence to prevent his little friend from straying off the reservation.*

*It was 1:30 a.m. and as the CISO drove back over the Williamsburg Bridge toward the Brooklyn-Queens Expressway and home, he began to think about the process he would have to adopt to redesign the IT function. The EBK specified the following six common work functions for system and application security design:*

1. *Specify the enterprise and IT system or application security policies, standards, and best practices*

2. *Specify security requirements for the IT system or application*

3. *Author an IT system or application security plan in accordance with the enterprise and IT system or application security policies*

4. *Identify standards against which to engineer the IT system or application*

5. *Develop processes and procedures to mitigate the introduction of vulnerabilities during the engineering process*

6. *Integrate applicable information security requirements, controls, processes, and procedures into IT system and application design specifications in accordance with established standards, policies, procedures, guidelines, directives, regulations, and laws (statutes)*

*As with the rest of the design functions in the EBK, these were a mix of management and technical activities.*

# Security Policies and Design

From an application and system security standpoint, it is vitally important to ensure that every activity and task within the assurance process can be related to an established policy. The ability to establish an explicit relationship between a given policy and the actions that are designed to implement that policy is a necessary element of the overall application and system security process, because those policies guarantee that application and system security operations will be correctly aligned with the overall security requirements of the organization.

Application and system security entails the use of defined policies, procedures, tools, and standards to monitor, test, and review software within its operational environment in order to detect vulnerabilities or violations. For that reason, the application and system security function should be executed on a continuous basis. Application and system security should be a proactive, rather than a reactive function; it should identify and address any latent security and control weaknesses present within the software, the data it processes, or its associated policies.

Vulnerabilities arise from defects in application software, operating system software, network or device software, or configurations. Accordingly, the application and system security process is not just limited to the software that the user can see, but extends into the operating system and even the environment where the system operates. Besides the functioning of the software and system itself, the operating environment that surrounds that system also has to be monitored in order to identify security threats, exposures, vulnerabilities, and violations as they arise. This part of the process is usually termed "threat identification." Threats are often identified using threat models, which are formal abstract-modeling techniques that are used to visualize the state of a given problem space.

## Building the Operational Framework

In order to ensure repeatable application and system assurance practice, the organization needs to define stable operational elements and structural relationships that will allow a specific control model to be tailored at the desired level of detail, for each project. The outcome of that tailoring process is a set of distinct activities, which is the actual realization of the requirements of the process for that project. In order to ensure correctness, however, a standard framework of common operational processes has to be created. This framework can be based on a general lifecycle standard, like ISO 12207, or ISO 15288, or the DHS Common Body of Knowledge to Develop, Sustain, and Acquire Software (DHS-CBK). A framework can also be developed from scratch for application to a specific organizational situation; however that requires a lot of additional expertise and effort.

Next, a set of well-defined and commonly understood activities have to be developed for each of those common operational processes. The purpose of those activities is to operationalize each of the process areas. These activities traditionally constitute the generic best practice ways to carry out each of the processes in the framework. Finally, unique, individual tasks are tailored to implement the activities that are specified in the model. Those tasks must produce known and explicit outcomes, and they must ensure that the desired security functionality or practice is built into the lifecycle for that project. Likewise, each of those tailored tasks should be directly traceable to the intents and purposes of the generic activity specifications in the framework.

At this juncture an essential qualification is necessary. Because no two organizations do business in exactly the same way, each individual application and system security process is executed differently in its particulars. For that reason, organizations need to tailor the implementation of those processes in a way that makes the most sense for them. Although they can use a standardized framework to guide the establishment of a coherent set of lifecycle processes, tailoring is always required.

The generic framework describes an optimum process for developing and maintaining application and system software. The actual tailoring process is carried out by identifying unique project-specific issues, problems, and criteria and making the necessary adjustments to fit those criteria. Developing the routine individual practices for each project within that standard framework lets planners build security directly into the lifecycle at the time it is defined for each individual project.

The standard framework serves as a tangible and practical basis for ensuring consistent understanding and execution of the process as a whole. It also provides a stable basis for considering where application and system security practices should be carried out.

Thus, the tailoring of a standard model of security like this lets the organization coordinate the assurance of application and system assurance from a single, standard, best practice-oriented framework of processes, activities, and tasks. At the same time, the approach allows the actual day-to-day practices themselves to be explicitly designed to realize each of the project's specific security goals.

## Coordination of the Process and Planning For Security

A standardized framework model serves as the essential basis for effective management of a software operation, because the framework communicates the explicit policies and procedures that define and relate all of the components in that particular operation. If the organization doesn't know what its processes are, it will be difficult to put tangible measures in place to implement them. Consequently, well-defined policies and procedures are a necessity in order to insure that the project is moving along as planned.

Because of the intangible and creative nature of software work, managers rarely know as much about what is actually happening within the process they manage. The problem can be better understood by looking at Figure 20-1, which is a representation of the typical oversight responsibility of an IT manager. As can be seen, the sheer amount of presence that is necessary to be able to monitor and then subsequently control the work of multiple complex projects almost precludes any form of effective supervision.

The problem with IT operations is that they are both complex and abstract. A standardized framework provides the point of reference that is needed in order to develop the tangible information flows that will let the supervisor see into the project itself. Managers should have practical visibility into the processes that they are supervising in order to run them effectively. Otherwise, the performance of the work could neither be assessed nor effectively directed.

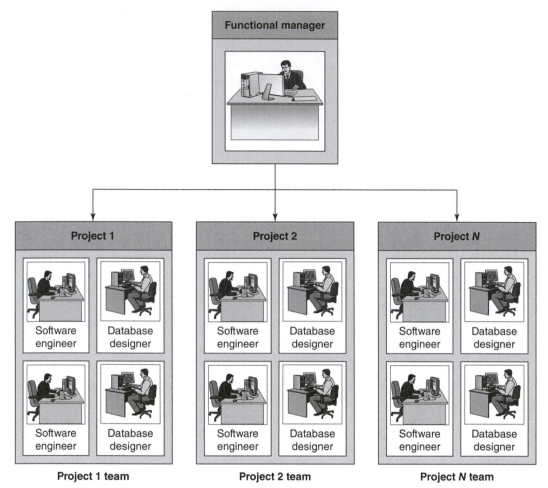

**Figure 20-1** Responsibility of a software manager

*© Cengage Learning 2012*

The key to effective control of the application and system development and maintenance process lies in getting essential information in front of decision makers when they need to make a decision. A comprehensive process framework lets planners think through and establish where, when, and how review activities will take place as well as who will receive the products of each review. Having a rich source of information about the internal functioning of each of the elements of a project provides a substantial advantage for any IT manager.

**Specification of Operational Duties for Security**  Since the application and system security function is important to the overall security of the organization, a reliable process has to be established to ensure that routine application and system security is done correctly. A variety of substantive artifacts have to be developed in order to underwrite that assurance.

An organizationally standard procedure manual is always required. It details the steps that are necessary to execute every routine activity in the application and system security process. The manual should itemize all of the expected results from that activity as well as some way to determine that they have been accomplished. In particular, a complete specification of procedure ensures a high degree of organizational control over the electronic elements of the system. That is because automated security functions can be developed and embedded directly into the functioning of the operating system. What is more, controlling operations at the operating system level makes the management of all system resources much more efficient.

Once all of the procedures for ensuring application and system software security have been defined, a tangible set of organizationally sanctioned tools and protocols for applying them have to be referenced to each of those activities. That description should include the point in the process where the activity should be carried out, as well as a specific way to evaluate and report the effectiveness of each activity. The specification of tools and protocols is important to the overall assurance of application and system security because so much of the actual assurance work takes place in the electronic domain.

Next, an assignment of roles and responsibilities has to be done for each of those activities. That specification is necessary because all of the relevant members of the organization have to know precisely what activities they have to perform to ensure their part of the application and system security process. This requirement also implies the need for a comprehensive program to build awareness of correct practice, including a formal employee education and training program. Every employee's assigned responsibilities should be documented as well as an explicit enforcement mechanism for every job title. Enforcement should then take place on a continuous basis and as an organization-wide commitment, in order to ensure the disciplined performance of the security work.

**Assuring Applications in Particular** The easiest way to secure an application is to ensure that security vulnerabilities are not created in the first place; however, most developers focus on functionality, rather than security. Since it is possible to write a program that operates properly, but which is insecure, the fact that properly functioning code is not necessarily secure code has to be kept in mind when the application is created. Both of these issues should be addressed in the testing and review processes that take place while the code is under development.

Application assurance in particular has become an increasingly critical area of concern because of the Internet. Applications no longer operate in isolation; the many interactions of applications have to be assured, both within the enterprise's own operating environment, as well as from the actions of external agents. This assurance is gained by first identifying threats and then ensuring against application vulnerabilities by either patching them or reconfiguring the system to prevent exploitation. The primary means for external attack against application and system comes through exploitation of faults in the application layer of the network. Those faults are exploited in one of two ways: they can be the subject of a direct attack by outsiders over the network, or they can be attacked from within the machine by insertion of malicious code.

In the case of applications, the primary aim of the security function is to minimize any potential harm that might occur through malicious action or misuse of the software. As such, application security primarily comprises the substantive actions that are taken to secure applications themselves, as well as the practices that are undertaken to ensure their continuously secure operation. The goal is to minimize the likelihood that malicious people will be able to modify, delete, or steal information of value that is associated with a given application.

## The CISO Takes a Meeting

*The CISO was back in Jersey City in the middle of the night getting his report from the weird little hacker he had "hired" to test the security of the company's applications and systems. He was not worried that he was standing in the middle of the Journal Square PATH station after midnight, because the network security manager was there to provide the buffer. The CISO had driven rather than taken the PATH train over from 33rd Street and he intended to go back home the same way. The hacker himself was lurking out by the statue of Jackie Robinson, refusing to come into the building, so the CISO and the network security manager went out in the mild spring night to meet him there.*

*As usual, the hacker refused to speak to the CISO, but since he was talking to the person the CISO was standing next to, the message got across. The hacker had had a field day. He had been able to read, add, delete, and modify data in almost every file he had tried to access. Next, he had put a sniffer on the company's VPN that drew him a roadmap of how to crash the entire company network. Then, just for the fun of it, he sat there under Jackie Robinson's outstretched arms and did a remote termination of somebody's running application. That event must have been very puzzling to whoever was running that application in Melbourne, Australia. Finally he had dropped a rootkit into the operating system that, among other things, had let him print out the contents of the CIO's e-mail archive. He had even included the entire e-mail directory of the CEO in his final report, just to make the point.*

*The worst part was that the hacker had just tunneled in through the company's firewall by connecting over standard TCP and encapsulating in SSL tunnels. All he had to do was use packets aimed at these services. Because they were HTTP and HTTPS, the packets simply passed through the firewall without being identified. He had then run a series of SQL injection and cross-site scripting exploits. Being a purist, he had stopped there. It was clear that the company's systems were exploitable through simple application layer attacks. The 783 other types of exploits listed in DHS's Common Vulnerability Enumeration were unnecessary. He had confirmed the CISO's worst fears.*

*The little guy handed the network security manager a huge printed report, and the network security manager thanked him and handed the hacker a little envelope in true New Jersey fashion. The network security manager also told the little guy that he was going to look carefully the next day to make sure that none of the company's systems had been added to the hacker's bot-net and that the rootkit he had dropped into the operating system was removed. If he found out otherwise, all 250 pounds of the network security manager was going to pay the hacker a visit to personally discuss his lack of ethics. The little guy assured him that that would not happen, and then he scuttled off into the darkness.*

*The CISO didn't want to gloat as he laid the contents of the CIO's e-mails in front of both the CIO and the CEO the next day. On the other hand, a deal was a deal, and if it took laying out the embarrassing details of the CIO's social life to get the organization going, he was more than happy to do that. Of course, revenge was a close second, motive-wise. Both of them had the same reaction: dawning horror followed by an urgent need to do something about the problem. And, of course, the copies that the CISO had of the personal communications between the CIO and her male friends suddenly made resource constraints less of a priority for her. The CISO had his top-down design plan in his briefcase and he walked through it with both the CIO and the CEO.*

*The implementation scheme was simple, and he was going to need the help of his usual team of security engineers. The Jacksonville security engineer, who everybody considered to be the CISO-in-waiting, was put in charge of the implementation project, with the Gaithersburg security engineer and the Corvallis security engineer as her assistants. The security engineer at the Singapore data center was designated as the Asian Rim coordinator. The Jacksonville security engineer had been living by the EBK's recommendations and she saw no need to change the game plan at that point. The EBK specifies the following 10 functions to implement system and application security:*

1. *Execute the enterprise and IT system or application security policies*
2. *Apply and verify compliance with identified standards against which to engineer the IT system or application*
3. *Perform processes and procedures to mitigate the introduction of vulnerabilities during the engineering process*
4. *Perform **configuration management** practices*
5. *Validate that engineered IT security and application security controls meet the specified requirements*
6. *Reengineer security controls to mitigate vulnerabilities identified during the operations phase*
7. *Ensure the integration of information security practices throughout the SDLC process*
8. *Document IT or application security controls addressed within the system*
9. *Adhere to secure coding practices*
10. *Implement and test backup-and-restore procedures for critical systems*

## Implementing the Process

Vulnerabilities are defects in application and system software that can be exploited by a threat. Defects happen in software because everyday software development and maintenance processes require extreme precision in both the logical and physical details of their execution. Thus, a great deals of oversight is necessary to ensure the correctness of the production process. For that reason, alone, the logical starting place in implementing an effective application and system security process is to ensure that managers of application and system security have full visibility into the processes they oversee. At a minimum, application and system security ensures that an appropriate development methodology is in place and that relevant standards of practice are employed as well as independently audited.

After the application and system security function has been designed, it is implemented in the operational environment. The day-to-day mission of the application and system security function is to scrutinize the actions of line organizations and bring any deviations in expected outcome to management's attention. As a result of that overall purpose, there are several important assumptions built into the application and system security process. First, application and system security is a monitoring and reporting tool; it is not responsible for actually doing application and system development and maintenance work. Nonetheless, it is always responsible for reviewing all development and maintenance plans for inclusion of required security practices.

Since it isn't possible to evaluate and test every artifact in the development process, the performance of the development and maintenance activities of the organization is charted through regularized review and testing of a defined set of deliverables. That review and testing takes place at pre-planned and mutually agreed-on entry and exit points in the various processes. Because the application and system security function is the organizational unit that is responsible for fulfilling that role, it should always participate in design and code inspections. In addition, application and system security reviews all test plans and test results for compliance with standards and adherence to plans. Finally, application and system security should audit the software configuration management operation to ensure its compliance with all required procedures. It is also responsible for registering non-concurrence where any non-compliance is identified. Because of this latter responsibility, application and system security should also have an effective enforcement mechanism to back it up.

## Human Considerations

As it is with most security functions, a number of the problems encountered by application and system security revolve around staffing, authority, and control issues. To do its job properly, the application and system security staff should be composed of software professionals who are specialists in securing applications and systems. Because application and system security inspects the work rather than actually producing it, the application and system security function often doesn't attract the sort of top-notch software people who usually tend to gravitate toward development. This fact has to be taken into account by the organization's top-level decision makers when they set up the application and system security operation.

The application and system security must also have an independent reporting line, because the application and system security management team is usually not capable of dealing with development managers. The problem is due to the fact that senior executives, who are more oriented toward production than they are security, are more likely to back the production units over the application and system security when non-concurrences are involved. Ultimately, the organization must make a commitment to be responsive to the recommendations of application and system security. A formal, organizationally sponsored and maintained problem resolution function must also be in place at the top of the organization. Application and system security's real dilemma is that it complicates the issue of group dynamics. Nobody likes to be criticized; therefore, an organizational awareness has to be created at the top that minimizes that kind of problem. That awareness is sometimes called a "security culture."

In addition, the configuration management and documentation processes have to be directly involved in the application and system security operation. Without the baselines put in place and documented by these other two processes, the application and system security practitioners would not have a point of reference for control. Established baselines are necessary because software development groups rarely produce documented security plans to judge progress. An established baseline of policies and practices is critical to the audit function.

## Establishing the Overall Operation

To establish the overall application and system security operation, the basic organizational framework must include a set of defined application and system security practices that are based on provably correct development methods and standards. Application and system security then uses those practices as a baseline for ensuring that security is built into the development and maintenance processes. Creating that framework is a critical function in the application and system security process, but it has to be customized to meet each project's unique needs. For this reason, the strategy for implementing security practices in each project must be planned at the outset.

The overall aim of application and system security is to enhance visibility into the development and maintenance processes. There have to be defined points in the application and system security process where the organization pauses to assess how well it is doing in ensuring that security is built into each development and maintenance project. To accomplish this, the application and system security function does regular evaluations to determine whether each project has followed the steps that were planned for it. For instance, appropriate coding discipline needs to be established and monitored, and a testing program must be defined, instituted, and performed independent from development. Ultimately, from a process standpoint, the application and system security function conducts in-process evaluations in order to chart the performance of the entire organizational control system.

The one simple rule for application and system security reporting is that it must not be done through the software development framework. There are a few simple guidelines for structuring an application and system security reporting system. Application and system security should not report to the project manager, but it should report to local management. Typically, there should be no more than one position between the application and system security function and the senior site manager. Consequently, application and system security should also have an advisory relationship to a senior executive.

## Launching the Program

There are eight steps required to launch an application and system security program. Step one is initiation, which requires defining the key application and system security leadership and operational roles and producing a formal organizational plan. The next step requires identification of the relevant application and system security issues. This is usually done in conjunction with the development project managers. In this process, the application and system security manager and staff must identify and prioritize the key application and system security issues.

The organization then writes the application and system security plan, which defines audit and control activities, and identifies required standards and practices. The application and system security plan is integrated with the software configuration management and project documentation plan. Once the plan has been developed, it is time for the organization to define the standard procedures to guide the application and system security function.

The next step is to formally establish the application and system security function itself. This normally involves training and in-house promotion of the application and system security program. Specifically, application and system security personnel must be trained in the requisite security methods. This requires an assignment of roles and responsibilities, the development of a schedule, the performance of monitoring activities, and the implementation of a problem resolution system. Finally, the application and system security program must be periodically audited to determine whether it is performing effectively and as intended. All of this is implemented by a plan.

# Establishing the Application and System Security Plan

Ensuring proper alignment between overall information security goals and the activities of application and system security requires a plan. That plan has to outline the explicit mechanisms that will be employed to carry out the activities and tasks that are required to ensure application and system security. Application and system security must be able to provide sufficient assurance that the organization's software and systems all conform to a set of specific security requirements. In addition, the application and system security function must warrant that those requirements all result from a formal plan. The first step in the planning process assumes that an application and system security process can be established and tailored to a given project. More importantly, the activities that are planned to ensure application and system security must be formally related to the security practices that comprise the overall information security process.

The plan must be documented, executed, and maintained as correct for its lifecycle. In order to ensure that correctness, the plan has to include a definition of any specific standards, methodologies, procedures, and tools that will be employed to ensure the application and system security activities. Along with documentation of security assurance practices, the procedures for contract review and coordination have to be itemized where software is purchased rather than developed. Finally, there has to be explicit specification of the procedures that will be followed for assigning resources, schedule, and responsibility for conducting the application and system security activities.

During the lifecycle of the project, the plan is used to carry out the required application and system security activities. If problems or non-conformances appear during the execution of the application and system security process, they are documented and then resolved through formal management channels. Because the outcomes of the application and system security process provide critical inputs to process improvement and other organizational activities, these results must be recorded and safely archived. Also, since they are important to the business functions that revolve around the development and the maintenance of the contract, the records of the application and system security work must be made easily accessible to conventional business managers. The mechanism for doing this should be itemized in the application and system security plan.

## Application and System Security Product Assurance

The application and system security assurance process has two separate but equally important focuses: product security and process security. The first focus is product security. In its actual day-to-day operation, application and system security is primarily an oversight function; therefore, the first step in the product focus is to confirm that the plans that are used to establish that oversight process are properly documented and meet the general practice requirements for monitoring and assurance.

In order to be correct, the plans must be mutually consistent and executed as required. Once the correctness and applicability of the plans has been assured, the application and system security process should then direct its attention to the products that are produced by the organization's routine development and maintenance activities. All of the products under application and system security control must be confirmed as compliant with previously defined specifications of requirements and the project's plans.

## Application and System Security Process Assurance

The ability to assure correct compliance with the process is the other side of application and system security and the one that has the greatest interest and payoff for the organization as a whole. Software lifecycle processes that are part of the project environment must be proven compliant with any of the application and system security standards and plans that are associated with that undertaking. This includes rigorous assurance of the routine application and system security practices specified for each project.

Every aspect of required application and system security practice must be ensured to comply with the requirements of the application and system security plan, including the development environment, the test environment, and the test libraries. In addition, because sub-contractors may be involved in the application and system security activity, pertinent prime contract requirements for application and system security have to be assured to have been passed down the supply chain. Moreover, all the sub-contractor software products must be proven to satisfy all application and system security requirements. To support this, a set of measures and evaluation criteria should be defined for both the application and system security product and the process space.

Ultimately, the success of any project depends on the quality of the people who carry out its component tasks. The application and system security function does not have a mandate to train personnel, but it does have the requirement to find out whether that group possesses the requisite knowledge and skills to meet project requirements and, if that is not the case, to recommend appropriate and sufficient training.

# Creating an Information-Based Management Process

*As was his frequent habit, the CISO was sitting with his chair turned to look out over the East River. He spent a lot of time sitting that way because the panorama of life in New York City was certainly more inspirational, from the standpoint of his creativity, than looking at a wall on the other side of his admittedly luxurious office. He had been sitting for some time, gazing off into the hinterlands of Queens and contemplating his next move. It would be an understatement to say that the implementation scheme that his team had prepared was met with some skepticism by the CEO and the CIO.*

*The main problem, as far as they were concerned, was one of control. Neither of them felt that the approach the team had chosen could be sufficiently managed. There was too much structure built into the definition and planning processes for the actual assurance work. In their minds, it would be impossible to monitor the innumerable company projects at the level of detail that would be required for the project managers to do any kind of direct management intervention if any type of change was required.*

*In turn, the CISO thought that that objection just demonstrated that neither the CEO nor the CIO had really understood the dynamic process that he was proposing. In his mind, it was a no-brainer that in implementing the tailored approach to assure correct practice in each project, activities should be built in that generated sufficient management data to ensure control. Moreover, since those activities would result in actual quantitative information, it would be possible to do the kind of management by exception that would allow everybody up and down the management food chain to exercise the appropriate control for their levels. The data coming out of the comparison of actual project outcomes against planned requirements would allow managers to concentrate on the few problem areas, while keeping the activities that were known to be on track with project aims on the back burner.*

*The issue was how to educate both the CEO and the CIO at the same time. Since the CISO could already see that routine evaluation activities would supply all the data he needed to prepare the sort of reports and graphs that the CEO loved, he decided to simply implement the evaluation process he was already planning. His process would require project managers to do regular inspection of each of their projects' processes in order to ensure that the controls they had deployed for each of their projects were effective in accomplishing desired security goals. These evaluations would typically be done on a routinely scheduled basis. With the decision being made, the CISO turned back to the computer that was built into the top of his desk to check the EBK in order to see what it said. The EBK specifies the following seven high-level functions for the evaluate perspective of system and application security:*

1. *Review new and existing risk management technologies to achieve an optimal enterprise risk posture*

2. *Review new and existing IT security technologies to support secure engineering across SDLC phases*

3. *Continually assess effectiveness of the information system's controls based on risk management practices and procedures*

4. *Assess and evaluate system compliance with corporate policies and architectures*

5. *Assess system maturation and readiness for promotion to the production stage*

6. *Collect lessons learned from integration of information security into the SDLC, and use to identify improvement actions*

7. *Collect, analyze, and report performance measures*

# Monitoring Security Status

The goal of the application and system security process is to evaluate the level of conformance of each project to its required security actions. Along with the mission of ensuring continuously correct security practice, application and system security also warrants the security of the organization's development and maintenance processes. Finally, application and system security assesses whether all of the risks and feasibility issues associated with those processes have been addressed and satisfied.

The organization calls on application and system security when it needs to determine whether a particular deliverable meets the requirements that were specified for it. Application and system security's principal purpose is to find out whether a given product is sufficiently consistent, complete, and correct in its development to proceed downstream to another phase in the process. As such, application and system security evaluations are almost always performed in an iterative fashion; the product is constantly evaluated for conformance to secure practice as its deliverables are refined and move downstream.

Application and system security seeks to catch and correct small errors before they propagate downstream. Since that capability demands a good eye for detail, it is usually done in teams rather than by individuals. Because security should be built in from the start of production, it is important to get the application and system security process started as early as possible in the overall lifecycle of each software product.

The determination to deploy a formal application and system security function should be a formal organizational decision which is based on evidence and supported by assessment. The application and system security processes themselves can range from highly informal to formal audit activities. Nonetheless, any security control process will only be as good as the degree of freedom that is granted to it by the organization. For that reason, the most effective application and system security processes normally involve a third party to do the actual assessment.

The application and system security process is formalized by a plan, which should be defined early and carefully refined as the project it is meant to regulate moves downstream. Also, intermediate range plans might emerge that reflect enhanced understanding as the real-world process of application and system security rolls out. These transitional plans must always be adapted to the overall aims of application and system security, which are to insure that the requisite security of a given deliverable can be confirmed.

## Launching a Comprehensive Evaluation Process

The rigor of the application and system security evaluation process should be based on a thorough analysis of the risks and criticality of the project's various components and processes. There are never enough resources to completely evaluate the security of every development and maintenance project; therefore, the project requirements are also used to determine how important it is. The rigor of the application and system security evaluation process is then traded off against the time and expense involved.

Based on that analysis and the determination that an application and system security program is even justified, the next step is to identify the lifecycle elements or deliverables to be evaluated. The process is formalized in an application and system security plan, which is the actual deliverable that comes out of this activity. The application and system security evaluation activity is then carried out based on this plan. These activities can range from a simple contract **risk assessment** activity to a full evaluation of the overall process itself. These activities can also include evaluating the design, code, integration scheme, or even the documentation.

## Implementing the Process

The first task in the process implementation stage is to determine whether the overall project actually warrants an application and system security process. This requirement is necessary because an application and system security evaluation represents overhead to the development process. During the time that the application and system security tasks are being done, no code gets written and no products get shipped. Any decision about undertaking an application and system security activity has to be cost-justified against the potential impact that failure in the software would have on the safety and security of the people using it.

The organization must also decide how independent the entity doing the application and system security evaluation has to be. The conventional criteria for judging this are: the potential of an undetected error to cause harm; the level of risk associated with the technology that will be used; and the availability of funds to support the assessment. These criteria are weighed against the costs and potential loss of productivity represented by an application and system security activity, keeping in mind that the more rigorous the activity, the greater the cost. If the organization determines from that trade-off analysis that the project warrants an application and system security evaluation, the next step is to set one up.

The unit that does the actual assessment is rarely the application and system security function itself. It is usually a third party or the developers themselves, due to the level of detail at which the assessment must be conducted. During the prior step, the decision was made about the degree of rigor based on criticality. If the project is critical enough to justify an independent evaluation agent, an agent with sufficient degrees of freedom has to be selected. This often involves obtaining the assessment from a third party.

Once the decision has been made about who will do the evaluation, the organization designates the specific project activities and deliverables that will be examined. This selection is based on the scope, size, and complexity of each of the target activities as well as how critical they are. Following that selection process, the precise evaluation activities and tasks are chosen and assigned to each target activity or deliverable. This includes a specific itemization of the associated methods, techniques, and tools for performing those tasks.

A formal application and system security evaluation plan is then written for each lifecycle activity to be examined and the evaluation procedures are specified. The plan itemizes each of the tasks that must be carried out to evaluate each of the lifecycle process or deliverables that are identified. This includes a precise stipulation of all of the resource and scheduling requirements, as well as an itemization of the roles and responsibilities for carrying out the process. Finally, the plan indicates who should get the reports that issue out of the process and assigns the responsibility for distributing them. This stipulation is meant to establish the essential feedback and resolution mechanisms.

**Targets for Evaluation** At a minimum, application and system security evaluates the security elements of the project requirements, the design and coding specifications, and the test plan. Ideally, this assessment is done independent from the development process. Some sort of evaluation activity is required in seven types of common project phases. Typically, the deliverables from the contract, process, requirements, design, code, integration, and documentation phases of the development and maintenance processes are assessed for compliance with security requirements. Walkthroughs or inspections, or combinations of both, are customarily employed to verify deliverables from five of these phases: contract, process, requirements, design, and documentation.

In a walkthrough, the review team is led through the deliverable by the designer or the programmer. While this happens, the reviewers might ask questions about items they encounter within that "Grand Tour," but the producer controls the logic of the process. Although walkthroughs are cheap and easy to conduct and they may be capable of detecting gross errors in the requirements or design, they should not be considered rigorous. They are best used as preliminary explorations rather than final determinations.

A more rigorous approach is the formal inspection, where a review team rigorously examines the artifact in an effort to identify any cracks. This is generally guided by an assessment checklist that is prepared in advance. Mitre Corporation's Common Vulnerability Enumeration is the current basis for formulating that checklist. The evaluations themselves range from the rigor of a code inspection all the way up to a strategic evaluation of the alignment of the artifact with business plans. The evaluation would normally identify any violations, missing requirements, breach of standards, logical inconsistencies in the build, and any other detectable faults or unspecified difficulties. Application and system security inspections are formal procedures that are usually based on some sort of explicit plan, and they always employ a pre-defined protocol. Since they are much more resource-intensive than walkthroughs, they should be used judiciously.

**Criteria for Evaluation**   There are a number of criteria that are used to judge whether a deliverable is complete, correct, consistent, and secure. Those criteria include critical things like determining whether the requirements cover all known security needs and whether there are adequate procedures in place to ensure control over the development process. Criteria can include specific things like whether roles and responsibilities for all parties have been stipulated and whether criteria have been provided for judging correctness of the build.

In addition to process criteria, there are also product criteria such as whether the software requirements are feasible and correct; whether the design is correct and consistent with and traceable to requirements; whether the design implements proper sequence of events, inputs, outputs, interfaces, logic flow, and error definition, isolation, and recovery; and whether the design implements critical security requirements correctly as shown by rigorous methods.

**Desk Checks**   In the coding phase, which is the place where most defects are actually created, the most common application and system security evaluation approach is the code inspection, which is commonly called a desk check. Even though this approach pre-dates the dinosaurs, it is still the most common practical method employed by the industry to verify individual segments of code and larger programming artifacts. Desk checks can be as informal as one programmer going into another's cubicle and asking to go through that person's work, or as formal as an acceptance audit of the source code, which is conducted at the termination of the project.

In the desk check, the reviewer, which is usually an individual but sometimes a team depending on the rigor required, executes the program in a virtual sense. This is accomplished by stepping through the code one line at a time, thinking through each step as the computer would. The goal of this operation is to detect any logical, physical, or syntactic errors, or any larger violations of programming standards. Even in this age of automation, desk checking is still considered to be the most effective method for evaluating code, because it can detect logical errors in program concept and structure that are impossible to find using automated program test suites and the other more sophisticated tools of the programmer's trade.

As a consequence, desk checks are still highly recommended and employed where a code deliverable alone is involved. Common criteria for desk checks include determining whether the code is traceable to design and requirements. Desk checks also determine whether the code is testable, correct, and compliant with requirements and coding standards and whether the code implements proper event sequence, consistent interfaces, correct data and control flow, completeness, and error definition, isolation, and recovery. More importantly the desk check will determine whether the code implements safety, security, and other critical requirements correctly.

**Integration Reviews**   A lot of security problems happen at the integration stage, so this is the place where the application and system security evaluation activities have the greatest impact. The application and system security evaluation process employs considerably greater stringency during the integration stage. In integration, the application and system security evaluation activity is customarily guided by a planned set of protocols which are normally determined during the creation of the development plan. These protocols define what will be tested, why it is being tested, and how that test is to be carried out. Often these testing protocols include a detailed description of the data to be employed, the environmental conditions that are necessary, and the anticipated results. They also usually specify how the tester should use these results to tell whether the test was passed.

Unless that specified protocol is basic and uncomplicated, a script or scenario is normally provided to guide the test procedure. The customary mechanism employed to do this is the standardized form and accompanying set of checklists. This form and checklist is then used to ensure that every test protocol, test script, and test case for the project is followed as required. Each of these protocols must furnish explicit and unmistakable direction as to the steps required to carry out the test. In addition, they should contain an approved set of individualized assurance cases as the means to categorically identify the requisite test data. In large projects, some sort of identification scheme is also used to guide the process of tracking test results back to their original design elements and their fundamental requirements.

Because integration is both a complex and critically important part of the process, the integration protocols have to "cover the waterfront". They should not only test how the final product typically works, but also ensure that the all of the documentation, procedures, and interfaces are thoroughly understood and can be used without difficulty by naïve end-users. The integration protocols should also look at how the artifact that is being evaluated handles every conceivable exception, including all the ways that a correct standard process can be presented to the system incorrectly.

Finally, those protocols should test how well the system traps real-world errors and handles the unanticipated events that might come up in normal, day-to-day activity (that is, anything feasibly covered by Murphy's First Law of computer operation). This requires such common sense activities as verifying the software's functioning under typical operating conditions. An example of this would be testing when the database is loaded that such things as exception handling under that normal operational load can be confirmed and that the normal security and disaster recovery controls are present and work correctly.

The ultimate condition that has to be ensured is that all software components and units of each software item have been completely and correctly integrated into the software or system function; that the hardware items, software items, and manual operations of the system have been completely and correctly integrated into the system; and that the integration tasks have been performed in accordance with an integration plan. As the application and system security evaluation process runs its course, each component that has been successfully evaluated has to be placed under configuration management.

## Assurance of Process

It is a cardinal principal that reliable software demands a reliable process. Thus, the application and system security evaluation process does not simply warrant that the software or system performs as it was designed or programmed to do. The process also guarantees that it will perform according to its specified requirements within the organization. Application and system security evaluation doesn't just involve looking at the artifact to see whether it works; it evaluates it to see whether it meets requirements within the actual operating environment. Application and system security evaluation establishes that a software or system product fully and correctly conforms to each functional and non-functional requirement stipulated for it. This means that the application and system security evaluation process is the one that warrants that the software product does what it was meant to do. Some sort of application and system security evaluation activity takes place during the entire routine construction process.

The plans to ensure lifecycle security, either as part of the general development process, or as a part of maintenance, are typically created during overall project planning. That usually amounts to preparing some form of comprehensive test plan as well as the protocols and data to be used to actually perform the process of evaluating the application and system security status of the development function. There has to be an explicit mechanism for collecting and disseminating the documentation generated throughout the lifecycle because it is the presence and uninterrupted accuracy of that documentation that provides the tangible evidence of application and system security. The application and system security evaluation documentation set must always provide a warranty of the correctness of the process as well as of all relevant data collected from it. It is not uncommon, particularly in the case of legacy software, for an organization to do an occasional retrospective application and system security evaluation of current systems.

Application and system security evaluation is also done if the software is sufficiently important to warrant it. Usually, the goal in this is to determine whether that software represents a mission-critical element. If so, the organization must always weigh the worst-case results of failure against the cost of doing the application and system security evaluation work. A system where failure could result in death or injury would be a likely candidate for all forms of application and system security evaluation. Systems where failure would not result in any drastic consequences are not likely to be as intensively evaluated.

The actual application and system security evaluation process is usually done by a team that may be composed of everyone from developers and users through independent consultants. The conduct of the application and system security evaluation is based on a formally documented evaluation plan. Normally, the involved parties select and describe a valid set of test requirements and the applicable assurance cases. The evaluators must ensure that whatever test requirements, cases, and specifications they define truly reflect the conditions for the intended situation. The evaluator agent then conducts the tests from that defined set of requirements, cases, and specifications. This may include such testing approaches as testing with stress, boundary, and singular inputs; testing the software product for its ability to isolate and minimize the effect of errors (e.g., graceful degradation upon failure, and request for operator assistance upon stress); and testing that the representative users can successfully achieve their intended tasks using the software product.

The purpose of these tests is to certify that the product undergoing application and system security evaluation satisfies the terms of its intended use. As discussed earlier, it is essential that this application and system security evaluation be done in the conditions of the target environment, not on a test bench.

# Getting the Participants on the Same Page

Joint review helps the business get on the same page with developers on any matter of importance. This activity usually revolves around getting and keeping consensus about the status of any product that is part of any given process. The joint review process can apply to anything from intermediate documentation elements right up to the complete and formal product itself.

Application and system security joint reviews are typically done using a formally stipulated set of processes and tools. They can be conducted at both the project and technical levels and are held throughout the lifecycle of the software or system artifact.

The primary purpose of joint review is to help the developing organization build a product that reflects the security aims of the business. For instance, a joint review is normally held to determine and evaluate the security performance of a particular project. Joint reviews help the developing organization to better understand what has to be done in order to ensure satisfaction of security goals from the business perspective. Using this process, it is possible for the business part of the organization to gain considerable insight into the new products that are under development. That insight will let both parties identify the associated risks and better manage their impact.

The joint review process uses a team approach to define, design, and evaluate work products. The team establishes a common set of evaluation criteria, assesses progress, and identifies the critical issues that are worth exploring. In addition, the group can bring up, discuss, and obtain common understanding and agreement on various relevant issues and recommendations as they arise. From that understanding, a collective decision can be reached about the optimum resolution to any given problem with security.

Ultimately, the outcomes of the joint review serve as the permanent repository for project issues, concerns, and their resolution. This produces a collaborative and constructive environment where members of each part of the organization can come to common understanding and resolution. These issues and recommendations can be shared and discussed between the business and the developer and used to support any necessary negotiations. For these reasons, joint review can provide a highly efficient and effective mechanism for bridging the inevitable differences between two different parts of the organization.

## Scheduling and Holding Joint Reviews

It is considered best practice to schedule joint reviews at predetermined milestones that are normally specified in the project plan which is developed at the beginning of each project. There is always a need to conduct joint reviews outside of the contract and the normal plan, and these reviews are usually called down as necessary by determination of either party. It isn't just the developer who might ask for a joint review activity.

No matter who calls for the reviews, they cost money and require allocations of funds for personnel, location, facilities, hardware, software, and tools. For this reason, joint reviews should be held based on a reasonable cost/benefit justification; they should not simply be held because one party or the other is feeling uncomfortable about the process. They should be held only after both parties have come to common agreement about the commitment of the resources necessary to carry it out.

In addition, it is an absolute prerequisite that both parties must reach consensus about how the review will be conducted. Whether it is formal or informal, joint reviews always produce action items. The standard rule for conducting joint reviews is that any documented action items or identified problem issuing out of a joint review has to be resolved.

That rule includes getting a formal, mutually agreed-on agenda for the meeting that specifies the particular items that will be covered by the review and the procedure that will be followed. This must stipulate both the products to be inspected and the events/problems that triggered the review. In addition, the scope, procedure, and entry and exit criteria for each item should be specified. In practice, the documented results or reports issuing out of the review are generally distributed to both parties. The party who performed the review can then endorse the results. If the results are approved, delegation of the responsibility for any action items is complete, and the joint review process is complete.

## Project Status Monitoring

Project status monitoring allows the producer and the customer to reach a common understanding concerning the security status and progress of an ongoing project. The artifacts most typically examined by this type of review include the project plans, schedules, standards, and guidelines.

Any and all mutually agreed-on action items that issue out of a status review must foster the advancement of project activities according to plan. Alternatively, an action item may serve to enhance global control of the project through adequate allocation of resources. Action items might also change project direction, or determine the need for alternate planning. Finally, action items can choose to evaluate and manage any issues associated with risks that might jeopardize the success of the project.

The most common form of joint review activity is the technical review. These are normally conducted at milestones in the development process or when an item specifically identified in the contract is produced. Their purpose is to determine whether the software product meets the specified criteria for security. They generate formal, documentary evidence that the product being inspected is correctly built and complies with any stipulated standards and specifications, including contract requirements. That assessment normally comes in the form of review reports for each phase of the development and maintenance process.

# Chapter Summary

- The application and system security process is defined by policies and passes through a lifecycle of five standard stages.

- The five lifecycle stages are: specification of requirements; design of the software or system; coding of the software; testing of the software; and acceptance and use of the software.

- Benchmarks are based on policies; they can be used to judge performance.

- Hidden functions are almost always malicious because they are intentionally hidden by somebody.

- Software comes in two functional categories: system and application.

- Defects that are introduced into a piece of software in the construction phase always constitute potential security vulnerability.

- In order to have a possibility of developing a successful, defect-free piece of software, a disciplined set of practices has to be adopted and followed.

- Software assurance, in the context of this text, warrants that the security and control features are collectively and individually free of vulnerabilities.

- Security architecture describes the formal design and approach that is used to build the system in such a way that it satisfies specified security requirements.

- The outcome of the process is an explicit understanding and documented description of every design element; what will be required to implement each function; and the inherent relationships between elements that are embodied in the design.

- A lot of the particulars of good architecture are oriented toward defining and implementing the modes of operation needed to adequately secure the product.

- Breaches can occur in a system unless adequate consideration is given to security issues during the development and implementation phases.

- The essence of defense-in-depth can only be assured through proper software design.

- Reliability is underwritten by the probability that a component or system will operate without failure for a given time, in a given environment.

- Risk analysis allows an organization to tell what software structural and development characteristics are predictive of vulnerabilities.

- The easiest and most effective way to obtain a security reliability estimate is to employ one of a number of useful modeling approaches to underwrite the understanding of system behavior.

- Application and system security monitors the security status of each project.

- Security status is determined by adherence to predetermined criteria, which define all aspects of correct product and process performance.

- The routine assessment of security activity produces quantitative data that can be used by managers to control the process.

## Key Terms

**Configuration management** Rational control of change based on a formal process.

**Risk assessment** The evaluation of the likelihood and impact of a given threat.

**Software assurance** The set of formal processes used to ensure confidence in software and systems.

**System development life cycle (SDLC)** A formal series of steps designed to produce properly functioning code that meets user requirements.

## Questions from the CIO

The CIO requires you to brief her on the current status of your investigation. This will be an important part of your continuing work on this project, since it is essential to be able to describe all of the ramifications of the software and system security function. Consequently, the CIO would like you to answer the following questions for her:

1. The essence of software and system assurance lies in the development of the right set of policies and procedures. Specifically, how do those two things aid security?

2. Defects cause vulnerabilities, but are defects vulnerabilities? If not, why not? Give an example.

3. What is the role of the configuration manager in subcontractor work? Why is that work important to security?

4. SQA and configuration management are the cornerstones of defect prevention. Why is that the case? What does each process contribute?

5. Why is defense-in-depth important in application and system software security? What does it provide and how easy is it to obtain? What are some of the obstacles?

6. The essence of operational assurance is the presence of reviews and inspections. How do these processes ensure operational assurance?

7. The purpose of operational analysis is to support decision making about how to react to problems. How exactly does operational assurance do that, and what is the primary element that underlies the process?

8. The conclusion of the problem resolution process must be authorized. Why is it important to do that? What would be the consequences if it were not?

9. Policies are essential to establishing and implementing the software and system assurance function. Why is that true? What would happen if a policy were not available to guide that implementation?

10. Problem resolutions should be conducted through a well-established and standard process. What is likely to happen if the process is not standardized?

# Hands-On Projects

The Gaithersburg facility of Humongous Holdings has been contracted by the air force to upgrade the flap control systems for the F-16 Fighting Falcon. Humongous has determined that about 100,000 source lines of code (SLOC) will have to be developed and/or modified. In addition, the condition of the existing legacy software in the aircraft is not known, and the customer wants formal documentation of the security of the interface between legacy and new software modules. The air force has contracted to supply a Specification of Requirements, a System Design Description and a Concept of Operations Document (COD). Humongous will be responsible for the following areas of assurance:

- Software and system interface design assurance
- Software security test planning
- Software security test description
- Software security test reporting

SQA and software configuration management will be part of the development effort. Here is some other information you may need:

- There are eight application interfaces involved.
- There will be a subcontract for modifications to some of the code.

- This is a life-critical application.
- There is a very high need for management visibility and control.
- Because it is a life-critical application, sufficient testing needs to be done to assure that the functional requirements have been reliably met.

The areas for concern are human safety, the level and formality of the design, and the unknown complexity that could exist in the interface code. On examining the project characteristics, the project manager requires you to address the following issues:

- Reliability metrics will be stressed during testing. Humongous needs to come up with six quantitative ways to measure reliability.
- There is a need for joint reviews for this project. Humongous must specify where.
- It will be important to track progress on the coding for this project. Suggest three ways to do that.
- Although the risk management practices will be used, there is no idea about where to apply them. Define the places in the process where risk assessments should be done.
- The program integration needs to be carefully controlled throughout that phase of the development effort. Justify why that should be done and suggest a method.
- Set up the review requirements to allow for in-process reviews of the execution of the project. These should be fully documented.

# Operating Scenario: Humongous Holdings

**Humongous Holdings, Inc. is a general holding company whose line of business is tailored to** finance and high-tech business. Humongous Holdings' various subsidiary companies are managed as one coordinated operation from offices in New York City. The centralization of policy and planning direction at one location has historically produced higher revenues, profit margins, and customer satisfaction. The necessary degree of coordination is enabled by a global, enterprise system that is managed from the New York location. That system provides secure telecommunications capability with embedded firewall protection, multi-carrier cellular access options, and automatic access point database updates for all connection types. It enables access to the enterprise's applications from any location on an as-needed basis. The system also provides integrated, any distance, seamless connectivity to Humongous' centralized information resources.

Humongous' business portfolio is concentrated in finance and advanced technology product development and services. Two closely held subsidiaries deal exclusively with the federal government. The line of business of one, which is based in Gaithersburg, Maryland, is component R&D and manufacture for advanced capability pods for the F16 Fighting Falcon and F18 Super Hornet. The other, based in Jacksonville, Florida, deals in R&D in advance fiber optic sensors for the navy. There is also a manufacturing facility in Detroit, Michigan that builds Leopard tanks for the Canadian army under license from the German government. Other close holdings in Humongous' empire include investment banks in Philadelphia, Pennsylvania, Memphis, Tennessee, Dallas, Texas, and Albuquerque, New Mexico and a commercial electronics R&D facility in Corvallis, Oregon. The Corvallis facility also does contract work for the Idaho National Laboratory. In addition to the closely held corporations, there are loosely held electronics manufacturing or service holdings in Pittsburgh, Pennsylvania, Houston, Texas, Des Moines, Iowa, Sioux Falls, South Dakota, Denver, Colorado and Bozeman, Montana. All of these serve the financial sector.

Finally, there are a number of loosely held international corporations in Mumbai, India, Sydney, Australia, and across the Pacific Rim, all concentrated in advanced technology. All computer services for that region are provided over a public/private VPN, which is maintained for that area in Singapore. The Singapore data center is actually owned and operated by Humongous as part of the company's global VPN, which is oveseen out of the New York office.

Information security executive management is also centralized in New York; however, there are small branch offices at each of the holdings that are staffed by security professionals who report directly to the executive managers in New York. Because of time differences, there is also a satellite security management function for the Far East that coordinates the activities of the Pacific Rim holdings under the general policy direction of the central offices. This operates independently from the U.S. operation in its day-to-day duties.

According to Humongous's charter, the primary business goal of the company's information processing function is to provide the "necessary information and analysis" that will enable the company's holdings to … "target the best business opportunities, create new business, and to deliver increased customer satisfaction." Humongous Holdings entered the market knowing that the ability to closely monitor its operation and deliver competitive business information quickly was going to be a prerequisite for its success. Its entire business model was based on the presumed ability to do that; since information was the key to company survival, that mission was laid out even before the technical capability for achieving it was in place.

Humongous Holdings' information processing operation delivers information and services to its various subsidiaries in two ways: hosted and embedded. The hosted model removes the burden of maintaining on-site data acquisition and management functions from the facility's operations managers while ensuring a secure and scalable worldwide environment. The embedded model allows each local facility to operate and maintain its own IT infrastructure, which is tailored around Humongous' enterprise systems to support that subsidiary's specific line of business and business operation.

# Subsidiaries

Humongous Holdings' customers are suppliers and manufacturers of complex custom or semi-custom products. These products are designed and priced by the subsidiary itself. Component suppliers typically do not sell off-the-shelf inventory that is built ahead of time. Contracts between the subsidiaries and their customers are always negotiated as part of the business process. Because of the high stakes involved in ensuring efficient financial transactions between the subsidiaries, local management of these holdings demands the utmost confidentiality, integrity, and availability for their data. As a result, security is one of the most important conditions for doing business; it actually exceeds performance issues in priority.

# Business Case: IT Operation

Humongous Holdings targets large customers who require custom and semi-custom components. Because these products must be developed, the subsidiaries rely on the RFP process to win business. Since the business itself involves custom development, the process typically must accommodate large numbers of engineering change orders. The company's current focus is on designing and building custom electronics, but other business verticals will be targeted in the future, especially health care electronics and data services. Estimates put the size of the health care market at 19,000 potential customers representing an initial market opportunity of several billion dollars.

A

Humongous Holdings relies on a centralized enterprise system called the Revenue Acquisition Manager (RAM) to coordinate the business outreach of its subsidiaries. That system is used universally, by all of Humongous' subsidiaries, to identify prospects, conduct sales efforts, create and deliver winning proposals, manage the subsequent requirements, and handle the fiduciary aspects of each project. The problems that RAM is meant to overcome include the inability to analyze bid requests to select the most promising opportunities, difficulty in keeping track of minor changes in specifications, no access to related organizational history, poor proposal tracking, inconsistent costing and pricing, and inefficiencies caused by manual document handling. The architecture of the systems embodies the following three large enterprise applications into a single enterprise-wide system, known collectively as the RAM Platform:

- Humongous Holdings Revenue Process Manager (HH-RPM) – This tool helps each subsidiary manage its business prospects. It contains a workflow engine and Web-based communication tools that are designed to help each business integrate design and pricing. It keeps track of all business proposal status and assists in managing the selling process.

- Humongous Holdings Knowledge Manager (HH-KM) – This tool helps to triage and analyze business opportunities, with decision support capabilities and analysis of financial performance, win/loss rates, and pricing. The idea here is to gather and analyze all available information to choose the best business prospects from among all the available opportunities. The Knowledge Manager uses historical information to prioritize opportunities and help the organization improve its response rates.

- Humongous Holdings Business Link (HH-BL) – This tool extends the collaboration between related subsidiaries, and between the subsidiaries and Humongous. Each application is itself a suite of products. For example, Revenue Process Manager includes an opportunity manager, a proposal manager, and a change-order manager. Knowledge Manager includes a performance analysis manager, a triage analysis manager, and a resource analysis manager.

Humongous Holdings knew that it could not have its subsidiaries on separate systems, since that complexity would prevent it from keeping track of its various lines of business. Separate systems would also far outstrip the ability of its small central staff to cope with the problems raised by separately evolving business ventures. For these reasons, it brought the relevant aspects of all of its ventures' business processes under the umbrella of a single system.

# Environmental Considerations

Humongous Holdings is a holding company, so it does not involve itself directly with the customer base of its subsidiaries; however, it wants to monitor that interface through quantitative data. The primary reason for that is that Humongous wants good data to base hold-or-fold business decisions on. The problem is that the complexity of tracking an unknown number of business transactions across a large variation of industries would completely overwhelm the company's relatively small central staff without considerable IT support. The problems that complexity and volume represent also cause considerable wear and tear on the IT security staff.

Naturally, Humongous wants to put strong process safeguards in place. Strategic security concerns include keeping all of the security functions in the organization aligned with organizational goals, dealing with changing events in the environment, making sure that the right people are involved in the decision making process, keeping the architecture of the business processes simple, and establishing a reliable response to market conditions.

In particular, maintaining alignment between its business processes and the company's overall vision is critical for Humongous Holdings' executive managers. Coordination and communication permeate the business operation. Keeping everyone in the business and its holdings on the same page, in terms of deciding where the company is and is not going, is a central theme of upper management. This capacity for working synchronously toward a common goal through strong communication and process discipline is the essence of Humongous Holdings' business model.

# Business Architecture

Every successful company depends on the right business architecture. For Humongous Holdings, this meant an architecture that blended general concerns about decision makers having data available to support informed decisions with the classic information security concerns about ensuring the confidentiality and integrity of that information. Thus, the front-end servers on Humongous' networks are simple and relatively inexpensive HP boxes. The back-end servers consist of a redundant set of about ten "really smoking" (in the words of the architect) application and database boxes that are responsible for carrying out the core functions of Humongous itself, as well as all of the various security applications that support the network infrastructure and its security subsystems.

This system architecture, and the way that the processing resources are allocated to it, makes upgrades and other kinds of changes, including security patches, straightforward. If it is necessary to do a small upgrade to an application in one of the front-end servers, the staff at the Humongous Holdings subsidiary can do it on site. If an upgrade or change is required that will involve the front-end servers as a whole, Humongous Holdings can do the necessary work on the front-end without affecting the overall security or integrity of the core functions. That scalable architecture also allows a major upgrade, which involves widespread changes in functionality or performance across the network, to be done in stages from the core functions outward with minimal risk.

Humongous Holdings uses COTS software when possible, but it does not hesitate to build its own components when necessary or to mitigate risk. Humongous Holdings' chief architect and the CIO are both former employees of a major Web search engine site/content provider. In four years back in the late 1990s, they watched that provider's usage go from 45,000 to 4,000,000 page views per day. With millions of people using the system, they learned quickly to take whatever security precautions were necessary to avoid being awakened in the middle of the night with a business-threatening problem.

Humongous Holdings' major concern about COTS products centers on its ability to ensure its security. That was particularly true when targeted bench-checks found inherent Trojan horses embedded in products that were acquired from an overseas source. When security is essential and the source of the code is in doubt, Humongous Holdings will build the necessary components in-house. Humongous Holdings' rule of thumb is that if the function is unimportant, COTS will do. If there is an actual or de facto security requirement for some aspect of the system, the COTS product will have to be proven secure. Otherwise, that component is a strong candidate for in-house implementation.

# Operations

The operations practice area is concerned with the day-to-day running of the business. Besides maintaining routine fiduciary control, it coordinates how the various stakeholders come together to cooperatively pursue corporate initiatives. In the case of security operations, the primary mission is to ensure that all new systems are built, launched, and deployed correctly. That implies all of the quality assurance (QA) and testing practices as well as security assurance. In order to identify security problems, the core security team, which is based in New York, holds a quarterly "security summit" event involving the security managers from all of the subsidiary sites. The aim of these summits is to address any implementation-level concerns as well as ensure that all projects are achieving their security metrics. The objectives of these meetings include:

- Coordinating the dialog between owners of front-end components and owners of back-end components. The outcome could be a written description of interface roles and responsibilities, which is captured in a formal organizational agreement.

- Resolving any communication or operational conflicts.

- Making sure that everyone is on track. In the words of one participant, they "will stop heaven and earth to resolve issues." The idea in these meetings is to do what it takes to make sure that everybody is on the same page.

# Data Collection, Metrics, and Tracking

Humongous Holdings uses security metrics as a key planning tool. For each protected item in its inventory, Humongous Holdings measures the:

- Projected number of threats with impact (as likelihood percent)
- New threats identified (as frequency)
- Actual number of incidents (as count)
- Time/date of incident
- Cost of incident
- Violations involving staff (as incident count)
- Number of software defects reported (as count)
- Number of software defects repaired (as percent)
- Cost of repair

These measures help Humongous Holdings determine how to allocate its security resources. Additionally, they ensure that Humongous' security operation is properly targeted and monitored. The measures also help alleviate executive-level prioritization battles by establishing a historical baseline for each item. That baseline, in turn, allows Humongous Holdings to make decisions about expansion of its holdings and other strategic directions.

# Structuring the Organization

In order to maintain up-to-date planning, documentation, and oversight of organization-wide security policy and procedure, Humongous has an executive management team and various ad-hoc task teams, which report to the CEO of the company. In some instances, for specific technology decisions the teams report to the CIO. Humongous Holdings has allocated a small percentage of its support staff resources to administrative coordination of the teams.

These resources constitute an elite group of Humongous Holdings' worldwide security employees. Although the personnel on the teams represent a low percentage of the total number of security staff, they are much more influential when it comes to formulating the shape of the overall security plan. This plan establishes Humongous' actual information security management system, which is strategic governance-oriented and affects the work of all of Humongous Holdings' security personnel.

The corporate CISO is responsible for providing quarterly status reports on the state of the security governance system and any emerging concerns. Since this artifact is considered a matter of board-level attention, it has a formal standing in the annual report, which is written at a high, non-technical level to promote understanding across the company.

# Organization Chart

Humongous Holdings is run like a typical corporation, as shown in Figure A-1.

Administrative IT operations at Humongous Holdings are client/server-based, with most new product development taking place in Java. This particularly applies to applications developed for the company's VPN. Security is important for development; there are frequent desk-checks of the code for all mission-critical elements, but this is mainly backroom stuff. None of the results is reported to top-level policy makers and none of this is used to update the prior requirements or design documentation. Staff is always trained ad-hoc only to the needs of a given project.

All acquisitions are by a "form letter" contract with suppliers and sub-contractors. Specifications of Requirements prior to acquisition are considered a waste of time and are not produced, except for expenditures over $100,000. RFPs are issued for acquisitions; however, they only provide customer-level detail. In most cases, Humongous chooses from among the people it has dealt with before and knows are reliable. A meeting between Humongous' "boss" programmer and the individual contractor follows to explain what is desired.

There is no formal policy on lifecycle for systems, either administrative or development. All systems are fully supported until they become too big a pain to maintain. When that happens, they are dropped. There is no plan or SOP for this. Decisions about the length of

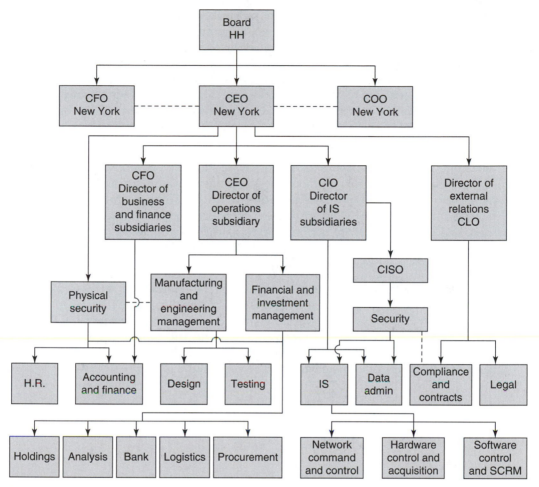

**Figure A-1** Organization chart

© Cengage Learning 2012

support, and whether Humongous or the supplier will support the finished product, are ad-hoc. They are dictated when the contract is negotiated, and they depend more on personalities than on sound business practice. The maintenance manager considers maintaining documentation to be for wimps, so none is produced after product installation. This is the one area of major security concern among Humongous' upper management.

Humongous' lifecycle model for new development is the Waterfall, although this is not strictly followed. All development goes through the major lifecycle stages, but project deadlines and terminal artifacts are artificial and not verified. Lifecycle documentation is neither produced nor updated. In general, Humongous outsources for its development needs; it buys its software for internal operations from the vendor that supplies the hardware for its networks. This is typically on an "open the box and install basis." There is no time to perform verification or acceptance tests on products acquired. There is also no management oversight, nor is this considered important. The general view of upper management is that "this stuff is too technical to understand."

Humongous does not employ any form of configuration or change management. Given the complexity of its legacy systems, this would be difficult to institute anyhow. The programming staff knows the interfaces and boundaries between systems. If this is ever an issue, the manager can just ask the programmer. New technology is thrown into the game as it is acquired. Eighty-five percent of Humongous' software assets are acquired software. There is some development for the financial end of the organization; Humongous' custom financial markets "all in one" enterprise package currently absorbs the majority of the programmer hours. As it approaches the end of the development lifecycle (it is in final tests prior to integration) a "bull and bear trading" addition is already being planned.

Staff that work on the new development projects are the corporation's hot-shots. The rest of the programming staff is kept occupied patching the administrative systems, and there is almost no communication between these two groups. Since the "all in one" system is designated as mission-critical software, there have been extensive testing, reviews, audits, verification, and validation activity performed on it by the programming staff. This has been mostly at the unit and integration testing level. The administrative systems are not considered important and are not monitored.

Managers of each functional area are responsible for contracts as well as general supervision. On the traditional IT side of the operation, Humongous employs three managers: one for development (83 analysts and 155 programmers); one for maintenance (10 analysts and 133 programmers); and one for operations (187 systems staff and 148 programmers). There are no supporting or quality management services. In that respect, IS security is managed as a separate function from the network and IT function.

# Glossary

**Acceptable behavior** Behavior that falls within the common norms of a group.

**Acceptable risk** A situation where either the likelihood or impact of an occurrence can be justified.

**Access control** All standardized controls utilized to ensure that only authorized individuals have access to protected data.

**Access privileges** The level of trust assigned an individual, expressed in terms of the types and levels of sensitivity of data the person has access to.

**Accountability** Assignment of specific responsibility to carry out a particular task or perform a specified behavior.

**Assessment** The process of determining the status of a target environment.

**Auditing** The process of generating proof and drawing conclusions from the evidence that can be attested to.

**Authentication** The process of establishing the identity and trust status of a person or process attempting to gain access.

**Authorization** The process of determining and assigning access privileges to all authenticated users and processes.

**Availability** A state of cybersecurity where all necessary information is accessible at the time it is needed.

**Awareness** Lowest level of training aimed at imparting general knowledge to the entire organization.

**Awareness (security)** General or company-wide recognition of the existence of a security requirement or concept.

**Barriers** Physical impediments to access.

**Baseline** The present status of the elements of the operating environment.

**Best practice** The commonly accepted best way to perform a task.

**Body of knowledge (BOK)** A collection of knowledge elements all related to the same purpose and which describe the practices for accomplishing a well-defined goal or doing a specific type of work.

**Bollards** Physical structures, usually made of cement or steel, that are designed to impede the progress of a vehicle or other large entity, like a tank.

**Boundaries** A perimeter that incorporates all items that will be secured.

**Breaches** Specific incidents of intrusion, unauthorized access, or misuse of information.

**Business impact analysis** Routine evaluation of the business environment in order to ensure continuing relevance of the continuity plan.

**Capability** The ability to perform a given set of tasks or execute a given behavior.

**Capability maturity** An increasing level of organizational competence.

**Certified Information Security Manager (CISM)** A certificate of personal competency in information security management granted by the International Systems Audit and Control Association (ISACA).

**Certified Information System Security Professional (CISSP)** A certificate of personal cybersecurity competency granted by the International Information Systems Security Certifications Consortium (ISC2).

**Chain of custody** A legal concept involving assurance that evidence is correct and has not been tampered with while being handled.

**Chief information officer (CIO)** The highest-level position in the information processing function; typically sets policy for the overall operation.

**CISO function** Usually the highest-level administrative position in the information security hierarchy, responsible for overall policy development and leadership of the IT security operation.

**Civil litigation** Court proceedings related to non-criminal legal action.

**Classification** The process of defining the level of sensitivity of information as a means of defining privileges to access it.

**Clearance level** An assigned level of trust determined after a standard, rigorous, and formal screening process.

**Common Criteria** An international standard for evaluating the security of a software product, e.g., ISO 15408.

**Competency** A description of a specific behavior, or set of behaviors, that a person should be able to carry out in order to be considered "competent."

**Competitive pressure** Ensuring the best deal by involving the maximum number of bidders.

**Completeness** A state in which all necessary criteria and requirements have been satisfied. In the case of the EBK, it refers to the mapping requirements for competencies.

**Compliance** Proven conformance with policy, procedure, standard, regulation, directive, or law.

**Compromise** A breakdown in organizational control leading to the loss of or harm to data.

**Computer forensics** The analysis of computer equipment to obtain evidence for civil or criminal proceedings.

**Confidentiality** A state of cybersecurity where information is protected from unauthorized access.

**Configuration** The specific array of software or hardware items that make up a component or system.

**Configuration management** Rational control of change based on a formal process.

**Consistent practice** Confidence that a given task or behavior will be executed for a specified period of time within a specific context.

**Constraints** Factors that might limit a solution.

**Contingency planning** Planning based on responding to scenarios; in the case of security, this is also known as "disaster planning."

**Continuity planning** Planning to ensure that critical functions and data of the organization are sustained in the event of disaster.

**Continuity strategy** Specific strategy to ensure continuity.

**Contractor and outsourced** Work that has been assigned to individuals who are employees of an entity whose services have been hired by the contracting company.

**Control framework** A collection of explicit controls designed to accomplish a purpose.

**Control objectives** Explicit behaviors implemented to achieve a desired outcome.

**Controls** Technical or managerial actions that are put in place to ensure a given and predictable outcome.

**Countermeasures** Technical or managerial actions taken to prevent loss of a defined set of information items.

**Crisis management** Another term for disaster planning.

**Criteria for evaluation** The basis specified by the acquirer for determining successful bidders.

**Cryptography** Literally means hidden writing; a method of hiding information in another item such as a webpage.

**Customer** The acquirer role.

**Data classification** The process of determining the sensitivity requirements of data; also the process of assigning a trust status to an individual (part of privilege setting).

**Data recovery coldsites** Alternative site that would allow migration of staff to ensure recovery with some loss of data.

**Data recovery hotsites** Alternative site that mirrors processing of a primary site in real time.

**Data recovery warmsites** Alternative site that provides the same capabilities of the primary site. However, data is backed up to the secondary site on a schedule so there will be losses based on optimum economic value calculations.

**Data retention policy** This policy sets a specific period of time to retain each record type, after which that particular record is erased from the system or archived in places that are difficult to access.

**Data security** A competency area of the EBK related to ensuring the confidentiality, integrity, and availability of enterprise data.

**Decision maker** The person in the organization authorized to make a specific decision.

**Decryption** The process of translating an encrypted message back to plaintext.

**Defense-in-depth** The arrangement of protection into increasingly stronger layers of security.

**Deliberate control** A level of security practice where all organizational decisions about security practice are based on data.

**Department of Homeland Security (DHS)** Federal agency charged with the overall protection of the national infrastructure.

**Design functions** In the EBK, these relate to the design of security related functionality; these can be technical, architectural, or work process related.

**Digital forensics** A specialized competency area of the EBK focused on the evidence gathering function, specifically targeted toward the collection of electronic evidence.

**Digital forensics professional** A person who practices digital forensics; implies specialized knowledge and training.

**Digital signatures** A hash value calculated from the plaintext of a message used to authenticate the sender by means of their public key information.

**Disaster impact classification** Prioritization of a disaster based on the harm it would cause.

**Disaster recovery plan** The specific steps the organization will take to recover its information processing function and data following a foreseen disaster.

**Disaster scenario** Assumptions about the course of a disaster embedded in the disaster recovery plan.

**Disciplined behavior** Ensuring a reliable response by an individual or group to a given event or situation.

**Discretionary access control (DAC)** A method of access control wherein the owner of the rights to the data can transfer or assign access privileges to other individuals.

**Doors and locks** Structural and mechanical barrier devices designed to control access.

**EBK framework** The overall conceptual model for the EBK.

**E-discovery** Request for and supplying of electronic evidence.

**Electronic evidence** Evidence that exists in electronic form in a computer or other digital media.

**Employee work functions** Activities specified for a given employee as part of their work assignment.

**Encryption** The process of converting a plaintext message into ciphertext readable only by the sender and the holder of a valid decryption key.

**Enforcement** The specific measures that will be taken to ensure compliance with a given requirement.

**Enterprise continuity** A competency area of the EBK related to ensuring the continuing survival of the business and that its data assets will be preserved in the event of a disaster.

**Escalation procedures** Procedures that allow the organization to respond in a disciplined fashion to an unforeseen event.

**Evaluate functions** In the EBK, these are equivalent to an internal audit of security functionality to assess the effectiveness of policies, procedures, programs, or controls in achieving security objectives.

**Evaluation** A process of gathering evidence and drawing conclusions about the correctness or quality of a given subject.

**Executive perspective** The policy layer perspective; most commonly involved in the development of strategic plans.

**Federal Information Security Management Act (FISMA)** Title three of the E-Government Act which mandates all procedural protections to ensure information security in all of the federal space.

**Fence systems** Barrier devices designed to prevent access to a physical space.

**Firewall** Firmware designed to ensure electronic access across a network; can be both reactive and proactive.

**Forensic analysis** Protocols for the analysis of data.

**Forensic investigation** The steps taken to gather and analyze digital evidence.

**Forensic laboratories** Used to conduct testing processes and procedures.

**Friendly termination** Separation from the company under good terms, usually to move to another job.

**Functional perspective** A dimension of the EBK focused on the various potential responsibilities of an EBK role. Common function perspectives are manage, design, implement, and evaluate.

**Functional requirements** Behaviors that the product must exhibit or perform.

**Functional role** The roles in cybersecurity work that are most directly involved in designing, implementing, and sustaining the mechanisms to ensure information.

**Gates** Barrier devices that are part of fence systems that can be used to regulate traffic flow.

**Generic role** Categorization of common functions and purposes into a single role label, which is a unique feature of the EBK.

**Governance** A condition that ensures that all organizational functions are adequately coordinated and controlled, typically enabled by strategic planning.

**Guards and patrols** Human-centered, physical security countermeasure.

**Hub** A component of a network that interconnects two components with each other.

**Identity management** The unique identifying data assigned to each individual who has been validated for access by system management; also the recording of maintenance of that data on the system.

**Implement functions** In the EBK, these involve tasks associated with the implementation of operational security measures, including programs, policies, and procedures.

**Incidents** Undesirable events associated with attacks or violations of information.

**Incident management** A dimension of the EBK focused on the specific steps designed to deal with a known event, typically supported by risk assessment and planning.

**Incident reporting** Process to alert organizations to potentially harmful security events.

**Incident response** The pre-planned set of steps defined in the incident response plan.

**Incident response policy** The general organizational guidelines for how to respond to incidents; meant to help dictate specific procedures.

**Informal practice** A level of security practice in which the organization informally acknowledges a set of defined practices for security.

**Information governance** The generic organizing and control principles that an organization uses to underwrite the management of its information function.

**Information security management system** A logical collection of controls assembled to ensure the confidentiality, integrity, and availability of organizational assets.

**Infrastructure** An architecture comprising all necessary components to accomplish a given purpose.

**Inspections** The least formal independent review process.

**Integrity** A state of cybersecurity where information can be shown to be accurate, correct, and trustworthy.

**Intrusion** An event involving unauthorized access, or a violation of the rules for information retrieval and use.

**Intrusion detection** Process employed to detect a penetration of secure space.

**Intrusion Detection System (IDS)** An automated system that identifies unauthorized attempts to access the system and responds according to preprogrammed instructions.

**Intrusion response** A targeted response to a violation of secure space; a countermeasure targeted to mitigate a particular type of event.

**IT security compliance professional** An executive position strictly devoted to ensuring compliance with policy, laws, directives, or regulations.

**IT security engineer** Cybersecurity role specifically devoted to development and maintenance of enterprise information security architectures (EISA).

**IT security operations and maintenance professional** Cybersecurity role devoted to monitoring and control of functioning of the day-to-day cybersecurity process.

**IT security professional** Cybersecurity role specifically oriented toward development and maintenance of the non-electronic aspects of the cybersecurity process.

**IT security training and awareness** A dimension of the EBK focused on ensuring that the workforce has adequate skills to perform assigned security functions.

**Job task analysis** A characterization of the specific functions that a given corporate role must carry out in order to fulfill the requirements of the position.

**Job title** A specific title used by an organization to describe a standard function carried out by an assigned person.

**Key** Authentication token for lock mechanism.

**Laws** Legal mandates dictated by a body with the authority to issue those mandates.

**Layered defense** Concentric defenses of increasing strength designed to put the most valuable assets behind the maximum degree of protection.

**Least privilege** The assurance that privileges will only allow an employee to access information needed to do a job properly.

**Legal and regulatory compliance** Specific practices to ensure that the organization complies with all applicable laws, regulations, directives, and standards.

**Location** A countermeasure in physical security based around optimum placement of protected space in the general environment.

**Manage functions** In the EBK, these are management activities such as overseeing technical and operational work from the highest levels. These functions ensure security system currency with the changing risk and threat environments.

**Management capability** The level of assessed competence of the management process.

**Mapping** Making an explicit and documented connection between two entities.

**Metrics** A measurement process which produces discrete objective data.

**Mitigation** Specific steps taken to decrease the impact of a given threat.

**Model** A comprehensive conceptual framework used to describe the elements of a generic process or entity.

**Motivation** The internal condition that activates or drives behavior.

**National Cyber Security Division (DHS-NCSD)** The division of DHS specifically tasked by the National Strategy with the protection of the U.S. cyber infrastructure.

**National Institute of Standards and Technology (NIST)** The body responsible for developing and promulgating standards for federal programs and federal government agencies.

**National Security Professional Development Program (NSPD)** The national strategy to ensure that all federal employees are adequately trained to carry out cybersecurity tasks.

**National Strategy to Secure Cyberspace** The national strategy to ensure the total protection of the American cyber infrastructure.

**Natural disasters** Events that are beyond human control, such as a flood or an earthquake.

**Negative problem space** The situation created when the satisfaction of one constraint would prevent the attainment of another.

**Network architecture** The specific arrangement of the components of a network.

**Network forensics** Analysis of physical components of a network.

**Non-electronic controls** Controls typically associated with ensuring continuity, compliance, physical, personnel, and secure software development in a cybersecurity solution.

**Non-functional requirements** Qualitative conditions that the product must satisfy.

**Operational controls** The control processes associated with day-to-day business operation.

**Operational duties** The activities that ensure the overall security of the system during routine operation.

**Operational security** The sustainment part of the cybersecurity process; ensures 24/7 protection of the assurance target.

**Operations** The day-to-day functioning of an organization's, mostly routine, well-defined practices.

**Optimum tradeoff** Finding an optimum relationship between recovery time and recovery point based on economic factors.

**Penetration testing** Testing that takes place with specific knowledge of the targeted environment; often used to test a specific defense.

**Performance measurement** Objective assessment process designed to provide quantitative data about the performance of a process.

**Perimeter** The area drawn around the protected space. Anything within the perimeter is protected, and anything outside is not protected.

**Perimeter controls** The countermeasures placed on the boundary between secure and unsecured space.

**Perimeter intrusion detection** Boundary countermeasures designed to identify penetrations of secure space.

**Personal data** Data about a single individual.

**Personally identifiable information (PII)** Data that can be used to identify a single individual.

**Personnel screening** A standard process that is employed to confirm basic details of employee history, which is applicable to all employees as part of the hiring process.

**Personnel security** A dimension of the EBK focused on ensuring that workers within the organization can be trusted, built around authentication, authorization, and monitoring.

**Personnel security strategy** The specific organizational approach to ensuring secure worker behavior.

**Perspective** As applied within the EBK, a perspective encompasses a given set of roles. There are three EBK perspectives, which represent policy, management, and operational layers.

**Physical access** Access to the tangible elements of the system, such as servers.

**Physical and environmental security** A dimension of the EBK focused on ensuring the security of the space within a security perimeter, also known as secured space.

**Physical security** The area of security devoted to protection of the physical space and the physical entities within it.

**Physical security controls** Physical countermeasures put in place to secure physical space. Guards, gates, and locks are examples of physical controls.

**Physical security professional** A specialist in physical security.

**Policy** An organization-wide directive on a given issue, which applies to all employees of the organization for a significant period of time.

**Preparedness plan** The organization's specific strategy to respond to foreseen disasters.

**Prioritization** Planning the order in which a threat will be addressed based on the potential harm it will cause.

**Privacy** Ensuring that all personal information about an individual is protected.

**Privacy professional** A specialist in protecting personal information.

**Privileges** The level of access authorization granted to a given individual.

**Proactive response** A response in advance of a potential incident.

**Problem resolution** A formal agreement process by which identified faults in an acquisition are resolved.

**Procedure** The specific activities that will be undertaken to satisfy some policy dictate.

**Procedure manual** A formal statement of the recommended approach to a given task or job requirement.

**Process dimension** The presence or absence of base practices which have been specified as necessary or correct.

**Process entropy** The tendency for organizational activities to become disorganized over time due to competitive pressure and technological change.

**Procurement** A dimension of the EBK focused on ensuring that products and services acquired by the organization are secure.

**Procurement contract** A legally enforceable agreement between a customer and a supplier to provide goods or services.

**Procurement professional** A specialist in acquisition.

**Professional certification** A formally recognized documentation of competency in an area of professional work.

**Public key infrastructure (PKI)** A public management authority who issues and certifies the validity of private and public keys; essential for public key encryption.

**Quantitative management** Decision making that is supported by empirically derived data.

**Reactive response** A response that takes place after an incident has occurred.

**Recognition** A level of security practice in which the organization generally recognizes the need for security.

**Recovery point objective (RPO)** The specific level of integrity that data will be restored following a disaster.

**Recovery time objective (RTO)** The specific time that the organization estimates will be required to achieve restoration of the system and its data.

**Redundancy** The approach of utilizing alternative sites as a means of ensuring against loss of data and functionality.

**Regulations** Requirements dictated by an agency or other legally constituted unit, which must be complied with; typically expressed in the form of a contract.

**Regulatory and standards compliance** A dimension of the EBK focused on ensuring that the organization complies with all relevant laws, directives, regulations, and standards.

**Request for proposal (RFP)** A formal notice issued to a potential supplier to provide a product or service at a specified price and within a specified time period.

**Residual risk** An intrinsic weakness that is currently not exploited by a threat.

**Restoration** The process of ensuring that data is restored to a desired level of integrity following a disaster.

**Rework** Additional work required to finalize a solution; usually results from a review.

**Risk** Likelihood that an identified weakness will be exploited by a known threat.

**Risk analysis** The assessment of the overall likelihood and impact of a threat.

**Risk assessment** The evaluation of the likelihood and impact of a given threat.

**Risk level** The degree of likelihood and impact that is considered acceptable before a response is required.

**Risk management** The process of placing a coherent set of countermeasures to mitigate all identified risks based on asset vulnerability and identified threats.

**Risk mitigation** A set of formal organizational processes that is designed to slow down or minimize the impact of an adverse event.

**Role** A generic area of security work, delineated by a common set of skills and functional purposes.

**Role-based access control (RBAC)** Access control model where rights to access are granted to individual organizational roles rather than people; particularly efficient for access control in large complex organizations.

**Router** A software and hardware item that is directly responsible for directing the flow of packets from one device to another over a network.

**Secure spaces** Specifically designated physical areas ensured by access controls.

**Security** Confidence that a given approach will produce dependable and intended outcomes.

**Security architecture** The specific framework of controls used by the organization.

**Security behavior** Behaviors designed to ensure the security of the individual and the organization.

**Security boundaries** The protected perimeter within which all individuals are assumed to be trusted—the separation between trusted and untrusted space.

**Security compliance officer (SCO)** The executive who is responsible for ensuring the compliance of all aspects of the organization involved in information processing, or cybersecurity, with laws, regulations, or directives.

**Security controls** Electronic or behavioral actions designed to prevent or mitigate an adverse event.

**Security incidents** Any happenings that could represent harm to information placed under the protection of the incident response function.

**Security management** Levels of security practice where security behaviors are planned and specified for all employees and then monitored for performance.

**Security metrics** Quantitative measures of security performance.

**Security monitoring** Reviews or tests undertaken recurrently to ensure a given situation.

**Security risk management** A dimension of the EBK focused on the identification, analysis, and mitigation of risks.

**Security solution** A specific architecture of controls designed to mitigate a given set of risks within a particular organizational context.

**Security strategy** The specific organization-wide approach to security; this is more directionally focused than it is detailed.

**Sensors** A form of access control, frequently electronic, that is designed to detect the presence of intruders.

**Separation of duties** The assurance that no one individual can control a process—primarily enforced by having different people carry out parts of the same function.

**Smart card** A token with computer-readable information inscribed on it that grants access to secure space.

**Software assurance** The set of formal processes used to ensure confidence in software and systems.

**Software development** The lifecycle process devoted to the creation of software; typically involves specification, design, code, test, and acceptance of software products.

**Software requirements specification (SRS)** A statement of all functional behaviors and nonfunctional qualities that must be provided to satisfy a particular software proposal.

**Standards** A formal statement of best practices promulgated by an agency with the formal authority to issue them.

**Statement of work (SOW)** The specification of work to be done to accomplish a given mission.

**Strategic alignment** Assurance that the security actions of the organization directly support its goals.

**Strategic governance** Large-scale process designed to ensure management control.

**Strategic management plan** The prescribed activities to achieve the long-range intentions of the organization.

**Strategic planning** The act of translating an organization's intended direction into specific steps along a particular timeline; strategic planning affects the entire organization for a significant period.

**Strategic security management** A dimension of the EBK focused on the development of strategies and policies to govern organizational directions for some defined period.

**Supplier** The role that provides a product or service.

**Supply chain** A hierarchical framework of entities that all work together to develop a product. Work at the bottom of the process is passed up to organizations that integrate those units into larger products.

**Switch** A low-level network device that determines the specific direction of a network packet from one segment to another.

**System and application security** The area of the EBK devoted to securing the lifecycle process by which system and application software is developed and sustained.

**System development life cycle (SDLC)** The well-defined set of steps that a system developer follows in the development and maintenance of an information system.

**System logs** Electronic files that provide step-by-step descriptions of the events that took place during a computer incident.

**Terminology** The terms used for a given purpose by a particular field or in a specific context.

**Third-party certification** Official recognition by an uninvolved party in the acquisition process that an organization has met a specified set of requirements.

**Threat** Adversarial action that could cause harm or an undesirable outcome.

**Threat analysis** Continuous operational analysis of the threat environment in order to identify any changes that will have to be planned for.

**Threat assessment** Formal process used to identify and characterize threats.

**Threat environment** The specific threats that are known to exist within a specific organizational context.

**Threat modeling** Representation of the risk environment using a commonly accepted graphic modeling approach such as data flow or UML.

**Training program** A formal skill development process aimed at increasing or ensuring the capability of a given group of people.

**Trust** The ability to authenticate a given individual or process as trustworthy.

**Umbrella framework** A comprehensive set of standard activities intended to explicitly define all required processes, activities, and tasks for a given field or application.

**Unfriendly termination** Separation from the company under circumstances where the party being terminated is likely to bear bad feelings.

**User privileges** The specific rights of access of a given user assigned by system management.

**Vandalism** The act of committing willful damage to an asset.

**Virtual private network (VPN)** A dedicated communication network that uses a public transmission system like the Internet.

**Vulnerabilities** Weaknesses, where threats are known to exist.

**Walkthrough** The most informal method of inspection, in which the producer takes the reviewers on a tour of the product. The primary value is educational; however, some insights might be obtained.

# Index